W9-AAW-605

PRAGUE
FIRST EDITION

Where to Stay and Eat
for All Budgets

Must-See Sights
and Local Secrets

Ratings You Can Trust

Fodor's Travel Publications   New York, Toronto, London, Sydney, Auckland
www.fodors.com

FODOR'S PRAGUE

Editor: Douglas Stallings

Editorial Production: Jacinta O'Halloran
Editorial Contributors: Mindy Kay Bricker, Collin Campbell, David Friday, Tim Gosling, Raymond Johnston, Frank Kuznik, Tomáš Kleisner, Philip Traynor
Maps: David Lindroth, *cartographer;* Bob Blake and Rebecca Baer, *map editors*
Design: Fabrizio La Rocca, *creative director;* Moon Sun Kim, *cover designer;* Guido Caroti, *art director;* Melanie Marin, *senior photo editor*
Production/Manufacturing: Robert B. Shields
Cover Photo: (Old Town Hall astronomical clock): Stuart Dee Photography

SPECIAL SALES

This book is available for special discounts for bulk purchases for sales promotions or premiums. Special editions, including personalized covers, excerpts of existing books, and corporate imprints, can be created in large quantities for special needs. For more information, write to Special Markets/Premium Sales, 1745 Broadway, MD 6-2, New York, New York 10019, or e-mail specialmarkets@randomhouse.com.

AN IMPORTANT TIP & AN INVITATION

Although all prices, opening times, and other details in this book are based on information supplied to us at press time, changes occur all the time in the travel world, and Fodor's cannot accept responsibility for facts that become outdated or for inadvertent errors or omissions. So **always confirm information when it matters,** especially if you're making a detour to visit a specific place. Your experiences—positive and negative—matter to us. If we have missed or misstated something, **please write to us.** We follow up on all suggestions. Contact the Prague editor at editors@fodors.com or c/o Fodor's at 1745 Broadway, New York, New York 10019.

PRINTED IN THE UNITED STATES OF AMERICA

10 9 8 7 6 5 4 3 2 1

DESTINATION PRAGUE

Since the fall of the Communist regime in 1989, the Czech Republic has become a thriving democracy that offers visitors some of Europe's most alluring attractions. The "hundred-spired" capital city of Prague—one of Europe's best-preserved architectural cityscapes—was largely untouched by World War II. Listen to the Czech Philharmonic Orchestra perform in the almost acoustically perfect neo-Renaissance Rudolfinum. Take a boat trip down the Vltava River, which lazily snakes through the city, or climb up to Prague Castle for a panoramic view. Feel like taking it easy? Grab an outdoor table at any of the numerous cafés and watch the sunset while nursing a refreshing Czech beer. Beyond Prague, medieval castles perch quietly near lost-in-time baroque and Renaissance villages, waiting for you to discover them. For outdoor enthusiasts, the country's rolling pine forests, rock outcroppings, and gentle green mountains provide all the fresh air and opportunities for exercise you need in any season. Have a fabulous trip!

Tim Jarrell, Publisher

CONTENTS

On the Road with Fodor's *F7*
About this Book *F12*
What's Where *F15*
Great Itineraries *F18*
When to Go *F21*

On the Calendar *F22*
Pleasures & Pastimes *F25*
Fodor's Choice *F28*
Smart Travel Tips *F33*

(1) Exploring Prague   *1*

Staré Město (Old Town) *2*
Josefov (Jewish Quarter) *14*
Malá Strana (Lesser Quarter) *18*
Hradčany (Castle Area) *27*
Pražský Hrad (Prague
    Castle) *30*

Nové Město (New Town) &
    Vyšehrad *39*
Vinohrady *47*
Letná & Holešovice *49*
Troja *50*
Žižkov *51*

(2) Where to Eat   *52*

Staré Město (Old Town) *54*
Malá Strana (Lesser Quarter) *63*
Hradčany *65*
Nové Město (New Town)
    & Vyšehrad *66*

Vinohrady *69*
Letná & Holešovice *71*
Žižkov *71*
Cafés *72*

(3) Where to Stay   *74*

Staré Město (Old Town) *75*
Malá Strana (Lesser
    Quarter) *81*
Hradčany *85*
Nové Město (New Town) *86*

Vinohrady *88*
Smíchov *89*
Žižkov *91*
Eastern Suburbs *92*
Western Suburbs *92*

(4) Nightlife & the Arts   *94*

Nightlife *95*
Performing Arts *108*

Late-Night Bites *123*

(5) Sports & the Outdoors   *125*

Parks & Playgrounds *126*

Sports & Activities *127*

(6) Shopping   *135*

Major Shopping Districts *136*
Department Stores *137*
Shopping Malls *140*

Street Markets *140*
Specialty Stores *141*

⑦ **Day-Trips from Prague**   *157*

Kutná Hora *160*
Karlštejn *164*
Křivoklát *167*
Český Šternberk *169*
Konopiště *171*

Lidice *172*
Terezín *174*
Měník *176*
Orlík *177*

⑧ **Southern Bohemia**   *179*

Tábor *180*
Písek *183*
Třeboň *184*
Jindřichův Hradec *186*

Hluboká nad Vltavou *189*
České Budějovice *190*
Český Krumlov *192*
Rožmberk nad Vltavou *197*

⑨ **Western Bohemia**   *198*

Karlovy Vary *200*
Cheb *208*
Františkovy Lázně *211*

Mariánské Lázně *212*
Plzeň *216*

⑩ **Moravia**   *220*

Jihlava *223*
Třebíč *224*
Telč *225*
Château Vranov nad Dyjí *227*
Znojmo *228*
Mikulov *229*

Valtice *231*
Brno *232*
Slavkov U Brna *242*
Kroměříž *243*
Moravský Kras *244*
Olomouc *245*

Understanding Prague & the Czech Republic   *249*

Prague at a Glance *250*
Time's Magpie *252*
A Short History of the Czech Republic *255*

The Czechs & their Beer *259*
Books & Movies *262*
Czech Vocabulary *265*

Index   *269*

Maps

Czech Republic *F9*
Prague Overview *F10–F11*
Central Prague *4–5*
Prague Castle *31*
Where to Eat in Prague *60–61*
Where to Stay in
    Prague *82–83*
Prague Nightlife *96–97*
Prague Performing
    Arts *110–111*

Shopping in Staré Město &
    Nové Město *138–139*
Day-Trips from Prague *159*
Kutná Hora *161*
Southern Bohemia *181*
Český Krumlov *193*
Western Bohemia *200*
Karlovy Vary *202*
Moravia *222*
Brno *234*

CloseUps

What's Free *7*
Tourist Traps *15*
Vacláv Havel *45*
Karel Čapek *47*
On the Menu *58–59*
Good Food on the Go *67*
Pub Etiquette *102*
Mozart in Prague *113*

Day Spas *128*
Prague Blitz Tour *142–143*
Guided Day Tours from
    Prague *166*
Guided Day Tours to Southern
    Bohemia *187*
Guided Day Tours to Western
    Bohemia *204*

ON THE ROAD WITH FODOR'S

A trip takes you out of yourself. Concerns of life at home completely disappear, driven away by more immediate thoughts—about, say, what marvels will beguile the next day, or where you'll have dinner. That's where Fodor's comes in. We make sure that you know all your options, so that you don't miss something that's around the next bend just because you didn't know it was there. Because the best memories of your trip might well have nothing to do with what you came to Prague to see, we guide you to sights large and small all over the region. You might set out to see St. Vitus's Cathedral, but back at home you find yourself unable to forget the views of the Charles Bridge while you were dining at Kampa Park or the trip you took to the startling Bone Church in Sedlec. With Fodor's at your side, serendipitous discoveries are never far away.

Our success in showing you every corner of Prague is a credit to our extraordinary writers. Although there's no substitute for travel advice from a good friend who knows your style, our contributors are the next best thing—the kind of people you would poll for travel advice if you knew them.

Mindy Kay Bricker is a freelance journalist based in Prague, where she writes about travel, entertainment, shopping, and nightlife for travel books and for London-based publications like *EasyJet In-Flight* magazine and *Bradmans Business Travel Guide*. She also reports on women's issues in the region for the Web site New York's Women's eNews.

Born and raised in Northern Ontario, **David Friday** first went to Prague in 1997, choosing it as an exciting base from which to research the Slovak branch of his family tree. Since that time he has spent a large part of his life in Prague, writing for several publications, including the *Prague Post* and the *Prague Tribune*. Previously, he had written educational materials and

spoken publicly on food and health issues in his home country. David credits his time spent in the Czech Republic and other countries of Central and Eastern Europe with enhancing his interests in architectural preservation and its role in the urban evolution of historically important cities. He wrote two chapters for this book, "Where to Eat" and "Day Trips from Prague."

Tim Gosling pole-vaulted over the English Channel and sprinted to Central Europe in 1997. He was Managing Editor of the city guide *Prague In Your Pocket* and has also written guides to cities in Albania, Croatia, and Slovakia. He currently works as a freelance journalist and editor in Prague. A keen amateur sportsman—when his aging knees allow—he fantasizes about world championship medals from his Letná home. Fittingly, he wrote the "Sports & the Outdoors" chapter for this book as well as "A Short History of the Czech Republic" and the "Books & Movies" section.

Raymond Johnston moved to Prague at the end of 1996 with money from an unproduced screenplay about aimless youths in the dreary high-rise housing of Prague's outer neighborhoods. He has traveled extensively around Central Europe in search of castles, ruins, interesting small towns, and microbreweries. His work as a journalist and freelance writer includes articles on travel, entertainment, and the Internet, as well the occasional celebrity interview. Before moving to Europe he earned degrees in journalism and cinema and has worked behind the scenes in television and radio. He currently writes and edits for the *Prague Post*. He wrote the "Nightlife & the Arts" and "Moravia" chapters of this guide, as well as the essay on Czech beer.

Tomáš Kleisner has a background as an academic historian, specializing in baroque architecture, which he studied at the Charles University in Prague. He's a regular contributor to various journals dealing with Czech period architecture, restoration, and conservation. He acts as a consultant for building restoration in Prague, and his wide background knowledge of the Czech capital city and its history and culture have also led him to contribute to various popular guidebooks to Prague and the Czech republic. This is his second appearance with Fodor's guides. He contributed "On the Calendar," "Smart Travel Tips," "Southern Bohemia," and the section on the Czech language to this book.

Frank Kuznik is the culture and features editor of the *Prague Post,* the capital city's English-language weekly. A veteran of almost three decades in journalism, Kuznik has been the editor of city magazines in Milwaukee and Detroit, as well as alternative news weeklies in Washington, D.C., and Cleveland. He relocated to Europe in early 2002, where he continues to work as an editor and writer. He often contributes travel articles on Central and Eastern European destinations to U.S. publications. He contributed the Old Town, Josefov, and Charles Bridges sections of "Exploring Prague."

Philip Traynor, a former editor and writer with CNN.com, moved to Prague in 2002 to work as a copy editor for the *Prague Post.* Although born and raised in the warm climate of Atlanta, Georgia, his love of traveling has driven him to brave the chilly Central European winters in his search for the architectural and cultural gems of the Czech Republic. He contributed a number of chapters to this book, including sections of "Exploring Prague," the "Western Bohemia" chapter, and many of the front-of-the-book sections.

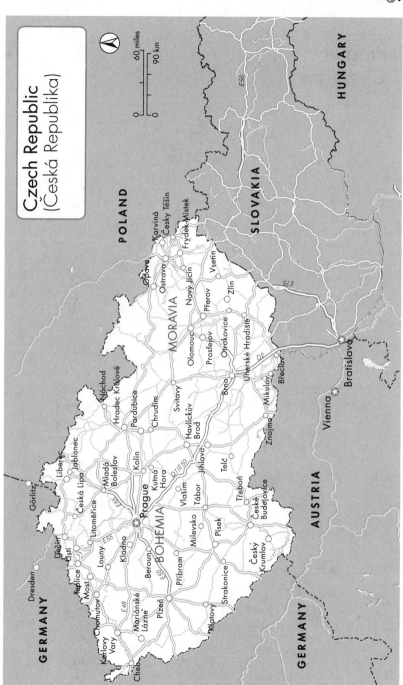

Czech Republic
(Česká Republika)

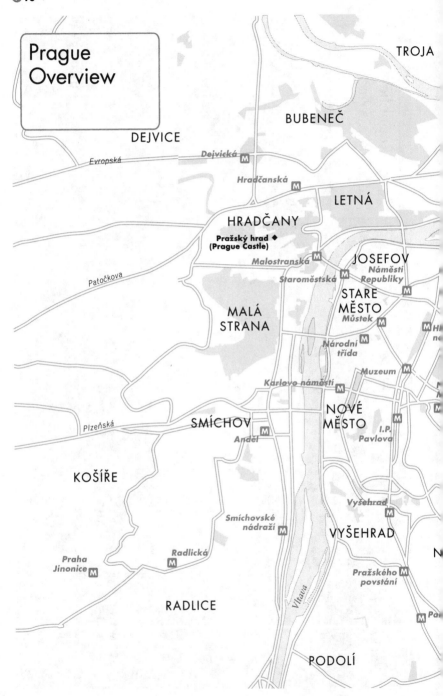

Prague
Overview

TROJA

BUBENEČ

DEJVICE

Evropská

Dejvická Ⓜ

Hradčanská Ⓜ

LETNÁ

HRADČANY

Pražský hrad ◆
(Prague Castle)

Patočkova

Malostranská Ⓜ

JOSEFOV

Náměstí
Republiky

Staroměstská Ⓜ

STARE
MĚSTO

Ⓜ

MALÁ
STRANA

Můstek Ⓜ

Ⓜ H
ne

Národní
třída Ⓜ

Muzeum Ⓜ

Karlovo náměstí Ⓜ

Plzeňská

SMÍCHOV

Anděl Ⓜ

NOVÉ
MĚSTO

Ⓜ

I.P.
Pavlova

Ⓜ

KOŠÍŘE

Vyšehrad Ⓜ

Smíchovské
nádraží Ⓜ

VYŠEHRAD

Praha
Jinonice Ⓜ

Radlická
Ⓜ

N

Pražského Ⓜ
povstání

RADLICE

Vltava

Ⓜ Pa

PODOLÍ

ABOUT THIS BOOK

There's no doubt that the best source for travel advice is a like-minded friend who's just been where you're headed. But with or without that friend, you'll have a better trip with a Fodor's guide in hand. Once you've learned to find your way around its pages, you'll be in great shape to find your way around your destination.

SELECTION

Our goal is to cover the best properties, sights, and activities in their category, as well as the most interesting communities to visit. We make a point of including local food-lovers' hot spots as well as neighborhood options, and we avoid all that's touristy unless it's really worth your time. You can go on the assumption that everything you read about in this book is recommended wholeheartedly by our writers and editors. Flip to On the Road with Fodor's to learn more about who they are. It goes without saying that no property mentioned in the book has paid to be included.

RATINGS

Orange stars ★ denote sights and properties that our editors and writers consider the very best in the area covered by the entire book. These, the best of the best, are listed in the Fodor's Choice section in the front of the book. Black stars ★ highlight the sights and properties we deem Highly Recommended, the don't-miss sights within any region. Fodor's Choice and Highly Recommended options in each region are usually listed on the title page of the chapter covering that region. Use the index to find complete descriptions. In cities, sights pinpointed with numbered map bullets ❶ in the margins tend to be more important than those without bullets.

SPECIAL SPOTS

Pleasures & Pastimes focuses on types of experiences that reveal the spirit of the destination. Watch for Off the Beaten Path sights. Some are out of the way, some are quirky, and all are worth your while. If the munchies hit while you're exploring, look for Need a Break? suggestions.

TIME IT RIGHT

Wondering when to go? Check On the Calendar up front and chapters' Timing sections for weather and crowd overviews and best days and times to visit.

SEE IT ALL

Use Fodor's exclusive Great Itineraries as a model for your trip. (For a good overview of the entire destination, follow those that begin the book, or mix regional itineraries from several chapters.) In cities, Good Walks guide you to important sights in each neighborhood; ☞ indicates the starting points of walks and itineraries in the text and on the map.

BUDGET WELL

Hotel and restaurant price categories from ¢ to $$$$ are defined in the opening pages of each chapter—expect to find a balanced selection for every budget. For attractions, we always give standard adult admission fees; reductions are usually available for children, students, and senior citizens. Look in Discounts & Deals in Smart Travel

Tips for information on destination-wide ticket schemes. Want to pay with plastic? AE, DC, MC, V following restaurant and hotel listings indicate whether American Express, Diners Club, MasterCard, or Visa are accepted.

BASIC INFO	Smart Travel Tips lists travel essentials for the entire area covered by the book; city- and region-specific basics end each chapter. To find the best way to get around, see the transportation section; see individual modes of travel ("Car Travel," "Train Travel") for details. We assume you'll check Web sites or call for particulars.
ON THE MAPS	Maps throughout the book show you what's where and help you find your way around. Black and orange numbered bullets ❶ ① in the text correlate to bullets on maps.
BACKGROUND	In general, we give background information within the chapters in the course of explaining sights as well as in CloseUp boxes and in Understanding Prague at the end of the book. To get in the mood, review the suggestions in Books & Movies. The Language section can be invaluable.
FIND IT FAST	Within the Exploring Prague chapter, sights are grouped by neighborhood. Where to Eat and Where to Stay are also organized by neighborhood—Where to Eat is further divided by cuisine type. The Nightlife & the Arts and Sports & the Outdoors chapters are arranged alphabetically by entertainment type. Within Shopping, a description of the city's main shopping districts is followed by a list of specialty shops grouped according to their focus. The remaining chapters focus on side-trips from Prague. The Day-Trips from Prague chapter contains cities and castles that can be visited easily as day-trips from Prague. Southern Bohemia covers the southern part of the Czech Republic, where some destinations require overnight stays. Western Bohemia concentrates on popular spa towns that are mostly west of Prague and can be reached on day tours but also offer comfortable overnight accommodations. The chapter on Moravia covers the area southeast of Prague, but these destinations will require an overnight visit, so we've given you ample recommendations for hotels and other accommodations. All these chapters are subdivided by town, and the towns are covered in logical geographical order. Heads at the top of each page help you find what you need within a chapter.
DON'T FORGET	Restaurants are open for lunch and dinner daily unless we state otherwise; we mention dress only when there's a specific requirement and reservations only when they're essential or not accepted—it's always best to book ahead. Hotels have private baths, phone, TVs, and air-conditioning and operate on the European Plan (a.k.a. EP, meaning without meals). We always list facilities but not whether you'll be charged extra to use them, so when pricing accommodations, find out what's included.

SYMBOLS

Many Listings

★ Fodor's Choice
★ Highly recommended
⊠ Physical address
✛ Directions
🖆 Mailing address
☎ Telephone
🖷 Fax
⊕ On the Web
✎ E-mail
💷 Admission fee
☉ Open/closed times
► Start of walk/itinerary
Ⓜ Metro stations
▭ Credit cards

Outdoors

🏌 Golf
⚑ Camping

Hotels & Restaurants

🏨 Hotel
🛏 Number of rooms
♨ Facilities
🍴 Meal plans
✕ Restaurant
🍴 Reservations
👗 Dress code
🚬 Smoking
🍸 BYOB
✕🏨 Hotel with restaurant that warrants a visit

Other

🐾 Family-friendly
🔌 Contact information
⇨ See also
⊠ Branch address
☞ Take note

Holešovice

This gritty suburb, while lacking the charm of the city center, has several redeeming sites. Veletržní palác, which contains the National Gallery's Sbírka moderního a soucasného umění (Collection of Modern & Contemporary Art), displays a wide-ranging collection of 20th-century Czech art. Výstaviště, an exhibition ground, is worth finding in order to enter the Lapidarium, which showcases monuments that were once scattered throughout the city. Next to Výstaviště is Stromovka, a tree-filled park that includes a small arcade with a Ferris wheel and other rides.

Hradčany

The Castle district is known for being the seat of Prague Castle, and its sights can easily take up most of a day. St. Vitus's Cathedral, which sits in the castle proper, with its Gothic flying buttresses, spires, and towers, looms high over the area. The history of Prague is irrevocably intertwined with that of the castle, which was founded in the 9th century, though it has been rebuilt numerous times, including a reconstruction after a massive fire in 1541. As a result, the structure incorporates many different architectural styles that reach all the way back to the Romanesque period. At night, floodlights light up the area, giving the impression to riverside onlookers that the castle is floating above the city.

Josefov

The Jewish Quarter's ghetto survived for more than 600 years until it was torn down in the 19th century. However, its history is revealed in the Old Jewish Cemetery, packed with thousands of tilting headstones, and in the synagogues that dot the neighborhood. The Old-New Synagogue, constructed around 1270, is the oldest in Europe. The Jewish Museum, which comprises five different buildings, has collections of Czechoslovak Jewish property confiscated and preserved, ironically, by Hitler. Today, art nouveau structures have replaced the former ghetto buildings, and some of the city's finest shopping can be had along Pařížká street.

Letná

Known for its sprawling park that overlooks the eastern half of the city and a bend of the Vltava River, this area is where the largest demonstration that led to 1989's "Velvet Revolution" took place. At that time, around a million protestors gathered to denounce Communism; now, citizens happily rollerblade, ride bicycles, and walk their dogs around the green pathways in the park. Perched on a cliff is a creaking, enormous metronome that replaced a 98-foot-high monument to Stalin, which was destroyed in the 1960s. The nearby National Technical Museum contains various models of Škoda Autos through the years, along with steam trains, airplanes, motorcycles, and even a coal mine underneath the building.

Nové Město

"New" is always a relative term, and that's no less the case for Prague's New Town, which was planned by Charles IV in the 14th century. Wenceslas Square, a commercialized grand boulevard lined with shops, restaurants, and hotels, forms the backbone of New Town. Although heavily visited by locals and tourists, it's worth seeing not only for its scale, but also for the National Museum, which sits at the top of the square like a king on his throne. Two doors over is the State Opera house with its intense red plush, gilding, and original interior artwork. Back down the square, follow Národní street to reach the blue-and-gold topped National Theater, a source of Czech cultural pride. It's also a part of town where you can find a good bit of the city's nightlife.

Malá Strana

The Lesser Quarter is full of winding cobblestone streets and baroque buildings, including numerous foreign embassies and stately palaces. Virtually untouched since the 18th century, the area seems to have a surprise at every turn. Go left and you will find sculpted house signs, which are works of art in their own right; go right, and you will be greeted by a statue of a saint holding a golden staff at the entrance to a church. When you feel like taking a break, grab a sandwich and look for one of the "secret" gardens that are tucked into the neighborhood.

Smíchov

A former industrial center, Smíchov is now home to several large office centers, multiplex cinemas, and a major shopping mall. Still, it betrays hints of what it used to be in days long gone by in Bertramka, a villa that once housed Wolfgang Amadeus Mozart. The Prague Metro's first station, Anděl, is here as well; though most of the Communist-era art that once decorated it were removed in the early 1990s, some remaining murals can still be seen on the platforms below.

Staré Město

Old Town Square is the center of tourist activity in Prague, so it's usually full of people from virtually every nation on earth, all gazing upward to view its many sights. The 15th-century astronomical clock, which is on one side of the town hall, has a procession of 12 apostles that make their rounds when certain hours strike. Meanwhile, the Church of Our Lady before Týn's Gothic spires and solid gold effigy of the Virgin Mary keep watch over onlookers as the rococo, Romanesque, and art nouveau buildings that surround the square. Follow the narrow streets leading out of the square for a stroll on the same pathways as the city's medieval architects designed. It's here you can find some of the most atmospheric (and expensive) hotels, not to mention many restaurants and pubs, some of them quite good. Undoubtedly, this is one of the more touristy parts of town.

Vinohrady

True to its name—which means vineyards—Vinohrady's fields were known for producing various vintages in the 17th century. Although the area has been transformed into an upscale, residential neighborhood with tree-lined streets and several parks, it offers grape-lovers plenty of wine bars and shops. Drop by the Dvořák Museum, housed in a red-and-yellow baroque villa, to view the piano, viola, scores, photos, and memorabilia of the 19th-century Czech composer. Later, walk over to Náměstí Míru (Peace Square) for a peek at the neo-Gothic Church of St. Ludmila and its twin 200-foot-high octagonal spires. Just to the left of the front doors of the church is the Vinohrady Theater, topped by two massive statues symbolizing drama and opera. Cafés and restaurants abound in this neighborhood, and you shouldn't hesitate to sit down and soak in some of the atmosphere while you are walking around.

Vyšehrad

Upriver from the Charles Bridge, the compact district Vyšehrad is known for its castle that sits perched above the Vltava's waters. A cemetary holding the nation's finest writers, composers, and artists is on the grounds and well worth a look, as are the stunning views from the castle's ramparts. Below the walls, near the waterfront, are several Cubist homes.

Žižkov

This working-class area supposedly has more bars than any other Prague neighborhood. Check out the rocketlike TV tower and its enormous metal babies—constructed by a local artist—climbing the pillars. A high-speed elevator brings you to a viewing platform, affording a bird's-eye view of the city and of massive courtyards not seen from street level. Afterward, head to the top of Vítkov hill to see the largest equestrian statue in the world, a bronze horse with the one-eyed General Jan Žiža, who led the Hussites to victory in 1420 over the emperor's Catholic crusaders. Though it's been cleaned up in recent years, there are still some gritty areas; you can also find several of the more reasonably priced hotels in this quarter.

Other Neighborhoods

Dejvice, home to some of the city's largest and most impressive villas, and **Střešovice** are suburbs to the north and west of the main part of the city; and a few hotels in these neighborhoods are near the Metro lines and may be attractive to those primarily interested in saving money and willing to take a long Metro ride into town. **Libeň** and **Stodůlky** are eastern suburbs and also have a few lodging options that are still reachable by public transportation. **Zličín** is a rather distant suburb, but it's the place to head if you want to see a real suburban-style mall (and Prague's large Ikea store); it's at the end of the city's B Metro line. **Troja** is north of the city, where you can find the Prague zoo and the Troja Château. **Nusle,** in the southern valley, is where you'll find the Nusle Bridge, a 1970s structure that helps link the southern and eastern housing blocs to the center. **Karlín,** on the east bank of the Vltava and hit hard by the 2002 floods, quickly recovered. Other neighborhoods where tourists sometimes end up include **Bohnice, Bubeneč, Vršovice,** and **Vysočansky.**

If You Have 3 Days

If you have only three days to spend in Prague, you'll probably not want to stray far. The city has plenty to keep you busy for a short trip, and three days will give you time to explore the beauties and wonders of the Old Town, New Town, Malá Strana, and Hradčany.

Day 1: On the first day—particularly if your plane lands early—beat the crowds and get an early start to Prague Castle, whose grounds contains the towering St. Vitus's Cathedral and the Golden Lane, a row of miniscule cottages built along one of the Castle's walls. Later, relax in the nearby Royal Gardens.

Day 2: On the second day, be sure to take in the sights on Old Town Square, including the Astronomical Clock and the Gothic Church of Our Lady before Týn. Climb to the top of the clock tower for a commanding view of the area. If you have time afterward, explore the streets that radiate from the square or take a walk down Wenceslas Square.

Day 3: On the third day, walk across the baroque, statue-adorned Charles Bridge on your way to Malá Strana, home to numerous embassies and palaces; the bridge is less busy early in the morning, so head there early if you want to take some pictures without crowds of people. In the Church of Our Lady Victorious be sure to see an odd effigy, the Holy Infant of Prague, a wax doll dressed in ceremonial garb. Legend holds that the figure has performed miraculous cures.

If You Have 7 Days

Plan to spend three full days exploring Prague, as suggested above. You can easily spend a day each in the Old Town, Malá Strana, and Hradčany.

Day 4: For an easy day-trip, visit the well-preserved medieval mining town of Kutná Hora, whose rich deposits of silver put it on the map in the 13th century. Tours of the mines, which were once the deepest in the country, offer a respite from the summer heat. The St. Barbara Church, built with the miner's donations and named after their patron saint, has many colorful murals depicting mining scenes; outside, the Gothic structure's three tent-shape spires rise above lines of flying buttresses. Be sure to save time either before or after Kutna Hora to visit the suburb of Sedlec to see the eerie Bone Church; since the train from Prague stops first in Sedlec, it often makes sense to see the Bone Church first, and then head into town for some touring and lunch.

Day 5: Take a trip to southern Bohemia to soak up the Renaissance charm of Český Krumlov, which is surely one of the most beautiful cities in the Czech Republic. Built around loops of the Vltava River, the town is listed as second in importance on UNESCO's list of World Heritage Sites, behind only Venice. Keep an eye out for the Mansion Tower, a spectacular green-and-pink Renaissance structure that juts into the sky. Take a hike up to Hrad Krumlov, the castle towering above the city's streets. At times the number of tourists can be a bit overwhelming, but you'll understand once you set foot in this lovely city. Although your time in the Czech Republic is short, for a less frenetic pace, you can spend the night, which might be recommendable if you take public transportation, which can take more than three hours each way from Prague.

Day 6: If you decided to spend the night in Český Krumlov, spend some extra hours strolling and shopping in the morning before you head back to Prague. If you returned to Prague last night, take a half-day to travel to 14th-century Karlštejn Castle. You can make an easy half-day trip of it if you leave fairly early in the morning, and then you'll have the afternoon to stroll and shop when you return to Prague.

Day 7: If you aren't yet tired of traveling, take a day-trip to see one of the Czech Republic's best spa towns, Karlovy Vary in Western Bohemia, which is one of the most famous spa destinations in Europe. Check out the historic city center and then take a soak in the thermal waters before you head back to Prague for the night.

If You Have 10 Days

In a country with as many amazing historical sights and as much natural beauty as the Czech Republic, having 10 days to explore will keep your eyes and feet busy. When you are ready to leave Prague and head south, consider a rental car so that you can see a bit more of the countryside than you would if you limited yourself to trains and buses. Use the itineraries below to keep you on track as you discover what the nation has to offer. Spend your first five days touring Prague, Kutná Hora, and Karlstejn Castle.

Day 6: Visit the former Nazi holding camp at Terezín, established in 1941. The town's quiet streets are a chilling reminder of the 140,000 men, women and children held here, most of whom were later sent to death camps. Red Cross officials visited Terezín twice, only to be fooled by the Nazis, who had set up a staged, flourishing Jewish community. Wittman Tours, a company that specializes in touring Jewish historical sights in the Czech Republic, operates good day-long bus tours of Terezín from Prague, or you can easily do it yourself on the train or bus.

Day 7: Now it's time to head south to Cěský Krumlov. If you've rented a car, you can make the trip in about two hours; by train or bus, it's going to be more like three or more hours. Certainly spend the night here after touring so that you can enjoy walking the quieter streets tomorrow morning.

Day 8: Take a trip to Tábor, which was founded by religious radicals in 1420. Be sure to purchase a map, as the town's labyrinthine layout—designed to confuse enemies—can have you walking in circles. Drop down into the tunnels that run beneath the main square for an interesting take on the town from the bottom up. Spend tonight in one of Tábor's small pensions, or if you are doing the trip by public transit, you can return to Prague for the night.

Day 9: This morning, you have a choice to make, and this is where a car will give you more options. You could head west to take the waters in the spa town Karlovy Vary, where the springs are reputed to help cure digestive disorders. The town is known not only for its water, but also for Moser glass and fine china. For a chance at celebrity-spotting, visit the town in July during the annual Karlovy Vary Film Festival. Or you might head east toward Moravia to do some spelunking in the Moravian caves. Make your way to the Punkevní jeskyně, one of the largest in the country. But be careful not to fall into the Macocha Abyss, a 459-foot-deep hole formed, partly, by the collapse of the ceiling of a cave. If you're using public transit, you need to rise early and take a bus to Brno, then catch a train to nearby Blansko. From there, local buses run to the caves. Either way, an overnight stay will be in order.

Day 10: How you spend your last day in the Czech Republic will depend on the choice you made on Day 9. If you went to Karlovy Vary, you can sleep in before heading back to Prague. If you're driving, consider a stop to see towering Střkov Castle or the moving memorial at Lidice. If you went west, you might wish to make a short detour to Telč, which has an impressive Gothic and Renaissance main square as well as an interesting château. Either way, plan to arrive in Prague in time to drop off your rental car and have a relaxing dinner before your flight home tomorrow.

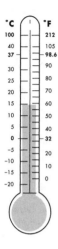

Prague is beautiful year-round, but it's busiest in summer and during the Christmas and Easter holidays. Spring offers generally good weather with a more relaxed level of tourism, as flowers are blossoming, historical sights are open longer, and the Prague Spring Music Festival is in full swing. During the busy Easter season you can watch a ritual with pagan roots, in which men with willow branches strike women in order to keep them fertile; the women reply by splashing their tormentors with water. When fall arrives, trees take on red-and-gold hues, and Czechs head to the woods to pick their beloved mushrooms. In winter you encounter fewer visitors and find much cheaper hotels; you also have the opportunity to see Prague breathtakingly covered in snow, but it can get very cold and dark, as the sun tends to set by 5, and many days are overcast. Also, some castles and museums outside Prague close for the season. January and February generally bring the best skiing in Bohemia's mountains—and great difficulty in finding a room. If you're not a skier, try visiting the mountains in late spring (April or May) or fall, when the colors are dazzling and you have the hotels and restaurants nearly to yourself. In much of the rest of Bohemia and Moravia, even in midsummer, the number of visitors is far smaller than in Prague, and trips to the towns that dot the countryside can be a welcome break from the long lines and crowded areas of the Golden City.

Climate

The Czech Republic is known for its breathtaking historical sights and not its weather—and for good reason. Winters can be bone-chillingly cold, with dark, overcast days. The maximum average temperature in December and January is 32° F, and temperatures frequently drop to the low 20s F. Things brighten up considerably in the spring and summer seasons. The days peak in July with around 10 hours of sunshine per day. Showers are infrequent and usually light and short, while temperatures hover in the high 70s F. Fall brings with it fewer crowds and slightly cooler temperatures in the 60s F, as well as a riotous display of color on the foliage in parts of the city and countryside.

PRAGUE

Jan.	36F	2C	May	66F	19C	Sept.	68F	20C
	25	– 4		46	8		50	10
Feb.	37F	3C	June	72F	22C	Oct.	55F	13C
	27	– 3		52	11		41	5
Mar.	46F	8C	July	75F	24C	Nov.	46F	8C
	32	0		55	13		36	2
Apr.	58F	14C	Aug.	73F	23C	Dec.	37F	3C
	39	4		55	13		28	– 2

The top seasonal events in Prague and the rest of the Czech Republic are listed below, and any one of them could provide the stuff of lasting memories. For contact information about most of these festivals, inquire at the Prague Tourist office or the local visitor information centers.

ONGOING

Late Feb.–late Mar.

Prague holds the St. Matthew's Fair, an annual children's fair at the Výstaviště exhibition grounds. It opens on St. Matthew's day February 24 and runs for most of the next four weeks. An ancient traditional fair has now been replaced by a giant fun fair, which occupies a large space in the Prague exhibition grounds. Come here for every variety of noisy mechanical fairground attraction. The flashing lights and volume of noise will satisfy the most demanding of children who will also want to buy from the eye-catching selection of sweet and refreshment stalls.

July–Sept.

The old stone walls and ramparts surrounding the courtyard of the Old Burgrave's Hall in Prague Castle create the perfect backdrop for the Letní shakespearovské slavnosti (Summer Shakespeare Festival), which includes several evenings of open-air Shakespeare performances. Drawing on the talents of many performers from Prague's professional theaters, the festival company usually presents two plays during the three-month season. Performances begin at 8:30.

WINTER

Dec. 5

One of the most important celebrations in Prague is the Eve of the Festival of St. Nicolas. Beginning in the late afternoon and continuing throughout the rest of the evening, this is one of the main Christmas-season celebrations in Prague. Although activities are focused mainly around the Old Town Square, you can find that Mikuláš and his entourage will also be at most of the Christmas markets, street corners, and even on the metro. This is the evening when small children are brought out to meet the jolly, white-bearded saint himself and his accompanying angels and sometimes terrifying devils. If they have been good, then the angels reward them with some sweets from their baskets, but if they have been bad, a devil may well try to take them away in a sack. All this provides as much fun for the grown-ups as it does for the kids, and the surrounding cacophony of fire crackers and the intoxicating bouquet of mulled wine helps make it a festive evening.

Late Jan.

Prague hosts the FebioFest International Film, Television & Video Festival at the end of January, which lasts for about 10 days. The festival has grown into an extremely popular and wide-ranging celebration of international film. Special prices at several main cinemas pull in the crowds to every event. Throughout the festival, films are shown from mid-morning to well past midnight, and the range on offer is vast. From Third-World art films to cult blockbusters, you find just about every kind of movie. Old black-and-white films jostle for attention with the latest lesbian or gay frivolity. Most venues offer a simultaneous translation into English at each showing. A detailed guide is available, and advance booking is a good idea since lines can be long.

Feb.	The Best of Czech Opera Festival, a bi-annual festival in odd-numbered years, provides opera lovers with an unparalleled opportunity to experience the full range of Czech operatic theater productions. For two weeks Prague's opera houses play host to the country's many regional companies, who relish this chance to bring their best productions and artists to the capital. This gives a chance to everybody to shine, and the final concert evening sees the presentation of several respected awards for operatic achievement. The repertoire varies from the familiar to the frankly obscure.

SPRING

Mar.	Prague and Brno jointly host the Days of European Film, an 11-day film festival focusing on the latest European releases.
Late Mar.	English-language and world authors appear at the Prague Writers' Festival, a four-day celebration of the written word that draws international writers for a series of readings and literary discussions.
Apr.	Eastertime brings two festivals of sacred music to Prague, Musica Ecumenica and Musica Sacra Praga.
Apr.	Brno puts on an Easter Spiritual Music Festival each year during Easter week.
May	The annual Prague Spring International Music Festival is undoubtedly the most significant cultural festival of the year. Opening with the customary performance of Smetana's "Má vlast" on the anniversary of the composer's death, the festival presents three weeks of world-class music-making throughout Prague. Internationally renowned performers gather in Prague's magnificent concert halls and churches to play music from the entire classical repertoire. Tickets are in high demand, but prices are relatively modest, and there are usually some seats available on most performance days.
Late May	Thousands of runners fill the city's streets for the Prague Marathon, which tends to draw a wide, international group of long-distance runners.

SUMMER

June	The international dance festival Tanec Praha hits the capital and brings together important representatives in European contemporary dance to a variety of venues throughout the city. This gathering of young

	dancers creates a heady atmosphere for those whose interest is in the modern dance form and it's a chance to compare the various styles of performances now in vogue.
Mid-June–mid-Aug.	The **Janáček Festival of Music** takes place in Olomouc each summer at Hukvaldy Castle. Janáček's birthplace (still preserved) provides the peg on which to hang a richly varied annual festival of music making. Naturally enough, the Master's own works are a chief feature, but performers are drawn from around the country. In addition to concerts, there are visiting drama and opera companies.
Late Aug.	Prague's two-week **Verdi Festival** is always staged at the State Opera and showcases performances of several of the master's operas during a two-week period starting in mid-August.
FALL	
Mid-Sept.	The two-week **Prague Autumn International Music Festival** is the last major European music festival of the summer season. It's a chance to see a wide range of international performers and orchestras perform a range of Czech and international music.
Late Oct.	An early fall highlight is always the **International Jazz Festival,** a weeklong series of performances by international jazz artists.
Nov.	Prague stokes the cultural fires against the approach of winter with the **Czech Press Photo Exhibition.** An exciting variety of work from the professional lenses of the many Czech photographers is always on display at this large photography exhibition. The aim is to stimulate press photographers to do work beyond their normal realm, and the results are usually well worth watching. A jury of top professionals awards prizes.
Nov.	Jewish musical groups gather from all over the world for the month-long **Musica Iudaica International Music Festival,** a festival of Jewish music.

PLEASURES & PASTIMES

Bicycling Czechs are avid cyclists, and it's not uncommon to see a cyclist, dressed in a store-bought team jersey, pedaling like mad to stay out of the way of Prague's notoriously bad drivers. The flatter areas of southern Bohemia and Moravia are ideal for biking. Outside the larger towns, quiet roads stretch for miles. The hillier terrain of northern Bohemia makes it popular with mountain-biking enthusiasts. Not many places rent bikes, though.

Boating & Sailing The country's main boating area is the enormous series of dams and reservoirs along the Vltava south of Prague. The most popular reservoir is Slapy, an hour's drive due south of the capital, where it's possible to rent small paddleboats or relax and swim on a hot day. Rowboats are available for rent along Prague's Vltava in summertime.

Castles & Châteaux More than 2,000 castles, manor houses, and châteaux collectively form a precious and not-to-be-missed part of the country's cultural and historical heritage. Grim ruins glower from craggy hilltops, and fantastical Gothic castles guard ancient trade routes. Hundreds of noble houses—Renaissance, baroque, and Empire—dot the countryside. Their former bourgeois and aristocratic owners were expelled in the anti-German reaction of 1945–46 or forced out by the Communists. Today, many of their valuable old seats stand in near ruin, and just as many more have been returned to the care of the original owners. Others remain in state hands as museums, homes for the elderly, or conference centers. More sights than ever are now open to the public. Picture galleries, rooms full of historic furniture, exquisite medieval stonework, and baroque chapels—all speak of a vanished way of life whose remnants survive in every town and village of Bohemia and Moravia. Within Prague itself, Malá Strana is home to numerous palaces and stately embassies.

Dining The quality of restaurant cuisine and service is increasingly improving as more variety and competition arrives on the dining scene. Pizza, still thought of in some places in the city—and many in the countryside—to be made of ketchup and cheese, is now available with true marinara sauce and with a wide range of flavors and toppings. In the capital, where hundreds of restaurants compete for an increasingly discriminating international clientele, a good restaurant can usually be found by simply observing whether or not the place is packed, as those not up to snuff contain only lonely, chain-smoking staff. The traditional dishes—roast pork or duck with dumplings, or broiled meat with sauce—can be light and tasty when well prepared. Grilled pond trout appears on most menus and is often excellent. However, you're not limited to eating only Czech specialties, as the city contains international cuisine such as French, Cuban, Pakistani, Italian, and many others. Restaurants generally fall into three categories. A *pivnice* or *hospoda* (beer hall) usually offers a simple, inexpensive menu of goulash or pork with dumplings. The atmosphere tends to be friendly and casual, and you can expect to share a table. More attractive, and more expensive, are the *vinárna* (wine cellars) and the *restaurace* (restaurants), which serve a full menu. Wine cellars, some occupying Romanesque basements, can be a real treat. Ignoring the familiar fast-food outlets that are now a common sight, the quickest and cheapest dining option is the *lahůdky* (snack bar or deli). In larger towns, the *kavárna* (café) and *čajovna* (teahouse) are ever more popular—and welcome—additions to the dining scene.

Hiking

The Czech Republic has 40,000 km (25,000 mi) of well-kept, -marked, and -signposted trails both in the mountainous regions and leading through beautiful countryside from town to town. The most scenic areas are the Beskydy range in northern Moravia and the Krkonoše range (Giant Mountains) in northern Bohemia. The rolling Šumava hills of southern Bohemia are also excellent hiking territory, and the environment there is the purest in the country. You can find colored markings denoting trails on trees, fences, walls, rocks, and elsewhere. The main paths are marked in red, others in blue and green, while the least important trails are marked in yellow. Hiking maps can be found in almost any bookstore; look for the large-scale *Soubor turistických* maps. Within Prague, parks such as Stromovka or Divoká Sarka, offer numerous trails and beautiful, tree-laden scenery; the latter also contains a swimming pool.

Shopping

In Prague, Karlovy Vary, and elsewhere in Bohemia, look for elegant and unusual crystal and porcelain. Bohemia is also renowned for the quality and deep-red color of its garnets; keep an eye out for beautiful garnet rings and brooches. You can also find excellent ceramics, especially in Moravia, as well as other folk artifacts, such as printed textiles, lace, hand-knit sweaters, and painted eggs. There are attractive crafts stores throughout the Czech Republic. In Karlovy Vary buy the strange pipelike drinking mugs used in the spas; vases left to petrify in the mineral-laden water; and Becherovka, a tasty herbal aperitif that makes a nice gift to take home.

Skiing

The two main skiing areas in the Czech Republic are the Giant Mountains in northern Bohemia and, especially for cross-country skiing, the Šumava hills of southern Bohemia. Lifts operate from January through March. In both areas you can find a number of organizations renting skis—although supplies may be limited and lines may be long.

Wine & Beer

Czechs are reputed to drink more beer per capita than any other people on earth; small wonder, as many connoisseurs rank Bohemian lager-style beer as the best in the world. This cool, crisp brew was invented in Plzeň in 1842, although Czech beer had already been brewed for centuries prior to that time. Aside from the world-famous Plzeňský Prazdroj (Pilsner

Urquell) and milder Budvar (the original Budweiser) brands, some typical beers are the slightly bitter Krušovice; the fruity Radegast; and the sweeter, Prague-brewed Staropramen. *Světlé pivo,* or light beer, is most common, although many pubs also serve *černé* (dark), which is often slightly sweeter than the light variety.

Czechs also produce quite drinkable wines: peppy, fruity whites and mild, versatile reds. Southern Moravia, with comparatively warm summers and rich soil, grows the bulk of the wine harvest. Look for the Mikulov and Znojmo regional designations. Favorite white varietals are Müller-Thurgau, with a fine muscat bouquet and light flavor, and Neuburské, yellow-green in color and with a dry, smoky bouquet. Rulandské bílé, a semidry burgundylike white, has a flowery bouquet and full-bodied flavor. Belying the notion that northerly climes are more auspicious for white than red grapes, northern Bohemia's scant few hundred acres of vineyards produce reliable reds and the occasional jewel. Frankovka is fiery red and slightly acidic, while the cherry-red Rulandské červené is an excellent, drier choice. Vavřinecké is dark and slightly sweet.

FODOR'S CHOICE

LODGING

$$$$	**Andel's Hotel Prague,** Smíchov. Modern, minimalist chic abounds at one of the city's trendiest hostelries, which is right next to the city's biggest mall.
$$$$	**Aria Hotel,** Malá Strana. The bland façade simply does not prepare you for Prague's best luxury boutique hotel, which has the city's best hotel view from its rooftop terrace.
$$$$	**Carlo IV,** Nové Město. Once you get past the snooty front-desk clerks, you'll discover one of the city's most beautiful hotels—inside and out—and an attention to detail that makes your experience memorable.
$$$$	**Hotel Palace Praha,** Nové Město. This coveted address for the well-heeled is also one of Prague's most conveniently located hotels.
$$–$$$	**Grandhotel Pupp,** Karlovy Vary. The hotel of choice for movie stars during the Karlovy Vary film festival will make nonactors will feel like royalty as well by the well-appointed rooms, attentive staff, and lush surroundings.
$$–$$$	**Hotel Růže,** Česky Krumlov. An excellent hotel now, the building was once a Renaissance-era monastery; some of the tastefully decorated rooms have drop-dead views of the castle.
$$$	**Romantik Hotel U Raka,** Hradčany. This small guesthouse in the ancient, winding streets of Nový Svét is an ideal romantic retreat, and it's even within walking distance of Prague Castle.
$$	**Hotel Roma,** Malá Strana. In a city where fair rates are often a laughable notion, the Roma is actually worth the price, making it Prague's best moderately priced hotel.
$$	**Tři Lilie,** Františkovy Lázně. This sanitorium and hotel has what few hotels in the country have—air conditioning. As if that wasn't reason enough to stay, the hotel is centrally located in lovely Františkovy Lázně, a less frenetic alternative to Karlovy Vary.
$	**Hotel Embassy,** Karlovy Vary. The intimate setting and personal service make this less grand alternative to Karlovy Vary's Grandhotel Pupp an equally enchanting place to stay.
¢	**Pension 189 Karel Bican,** Tábor. You'd be hard-pressed to find a nicer pension in southern Bohemia than this family-run gem, where the

level of comfort far exceeds what you might expect for the modest pricetag.

RESTAURANTS

$$$$ | **Kampa Park,** Malá Strana. The rich and famous have all dined here, and for good reason: a wonderful view of the Charles Bridge and stupendous, contemporary cuisine.

$$$–$$$$ | **C'est La Vie,** Malá Strana. Excellent restaurants seem to sprout up everywhere in Kampa, and this one, with an inviting stone terrace next to the Vltava, is no exception; the menu blends ingredients and cooking styles from France and Asia.

$$–$$$$ | **Allegro,** Staré Město. The Four Seasons Hotel's Italian restaurant is simply one of the best in the entire Czech Republic. Try to get a seat on the outdoor terrace if it's open.

$$–$$$$ | **Pravda,** Josefov. One of Prague's slick, Asian-inspired bistros, this upscale restaurant in the city's old Jewish quarter is even better than when it first opened.

$$–$$$$ | **Zahrada v opeře,** Nové Město. A romantic setting and a menu that blends delicious, creative cuisine with fair prices, is a combination that's hard to beat in Prague.

$–$$ | **Kavárna Slavia,** Staré Město. Prague's most famous café nurtured the souls of dissident writers and musicians during the dark Communist period; it's no wonder, since it has one of the best views in town. The food's good, too, which is an added bonus.

¢–$ | **Na Louži,** Český Krumlov. This pub is your best bet for a simple, satisfying meal in Česky Krumlov.

PERFORMING ARTS

Archa Theater, Nové Město. Prague's main venue for modern theater, dance, and music, the Archa also presents some performances in English; others are English-friendly.

Národní divadlo, Nové Město. A symbol of the country's cultural revival, the National Theater, dominates the bank of the river on which it stands. Its star-studded roof represents the peak all artists should strive for.

Rudolfinum, Staré Město. The neo-Renaissance performance space has excellent acoustics and hosts the Czech Philharmonic.

NIGHTLIFE

AghaRTA, Nové Město. Though small, this is one of the best places in the city to see local jazz acts.

Pivovarský dům, Nové Město. Many brewpubs in Prague are more historic; few are better.

Roxy, Staré Město. Part performance space, part nightclub, Roxy is one of the best clubs in the city for live music.

SHOPPING

Art Deco Gallery Shop, Malá Strana. Although tiny, this shop is one of the city's best resources for art-deco antiques.

Artěl, Vinohrady. The American owner of this store produces pieces that are a combination of modern and antique.

Klára Nademlýnská, Staré Město. The fashionable clothes from this popular Czech designer can be both funky and conservative; costume-jewelry designs are inexpensive and good.

Qubus Design, Staré Město. Shop here only if you are looking for the best and latest Czech innovations in design for the home.

Swarovksi Bohemia, Staré Město. Beautiful but still mid-range crystal jewelry is the staple in this small store.

Tatiana, Staré Město. This designer's specialty is sexy evening and party wear, plus great accessories.

CHURCHES & RELIGIOUS BUILDINGS

Bazilika svatého Jiří, Pražský Hrad. The best-preserved Romanesque relic in the country, St. George's Basilica, looks much as it did following a remodeling in the 12th century. The structure's golden yellow walls and small arched windows create a peaceful place in which to take a break from the city outside.

Chrám svaté Barbory, Kutná Hora. This three-peaked Gothic church is one of Bohemia's most striking.

Chrám svatého Mikuláše, Malá Strana. A religious experience in every sense of the term, St. Nicholas's Church is one of Europe's great tributes to high baroque.

Chrám svatého Víta, Pražský Hrad. The spiritual heart of Prague, the Gothic St. Vitus's Cathedral, stands proudly over the grounds of the castle. At night, floodlights on the looming structure give viewers the impression that the spires of the building are floating above the river and city below.

Kostel Sv. Mikuláše, Hradčany. Lit up at night or in daylight, the Baroque, dome-topped St. Nicholas Church stands tall over the rest of the surrounding buildings in Hradčany. Drop inside for a look at its lurid, colorful interior adorned with flying golden angels and other vivid decorations.

Kostnice, Sedlec. Almost every surface in this eerie church—one of the Czech Republic's most ghoulish landmarks—is covered with human bones.

Hřbitov, Vyšehrad. The Vyšehrad Cemetary contains some of the country's best-known artists, writers and musicians. The elaborate monuments and intricate headstones are works of art in their own right.

Karlův most, Staré Město. Take a five-minute stroll or spend hours exploring Prague's religious and social history on the Charles Bridge. Particularly magical at night, when the crowds have thinned and the city lights are shimmering on the river.

Královská zahrada, Pražský Hrad. A good place to rest your feet is in the Royal Gardens just below Prague Castle. Dotted with statues and Renaissance-era structures, the sloping lawns give a commanding view of Prague.

Morový sloup, Olomouc. This towering plague column is the finest example of the Olomouc baroque style and dates to the early 18th century.

Obecní dům, Staré Město. A grand monument to art nouveau, lavishly ornate inside and out, with the marvelous contrast of the attached Gothic Prašná brána (Powder Tower).

Pilsner Urquell Brewery, Plzeň. Get some respect from the Czechs by learning a bit about brewing culture. After the tour, drop into a local pub and engage the locals in a debate over what brand is the finest. Be prepared to sample the full range of the nation's beer stock before your opinion will be taken seriously.

Staroměstské náměstí, Staré Město. For a one-stop combination of architecture, history, and sheer spectacle, there's no better place in the entire country than Prage's Old Town Square.

Starý židovský hřbitov, Josefov. A sobering and unforgettable sight, Prague's Old Jewish Cemetery, marks centuries of discrimination and, ultimately, triumph over adversity.

Château Lednice na Moravé, Lednice. This extravagant neo-Gothic château, built by the Liechtensteins in the late 18th century was long neglected by the Communists; it is now being magnificently restored and has been a World Heritage Site since 1996.

Český Šternberk. One of the country's great Gothic castles is still inhabited by its namesake owners, making it less of a museum piece than you are likely to see anywhere else.

Hluboká nad Vltavou. If you think this castle, which was built by the Schwarzenberg family, looks familiar, it may be becuase it was modeled closely on Windsor Castle, the home of the British royal family near London.

Kroměříž Châteaux. The former summer palace of the archbishop of Olomoc is one of the country's most opulent; its gardens are among the finest you'll see in Central Europe.

Villa Tugendhat, Brno. This cool, modernist structure was designed by Bauhaus architect Ludwig Mies van der Rohe. Though it's still in the midst of a long-term renovation project, you'll definitely appreciate the chance to peak inside.

Zámek Konopiště, Benešov. The summer residence of the Hapsburg's has an impressive interior, and an especially impressive taxidermy collection, a monument to Archduke Franz Ferdinand.

MUSEUMS

Lobkovický palác, Pražský Hrad. An overview of Czech history from the nation's beginning to the mid-19th century can be found at the Lobkowicz Palace. Copies of the crown jewels are on display, but it's the vast collection of Bibles, coins, weapons, royal decrees, paintings, and statues that stand out.

SPORTS & THE OUTDOORS

Cybex, Karlín. The Prague Hilton's health club is the city's best; it also has one of the best day spas for pampering.

HC Sparta Praha. Prague's favorite hockey team still draws the best young players.

Jelení skok, Karlovy Vary. Western Bohemia's most famous spa town offers nature lovers plenty of hiking trails; a great overview can be had at Jelení skok (Stag's Leap), where you will find the symbol of the town—a bronze statue of a deer perched on an outcropping.

Punkevní jeskyně, Skalní mlýn. Whether you are a spelunker or not, you'll enjoy this magnificent cave in the Moravian Karst, which includes the deepest river in the region, on which you can take a boat trip.

SMART TRAVEL TIPS

Finding out about your destination before you leave home means you won't squander time organizing everyday minutiae once you've arrived. You'll be more streetwise when you hit the ground as well, better prepared to explore the aspects of Prague that drew you here in the first place. The organizations in this section can provide information to supplement this guide; contact them for up-to-the-minute details, and consult the A to Z sections that end the side trips chapters for facts on the various topics as they relate to the areas around Prague and the rest of the Czech Republic. Happy landings!

ADDRESSES

Prague is divided into 10 postal districts, with the most popular tourist attractions being mostly in Prague 1 (the city center, which includes the Old Town, much of the New Town, and Mala Strana), Prague 2 (the area south of the city center), and Prague 3 (the area east of the city center). Residents often refer to the districts to orient themselves geographically ("x is in Prague 1" or "y is in Prague 7"), but the more useful (and specific) neighborhood names also appear on many street corners.

Navigating Prague is relatively simple once you know some basic vocabulary: *ulice* (street, abbreviated to ul., commonly dropped in printed addresses); *náměstí* (square, abbreviated to nám.); and *třída* (avenue). In most towns, each building has two numbers, a confusing practice with historic roots. In Prague, the blue tags mark the street address (usually); in Brno, ignore the blue tags and go by the white ones. The European custom of naming streets conforms to no geographic method, and the names themselves reflect the importance of national figures. Street names usually appear on plaques mounted on the buildings at each intersection, so look up to find them as they are sometimes difficult to locate.

AIR TRAVEL TO & FROM PRAGUE

ČSA (Czech Airlines), the Czech national carrier, offers the only nonstop flights from the United States (from New York–JFK

Addresses
Air Travel to & from Prague
Airports & Transfers
Business Hours
Bus Travel in the Czech Republic
Car Rental
Car Travel
Children in Prague
Concierges
Consumer Protection
Customs & Duties
Disabilities & Accessibility
Discounts & Deals
Electricity
Embassies
Emergencies
English-Language Media
Etiquette & Behavior
Gay & Lesbian Travel
Health
Holidays
Insurance
Language
Mail & Shipping
Money Matters
Packing
Passports & Visas
Public Transit in Prague
Restrooms
Safety
Senior-Citizen Travel
Shopping
Sightseeing Tours
Taxes
Taxis
Telephones
Time
Tipping
Tours & Packages
Train Travel
Travel Agencies
Visitor Information
Web Sites

and Newark) to Prague, with six flights a week most times (daily flights during the busiest season). Most major U.S.-based airlines fly to Prague only through codeshare arrangements with their European counterparts. However, all the major European airlines fly there, so it's usually easy to connect through a major European airport (such as London–Heathrow, Amsterdam, or Vienna) and continue to Prague; indeed, flights between the U.K. and Prague are numerous and frequent, including some on very cheap discount airlines, though in London most of these leave from Gatwick or Stansted airports rather than Heathrow, making them less attractive options for Americans. Fares from the U.S. tend to rise dramatically during the busy summer season, particularly from June through August or September. There are many discounts during the slow winter months. Czech Airlines also flies to Ostrava and Karlovy Vary from Prague, though it's usually more cost-effective to drive or take a bus or train.

BOOKING

When you book, look for nonstop flights and remember that "direct" flights stop at least once. Try to avoid connecting flights, which require a change of plane. Two airlines may operate a connecting flight jointly, so ask whether your airline operates every segment of the trip; you may find that the carrier you prefer flies you only part of the way. To find more booking tips and to check prices and make online flight reservations, log on to www.fodors.com.

CARRIERS

🛪 To & From Prague **Aer Lingus** ☎ 221-667-407 in Prague, 800/474-7424 in U.S., 0845-084-4444 in U.K. ⊕ www.aerlingus.ie. **Air Canada** ☎ 888-247-2262 in Canada, 224-810-181 in Prague ⊕ www.aircanada.ca. **Air France** ☎ 221-662-662 in Prague, 800/237-2747 in U.S., 0845/084-5111 in U.K. ⊕ www.airfrance.com. **Alitalia** ☎ 221-629-150 in Prague, 800/223-5730 in U.S., 0870/544-8259 in U.K. ⊕ www.alitaliausa.com, in U.S.; www.alitalia.co.uk, in U.K. **American Airlines** ☎ 224-234-985 in Prague, 800/433-7300 in U.S., 0845/778-9789 in U.K. ⊕ www.aa.com. **Austrian Airlines** ☎ 220-116-272 in Prague, 800/843-0002 in U.S., 0870/1-242-625 in U.K. ⊕ www.austrianair.com, in U.S.; www.austrianairlines.co.uk, in U.K. **British Airways** ☎ 222-114-444 in Prague, 800/247-9297 in U.S., 0870/850-9850 in U.K. ⊕ www.britishairways.com. **BMI Baby** ☎ 0870/264-2229 in U.K. ⊕ www.bmibaby.com. **Continental** ☎ 221-665-133 in Prague, 800/231-0856 in U.S., 0845/607-6760 in U.K. ⊕ www.continental.com. **Czech Airlines ČSA** ☎ 239-007-007 in Prague, 800/223-2365 in U.S., 0870/4443-747 in U.K. ⊕ www.csa.cz. **Delta** ☎ 224-946-733 in Prague, 800/241-4141 in U.S., 0800/414-767 in U.K. ⊕ www.delta.com. **EasyJet** ⊕ www.easyjet.com. **Eurowings** ☎ 223-536-242 in Prague ⊕ www.eurowings.com. **Jet2** ☎ 0871-226-1-737 in U.K., 257-187-100 in Prague ⊕ www.jet2.com. **Finnair** ☎ 222-252-448 in Prague, 800/950-5000 in U.S., 0870/241-4411 in U.K. ⊕ www.finnair.com. **Germanwings** ☎ 800-142-287, 208-321-7255 in U.K. ⊕ www.germanwings.com. **KLM** ☎ 233-090-933 in Prague, 800/225-2525 in U.S., 0870/507-4074 in U.K. ⊕ www.klm.com. **LOT** ☎ 222-317-524 in Prague, 800/223-0593 in U.S., 0870-414-0088 in U.K. ⊕ www.lot.com. **Lufthansa** ☎ 220-114-456 in Prague, 800/645-3880 in U.S., 870/8377-747 in U.K. ⊕ www.lufthansa.com. **SAS** ☎ 220-116-031 in Prague, 800/221-2350 in U.S., 0870/607-27727 in U.K. ⊕ www.scandinavian.net. **Malév Hungarian Airlines** ☎ 224-224-471 in Prague, 212/566-9944 or 800/223-6884 in U.S., 870/909-0577 in U.K. ⊕ www.malev.hu. **Smart Wings** ☎ 00800-17-18-19-20 in Denmark, France, Italy, the Netherlands, Spain, Switzerland, and Prague ⊕ www.smartwings.net. **Swiss International Airline** ☎ 221-990-444 in Prague, 877/359-7947 in U.S., 0845/601-0956 in U.K. ⊕ www.swiss.com. **United** ☎ 800/538-2929 in U.S., 0845/844-4777 in U.K. ⊕ www.ual.com.

🛪 Within the Czech Republic **Aerotaxi** ☎ 286-922-774 in Prague ⊕ www.aerotaxisro.cz.

CHECK-IN & BOARDING

Always **find out your carrier's check-in policy.** Plan to arrive at the airport about two hours before your scheduled departure time for domestic flights and 2½ to 3 hours before international flights. You may need to arrive earlier if you're flying from one of the busier airports or during peak air-traffic times. To avoid delays at airport-security checkpoints, try not to wear any metal. Jewelry, belt and other buckles, steel-toe shoes, barrettes, and underwire bras are among the items that can set off detectors.

Assuming that not everyone with a ticket will show up, airlines routinely overbook planes. When everyone does, airlines ask for volunteers to give up their seats. In return, these volunteers usually get a several-hundred-dollar flight voucher, which can be used toward the purchase of another ticket, and are rebooked on the next flight out. If there are not enough volunteers, the airline must choose who will be denied boarding. The first to get bumped are passengers who checked in late and those flying on discounted tickets, so get to the gate and check in as early as possible, especially during peak periods.

Always **bring a government-issued photo ID** to the airport; even when it's not required, a passport is best.

CUTTING COSTS

The least expensive airfares to Prague are almost always on European budget carriers like EasyJet that fly from secondary airports. What this means for Americans is not only a change of airline but also a change of airports, so you must carefully consider whether flight connections can be timed so that you can transfer from one airport to another without an additional overnight stay. Consider both the money you will save by booking a cheaper airfare to London as well as a cheap airfare from London to Prague, but don't forget the cost of transferring from London–Heathrow, where almost all flights from the U.S. land at another of London's airports. Also consider limits on both carry-on and checked baggage, which are much more stringent on these budget carriers than they are on large international carriers. Other cheap flights are priced for round-trip travel and must usually be purchased in advance. Airlines generally allow you to change your return date for a fee; most low-fare tickets, however, are nonrefundable. It's smart to call a number of airlines and check the Internet; when you are quoted a good price, book it on the spot—the same fare may not be available the next day, or even the next hour. Always check different routings and look into using alternate airports. Also, price off-peak flights, which may be significantly less expensive than others. Travel agents, especially low-fare specialists (⇨ Discounts & Deals), are helpful.

Consolidators are another good source. They buy tickets for scheduled flights at reduced rates from the airlines, then sell them at prices that beat the best fare available directly from the airlines. Many also offer reduced car-rental and hotel rates. Sometimes you can even get your money back if you need to return the ticket. Carefully read the fine print detailing penalties for changes and cancellations, purchase the ticket with a credit card, and confirm your consolidator reservation with the airline.

🛩 Consolidators **AirlineConsolidator.com** ☎ 888/468-5385 ⊕ www.airlineconsolidator.com, for international tickets. **Best Fares** ☎ 800/880-1234 or 800/576-8255 ⊕ www.bestfares.com; $59.90 annual membership. **Cheap Tickets** ☎ 800/377-1000 or 800/652-4327 ⊕ www.cheaptickets.com. **Expedia** ☎ 800/397-3342 or 404/728-8787 ⊕ www.expedia.com. **Hotwire** ☎ 866/468-9473 or 920/330-9418 ⊕ www.hotwire.com. **Now Voyager Travel** ✉ 45 W. 21st St., Suite 5A New York, NY 10010 ☎ 212/459-1616 🖷 212/243-2711 ⊕ www.nowvoyagertravel.com. **Onetravel.com** ⊕ www.onetravel.com. **Orbitz** ☎ 888/656-4546 ⊕ www.orbitz.com. **Priceline.com** ⊕ www.priceline.com. **Travelocity** ☎ 888/709-5983, 877/282-2925 in Canada, 0870/876-3876 in U.K. ⊕ www.travelocity.com.

ENJOYING THE FLIGHT

State your seat preference when purchasing your ticket, and then repeat it when you confirm and when you check in. For more legroom, you can request one of the few emergency-aisle seats at check-in, if you're capable of moving obstacles comparable in weight to an airplane exit door (usually between 35 pounds and 60 pounds)—a Federal Aviation Administration requirement of passengers in these seats. Seats behind a bulkhead also offer more legroom, but they don't have underseat storage. Don't sit in the row in front of the emergency aisle or in front of a bulkhead, where seats may not recline.

Ask the airline whether a snack or meal is served on the flight. If you have dietary concerns, request special meals when booking. These can be vegetarian, low-cholesterol, or kosher, for example. It's a good idea to pack some healthful snacks and a small (plastic) bottle of water in your carry-on bag. On long flights, try to maintain a normal routine, to help fight jet lag. At night, get some sleep. By day, eat light meals, drink water (not alcohol), and **move around the cabin** to stretch your legs. For additional jet-lag tips consult *Fodor's FYI: Travel Fit & Healthy* (available at bookstores everywhere).

Smoking policies vary from carrier to carrier. Many airlines prohibit smoking on all of their flights; others allow smoking only on certain routes or certain departures. Ask your carrier about its policy.

FLYING TIMES

A nonstop flight from New York to Prague takes about 8 hours, but the entire trip can take considerably longer (12 to 14 hours, for example) if you must change planes in Europe. The flight from London to Prague takes about 2 hours; the flight from Vienna to Prague takes less than an hour.

HOW TO COMPLAIN

If your baggage goes astray or your flight goes awry, complain right away. Most carriers require that you **file a claim immediately.** The Aviation Consumer Protection Division of the Department of Transportation publishes *Fly-Rights,* which discusses airlines and consumer issues and is available online. You can also find articles and information on mytravelrights.com, the Web site of the nonprofit Consumer Travel Rights Center.

⨍ Airline Complaints **Aviation Consumer Protection Division** ⊠ U.S. Department of Transportation, Office of Aviation Enforcement and Proceedings, C-75, Room 4107, 400 7th St. SW, Washington, DC 20590 ☎ 202/366-2220 ⊕ airconsumer.ost.dot.gov. **Federal Aviation Administration Consumer Hotline** ⊠ for inquiries: FAA, 800 Independence Ave. SW, Washington, DC 20591 ☎ 800/322-7873 ⊕ www.faa.gov.

RECONFIRMING

Check the status of your flight before you leave for the airport. You can do this on your carrier's Web site by linking to a flight-status checker (many Web booking services offer these), or by calling your carrier or travel agent. Always confirm international flights at least 72 hours ahead of the scheduled departure time.

AIRPORTS & TRANSFERS

Ruzyně Airport is 20 km (12 mi) northwest of the downtown area. It's small but easily negotiated. A still-expanding main terminal has eased traffic flow. The trip to downtown is a straight shot down Evropská Boulevard and takes approximately 20 minutes. The road is not usually busy, but anticipate an additional 20 minutes during rush hour (7 AM–9 AM and 3 PM–6 PM). Brno and Ostrava airports handle domestic flights only. Karlovy Vary airport offers flights to Prague and Moscow.

⨍ Airport Information **Brno-Tuřany Airport** ☎ 545-521-310 ⊕ www.airport-brno.cz. **Karlovy Vary Airport** ☎ 353-360-611 ⊕ www.airport-k-vary.cz. **Ostrava Airport** ☎ 597-471-117 ⊕ www.airport-ostrava.cz. **Ruzyně Airport** ☎ 220-111-111 ⊕ www.csl.cz.

AIRPORT TRANSFERS

The Cedaz minibus shuttle links the airport with náměstí Republiky (Republic Square, just off the Old Town). It runs hourly, more often at peak periods, between 5:30 AM and 9:30 PM daily and makes an intermediate stop at the Dejvická metro station. The one-way fare is 90 Kč. You can also take a Cedaz minibus directly to your hotel for 370 Kč—650 Kč, which is sometimes less than the taxi fare. Regular municipal bus service (Bus 119) connects the airport and the Dejvická station; the fare is 12 Kč (15 Kč if purchased from the driver), and the ticket is transferrable to trams or the metro. From Dejvická you can take the metro to the city center. To reach Wenceslas Square, get off at the Můstek station.

The transportation company FIX has the monopoly on airport taxis, and these are your only choice if you want a taxi. Technically, though, these cars charge a fixed rate based on zones. The fees range from 120 Kč to 870 Kč for travel into the city. Be sure to find out how much it will cost—preferably in writing from their airport representative—before entering the car, because overcharging is a problem. The ride should cost 500 Kč–700 Kč.

You can call a taxi on your own; the rates might be a little cheaper than if you use a FIX car, but beware of dishonest taxi drivers. Prague Airport Shuttle offers offers transport to your hotel for a fixed price between 650 Kč and 1,200 Kč, depending on the number of passengers (1–8). The company promises to wait up to an hour from your originally scheduled arrival if your flight is delayed or if customs and immigration are slow. Reservations must be made advance via e-mail.

F Taxis & Shuttles **Cedaz** ☏ 220-114-296 ⊕ www. aas.cz/cedaz. **AAA Radiotaxi** ☏ 14014 ⊕ www. aaataxi.cz. **Prague Airport Shuttle** ☏ 602-395-421 ⊕ www.prague-airport-shuttle.com.

BUSINESS HOURS

BANKS & OFFICE

Though hours vary, most banks are open weekdays from 8 to 5. Private currency exchange offices usually have longer hours, and some are open all night.

GAS STATIONS

Gas stations on the main roads are open 24 hours a day.

MUSEUMS & SIGHTS

It used to be that many sights outside the large towns, including most castles, were open daily except Monday only from May through September and in April and October were open only on weekends. Lately the trend is toward a longer season, although off-season hours may change capriciously, and many places still close from November to March.

PHARMACIES

Though hours vary, most pharmacies are open from 8 to 5 on weekdays and from 8 to noon on Saturday. Opening hours are sometimes longer in Prague and Brno. Outside of Prague, every district town has a pharmacy open 24 hours.

SHOPS

Stores are open weekdays from 9 to 6. Some grocery stores open at 6 AM. Western-operated supermarkets are open much longer hours and on weekends; some larger supermarkets never close. Department stores often stay open until 7 PM. Outside Prague, most stores close for the weekend at noon on Saturday, although you can usually find a grocery open nights and weekends.

BUS TRAVEL IN THE CZECH REPUBLIC

The Czech complex of regional bus lines known collectively as ČSAD operates its dense network from the sprawling Florenc station. For information about routes and schedules, call, consult the confusingly displayed timetables posted at the station, or visit the information window in the lower level lobby, which is open daily from 6 AM to 9 PM. The company's Web site will give you bus and train information in English (click on the British flag).

F Bus Lines **ČSAD** Florenc station ✉ Křižíkova, Karl'n ☏ 900-144-444, 224-214-990 for route and schedule information ⊕ www.jizdnirady.cz **M** Line B and C: Florenc

CAMERAS & PHOTOGRAPHY

In general, people are pleased to be photographed, but ask first. Never photograph Gypsies, however colorful their attire, without explicit permission and payment clearly agreed upon. Photographing anything military, assuming you'd want to, is usually prohibited. The *Kodak Guide to Shooting Great Travel Pictures* (available at bookstores everywhere) is loaded with tips.

F Photo Help **Kodak Information Center** ☏ 800/242-2424 ⊕ www.kodak.com.

EQUIPMENT PRECAUTIONS

Don't pack film or equipment in checked luggage, where it is much more susceptible to damage. X-ray machines used to view checked luggage are extremely powerful and therefore are likely to ruin your film. Try to ask for hand inspection of film, which becomes clouded after repeated exposure to airport X-ray machines, and keep videotapes and computer disks away from metal detectors. Always keep film, tape, and computer disks out of the sun. Carry an extra supply of batteries, and be prepared to turn on your camera, camcorder, or laptop to prove to airport security personnel that the device is real.

FILM & DEVELOPING

Major brands of film are available in Prague, and 24-hour developing is the rule rather than the exception. The variable is cost—prices fluctuate widely from place to place.

VIDEOS & DVDS

Due to differing television systems, pre-recorded VHS tapes and DVDs bought in Central and Eastern Europe (which use the SECAM standard—the same one used in France) are not compatible with either U.S. machines (which use the NTSC standard) or British machines (which use the PAL standard). Generally, any blank tape may be used by your video recorder as the signal is laid down by your machine during recording, but the recording can only be played back on NTSC equipment, which is the U.S. standard.

CAR RENTAL

Several major agencies have offices at the airport and also in the city. Prices can differ greatly, so be sure to shop around. Major firms like Avis and Hertz offer Western makes starting at around $45 per day or $300 per week, which includes insurance, damage waiver, and V.A.T. (value-added tax); cars equipped with automatic transmission and air-conditioning are available, but are generally much more expensive. It's best to reserve your rental car before you leave home, and it may be less expensive as well. Smaller local companies, on the other hand, can rent Czech cars for significantly less, but the service and insurance coverage may be inferior. A surcharge of 5%–12% applies to rental cars picked up at Prague's Ruzyně Airport.

🚗 Major Agencies **Alamo** ☎ 800/522-9696 ⊕ www.alamo.com. **Avis** ☎ 800/331-1084, 800/879-2847 in Canada, 0870/606-0100 in U.K., 02/9353-9000 in Australia, 09/526-2847 in New Zealand ⊕ www.avis.com. **Budget** ☎ 800/527-0700, 0870/156-5656 in U.K. ⊕ www.budget.com. **Dollar** ☎ 800/800-6000, 0800/085-4578 in U.K. ⊕ www.dollar.com. **Hertz** ☎ 800/654-3001, 800/263-0600 in Canada, 0870/844-8844 in U.K., 02/9669-2444 in Australia, 09/256-8690 in New Zealand ⊕ www.hertz.com.

🚗 Local Offices **Alamo** ⊠ Ruzyně Airport, Ruzyně ☎ 220-114-554 ⊠ Masarykovo nábřezí 4, Nové Město ☎ 224-923-719. **Avis** ⊠ Ruzyně Airport, Ruzyně ☎ 235-362-420 ⊠ Klimentská 46, Nové Město ☎ 221-851-225. **Budget** ⊠ Ruzyně Airport, Ruzyně ☎ 220-113-253 ⊠ Hotel Inter-Continental, Nám. Curieových 5, Staré Město ☎ 602-165-108. **Europcar** ⊠ Ruzyně Airport, Ruzyně ☎ 235-364-531 ⊠ Pařížská 28, Staré Město ☎ 224-811-290

⊕ www.europcar.cz. **Hertz** ⊠ Ruzyně Airport, Ruzyně ☎ 233-324-714 ⊠ Karlovo nám. 28, Nové Město ☎ 222-231-010 ⊠ Diplomat Hotel, Evropská 15, Dejvice ☎ 224-394-174.

CUTTING COSTS

For a good deal, book through a travel agent who will shop around.

Do look into wholesalers, companies that do not own fleets but rent in bulk from those that do and often offer better rates than traditional car-rental operations. Prices are best during off-peak periods. Rentals booked through wholesalers often must be paid for before you leave home.

🚗 Wholesalers **Auto Europe** ☎ 207/842-2000 or 800/223-5555 🖶 207/842-2222 ⊕ www.autoeurope.com. **Destination Europe Resources** (DER) ⊠ 9501 W. Devon Ave., Rosemont, IL 60018 ☎ 800/782-2424 🖶 800/282-7474 ⊕ www.der.com. **Europe by Car** ☎ 212/581-3040 or 800/223-1516 🖶 212/246-1458 ⊕ www.europebycar.com. **Kemwel** ☎ 877/820-0668 or 800/678-0678 🖶 207/842-2147 ⊕ www.kemwel.com

INSURANCE

When driving a rented car you are generally responsible for any damage to or loss of the vehicle. Collision policies that car-rental companies sell for European rentals typically do not cover stolen vehicles. Before you rent—and purchase collision or theft coverage—see what coverage you already have under the terms of your personal auto-insurance policy and credit cards. Collision-damage waivers must be purchased in the Czech Republic, so car rentals are liable to be more expensive than in the West. It's advised to check that any advertised prices apply to visitors and not only locals.

REQUIREMENTS & RESTRICTIONS

Drivers from the U.S., Canada, U.K., Australia, and New Zealand need no international driving permit to rent a car in the Czech Republic, only a valid domestic license, along with the vehicle registration. If you intend to drive across a border, **ask about restrictions on driving into other countries.** The minimum age required for renting is usually 21 or older, and some companies also have maximum ages; be sure to inquire when making your arrangements. The Czech Republic requires that you will have held your driver's license for at least a year before you can rent a car.

SURCHARGES

Before you pick up a car in one city and leave it in another, ask about drop-off charges or one-way service fees, which can be substantial. Also inquire about early-return policies; some rental agencies charge extra if you return the car before the time specified in your contract while others give you a refund for the days not used. To avoid a hefty refueling fee, fill the tank just before you turn in the car, but be aware that gas stations near the rental outlet may overcharge. It's almost never a deal to buy the tank of gas that's in the car when you rent it; the understanding is that you'll return it empty, but some fuel usually remains.

CAR TRAVEL

Traveling by car is the easiest and most flexible way to see the Czech Republic; however, if you intend to visit only Prague, you can—and should—do without a car. The city center is congested and difficult to navigate, and you can save yourself a lot of hassle by sticking to public transportation.

A permit is required to drive on expressways and other four-lane highways. Permits cost 150 Kč for 10 days, 250 Kč for one month, and 900 Kč for one year and are sold at border crossings, some service stations, and all post offices.

EMERGENCY SERVICES

🚗 **Autoklub Bohemia Assistance** ☎ 1240 ⊕ www. aba.cz. **ÚAMK Emergency Roadside Assistance** ☎ 1230 ⊕ www.uamk.cz

GASOLINE

Gas stations are easy to come by on major thoroughfares and near large cities. Many are open around the clock. At least two grades of gasoline are sold, usually 90–93 octane (regular) and 94–98 octane (super). Lead-free gasoline is now available in most gas stations. The average cost of a gallon of gasoline is at least twice the cost of gasoline in the U.S.

PARKING

Parking is permitted in the city center on a growing number of streets with parking meters or in the few small lots within walking distance of the historic center—but parking spaces are scarce. A meter with a green stripe lets you park up to six hours; an orange-stripe meter gives you two. (Use change in the meters.) A sign with a blue circle outlined in red with a diagonal red slash indicates a no-parking zone. Avoid the blue-marked spaces, which are reserved for local residents. Violators may find a "boot" immobilizing their vehicle. If your hotel offers parking, you will have to pay a daily rate.

There's an underground lot at náměstí Jana Palacha, near Old Town Square. There are also park-and-ride (P+R) lots at some suburban metro stations, including Skalka (Line A), Zličín and Černý Most (Line B), and Nádraží Holešovice and Opatov (Line C).

ROAD CONDITIONS

The Prague city center is mostly a snarl of traffic, one-way cobblestone streets, and tram lines. If you plan to drive outside the capital, there are few four-lane highways, but most of the roads are in reasonably good shape, and traffic is usually light. Roads can be poorly marked, however, so before you start out, buy one of the inexpensive multilingual auto atlases available at any bookstore.

ROAD MAPS

In the Czech Republic, the ubiquitous 24-hour gas stations often sell road maps, or try a bookstore, such as Jan Kanzelsberger Bookshop, which has a good selection of hiking maps and auto atlases. The Kiwi bookstore specializes in selling maps.

🚗 **Jan Kanzelsberger Bookshop** ✉ Václavské nám. 42, Nové Město ☎ 224-217-335. **Kiwi** ✉ Jungmannova 23, Nové Město ☎ 224-948-455 ⊕ www.kiwick.cz.

RULES OF THE ROAD

The Czech Republic follows the usual Continental rules of the road. A right turn on red is permitted only when indicated by a green arrow. Signposts with yellow diamonds indicate a main road where drivers have the right of way. The speed limit is 130 kph (78 mph) on four-lane highways, 90 kph (56 mph) on open roads, and 50 kph (30 mph) in built-up areas. Seat belts are compulsory, and drinking before driving is absolutely prohibited. Passengers under 12 years of age, or less than 150 cm (5 feet) in height, must ride in the back seat.

CHILDREN IN PRAGUE

Children in the Czech republic generally receive considerate attention from their families and other grown-ups. However, this largely depends on the child's own sense of appropriate behavior. In public, Czech children are noticeably quiet, polite, and well-behaved. It is, therefore, seen as something of an anomaly if foreign children behave noisily or discourteously in public places and on public transport. Generally, restaurants are child-friendly.

If you are renting a car, don't forget to arrange for a car seat when you reserve. For general advice about traveling with children, consult *Fodor's FYI: Travel with Your Baby* (available in bookstores everywhere).

BABYSITTING

Tetty Childcare Agency offers a comprehensive child-care service, including babysitting, daily care, and special individual programs. It's an international nursery and preschool with a large number of qualified babysitters and child minders throughout Prague. Sweet Baby charges 150 Kč for the first three hours, and then 100 Kč for every hour thereafter. If you return after 10 PM you're obliged to pay for a taxi home for the babysitter. Generally, Prague babysitting agencies most frequently send young women or university students.

Agencies **Tetty** ✉ Muchova 11, Bubeneč ☎ 233-340-766. **Sweet Baby** ✉ Tachovské nám. 90/2, Žižkov ☎ 608-802-060.

DINING

Cihelna restaurant in Prague has an indoor play area to occupy children while their parents eat.

Cihelna ✉ Cihelná 2b, Malá Strana ☎ 257-535-534.

FLYING

If your children are two or older, ask about children's airfares. As a general rule, infants under two not occupying a seat fly at greatly reduced fares or even for free. But if you want to guarantee a seat for an infant, you have to pay full fare. Consider flying during off-peak days and times; most airlines will grant an infant a seat without a ticket if there are available seats. When booking, confirm carry-on allowances if you're traveling with infants. In general, for babies charged 10% to 50% of the adult fare you are allowed one carry-on bag and a collapsible stroller; if the flight is full, the stroller may have to be checked or you may be limited to less.

Experts agree that it's a good idea to use safety seats aloft for children weighing less than 40 pounds. Airlines set their own policies: if you use a safety seat, U.S. carriers usually require that the child be ticketed, even if he or she is young enough to ride free, because the seats must be strapped into regular seats. And even if you pay the full adult fare for the seat, it may be worth it, especially on longer trips. Do **check your airline's policy about using safety seats during takeoff and landing.** Safety seats are not allowed everywhere in the plane, so get your seat assignments as early as possible.

When reserving, request children's meals or a freestanding bassinet (not available at all airlines) if you need them. But note that bulkhead seats, where you must sit to use the bassinet, may lack an overhead bin or storage space on the floor.

LODGING

Most hotels in Prague allow children under a certain age to stay in their parents' room at no extra charge, but others charge for them as extra adults; be sure to find out the cutoff age for children's discounts. Some spa hotels don't allow children under 12.

The Accor group, which owns the Novotel, Mercure, Ibis, and Sofitel chains, has hotels in Prague and allows up to two children under 12 to stay free in their parents' room.

Young visitors to Prague will enjoy staying at one of the city's picturesque floating "botels." For further information contact the Czech Tourist Authority. Prague's luxurious Palace and Savoy hotels, managed by Vienna International, allow children under 12 to stay free in their parents' room.

Best Choices **Accor Hotels** 🌐 www.accorhotels.com.

SIGHTS & ATTRACTIONS

Places that are especially appealing to children are indicated by a rubber-duckie icon (🦆) in the margin.

SUPPLIES & EQUIPMENT

Popular brands of disposable diapers such as Huggie's and Pamper's are available anywhere; try one of the international supermarket chains, such as Tesco.

CONCIERGES

Concierges, found in many hotels, can help you with theater tickets and dinner reservations: a good one with connections may be able to get you seats for a hot show or prime-time dinner reservations at the restaurant of the moment. You can also turn to your hotel's concierge for help with travel arrangements, sightseeing plans, services ranging from aromatherapy to zipper repair, and emergencies. **Always tip** a concierge who has been of assistance (⇨ Tipping).

CONSUMER PROTECTION

Whether you're shopping for gifts or purchasing travel services, **pay with a major credit card** whenever possible, so you can cancel payment or get reimbursed if there's a problem (and you can provide documentation). If you're doing business with a particular company for the first time, contact your local Better Business Bureau and the attorney general's offices in your state and (for U.S. businesses) the company's home state as well. Have any complaints been filed? Finally, if you're buying a package or tour, always consider travel insurance that includes default coverage (⇨ Insurance).

🏢 BBBs **Council of Better Business Bureaus** ✉ 4200 Wilson Blvd., Suite 800, Arlington, VA 22203 ☎ 703/276-0100 📠 703/525-8277 ⊕ www.bbb.org.

CUSTOMS & DUTIES

When shopping abroad, keep receipts for all purchases. Upon reentering the country, **be ready to show customs officials what you've bought.** Pack purchases together in an easily accessible place. If you think a duty is incorrect, appeal the assessment. If you object to the way your clearance was handled, note the inspector's badge number. In either case, first ask to see a supervisor. If the problem isn't resolved, write to the appropriate authorities, beginning with the port director at your point of entry.

IN THE CZECH REPUBLIC

The export of items considered to have historical value is not allowed. To be exported, an antique or work of art must have an export certificate. Reputable shops should be willing to advise customers on how to comply with the regulations. If a shop can't provide proof of the item's suitability for export, be wary. The authorities do not look kindly on unauthorized "export" of antiques, particularly of baroque religious pieces. Under certain circumstances, the value-added tax (V.A.T.) on purchases over 2,500 Kč can be refunded if the goods are taken out of the country within 30 days, and you can get a cash refund in U.S. dollars or euros at the airport.

IN AUSTRALIA

Australian residents who are 18 or older may bring home A$400 worth of souvenirs and gifts (including jewelry), 250 cigarettes or 250 grams of cigars or other tobacco products, and 1,125 ml of alcohol (including wine, beer, and spirits). Residents under 18 may bring back A$200 worth of goods. Members of the same family traveling together may pool their allowances. Prohibited items include meat products. Seeds, plants, and fruits need to be declared upon arrival.

🏢 **Australian Customs Service** 🏢 Regional Director, Box 8, Sydney, NSW 2001 ☎ 02/9213-2000 or 1300/363-263, 02/9364-7222 or 1800/020-504 quarantine-inquiry line 📠 02/9213-4043 ⊕ www. customs.gov.au.

IN CANADA

Canadian residents who have been out of Canada for at least seven days may bring in C$750 worth of goods duty-free. If you've been away fewer than seven days but more than 48 hours, the duty-free allowance drops to C$200. If your trip lasts 24 to 48 hours, the allowance is C$50. You may not pool allowances with family members. Goods claimed under the C$750 exemption may follow you by mail; those claimed under the lesser exemptions must accompany you. Alcohol and tobacco products may be included in the seven-day and 48-hour exemptions but not in the 24-hour exemption. If you meet the age requirements of the province or territory through which you reenter Canada, you may bring in, duty-free, 1.5 liters of wine *or* 1.14 liters (40 imperial ounces) of liquor *or* 24 12-ounce cans or bottles of beer or ale. Also, if you meet the local age requirement for tobacco products, you may bring in, duty-free, 200 cigarettes and 50 cigars. Check ahead of time with the Canada Customs and Revenue Agency or the Department of Agriculture for policies regarding meat products, seeds, plants, and fruits.

You may send an unlimited number of gifts (only one gift per recipient, however) worth up to C$60 each duty-free to Canada. Label the package UNSOLICITED GIFT—VALUE UNDER $60. Alcohol and tobacco are excluded.

🇨🇦 **Canada Customs and Revenue Agency** ✉ 2265 St. Laurent Blvd., Ottawa, Ontario K1G 4K3 ☎ 800/461-9999 in Canada, 204/983-3500, 506/636-5064 ⊕ www.ccra.gc.ca.

IN NEW ZEALAND

All homeward-bound residents may bring back NZ$700 worth of souvenirs and gifts; passengers may not pool their allowances, and children can claim only the concession on goods intended for their own use. For those 17 or older, the duty-free allowance also includes 4.5 liters of wine or beer; one 1,125-ml bottle of spirits; and either 200 cigarettes, 250 grams of tobacco, 50 cigars, *or* a combination of the three up to 250 grams. Meat products, seeds, plants, and fruits must be declared upon arrival to the Agricultural Services Department.

🇳🇿 **New Zealand Customs** ✉ Head office: The Customhouse, 17–21 Whitmore St., Box 2218, Wellington ☎ 09/300-5399 or 0800/428-786 ⊕ www.customs. govt.nz.

IN THE U.K.

If you are a U.K. resident and your journey was wholly within the European Union (which now includes the Czech Republic), you probably won't have to pass through customs when you return to the United Kingdom. If you plan to bring back large quantities of alcohol or tobacco, check EU limits beforehand. In most cases, if you bring back more than 200 cigars, 3,200 cigarettes, 400 cigarillos, 10 liters of spirits, 110 liters of beer, 20 liters of fortified wine, and/or 90 liters of wine, you have to declare the goods upon return. Prohibited items include unpasteurized milk, regardless of country of origin.

🇬🇧 **HM Customs and Excise** ✉ Portcullis House, 21 Cowbridge Rd. E, Cardiff CF11 9SS ☎ 0845/010-9000 or 0208/929-0152 for information, 0208/929-6731 or 0208/910-3602 complaints ⊕ www.hmce.gov.uk.

IN THE U.S.

U.S. residents who have been out of the country for at least 48 hours may bring home, for personal use, $800 worth of foreign goods duty-free, as long as they haven't used the $800 allowance or any part of it in the past 30 days. This exemption may include 1 liter of alcohol (for travelers 21 and older), 200 cigarettes, and 100 non-Cuban cigars. Family members from the same household who are traveling together may pool their $800 personal exemptions. For fewer than 48 hours, the duty-free allowance drops to $200, which may include 50 cigarettes, 10 non-Cuban cigars, and 150 ml of alcohol (or 150 ml of perfume containing alcohol). The $200 allowance cannot be combined with other individuals' exemptions, and if you exceed it, the full value of all the goods will be taxed. Antiques, which U.S. Customs & Border Protection defines as objects more than 100 years old, enter duty-free, as do original works of art done entirely by hand, including paintings, drawings, and sculptures. This doesn't apply to folk art or handicrafts, which are in general dutiable.

You may also send packages home duty-free, with a limit of one parcel per addressee per day (except alcohol or tobacco products or perfume worth more than $5). You can mail up to $200 worth of goods for personal use; label the package PERSONAL USE and attach a list of its contents and their retail value. If the package contains your used personal belongings, mark it AMERICAN GOODS RETURNED to avoid paying duties. You may send up to $100 worth of goods as a gift; mark the package UNSOLICITED GIFT. Mailed items do not affect your duty-free allowance on your return.

To avoid paying duty on foreign-made high-ticket items you already own and will take on your trip, register them with Customs before you leave the country. Consider filing a Certificate of Registration for laptops, cameras, watches, and other digital devices identified with serial numbers or other permanent markings; you can keep the certificate for other trips. Otherwise, bring a sales receipt or insurance form to show that you owned the item before you left the United States.

For more about duties, restricted items, and other information about international travel, check out U.S. Customs and Border Protection's online brochure, *Know Before You Go.*

U.S. Customs & Border Protection ✉ For inquiries and equipment registration, 1300 Pennsylvania Ave. NW, Washington, DC 20229 ⊕ www.cbp. gov ☎ 877/287-8667 or 202/354-1000 ✉ For complaints, Customer Satisfaction Unit, 1300 Pennsylvania Ave. NW, Room 5.2C, Washington, DC 20229.

DISABILITIES & ACCESSIBILITY

Provisions for travelers with disabilities in the Czech Republic are extremely limited; probably the best solution is to travel with a companion who can help you. Although many hotels, especially large American or international chains, offer some wheelchair-accessible rooms, special facilities at museums and restaurants and on public transportation are difficult to find.

Local Resources Sdružení zdravotné postižených (Association of Disabled Persons) ✉ Karlínské nám. 12, Prague ☎ 224-815-914 ⊕ www.czechia.com/szdp.

LODGING

Most hotels take few or no measures to accommodate travelers with disabilities. Your best bets are newer hotels and international chains.

RESERVATIONS

When discussing accessibility with an operator or reservations agent, ask hard questions. Are there any stairs, inside *or* out? Are there grab bars next to the toilet *and* in the shower/tub? How wide is the doorway to the room? To the bathroom? For the most extensive facilities meeting the latest legal specifications, opt for newer accommodations. If you reserve through a toll-free number, consider also calling the hotel's local number to confirm the information from the central reservations office. Get confirmation in writing when you can.

SIGHTS & ATTRACTIONS

Most tourist attractions in Prague pose significant problems to travelers with mobility problems. Many are historic structures without ramps or other means to improve accessibility. Streets are often cobblestone, and potholes are common. Many streets in Prague's Staré Meš to are pedestrian-only.

TRANSPORTATION

A few Czech trains are equipped with carriages for travelers using wheelchairs. Some stations on the Prague metro have elevators, and there are two lines of accessible buses, but the system is light-years from being barrier-free. Outside of Prague, public transportation is difficult, if not impossible, for many travelers with disabilities.

Complaints Aviation Consumer Protection Division (⇨ Air Travel) for airline-related problems. **Departmental Office of Civil Rights** ✉ For general inquiries, U.S. Department of Transportation, S-30, 400 7th St. SW, Room 10215, Washington, DC 20590 ☎ 202/366-4648 🖷 202/366-9371 ⊕ www.dot. gov/ost/docr/index.htm. **Disability Rights Section** ✉ NYAV, U.S. Department of Justice, Civil Rights Division, 950 Pennsylvania Ave. NW, Washington, DC 20530 🖷 ADA information line 202/514-0301, 800/514-0301, 202/514-0383 TTY, 800/514-0383 TTY ⊕ www.ada.gov. **U.S. Department of Transportation Hotline** 🖷 For disability-related air-travel problems, 800/778-4838 or 800/455-9880 TTY.

TRAVEL AGENCIES

In the United States, the Americans with Disabilities Act requires that travel firms serve the needs of all travelers. Some agencies specialize in working with people with disabilities.

Travelers with Mobility Problems Access Adventures/B. Roberts Travel ✉ 206 Chestnut Ridge Rd., Scottsville, NY 14624 🖷 585/889-9096 ⊕ www.brobertstravel.com ✎ dltravel@prodigy. net, run by a former physical-rehabilitation counselor. **CareVacations** ✉ No. 5, 5110-50 Ave., Leduc, Alberta, Canada T9E 6V4 🖷 780/986-6404 or 877/

478-7827 🖷 780/986-8332 ⊕ www.carevacations.com, for group tours and cruise vacations. **Flying Wheels Travel** ✉ 143 W. Bridge St., Box 382, Owatonna, MN 55060 ☎ 507/451-5005 🖷 507/451-1685 ⊕ www.flyingwheelstravel.com.

🔢 **Travelers with Developmental Disabilities** **New Directions** ✉ 5276 Hollister Ave., Suite 207, Santa Barbara, CA 93111 ☎ 805/967-2841 or 888/967-2841 🖷 805/964-7344 ⊕ www.newdirectionstravel.com. **Sprout** ✉ 893 Amsterdam Ave., New York, NY 10025 ☎ 212/222-9575 or 888/222-9575 🖷 212/222-9768 ⊕ www.gosprout.org.

DISCOUNTS & DEALS

The International Student I.D. Card often entitles the holder to discounts on museum and gallery entrance fees.

You can also purchase a Prague Card. The basic card costs an extraordinarily steep €35. In truth, for the typical visitor this is simply not a good deal. The discounts and free admissions offered (even though the card grants you three days of free use of the city's public transport system) don't make it worth the high price. Most people find it more cost-advantageous to pay for everything individually.

Be a smart shopper and compare all your options before making decisions. A plane ticket bought with a promotional coupon from travel clubs, coupon books, and direct-mail offers or purchased on the Internet may not be cheaper than the least expensive fare from a discount ticket agency. And always keep in mind that what you get is just as important as what you save.

🔢 **Prague Card** ⊕ www.praguecard.info.

DISCOUNT RESERVATIONS

To save money, look into discount reservations services with Web sites and toll-free numbers, which use their buying power to get a better price on hotels, airline tickets (⇨ Air Travel), even car rentals. When booking a room, always **call the hotel's local toll-free number** (if one is available) rather than the central reservations number—you'll often get a better price. Always ask about special packages or corporate rates.

When shopping for the best deal on hotels and car rentals, look for guaranteed exchange rates, which protect you against a falling dollar. With your rate locked in, you won't pay more, even if the price goes up in the local currency.

🔢 **Airline Tickets** **Air 4 Less** ☎ 800/AIR4LESS; low-fare specialist.

🔢 **Hotel Rooms** **Accommodations Express** ☎ 800/444-7666 or 800/277-1064 ⊕ www.acex.net. **Hotels.com** ☎ 800/246-8357 ⊕ www.hotels.com. **International Marketing & Travel Concepts** ☎ 800/790-4682 ⊕ www.imtc-travel.com. **Steigenberger Reservation Service** ☎ 800/223-5652 ⊕ www.srs-worldhotels.com. **Turbotrip.com** ☎ 800/473-7829 ⊕ www.turbotrip.com.

PACKAGE DEALS

Don't confuse packages and guided tours. When you buy a package, you travel on your own, just as though you had planned the trip yourself. Fly/drive packages, which combine airfare and car rental, are often a good deal. In cities, ask the local visitor's bureau about hotel and local transportation packages that include tickets to major museum exhibits or other special events. If you **buy a rail/drive pass,** you may save on train tickets and car rentals. All Eurailpass holders get a discount on Eurostar fares through the Channel Tunnel and often receive reduced rates for buses, hotels, ferries, sightseeing cruises, and car rentals.

Both Czech Airlines and Austrian Airlines offer good-value hotel-and-air packages to Prague, particularly int he off-season. The online discounter Go-Today.com usually has discounted tarvel packages to Prague, though flights often require a transfer in Europe and hotels are usually not in the city center (booking reservations by telephone incurs an additional $20 fee).

🔢 **Austrian Air Vactions** ☎ 800/790-4682 or 404/240-0949 ⊕ www.austrian-airvacations.com **ČSA Airtours** ☎ 800/224-2365 or 212/765-6588 ⊕ usa.csa.cz **Go-Today.com** ☎ 425-487-9632 ⊕ www.go-today.com

ELECTRICITY

To use electric-powered equipment purchased in the U.S. or Canada, **bring a converter and adapter.** The electrical current in Eastern and Central Europe is 220 volts, 50 cycles alternating current (AC); wall outlets generally take plugs with two round prongs.

If your appliances are dual-voltage, you'll need only an adapter. Don't use 110-volt outlets marked FOR SHAVERS ONLY for high-wattage appliances such as blow-dryers. Most laptops operate equally well on 110 and 220 volts and so require only an adapter.

EMBASSIES

⚑ Australia Australian Consulate ✉ Klimentská 10, Nové Město ☎ 296-578-350.

⚑ Canada Canadian Embassy ✉ Mickiewiczova 6, Hradčany ☎ 272-101-890, ⊕ www.canada.cz.

⚑ New Zealand New Zealand Consulate ✉ Dykova 19, Vinohrady ☎ 222-514-672.

⚑ United Kingdom U.K. Embassy ✉ Thunovská 14, Malá Strana ☎ 257-530-278 ⊕ www.britain.cz.

⚑ United States U.S. Embassy ✉ Tržiště 15, Malá Strana ☎ 257-530-663 ⊕ www.usembassy.cz.

EMERGENCIES

⚑ Doctors & Dentists Dentist Referrals ✉ Palackého 5, Nové Město ☎ 224-946-981 24-hr emergency service. **Lékařská služba první pomoci** (District first-aid clinic) ✉ Palackého 5, Nové Město ☎ 224-946-982.

⚑ Emergency Services Ambulance ☎ 155. **Autoklub Bohemia Assistance** ☎ 1240 ⊕ www.aba.cz. **Federal Police** ☎ 158. **Prague city police** ☎ 156. **ÚAMK Emergency Roadside Assistance** ☎ 1230 ⊕ www.uamk.cz.

⚑ Hospitals American Medical Center ✉ Janovského 48, Holešovice ☎ 220-807-756 24-hr service. **Canadian Medical Clinic** ✉ Veleslavínská 1, Veleslavín ☎ 235-360-133. **Na Homolce Hospital** ✉ Roentgenova 2, Motol ☎ 257-272-146 weekdays [foreigners' department], 257-211-111, 257-272-191.

⚑ 24-Hour Pharmacies Lékárna U Anděla ✉ Štefánikova 6, Smíchov ☎ 257-320-918. **Lékárna** ✉ Belgická 37, Nové Město ☎ 222-513-396.

ENGLISH-LANGUAGE MEDIA

In the city center nearly every bookstore carries a few guidebooks and paperbacks in English. Street vendors on Wenceslas Square and Na Příkopě carry leading foreign newspapers and periodicals.

BOOKS

⚑ Bookstores Globe ✉ Pštrossova 6, Nové Město ☎ 224-934-203. **Anagram** ✉ Týn 4, Staré Město ☎ 224-895-737. **Big Ben** ✉ Malá Štupartská 5, Staré Město ☎ 224-826-565.

NEWSPAPERS & MAGAZINES

To find out what's on and to get the latest tips for shopping, dining, and entertainment, consult Prague's weekly English-language newspaper, the **Prague Post** (⊕ www.praguepost.com). It prints comprehensive entertainment listings and can be bought at most downtown newsstands as well as in major North American and European cities. If you take a Czech Airlines flight, you may be able to pick up a free copy as you board. The **Prague Tribune** (⊕ www.prague-tribune.cz) is a business and lifestyle magazine published monthly. **Prague In Your Pocket** (⊕ www. inyourpocket.com) is a badly spelled bi-monthly, though perhaps its thorough listings for all forms of entertainment and hotels are more accurate than its Czech nomenclature would lead you to believe. At a quarter of the price of *In Your Pocket*, an original Czech publication **Kulturní přehled** (Culture Preview) will give you a monthly culture round-up and the chance to exercise some straightforward local language skills.

ETIQUETTE & BEHAVIOR

Czechs are very keen on hand-shaking on meeting and parting, kissing is reserved for family members and close friends. On entering a shop it's usual to say hello (*Dobrý den*) to the shop keeper. It's considered rude to speak too loudly in public, particularly in restaurants and railway trains. All men's headgear should be removed on entering a church. It's customary for young people to give up their seats on public transport for senior citizens, mothers with small children, and any person with a physical disability. No hostess will be offended by a gift of flowers, a box of chocolates, or a bottle of wine when you're visiting them in their own home.

BUSINESS ETIQUETTE

As in other European countries, etiquette is important. Always arrive for a business meeting or a meal on time; in Prague, punctuality is viewed as a sign of reliability and responsibility. Handshakes begin and end every meeting. Your Czech counterpart will say his or her surname as he shakes your hand for the first time. You can do the same. It's also customary during or after a meeting to exchange business cards. Czechs do not quickly get on first-name terms so addressing somebody by a formal title (e.g., Mr., Mrs., or Doctor) is expected. Cordial formality is the best attitude to maintain. In meetings, many people tend to make their points in a roundabout, drawn-out, or subtle manner. Let them do so, and do not push. The aggressive, get-to-the-bottom-line approach favored in the U.S. can be seen as pushy and suspect in the Czech Republic. Business lunches, held one-on-one so as to get to know a partner or prospect better, are not yet a common practice and may make your Czech counterpart uncomfortable. It's better to invite a small group and, of course, pick up the tab. The good news is that no one will bat an eye if you order beer or wine with a meal; it's normal and customary. The bad news (or good, depending on your habits) is that smoking is widespread. It's best, of course, to turn off cell phones during any business meeting, but if you must take a call, excuse yourself and leave the room.

GAY & LESBIAN TRAVEL

The Czech Republic is one of the most liberal countries in Eastern Europe, and Prague in particular fosters a growing gay and lesbian scene. Prague does not have one particular gay neighborhood, but there are a lot of bars and clubs in Staré Město and Nové Město (Praha 1), Vinohrady (Praha 2), and Žižkov (Praha 3). Rainbow Travel, a gay-owned company, offers personalized tours; however, because the tours are private, the costs are high unless you're traveling with a group, which makes the services more cost-effective.

◪ Gay- & Lesbian-Friendly Travel Agencies **Different Roads Travel** ⊠ 8383 Wilshire Blvd., Suite 520, Beverly Hills, CA 90211 ☎ 323/651-5557 or 800/429-8747 (Ext. 14 for both) ⊟ 323/651-5454 ✐ lgernert@tzell.com. **Kennedy Travel** ⊠ 130 W. 42nd St., Suite 401, New York, NY 10036 ☎ 212/840-8659 or 800/237-7433 ⊟ 212/730-2269 ⊕ www.kennedytravel.com. **Now, Voyager** ⊠ 4406 18th St., San Francisco, CA 94114 ☎ 415/626-1169 or 800/255-6951 ⊟ 415/626-8626 ⊕ www.nowvoyager.com. **Rainbow Travel** ⊠ Lidická 569, Roztoky ☎ 220-910-855 ⊕ www.rainbowtravel.cz. **Skylink**

Travel & Tour/Flying Dutchmen Travel ⊠ 1455 N. Dutton Ave., Suite A, Santa Rosa, CA 95401 ☎ 707/546-9888 or 800/225-5759 ⊟ 707/636-0951; serves lesbian travelers.

◪ Web Sites **Prague** ⊕ http://prague.gayguide.net.

HEALTH

You may gain weight, but there are few other serious health hazards for the traveler in the Czech Republic. Tap water may taste bad but is drinkable (though see the precautions below); when it runs rusty out of the tap or the aroma of chlorine is overpowering, it might help to have some iodine tablets or bottled water handy. Buy bottled water, particularly if staying in an older home or hotel.

Vegetarians and those on special diets may have a problem with the heavy local cuisine, which is based largely on pork and beef. To prevent your vitamin intake from dropping to danger levels, buy fresh fruits and vegetables at seasonal street markets.

Tick-borne Lyme disease is a risk in the woodlands of the Czech Republic. Schedule vaccinations well in advance of departure because some require several doses, and others may cause uncomfortable side effects.

To avoid problems clearing customs, diabetic travelers carrying needles and syringes should have on hand a letter from their physician confirming their need for insulin injections.

OVER-THE-COUNTER REMEDIES

Pharmacies in Prague carry a variety of non-prescription as well as prescription drugs.

HOLIDAYS

January 1; Easter Monday; May 1 (Labor Day); May 8 (Liberation Day); July 5 (Sts. Cyril and Methodius Day); July 6 (Jan Hus Day); September 28 (Day of Czech Statehood); October 28 (Czech National Day); November 17 (Day of a Struggle for Liberty and Democracy); and December 24, 25, and 26.

INSURANCE

The most useful travel-insurance plan is a comprehensive policy that includes coverage for trip cancellation and interruption, default, trip delay, and medical expenses (with a waiver for preexisting conditions).

Without insurance you'll lose all or most of your money if you cancel your trip, regardless of the reason. Default insurance covers you if your tour operator, airline, or cruise line goes out of business—the chances of which have been increasing. Trip-delay covers expenses that arise because of bad weather or mechanical delays. Study the fine print when comparing policies.

If you're traveling internationally, a key component of travel insurance is coverage for medical bills incurred if you get sick on the road. Such expenses aren't generally covered by Medicare or private policies. U.K. residents can buy a travel-insurance policy valid for most vacations taken during the year in which it's purchased (but check preexisting-condition coverage). British and Australian citizens need extra medical coverage when traveling overseas.

Always **buy travel policies directly from the insurance company**; if you buy them from a cruise line, airline, or tour operator that goes out of business you probably won't be covered for the agency or operator's default, a major risk. Before making any purchase, review your existing health and home-owner's policies to find what they cover away from home.

📋 Travel Insurers In the U.S.: **Access America** ✉ 2805 N. Parham Rd., Richmond, VA 23294 ☎ 800/284-8300 🖷 804/673-1491 or 800/346-9265 ⊕ www.accessamerica.com. **Travel Guard International** ✉ 1145 Clark St., Stevens Point, WI 54481 ☎ 715/345-0505 or 800/826-1300 🖷 800/955-8785 ⊕ www.travelguard.com.

📋 In the U.K.: **Association of British Insurers** ✉ 51 Gresham St., London EC2V 7HQ ☎ 020/7600-3333 🖷 020/7696-8999 ⊕ www.abi.org.uk. In Canada: **RBC Insurance** ✉ 6880 Financial Dr., Mississauga, Ontario L5N 7Y5 ☎ 800/668-4342 or 905/816-2400 🖷 905/813-4704 ⊕ www.rbcinsurance.com. In Australia: **Insurance Council of Australia** ✉ Insurance Enquiries and Complaints, Level 12, Box 561, Collins St. W, Melbourne, VIC 8007 ☎ 1300/780808 or 03/9629-4109 🖷 03/9621-2060 ⊕ www.iecltd.com.au. In New Zealand: **Insurance Council of New Zealand** ✉ Level 7, 111–115 Customhouse Quay, Box 474, Wellington ☎ 04/472-5230 🖷 04/473-3011 ⊕ www.icnz.org.nz.

LANGUAGE

Czech, a Slavic language closely related to Slovak and Polish, is the official language of the Czech Republic. Learning English is popular among young people, but German is still the most useful language for tourists, especially outside Prague.

MAIL & SHIPPING

It takes two days for letters and postcards to reach the U.K., five to seven days to reach Australia, and a week to reach the U.S. Remember to pay a little extra for airmail otherwise your letters will be sent by ship. The opening hours of post offices vary—the smaller the place, the shorter the hours. Most post offices are open from 8 AM to 7 PM on weekdays and 8 AM to noon on Saturday. The main post office in Prague is open 24 hours, with a 30-minute break after midnight.

📋 Post Offices **Prague Main Post Office** ✉ Jindřišská ul. 14 ⊕ www.cpost.cz

OVERNIGHT SERVICES

Česká pošta runs an Express Mail Service. You can post your EMS parcel at any post office, and Česká pošta can supply forms for customs clearance. Maximum weight is 30 kg (20 kg to Australia), sending a parcel of 1 kg costs now between 800 Kč (to the U.K.) and 1,200 Kč (to Australia and New Zealand). Delivery times vary between one and five days, though material is often delayed by American customs. You may not send currency, travel checks, precious metals, or stones through Express Mail. Not every post office offers a pickup service. Most other international express carriers also serve the Czech Republic.

📋 **DHL** ☎ 800-103-000 ⊕ www.dhl.cz. **EMS** ☎ 800-104-410 ⊕ www.cpost.cz. **Fed Ex** ☎ 800-133-339 ⊕ www.inspekta.cz/fedex. **UPS** ☎ 800-181-111 ⊕ www.ups.com.

POSTAL RATES

At this writing, postcards to the United States and Canada cost 12 Kč, letters up to 20 grams in weight 14 Kč. Postcards to Great Britain cost 9 Kč, letters 9 Kč. You can buy stamps at post offices, hotels, newsstands, and shops that sell postcards.

RECEIVING MAIL

If you don't know where you'll be staying, American Express mail service is a great convenience, available at no charge to anyone holding an American Express credit card or carrying American Express traveler's checks. There are several offices in Prague. You can also have mail held *poste restante* (general delivery) at post offices in major towns, but the letters should be marked *Pošta 1,* to designate the city's main post office; in Prague, the poste restante window is at the main post office. You'll be asked for identification when you collect your mail.

◪ **American Express** ✉ Václavské nám. 56, Nové Město ☎ 224-219-992 ⊕ www.americanexpress. com ✉ Staroměstské náměstí 5, Staré Město ☎ 224-818-388.

SHIPPING PARCELS

Some major stores can make their own arrangements to ship purchases home on behalf of their customers. A number of freight and cargo services operate international delivery services, and these can generally be relied upon. An average shipping time to the U.S. is 21 days (4 days for air cargo), 40 days to Australia and to New Zealand. There's no reason not to use the reliable Česká pošta, which delivers anything up to 30 kg (20 kg to Australia and New Zealand).

◪ **Art Trans** ✉ Nám. Interbrigády 1, Bubeneč ☎ 233-336-076 ⊕ www.shipping.cz. **Fix Box Air Shipping** ✉ Sudoměřská 26, Žižkov ☎ 222-720-456 ⊕ www.fixbox.cz.

MONEY MATTERS

Although the Czech Republic is still generally a bargain by Western standards, Prague remains the exception. Hotel prices in particular are often higher than the facilities would warrant, but prices at tourist resorts outside the capital are lower and, in the outlying areas and off the beaten track, very low. Unfortunately, many museums, castles, and certain clubs charge a higher entrance fee for foreigners than they charge for Czechs. A few hotels still follow this practice, too.

Prices throughout this guide are given for adults. Substantially reduced fees are almost always available for children, students, and senior citizens. For information on taxes, *see* Taxes.

ATMS

ATMs are common in Prague and most towns in the Czech Republic and more often than not are part of the Cirrus and Plus networks; outside of urban areas, machines are scarce and you should plan to carry enough cash to meet your needs.

In Czech, an ATM is a *bankomat,* and a PIN is also a PIN, just as in English.

CREDIT CARDS

Visa, MasterCard, and American Express are widely accepted by major hotels and stores, Diners Club less so. Smaller establishments and those off the beaten track are less likely to accept a wide variety of credit cards.

Throughout this guide, the following abbreviations are used: **AE**, American Express; **DC**, Diners Club; **MC**, MasterCard; and **V**, Visa.

◪ Reporting Lost Cards **American Express** ☎ 222-800-222 **Diners Club** ☎ 267-197-450 **MasterCard** ☎ 800-142-494 **Visa** ☎ 224-125-353

CURRENCY

The unit of currency in the Czech Republic is the koruna, or crown (Kč), which is divided into 100 haléřů, or hellers. There are (little-used) coins of 50 hellers; coins of 1, 2, 5, 10, 20, and (rarely) 50 Kč; and notes of 50, 100, 200, 500, 1,000, 2,000, and 5,000 Kč. Notes of 1,000 Kč and up may not always be accepted for small purchases.

CURRENCY EXCHANGE

Try to avoid exchanging money at hotels or private exchange booths, including the ubiquitous Chequepoint and Exact Change booths. They routinely take commissions of 8% to 10%. The best places to exchange are at bank counters, where the commissions average 1% to 3%, or at ATMs. The koruna is fully convertible, which means it can be purchased outside the country and exchanged into other currencies. Of course, never change money with people on the street. Not only is it illegal, you will almost definitely be ripped off.

One currency exchange service does offer rates as good as you will get anywhere. It's just off Old Town Square and is called Exchange. There is a minimum you can exchange, however. At this writing it was €150 or $200.

Happily, the exchange rates offered by the currency exchange windows at the Prague airport are no worse than you will find anywhere, if not quite as good as those at banks. However, you will still usually get a better rate from one of the airport ATMs, which you can see past baggage claim.

At this writing the exchange rate was around 24 Kč to the U.S. dollar, 20 Kč to the Canadian dollar, 46 Kč to the pound sterling, and 32 Kč to the euro.

For the most favorable rates, **change money through banks.** Although ATM transaction fees may be higher abroad than at home, ATM rates are excellent because they're based on wholesale rates offered only by major banks. You won't do as well at exchange booths in airports or rail and bus stations, in hotels, in restaurants, or in stores. To avoid lines at airport exchange booths, get a bit of local currency before you leave home.

🏧 **Exchange Services Exchange** ⊠ 2 na. Franze Kafka **International Currency Express** ⊠ 427 N. Camden Dr., Suite F, Beverly Hills, CA 90210 ☎ 888/278-6628 orders 🖷 310/278-6410 ⊕ www.foreignmoney.com. **Travel Ex Currency Services** ☎ 800/287-7362 orders and retail locations ⊕ www.travelex.com

TRAVELER'S CHECKS

Do you need traveler's checks? It depends on where you're headed. If you're going to rural areas and small towns, go with cash; traveler's checks are best used in cities. Lost or stolen checks can usually be replaced within 24 hours. To ensure a speedy refund, buy your own traveler's checks—don't let someone else pay for them: irregularities like this can cause delays. The person who bought the checks should make the call to request a refund.

PACKING

Don't worry about packing lots of formal clothing. Jeans are common, and casual dress is the norm except for concerts or the opera and a few high-end restaurants, when a sports jacket or suit for men is the norm. Everywhere else, you will feel comfortable in casual pants or jeans. Be aware that few Europeans wear shorts in the summer unless they are taking part in sporting events, hiking, or at the beach.

Prague enjoys all the extremes of an inland climate, so plan accordingly. In the higher elevations of the Czech Republic, winter can last until April, and even in summer the evenings will be on the cool side.

Many areas are best seen on foot, so take a pair of sturdy walking shoes and be prepared to use them. High heels will present considerable problems on the cobblestone streets of Prague.

Some items that you take for granted at home are occasionally unavailable or of questionable quality in Eastern and Central Europe, though the situation has been steadily improving. Toiletries and personal-hygiene products have become relatively easy to find, but it's always a good idea to bring necessities when traveling in rural areas.

In your carry-on luggage, pack an extra pair of eyeglasses or contact lenses and enough of any medication you take to last a few days longer than the entire trip. You may also ask your doctor to write a spare prescription using the drug's generic name, as brand names may vary from country to country. In luggage to be checked, **never pack prescription drugs, valuables, or undeveloped film.** And don't forget to carry with you the addresses of offices that handle refunds of lost traveler's checks. Check *Fodor's How to Pack* (available at online retailers and bookstores everywhere) for more tips.

To avoid customs and security delays, carry medications in their original packaging. Don't pack any sharp objects in your carry-on luggage, including knives of any size or material, scissors, nail clippers, and corkscrews, or anything else that might arouse suspicion.

To avoid having your checked luggage chosen for hand inspection, don't cram bags full. The U.S. Transportation Security Administration suggests packing shoes on top and placing personal items you don't want touched in clear plastic bags.

CHECKING LUGGAGE

You're allowed to carry aboard one bag and one personal article, such as a purse or a laptop computer. Make sure what you carry on fits under your seat or in the overhead bin. Get to the gate early, so you can board as soon as possible, before the overhead bins fill up.

Baggage allowances vary by carrier, destination, and ticket class. On international flights, you're usually allowed to check two bags weighing up to 70 pounds (32 kilograms) each, although a few airlines allow checked bags of up to 88 pounds (40 kilograms) in first class. Some international carriers don't allow more than 66 pounds (30 kilograms) per bag in business class and 44 pounds (20 kilograms) in economy. On domestic flights, the limit is usually 50 to 70 pounds (23 to 32 kilograms) per bag. In general, carry-on bags shouldn't exceed 40 pounds (18 kilograms). Most airlines won't accept bags that weigh more than 100 pounds (45 kilograms) on domestic or international flights. Expect to pay a fee for baggage that exceeds weight limits. Check baggage restrictions with your carrier before you pack.

Airline liability for baggage is limited to $2,500 per person on flights within the United States. On international flights it amounts to $9.07 per pound or $20 per kilogram for checked baggage (roughly $640 per 70-pound bag), with a maximum of $634.90 per piece, and $400 per passenger for unchecked baggage. You can buy additional coverage at check-in for about $10 per $1,000 of coverage, but it often excludes a rather extensive list of items, shown on your airline ticket.

Before departure, itemize your bags' contents and their worth, and label the bags with your name, address, and phone number. (If you use your home address, cover it so potential thieves can't see it readily.) Include a label inside each bag and **pack a copy of your itinerary.** At check-in, make sure each bag is correctly tagged with the destination airport's three-letter code. Because some checked bags will be opened for hand inspection, the U.S. Transportation Security Administration recommends that you leave luggage unlocked or use the plastic locks offered at check-in. TSA screeners place an inspection notice inside searched bags, which are re-sealed with a special lock.

If your bag has been searched and contents are missing or damaged, file a claim with the TSA Consumer Response Center as soon as possible. If your bags arrive damaged or fail to arrive at all, file a written report with the airline before leaving the airport.

🗂 Complaints **U.S. Transportation Security Administration Contact Center** ☎ 866/289-9673 ⊕ www.tsa.gov.

PASSPORTS & VISAS

When traveling internationally, carry your passport even if you don't need one (it's always the best form of ID) and **make two photocopies of the data page** (one for someone at home and another for you, carried separately from your passport). If you lose your passport, promptly call the nearest embassy or consulate and the local police.

U.S. passport applications for children under age 14 require consent from both parents or legal guardians; both parents must appear together to sign the application. If only one parent appears, he or she must submit a written statement from the other parent authorizing passport issuance for the child. A parent with sole authority must present evidence of it when applying; acceptable documentation includes the child's certified birth certificate listing only the applying parent, a court order specifically permitting this parent's travel with the child, or a death certificate for the nonapplying parent. Application forms and instructions are available on the Web site of the U.S. State Department's Bureau of Consular Affairs (⊕ travel.state.gov).

ENTERING THE CZECH REPUBLIC

Be sure to verify entrance requirements at the time you purchase your tickets or at least a month before you're scheduled to leave; they can and do change. At this writing, U.S. citizens need only a valid passport to visit the Czech Republic as tourists. British citizens holding a full British passport do not require a visa to enter the Czech Republic; however, persons holding British Overseas Citizens passports require a visa. Citizens of Australia, Canada, New Zealand, and the U.S. may stay for 90 days without a visa. Long-term and work visas for all foreigners now must be obtained from outside the country. Those interested in working or living in the Czech Republic are advised to contact the Czech embassy or consulate in their home country well in advance of their trip.

PASSPORT OFFICES

The best time to apply for a passport or to renew is in fall and winter. Before any trip, check your passport's expiration date, and, if necessary, renew it as soon as possible.

Australian Citizens Passports Australia Australian Department of Foreign Affairs & Trade ☎ 131-232 ⊕ www.passports.gov.au.

Canadian Citizens Passport Office ✉ To mail in applications: 200 Promenade du Portage, Hull, Québec J8X 4B7 ☎ 819/994-3500 or 800/567-6868 ⊕ www.ppt.gc.ca.

New Zealand Citizens New Zealand Passports Office ☎ 0800/22-5050 or 04/474-8100 ⊕ www.passports.govt.nz.

U.K. Citizens U.K. Passport Service ☎ 0870/521-0410 ⊕ www.passport.gov.uk.

U.S. Citizens National Passport Information Center ☎ 877/487-2778, 888/874-7793 TDD/TTY ⊕ travel.state.gov.

PUBLIC TRANSIT IN PRAGUE

Prague's extensive public transit system, which includes a clean and reliable underground subway system—called the metro—as well as bus and streetcar network allows for fast, efficient travel throughout the city. Metro stations are marked with an inconspicuous M sign. A refurbished old tram, No. 91, travels through the Old Town and Lesser Quarter on summer weekends. Beware of pickpockets, who often operate in large groups on crowded trams and metro cars.

FARES & SCHEDULES

The basic, transferrable ticket costs 12 Kč. It permits one hour's travel throughout the metro, tram, and bus network between 5 AM and 8 PM on weekdays, or 90 minutes' travel at other times. Single-ride tickets cost 8 Kč and allow one 15-minute ride on a tram or bus, without transfer, or a metro journey of up to four stations lasting less than 30 minutes (transfer between lines is allowed). You can also buy a one-day pass allowing unlimited use of the system for 70 Kč, a 3-day pass for 200 Kč, a 7-day pass for 250 Kč, or a 15-day pass for 280 Kč. The passes can be purchased at the main metro stations, from ticket machines, and at some newsstands in the center. A pass is not valid until stamped in the orange machines in metro stations or aboard trams *and* the required information is entered on the back (there are instructions in English).

The metro shuts down at midnight, but Trams 50 to 59 and Buses 500 and above run all night. Night trams run at 40-minute intervals, and all routes intersect at the corner of Lazarská and Spálená streets in the New Town, near the Národní třída metro station. Schedules and regulations in English are on the transportation department's official Web site. Travel Information Centres provide all substantial information about public transport operation, routes, timetables, etc. There are six of them located at the airport and at five major metro stations.

PAYING

Validate your metro ticket at an orange machine before descending the escalator. Trains are patrolled often; the fine for riding without a valid ticket is 800 Kč. Tickets for buses are the same as those used for the metro, although you validate them at machines inside the bus or tram. Tickets (*jízdenky*) can be bought at hotels, some newsstands, and from dispensing machines in the metro stations.

Transit Information Web Sites Dopravní Podnik ⊕ www.dp-praha.cz.

Transit Information Centers Anděl ☎222-646-055. **Černý most** ☎222-647-450. **Muzeum** ☎222-623-777. **Mustek** ☎222-646-350. **Nádraží Holešovice** ☎220-806-790. **Ruzyně airport** ☎220-115-404.

Lost & Found Lost & Found ✉ Karoliny Světlé 5, Staré Město ☎ 222-623-371 or 224-235-085.

RESTROOMS

Public restrooms are more common, and cleaner, than they used to be in the Czech

Republic. You nearly always have to pay 2 Kč to 10 Kč to the attendant. Restaurant and bar toilets are generally for customers only, but as prices are low, this isn't a significant burden.

SAFETY

Don't wear a waist pack, which pegs you as a tourist. Distribute your cash and any valuables (including your credit cards and passport) between a deep front pocket, an inside jacket or vest pocket, and a hidden money pouch. Do not reach for the money pouch once you're in public.

Crime rates are still relatively low in Prague, but travelers should beware of pickpockets in crowded areas, especially on public transportation, at railway stations, and in big hotels. In general, always keep your valuables with you—in open bars and restaurants, purses hung on or placed next to chairs are easy targets. Make sure your wallet is safe in a buttoned pocket, or watch your handbag.

In the Czech Republic, except for widely scattered attacks against people of color, violent crime against tourists is extremely rare. Pickpocketing and bill-padding are the most common complaints.

LOCAL SCAMS

To avoid potential trouble in the Czech Republic: ask taxi drivers what the approximate fare will be before getting in, and ask for a receipt (*paragon*); carefully look over restaurant bills; be extremely wary of handing your passport to anyone who accosts you with a demand for ID; and never exchange money on the street.

WOMEN IN PRAGUE

If you carry a purse, choose one with a zipper and a thick strap that you can drape across your body; adjust the length so that the purse sits in front of you at or above hip level. (Don't wear a money belt or a waist pack.) Store only enough money in the purse to cover casual spending. Distribute the rest of your cash and any valuables between deep front pockets, inside jacket or vest pockets, and a concealed money pouch.

It isn't wise for a woman to go alone to a bar or nightclub or to wander the streets late at night. When traveling by train at night, seek out compartments that are well-populated.

SENIOR-CITIZEN TRAVEL

To qualify for age-related discounts, mention your senior-citizen status up front when booking hotel reservations (not when checking out) and before you're seated in restaurants (not when paying the bill). Be sure to have identification on hand. When renting a car, ask about promotional car-rental discounts, which can be cheaper than senior-citizen rates.

🚩 **Educational Programs Elderhostel** ✉ 11 Ave. de Lafayette, Boston, MA 02111-1746 ☎ 877/426-8056, 978/323-4141 international callers, 877/426-2167 TTY 🖷 877/426-2166 ⊕ www.elderhostel.org. **Interhostel** ✉ University of New Hampshire, 6 Garrison Ave., Durham, NH 03824 ☎ 603/862-1147 or 800/733-9753 🖷 603/862-1113 ⊕ www.learn.unh.edu.

SHOPPING

Bargaining is not an acceptable practice in Prague.

SMART SOUVENIRS

Folk-style pottery—which is often small and highly decorative—makes for an interesting and unusual contrast to the ubiquitous crystal. Clever, colorful, and attractive handmade wooden toys, wind-up tin plate toys, and folk dolls are as happily received by adults as the 2- to 10-year-olds they are made for. Most toys are fairly inexpensive, priced between 100 and 500 Kč, but there are small items for as little as 5 Kč, and high-end hand-made electric trains costing several thousand koruna. The local herb liqueur Becherovka may be an acquired taste, but is always attractively bottled in various sizes and can be bought boxed with matching glasses. A special place in Czech affections is held for the art nouveau designs of the Czech artist Alfons Mucha. A wide selection of high-quality prints and subtle souvenirs bearing these beautiful images will appeal to almost anybody with a sense of style.

🚩 **Hracky/Toys** ✉ Pohořelec 24, Pohořelec ☎ 233-359-127. **Mucha Museum** ✉ Panská 7, Nové Město ☎ 224-216-415 ⊕ www.mucha.cz.

SIGHTSEEING TOURS

BOAT TOURS

You can take a 30- to 60-minute boat trip along the Vltava year-round from several boat companies that are based on the quays near the Malá Strana side of the Charles Bridge. It's not really necessary to buy tickets in advance, though you can; boats leave as they fill up. One of the cruise companies stands out, and it's on the Old Town side of the bridge. Prague-Venice Cruises operates restored, classic canal boats from late 19th century; the company operates one larger boat that holds 35 passengers and 8 smaller boats that hold 12 passengers. Take one of the smaller boats—particularly one of the uncovered ones—if you can for a more intimate narrated cruise of about 45 minutes along the Vltava and nearby canals; refreshments are included in all cruises. You actually set sail from beneath the last remaining span of Judith's Bridge (the Roman-built precursor to the Charles Bridge). Look for the touts in sailor suits right before the bridge; they will direct you to the ticket office. Cruises are offered daily from 10:30 to 6 from November through February, until 8 from March through June and September through October, and until 11 in July and August. Cruises cost 270 Kč.

Prague-Venice Cruises ⊠ Krizovnicke nam. 3, Staré Město ☎ 603-819-947 ⊕ www.prague-venice.cz

BUS TOURS

Čedok offers a 3½-hour "Grand City Tour," a combination bus and walking venture that covers all the major sights with commentary in English. It departs daily at 9:30 AM year-round, and also at 2 PM from April through October, from opposite the Prašná brána (Powder Tower) on Republic Square, near the main Čedok office. The price is about 750 Kč. "Historic Prague on Foot" is a slower-paced, three-hour walking tour for 400 Kč. From April through October, it departs Republic Square on Wednesday, Friday, and Sunday at 9:30 AM; in the off-season, it departs Friday at 9:30 AM. More tours are offered, especially in summer, and the schedules may well vary according to demand. You can also contact Čedok's main office to arrange a personalized walking tour. Times and itineraries are negotiable; prices start at around 500 Kč per hour.

Very similar tours by other operators also depart daily from Republic Square,

Národní třída near Jungmannovo náměstí, and Wenceslas Square. Prices are generally a couple hundred crowns less than for Čedok's tours.

Čedok ⊠ Na Příkopě 18, Nové Město ☎ 224-197-111 ⊕ www.cedok.cz. **Precious Legacy Tours** ⊠ Maiselova 16, Josefov ☎ 222-320-398 ⊕ www.legacytours.cz. **Travel Plus** ⊠ Na příkopě 24, Nové Město ☎ 224-227-989 ⊕ www.travel.cz. **Wittmann Tours** ⊠ Mánesova 8, Vinohrady ☎ 222-252-472 ⊕ www.wittmann-tours.com. **Wolff Travel** ⊠ Dykova 31, Vinohrady ☎ 222-511-333 ⊕ www.wolff-travel.com.

PRIVATE GUIDES

Tours of Prague come under the supervision of Prague Information Service, which is reliable and always informative. The company organizes walking tours in Prague's city center and in the outskirts, including excursions from Prague. Arrangements can be made with them for many tailor-made tours. Nonregistered guides can also be found, but unless they come with a personal recommendation from someone you trust, their services cannot be guaranteed.

We can recommend one private guide from personal experience. His name is Jaroslav "Jay" Pesta, and he's an intelligent, informative, and reliable guide who speaks excellent English (and also German). Jay offers a wide range of touring options, or he can design a personalized tour around your interests. He'll lead you around Prague on a full-day private walking tour for around 1000 Kč per person (less if you want a half-day tour), and the experience is much more enjoyable than a bus tour with a large group. We recommend him highly. The best and easiest way to contact him is through his web site.

Jay Pesta ⊠ Krizovnicke nam. 3, Staré Město ☎ 603-819-947 ⊕ www.prague-venice.cz **Prague Information Service** ⊠ Staromestské náměstí, Staré Město ☎ 236-002-569 ⊕ www.pis.cz.

WALKING TOURS

Themed walking tours are very popular in Prague. You can choose from tours on medieval architecture, "Velvet Revolution walks," visits to Communist monuments, and any number of pub crawls. Each year, four or five small operators do these tours, which generally last a couple of hours and cost 200 Kč to 300 Kč. Inquire at Prague Information Service or a major ticket agency for the current season's offerings.

A special guide service is available in the Czech Republic, designed to examine and explain the country's Jewish history. The company, Wittmann Tours, offers several different tours within Prague and also outside, including the Terezín concentration camp.

☑ Wittmann Tours ⊠ Mánesova 8, Vinohrady ☎ 222-252-472 ⊕ www.wittmann-tours.com.

STUDENTS IN PRAGUE

CKM (Cestovni Kancelář Mládeže) and GTS International provide information on travel bargains within the Czech Republic and abroad to students, travelers under 26, and teachers. KMC, the Young Travelers' Club, issues IYH cards (150 Kč for those under 26, 200 Kč for others) and books hostel beds throughout the country.

☑ CKM ⊠ Mánesova 77, Vinohrady ☎ 222-721-595 ⊕ www.ckm-praha.cz. **GTS International** ⊠ Ve Smečkách 33, Nové Město ☎ 222-211-204 ⊕ www.gtsint.cz. **KMC** (Young Travelers' Club) ⊠ Karoliny Světlé 30, Staré Město ☎ 222-221-328 ⊕ www.kmc.cz.

☑ IDs & Services STA Travel ⊠ 10 Downing St., New York, NY 10014 ☎ 212/627-3111, 800/777-0112 24-hr service center ☎ 212/627-3387 ⊕ www.sta.com. **Travel Cuts** ⊠ 187 College St., Toronto, Ontario M5T 1P7, Canada ☎ 800/592-2887 in U.S., 416/979-2406 or 866/246-9762 in Canada ☎ 416/979-8167 ⊕ www.travelcuts.com.

TAXES

The airport departure tax, which is included in the price of airline tickets, is now 550 Kč; the hotel tax rate is 5% and is usually included in your room price (ask if you are not sure).

VALUE-ADDED TAX

The Czech V.A.T. is called DPH (daň z přidané hodnoty), and there are two rates. The higher one (19%) covers nearly everything—gifts, souvenirs, clothing, and food in restaurants. Food in grocery stores and books are taxed by 5%. Exported goods are exempt from the tax, which can be refunded. All tourists outside the EU are en-

titled to claim the tax back if they spend over 2,500 Kč in one shop on the same day. The goods need to be exported within two months from the end of the purchase month. Global Refund processes V.A.T. refunds in the Czech Republic and will give you your refund in cash (U.S. dollars or euros) from a booth at the airport just past passport control; be aware that the Czech Republic does *not* provide a postage-paid mailer for V.A.T. refund forms, unlike most other European countries.

When making a purchase, **ask for a V.A.T. refund form** and find out whether the merchant gives refunds—not all stores do, nor are they required to. Have the form stamped like any customs form by customs officials when you leave the country or, if you're visiting several European Union countries, when you leave the EU. Be ready to show customs officials what you've bought (pack purchases together, in your carry-on luggage); budget extra time for this. After you're through passport control, take the form to a refund-service counter for an on-the-spot refund, or mail it to the address on the form (or the envelope with it) after you arrive home.

A service processes refunds for most shops. You receive the total refund stated on the form. Global Refund is a Europe-wide service with 210,000 affiliated stores and more than 700 refund counters—located at major airports and border crossings. Its refund form is called a Tax Free Check. The service issues refunds in the form of cash, check, or credit-card adjustment. If you don't have time to wait at the refund counter, you can mail in the form instead.

☑ V.A.T. Refunds Global Refund ⊠ Grafická 14, Praha 5 ☎ 800-186-238 ⊠ 99 Main St., Suite 307, Nyack, NY 10960 ☎ 800/566-9828 ☎ 845/348-1549 ⊕ www.globalrefund.com.

TAXIS

Dishonest taxi drivers are the shame of the nation. Luckily you probably won't need to rely on taxis for trips within the city center (it's usually easier to walk or take the subway). Typical scams include drivers doctoring the meter or simply failing to turn the meter on and then demanding an exorbitant sum at the end of the ride. In an honest cab, the meter starts at 30 Kč and increases by 25 Kč per km (½ mi) or 4 Kč per minute at rest. Most rides within town should cost no more than 100 Kč to 200 Kč. To minimize the chances of getting ripped off, avoid taxi stands in Wenceslas Square, Old Town Square, and other heavily touristed areas. The best alternative is to phone for a taxi in advance. Many radio-taxi firms have English-speaking operators.

⌂ Taxi Companies AAA Taxi ☎ 233-113-311 ⊕ www.aaa.radiotaxi.cz. **Profitaxi** ☎ 261-314-151.

TELEPHONES

Now that most people in Prague have mobile phones, working phone booths are harder to find. If you can't find a booth, the telephone office of the main post office is the best place to try. Once inside, follow signs for TELEGRAF/TELEFAX.

AREA & COUNTRY CODES

The country code for the Czech Republic is 420. There are no regional codes but rather a nationwide nine-digit standard. Prefixes 601 to 777 denote mobile phones and are not considered local calls.

When dialing out of the country, the country code is 1 for the United States and Canada, 61 for Australia, 64 for New Zealand, and 44 for the United Kingdom.

DIRECTORY & OPERATOR ASSISTANCE

You can reach an English-speaking operator from one of the major long-distance services on a toll-free number. The operator will connect your collect or credit-card call at the carrier's standard rates. In Prague, many phone booths allow direct international dialing.

INTERNATIONAL CALLS

The international dialing code is 00. For calls to the United States, Canada, or the United Kingdom, dial the international operator. Otherwise, ask the receptionist at any hotel to put a call through for you, but the surcharges and rates will be tremendously high.

With the prepaid Karta X (300 Kč to 1,000 Kč), rates to the U.S. are roughly 13 Kč per minute; a call to the U.K. costs about 12 Kč per minute. The cards are available at many money-changing stands and can work with any phone once you enter a 14-digit code. You do not need to find a booth with a card slot to use the cards.

⌂ Other Contacts International Operator ☎ 133004. **International Directory Assistance** ☎ 1181.

LOCAL CALLS

Coin-operated pay phones are hard to find. Most newer public phones operate only with a special telephone card, available from post offices and some newsstands in denominations of 150 Kč and up. Since the boom in mobile phone use, both the cards and working pay phones are harder to find. A short call within Prague costs a minimum of 4 Kč from a coin-operated phone or the equivalent of 3.5 Kč (1 unit) from a card-operated phone. The dial tone is a series of alternating short and long buzzes.

LONG-DISTANCE SERVICES

AT&T, MCI, and Sprint access codes make calling long-distance relatively convenient, but you may find the local access number blocked in many hotel rooms. First ask the hotel operator to connect you. If the hotel operator balks, ask for an international operator, or dial the international operator yourself. One way to improve your odds of getting connected to your long-distance carrier is to travel with more than one company's calling card (a hotel may block Sprint, for example, but not MCI). If all else fails, call from a pay phone.

⌂ Access Codes Long-Distance Access Numbers AT&T ☎ 0/042-000-101. **BT Direct** ☎ 0/042-004-401. **CanadaDirect** ☎ 0/042-000-151. **MCI** ☎ 0/042-000-112. **Sprint** ☎ 0/042-087-187.

TIME

The Czech Republic is on Central European Time (CET), one hour ahead of Greenwich Mean Time and six hours ahead of the Eastern time zone of the United States.

TIPPING

Service is usually not included in restaurant bills. Round the bill up to the next multiple of 10 (if the bill comes to 83 Kč, for example, give the waiter 90 Kč); 10%

is considered appropriate in all but the most expensive places. Tip also in pubs by rounding up to the next multiple of 10. Tip porters who bring bags to your rooms 40 Kč total. For room service, a 20 Kč tip is enough. In taxis, round the bill up by 10%. Give tour guides and helpful concierges between 50 Kč and 100 Kč for services rendered.

TOURS & PACKAGES

Because everything is prearranged on a prepackaged tour or independent vacation, you spend less time planning—and often get it all at a good price.

BOOKING WITH AN AGENT

Travel agents are excellent resources. But it's a good idea to collect brochures from several agencies, as some agents' suggestions may be influenced by relationships with tour and package firms that reward them for volume sales. If you have a special interest, find an agent with expertise in that area; the American Society of Travel Agents (ASTA; ➪ Travel Agencies) has a database of specialists worldwide; you can log on to the group's Web site to find one near you.

Make sure your travel agent knows the accommodations and other services of the place being recommended. Ask about the hotel's location, room size, beds, and whether it has a pool, room service, or programs for children, if you care about these. Has your agent been there in person or sent others whom you can contact?

Do some homework on your own, too: local tourism boards can provide information about lesser-known and small-niche operators, some of which may sell only direct.

BUYER BEWARE

Each year consumers are stranded or lose their money when tour operators—even large ones with excellent reputations—go out of business. So check out the operator. Ask several travel agents about its reputation, and try to **book with a company that has a consumer-protection program.** (Look for information in the company's brochure.) In the United States, members of the United States Tour Operators Asso-

ciation are required to set aside funds ($1 million) to help eligible customers cover payments and travel arrangements in the event that the company defaults. It's also a good idea to choose a company that participates in the American Society of Travel Agents' Tour Operator Program; ASTA will act as mediator in any disputes between you and your tour operator.

Remember that the more your package or tour includes, the better you can predict the ultimate cost of your vacation. Make sure you know exactly what is covered, and beware of hidden costs. Are taxes, tips, and transfers included? Entertainment and excursions? These can add up.

🔁 Tour-Operator Recommendations **American Society of Travel Agents** (➪ Travel Agencies). **National Tour Association** (NTA) ✉ 546 E. Main St., Lexington, KY 40508 ☎ 859/226-4444 or 800/682-8886 📠 859/226-4404 🌐 www.ntaonline.com. **United States Tour Operators Association** (USTOA) ✉ 275 Madison Ave., Suite 2014, New York, NY 10016 ☎ 212/599-6599 📠 212/599-6744 🌐 www.ustoa.com.

TRAIN TRAVEL

International trains arrive at and depart from either of two stations: the main station, Hlavní nádraží, is about 500 yards east of Wenceslas Square via Opletalova or Washingtonova Street. Then there's the suburban Nádraží Holešovice, about 2 km (1 mi) north of the city center. This is an unending source of confusion—always make certain you know which station your train is using. Note also that trains arriving from the west usually stop at Smíchov station, on the west bank of the Vltava, before continuing to the main station. Prague's other central train station, Masarykovo nádraží, serves mostly local trains but has an international ticket window that is often much less crowded than those at the main station.

For train times, consult timetables in a station or get in line at the information office upstairs at the main station (for domestic trains, open daily 3 AM to 11:45 PM) or downstairs near the exits under the ČD Centrum sign (open daily 6 AM to 7:30 PM). The main Čedok office also provides train information and issues tickets.

Wenceslas Square is a convenient five-minute walk from the main station (best not undertaken late at night), or you can take the subway (Line C) one stop in the Háje direction to Muzeum. A taxi ride from the main station to the center should cost about 100 Kč, but the station cabbies are known for overcharging. To reach the city center from Nádraží Holešovice, take the metro (Line C) four stops to Muzeum; a taxi ride should cost roughly 200 Kč to 250 Kč.

The state-run rail system is called České dráhy (ČD). On longer runs, it's not really worth taking anything less than an express (*rychlík*) train, marked in red on the timetable. Tickets are still very inexpensive: a second-class ticket from Prague to Brno cost 294 Kč at this writing. First-class is considerably more spacious and comfortable and well worth the cost (50% more than a standard ticket). A 40 Kč to 60 Kč supplement is charged for the excellent international expresses, EuroCity (EC) and InterCity (IC), and for domestic SuperCity (SC) schedules. A 20 Kč supplement applies to reserved seats on domestic journeys. If you haven't bought a ticket in advance at the station (mandatory for seat reservations), you can buy one aboard the train from the conductor. On timetables, departures (*odjezd*) appear on a yellow background; arrivals (*příjezd*) are on white. It's possible to book sleepers (*lůžkový*) or the less-roomy couchettes (*lehátkový*) on most overnight trains. You do not need to validate your train ticket before boarding.

▪️ Čedok ✉ Na Příkopě 18, Staré Město ☎ 224-197-111 ⊕ www.cedok.cz.
▪️ Train Stations Hlavní nádraží ✉ Wilsonova ul., Nové Město ☎ 224-224-200 schedules and fares ⊕ www.cd.cz. **Masarykovo nádraží** ✉ Hybernská 13, Nové Město. **Nádraží Holešovice** ✉ Vrbenskéhoo, Holešovice.

CUTTING COSTS

To save money, **look into rail passes.** But be aware that if you don't plan to cover many miles, you may come out ahead by buying individual tickets

The Eurail Pass and the Eurail Youthpass are not valid for travel within the Czech

Republic, and most rail passes, such as the Czech Flexipass, will wind up costing more than what you'd spend buying tickets on the spot, particularly if you intend to travel mainly in the Czech Republic, since international tickets normally are more expensive. The European East Pass, for example, is good for first-class travel on the national railroads of the Czech Republic, Austria, Hungary, Poland, and Slovakia. The pass allows five days of unlimited travel within a one-month period for $220, and it must be purchased from Rail Europe before your departure. The many Czech rail passes available are useful chiefly to regular travelers. A discount applies to any group of 2 to 15 people traveling second class (*sleva pro skupiny*). It's always cheaper to buy a return ticket. Foreign visitors will find it easiest to inquire at the international booking offices of major stations for the latest discounts and passes that will apply to them.

▪️ Rail Europe ✉ 226–230 Westchester Ave., White Plains, NY 10604 ☎ 877/257-2887 ⊕ www.raileurope.com ✉ 2087 Dundas E, Suite 106, Mississauga, Ontario, Canada L4X 1M2 ☎ 800/361-7245.

TRAVEL AGENCIES

A good travel agent puts your needs first. Look for an agency that has been in business at least five years, emphasizes customer service, and has someone on staff who specializes in your destination. In addition, **make sure the agency belongs to a professional trade organization.** The American Society of Travel Agents (ASTA) has more than 10,000 members in some 140 countries, enforces a strict code of ethics, and will step in to mediate agent-client disputes involving ASTA members. ASTA also maintains a directory of agents on its Web site. (If a travel agency is also acting as your tour operator, *see* Buyer Beware *in* Tours & Packages.)

Travel agencies can be useful for visitors to Prague; they can provide you with information and then book your tickets. American Express and Thomas Cook, two big international agencies, have convenient offices in Prague. For bus tickets to just about anywhere in Europe, Bohemia Tour is useful. Čedok, the ubiquitous Czech travel agency, provides general tourist information and city maps. Čedok will also exchange money, book accommodations, arrange guided tours, and book passage on airlines, buses, and trains. You can pay for Čedok services, including booking rail tickets, with any major credit card. Note limited weekend hours. The main office is open weekdays from 8:30 to 6 and Saturday from 9 to 1.

In the U.S., an agency like Tatra Travel, which specializes in Eastern and Central Europe, can save you money booking nonstop flights to the Czech Republic; the agency also can book Czech Airlines travel packages.

🛃 Local Agent Referrals **American Society of Travel Agents (ASTA)** ✉ 1101 King St., Suite 200, Alexandria, VA 22314 ☎ 703/739-2782 or 800/965-2782 24-hr hotline 🖶 703/684-8319 ⊕ www. astanet.com. **Association of British Travel Agents** ✉ 68-71 Newman St., London W1T 3AH ☎ 020/7637-2444 🖶 020/7637-0713 ⊕ www.abta.com. **Association of Canadian Travel Agencies** ✉ 130 Albert St., Suite 1705, Ottawa, Ontario K1P 5G4 ☎ 613/237-3657 🖶 613/237-7052 ⊕ www.acta.ca. **Australian Federation of Travel Agents** ✉ Level 3, 309 Pitt St., Sydney, NSW 2000 ☎ 02/9264-3299 or 1300/363-416 🖶 02/9264-1085 ⊕ www.afta.com. au. **Travel Agents' Association of New Zealand** ✉ Level 5, Tourism and Travel House, 79 Boulcott St., Box 1888, Wellington 6001 ☎ 04/499-0104 🖶 04/499-0786 ⊕ www.taanz.org.nz.

🛃 Prague Travel Agencies **American Express** ✉ Václavské nám. 56, Nové Město ☎ 224-219-992 ✉ Na příkopě 19, Nové Město ☎ 222-800-800. **Čedok** ✉ Na Příkopě 18, Staré Město ☎ 224-197-111 ⊕ www.cedok.cz. **Prague International** ✉ Senovážné náměstí 23, Nové Město ☎ 224-142-431 ⊕ www.pragueinternationalcz.

🛃 U.S. Travel Agencies **Tatra Travel** ✉ 212 E. 51 St., New York, NY ☎ 212/486-0533 ⊕ www. tatratravel.com.

VISITOR INFORMATION

Learn more about foreign destinations by checking government-issued travel advisories and country information. For a broader picture, consider information from more than one country.

🛃 Before You Leave **Czech Tourist Authority** In U.S. ✉ 1109-1111 Madison Ave., New York, NY 10028 ☎ 212/288-0830 🖶 212/288-0971 ⊕ www. czechcenter.com ✉ In Canada ✉ Czech Airlines office, Simpson Tower, 401 Bay St., Suite 1510, Toronto, Ontario M5H 2YA ☎ 416/363-9928 🖶 416/363-0239 ⊕ www.czechtourism.com In U.K. ✉ 13 Harley St., London W1G 9QG ☎ 020/7307-5180 🖶 020/7323-3709 ⊕ www.czechcentre.org.uk.

🛃 In Prague **Czech Tourist Authority** ✉ Rytířská 31, Staré Město ☎ 221-610-252 🖶 221-610-282 ⊕ www.czechcentre.cz. **Prague Information Service (PIS)** ✉ Staroměstská radnice [Old Town Hall], Staré Město ☎ 224-482-562 ⊕ www.pis.cz ✉ Na Příkopě 20, Nové Město ☎ No phone ✉ Hlavní nádraží, lower hall, Staré Město ☎ No phone ✉ Malostranská mostecká věž, Malá Strana ☎ No phone.

🛃 Government Advisories **U.S. Department of State** ✉ Overseas Citizens Services Office, 2100 Pennsylvania Ave. NW, 4th fl., Washington, DC 20520 ☎ 202/647-5225 interactive hotline, 888/407-4747 ⊕ www.travel.state.gov. **Consular Affairs Bureau of Canada** ☎ 800/267-6788 or 613/944-6788 ⊕ www. voyage.gc.ca. **U.K. Foreign and Commonwealth Office** ✉ Travel Advice Unit, Consular Division, Old Admiralty Bldg., London SW1A 2PA ☎ 0870/606-0290 or 020/7008-1500 ⊕ www.fco.gov.uk/travel. **Australian Department of Foreign Affairs and Trade** ☎ 300/139-281 travel advice, 02/6261-1299 Consular Travel Advice Faxback Service ⊕ www.dfat.gov.au. **New Zealand Ministry of Foreign Affairs and Trade** ☎ 04/439-8000 ⊕ www.mft.govt.nz.

WEB SITES

Do check out the World Wide Web when planning your trip. You'll find everything from weather forecasts to virtual tours of famous cities. Be sure to visit Fodors.com (⊕ www.fodors.com), a complete travel-planning site. You can research prices and book plane tickets, hotel rooms, rental cars, vacation packages, and more. In addition, you can post your pressing questions in the Travel Talk section. Other planning tools include a currency converter and weather reports, and there are loads of links to travel resources.

🛃 Suggested Web Sites **Czech Tourist Authority** ⊕ www.visitczechia.cz.

EXPLORING PRAGUE

1

MOST ATMOSPHERIC SQUARE
Staroměstské náměstí, *Staré Město* ⇨*p.13*

A MOST WITH THE MOST
Karlův most, *Malá Strana* ⇨*p.21*

BEST BAROQUE CHURCH
Kostel Sv. Mikuláše, *Malá Strana* ⇨*p.20*

PRAGUE'S SPIRITUAL HEART
Chrám svatého Víta, *Pražsky Hrad* ⇨*p32*

BEST MUSEUM
Lobkovický palác, *Pražsky Hrad* ⇨*p.37*

RESTING PLACE OF FAMOUS SOULS
Vyšehrad Hřbitov, *Vyšehrad* ⇨*p.46*

MOST SOBERING SIGHT
Starý Židovský hřbitov, Josefov ⇨*p.17*

By Frank
Kuznik & Philip
Traynor

THE SPINE OF THE CITY IS THE RIVER VLTAVA (also known by its German name, Moldau), which runs through the city from south to north with a single sharp curve to the east. Prague originally comprised five independent towns, represented today by its main historic districts: Hradčany (Castle Area), Malá Strana (Lesser Quarter), Staré Město (Old Town), Nové Město (New Town), and Josefov (Jewish Quarter).

Hradčany, the seat of Czech royalty for hundreds of years, has as its center the Pražský hrad (Prague Castle), which overlooks the city from its hilltop west of the Vltava. Steps lead down from Hradčany to the Lesser Quarter, an area dense with ornate mansions built by 17th- and 18th-century nobility.

Karlův most (Charles Bridge) connects the Lesser Quarter with the Old Town. A few blocks east of the bridge is the district's focal point, Staroměstské náměstí (Old Town Square). The Old Town is bounded by the curving Vltava and three large commercial avenues: Revoluční to the east, Na Příkopě to the southeast, and Národní třída to the south. North of Old Town Square, the diminutive Jewish Quarter fans out around the wide avenue called Pařížská.

Beyond the Old Town to the south is the New Town, a highly commercial area that includes the city's largest square, Karlovo náměstí (Charles Square). Roughly 1 km (½ mi) farther south is Vyšehrad, an ancient castle high above the river.

On a promontory to the east of Václavské náměstí (Wenceslas Square) stretches Vinohrady, once the favored neighborhood of well-to-do Czechs. Bordering Vinohrady are the neighborhoods of Žižkov to the north and Nusle to the south. On the west bank of the Vltava lie many older residential neighborhoods and several sprawling parks. About 3 km (2 mi) from the center in every direction, Communist-era housing projects begin their unsightly sprawl.

STARÉ MĚSTO (OLD TOWN)

a good
walk

Numbers in the text correspond to numbers in the margin and on the Central Prague map.

The north end of Wenceslas Square, which ends in a T with a wide pedestrian walkway and upscale shopping strip, is a good place to begin a tour of Old Town. This intersection marks the border between the old and new worlds in Prague. A quick glance around shows the often-jarring juxtaposition: centuries-old buildings cheek-by-jowl with modern retail names like United Colors of Benneton and McDonald's.

Start on the perimeter of Old Town by turning right at the tall, art deco Koruna complex onto **Na Příkopě** ❶ ▶. A short detour down the first street on your left, Havířská ulice, brings you to the 18th-century **Stavovské divadlo** ❷. Part of the National Theater complex of stages, this theater appears relatively plain outside, but glitters with refurbished baroque beauty inside.

Return to Na Příkopě, turn left, and continue to the end of the street. On weekdays between 8 AM and 5 PM, it's well worth taking a peek at the stunning interior of the Živnostenská banka (Merchant's Bank), at No. 20. A little farther on, crane your neck at the Česká národní banka (No. 32), where atop the building you can see a Central European version of Lady Liberty running with a lion.

Na Příkopě ends abruptly at náměstí Republiky (Republic Square), an important New Town transportation hub (with a busy metro stop). Two buildings, built centuries apart but both monumental and stunning, anchor the area. Hundreds of years of grime have not diminished the majesty of the Gothic **Prašná brána** ❸, with its stately spires looming above the square. Adjacent to this tower, the rapturous art nouveau **Obecní dům** ❹ concert hall and municipal center looks like a brightly decorated confection.

Walk through the archway of the massive Prašná brána and down the formal **Celetná ulice** ❺, the first leg of the so-called Royal Way. Monarchs favored this route primarily because the houses along Celetná were among the city's finest, providing a suitable backdrop to the coronation procession. The Cubist building at Celetná 34 is **Dům U černé Matky Boží** ❻, the House of the Black Madonna, now a museum. You can see the Madonna mounted in a niche cut in the corner of the building.

After a few blocks, Celetná opens onto **Staroměstské náměstí** ❼, the busy hub of Old Town, surrounded by dazzling architecture on all sides. On the east side of the square, the double-spired **Kostel Panny Marie před Týnem** ❽, rises from behind a row of patrician houses. To the immediate left of this church, at No. 13, is Dům U Kamenného zvonu (House at the Stone Bell), a baroque town house that has been stripped down to its original Gothic elements.

Next door stands the gorgeous pink-and-ocher **Palác Kinských** ❾, the subject of recent legal battles by a descendant of the original owners, who hopes to reclaim the property. At this end of the square, you can't help noticing the expressive **Jan Hus monument** ❿. At this point, you may wish to take a detour to see the National Gallery's Gothic art collection at **Klášter svaté Anežky České** ⓫. Go northeast from the square up Dlouha Street, and then straight along Kozi Street all the way until it ends at U Milosrdných. If your tastes run more to commerce than art, take a stroll instead up Pařížská street out of the north end of the square, which has some of the most glamorous stores—and storefronts—in the city.

Return to Staroměstské náměstí, and just beyond the Jan Hus monument is the Gothic **Staroměstská radnice** ⓬, which, with its impressive 200-foot tower, gives the square its sense of importance. As the hour approaches, join the crowds milling below the tower's 15th-century astronomical clock for a brief but spooky spectacle taken straight from the Middle Ages involving a skeleton, the 12 apostles, and a forbidding-looking Turk; this happens every hour on the hour and tends to draw large crowds of onlookers. The square's second church, the baroque **Kostel svatého Mikuláše** ⓭, is not to be confused with the Lesser Quarter's similarly named Chrám svatého Mikuláše on the other side of the river.

4 <

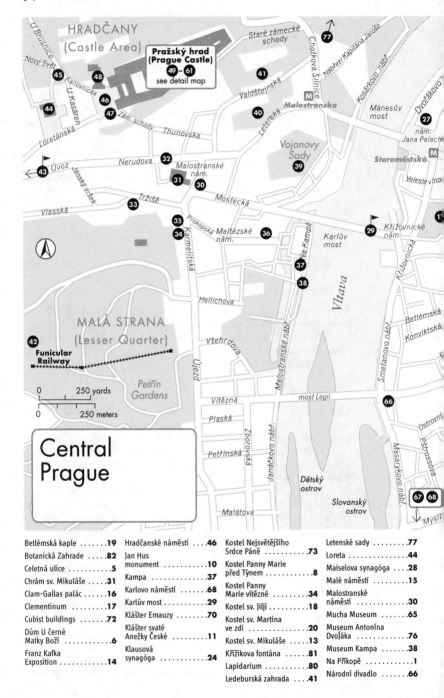

Betlémská kaple **19**

Botanická Zahrade **82**

Celetná ulice **5**

Chrám sv. Mikuláše ... **31**

Clam-Gallas palác **16**

Clementinum **17**

Cubist buildings **72**

Dům U černé
Matky Boží **6**

Franz Kafka
Exposition **14**

Hradčanské náměstí ... **46**

Jan Hus
monument **10**

Kampa **37**

Karlovo náměstí **68**

Karlův most **29**

Klášter Emauzy **70**

Klášter svaté
Anežky České **11**

Klausová
synagóga **24**

Kostel Nejsvětějšího
Srdce Páně **73**

Kostel Panny Marie
před Týnem **8**

Kostel Panny
Marie vítězné **34**

Kostel sv. Jiljí **18**

Kostel sv. Martina
ve zdi **20**

Kostel sv. Mikuláše ... **13**

Křížíkova fontána **81**

Lapidarium **80**

Ledeburská zahrada ... **41**

Letenské sady **77**

Loreta **44**

Maiselova synagóga ... **28**

Malé náměstí **15**

Malostranské
náměstí **30**

Mucha Museum **65**

Museum Antonína
Dvořáka **76**

Museum Kampa **38**

Na Příkopě **1**

Národní divadlo **66**

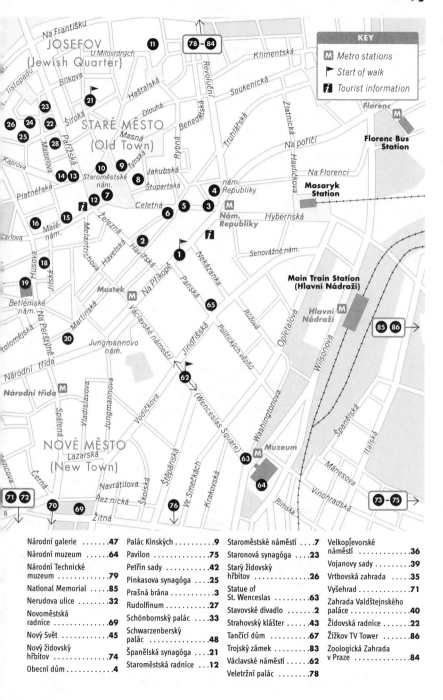

Národní galerie **47**

Národní muzeum **64**

Národní Technické
muzeum **79**

National Memorial **85**

Nerudova ulice **32**

Novoměstská
radnice **69**

Nový Svět **45**

Nový židovský
hřbitov **74**

Obecní dům **4**

Palác Kinských **9**

Pavilon **75**

Petřín sady **42**

Pinkasova synagóga **25**

Prašná brána **3**

Rudolfinum **27**

Schönbornský palác **33**

Schwarzenberský
palác **48**

Španělská synagóga **21**

Staroměstská radnice . . .**12**

Staroměstské náměstí **7**

Staronová synagóga **23**

Starý židovský
hřbitov **26**

Statue of
St. Wenceslas **63**

Stavovské divadlo **2**

Strahovský klášter **43**

Tančící dům **67**

Trojský zámek **83**

Václavské náměstí **62**

Veletržní palác **78**

Velkopřevorské
náměstí **36**

Vojanovy sady **39**

Vrtbovská zahrada **35**

Vyšehrad **71**

Zahrada Valdštejnského
paláce **40**

Židovská radnice **22**

Žižkov TV Tower **86**

Zoologická Zahrada
v Praze **84**

You'll find the **Franz Kafka Exposition** ⑭ adjoining Kostel svatého Mikuláše on náměstí Franze Kafky, a little square that used to be part of U Radnice Street. Turn left and continue along U Radnice proper a few yards until you come to **Malé náměstí** ⑮, a minisquare with arcades on one side. Look for tiny Karlova ulice, which begins in the southwest corner of the square, and take another quick right to stay on it (watch the signs—this medieval street seems designed to confound the visitor). If you're a tried-and-true fan of 20th-century Czech art, you could stop at the České muzeum výtvarných umění (Czech Museum of Fine Arts), but you're more likely to want to pause and inspect the exotic **Clam-Gallas palác** ⑯, behind you at Husova 20. You can recognize it easily: look for the Titans in the doorway holding up what must be a very heavy baroque façade. A block north, the street opens onto Mariánské náměstí, where you'll find the entrance to the mammoth **Clementinum** ⑰.

Head the other way down Husova for a glimpse of ecstatic baroque stuffed inside somber Gothic at the **Kostel svatého Jiljí** ⑱, at No. 8. Continue walking along Husova to Na Perštýně, and look up. You can see a sculpture of a man hanging from a building. "Hanging Out" is by David Černý, the art prankster also responsible for the upside-down horse hanging in the Lucerna pasáž on Wenceslas Square. A right turn puts you on a quiet square, Betlémské náměstí, where you'll find the most revered of all Hussite churches in Prague, the **Betlémská kaple** ⑲.

Return to Na Perštýně and continue walking to the right. As you near the back of the buildings of the busy Národní třída (National Boulevard), turn left at Martinská ulice. At the end of the street, the forlorn but majestic church **Kostel svatého Martina ve zdi** ⑳ looks as if it got lost. Walk around the church to the left, through a little archway of apartments and a courtyard with shops and restaurants, onto the bustling Národní třída. To the left, a five-minute walk away, lies Wenceslas Square and the starting point of this walk.

There's no public transit in the Old Town, so walking is really the most practical way to get around; you could take a cab, but it's not really worth it. It takes only about 15 to 20 minutes to walk from Náměstí Republiky to Staroměstská. If you're coming to the Old Town from another part of Prague, three Metro stops circumscribe the area: Staroměstská on the west, Náměstí Republiky on the east, and Můstek on the south, at the point where Old Town and Wenceslas Square meet.

TIMING   Wenceslas Square and Old Town Square are busy with activity around-the-clock almost year-round. If you're in search of a little peace and quiet, you can find the streets at their most subdued on early weekend mornings or when it's cold. The streets in this walking tour are reasonably close together and can be covered in a half-day. Remember to be in the Old Town Square just before the hour if you want to see the astronomical clock in action.

What to See

⑲ **Betlémská kaple** (Bethlehem Chapel). The original church was built at the end of the 14th century, and the Czech religious reformer Jan Hus was a regular preacher here from 1402 until his exile in 1412. After the

WHAT'S FREE

TROLLING THE ATMOSPHERIC STREETS OF OLD TOWN is always free, as is one of the city's most popular attractions, the Astronomical Clock. You can explore the grounds and gardens of Prague Castle without a charge, including the Královský letohrádek (Royal Summer Palace, also known as the Belvedere) that sits in the eastern end of the Royal Gardens and is considered one of the most beautiful Renaissance structures north of the Alps. St. Vitus's Cathedral, inside the Castle walls, does not charge for visits to the western third of the structure, including the façade and the two towers you can see from outside. You must pay for most other sights within Prague Castle.

The National Museum, at the top of Wenceslas Square, contains collections of rocks and minerals as well as plenty of musty stuffed animals; admission is free on the first Monday of the month. An exposition on the history of the Czech lands from the 4th century BC to the mid-19th century at the Lobkovický palác (Lobowitz Palace) charges no fee on the first Wednesday of the month. Inside Vyšehrad, Hřbitov cemetery, the final resting place for many of the country's famous writers, academics, musicians, and actors, is open without a charge. In the upscale neighborhood Vinohrady, Nový židovský hřbitov, or the New Jewish Cemetary, has no fee; Franz Kafka's grave, marked by a thin, white tombstone, can be found here.

Thirty Years' War, the church fell into the hands of the Jesuits and was finally demolished in 1786. Excavations carried out after World War I uncovered the original portal and three windows, and the entire church was reconstructed during the 1950s. Although little remains of the first church, some remnants of Hus's teachings can still be read on the inside walls. A word of warning: even though regular hours are posted, the church is not always open at those times. It's worth visiting, but only if you're in the immediate neighborhood. ⊠ Betlémské nám. 5, Staré Město ⊑ 50 Kč ☉ Tues.–Sun. 10–6:30.

⑤ Celetná ulice. Most of this street's façades indicate the buildings are from the 17th or 18th century, but appearances are deceiving: many of the houses in fact have parts that date back to the 12th century. Be sure to look above the street-level storefronts to see the fine examples of baroque detail.

⑯ Clam-Gallas palác (Clam-Gallas Palace). The beige-and-brown palace, the work of Johann Bernhard Fischer von Erlach, the famed Viennese architectural virtuoso of the day, was begun in 1713 and finally finished in 1729. Enter the building for a glimpse of the battered but finely carved staircase, the work of the master himself, and of the Italian frescoes—

featuring Apollo—that surround it. Clam-Gallas palác is now used for art exhibitions and concerts. If you don't see anyone selling tickets at a table on the street, go inside and up to the desk on the second floor. ⊠ *Husova 20, Staré Město* ☎ *No phone* ⊕ *www.ahmp.cz/eng* ⊙ *Tues.–Sun. 10–6.*

⑰ Clementinum. The origins of this massive complex date back to the 12th and 13th centuries, but it's best-known as the stronghold of the Jesuits, who occupied it for more than 200 years beginning in the early 1600s. Very little of the complex is open to the public, but what you can see is well worth a visit. The Jesuits built a resplendent library, with fabulous ceiling murals that depict the three levels of knowledge with the "Dome of Wisdom" as a centerpiece. Next door, the Mirror Chapel is as dazzling as its name implies, with acoustics to match. Mozart played here, and the space is still used for occasional chamber music concerts. The Astronomical Tower in the middle of the complex was used by Johannes Kepler, and for centuries afterward functioned as the "Prague Meridian" where the time was set each day. At high noon, a timekeeper would appear on the balcony and wave a flag that could be seen from the Castle, where a cannon was fired to mark the hour. ⊠ *Mariánské náměstí 4, Staré Město* ☎ *224–813–892* 🎟 *100 Kč* ⊙ *Mar.–Dec., weekdays 2–7, weekends 10–7.*

⑥ Dům U černé Matky Boží (House of the Black Madonna). In the second decade of the 20th century, young Czech architects boldly applied Cubism's radical reworking of visual space to architecture and design. This museum, refurbished and now run by the National Gallery, showcases fine examples of every genre. The building itself is Cubist, designed by Josef Gočár. Inside, there are three floors of paintings, sculptures, drawings, furniture, and other "applied arts" in the Cubist style. And don't miss the gift shop, which while pricey is worth discovering for some of the oddest-looking home furnishings you've ever seen. ⊠ *Celetná 34, Staré Město* ☎ *224–211–732* ⊕ *www.ngprague.cz* 🎟 *100 Kč* ⊙ *Tues.–Sun. 10–6.*

⑭ Franz Kafka Exposition. Kafka came into the world on July 3, 1883, in a house next to the Kostel svatého Mikuláše (Church of St. Nicholas). For years the writer was only grudgingly acknowledged by the Communist cultural bureaucrats, reflecting the traditionally ambiguous attitude of the Czech government toward his work. As a German and a Jew, moreover, Kafka could easily be dismissed as standing outside the mainstream of Czech literature. Following the 1989 revolution, however, Kafka's popularity soared, and his works are now widely available in Czech. Though only the portal of the original house remains, inside the building is a fascinating little exhibit (mostly photographs) on Kafka's life, with commentary in English. ⊠ *Náměstí Franze Kafky 3, Staré Město* 🎟 *50 Kč* ⊙ *Tues.–Fri. 10–6, Sat. 10–5, Sun. 10–6.*

need a break?

Just a few doors south of the Kafka house, tucked under the portico, **Bar U Radnice** (⊠ U Radnice 2) is a comfortable nook that offers coffee, tea, hot chocolate, and soft drinks along with a tasty selection of cakes, baguettes and salads.

⑩ Jan Hus monument. Few memorials have elicited as much controversy as this one, which was dedicated in July 1915, exactly 500 years after Hus was burned at the stake in Constance, Germany. Some maintain that the monument's Secessionist style (the inscription seems to come right from turn-of-the-20th-century Vienna) clashes with the Gothic and baroque of the square. Others dispute the romantic depiction of Hus, who appears here in flowing garb as tall and bearded. The real Hus, historians maintain, was short and had a baby face. Still, no one can take issue with the influence of this fiery preacher, whose ability to transform doctrinal disputes, both literally and metaphorically, into the language of the common man made him into a religious and national symbol for the Czechs. ⊠ *Staroměstské náměstí, Staré Město.*

⑪ Klášter svaté Anežky České (St. Agnes's Convent). Situated near the river between Pařížská and Revoluční streets, this peaceful complex has Prague's first buildings in the Gothic style, built between the 1230s and the 1280s. The convent now provides a fitting home for the National Gallery's marvelous collection of Czech Gothic art, including altarpieces, portraits, and statues. ⊠ *U Milosrdných 17, Staré Město* ☎ *224–810–628* ⊕ *www.ngprague.cz* ⊠ *100 Kč* ☉ *Tues.–Sun. 10–6.*

★ ⑧ Kostel Panny Marie před Týnem (Church of the Virgin Mary Before Týn). The exterior of the church is one of the best examples of Prague Gothic and is in part the work of Peter Parler, architect of the Charles Bridge and Chrám svatého Víta (St. Vitus's Cathedral). Construction of its twin black-spire towers was begun later, by King Jiří of Poděbrad in 1461, during the heyday of the Hussites. Jiří had a gilded chalice, the symbol of the Hussites, proudly displayed on the front gable between the two towers. Following the defeat of the Czech Protestants by the Catholic Hapsburgs, the chalice was removed and eventually replaced by a Madonna. As a final blow, the chalice was melted down and made into the Madonna's glimmering halo (you still can see it by walking into the center of the square and looking up between the spires). The entrance to the church is through the arcades on Old Town Square, under the house at No. 604.

Much of the interior, including the tall nave, was rebuilt in the baroque style in the 17th century. Some Gothic pieces remain, however: look to the left of the main altar for a beautifully preserved set of early Gothic carvings. The main altar itself was painted by Karel Škréta, a luminary of the Czech baroque. Before leaving the church, look for the grave marker (tucked away to the right of the main altar) of the great Danish astronomer Tycho Brahe, who came to Prague as "Imperial Mathematicus" in 1599 under Rudolf II. As a scientist, Tycho had a place in history that is assured: Johannes Kepler (another resident of the Prague court) used Tycho's observations to formulate his laws of planetary motion. But it is myth that has endeared Tycho to the hearts of Prague residents. The robust Dane, who was reportedly fond of duels, is said to have lost part of his nose in one (take a closer look at the marker). He quickly had a wax nose fashioned for everyday use but preferred to parade around on holidays and festive occasions sporting a bright silver one; later examination proved that it was, in fact, copper. ⊠ *Staroměstské náměstí, between Celetná and Týnská, Staré Město* ☉ *Weekdays 9–1.*

⑱ Kostel svatého Jiljí (Church of St. Giles). This church was an important outpost of Czech Protestantism in the 16th century. The exterior is a powerful example of Gothic architecture, including the buttresses and a characteristic portal. The interior, as in many important Czech churches, is baroque, with a design by Johann Bernhard Fischer von Erlach and sweeping frescoes by Václav Reiner. The interior can be viewed during the day from the vestibule or at the evening concerts held several times a week. ⊠ *Husova 8, Staré Město* ✆ *Weekdays 9–5.*

⑳ Kostel svatého Martina ve zdi (Church of St. Martin-in-the-Wall). It was here in 1414 that Holy Communion was first given to the Bohemian laity in the form of both bread and wine, in defiance of the Catholic custom of the time, which dictated that only bread was to be offered to the masses, with wine reserved for the priests and clergy. From then on, the chalice came to symbolize the Hussite movement. The church is open for evening concerts, held several times each week, but that's the only time you'll be able to see the interior. ⊠ *Martinská ulice, Staré Město.*

need a break? In the Platýz courtyard immediately east of the church (also accessible from Národní), **Káva Káva Káva** (⊠ Národní třída 37) offers one of the best selections of coffee in town, along with a small assortment of pastries and desserts. You can access the Internet for free if you spend 60 Kč or more during designated hours.

⑬ Kostel svatého Mikuláše (Church of St. Nicholas). Designed in the 18th century by Prague's own master of late baroque, Kilian Ignaz Dientzenhofer, this church is probably less successful in capturing the style's lyric exuberance than its namesake across town, the Chrám svatého Mikuláše. Still, Dientzenhofer utilized the limited space to create a well-balanced structure. The interior is compact, with a beautiful but small chandelier and an enormous black organ that seems to overwhelm the rear of the church. The church hosts almost continuous afternoon and evening tourist concerts. ⊠*Staroměstské náměstí, Staré Město* ✆ *Apr.–Oct., Mon. noon–4, Tues.–Sat. 10–4, Sun. noon–3; Nov.–Mar., Tues., Fri., and Sun. 10–noon; Wed. 10–4.*

⑮ Malé náměstí (Small Square). Note the iron fountain dating from around 1560 in the center of the square. The colorfully painted house at No. 3, originally a hardware store, is not as old as it looks, but here and there you can find authentic Gothic portals and Renaissance sgraffiti that betray the square's true age.

❶ Na Příkopě. The name means "At the Moat" and harks back to the time when the street was indeed a moat separating the Old Town from the New Town. Today the pedestrian zone Na Příkopě is prime shopping territory. Sleek modern buildings have been sandwiched between baroque palaces, with the latter cut up inside to accommodate casinos, fast-food restaurants, and, at No. 10, the Museum of Communism. The new structures all look the same inside, but at the end of the block, Slovanský dům (No. 22) is worth a look. The former site of both the Gestapo and Communist Party offices, this late-18th-century structure has been tastefully refurbished and now houses fashionable boutiques, tony restaurants, and one of the city's better multiplex cinemas.

④ **Obecní dům** (Municipal House). The city's art nouveau showpiece still
FodorsChoice fills the role it had when it was completed in 1911: it's a center for con-
★ certs, rotating art exhibits, and café society. The mature art nouveau style recalls the lengths the Czech middle classes went to at the turn of the 20th century to imitate Paris, then the epitome of style and glamour. Much of the interior bears the work of Alfons Mucha, Max Švabinský, and other leading Czech artists. Mucha decorated the Hall of the Lord Mayor upstairs with impressive, magical frescoes depicting Czech history; unfortunately it's not open to the public. The beautiful **Smetanova síň** (Smetana Hall), which hosts concerts by the Prague Symphony Orchestra as well as international players, is on the second floor. The ground-floor restaurants are touristy but lovely, with glimmering chandeliers and exquisite woodwork. There's also a beer hall in the cellar with decent food and superbly executed ceramic murals on the walls. ⊠ *Náměstí Republiky 5, Staré Město* ☎ *222–002–100* ⊕ *www. obecnidum.cz* ⊗ *Information center and box office daily 10–6.*

need a break? If you prefer subtle elegance, head around the corner from Obecní dům to the café at the **Hotel Paříž** (⊠ U Obecního domu 1, Staré Město ☎ 224–222–151), a Jugendstil jewel tucked away on a relatively quiet street.

⑨ **Palác Kinských** (Kinský Palace). This exuberant building, built in 1765 from Kilian Ignaz Dientzenhofer's design, is considered one of Prague's finest late-baroque structures. With its exaggerated pink overlay and numerous statues, the façade looks extreme when contrasted with the more staid baroque elements of other nearby buildings. (The interior, however, was "modernized" under Communism.) The palace once housed a German school—where Franz Kafka was a student for nine misery-laden years—and presently contains the National Gallery's graphics collection. It was from this building that Communist leader Klement Gottwald, flanked by his Slovak comrade Vladimír Clementis, first addressed the crowds after seizing power in February 1948—an event recounted in the first chapter of Milan Kundera's novel *The Book of Laughter and Forgetting.* ⊠ *Staroměstské náměstí 12, Staré Město* ☎ *224–210–758* ⊕ *www.ngprague.cz* ⊠ *100 Kč* ⊗ *Tues.–Sun. 10–6.*

③ **Prašná brána** (Powder Tower). Construction of the tower, which replaced one of the city's 13 original gates, was begun by King Vladislav II of Jagiello in 1475. At the time, the kings of Bohemia maintained their royal residence next door, on the site of the current Obecní dům, and the tower was intended to be the grandest gate of all. But Vladislav was Polish and thus heartily disliked by the rebellious Czech citizens of Prague. Nine years after he assumed power, fearing for his life, he moved the royal court across the river to Prague Castle. Work on the tower was abandoned, and the half-finished structure was used for storing gunpowder—hence its odd name—until the end of the 17th century. The oldest part of the tower is the base. The golden spires were not added until the end of the 19th century. Climb to the top for a striking view of the Old Town and Prague Castle in the distance. ⊠ *Náměstí Republiky, Staré Město* 📷 *40 Kč* ⊙ *Apr.–Oct., daily 10–6.*

off the
beaten
path

MUZEUM HLAVNÍHO MěSTA PRAHY (Museum of the City of Prague) – The high point of this museum is a paper model of Prague that shows what the city looked like before the Jewish ghetto was destroyed in a massive fire in 1689. Display boards—not all are in English—trace the history of the city from its origins through the 17th century. Though in the Nové Město, the trek over to this out-of-the-way museum is easier from Old Town, since it's near the Florenc Metro station. ⊠ *Na Poříčí 52, Nové Město* ☎ *224–816–772* 📷 *30 Kč* ⊙ *Tues.–Sun. 9–6* Ⓜ *Lines B & C: Florenc.*

★ ⓬ **Staroměstská radnice** (Old Town Hall). This is one of Prague's magnets: hundreds of people gravitate to it throughout the day to see the hour struck by the mechanical figures of the **astronomical clock.** Just before the hour, look to the upper part of the clock, where a skeleton begins by tolling a death knell and turning an hourglass upside down. The Twelve Apostles parade momentarily, and then a cockerel flaps its wings and crows, piercing the air as the hour finally strikes. To the right of the skeleton, the dreaded Turk nods his head, seemingly hinting at another invasion like those of the 16th and 17th centuries. This small spectacle doesn't clue viewers in to the way this 15th-century marvel indicates the time—by the season, the zodiac sign, and the positions of the sun and moon. The calendar under the clock dates from the mid-19th century.

The Old Town Hall served as the center of administration for the Old Town beginning in 1338, when King John of Luxembourg first granted the city council the right to a permanent location. The impressive 200-foot **Town Hall Tower,** where the clock is mounted, was first built in the 14th century and given its current late-Gothic appearance around 1500 by the master Matyáš Rejsek. For a rare view of the Old Town and its maze of crooked streets and alleyways, climb the ramp or ride the elevator to the top of the tower.

If you walk around the hall to the left, you can see it's actually a series of houses jutting into the square; they were purchased over the years and successively added to the complex. On the other side, jagged stonework reveals where a large, neo-Gothic wing once adjoined the tower until it was destroyed during fighting between townspeople and Nazi troops in May 1945.

Guided tours (most guides speak English, and English texts are on hand) of the Old Town Hall depart from the main desk inside. Previously unseen parts of the tower were opened to the public in 2002, and you can now see the inside of the famous clock. ⊠ *Staroměstské náměstí, Staré Město* ⊙ *May–Sept., Tues.–Sun. 9–6, Mon. 11–6; Oct.–Apr., Tues.–Sun. 9–5, Mon. 11–5* 📷 *Tower 40 Kč, tours 50 Kč.*

need a break? One of the best rooftop views in the city is at **Hotel U Prince** (✉ Staroměstká náměstí 29), diagonally opposite the astronomical clock. Go in the arched entryway to the right and walk all the way to the back, where a golden angel with a trumpet stands watch over a glass-door lift. Take the lift to the rooftop bar, which has covered seating and portable heaters running in cold weather.

❼ Staroměstské náměstí (Old Town Square). There are places that, on first glimpse, stop you dead in your tracks in sheer wonder. Old Town Square is one such place. Long the heart of the Old Town, the square grew to its present proportions when the city's original marketplace was moved away from the river in the 12th century. Its shape and appearance have changed little over the years. During the day the square is festive, as musicians vie for the favor of onlookers and artists display renditions of Prague street scenes. In summer the south end of the square is taken over by sprawling outdoor restaurants. During the Easter and Christmas seasons, Old Town Square is filled with wooden booths of vendors selling everything from simple wooden toys to fine glassware. At night, the gaudily lit towers of the Church of the Virgin Mary Before Týn rise gloriously over the glowing baroque façades.

FodorsChoice ★

During the 15th century the square was the focal point of conflict between Czech Hussites and German Catholics. In 1422 the radical Hussite preacher Jan Želivský was executed here for his part in storming the New Town's town hall three years earlier. In the 1419 uprising, three Catholic consuls and seven German citizens were thrown out the window—the first of Prague's many famous defenestrations. Within a few years, the Hussites had taken over the town, expelled the Germans, and set up their own administration.

Twenty-seven white crosses set flat in the paving stones in the square, at the Old Town Hall's base, mark the spot where 27 Bohemian noblemen were killed by the Hapsburgs in 1621 during the dark days following the defeat of the Czechs at the Battle of White Mountain. The grotesque spectacle, designed to quash any further national or religious opposition, took some five hours to complete, as the men were put to the sword or hanged one by one.

One of the most interesting houses on the Old Town Square juts out into the small extension leading into Malé náměstí. The house, called **U Minuty** (✉ 3 Staroměstské náměstí, Staré Město), with its 16th-century Renaissance sgraffiti of biblical and classical motifs, was the home of the young Franz Kafka in the 1890s.

❷ Stavovské divadlo (Estates Theater). Built in the 1780s in the classical style, this handsome theater was for many years a beacon of Czech-language culture in a city long dominated by the German variety. It's probably best known as the site of the world premiere of Mozart's opera *Don Giovanni* in October 1787, with the composer himself conducting. Prague audiences were quick to acknowledge Mozart's genius: the opera was an instant hit here, though it flopped nearly everywhere else in Europe. Mozart wrote most of the opera's second act in Prague at the Villa Bertramka, where he was a frequent guest. You must attend a performance here to see inside. ⊠ *Ovocný tř. 1, Staré Město* ☎ *224–215–001* box office ⊕ *www.narodni-divadlo.cz.*

JOSEFOV (JEWISH QUARTER)

Prague's Jews survived centuries of discrimination, but two unrelated events of modern times have left their historic ghetto little more than a collection of museums. Around 1900, city officials decided for hygienic purposes to raze the minuscule neighborhood—it had ceased to be a true ghetto with the political reforms of 1848–49, and by this time the majority of its residents were poor Gentiles—and pave over its crooked streets. Only some of the synagogues, the town hall, and the cemetery survived this early attempt at urban renewal. The second event was the Holocaust. Under Nazi occupation, a staggering percentage of the city's Jews were deported or murdered in concentration camps. Of the 35,000 Jews living in Prague before World War II, only about 1,200 returned to resettle the city after the war. The community is still tiny. Only a scant few Jews, mostly elderly, live in the "ghetto" today.

Treasures and artifacts of the ghetto are now the property of the **Židovské muzeum v Praze** (Prague Jewish Museum), which includes the Old Jewish Cemetery and collections installed in four surviving synagogues and the Ceremony Hall. (the Staronová synagóga, or Old-New Synagogue, a functioning house of worship, technically does not belong to the museum, but the Prague Jewish Community oversees both.) The museum was founded in 1906 but traces the vast majority of its holdings to the Nazis' destruction of 150 Jewish communities in Bohemia and Moravia. Dedicated museum workers, nearly all of whom were to die at Nazi hands, gathered and cataloged the stolen artifacts under German supervision. Exhibitions were even held during the war. A ticket good for all museum sites may be purchased at any of the synagogues but the Old-New Synagogue; single-site tickets apply only at the Old-New Synagogue and during occasional exhibits at the Spanish Synagogue. All museum sites are closed on Saturday and Jewish holidays.

a good walk

To reach the Jewish Quarter, leave Old Town Square via handsome Pařížská ulice, centerpiece of the urban renewal effort, and head north toward the river. The sudden appearance of a cluster of ancient buildings marks the ghetto. Take a right on Široká and stroll two blocks down to the recently restored **Španělská synagóga** ㉑ ▶. The man perched on a headless figure on the north side of the traffic circle is Franz Kafka, sculptor Jaroslav Róna's monument to noted writer. Head back the other way, past Pařížská, turn right on Maiselova, and you come to the **Židovská radnice** ㉒, which is now the Jewish Community Center. Adjoining it on Červená is the 16th-century High Synagogue. Across the street, at Červená 2, you see the **Staronová synagóga** ㉓, the oldest surviving synagogue in Prague.

Go west on the little street U starého hřbitova. The main museum ticket office is at the **Klausová synagóga** ㉔ at No. 3A. Separated from the synagogue by the exit gate of the Old Jewish Cemetery is the former building of the Jewish Burial Society, Obřadní síň, which exhibits traditional Jewish funeral objects.

TOURIST TRAPS

L IKE EVERY EUROPEAN CITY OVERRUN WITH TOURISTS, *Prague has its share of come-ons, overpriced attractions designed primarily to pull in people who don't know the local scene but are itching to spend money. The gimmicks are comparatively tame here, and unless your tastes run to casinos and girlie bars, you're unlikely to wake up with a hangover and an empty wallet. But there are a few guidelines worth keeping in mind.*

Generally speaking, anything being hustled on the streets is not worth the money. The boys in wigs and period costumes promoting chamber concerts in front of Obecni dům may seem charming, but for the same amount of money you can see a really first-rate orchestra at the Rudolfinum. The same goes for many of the daily church concerts, known derisively among locals as "tourist music." A sure tip-off that you're at amateur hour: Any bill that includes both Vivaldi's "Four Seasons" and Mozart's "Eine Kleine Nachtmusik."

Na Příkopě, the street that runs between Obecni dům and Wenceslas Square, is a veritable gauntlet of gimmicks. Along with a steady stream of leafleteers and kiosks for guided tours, you can find the Museum of Communism, an uninspired collection of posters, documents, and memorabilia. The better secondhand bookstores and antique shops have collections every bit as interesting, but you won't know that until you've paid the 180 Kč admission.

A two-block detour down Panská brings you to the Mucha Museum, which has a few genuinely interesting pieces. But do you really need to pay 120 Kč to see them, when a walk through St. Vitus Cathedral or Obecni dům offers larger and better examples of Mucha's work?

The best of what Prague has to offer is old, traditional, and administered by grouches. If something seems too slick or easy, you've wandered into the tourist zone.

Return to Maiselova and follow it to Široká. Turn right to find the **Pinkasova synagóga** ㉕, a handsome Gothic structure. Here also is the entrance to the Jewish ghetto's most astonishing sight, the **Starý židovský hřbitov** ㉖.

For a small detour, head down Široká street to the **Rudolfinum** ㉗ concert hall and gallery; across the street is the Uměleckoprůmyslové muzeum (Museum of Decorative Arts). Both are notable neo-Renaissance buildings.

Return to Maiselova once more and turn right in the direction of the Old Town. Look in at the displays of Czech Jewish history in the **Maiselova synagóga** ㉘.

TIMING The Jewish Quarter is one of the most popular areas in Prague, especially in the height of summer, when its tiny streets are jammed to bursting with tourists almost all the time. The best time for a quieter visit is early morning when the museums and cemetery first open. The area itself is very compact, and a fairly thorough tour should only take half a day, but don't go on the Sabbath (Saturday), when all the museums are closed.

What to See

㉔ Klausová synagóga (Klausen Synagogue). This baroque former synagogue was built at the end of the 17th century in the place of three small buildings (a synagogue, school, and ritual bath) that were destroyed in a fire that devastated the ghetto in 1689. Inside, displays of Czech Jewish traditions emphasize celebrations and daily life. In the neo-Romanesque **Obřadní síň** (Ceremony Hall), which adjoins the Klausen Synagogue, the focus is on rather grim subjects: Jewish funeral paraphernalia, old gravestones, and medical instruments. Special attention is paid to the activities of the Jewish Burial Society through many fine objects and paintings. ☒ *U starého hřbitova 3A, Josefov* ☏ *224–819–456* ⊕ *www. jewishmuseum.cz* ☑ *Combined ticket to museums and Old-New Synagogue 500 Kč; museums only, 300 Kč* ☉ *Apr.–Oct., Sun.–Fri. 9–6; Nov.–Mar., Sun.–Fri. 9–4:30.*

㉘ Maiselova synagóga (Maisel Synagogue). Here, the history of Czech Jews from the 10th to the 18th century is illustrated with the aid of some of the Prague Jewish Museum's most precious objects, including silver Torah shields and pointers, spice boxes, and candelabra; historic tombstones; and fine ceremonial textiles, including some donated by Mordechai Maisel to the synagogue he founded. The richest items come from the late 16th and early 17th centuries—a prosperous era for Prague's Jews. ☒ *Maiselova 10, Josefov* ☏ *224–819–456* ⊕ *www.jewishmuseum.cz* ☑ *Combined ticket to museums and Old-New Synagogue 500 Kč; museums only, 300 Kč* ☉ *Apr.–Oct., Sun.–Fri. 9–6; Nov.–Mar., Sun.–Fri. 9–4:30.*

㉕ Pinkasova synagóga (Pinkas Synagogue). This synagogue has two particularly moving testimonies to the appalling crimes perpetrated against the Jews during World War II. One tribute astounds by sheer numbers: the inside walls are covered with nearly 80,000 names of Bohemian and Moravian Jews murdered by the Nazis. Among them are the names of the paternal grandparents of former U.S. Secretary of State Madeleine Albright, who learned of their fate only in 1997. There's also an exhibition of drawings made by children at the Nazi concentration camp Terezín. The Nazis used the camp for propaganda purposes to demonstrate their "humanity" toward the Jews, and prisoners were given relative freedom to lead "normal" lives. However, transports to death camps in Poland began in earnest in 1944, and many thousands of Terezín prisoners, including many of these children, eventually perished. The entrance to the old Jewish cemetery is through this synagogue. ☒ *Široká 3, Josefov* ☏ *224–819–456* ⊕ *www.jewishmuseum.cz* ☑ *Combined ticket to museums and Old-New Synagogue 500 Kč; museums only, 300 Kč* ☉ *Apr.–Oct., Sun.–Fri. 9–6; Nov.–Mar., Sun.–Fri. 9–4:30.*

㉗ Rudolfinum. Thanks to a thorough makeover and exterior sandblasting, this neo-Renaissance monument designed by Josef Zítek and Josef Schulz presents some of the cleanest, brightest stonework in the city. Completed in 1884 and named for then–Hapsburg Crown Prince Rudolf, the rather low-slung sandstone building was meant to be a combination concert hall and exhibition gallery. After 1918 it was converted into the parliament of the newly independent Czechoslovakia until German invaders reinstated the concert hall in 1939. Czech writer Jiří Weil's novel *Mendelssohn*

Is on the Roof tells of the cruel farce that ensued when officials ordered the removal of the Jewish composer's statue from the roof balustrade. Now the Czech Philharmonic has its home base here. The 1,200-seat **Dvořákova síň** (Dvořák Hall) has superb acoustics (the box office faces 17 listopadu). To see the hall, you must attend a concert.

Behind Dvořák Hall is a set of large exhibition rooms, the **Galerie Rudolfinum** (⊕ www.galerierudolfinum.cz) an innovative, state-supported gallery for rotating shows of contemporary art. Four or five large shows are mounted here annually, showcasing excellent Czech work along with occasional international artists such as photographer Cindy Sherman. ⊠ *Náměstí Jana Palacha, Josefov* ☎ *224–893–111 box office, 224–893–205 gallery* ⊕ *www.czechphilharmonic.cz* ☼ *Gallery Tues.–Sun. 10–6* ⌫ *Gallery 100 Kč.*

★ ㉑ **Španělská synagóga** (Spanish Synagogue). A domed Moorish-style synagogue was built in 1868 on the site of the Altschul, the city's oldest synagogue. Here, the historical exposition that begins in the Maisel Synagogue continues, taking the story up to the post–World War II period. The displays are not that compelling, but the building's painstakingly restored interior definitely is. ⊠ *Vězeňská 1, Josefov* ☎ *224–819–456* ⊕ *www.jewishmuseum.cz* ⌫ *Combined ticket to museums and Old-New Synagogue 500 Kč; museums only, 300 Kč* ☼ *Apr.–Oct., Sun.–Fri. 9–6; Nov.–Mar., Sun.–Fri. 9–4:30.*

> **need a break?** For first-rate Czech cuisine and beer, it would be hard to beat **Kolkovna** (⊠ V Kolkovné 8), opposite the Spanish synagogue. The front room, with a lively bar and wide doors that open onto the street, is particularly nice in the summer.

★ ㉓ **Staronová synagóga** (Old-New Synagogue, or Altneuschul). Dating from the mid-13th century, this is one of the most important works of early Gothic in Prague. The odd name recalls the legend that the synagogue was built on the site of an ancient Jewish temple and that stones from the temple were used to build the present structure. The oldest part of the synagogue is the entrance, with its vault supported by two pillars. The synagogue has not only survived fires and the razing of the ghetto at the end of the last century but also emerged from the Nazi occupation intact; it's still in active use. As the oldest synagogue in Europe that still serves its original function, it's a living storehouse of Bohemian Jewish life. Note that men are required to cover their heads inside and that during services men and women sit apart. ⊠ *Červená 2, Josefov* ☎ *224–819–456* ⊕ *www.jewishmuseum.cz* ⌫ *Combined ticket to Old-New Synagogue and museums 500 Kč; Old-New Synagogue only, 200 Kč* ☼ *Apr.–Oct., Sun.–Fri. 9–6; Nov.–Mar., Sun.–Fri. 9–4:30.*

㉖ **Starý židovský hřbitov** (Old Jewish Cemetery). This unforgettably melancholy sight not far from the busy city was, from the 15th century to 1787, the final resting place for all Jews living in Prague. The confined space forced graves to be piled one on top of the other. Tilted at crazy angles, the 12,000 visible tombstones are but a fraction of countless thousands more buried below. Walk the path amid the gravestones; the relief sym-

Fodor'sChoice
★

bols you see represent the names and professions of the deceased. The oldest marked grave belongs to the poet Avigdor Kara, who died in 1439; the grave is not accessible from the pathway, but the original tombstone can be seen in the Maisel Synagogue. The best-known marker is that of Jehuda ben Bezalel, the famed Rabbi Loew (died 1609), a chief rabbi of Prague and profound scholar who is credited with creating the mythical Golem. Even today, small scraps of paper bearing wishes are stuffed into the cracks of the rabbi's tomb in the hope he will grant them. Loew's grave lies near the exit. ⊠ *Široká 3, enter through Pinkasova synagóga, Josefov* ☎ *224–819–456* ⊕ *www.jewishmuseum.cz* ⊠ *Combined ticket to museums and Old-New Synagogue 500 Kč; museums only, 300 Kč* ⊙ *Apr.–Oct., Sun.–Fri. 9–6; Nov.–Mar., Sun.–Fri. 9–4:30.*

㉒ **Židovská radnice** (Jewish Town Hall). The hall was the creation of Mordechai Maisel, an influential Jewish leader at the end of the 16th century. It was restored in the 18th century and given its clock and bell tower at that time. A second clock, with Hebrew numbers, keeps time counterclockwise. Now the Jewish Community Center, the building also houses a kosher restaurant, Shalom. ⊠ *Maiselova 18, Josefov* ☎ *222–319–012.*

MALÁ STRANA (LESSER QUARTER)

One of Prague's most exquisite neighborhoods, the Lesser Quarter (or Little Town) was established in 1257 and for years was where the merchants and craftsmen who served the royal court lived. Today, the area is home to many embassies, Czech government offices, historical attractions, and occasional galleries mixed in with the usual glut of pubs, restaurants, and souvenir shops. Though not nearly as confusing as the labyrinth of Old Town, the streets in the Lesser Quarter rise from river level nearly 400 vertical meters to the Castle, so be prepared for a climb. Pausing along the way will not only give you a chance to catch your breath but afford you views of the colorful jumble of terra cotta–tile rooftops and, occasionally, the spires of city center beyond.

a good walk

Begin your tour on the Old Town side of **Karlův most** ㉙ ➤, which you can reach by foot in about 10 minutes from the Old Town Square. Rising above it is the majestic Staroměstská mostecká věž, one of the finest medieval towers in Europe. The sides are covered with sculptures of emperors, saints, and above the archway on the eastern side of the tower, a row of carved emblems depicting the territories under the rule of King Charles IV. The climb of 138 steps up to the viewing gallery is worth the effort for the view you get of the Old Town and, across the river, of the Lesser Quarter and Prague Castle.

It's worth pausing to take a closer look at some of the statues as you walk across Karlův most toward the Lesser Quarter. As you approach the western end you'll see Kampa Island below on the left, separated from the mainland by an arm of the Vltava known as Čertovka (Devil's Stream).

By now you are almost at the end of the bridge. In front of you is the striking conjunction of the two Malá Strana bridge towers, the lower one Gothic, the taller one Romanesque. Together they frame the baroque flamboyance of Chrám svatého Mikuláše in the distance. This is a dramatic sight anytime, but particularly impressive at night. For that matter, the best time to walk across the bridge is at night, after the crowds dwindle and the river shimmers with the reflections of city lights.

Walk under the gateway of the towers into the little uphill street called Mostecká. You have now entered the Lesser Quarter. There are immediately any number of side streets to explore, each with unexpected discoveries. Making a hairpin turn to the right as soon you get off the bridge will drop you into a charming, less-traveled neighborhood where you can follow the Čertovka and, depending on the water level, see big wooden water wheels in action. Or continue up Mostecká to the rectangular **Malostranské náměstí** ㉚, the district's transportation hub. Packed with modern storefronts and restaurants on the street level, the buildings surrounding the square have façades dating back to the Renaissance on the upper levels. Up and slightly behind the square stands **Chrám svatého Mikuláše** ㉛.

Nerudova ulice ㉜ runs up from the square toward Prague Castle. Lined with a mix of shops, restaurants, churches, and the occasional embassy, it will take you to the huge twin set of staircases that lead up to the castle, or beyond, to Strahovský klášter. A tiny passageway at No. 13, on the left-hand side as you go up, drops you down to Tržiště ulice and the **Schönbornský palác** ㉝, one of Franz Kafka's residences, now the embassy of the United States. Tržiště winds down to the quarter's busy main street, Karmelitská, where the famous Infant Jesus of Prague resides in the **Kostel Panny Marie vítězné** ㉞. A few doors away, closer to Tržiště, is a quiet oasis, the **Vrtbovská zahrada** ㉟. Tiny Prokopská ulice leads off of Karmelitská, past the former Church of St. Procopius (now converted, oddly, into an apartment block), and into Maltézské náměstí (Maltese Square), a characteristically noble compound.

Take the left just before the square and then an immediate right onto Láeňská, and you'll be at **Velkopřevorské náměstí** ㊱ (Grand Priory Square), which is lined with fine baroque buildings. Or continue through Maltese Square, then turn left (before Nebovidská) onto the small side street that becomes a footbridge across the creeklike Čertovka to the island of **Kampa** ㊲, with its broad lawns, river views, and Czech modern-art showcase, **Museum Kampa** ㊳. Head north, keeping the river on your right, and you pass through a small square of shops and restaurants before passing underneath Karlův most. Continue following the street U lužického semináře and you come to a quiet walled garden, **Vojanovy sady** ㊴. To the northwest, hiding off busy Letenská ulice near the Malostranská metro station, is **Zahrada Valdštejnského paláce** ㊵, a more formal garden with an unbeatable view of Prague Castle looming above. A bit farther north is another garden, the baroque **Ledeburská zahrada** ㊶.

Another walking option is to take the south entrance out of Kampa park and follow Říční street back to Karmelitská, which puts you at the foot of Petřín Hill, at the top of which is **Petřin sady** ㊷. Cross the street and walk up the short flight of steps, and on your left you see Olbram

Zoubek's powerful memorial to the victims of Communism. The broad, steep steps are deliberately difficult to climb as you make your way up to the tortured figure whose body and soul disintegrate in a series of statues receding up the incline. To your right, you can find the entrance to the funicular, which you can ride to the top of the hill and the park's attractions.

TIMING The heat builds up in this area during the day—as do the crowds—so it's best visited before noon, or in late afternoon and early evening. The basic walk described here could take anywhere from two hours to the better part of a day, depending on how much dining, shopping, and exploring you do along the way. There are plenty of cafés along literally every block to stop, sip coffee or tea and people-watch, and a wealth of gardens and parks in which to rest in the shade. The trip up Petřin can add two hours to a half-day, depending how much exploring you do at the top and on the hillside. Going to Bertramka will add at least a half day.

What To See

31 **Chrám svatého Mikuláše** (Church of St. Nicholas). With its dynamic
Fodor'sChoice curves, this church is one of the purest and most ambitious examples
★ of high baroque. The celebrated architect Christoph Dientzenhofer began the Jesuit church in 1704 on the site of one of the more active Hussite churches of 15th-century Prague. Work on the building was taken over by his son Kilian Ignaz Dientzenhofer, who built the dome and presbytery. Anselmo Lurago completed the whole in 1755 by adding the bell tower. The juxtaposition of the broad, full-bodied dome with the slender bell tower is one of the many striking architectural contrasts that mark the Prague skyline. Inside, the vast pink-and-green space is impossible to take in with a single glance. Every corner bristles with movement, guiding the eye first to the dramatic statues, then to the hectic frescoes, and on to the shining faux-marble pillars. Many of the statues are the work of Ignaz Platzer, and in fact they constitute his last blaze of success. Platzer's workshop was forced to declare bankruptcy when the centralizing and secularizing reforms of Joseph II toward the end of the 18th century brought an end to the flamboyant baroque era. The tower, with an entrance on the side of the church, is open in summer. The church also hosts chamber music concerts during the summer, which have their charm in this eye-popping setting but do not reflect the true caliber of classical music in Prague. For that, check the schedule posted across the street at **Líchtenský palác,** where the faculty of HAMU, the city's premier music academy, often give performances. ⊠ *Malostranské náměstí, Malá Strana* ⊡ *50 Kč* ☉ *Daily 9–4:30 for sightseeing, 8:30–9:00 AM for prayer; no admission charge.*

🄫 **37** **Kampa.** Prague's largest island is cut off from the "mainland" by the narrow Čertovka streamlet. The name Čertovka, or Devil's Stream, reputedly refers to a cranky old lady who once lived on Maltese Square (given the river's present filthy state, the name is certainly appropriate). The well-kept lawns of the **Kampa Gardens,** which occupy much of the island, took a beating during the 2002 floods, as did the retaining wall that runs along the river. As a result, it's less picturesque than it once was, but an excellent place to get a sense of how extensive the flood damage was. Restoration of the area has been slow, partly due to construction of a flood wall that will hopefully avert future tragedies.

need a break?

A brief walk across the footbridge on the west side of Kampa Park will bring you to **Restaurace Nostitz** (⊠ Nosticova 2a), a cozy retreat for coffee or lunch indoors, or if the weather is warm, a cold drink on the shaded, spacious patio.

❷ **Karlův most** (Charles Bridge). The view from the foot of the bridge on
Fodor'sChoice the Old Town side is nothing short of breathtaking, encompassing the
★ towers and domes of the Lesser Quarter and the soaring spires of St. Vitus's Cathedral to the northwest. This heavenly vision changes subtly in perspective as you walk across the bridge, attended by the host of baroque saints that decorate the bridge's peaceful Gothic stones. At night its drama is spellbinding: St. Vitus's Cathedral lit in a ghostly green, the castle in monumental yellow, and the Church of St. Nicholas in a voluptuous pink, all viewed through the menacing silhouettes of the bowed statues and the Gothic towers. Night is absolutely the best time to visit the bridge, which is choked with tourists, vendors, and beggars by day. The later the hour, the thinner the crowds—though the bridge is never truly empty, especially in summer. Tourists with flash cameras are there all hours of the night, and as dawn is breaking, revelers from the dance clubs at the east end of the bridge are usually weaving their way homeward, singing loudly and talking about where to go for breakfast.

When the Přemyslid princes set up residence in Prague in the 10th century, there was a ford across the Vltava at this point—a vital link along one of Europe's major trading routes. After several wooden bridges and the first stone bridge had washed away in floods, Charles IV appointed the 27-year-old German Peter Parler, the architect of St. Vitus's Cathedral, to build a new structure in 1357. After 1620, following the defeat of Czech Protestants by Catholic Hapsburgs at the Battle of White Mountain, the bridge became a symbol of the Counter-Reformation's vigorous re-Catholicization efforts. The many baroque statues that began to appear in the late 17th century, commissioned by Catholics, eventually came to symbolize the totality of the Austrian (hence Catholic) triumph. The Czech writer Milan Kundera sees the statues from this perspective: "The thousands of saints looking out from all sides, threatening you, following you, hypnotizing you, are the raging hordes of occupiers who invaded Bohemia 350 years ago to tear the people's faith and language from their hearts."

The religious conflict is less obvious nowadays, leaving only the artistic tension between baroque and Gothic that gives the bridge its allure. It's worth pausing to take a closer look at some of the statues as you walk toward the Lesser Quarter. The third on the right, a bronze crucifix from the mid-17th century, is the oldest of all. It's mounted on the location of a wooden cross destroyed in a battle with the Swedes (the golden Hebrew inscription was reputedly financed by a Jew accused of defiling the cross). The fifth on the left, which shows St. Frances Xavier carrying four pagan princes (an Indian, Moor, Chinese, and Tartar) ready for conversion, is an outstanding piece of baroque sculpture. Eighth on the right is the statue of St. John of Nepomuk, who according to legend was wrapped in chains and thrown to his death from this bridge. Touching the statue is supposed to bring good luck or, according to some versions of the story, a return visit to Prague. On the left-hand side, sticking out from the bridge between the 9th and 10th statues (the latter has a wonderfully expressive vanquished Satan), stands a Roland (Bruncvík) statue. This knightly figure, bearing the coat of arms of the Old Town, was once a reminder that this part of the bridge belonged to the Old Town before Prague became a unified city in 1784.

In the eyes of most art historians, the most valuable statue is the 12th on the left, near the Lesser Quarter end. Mathias Braun's statue of St. Luitgarde depicts the blind saint kissing Christ's wounds. The most compelling grouping, however, is the second from the end on the left, a work of Ferdinand Maxmilian Brokoff (son of Johann) from 1714. Here the saints are incidental; the main attraction is the Turk, his face expressing extreme boredom at guarding the Christians imprisoned in the cage at his side. When the statue was erected, just 31 years after the second Turkish siege of Vienna, it scandalized the Prague public, who smeared it with mud. A half-dozen of the 30 bridge sculptures are 19th-century replacements for originals damaged in wars or sunk in a 1784 flood. All but a couple of the bridge's surviving baroque statues, including St. Luitgarde and the Turk, have been replaced by modern copies. The 17th- and 18th-century originals are in safer quarters, protected from Prague's acidic air. Several, including St. Luitgarde, can be viewed in the Lapidarium museum at the Výstaviště exhibition grounds in Prague 7; a few more occupy a man-made cavern at Vyšehrad.

Staroměstská mostecká věž (Old Town Bridge Tower), at the bridge entrance on the Old Town side, is where Peter Parler, the architect of the Charles Bridge, began his bridge building. The carved façades he designed for the sides of the tower were destroyed by Swedish soldiers in 1648, at the end of the Thirty Years' War. The sculptures facing the Old Town, however, are still intact (although some are recent copies); they depict an old and gout-ridden Charles IV with his son, who later became Wenceslas IV. Above them are two of Bohemia's patron saints, Adalbert of Prague and Sigismund. The top of the tower offers a spectacular view of the city for 50 Kč; it's open daily from 10 to 5, until 7 in summer.

> **need a break?**
>
> Just half a block off teeming Mostecká, the **Bakeshop Diner** (✉ Lázeňská 19) offers a quiet haven for coffee, tea, and a light lunch or breakfast. The omelets and pastries are some of the best in town, plus there's always a thoughtful selection of English-language newspapers.

㉞ Kostel Panny Marie vítězné (Church of Our Lady Victorious). This aging but well-appointed church on the Lesser Quarter's main street is the unlikely home of Prague's most famous religious artifact, the *Pražské*

Jezulátko (Infant Jesus of Prague). Originally brought to Prague from Spain in the 16th century, this wax doll is renowned worldwide for bestowing miracles on many who have prayed for its help. A measure of how powerful the attraction is lies in the prayerbooks on the kneelers in front of the statue, which have prayers of intercession in 20 different languages. The "Bambino," as he's known locally, has an enormous and incredibly ornate wardrobe, some of which is on display in a museum upstairs. Nuns from a nearby convent change the outfit on the statue regularly. Don't miss the souvenir shop (accessible via a doorway to the right of the main altar), where you can find that the Bambino's custodians are no slouches at marketing. Alas, the Infant's miraculous powers do not ward off petty theft: as a sign in the vestibule warns, BE AWARE OF PICKPOCKETS WHILE PRAYING! ⊠ *Karmelitská 9A, Malá Strana* ≋ *Free* ☉ *Mon.–Sat. 9:30–5:30, Sun. 1–6.*

㊶ Ledeburská zahrada (Ledeburg Garden). Rows of steeply banked baroque gardens rise behind the palaces of Valdštejnská ulice. This one is a climb if you enter from the street side, but the many shady arbors and niches are well worth it. The garden, with its frescoes and statuary, was restored with support from a fund headed by Czech president Václav Havel and Charles, Prince of Wales. Renovation seems to be never-ending at the lower entrance, but don't be deterred by the barriers and construction equipment—press on, through the courtyard and up the stairs. You can also enter directly from the upper, south gardens of Prague Castle in the summer. ⊠ *Valdštejnské nám. 3, Malá Strana* ≋ *70 Kč* ☉ *Daily 10–6.*

㉚ Malostranské náměstí (Lesser Quarter Square). The arcaded houses on the east and south sides of the square, dating from the 16th and 17th centuries, exhibit a mix of baroque and Renaissance elements. The Czech Parliament resides partly in the gaudy yellow-and-green palace on the square's north side, partly in the street behind the palace, Sněmovní. The huge bulk of the Church of St. Nicholas divides the lower, busier section—buzzing with restaurants, street vendors, clubs, and shops—from the quieter, upper part.

㊳ Museum Kampa. The spotlit jewel on Kampa Island is a remodeled mill house that now displays a private collection of paintings by Czech artist František Kupka and first-rate temporary exhibitions by both Czech and foreign artists. The museum was hit hard by the 2002 flood waters, which rose up 6 meters in the building and courtyard (you can still see the high-water marks if you look on the inner courtyard walls). But it has come back quickly and in fine fashion, now including an elegant restaurant with an outdoor patio that offers a splendid view of the river and historic buildings on the opposite bank. You won't be able to miss Židlé, a huge sculpture of a chair on the breakwall, a replacement for a smaller version that was swept away during the floods. ⊠ *U Sovových mlýnů 2, Malá Strana,* ☎ *257–786–147* ⊕ *www.museumkampa.cz* ≋ *100 Kč* ☉ *Tues.–Sun. 10–5.*

㉜ Nerudova ulice. This steep little street used to be the last leg of the Royal Way walked by the king before his coronation, though he made the ascent on horseback, not huffing and puffing on foot. It was named for the 19th-century Czech journalist and poet Jan Neruda (after whom Chilean poet Pablo Neruda renamed himself). Until Joseph II's administrative reforms in the late 18th century, house numbering was unknown in Prague. Each house bore a name, depicted on the façade, and these are particularly prominent on Nerudova ulice. No. 6, **U červeného orla** (At the Red Eagle), proudly displays a faded painting of a red eagle. No. 12 is known as **U tří housliček** (At the Three Fiddles); in the early 18th century, three generations of the Edlinger violin-making family lived here. Joseph II's scheme numbered each house according to its position in its "town" (here the Lesser Quarter) rather than its sequence on the street. The red plates record the original house numbers; the blue ones are the numbers used in addresses today. To confuse the tourist, many architectural guides refer to the old, red-number plates.

Two palaces break the unity of the burghers' houses on Nerudova ulice. Both were designed by the adventurous baroque architect Giovanni Santini, one of the Italian builders most in demand by wealthy nobles of the early 18th century. The **Morzin Palace,** on the left at No. 5, is now the Romanian Embassy. The fascinating façade, with an allegory of night and day, was created in 1713 and is the work of Ferdinand Brokoff, of Charles Bridge statue fame. Across the street at No. 20 is the **Thun-Hohenstein Palace,** now the Italian Embassy. The gateway with two enormous eagles (the emblem of the Kolovrat family, who owned the building at the time) is the work of the other great Charles Bridge statue sculptor, Mathias Braun. Santini himself lived at No. 14, the **Valkoun House.**

The archway at Nerudova 13 hides one of the many winding passageways that give the Lesser Quarter its enchantingly ghostly character at night. Higher up the street at No. 33 is the **Bretfeld Palace,** a rococo house on the corner of Jánský vršek. The relief of St. Nicholas on the façade is the work of Ignaz Platzer, a sculptor known for his classic and rococo work, but the building is valued more for its historical associations than for its architecture: this is where Mozart, his lyricist partner Lorenzo da Ponte, and the aging but still infamous philanderer and music lover Casanova stayed at the time of the world premiere of *Don Giovanni* in 1787.

need a break? Nerudova ulice is filled with little restaurants and snack bars and offers something for everyone. At the bottom of the street, **U Kocoura** (✉ Nerudova 2) is a classic local pub, with long tables, a boisterous clientele, and the original Budweiser (Budvar in Czech) on tap.

Nerudova ulice eventually turns into Úvoz. For a sensational view of the city, continue up the street until it turns into Úvoz. At No. 40, go through the gateway on your left and follow the path up to **Oživlé Dřevo** (✉ Úvoz 40), which is situated in front of Strahovský klášter. The outdoor tables overlook Petrin hill, Malá Strana, and the city beyond. In nice weather, it's one of the most pleasant outdoor spots in the city.

⏱ ㊷ **Petřín sady.** For a superb view of the city—from a somewhat less touristed perch—the top of Petřín Hill is a charming playground for children and adults alike. You can find Prague's own miniature version of the Eiffel Tower, which was restored in 2002. The park is laced with footpaths, with several buildings clustered together near the tower—just keep going gradually upward until you reach the base, where you can also find a mirror maze (*bludiště*) in a small structure, and the seemingly abandoned svatý Vavřinec (St. Lawrence) church. The area is beautifully peaceful and well worth an afternoon's wandering. You can walk up from Karmelitská ulice or Újezd down in the Lesser Quarter or ride the funicular railway from U lanové dráhy ulice, off Újezd; you can also stroll over from Stahov klášter. Regular public-transportation tickets are valid on the funicular. Just be aware that lines for the funicular can be very long on a clear day, and they move very slowly (if the line is very far outside the terminal door, you're in for at least a 30-minute wait, if not longer). For the descent, take the funicular or meander on foot down through the stations of the cross on the pathways leading back to the Lesser Quarter. A number of paths meander down the face of the hillside through fruit orchards, and finally back to Karmelitská; a wide path goes to Strahov Monastery. The funicular is run as an extension of the tram system, and it's an attraction in itself. The station at the top opens onto a rose garden, a lovely place in the summer months.

As you exit the funicular at the top of Petřín Hill, the rounded dome off to your left is **Štefánik Observatory** (☎ 257–320–540 ⊕ www.observatory.cz), a working astronomical facility with some fine displays (though not many in English). Both day and night telescope viewing are available. A large children's play area in Petřín sady is dominated by the **Petřiinská razhelda** (Petřín Tower; ☎ 257–320–112), a one-fifth replica of the Eiffel Tower with a marvelous view of the city from the top. This is not an attraction for the timid; the only way to the viewing platforms is via a circular stairway that wraps around the outside of the tower, a safe but vertiginous ascent. For the hardy, the views are well worth the climb. A stone's throw from the Petřín Tower, the **Bludiste na Petřína** (Mirror Maze; ☎ 257–315–212) is an amusement park attraction with, as the name suggests, a variety of amusingly distorted mirrors. It's great fun for the kids. ⊠ *Petřín Hill* 🎫 *Observatory 30 Kč; Tower 50 Kč; Maze 40 Kč* 🕙 *Observatory Jan.–Feb., Tues.–Fri. 6–10 PM, weekends 10–noon and 2–8; Mar., Tues.–Fri. 7–9 PM, weekends 10–noon, 2–6, and 7–9; Apr.–Aug., Tues.–Fri. 2–7 and 9–11, weekends 10–noon,2–7, and 9–11; Sept., Tues.–Fri. 2–7 and 9–11, weekends 10–noon, 2–6, and 8–10; Oct. Tues.–Fri. 7–9, weekends 10–noon, 2–6, and 7–9; Nov. and Dec., Tues.–Fri. 6–8, weekends 10–noon and 2–8. Tower & Maze Jan.–Mar., Nov., and Dec., weekends 10–5; Apr. and Sept.–Oct., daily 10–5; May–Aug., daily 10–10.*

㉝ **Schönbornský palác** (Schönborn Palace). Franz Kafka had an apartment in this massive baroque building at the top of Tržiště ulice in mid-1917, after moving from Zlatá ulička, or Golden Lane. The heavily guarded U.S. Embassy now occupies this prime location. This is not a good area to linger; the Czech police take the threat of terrorist acts against American targets very seriously, and if you hang around with no apparent purpose, you can be approached and questioned. ⊠ *Tržiště at Vlašská, Malá Strana.*

36   **Velkopřevorské náměstí** (Grand Priory Square). This square lies just south and slightly west of the Charles Bridge, next to the Čertovka. The Grand Prior's Palace fronting the square is considered one of the finest baroque buildings in the Lesser Quarter, though it's now part of the Embassy of the Sovereign Military Order of Malta—the contemporary (and very real) descendant of the Knights of Malta—and no longer open to the public. Opposite is the flamboyant orange-and-white stucco façade of the Buquoy Palace, built in 1719 by Giovanni Santini and the present home of the French Embassy. The so-called **John Lennon Peace Wall,** leading to a bridge over the Čertovka, was once a kind of monument to youthful rebellion, emblazoned with a large painted head of the former Beatle. But Lennon's visage is nowhere to be seen these days; the wall is usually covered instead with political and music-related graffiti.

39   **Vojanovy sady** (Vojan Park). Once the gardens of the Monastery of the Discalced Carmelites, later taken over by the Order of the English Virgins, and now part of the Ministry of Finance, this walled garden, with its weeping willows, fruit trees, and benches, makes another peaceful haven in summer. The flood waters of 2002 reached this area, too; you can see lower portions of some walls still stripped away. Exhibitions of modern sculptures are occasionally held here, contrasting sharply with the two baroque chapels and the graceful Ignaz Platzer statue of John of Nepomuk standing on a fish at the entrance. At the other end of the park, you can find a terrace with a formal rose garden and a peacock that likes to preen for visitors. The park is surrounded by the high walls of the old monastery and new Ministry of Finance buildings, with only an occasional glimpse of a tower or spire to remind you that you're in Prague. ⊠ *U lužického semináře, between Letenská ulice and Míšeňská ulice, Malá Strana* ⊙ *Nov.–Mar., daily 8–5; Apr.–Oct., daily 8–7.*

need a break?   Immediately north of the entrance to the Vojanovy sady, you can find **Restaurace Vojanův Dvůr** (⊠ U ležiokého semináře 23), which offers a full Czech menu and has a great summer patio.

★ **35**   **Vrtbovská zahrada** (Vrtba Garden). An unobtrusive door on noisy Karmelitská hides the entranceway to a fascinating oasis that also has one of the best views over the Lesser Quarter. The street door opens onto the intimate courtyard of the Vrtbovský palác (Vrtba Palace), which is now private housing. Two Renaissance wings flank the courtyard; the left one was built in 1575, the right one in 1591. The owner of the latter house was one of the 27 Bohemian nobles executed by the Hapsburgs in 1621 before the Old Town Hall. The house was given as confiscated property to Count Sezima of Vrtba, who bought the neighboring property and turned the buildings into a late-Renaissance palace. The Vrtba Garden, created a century later, reopened in summer 1998 after an excruciatingly long renovation. This is the most elegant of the Lesser Quarter's public gardens, built in five levels rising behind the courtyard in a wave of statuary-bedecked staircases and formal terraces to reach a seashell-decorated pavilion at the top. In summer it's a popular spot for weddings, receptions, and occasional concerts. (The fenced-off garden immediately behind and above belongs to the U.S. Embassy.)

The powerful stone figure of Atlas that caps the entranceway in the courtyard and most of the other classically derived statues are from the workshop of Mathias Braun, perhaps the best of the Czech baroque sculptors. ⊠ *Karmelitská 25, Malá Strana* 🎟 *40 Kč* ⊘ *Apr.–Oct., daily 10–6.*

off the beaten path

VILLA BERTRAMKA – Mozart fans won't want to pass up a visit to this villa, where the great composer stayed on several occasions as a guest of art patrons František and Josefina Dušek. The small, well-organized W. A. Mozart Museum is packed with musical memorabilia, including a flyer for a performance of *Don Giovanni* in 1788, only months after the opera's world premiere at the Estates Theater. Also on hand is a handsome collection of period instruments, several purportedly played by the master. Summer concerts here are pricey but unmatchable in atmospherics. Take Tram No. 12 from Karmelitská south (or ride metro Line B) to the Anděl metro station. From there, a 10-minute walk west on Plzeňská past the shopping malls will bring you within sight of the Hotel Movenpick; Bertramka is up and behind the hotel. ⊠ *Mozartova ulice 169, Smíchov* 🕾 *257–327–732* ⊕ *www.bertramka.cz* 🎟 *90 Kč* ⊘ *Apr.–Oct., daily 9:30–6; Nov.–Mar., daily 9:30–5.*

★ ☾ ㊵ **Zahrada Valdštejnského paláce** (Wallenstein Palace Gardens). Albrecht von Wallenstein, onetime owner of the house and gardens, began a meteoric military career in 1622, when the Austrian emperor Ferdinand II retained him to save the empire from the Swedes and Protestants during the Thirty Years' War. Wallenstein, wealthy by marriage, offered to raise 20,000 men at his own cost and lead them personally. Ferdinand II accepted and showered Wallenstein with confiscated land and titles. Wallenstein's first acquisition was this enormous area. Having knocked down 23 houses, a brick factory, and three gardens, in 1623 he began to build his magnificent palace with its idiosyncratic high-walled gardens and superb, vaulted Renaissance *sala terrena* (room opening onto a garden). Walking around the formal paths, you come across numerous fountains and statues depicting figures from classical mythology or warriors dispatching a variety of beasts. But the most amazing piece of sculpture work is "The Grotto," a huge dripstone wall packed with imaginative rock formations and what's billed as "illusory hints of secret corridors." Next to the wall, an aviary houses some rather large owls (look up, they're usually perched in the upper reaches). Most of the palace itself now serves the Czech Senate as meeting chamber and offices. The palace's cavernous former *Jízdárna,* or riding school, now hosts occasional art exhibitions. ⊠ *Letenská 10, Malá Strana* 🎟 *Free* ⊘ *Apr. 1–Oct. 31, daily 10–6.*

HRADČANY (CASTLE AREA)

To the west of Prague Castle is the residential Hradčany (Castle Area), the town that during the early 14th century emerged out of a collection of monasteries and churches. The concentration of history packed into Prague Castle and Hradčany challenges those not versed in the ups and downs of Bohemian kings, religious uprisings, wars, and oppression. The picturesque area surrounding Prague Castle, with its breathtaking vistas of the Old Town and the Lesser Quarter, is ideal for just wandering. But the castle itself, with its broad history and architecture, is difficult to appreciate fully without investing a little more time.

Take the metro to Malostranská and then switch to a tram that takes you to Malostranské náměstí. You exit at the Chrám Sv. Mikuláše (St. Nicholas Church; see ⇨ Mala Strana, *above*), which fills a large section of the square. Finished in 1761, the baroque structure houses many statues, frescoes, and paintings as well as an organ that was played by Mozart in 1787. To one side of the church is Nerudova ulice, which runs west from the square. Along this slender street are some of the city's best house signs, such as the one at the home of Jan Neruda, a poet and journalist after whom the route is named. Look for his house, At the Two Suns, at No. 47. Other notable emblems, among others, are at the White Swan (No. 49), the Green Lobster (No. 43), and the Three Fiddles (No. 12).

At the western (upper) end of the street, look for a flight of stone steps guarded by two saintly statues. Take the stairs up to Loretánská ulice, and enjoy panoramic views of the church and the Lesser Quarter. At the top of the steps, turn left and walk a couple hundred yards until you come to a dusty, elongated square named Pohořelec (Scene of Fire), which suffered tragic fires in 1420, 1541, and 1741. Go through the inconspicuous gateway at No. 8 and up the steps, and you find yourself in the courtyard of one of the city's richest monasteries, the **Strahovský klášter** ㊸ ▶.

Retrace your steps to Loretánské náměstí, the square at the head of Loretánská ulice that's flanked by the feminine curves of the baroque church **Loreta** ㊹. Across the road, the 29 half pillars of the Černínský palác (Černín Palace) now mask the Czech Ministry of Foreign Affairs. At the bottom of Loretánské náměstí, a little lane trails to the left into the area known as **Nový Svět** ㊺; the name means "New World," though the district is as old-world as they come. Turn right onto the street Nový Svět. Around the corner you get a tantalizing view of the cathedral through the trees. Walk down the winding Kanovnická ulice past the Austrian Embassy and the dignified but melancholy Kostel svatého Jana Nepomuckého (Church of St. John of Nepomuk). At the top of the street on the left, the rounded, Renaissance corner house, Martinický palác, catches the eye with its detailed sgraffiti decorations. Martinický palác opens onto **Hradčanské náměstí** ㊻, with its grandiose gathering of Renaissance and baroque palaces. To the left of the bright yellow Arcibiskupský palác (Archbishop's Palace) on the square is an alleyway leading down to the Sternberg Palace, which houses the **Národní galerie** ㊼ and its collections of European art. Across the square, the handsome *sgraffito* sweep of **Schwarzenberský palác** ㊽ beckons; this is the building you saw from the back side at the beginning of the tour.

TIMING To do justice to the subtle charms of Hradčany, allow at least two hours just for ambling and admiring the passing buildings and views of the city. The Strahovský klášter halls need about a half-hour to take in, more if you tour the small picture gallery there, and the Loreta and its treasures need at least that length of time. The Národní galerie in the Šternberský palác deserves at least a couple of hours. Keep in mind that several places are not open on Monday.

What to See

46 **Hradčanské náměstí** (Hradčany Square). With its fabulous mixture of baroque and Renaissance houses, topped by the castle itself, the square had a prominent role (disguised, ironically, as Vienna) in the film *Amadeus,* directed by the then-exiled Czech director Miloš Forman. The house at No. 7 stood in for Mozart's residence, where the composer was haunted by the masked figure he thought was his father. Forman used the flamboyant rococo Arcibiskupský palác (Archbishop's Palace), on the left as you face the castle, as the Viennese archbishop's palace. The plush interior, shown off in the film, is open to the public only one day each year, on Maundy Thursday. No. 11 was home for a brief time after World War II to a little girl named Marie Jana Korbelová, who is better known as Madeleine Albright.

★ **44** **Loreta** (Loreto Church). The church's seductive lines were a conscious move on the part of Counter-Reformation Jesuits in the 17th century who wanted to build up the cult of Mary and attract the largely Protestant Bohemians back to the church. According to legend, angels had carried Mary's house from Nazareth and dropped it in a patch of laurel trees in Ancona, Italy. Known as *Loreto* (from the Latin for laurel), it immediately became a center of pilgrimage. The Prague Loreto was one of many symbolic reenactments of this scene across Europe, and it worked: pilgrims came in droves. The graceful façade, with its voluptuous tower, was built in 1720 by Kilian Ignaz Dientzenhofer, the architect of the two St. Nicholas churches in Prague. Most spectacular of all is a small exhibition upstairs displaying the religious treasures presented to Mary in thanks for various services, including a monstrance studded with 6,500 diamonds. ⊠ *Loretánské náměstí 7, Hradčany* 🕾 *80 Kč* ☉ *Tues.–Sun. 9–12:15 and 1–4:30.*

★ **47** **Národní galerie** (National Gallery). Housed in the 18th-century Šternberský palác (Sternberg Palace), this collection, though impressive, is fairly limited compared to relatively nearby museums in Germany and Austria. During the time when Berlin, Dresden, and Vienna were building up superlative old-master galleries, Prague languished, neglected by her Viennese rulers—one reason why the city's museums lag behind. Works by Rubens and Rembrandt are on display; some other key pieces in the collection wait in the wings. Other branches of the National Gallery are scattered around town. ⊠ *Hradčanské náměstí 15, Hradčany* 🕾 *233–090–570* ⊕ *www.ngprague.cz* 🕾 *60 Kč* ☉ *Tues.–Sun. 10–6.*

★ **45** **Nový Svět.** This picturesque, winding little alley, with façades from the 17th and 18th centuries, once housed Prague's poorest residents; now many of the homes are used as artists' studios. The last house on the street, No. 1, as the home of the Danish-born astronomer Tycho Brahe. Living so close to the Loreto, so the story goes, Tycho was constantly disturbed during his nightly stargazing by the church bells. He ended up complaining to his patron, Emperor Rudolf II, who instructed the Capuchin monks to finish their services before the first star appeared in the sky.

❹⑧ Schwarzenberský palác (Schwarzenberg Palace). This boxy palace with its extravagant sgraffito façade is the **Vojenské historické muzeum** (Military History Museum), one of the largest of its kind in Europe. The beautifully decorated exterior is all that is on display while the interior undergoes a long-term renovation that is not expected to be finished until 2007. ✉ *Hradčanské náměstí 2, Hradčany* ⊕ *www.militarymuseum.cz.*

★ ❹③ Strahovský klášter (Strahov Monastery). Founded by the Premonstratensian order in 1140, the monastery remained in its hands until 1952, when the Communists suppressed all religious orders and turned the entire complex into the **Památník národního písemnictví** (Museum of National Literature). The major building of interest is the **Strahov Library,** with its collection of early Czech manuscripts, the 10th-century Strahov New Testament, and the collected works of famed Danish astronomer Tycho Brahe. Also of note is the late-18th-century **Philosophical Hall.** Engulfing its ceilings is a startling sky-blue fresco that depicts an unusual cast of characters, including Socrates' nagging wife, Xanthippe; Greek astronomer Thales, with his trusty telescope; and a collection of Greek philosophers mingling with Descartes, Diderot, and Voltaire. On the premises is the order's small art gallery, highlighted by late-Gothic altars and paintings from Rudolf II's time. There are no tours in English, unfortunately, but you can get pamphlets in English. ✉ *Strahovské nádvoří 1/132, Hradčany* ☎ *220–516–671 to arrange tours* 🎟 *Library tour 50 Kč, gallery tour 30 Kč* ☉ *Gallery Tues.–Sun. 9–noon and 12:30–5; library daily 9–noon and 1–5.*

PRAŽSKÝ HRAD (PRAGUE CASTLE)

Numbers in the text correspond to numbers in the margin and on the Prague Castle (Pražský hrad) map.

Despite its monolithic presence, Prague Castle is not a single structure but rather a collection of buildings dating from the 10th to the 20th century, all linked by internal courtyards. The most important structures are **Chrám svatého Víta** ❺④, clearly visible soaring above the castle walls, and the **Královský palác** ❺⑤, the official residence of kings and presidents and still the center of political power in the Czech Republic. The castle is compact and easy to navigate. Be forewarned: in summer, the castle, especially Chrám svatého Víta, is hugely popular. **Zlatá ulička** ❺⑨ became so crowded that in 2002 a separate admission fee was imposed for it.

TIMING   The castle is at its mysterious best in early morning and late evening, and it's incomparable when it snows. The cathedral deserves an hour, as does the Královský palác, while you can easily spend an entire day taking in the museums, the views of the city, and the hidden nooks of the castle. Remember that some sights, such as the Lobkovický palác and the National Gallery branch at Klášter svatého Jiří, are not open on Monday.

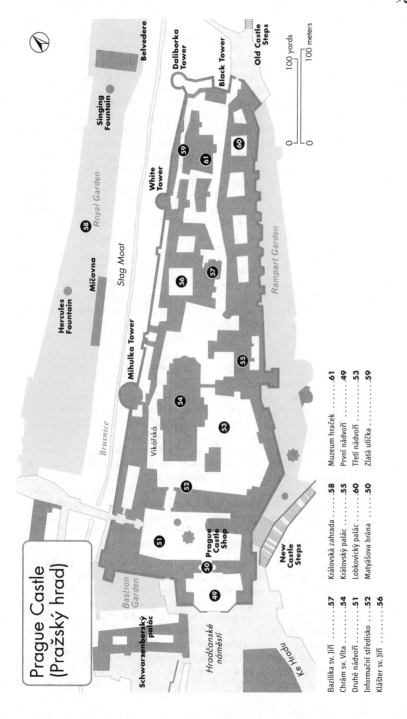

Prague Castle (Pražský hrad)

Belvedere

Daliborka Tower

Black Tower

Old Castle Steps

Singing Fountain

Royal Garden

White Tower

Hercules Fountain

Míčovna

Stag Moat

Brusnice

Mihulka Tower

Vikářská

Rampart Garden

0 — 100 yards

0 — 100 meters

Schwarzenberský palác

Bastion Garden

Hradčanské náměstí

K Hradu

Prague Castle Shop

New Castle Steps

Bazilika sv. Jiří **57**

Chrám sv. Víta **54**

Druhé nádvoří **51**

Informační středisko **52**

Klášter sv. Jiří **56**

Královská zahrada **58**

Královský palác **55**

Lobkovický palác **60**

Matyášova brána **50**

Muzeum hraček **61**

První nádvoří **49**

Třetí nádvoří **53**

Zlatá ulička **59**

What to See

⑤⑦ Bazilika svatého Jiří (St. George's Basilica). This church was originally built
FodorśChoice　in the 10th century by Prince Vratislav I, the father of Prince (and St.)
★　　　　Wenceslas. It was dedicated to St. George (of dragon fame), who it was
believed would be more agreeable to the still largely pagan people. The
outside was remodeled during early baroque times, although the striking rusty-red color is in keeping with the look of the Romanesque edifice. The interior looks more or less as it did in the 12th century and is
the best-preserved Romanesque relic in the country. The effect is at once
barnlike and peaceful, the warm golden yellow of the stone walls and
the small arched windows exuding a sense of enduring harmony. The house-
shaped painted tomb at the front of the church holds the remains of the
founder, Vratislav I. Up the steps, in a chapel to the right, is the tomb
Peter Parler designed for St. Ludmila, the grandmother of St. Wenceslas.
✉ *Náměstí U sv. Jiří, Pražský Hrad* ☎ *224–373–368 castle information*
⊕ *www.prague-info.cz* ✉ *Requires 2-day castle ticket for 350 Kč, or a*
separate 50Kč charge ☉ *Apr.–Oct., daily 9–5; Nov.–Mar., daily 9–4.*

⑤④ Chrám svatého Víta (St. Vitus's Cathedral). With its graceful, soaring tow-
FodorśChoice　ers, this Gothic cathedral—among the most beautiful in Europe—is the
★　　　　spiritual heart not only of Prague Castle but of the entire country. It
has a long and complicated history, beginning in the 10th century and
continuing to its completion in 1929. If you want to hear its history in
depth, English-speaking guided tours of the cathedral and the Královský
palác can be arranged at the information office across from the cathedral entrance.

Once you enter the cathedral, pause to take in the vast but delicate beauty
of the Gothic and neo-Gothic interior glowing in the colorful light that
filters through the startlingly brilliant stained-glass windows. This western third of the structure, including the facade and the two towers you
can see from outside, was not completed until 1929, following the initiative of the Union for the Completion of the Cathedral, set up in the
last days of the 19th century. Don't let the neo-Gothic illusion keep you
from examining this new section. The six stained-glass windows to
your left and right and the large rose window behind are modern mas-
terpieces. Take a good look at the third window up on the left. The familiar art nouveau flamboyance, depicting the blessing of Sts. Cyril and
Methodius (9th-century missionaries to the Slavs), is the work of the
Czech father of the style, Alfons Mucha. He achieved the subtle color-
ing by painting rather than staining the glass.

If you walk halfway up the right-hand aisle, you will find the **Svatová-
clavská kaple** (Chapel of St. Wenceslas). With a tomb holding the saint's
remains, walls covered in semi-precious stones, and paintings depicting
the life of Wenceslas, this square chapel is the ancient heart of the cathedral. Stylistically, it represents a high point of the dense, richly decorated
though rather gloomy Gothic favored by Charles IV and his successors.
Wenceslas (the "good king" of Christmas-carol fame) was a determined
Christian in an era of widespread paganism. Around 925, as prince of
Bohemia, he founded a rotunda church dedicated to St. Vitus on this
site. But the prince's brother, Boleslav, was impatient to take power, and

he ambushed and killed Wenceslas in 929 (or 935 according to some experts) near a church at Stará Boleslav, northeast of Prague. Wenceslas was originally buried in that church, but his grave produced so many miracles that he rapidly became a symbol of piety for the common people, something that greatly irritated the new Prince Boleslav. Boleslav was finally forced to honor his brother by reburying the body in the St. Vitus Rotunda. Shortly afterward, Wenceslas was canonized.

The rotunda was replaced by a Romanesque basilica in the late 11th century. Work was begun on the existing building in 1344. For the first few years the chief architect was the Frenchman Mathias d'Arras, but after his death in 1352 the work was continued by the 22-year-old German architect Peter Parler, who went on to build the Charles Bridge and many other Prague treasures.

The small door in the back of the chapel leads to the **Korunní komora** (Crown Chamber), the repository of the Bohemian crown jewels. It remains locked with seven keys held by seven important people (including the president) and is definitely not open to the public.

A little beyond the Chapel of St. Wenceslas on the same side, stairs lead down to the underground **royal crypt,** interesting primarily for the information it provides about the cathedral's history. As you descend the stairs, you can see parts of the old Romanesque basilica and portions of the foundations of the rotunda. Moving around into the second room, you'll find a rather eclectic group of royal remains ensconced in new sarcophagi dating from the 1930s. In the center is Charles IV, who died in 1378. Rudolf II, patron of Renaissance Prague, is entombed at the rear in the original tin coffin. To his right is Maria Amalia, the only child of Empress Maria Theresa to reside in Prague. Ascending the wooden steps back into the cathedral, you'll come to the white-marble **Kralovské mausoleum** (Royal Mausoleum), atop which lie stone statues of the first two Hapsburg kings to rule in Bohemia, Ferdinand I and Maximilian II, and of Ferdinand's consort, Anne Jagiello.

The cathedral's **Kralovské oratorium** (Royal Oratory) was used by the kings and their families when attending mass. Built in 1493, the work is a perfect example of late Gothic, laced on the outside with a stone network of gnarled branches very similar in pattern to the ceiling vaulting in the Králoský palác. The oratory is connected to the palace by an elevated covered walkway, which you can see from outside.

A few more steps toward the east end, you can't fail to catch sight of the ornate silver **sarcophagus of St. John of Nepomuk.** According to legend, when Nepomuk's body was exhumed in 1721 to be reinterred, the tongue was found to be still intact and pumping with blood. This strange tale served a highly political purpose. The Catholic Church and the Hapsburgs were seeking a new folk hero to replace the Protestant forerunner Jan Hus, whom they despised. The 14th-century priest Nepomuk, killed during a power struggle with King Václav IV, was sainted and reburied a few years later with great ceremony in the 3,700-pound silver tomb, replete with angels and cherubim; the tongue was enshrined in its own reliquary.

The eight chapels around the back of the cathedral are the work of the original architect, Mathias d'Arras. A number of old tombstones, including some badly worn grave markers of medieval royalty, can be seen within, amid furnishings from later periods. Opposite the wooden relief, depicting the looting of the cathedral by Protestants in 1619, is the **Valdštejnská kaple** (Wallenstein Chapel). Since the 19th century, the chapel has housed the Gothic tombstones of its two architects, d'Arras and Peter Parler, who died in 1352 and 1399, respectively. If you look up to the balcony, you can just make out the busts of these two men, designed by Parler's workshop. The other busts around the triforium depict royalty and other VIPs of the time.

The Hussite wars in the 15th century put an end to the first phase of the cathedral's construction. During the short era of illusory peace before the Thirty Years' War, the massive south tower was completed, but lack of money quashed any idea of finishing the building, and the cathedral was closed by a wall built across from the Chapel of St. Wenceslas. Not until the 20th century was the western side of the cathedral, with its two towers, completed in the spirit of Parler's conception.

A key element of the cathedral's teeming, rich exterior decoration is the **Last Judgment mosaic** above the ceremonial entrance, called the Golden Portal, on the south side. The use of mosaic is quite rare in countries north of the Alps; this work, dating from the 1370s, is made of 1 million glass and stone chunks. The once-clouded glass now sparkles again thanks to many years of restoration funded by the Getty Conservation Institute, which was finished in 2001. The central field shows Christ in glory, adored by Charles IV and his consort, Elizabeth of Pomerania, as well as several saints; the risen dead and attendant angels are on the left; and on the right the flames of Hell lick around the figure of Satan. ⊠ *St. Vitus's Cathedral, Pražský Hrad* ☎ *224–373–368 castle information* ⊕ *www.prague-info.cz* ⊠ *Western section free; chapels, crypt, and tower require 2-day castle ticket for 220 Kč–350 Kč* ☉ *Apr.–Oct., daily 9–5; Nov.–Mar., daily 9–4.*

⑤ Druhé nádvoří (Second Courtyard). Empress Maria Theresa's court architect, Nicolò Pacassi, received the imperial approval to remake the castle in the 1760s, as it was badly damaged by Prussian shelling during the Seven Years' War in 1757. The Second Courtyard was the main victim of Pacassi's attempts at imparting classical grandeur to what had been a picturesque collection of Gothic and Renaissance styles. Except for the view of the spires of St. Vitus's Cathedral, the exterior courtyard offers little for the eye to feast upon. This courtyard also houses the rather gaudy **Kaple svatého Kříže** (Chapel of the Holy Cross), with decorations from the 18th and 19th centuries, which now serves as a souvenir and ticket stand.

Built in the late 16th and early 17th century, the Second Courtyard was originally part of a reconstruction program commissioned by Rudolf II, under whom Prague enjoyed a period of unparalleled cultural development. Once the Prague court was established, the emperor gathered around him some of the world's best craftsmen, artists, and scientists, including the brilliant astronomers Johannes Kepler and Tycho Brahe.

Rudolf II amassed a large and famed collection of fine and decorative art, scientific instruments, philosophic and alchemical books, natural wonders, coins, and everything else under the sun. The bulk of the collection was looted by the Swedes during the Thirty Years' War, removed to Vienna when the imperial capital returned there after Rudolf's death, or auctioned off during the 18th century. Artworks that survived the turmoil, for the most part acquired after Rudolf's time, are displayed in the **Obrazárna** (Picture Gallery), on the left side of the courtyard as you face St. Vitus's. In rooms elegantly redecorated by the official castle architect, Bořek Šípek, there are good Renaissance, mannerist, and baroque paintings that hint at the luxurious tastes of Rudolf's court. Across the passageway by the gallery entrance is the **Císařská konírna** (Imperial Stable), where temporary exhibitions are held. The passageway at the northern end of the courtyard forms the northern entrance to the castle and leads out over a luxurious ravine known as the **Jelení příkop** (Stag Moat), which can be entered either here or at the lower end via the metal catwalk off Chotkova ulice, when it isn't closed for sporadic renovations. ⊠ *Obrazárna: 2nd Courtyard, Pražský Hrad* ☎ *224–373–368 castle information* ⊕ *www.prague-info.cz* ✑ *Courtyard free; Picture Gallery 100 Kč* ⊙ *Picture Gallery daily 10–6.*

52 **Informační středisko** (Castle Information Office). This is the place to come for entrance tickets, guided tours, headphones for listening to recorded tours in English, tickets to cultural events held at the castle, and money changing. You can wander around a great deal of the Castle for free, and this is an enticing option if you want to save money; you can still enter St. Vitus's, though you won't be able to get close to the oldest parts. There are two ticketing options. The cheaper allows entrance to St. Vitus's Cathedral (the oldest parts and the tower), the Royal Palace, and Golden Lane, and this will provide more than enough Castle-visiting for most people; a more expensive ticket includes St. George's Basilica, the powder tower, and an extensive exhibit on the history of the Castle. Tickets are valid for 2 days. You can also pay separately for Golden Lane and St. George's Basilica. Other attractions include the National Gallery and Toy Museum, which have separate admission charges. If you just want to walk through the castle grounds, note that the gates close at midnight from April through October and at 11 PM the rest of the year, while the gardens are open from April through October only. ⊠ *Třetí nádvoří, across from entrance to St. Vitus's Cathedral, Pražský Hrad* ☎ *224–373–368* ⊕ *www.prague-info.cz* ✑ *2-day castle tickets 220 Kč–350 Kč; Golden Lane 50 Kč; St. George's Basilica 50 Kč; English-language guided tours 400 Kč for up to 5 people, 60 Kč per additional person, advance booking recommended; grounds and gardens free* ⊙ *Apr.–Oct., daily 9–5; Nov.–Mar., daily 9–4.*

56 **Klášter svatého Jiří** (St. George's Convent). The first convent in Bohemia was founded here in 973 next to the even older St. George's Basilica. The National Gallery collections of Czech mannerist and baroque art are housed here. The highlights include the voluptuous work of Rudolf II's court painters, the giant baroque religious statuary, and some fine paintings by Karel Škréta and Petr Brandl. Although inside Prague Castle, this museum has a separate admission. ⊠ *Náměstí U sv. Jiří, Pražský Hrad* ☎ *257–320–536* ⊕ *www.ngprague.cz* ☜ *100 Kč* ☉ *Tues.–Sun. 10–6.*

58 Královská zahrada (Royal Garden). This peaceful swath of greenery affords an unusually lovely view of St. Vitus's Cathedral and the castle's walls and bastions. Originally laid out in the 16th century, it endured devastation in war, neglect in times of peace, and many redesigns, reaching its present parklike form early in the 20th century. Luckily, its Renaissance treasures survive. One of these is the long, narrow **Míčovna** (Ball Game Hall), built by Bonifaz Wohlmut in 1568, its garden front completely covered by a dense tangle of allegorical sgraffiti.

FodorśChoice
★

The **Královský letohrádek** (Royal Summer Palace, also known as the Belvedere), at the garden's eastern end, deserves its usual description as one of the most beautiful Renaissance structures north of the Alps. Italian architects began it; Wohlmut finished it off in the 1560s with a copper roof like an upturned boat's keel riding above the graceful arcades of the ground floor. During the 18th and 19th centuries, military engineers tested artillery in the interior, which had already lost its rich furnishings to Swedish soldiers during their siege of the city in 1648. The Renaissance-style *giardinetto* (little garden) adjoining the summer palace centers on another masterwork, the Italian-designed, Czech-cast Singing Fountain, which resonates to the sound of falling water. ⊠ *U Prašného mostu ulice and Mariánské hradby ulice near Chotkovy Park, Pražský Hrad* ☎ *224–373–368 castle information* ⊕ *www.prague-info.cz* ☜ *Free* ☉ *Apr.–Oct., daily 10–5:45.*

55 Královský palác (Royal Palace). The palace is an accumulation of the styles and add-ons of many centuries. The best way to grasp its size is from within the **Vladislavský sál** (Vladislav Hall), the largest secular Gothic interior space in Central Europe. The enormous hall was completed in 1493 by Benedikt Ried, who was to late-Bohemian Gothic what Peter Parler was to the earlier version. The room imparts a sense of space and light, softened by the sensuous lines of the vaulted ceilings and brought to a dignified close by the simple oblong form of the early Renaissance windows. In its heyday, the hall was the site of jousting tournaments, festive markets, banquets, and coronations. In more recent times, it has been used to inaugurate presidents, from the Communist Klement Gottwald in 1948 to Václav Havel in 1989, 1993, and 1998, and Václav Klaus in 2003.

From the front of the hall, turn right into the rooms of the **Česká kancelář** (Bohemian Chancellery). This wing was built by the same Benedikt Ried only 10 years after the hall was completed, but it shows a much stronger Renaissance influence. Pass through the Renaissance portal into the last chamber of the chancellery. This room was the site of the second defenestration of Prague, in 1618, an event that marked the beginning of the Bohemian rebellion and, ultimately, the Thirty Years' War. This peculiarly Bohemian method of expressing protest (throwing someone out a window) had first been used in 1419 in the

New Town Hall, during the lead-up to the Hussite wars. Two hundred years later the same conflict was reexpressed in terms of Hapsburg-backed Catholics versus Bohemian Protestants. Rudolf II had reached an uneasy agreement with the Bohemian nobles, allowing them religious freedom in exchange for financial support. But his next-but-one successor, Ferdinand II, was a rabid opponent of Protestantism and disregarded Rudolf's tolerant "Letter of Majesty." Enraged, the Protestant nobles stormed the castle and chancellery and threw two Catholic officials and their secretary, for good measure, out the window. Legend has it they landed on a mound of horse dung and escaped unharmed, an event the Jesuits interpreted as a miracle. The square window in question is on the left as you enter the room.

At the back of the Vladislav Hall, a staircase leads up to a gallery of the **Kaple všech svatých** (All Saints' Chapel). Little remains of Peter Parler's original work, but the church contains some fine works of art. The large room to the left of the staircase is the **Stará sněmovna** (council chamber), where the Bohemian nobles met with the king in a kind of prototype parliament. The descent from Vladislav Hall toward what remains of the **Romanský palác** (Romanesque Palace) is by way of a wide, shallow set of steps. This **Jezdecké schody** (Riders' Staircase) was the entranceway for knights who came for the jousting tournaments. ⊠ *Royal Palace, Třetí nádvoří, Pražský Hrad* ☎ *224–373–368 castle information* ⊕ *www.prague-info.cz* ✉ *Requires 2-day castle ticket, 220 Kč–350 č* ☉ *Apr.–Oct., daily 9–5; Nov.–Mar., daily 9–4.*

60 **Lobkovický palác** (Lobkowicz Palace). From the beginning of the 17th century until the 1940s, this building was the residence of the powerful Catholic Lobkowicz family. It was supposedly to this house that the two defenestrated officials escaped after landing on a dung hill in 1618. During the 1970s the building was restored to its early baroque appearance and now houses the National Museum's permanent exhibition on Czech history. If you want to get a chronological understanding of Czech history from the beginnings of the Great Moravian Empire in the 9th century to the Czech national uprising in 1848, this is the place. Copies of the crown jewels are on display here, but it's the rich collection of illuminated Bibles, old musical instruments, coins, weapons, royal decrees, paintings, and statues that makes the museum well worth visiting. Detailed information on the exhibits is available in English. Although inside Prague Castle, this museum has a separate admission. ⊠ *Jiřská 3, Pražský Hrad* ⊕ *www.nm.cz* ✉ *40 Kč* ☉ *Tues.–Sun. 9–5.*

Fodor's Choice
★

need a break? You can take a break for a coffee, pastry, or even lunch and enjoy one of the loveliest views of the city from the outdoor terrace of the **Lobkowicz Palace Café** (⊠ Lobkovický palác, Jirska 3, Pražský Hrad ☎ 602–595–998), which serves a full (though somewhat expensive) menu of delicious sandwiches, beverages, and desserts. It's a lovely and quite beautiful place to while away an hour.

50 **Matyášova brána** (Matthias Gate). Built in 1614, the stone gate once stood alone in front of the moats and bridges that surrounded the castle.

Under the Hapsburgs, the gate survived by being grafted as a relief onto the palace building. As you go through it, notice the ceremonial white-marble entrance halls on either side that lead up to President Václav Klaus's reception rooms (which are only rarely open to the public).

61 Muzeum hraček (Toy Museum). The building that once belonged to a high royal official called the Supreme Burgrave houses a private collection of modern dolls and other toys, somewhat incongruous to the historical surroundings but fun for those who still love Barbie. Enter at the eastern entrance to the castle. Although inside Prague Castle, this museum has a separate admission charge. ✉ *Jiřská ulice, Pražský Hrad* ⊕ *www.muzeumhracek.cz* ▨ *40 Kč* ☉ *Daily 9:30–5:30.*

49 První nádvoří (First Courtyard). The main entrance to Prague Castle from Hradčanské náměstí is a little disappointing. Going through the wrought-iron gate, guarded at ground level by Czech soldiers and from above by the ferocious *Battling Titans* (a copy of Ignaz Platzer's original 18th-century work), you enter this courtyard, built on the site of old moats and gates that once separated the castle from the surrounding buildings and thus protected the vulnerable western flank. The courtyard is one of the more recent additions to the castle, designed by Maria Theresa's court architect, Nicolò Pacassi, in the 1760s. Today it forms part of the presidential office complex. Pacassi's reconstruction was intended to unify the eclectic collection of buildings that made up the castle, but the effect of his work is somewhat flat.

53 Třetí nádvoří (Third Courtyard). The contrast between the cool, dark interior of St. Vitus's Cathedral and the brightly colored Pacassi façades of the Third Courtyard just outside is startling. The courtyard's clean lines are the work of Slovenian architect Josip Plečnik in the 1930s, but the modern look is a deception. Plečnik's paving was intended to cover an underground world of house foundations, streets, and walls dating from the 9th through 12th centuries and rediscovered when the cathedral was completed. (You can see a few archways through a grating in a wall of the cathedral.) Plečnik added a few eclectic features to catch the eye: a granite obelisk to commemorate the fallen of the First World War, a black-marble pedestal for the Gothic statue of St. George (a copy of the National Gallery's original statue), the inconspicuous entrance to his Bull Staircase leading down to the south garden, and the peculiar golden ball topping the eagle fountain near the eastern end of the courtyard.

59 Zlatá ulička (Golden Lane). An enchanting collection of tiny, ancient, brightly colored houses crouched under the fortification wall looks remarkably like a set for *Snow White and the Seven Dwarfs*. Legend has it that these were the lodgings of the international group of alchemists whom Rudolf II brought to the court to produce gold. The truth is a little less romantic: the houses were built during the 16th century for the castle guards, who supplemented their income by practicing various crafts. By the early 20th century, Golden Lane had become the home of poor artists and writers. Franz Kafka, who lived at No. 22 in 1916 and 1917, described the house on first sight as "so small, so dirty, impossible to live in and lacking everything necessary." But he soon came to love the place. As he wrote to his fiancée: "Life here is something special . . . to close out the world not just by shutting the door to a room or apartment but to the whole house, to step out into the snow of the silent lane." The lane now houses tiny stores selling books, music, and crafts and has become so popular that a separate admission fee is now charged. The houses are charming, but crowds can be uncomfortable; and you simply can't escape the fact that you are actually paying money for the priviliege to shop in fairly touristy little stores. This is easier to laugh off if you're purchased a combination ticket to the palace, which always includes Golden Lane, but if you are thinking of paying a separate fee, think hard. Within the walls above Golden Lane, a timber-roof **corridor** (enter between No. 23 and No. 24) is lined with replica suits of armor and weapons (some of it for sale), mock torture chambers, and the like. A shooting range allows you to fire five bolts from a crossbow for 50 Kč. ⊠ *Pražský Hrad* ☎ *224–373–368* ⊕ *www.prague-info.cz* ✉ *50 Kč; included in combination 2-day Castle ticket for 220 Kč–350 Kč* ⊙ *Golden Lane Apr.–Oct., daily 9–5; Nov.–Mar., daily 9–4. Golden Lane Corridor Apr.–Oct., Tues.–Sun. 10–5, Mon. 1–5; Nov.–Mar., Tues.–Sun. 10–4, Mon. 1–4.*

NOVÉ MĚSTO (NEW TOWN) & VYŠEHRAD

To this day, Charles IV's building projects are tightly woven into the daily lives of Praguers. His most extensive scheme, the New Town, is still such a lively, vibrant area you may hardly realize that its streets, Gothic churches, and squares were planned as far back as 1348. With Prague fast outstripping its Old Town parameters, Charles IV extended the city's fortifications. A high wall surrounded the newly developed 2½ square km (1½ square mi) area south and east of the Old Town, tripling the walled territory on the Vltava's right bank. The wall extended south to link with the fortifications of the citadel called Vyšehrad. In the mid-19th century, new building in the New Town boomed in a welter of Romantic and neo-Renaissance styles, particularly on Wenceslas Square and avenues such as Vodičkova, Na Poříčí, and Spálená. One of the most important structures was the Národní divadlo (National Theater), meant to symbolize in stone the revival of the Czechs' history, language, and sense of national pride. Both preceding and following Czechoslovak independence in 1918, modernist architecture entered the mix, particularly on the outer fringes of the Old Town and in the New Town. One of modernism's most unexpected products was Cubist architecture, a form unique to Prague, which produced four notable examples at the foot of ancient Vyšehrad.

a good walk

Václavské náměstí ⊕ ☞ is a long, gently sloping boulevard rather than an actual square. Although highly commercial, it's worth walking down its length, if only to experience the hustle and bustle of everyday Czech life as well as the various architectural styles that are represented there. This walk will begin from the top of the boulevard, so first take the metro to the Museum stop, where you will pop out within view of the **Statue of St. Wenceslas** ⊕, a patron saint on horseback, which stands here along with statues of various other saints, one of which—Ludmila—is

Wenceslas's grandmother. The **Národní muzeum** ⑥, which caps the square, is a massive neo-Renaissance structure finished in 1890; take a tour only if you're interested in viewing dusty stuffed animals and one of Europe's largest collections of rocks. Heading down the square, back toward the Old Town, the Supich Building, built in the early 20th century, stands at No. 38; note the Assyrian masks on its façade. Across the square, the Hotel Europa, at No. 25, has preserved most of its interior and exterior art nouveau features.

Work by the Czech artist whose name is synonymous with art nouveau is on show just a block off Václavské náměstí, at the **Mucha Museum** ⑥. To reach the museum, turn right on Jindřišská, and notice the Assicurazioni Generali building on your immediate left. Franz Kafka put in 10 months here in 1906–07 as an insurance clerk. After touring the museum, return to Wenceslas Square via Jindřišská. Back on the square, the Wiehl House, dating from 1896, is a neo-Renaissance building with color-laden sgraffito at the corner of Vodičkova and Václavske Náměstí. At No. 8, you may wish to take a look at the interior of the Adam Pharmacy, which is done in a Cubist style.

At the foot of the square, turn left down 28 Řijna to Jungmannovo náměstí, a small square named for the linguist and patriot Josef Jungmann (1773–1847). In the courtyard off the square, at No. 18, have a look at the Kostel Panny Marie Sněžné (Church of the Virgin Mary of the Snows). Building on the church ceased during the Hussite wars, leaving a very high, foreshortened façade that never grew into the monumental structure planned by Charles IV. Beyond it lies a quiet sanctuary, the walled Františkánská zahrada (Franciscan Gardens). From Jungmannovo náměstí, 28 Řijna becomes Národní třída, a busy shopping street that continues about ¾ km (½ mi) to the river. Continue your walk toward the river, stopping for a look at the art nouveau Praha House at No. 7, which displays its name in gilt letters at the top. The **Národní divadlo** ⑥ (National Theater), a symbol of Czech cultural pride, stands proudly facing the Vltava River. From the theater, follow the embankment, Masarykovo nábřeží, south toward Vyšehrad. Note the art nouveau architecture of No. 32, the amazingly eclectic design by Kamil Hilbert at No. 26, and the tile-decorated Hlahol building at No. 16. Opposite, on a narrow island, is a 19th-century, yellow-and-white ballroom-restaurant, Žofín.

Straddling an arm of the river at Myslíkova ulice are the modern Galerie Mánes (1928–1930) and its attendant 15th-century water tower; it was from a lookout on the sixth floor that Communist-era secret police used to observe Václav Havel's apartment at Rašínovo nábřeží 78. This building, still part-owned by the former president, and the adjoining **Tančící dům** ⑥ are on the far side of a square named Jiráskovo náměstí after the historical novelist Alois Jirásek. From this square, Resslova ulice leads uphill four blocks to a much larger, parklike square, **Karlovo náměstí** ⑥. On the park's northern end is the **Novoměstská radnice** ⑥. Just south of the square is the Benedictine **Klášter Emauzy** ⑦. For a side trip that encompasses some of the city's Cubist architecture, walk to Palackého náměstí via Na Moráni street at the southern end of Karlovo náměstí. The riverfront square has a (melo)dramatic monument to the 19th-century historian František Palacký, "awakener of the nation," and the view from here of the Klášter Emauzy is lovely. The houses grow less attractive south of here, so you may wish to hop a tram (No. 3, 16, or 17 at the stop on Rašínovo nábřeží) and ride one stop to Výtoň, at the base of the **Vyšehrad** ⑦ citadel. Walk under the railroad bridge on Rašínovo nábřeží to find the closest of four nearby **Cubist houses** ⑫. Another lies just a minute's walk farther along the embankment; two more are on Neklanova, a couple of minutes' walk "inland" on Vnislavova. To get up to the fortress, make a hard left onto Vratislavova (the street right before Neklanova), an ancient road that runs tortuously up into the heart of Vyšehrad. If you prefer to go directly to Vyšehrad, take the Metro to Vyšehrad from Karlovo náměstí. Following the signs to the castle, you will walk through a small neighborhood before seeing the high stone walls of the citadel.

TIMING   You might want to divide the walk into two parts, first taking in the busy New Town between Václavské náměstí and Karlovo náměstí, then doing Vyšehrad and the Cubist houses as a separate trip on a different day, or at least after a fortifying lunch. The castle grounds can easily absorb several hours. Vyšehrad is open every day, year-round, and the views are stunning on a clear day or evening.

What to See

★ ⑫ **Cubist buildings.** Bordered to the north by Nové Město and to the south by Nusle, the Vyšehrad neighborhood is mostly known and visited for its citadel that sits high above the river on a rocky outcropping. However, fans of 20th-century architecture can find some Cubist gems between the area's highwaylike riverfront street and the homes that dot the hills on the other side. Born of zealous modernism, Prague's Cubist architecture followed a great Czech tradition in that it fully embraced new ideas while adapting them to existing artistic and social contexts. Between 1912 and 1914, Josef Chochol (1880–1956) designed several of the city's dozen or so Cubist projects. His apartment house **Neklanova 30**, on the corner of Neklanova and Přemyslova, is a masterpiece in dingy concrete. The pyramidal, kaleidoscopic window mouldings and roof cornices are completely novel while making an expressive link to baroque forms; the faceted corner balcony column elegantly alludes to Gothic forerunners. On the same street, at **Neklanova 2**, is another apartment house attributed to Chochol; like the building at Neklanova 30, it uses pyramidal shapes and the suggestion of Gothic columns. Nearby, Chochol's **villa,** on the embankment at Libušina 3, has an undulating effect created by smoothly articulated forms. The wall and gate around the back of the house use triangular moldings and metal grating to create an effect of controlled energy. The **three-family house,** about 100 yards away from the villa at Rašínovo nábřeží 6–10, was completed slightly earlier, when Chochol's Cubist style was still developing. Here, the design is touched with baroque and neoclassical influence, with a mansard roof and end gables.

⑥⑧ **Karlovo náměstí** (Charles Square). This square began life as a cattle market, a function chosen by Charles IV when he established the New Town in 1348. The horse market (now Wenceslas Square) quickly overtook it as a livestock-trading center, and an untidy collection of shacks accumulated here until the mid-1800s, when it became a green park named for its patron. ✉ *Bounded by Řeznická on the north, U Nemocnice on the south, Karlovo náměstí on the west, and Vodičkova on the east, Nové Město.*

need a break? If you've had your fill of goulash and would like to try some of the city's other offerings, walk up Ječná Street from Karlovo náměstí a few blocks to Melounová 2. Here you find the Mexican restaurant **Banditos** (☎ 251–560–513 🖃 No credit cards), offering tasty chicken, beef, and vegetarian dishes, as well as numerous cool cocktails to wash everything down. It doesn't open until noon on weekends.

⑦ Klášter Emauzy (Emmaus Monastery). Another of Charles IV's gifts to the city, the Benedictine monastery sits south of Karlovo náměstí. It's often called Na Slovanech, literally "At the Slavs'," in reference to its purpose when established in 1347: the emperor invited Croatian monks here to celebrate mass in Old Slavonic and thus cultivate religion among the Slavs in a city largely controlled by Germans. A faded but substantially complete cycle of Biblical scenes by Charles's court artists lines the four cloister walls. The frescoes, and especially the abbey church, suffered heavy damage from a raid by Allied bombers on February 14, 1945; it's believed they may have mistaken Prague for Dresden, 121 km (75 mi) away. The church lost its spires, and the interior remained a blackened shell until a renovation was begun in 1998; while the reconstruction work is ongoing, the church reopened to the public in 2003. ✉ *Vyšehradská 49, cloister entrance on left at rear of church, Vyšehrad* 🎟 *10 Kč ⊘ Weekdays 9–4.*

★ ㏝ Mucha Museum. For decades it was almost impossible to find an Alfons Mucha original in the homeland of this famous Czech artist, until, in 1998, this private museum opened with nearly 100 works from his long career. What you expect to see is here—the theater posters of actress Sarah Bernhardt, the magazine covers, and the luscious, sinuous art nouveau designs. There are also paintings, photographs taken in Mucha's studio (one shows Paul Gauguin playing the piano in his underwear), and even Czechoslovak banknotes designed by the artist. ✉ *Panská 7, 1 block off Wenceslas Sq., across from Palace Hotel, Nové Město* ☎ *221–451–335 ⊕ www.mucha.cz* 🎟 *120 Kč ⊘ Daily 10–6.*

㏞ Národní divadlo (National Theater). The idea for a Czech national theater began during the revolutionary decade of the 1840s. In a telling display of national pride, donations to fund the plan poured in from all over the country, from people of every socioeconomic stratum. The cornerstone was laid in 1868, and the "National Theater generation" who built the neo-Renaissance structure became the architectural and artistic establishment for decades to come. Its designer, Josef Zítek (1832–1909), was the leading neo-Renaissance architect in Bohemia. The nearly finished interior was gutted by a fire in 1881, and Zítek's onetime student Josef Schulz (1840–1917) saw the reconstruction through

Fodor'sChoice ★

to completion two years later. Statues representing Drama and Opera rise above the riverfront side entrances; two gigantic chariots flank figures of Apollo and the nine Muses above the main façade. The performance space itself is filled with gilding, voluptuous plaster figures and plush upholstery. Next door is the modern (1970–80) Nová scéna (New Stage), where the popular Magic Lantern black-light shows are staged. The Národní divadlo is one of the best places to see a performance; ticket prices start as low as 30 Kč, and you have to buy a ticket if you want to see inside because there are no public tours. ⊠ *Národní tř. 2, Nové Město* ☎ *224–901–448 box office* ⊕ *www.narodni-divadlo.cz.*

64 **Národní muzeum** (National Museum). This imposing structure, designed by Prague architect Josef Schulz and built between 1885 and 1890, does not come into its own until it is bathed in nighttime lighting. By day the grandiose edifice seems an inappropriate venue for a musty collection of stones and bones, minerals, and coins. This museum is only for dedicated fans of the genre. ⊠ *Václavské náměstí 68, Nové Město* ☎ *224–497–111* ⊕ *www.nm.cz* 🎟 *80 Kč* ⊙ *May–Sept., daily 10–6; Oct.–Apr., daily 9–5; except for 1st Tues. of each month, when it's closed.*

69 **Novoměstská radnice** (New Town Hall). At the northern edge of Karlovo náměstí, the New Town Hall has a late-Gothic tower similar to that of the Old Town Hall, as well as three tall Renaissance gables. The first defenestration in Prague occurred here on July 30, 1419, when a mob of townspeople, followers of the martyred religious reformer Jan Hus, hurled Catholic town councillors out the windows. Historical exhibitions and contemporary art shows are held regularly in the gallery, and you can climb the tower for a view of the New Town. ⊠ *Karlovo náměstí at Vodičkova, Nové Město* 🎟 *Tower 20 Kč; gallery admission varies by exhibition* ⊙ *Tower May–Sept., Tues.–Sun. 10–6; gallery Tues.–Sun. 10–6.*

★ **63** **Statue of St. Wenceslas.** Josef Václav Myslbek's huge equestrian grouping of St. Wenceslas with other Czech patron saints around him is a traditional meeting place at times of great national peril or rejoicing. In 1939, Praguers gathered to oppose Hitler's takeover of Bohemia and Moravia. It was here also, in 1969, that the student Jan Palach set himself on fire to protest the bloody invasion of his country by the Soviet Union and other Warsaw Pact countries in August of the previous year. The invasion ended the "Prague Spring," a cultural and political movement emphasizing free expression, which was supported by Alexander Dubček, the popular leader at the time. Although Dubček never intended to dismantle Communist authority completely, his political and economic reforms proved too daring for fellow comrades in the rest of Eastern Europe. In the months following the invasion, conservatives loyal to the Soviet Union were installed in all influential positions. The subsequent two decades were a period of cultural stagnation. Hundreds of thousands of Czechs and Slovaks left the country, a few became dissidents, and many more resigned themselves to lives of minimal expectations and small pleasures. ⊠ *Václavské náměstí, Nové Město.*

★ ⑰ **Tančící dům** (Dancing House). This whimsical building was partnered into life in 1996 by architect Frank Gehry (of Guggenheim Museum in Bilbao fame) and his Croatian-Czech collaborator Vlado Milunic. A wasp-waisted glass-and-steel tower sways into the main structure as though they were a couple on the dance floor—a "Fred and Ginger" effect that gave the wacky, yet somehow appropriate, building its nickname. The French restaurant La Perle de Prague occupies the top floors, and there's a café at street level. ✉ *Rašínovo nábř. 80, Nové Město.*

★ ⑫ **Václavské náměstí** (Wenceslas Square). You may recognize this spot from your television set, for it was here that some 500,000 students and citizens gathered in the heady days of November 1989 to protest the policies of the former Communist regime. The government capitulated after a week of demonstrations, without a shot fired or the loss of a single life, bringing to power the first democratic government in 40 years (under playwright-president Václav Havel). Today this peaceful transfer of power is half-ironically referred to as the "Velvet" or "Gentle" Revolution (*něžná revoluce*). It was only fitting that the 1989 revolution should take place on Wenceslas Square: throughout much of Czech history, the square has served as the focal point for popular discontent. The long "square"—which is really a broad, divided boulevard not unlike the Champs Elysées in Paris—was first laid out by Charles IV in 1348 as a horse market at the center of the New Town.

At No. 25, the **Hotel Europa** (✉ Vaclavske náměstí 25) is an art nouveau gem, with elegant stained glass and mosaics in the café and restaurant. The terrace is an excellent spot for people-watching. Note in particular the ornate sculpture work of two figures supporting a glass egg on top of the building and the ornate exterior mural. In 1906, when the hotel opened, this was a place for the elite; now the rooms reflect a sense of sadly faded grandeur.

🕑 ⑦ **Vyšehrad.** Bedřich Smetana's symphonic poem *Vyšehrad* opens with four bardic harp chords that seem to echo the legends surrounding this ancient fortress. Today, the flat-top bluff standing over the right bank of the Vltava is a green, tree-dotted expanse showing few signs that splendid medieval monuments once made it a landmark to rival Prague Castle.

The historical father of Vyšehrad, the "High Castle," is Vratislav II (ruled 1061–92), a Přemyslid duke who became first king of Bohemia. He made the fortified hilltop his capital, but under subsequent rulers, it fell into disuse until the 14th century, when Charles IV transformed the site into an ensemble of palaces, the Gothicized main church, battlements, and a massive gatehouse called *Špička,* whose scant remains are on V Pevnosti ulice. By the 17th century, royalty had long since departed, and most of the structures they built were crumbling. Vyšehrad was turned into a fortress.

Vyšehrad's place in the modern Czech imagination is largely thanks to the National Revivalists of the 19th century, particularly writer Alois Jirásek (1851–1930), who mined medieval chronicles for legends and facts to glorify the early Czechs. In his rendition, Vyšehrad was the court of the prophetess-ruler Libuše, who had a vision of her husband-to-be,

VACLÁV HAVEL

VACLÁV HAVEL, a playwright who became the first president of the Czech Republic, became famous during the Velvet Revolution that began on November 17, 1989; the six-week-long peaceful protest against the Communist government led to the demise of the Communists after 40 years of authoritarian rule. A committee of opposition groups, the Civic Forum, was formed and led by Havel, who addressed the masses gathering in Wenceslas Square. In December 1989 he was elected president of Czechoslovakia and later resigned from the position, saying that he could not fulfill the oath of allegiance to the country in a way that would mesh with his convictions. He left public life but returned in January 1993, when he was elected the first president of the Czech Republic, a country formed by the split of Czechoslovakia into the Czech and Slovak republics. He stepped down in ill health in February 2003 after serving two five-year terms.

Decades earlier, after the invasion of Czechoslovakia in 1968 by Soviet troops, who quashed the "Prague Spring" reform movement, Havel's plays had been banned. In 1977, he became a founding member and primary spokesperson for the Charter 77 human rights manifesto, which called on the government to adhere to obligations in the Helsinki Agreement. He was also a member of the Committee for the Defense of the Unjustly Prosecuted, founded by a group of Charter 77 signatories. He was jailed from 1979 to 1983 and again in 1989 for political activities. It was during this period that, he says, he endured conditions in jail that led to the deterioration of his health. A former chain-smoker, he underwent an operation to have half of his right lung removed in December 1996. He was hospitalized at least a dozen times since 1993.

the ploughman Přemysl—father of the Přemyslid line—and of "a city whose glory shall reach the heavens" called Praha. (In truth, the Czechs first came to Vyšehrad around the beginning of the 900s, slightly later than the building of Prague Castle.)

Traces of the citadel's distant past can be found at every turn, and are reflected even in the structure chosen for the visitors' center, the remains of a Gothic stone fortification wall known as **Špička,** or Peak Gate, at the corner of V Pevnosti and U Podolského Sanatoria. Farther ahead is the sculpture-covered **Leopold Gate,** which stands next to brick walls enlarged during the 1742 occupation by the French. Out of the gate, a heavily restored **Romanesque rotunda,** built by Vratislav II in the 11th century, stands on the corner of K rotundě and Soběslavova. It's considered the oldest fully intact Romanesque building in the city. Down Soběslavova are the excavated foundations and a few embossed floor tiles from the late-10th-century **Basilika svatého Vavřince** (St. Lawrence Basilica). The foundations, discovered in 1884 while workers were creating a cesspool, are in a baroque structure at Soběslavova 14 (if it's locked, you can ask for the key at the refreshment stand just to the left of the basilica entrance; admission is 5 Kč). The remains are from one of the few early Medieval buildings to have survived in the area and are worth a look. On the west side of Vyšehrad, part of the fortifications stand next to the surprisingly confined foundation mounds of a medieval palace overlooking a ruined watchtower called **Libuše's Bath,** which precariously juts out of a rocky outcropping over the river. A nearby plot of grass hosts a statue of Libuše and her consort Přemysl, one of four large, sculpted images of couples from Czech legend by J. V. Myslbek (1848–1922), the sculptor of the St. Wenceslas monument.

The military history of the fortress and the city is covered in a small exposition inside the Cihelná brána Brick Gate, but the real attraction is the **casemates,** a long, dark passageway within the walls that ends at a dank hall used to store several original, pollution-scarred Charles Bridge sculptures. A guided tour into the casemates and the statue storage room starts at the military history exhibit; it has a separate admission fee.

With its neo-Gothic spires, **Kapitulní kostel svatých Petra a Pavla** (Chapter Church of Sts. Peter and Paul; ⊠ K rotundì 10, Vyšehrad ☏ 224–911–353) dominates the plateau as it has since the 11th century. Next to the church lies the burial ground of the nation's revered cultural figures. Most of the buildings still standing are from the 19th century, but scattered among them are a few older structures and some foundation stones of the medieval palaces. Surrounding the ruins are gargantuan, excellently preserved brick fortifications built from the 17th to the mid-19th century; their broad tops allow you to take in sweeping vistas up- and downriver. The church is open daily from 9 to noon and 1 to 5, with an admission charge of 10 Kč.

Fodor'sChoice
★ A concrete result of the national revival was the establishment of the **Hřbitov** (cemetery) in the 1860s, adjacent to the Church of Sts. Peter and Paul—it peopled the fortress with the remains of luminaries from the arts and sciences. The grave of Smetana faces the Slavín, a mausoleum for more than 50 honored men and women including Alfons Mucha, sculptor Jan Štursa, inventor František Křižík, and the opera diva Ema Destinnová. All are guarded by a winged genius who hovers above the inscription AČ ZEMŘELI, JEŠTĚ MLUVÍ ("Although they have died, they yet speak"). Antonín Dvořák (1841–1904) rests in the arcade along the north wall of the cemetery. Among the many writers buried here are Jan Neruda, Božena Němcová, Karel Čapek, and the Romantic poet Karel Hynek Mácha, whose grave was visited by students on their momentous November 17, 1989, protest march. ⊠ V Pevnosti 159/5b, Vyšehrad ☏ 241–410–348 ⊕ www.praha-vysehrad.cz ☉ Grounds daily. Casemates, military history exhibit, and St. Lawrence Basilica Apr.–Oct., daily 9:30–5:30; Nov.–Mar., daily 9:30–4:30. Cemetary Apr.–Oct. daily 8–6; Nov.–Mar. daily 8–4 🎫 Grounds and cemetary free; casemates tour 20 Kč; Military history exhibit 10 Kč; St. Lawrence Basilica 5 Kč Ⓜ Line C: Vyšehrad.

need a break? Grab an outdoor table at **V Vyšehrad rotundy** (⊠ K Rotunde 1) restaurant, right across from the Romanesque rotunda. Pasta, chicken, and pork dishes are available, and the restaurant stays open seven days a week.

KAREL ČAPEK

KAREL ČAPEK, a Czech author best known for introducing the word robot to the world, had his first major success as a playwright in 1921 with R. U. R. (Rossum's Universal Robots), a satire of the Czech agrarian system. His essay, "Why I Am Not a Communist," was published in1924, long before Communists took over the Czech Republic. Čapek wrote other, less successful works; however, the novel War with the Newts—a satire of dictatorships— and a series of interviews with the president of Czechoslovakia, Tomaš Garrique Masaryk, stand out. Čapek earned his master's degree in philosophy and was not only a writer but also an editor of the newspaper Lidové noviny (The People's Paper). He was born January 9, 1890, in Malé Svatoňovice near Trutnov in northeastern Bohemia. His father, Antonin Čapek, was a doctor; his mother, Božena Čapková, was a housewife.

When France and Britain signed the Munich Agreement, ordering Czechoslovakia to leave its border regions to Germany, Čapek was offered the possibility of exile in England. He chose to remain in Prague even though the decision meant risking his life. During the Nazi occupation, his writings were banned as anti-fascist. Čapek's works later suffered, posthumously, under the Communists as well.

His brother, Josef, was a painter who illustrated several of his brother's books; Josef's political caricatures led to his death in a Nazi concentration camp after the Germans occupied Czechoslovakia in 1939. Back problems afflicted Čapek for most of his life, and he eventually succumbed to pneumonia on December 25, 1938, at the age of 48. His works are still widely translated today.

VINOHRADY

From Riegrovy Park and its sweeping view of the city from above the National Museum, the eclectic apartment houses and villas of the elegant residential neighborhood called Vinohrady extend eastward and southward. The pastel-tint ranks of turn-of-the-20th-century apartment houses—many crumbling after years of neglect—are slowly but unstoppably being transformed into upscale flats, slick offices, eternally packed new restaurants, and all manner of shops unthinkable only a half decade ago. Much of the development lies on or near Vinohradská, the main street, which extends from the top of Wenceslas Square to a belt of enormous cemeteries about 3 km (2 mi) eastward. Yet the flavor of daily life persists: smoky old pubs still ply their trade on the quiet side streets; the stately theater, Divadlo na Vinohradech, keeps putting on excellent shows as it has for decades; and on the squares and in the parks nearly everyone still practices Prague's favorite form of outdoor exercise—walking the dog.

73 **Kostel Nejsvětějšího Srdce Páně** (Church of the Most Sacred Heart). If you had your fill of Romanesque, Gothic, and baroque, this church will give you a look at a startling art deco edifice. Designed in 1927 by Slovenian architect Josip Plečnik (the same architect commissioned to update Prague Castle), the church resembles a luxury ocean liner more than a place of worship. The effect was conscious: during the 1920s and 1930s, the avant-garde imitated mammoth objects of modern technology. Plečnik used many modern elements on the inside. Notice the hanging speakers, seemingly designed to bring the word of God directly to the ears of each worshipper. You may be able to find someone at the back entrance of the church who will let you walk up the long ramp into the fascinating glass clock tower. ⊠ *Náměstí Jiřího z Poděbrad, Vinohrady* 🎫 *Free* ☉ *Daily 10–5* Ⓜ *Line A: Jiřího z Poděbrad.*

⓴ Nový židovský hřbitov (New Jewish Cemetery). Tens of thousands of Czechs find eternal rest in Vinohrady's cemeteries. In this, the newest of the city's half-dozen Jewish burial grounds, you can find the modest **tombstone of Franz Kafka,** which seems grossly inadequate to Kafka's stature but oddly in proportion to his own modest ambitions. The cemetery is usually open, although guards sometimes inexplicably seal off the grounds. Men may be required to wear a yarmulke (you can buy one here if you need to). Turn right at the main cemetery gate and follow the wall for about 100 yards. Kafka's thin, white tombstone lies at the front of section 21. City maps may label the cemetery *Židovské hřbitovy.* ⊠ *Vinohradská at Jana Želivského, Vinohrady* 🎫 *Free* ☉ *June–Aug., Sun.–Thurs. 9–5, Fri. 9–1; Sept.–May, Sun.–Thurs. 9–4, Fri. 9–1* Ⓜ *Line A: Želivského.*

⓵ Pavilon. This gorgeous, turn-of-the-20th-century, neo-Renaissance, three-story market hall is one of the most attractive sites in Vinohrady. It used to be a major old-style market, a vast space filled with stalls selling all manner of foodstuffs plus the requisite grimy pub. After being spiffed up in the 1990s, it mutated into an upscale shopping mall. Those looking for gleaming designer pens or Italian shoes can find them here. Walk west two blocks down Vinohradská after exiting the metro. ⊠ *Vinohradská 50, Vinohrady* 🕿 *222–097–111* ☉ *Mon.–Sat. 8:30 AM–9 PM, Sun. noon–6* Ⓜ *Line A: Jiřího z Poděbrad.*

⓶ Muzeum Antonína Dvořáka (Antonín Dvořák Museum). The baroque red-and-yellow villa housing the museum displays the 19th-century Czech composer's scores, photographs, viola, piano, and other memorabilia. The statues in the garden date from about 1735; the house from 1720. Check the schedule for classical performances, as recitals are often held in the first floor of the two-story villa. ⊠ *Ke Karovu 20, Vinohrady* 🕿 *224–923–363* 🎫 *40 Kč* ☉ *Tues.–Sun. 10–7* Ⓜ *Line C: I. P. Pavlova.*

---

need a break?

Artyčok (⊠ Londýnská 49 🕿 222–524–110) has some of the city's best pizza. Slide into a seat on the outdoor patio, which is on a peaceful corner in the neighborhood, and try the eponymous artyčok pizza. The pizzeria doesn't take credit cards.

LETNÁ & HOLEŠOVICE

From above the Vltava's left bank, the large, grassy plateau called Letná gives you one of the classic views of the Old Town and the many bridges crossing the river. (To get to Letná from the Old Town, take Pařížská Street north, cross the Čechův Bridge, and climb the stairs.) Beer gardens, tennis, and Frisbee attract people of all ages, while amateur soccer players emulate the professionals of Prague's top team, Sparta, which plays in the stadium just across the road. A 10-minute walk from Letná, down into the residential neighborhood of Holešovice, brings you to a massive, gray-blue building whose cool exterior gives no hint of the treasures of Czech and French modern art that line its corridors. Just north along Dukelských hrdinů Street is Stromovka—a royal hunting preserve turned gracious park.

Numbers in the margin correspond to numbers on the Exploring Prague map.

⑧⓵ **Křížikova fontána** (Kříž Fountain). Still functioning, this pressurized water and colored-light show was originally built for the Jubilee Industrial Exhibition of 1891. Occasionally, live music is played with the lights, but more often recorded programs of film music, classics, or rock accompanies the dancing waters and lights. František Křížík, who built the fountain, was a famous inventor of his day and a friend of Thomas Edison. Live acts sometimes play along to the lights and water. ✉ *Výstaviště, exhibition grounds, Holešovice* ☎ *220–103–224* ⊕ *www.krizikovasfontana.cz* Ⓜ *Line C: Nádraží Holešovice.*

⑧⓪ **Lapidárium.** Come here to see a fascinating display of 11th- to 19th-century sculptures saved from torn-down buildings or the vicissitudes of Prague's weather. Some of the original Charles Bridge statues can be found here as well as a towering bronze monument to Field Marshall Radetsky, a leader of the 19th-century Austrian army. Pieces of a marble fountain that once stood in Old Town Square now occupy most of one room. For horse lovers, there are several fine equestrian statues inside. ✉ *Výstavisté 422, Holešovice* ☎ *233–375–636* ⊕ *www.nm.cz* 🎟 *20 Kč* ⊙ *Tues.–Fri. 12–6, weekends 10–6* Ⓜ *Line C: Vltavská.*

⑦⑦ **Letenské sady** (Letna Park). Come to this large, shady park for an unforgettable view of Prague's bridges. From the enormous cement pedestal at the center of the park, the largest statue of Stalin in Eastern Europe once beckoned to citizens on the Old Town Square far below. The statue was ripped down in the 1960s, when Stalinism was finally discredited. On sunny Sundays expatriates often meet up here to play ultimate Frisbee. Head east on Milady Horáové street after exiting the metro. ✉ *Letna* Ⓜ *Line A: Hradčanská.*

☾ ⑦⑨ **Národní Technické muzeum** (National Technical Museum). Planes, trains, and automobiles dating from the 19th through the 20th century can all be found within this museum's massive Transport Hall. The upper levels showcase technical advancements in cinematography and measuring time and also include a collection of astronomical instruments.

Underneath the structure, a reconstruction of a coal mine and its assortment of heavy machinery challenges the claustrophobic. ⊠ *Kostelní 42, Holešovice* ☎ *220–399–111* ⊕ *www.ntz.cz* ⊠ *60 Kč* ☉ *Tues.–Sun. 9–5* Ⓜ *Line C: Vltavská.*

⑦ **Veletržní palác** (Trade Fair Palace). The National Gallery's **Sbírka moderního a soucasného umění** (Collection of Modern and Contemporary Art) has become a keystone in the city's visual-arts scene since its opening in 1995. Touring the vast spaces of this 1920s Constructivist exposition hall and its comprehensive collection of 20th-century Czech art is the best way to see how Czechs surfed the forefront of the avant-garde wave until the cultural freeze following the Communist takeover in 1948. Also on display are works by Western European—mostly French—artists from Delacroix to the present. Especially noteworthy are the early Cubist paintings by Picasso and Braque. The 19th-century Czech art collection of the National Gallery was installed in the palace in summer 2000. Watch the papers and posters for information on traveling shows and temporary exhibits. The collection is divided into sections, so be sure to get a ticket for exactly what you want to see. ⊠ *Dukelských hrdinů 47, Holešovice* ☎ *224–301–111* ⊕ *www.ngprague.cz* ⊠ *One floor 100 Kč, 2 floors 150 Kč, 3 floors 200 Kč, special exhibits 40 Kč* ☉ *Tues., Wed., and Fri.–Sun. 10–6, Thurs. 10–9* Ⓜ *Line C: Vltavská.*

TROJA

North of Holešovice on the banks of the Vlatava, the City Gallery Prague has a branch at Troja Château. Nearby are the Prague Botanical Gardens and the zoo. This area makes a nice half-day trip if you want to get out of the city-center, but it's distant enough from the main part of town that it's hard to visit if you don't set aside several hours.

⑧ **Botanická zahrada** (Botanical Gardens). The garden's newest addition, a snaking 429-foot greenhouse that simulates three different environments, has been drawing large crowds ever since it opened to visitors in summer 2004. Its path first takes you through a semidesert environment, such as those found in Australia, then through a tunnel beneath a tropical lake and into a rain forest; you end up cooling off in a room devoted to plants found in tropical mountains. Sliding doors and computer-control climate systems help keep it all together. ⊠ *Nadvorni 134, Troja* ☎ *234–148–111* ⊕ *www.botgarden.cz* ⊠ *90 Kč* ☉ *Tues.–Sun. 9–7* Ⓜ *Line C: Nádraží Holešovice, then Bus 112.*

⑧ **Trojský zámek** (Troja Château). Built in the late 17th century for the Czech nobleman Count Šternberg, this sprawling summer residence is modeled on a classical Italian villa and had the first French-style gardens in Bohemia. Inside, rich frescoes in rooms that took more than 20 years to complete depict the stories of emperors. Outside, a sweeping staircase is adorned with statues of the sons of Mother Earth. ⊠ *U trojského zámku 1, Troja* ☎ *283–851–654* ⊕ *www.citygalleryprague.cz* ⊠ *120 Kč* ☉ *Apr.–Sept. 10–6; Oct.–Mar. 10–5* Ⓜ *Line C: Nádraží Holešovicé, then Bus 112.*

🐾 ⑳ **Zoologická zahrada v Praze** (Prague Zoo). Flora, fauna, and fresh air are the main things you can find in Prague's zoo. Hit hard by the floods in 2002, the zoo has been cleaned up and is a great break from the bustle of the city. Covering 160 acres on a slope overlooking the Vltava River, the zoo has thousands of animals representing 500 species. Take the chairlift for an outstanding view of the area. ⊠ *U trojského zámku 3, Troja* ☎ *296–112–111* ⊕ *www.zoopraha.cz* 🏷 *50 Kč* ☉ *May–Sept. 9–7; Oct.–Apr. 9–4* Ⓜ *Line C: Nádraží Holešovicé, then Bus 112.*

ŽIŽKOV

Žižkov is not a major draw for tourists. Named after Jan Žižka, a Hussite military commander who fought a battle here in 1420, the neighborhood has always been working-class. Until recently, it was fairly run-down and crumbling, though efforts are underway to spruce it up and to restore some of the early-20th-century housing stock. Progress has been mixed, and many parts of the area are still fairly run-down and grim-looking. You're most likely to end up here if you're looking for nightlife or budget hotels, but there are a couple of sights to visit. Don't be surprised to see scruffy gypsies if you come here.

⑳ **National Memorial.** Situated on Vítkov Hill, one of the high points in the city, this stone building's one outstanding feature is the largest equestrian statue in the world—a 16.5-ton metal structure of Hussite leader Jan Žižka on horseback. In the past, the 20th-century memorial was a final resting place for post-war presidents; now, the eerily quiet mausoleum is a popular spot for movie shoots. ⊠ *U Památníku, Žižkov* ☎ *222–781–676* ⊕ *www.nm.cz* 🏷 *150 Kč* ☉ *By appointment only* Ⓜ *Lines B & C: Florenc.*

⑳ **Žižkov TV Tower.** Looking like a rocket ready to blast off, the Žižkov TV Tower came under fire from area residents, who claimed it gave their children cancer soon after it began operating in 1990. The eighth-floor platform, reached by a high-speed elevator, gives a bird's-eye view of the numerous courtyards and apartment blocks that make up the city, but in truth, it's almost too tall to give a good view of the low-slung city. Once back down on the ground, look up its 709-foot grey steel legs at the bronze statues of babies crawling on the structure, which were created by local artist David Černy. ⊠ *Mahlerovy sady, Žižkov* ☎ *267–005–778* 🏷 *60 Kč* ☉ *Daily 10 AM–11 PM* Ⓜ *Lines B & C: Florenc.*

WHERE TO EAT

2

BEST INTERNATIONAL ITALIAN
Allegro in the Four Seasons Hotel,
Staré Město ⇨*p.62*

HIP DINING UNDER THE SPIRES
Pravda, *Staré Město* ⇨*p.57*

CHARMING AND UNPRETENTIOUS
C'est La Vie, *Malá Strana* ⇨*p.63*

WATERSIDE INSTITUTION
Kampa Park, *Malá Strana* ⇨*p.63*

ESSENTIAL PIT STOP
Kavarna Slavia, *Staré Město* ⇨*p.62*

BEST (UPSCALE) BANG FOR BUCK
Zahrada v opeře, *Nové Město* ⇨*p.66*

By David
Friday

THE HUNDREDS OF RESTAURANTS that have opened up since the mid-1990s have transformed Prague from a city where word of mouth led you to one of a limited number of nimbly found spots to a city where a leisurely walk, even outside of the center, can bring you past several inviting restaurants. Cutting-edge cuisine is still something of a rarity, save in the most expensive restaurants, but bearing in mind that nearly 50 years of Communism depleted both creativity and fresh ingredients from restaurants, great strides have been made in local kitchens.

Unfortunately, the Czech palate has not been particularly open-minded. Of new cuisines that have been introduced since the borders were opened and tastebuds challenged, only Mexican, which came in the early and mid-1990s, has been widely embraced; even then, there was the unfortunate period of "Czech-Mex" to suffer through. Local Chinese cuisine, where cabbage and carrots seem to find their way into everything, has also suffered an uncomfortable fusion. On other Asian fronts, two pioneers of Thai cuisine that opened in the late-1990s bore the brunt of educating people and shut down by 2002. Since then, two more Thai restaurants have opened and are receiving much more support.

The city center, particularly Old Town and Malá Strana in Prague 1, is densely packed with restaurants; indeed, the problem here is often too much choice. If you use your common sense when pausing to look at a menu—photographs of food, cartoon figures, and flags from several nations generally indicate a more touristy place—there's a higher probability of avoiding substandard fare for higher prices. In New Town, a cluster of restaurants has emerged over the last several years in the maze of streets behind the National Theatre, a sort of dining ghetto that offers a range of cuisines including French and Thai. Only two or three mostly Czech choices existed here in the early 1990s. Beyond this, and over the river, the Anděl area was a rather depressing postindustrial neighborhood as recently as the late 1990s; in the past few years, it has been completely transformed into a vibrant urban destination with all manner of pubs, pizzerias, and restaurants continuing to spring up. Though most of them are fine—and make a good respite after a busy shopping excursion—they don't offer anything exceptional that cannot be found in the center. Increasingly attractive restaurants are opening in the Vinohrady neighborhood on either side of (but not really on) Vinohradská Street. A walk here can bring you past several pleasant restaurants in a less hectic setting than downtown.

You can generally find lower prices outside the center, but this is by no means across the board. But you needn't worry too much: price levels are significantly less in Prague than in cities of Western Europe or North America. In addition, many restaurants serving international food have followed the Czech restaurant tradition and offer a selection of five to 10 quickly made lunchtime meals, on a *denní lístek* (daily menu), valid until 3 or 4 PM. Otherwise, main courses tend to be served without side orders, such as potatoes, rice, etc., so you'll be asked by the waitstaff to name your choice from a list of five to 10, or more, options listed in the menu. These days, out-and-out rip-offs have almost disappeared, but in the tourist-ridden areas, occasional bill-padding is sometimes still seen.

Though it's improving gradually, service in restaurants, overall, is still not up to Western standards. Delays are common at ordering or bill time, but service is usually only mildly annoying or bemusing rather than outright bad. You may find yourself waiting five or 10 minutes in an almost empty restaurant while the server wipes off every table in the room and changes the placemats before she acknowledges you. In the more expensive restaurants, slow or unfriendly service is uncommon, but smiles and friendliness are still not ubiquitous. Nevertheless, as youthful staff, educated in modern customer service, take over, smiles and attentiveness increase.

Traditional Czech food can be found in a *Český restaurace* (Czech restaurant) or *hospoda* (like a pub). The raison d'etre for the latter is beer, and though food is technically said to be secondary and offered on a limited menu, the line is blurry, and many hospodas are indistinguishable from restaurants. Another related word you may see is *hostinec*, an older form of the word *hospoda*. Both come from the route *host*, which means "guest." However, wherever beer is drunk in great quantities (which is most places), smoking usually accompanies, so plan ahead if you value the clean smell of your favorite T-shirt.

STARÉ MĚSTO (OLD TOWN)

ASIAN
$$$$

✕ **Barock.** It's certainly chic, and some call it pretentious, but there's no doubt that the food here is very good. Thai and Japanese dishes predominate, and there are other Asian and international choices. The burnished walls, fresh flowers, and black-and-white photographs of attractive people all add to hip charm. There's also a decent chance that you'll see a Czech actress or model dining nearby. ⊠ *Pařížská 24, Josefov* ☎ 222–329–221 ⊟ *AE, DC, MC, V* Ⓜ *Line A: Staroměstska.*

$–$$$

✕ **Orange Moon.** Thai, Burmese, and Indian dishes draw tourists and locals alike to this reasonably priced spot a short walk from Old Town Square. The space is not blessed with an abundance of natural light, but the blond wood, orange walls, and paper lamps have a relaxing and mood-boosting effect, along with the enticing aromas of jasmine and spice. Chicken soup with coconut milk and lemon grass, fresh squid in oyster sauce, and beef kebabs with Madras curry represent just three outstanding items from a consistently good menu. ⊠ *Ráova 5, Staré Město* ☎ 222–325–119 ⊟ *AE, DC, MC, V* Ⓜ *Line B: Náěstí Republiky.*

CONTEMPORARY
★ $$–$$$$

✕ **Le Terroir.** When the manager of a premier fish restaurant—who happens to know something about wine—finds the perfect spot to create a new restaurant from scratch, good things happen. This restaurant and wine shop boasts a cellar nine centuries old with one of Prague's widest wine selections, at more than 600 varieties. Clever design touches, such as the collage of earth samples from wine regions of Europe, and masterful lighting make the cellar a pleasure to dine in. From the smoked tuna with cucumber foam and arugula starter to the Domori-chocolate dessert, the menu is impeccable. ⊠ *Vejvodova 1, Staré Město* ☎ 602–889–118 ⊟ *AE, MC, V* Ⓜ *Line A: Můstek.*

Mealtimes Most restaurants in Prague are open from about 11 AM to 11 PM. This closing time is very regular with traditional Czech restaurants and *hospoda,* which seldom stay open beyond this; the kitchens in these restaurants usually shut down at 10 PM, and often earlier if it's a slow night, so it's a good idea to ask when you arrive. A growing number of restaurants serve the late-night crowd, especially in the city center and, more recently, in Vinohrady, but it's still a far cry from the likes of Paris or New York. Some Czech restaurants in neighborhoods outside of the center close on Sunday or open only for evening meals, but in the heavily touristed areas, one day of the week is like any other.

2

Menus Most restaurants post menus outside. Prix-fixe menus are not popular in the evening, but many restaurants offer a *denní lístek* (prix-fixe lunch) with five or six items that usually include a soup starter and/or dessert. If you want to try a traditional Czech meal, such as *svickova* (beef tenderloin) or *gulás* (much like the Hungarian version), you may find that it's only offered at lunchtime in most restaurants outside of Prague 1. However, if you do come across it on a dinner menu, it will likely be a larger portion (at a reasonably higher price) and may even include a slightly more elaborate presentation, such as with a mix of dumplings.

Reservations The need for a reservation varies with the season and the weather, perhaps more than other cities. When there are few tourists on the street (in Old Town and Malá Strana, most of the people on the street are tourists), the restaurants will likely follow suit, and you probably won't have a problem. If you have your heart set on a particular spot and it's a busier time, it's best to drop in or call ahead. Most of the restaurants below will understand English enough to take a reservation.

Smoking Smoking is very popular in Prague. Some of the more expensive restaurants have no-smoking sections, but few others do. In traditional Czech establishments, such as *hospody* (pubs) and *pivnice* (named after *pivo,* which means beer, is a place where beer is drunk, usually in high quantities), you may be overwhelmed by the amount of cigarette smoke.

What to Wear At most moderately priced and inexpensive restaurants, casual but neat dress is acceptable. In restaurant listings, we mention dress only when men are expected to wear a jacket or a jacket and tie, which is seldom the case.

Wine There's a reason why the Czech Republic is more famous for beer than for wine. Polite responses to first tastings of Czech wine akin to "Hmm, that's different," are not uncommon. However, with a little suspension of preconceptions and remembering the price, which is generally less than half the cost of foreign wines, you'll have less reason to complain. You can almost always order wines by the glass, though more expensive vintages are usually available in the bottle only. So called *archiví* (vintage) wines, though more expensive, are not necessarily better. Moravian wines, such as those from *Valtice,* are often better bets.

The most popular Czech whites are *Müller Thurgau* and *Ryzlink* (Riesling); of these, domestic Rieslings tend to be the better choice. After that, four of five varietals appear on menus, and these are hit and miss, so one is difficult to recommend; one exception, though it doesn't always make it onto the menu, is the light and sometimes floral *tramin,* made from the same grape used in the German wine *gewürtztraminer,* which tends to be better more often.

Two of the most popular reds are frankovka and svatovavřinecké. If you're in an inexpensive restaurant, you may find that the frankovkas are inferior, so try to avoid them unless they are all that's offered. After these, cabernet sauvignon is popular, but regardless of the variety, the Czech reds are generally lighter in body than the wines of, say, Australia, France, or California. Bohemia Sekt (go for the *suchý,* or dry) can hold its own against, if not surpass, sparkling wines from other countries, and it's definitely a good starter for a fun and memorable meal.

Most restaurants, aside from hospody, offer a selection of international wines.

Prices In medium and expensive restaurants, prices can be more than a third less than in a comparable U.S. restaurant. In traditional Czech restaurants and *hospoda,* especially outside the city center, price levels are even less, and can drop to a rock-bottom 45 Kč on the *denní lístek* (daily menu).

Watch for a "couvert," which may appear in smaller print on a menu. Though a bit annoying, it's legitimate and is meant to cover bread, a caddy of condiments, and/or service. Remember that side orders usually have to be ordered separately and so will be tabulated accordingly. Taxes are included with all meal prices listed in the menu.

WHAT IT COSTS in Czech koruna				
	$$$$	$$$	$$	$	¢
AT DINNER	over 500	300–500	150–300	100–150	under 100

Prices are per person for a main course at dinner and include 19% V.A.T.

Paying In a more traditional dining venue, such as a Czech *restaurace* or *hospoda,* it's possible that the person you ordered from will not be the person who tallies your bill. In that case, you may hear your waiter say *colega,* meaning a colleague will bring the bill. This situation is less likely in the more modern establishments. In the bulk of low- and mid-price restaurants, the waiter or bill person will tally your bill in front of you and stand by while you pull together the money to pay. If you want to do it the Czech way, quickly add a suitable amount for a tip on in your head, and say this new total when you hand over your money. If you need a bit of time, it's best to politely smile and say *moment prosím* (one moment please). Don't panic if you miss the moment; many people don't make the calculation quickly enough and just leave the money on the table. In the places frequented by tourists, particularly in the city center, the waiter (or a colleague) may expect this already and just leave the bill on the table for you.

Tipping in the Czech Republic has been based traditionally on rounding up the tab to a convenient number rather than calculating a percentage and adding it on, and in the *hospoda* around the city (especially out of the tourist area) this is still how it's done. For example, paying 150 Kč on a bill of 137 Kč would be perfectly acceptable (though locals might stop at 140 Kč). But as tourists, expatriates living in Prague, and traveling Czechs returning from vacation continue to exert their influence, a 10% tip is becoming the norm. A good rule of thumb to follow (particularly if the restaurant you're in seems to be frequented by foreigners) is to round the price up to a convenient number that leaves roughly 10%. In the more expensive restaurants, tip 15% or more, as in the West.

$$–$$$$
Fodor'sChoice
★
✕ **Pravda.** The slightly younger brother of Barock, Pravda is part of the slick trio of heavily Asian-inspired establishments owned by local restaurateur Tommy Sjöö. Potatoes pureed with wasabi and truffles accompany seared tuna, monk fish, and other delectables. Pravda is housed in a gorgeous turn-of-the-20th-century building that has undergone a complete restoration, so the setting these days is even nicer than it was when it first opened. ⊠ *Pařížská 17, Josefov* ☎ *222–326–203* ▤ *AE, DC, MC, V* Ⓜ *Line A: Staroměstská.*

$$–$$$$
✕ **V Zátiší.** A long-time favorite on the Prague upscale dining scene, this understated restaurant has not lost its appeal. It continues to please with upgraded Czech specialties, such as venison with vegetable cream sauce and chestnut dumplings, as well as the requisite Asian and seafood contingent. Service, as always, is very good. ⊠ *Liliová 1, at Betlémské nám., Staré Město* ☎ *222–222–025* ▤ *AE, MC, V* Ⓜ *Line B: Národní Třída.*

$–$$$
✕ **Ambiente–Pasta Fresca.** Offering up much more than pasta, the second member of the Ambiente chain has the trademark attentive service and the more impressive setting, thanks largely to its location under a high stone-rimmed vaulted ceiling in the cellar of a baroque-era building. It's one of the mainstays for the business crowd at lunchtime. Whenever you go, soft lighting, candles, and excellent service ensure a stress-free dining experience. ⊠ *Celetná 11, Staré Město* ☎ *222–322–865* ▤ *AE, DC, MC, V* Ⓜ *Line A or B: Můstek.*

CONTINENTAL
$$$–$$$$
✕ **Bellevue.** The first choice for visiting dignitaries and businesspeople blessed with expense accounts, Bellevue has creative, freshly prepared cuisine with a strong French influence. Typical dishes include roasted veal loin with a crust of black truffle, star anise, and fingerling potatoes with Girolle mushroom sauce. Window seats have stunning views of Prague Castle. The Sunday jazz brunch includes all the Bohemia sekt you can drink. ⊠ *Smetanovo nábř. 18, Staré Město* ☎ *222–221–449* ▤ *AE, MC, V* Ⓜ *Line A: Staroměstská.*

CZECH
★ $–$$$
✕ **Kolkovna.** For Czechs and expatriates living in Prague, this is one of the most popular spots to take people visiting from other countries for a true taste of Czech food without the stress associated with either tourist rip-offs or dingy neighborhoods. The wood-and-copper decor gives an appropriate brewery-type feeling, and you can wash down traditional meals—such as *svíčkova* (sliced sirloin beef in cream sauce), roast

ON THE MENU

TRADITIONAL CZECH FOOD is hearty, with big portions of meat and something starchy on the side such as dumplings or potatoes. Herbs and spices are not used heavily, though dill, marjoram, and caraway make frequent appearances, and garlic is used heavily in some dishes. Salt is used liberally. Aside from these, flavor comes from meat. The Czechs know what they're doing when it comes to smoking meat—the natural way—and smoked (uzený) pork makes its way into many meals, occasionally (though less frequently than a few years ago) even "vegetarian" ones.

Bramborák (bram-bohr-ahk). Available from fast-food stands throughout the city as well as in restaurants, this large (six- to eight-inch) potato pancake is flavored with marjoram and deep-fried.

Bezmasá jídla. This section of the menu lists dishes without meat. This is where you'll find čočky (stewed lentils), smažený sýr (fried cheese), and rizoto se zeleninou (risotto with vegetables).

Česnečka (ches-netch-kah). This Czech standby, garlic soup, is a thin—usually meatless—garlic-laced broth containing small pieces of potato, served with fried bread cubes.

Čočky (choch-kee). In this traditional vegetarian dish, green lentils are stewed with or without smoked meat. An egg and pickle are usually served with the true meatless version.

Cibulačka (tsi-boo-latch-kah). A close relative of česnečka—though a little less potent—this onion soup is usually served with bread; cheese is sprinkled on top. Unlike its French counterpart, it's not made from meat broth, so it's usually quite light.

Ďábělskě toasty (dya-byel-skeh). Devil's toasts are a mixture of cooked ground beef, tomatoes, onions, and peppers served on fried or toasted white bread. This starter is meant, as its name suggests, to be hot (as in spicy). By North American standards it doesn't deliver that big a punch, however, and more closely resembles a mildly spiced sloppy Joe. It may come with cheese melted on top.

Gulás (goo-laush). Like its Hungarian counterpart, Czech goulash is cubes of beef or pork, stewed and served in thin, juicy gravy. It's usually served with houskové knedliky (bread dumplings).

Hotová jídla (ho-to-vah yee'dla). This section of the menu lists dishes that are made ahead in the kitchen and ready to be served. This is where you can find the most traditional favorites svíčkova (stewed beef) and (goulash).

Jídla na objednávka (yee'dla na obe-yeh'dnahv-ka). This section of the menu lists dishes that are cooked to order. This is where you will find a selection of chicken and pork cutlets (referred to as chicken and pork steaks on menus), as well as beef steak, prepared in various ways. Usually, they differ in their use of ingredients, such as onions, garlic, mushrooms, or cheese.

Klobása (kloh-bah-sa). This smoked sausage, a mainstay of the občerstveni (fast-food stand) is also served in restaurants on its own or as an addition to certain types of gulás and soups.

Kulajda (koo-lie-dah). This traditional creamy soup with fresh or dried forest mushrooms is flavored with wine vinegar, caraway, and dill.

Livanečky (liv-ah-nech-kee). These griddle-cakes are made with a yeast-based batter and are usually served with blueberry sauce and whipped cream. They involve more work to make and thus are a little less common than palačinky but seem to be making a comeback on menus.

Moučníky (moe-ooch-nikkee). There's usually not a long list of desserts on any traditional Czech menu, but you might see palačinky, zmrzlina *(ice cream)*, compot *(fruit compote)*, or dort *(cake)*.

Nakládený Hermelín (nah-kla-den-ee). This favorite snack of cafés and pubs consists of a small round of hermelin, a soft cheese closely resembling camembert, which is pickled in oil, onions, and herbs and served with dark bread.

Ovocní knedlíky (o-voht-snee kned-lee-kee). These fruit dumplings are slightly bigger than golf balls and consist of a yeast-risen or soft-cheese dough filled with apricot, plum, strawberry, or in some cases blueberry. They are sometimes listed as desserts, but Czechs often eat them as a main meatless meal.

Palačinky (pala-ching-kee). Usually served with jam or ice cream inside and whipped cream on top, these pancakes resemble crêpes, but are made with a thicker batter.

Přílohy (pr'zhee-lo-hee). In traditional Czech restaurants, side orders aren't usually included with main courses, so look for them in this menu section. You're most likely to see hranolky *(French fries)*, Americké brambory *(literally, American potatoes; actually, fried potato wedges)*, and ryže *(rice)*.

Rizoto (riz-oh-toe). Unlike the Italian original, whose name it inherits, the rizoto found in most Czech restaurants is more like rice pilaf, a steamed dish. In the usual preparation, it is served se zeleninou *(with vegetables)*, which means frozen mixed vegetables are steamed along with the rice, and, adding to a somewhat disharmonious mixture, stretchy cheese is grated on top prior to service.

Smažný sýr (sma-zhe-nee see'r). A post-war and hence nontraditional staple of the Czech diet, this is literally translated as fried cheese. A thick slab of an Edam-like cheese is breaded and deep fried, ideally giving it a crusty shell and somewhat stretchy interior. This favorite is usually served with tartar sauce—which is meant to be liberally spread on top—and fries.

Studené předkrmy (stoo-den-eh pr'zhed-krmy). The section of cold appetizers on a Czech menu is typically a short one and usually includes utopenec *(pickled pork sandwich)*, tlačenka *(head cheese)*, and šunkova rolka *(ham roll with horseradish cream)*.

Svícková (svitch-koh-vah). Though technically this is the tenderloin cut of beef, on menus it means a dish consisting of two to four slabs of stewed beef, usually sirloin; in better restaurants you can get real tenderloin covered with a creamy sauce of pureed root vegetables, garnished with a dollop of whipping cream, cranberry sauce, and a slice of lemon. It's served with houskové knedlíky *(bread dumplings)*.

Teplé předkrmy (teh-pleh pr'zhed-kr-mee). Warm appetizers on the Czech menu ordinarily include topinka *(toasted or fried dark bread, rubbed with garlic cloves)*, and ďabělské toasty *(devil's toasts)*.

Utopenec (oo-toe-pen-etts). Literally translated as "drowned man." utopenec is uncooked pork sausage, which has been pickled in vinegar. It's not only a common appetizer in Czech restaurants, but along with tlacenka, is a ubiquitous beer-snack staple in Czech pubs.

Vepřo-knedlo-želo (veh-pr'zho-kne'dlo-zhe-lo). An affectionately shortened name for the three foods that appear on one plate, this popular family dish consists of pork, dumplings, and cabbage, the latter being stewed with a bit of caraway.

Zelňačka (zell-n'yatch-kah). Cabbage is the main ingredient in this hearty soup whose flavor is accentuated by smoked pork or sausage and caraway. It can be a filling meal in itself when served in a small round loaf of bread.

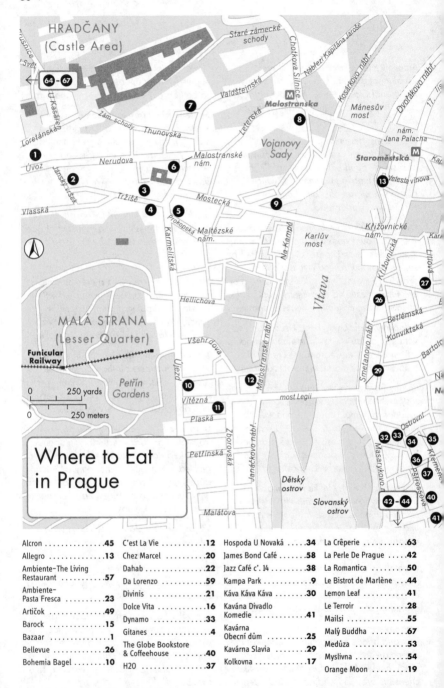

Where to Eat in Prague

Alcron	**45**
Allegro	**13**
Ambiente–The Living Restaurant	**57**
Ambiente–Pasta Fresca	**23**
Artičok	**49**
Barock	**15**
Bazaar	**1**
Bellevue	**26**
Bohemia Bagel	**10**
C'est La Vie	**12**
Chez Marcel	**20**
Dahab	**22**
Da Lorenzo	**59**
Divinis	**21**
Dolce Vita	**16**
Dynamo	**33**
Gitanes	**4**
The Globe Bookstore & Coffeehouse	**40**
H2O	**37**
Hospoda U Novaká	**34**
James Bond Café	**58**
Jazz Café c'. 14	**38**
Kampa Park	**9**
Káva Káva Káva	**30**
Kavána Divadlo Komedie	**41**
Kavárna Obecní dům	**25**
Kavárna Slavia	**29**
Kolkovna	**17**
La Crêperie	**63**
La Perle De Prague	**42**
La Romantica	**50**
Le Bistrot de Marlène	**44**
Lemon Leaf	**41**
Le Terroir	**28**
Mailsi	**55**
Malý Buddha	**67**
Medůza	**53**
Myslivna	**54**
Orange Moon	**19**

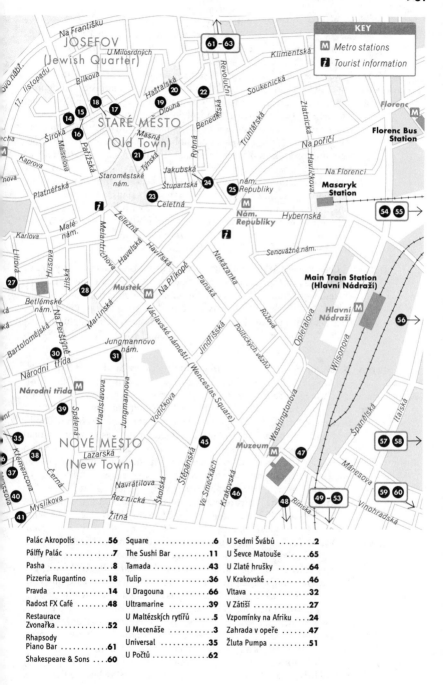

KEY

M Metro stations

ℹ️ Tourist information

Palác Akropolis **56**	Square **6**	U Sedmi Švábů **2**
Pálffy Palác **7**	The Sushi Bar **11**	U Ševce Matouše **65**
Pasha **8**	Tamada **43**	U Zlaté hrušky **64**
Pizzeria Rugantino **18**	Tulip **36**	V Krakovské **46**
Pravda **14**	U Dragouna **66**	Vltava **32**
Radost FX Café **48**	Ultramarine **39**	V Zátiší **27**
Restaurace Zvonařka **52**	U Maltézských rytířů **5**	Vzpomínky na Afriku **24**
	U Mecenáše **3**	Zahrada v opeře **47**
Rhapsody Piano Bar **61**	Universal **35**	Žluta Pumpa **51**
Shakespeare & Sons **60**	U Počtů **62**	

duck, and fried pork cutlets, or upgrades of traditional food, such as turkey steak with Roquefort sauce and walnuts—with a mug of tank-pushed Pilsner. ☒ *V Kolkovně, Staré Město* ☏ *224–818–701* ☰ *AE, MC, V* Ⓜ *Line A: Staroměstská.*

$–$$
Fodor'sChoice
★

✕ **Kavárna Slavia.** There are two main reasons to come to Café Slavia: to see the place that nurtured the ideals of prominent historical figures, and to see the great view, which is probably part of the reason they came. This legendary hangout for dissident writers and musicians—regular patrons have included composer Bedřich Smetana and playwright and former president Václav Havel—is possibly the most famous café in Prague. The interior looks a bit new these days thanks to a late-1990s renovation, but at least one aspect of life in the old days is captured in spirit by the large painting of "The Absinth Drinker." It's enough to come for a coffee or glass of wine, but the light snacks, salads, and main courses, which include gulaš and grilled turkey steak with broccoli, are reasonably priced, especially given the views of the Vltava, the National Theatre, and Prague Castle. ☒ *Smetanovo nábř. 1012/2, Staré Město* ☏ *224–220–957* ☰ *AE, MC, V* Ⓜ *Line B: Národní Třida.*

FRENCH
$$

✕ **Chez Marcel.** At this authentic French bistro on a quiet street you can get a little taste of that *other* riverside capital. French-owned and -operated, Chez Marcel has a small but reliable menu listing pâtés, salads, rabbit, and chicken, as well as some of the best steaks in Prague. The specials board usually has some tempting choices, such as salmon, beef daube, or foie gras. ☒ *Haštalská 12, Staré Město* ☏ *222–315–676* ☰ *No credit cards* Ⓜ *Line B: Náěstí Republiky.*

ITALIAN
$$–$$$$
Fodor'sChoice
★

✕ **Allegro.** Some of the best food in the country can be had at the top-rated restaurant in the Four Seasons Prague, thanks to chef Vito Mollica. Among the changing specialties are appetizers such as crispy sardines in a focaccia crust, *primi piatti* that include potato ratte cream soup with baccala brandade and crayfish, and *secondi piatti* such as šumava milk-fed lamb with a basil crust. Mollica celebrates the freshness of seasonal items such as mushrooms, truffles, and asparagus to the fullest, often devoting an entire section on the menu to them. In summer, the already good experience is heightened if you can manage a seat on the front of the terrace, which offers a spectacular view of the Charles Bridge. The international wine list features selections from the National Wine Bank. ☒ *Four Seasons Prague, Veleslavinova 21, Staré Město* ☏ *221–427–000* ⌁ *Reservations essential* ☰ *AE, DC, MC, V* Ⓜ *Line A: Staroměstska.*

★ $$–$$$

✕ **Divinis.** Feeling at once rustic and refined, casual but well-designed, this wine bar–restaurant was immediately noticed in an area more often associated with countless spires and cobbles than with good food. The friendly Italian owners offer the perfect venue for their carefully chosen selection of wines. Only a few items are listed on the menu, and the place is far from formal. The exact composition of the appetizer plate, which may include salamis, cheeses, and prosciutto, sometimes changes depending on what's in stock and the mood of the chef, but you can bet that if the delectables haven't been recently hauled in from carefully pinpointed regions of Italy, it's only because they had to be aged properly before being served. The menu changes twice-weekly but the five or six main courses listed usually include pasta, a red meat (such as rack of lamb), and fresh seafood, all of which are simply presented but delightful. The staff are happy to help you choose from over 250 bottles of mostly Italian wine on the wine list. ⊠ *Týnská 19, Staré Město* ☎ *224–808–318* ☐ *AE, DC, MC, V* Ⓜ *Line B: Náěstí Republiky.*

$–$$ ✕ **Pizzeria Rugantino.** Bright and spacious, this buzzing pizzeria serves up thin-crust pies; big, healthy salads; and good Italian bread. It can get quite loud when full, which is most nights. ⊠ *Dušní 4, Staré Město* ☎ *222–318–172* ☐ *No credit cards* ⊙ *No lunch Sun.* Ⓜ *Line A: Staroměstská.*

SEAFOOD ✕ **Alcron.** Czech chef Jiří Štift made a big splash on the local dining scene
★ **$$$$** when is all-seafood restaurant opened in 1998. It wasn't long before he began to gather up the culinary awards. Štift's talent in blending the simple and the exotic into a harmony that is never gimmicky comes through strongly in dishes like delicious smoked eel with black truffle and scrambled egg, a fabulous lobster bisque with artichoke poivrade and shellfish oil, and baby monk fish with Belgian endive and seared foie gras. There are often one or two tables free but the cozy 24-seat dining room can fill quickly, especially later in the evening, particularly on weekends. ⊠ *Radisson SAS Alcron Hotel, Štěpáská 40* ☎ *222–820–038* ☐ *AE, DC, MC, V* ⚙ *Reservations essential* Ⓜ *Line A: Můstek.*

MALÁ STRANA (LESSER QUARTER)

CONTEMPORARY ✕ **Kampa Park.** The first of a growing number of restaurants in the Kampa
$$$$ group under the guidance of Nils Jebens, who is now something of a
Fodor'sChoice local celebrity, Kampa Park scored one of the best locations in Prague
★ on the junction of the Vltava and the smaller Čertovka, which delineates Kampa Island. The food lives up to the location, and meals such as grilled octopus with celery puree, forest mushrooms, rukola (arugula), and glazed tomatoes keep guests coming back. The pièce-de-resistance is the riverside location with a stunning view of Charles Bridge. ⊠ *Na Kampě 8/b, Malá Strana* ☎ *257–532–685* ☐ *AE, DC, MC, V* Ⓜ *Line A: Malostranská.*

$$$–$$$$ ✕ **C'est La Vie.** This charming, informal restaurant honors its superb lo-
Fodor'sChoice cation, in a parkside nook on Kampa Island, by offering food that's just
★ as good as the setting. The menu offers several kinds of fresh fish and meats prepared with French and Asian influences, both in ingredients and cooking methods, from truffles to Tandoori. There's outdoor seating a few steps down on a stone terrace next to the river, where you can gaze across to the island or watch a variety of tour boats pass through the locks. ⊠ *Říční 1, Malá Strana* ☎ *257–321–511* ☐ *AE, DC, MC, V* Ⓜ *Line B: Národní Třida.*

★ **$$$–$$$$** ✕ **Pálffy Palác.** It's hard to choose the best attribute of this local hideaway set in the second story of a baroque palace at the foothills below Prague Castle. Owner Roman Řezniček has done his best to create an atmosphere of relaxed elegance and superlative dining. Amid the potted ferns and large bowls of fruit, you can order quail breast with sundried plums and apricot sauce, or salmon steak stuffed with lemon sole filets and Dublin bay prawns. As if the food weren't enough, the terrace looking over the lush castle ramparts and palace rooftops is one of the nicest settings—arguably *the* nicest—in the city for brunch. ✉ *Valdštejnská 14, Malá Strana* ☎ *257–530–522* ☰ *AE, MC, V* Ⓜ *Line A: Malostranská.*

$$–$$$$ ✕ **Bazaar.** Now a member of the Kampa group of restaurants, Bazaar is undoubtedly unique. The dramatic vaulted interior is an impressive and comfortable place to dine, but if the weather is even remotely nice, walk through the labyrinth of rooms and winding staircases, and you will eventually come to a fabulous rooftop garden, just a few stories below the castle. Here, Prague is splayed out before you, from the nearby palatial rooftops to virtually the entire right bank fading into the distance. Typical of the Kampa group, the wine list starts high, but the food is expertly prepared. Portion size isn't huge, but the dishes, including rack of lamb with pumpkin puree and cipollini onion, or tiger prawns with saffron risotto and grapefruit, show creativity. ✉ *Nerudova 40, Malá Strana* ☎ *257–535–050* ☰ *AE, DC, MC, V* Ⓜ *Line A: Malostranská.*

$$–$$$$ ✕ **Square.** The original restaurant in this space, Malostranska Kavarna, was visited by artists and writers the likes of Franz Kafka. The extinction of a historical favorite did not go unnoticed by preservationists and local café lovers. Indeed, Square is nothing like the former spot, particularly in price, but as a member of the Kampa Group of restaurants, that is no surprise. Also no surprise is the very good food, including sautéed octopus and roast suckling piglet with calvados reduction, which continues to impress. The stylish, modern interior does show off the natural arches nicely, and the large windows let you see and be seen, both of which are the point. ✉ *Malostranské nám., Malá Strana* ☎ *257–532–109* ☰ *AE, DC, MC, V* Ⓜ *Line A: Malostranská.*

CONTINENTAL ✕ **U Maltézských rytířů.** The tongue-twisting name means "At the Knights
$$–$$$ of Malta," a reference to the Catholic order whose embassy is nearby. The upstairs dining room and bar are cozy, but ask for a table in the deep cellar—then ask the proprietress to regale you with yarns about this ancient house. Some old favorites have been dropped from the menu, but you can still get good steaks, game, and fish. Dishes usually show a little more effort in their preparation than those found in ordinary, or less fancy, Czech restaurants. The roast duck breast, for example, a menu item common in Czech restaurants, comes marinated with ginger and served alongside smoked cabbage with apples and onion-potato gnocchi. ✉ *Prokopská 10, Malá Strana* ☎ *257–533–666* ☰ *AE, MC, V* Ⓜ *Line A: Malostranská.*

$$–$$$ ✕ **U Mecenáše.** Behind the stained-glass windows, the vaulted spaces of a 17th-century inn await. The oriental carpets are a bit worn, but with dark, high-back benches in the front room and cozy, elegant sofas and chairs in back, this place offers plenty of atmosphere for the money. From the aperitifs to the specialty steaks or beef Wellington to an after-dinner cognac (swirled lovingly in oversize glasses), the presentation is seamless. ✉ *Malostranské nám. 10, Malá Strana* ☎ *257–531–631* ☰ *AE, MC, V* Ⓜ *Line A: Malostranská.*

CZECH ✕ **U Sedmi Švábů.** Medieval decorations and waitresses in peasant dresses
¢–$$ serving beer and mead to diners seated at long wooden tables make this

theme restaurant worth a stop. Unusual menu items include millet pancakes with herbs, carp with garlic, flambéed venison skewer with rosehip sauce, and roast pork knuckle for two. Special multicourse "knight's feasts" are also available. Chicken, steaks, and other mundane dishes are available for the less adventuresome. ⊠ *Jánský vršek 14, Malá Strana* ☎ *257–531–645* ⊟ *AE, MC, V* Ⓜ *Line A: Malostranská.*

DELICATESSENS   ✕ **Bohemia Bagel.** One of the bellwether destinations for newly settled
¢–$ and seasoned expats (hence the popular bulletin board and near-Western prices), this sandwich shop and café serves up a variety of combinations on bagels made fresh every day. The bagels are not as chewy as those from New York or Montreal, but the combinations, such as lemon-pepper chicken or lox with cream cheese and capers, are fresh and tasty, and you can order them with a bottomless cup of coffee or soda. ⊠ *Újezd 16, Malá Strana* ☎ *257–310–694* ⊟ *No credit cards* Ⓜ *Line B: Národní Třida* ⊠ *Masná 2, Staré Město* ☎ *224–812–560* ⊟ *No credit cards* Ⓜ *Line A: Staroměstka.*

JAPANESE   ✕ **The Sushi Bar.** The wacky whale sculpture is gone, but this hip little
$$–$$$$ place—roughly across the river from the National Theatre—done up in aqua blue and pale wood is still a fun place to go. Given Prague's distance from the sea, the selection of sushi and sashimi is excellent. Though prices start low, the bill here can quickly reach stratospheric levels depending on how many dishes you choose. ⊠ *Zborovská 49, Malá Strana* ☎ *0603–244–882* ⊟ *DC, MC, V* Ⓜ *Line B: Národní Třida.*

MEDITERRANEAN   ✕ **Gitanes.** Outside, small clusters of flowers in terra-cotta planters lead
$–$$$ into a Mediterranean-inspired interior. The cozy dining room has colorfully painted arches, flowered table cloths, and Balkan music, all of which help to make you feel warmer inside. Spot-lit photos and paintings hip up the atmosphere and add to the glow. The food is mainly Balkan, including such festive treats as *muckalica* (a thick Balkan stew with chunks of pork, tomato, and peppers) and *cevapcici* (grilled ingots of spiced ground meat); or you can choose from a host of more popularly known dishes such as paella. ⊠ *Třiště 7, Malá Strana* ☎ *257–530–163* ⊟ *AE, DC, MC, V* Ⓜ *Line A: Malostranská.*

MIDDLE EASTERN   ✕ **Pasha.** This inviting spot not far from the Malostranská metro sta-
$$–$$$$ tion hits just the right notes of luxury and easiness. A rich sienna and cobalt interior complements the menu, which has both Middle Eastern and Mediterranean items, including fragrant couscous, grilled vegetables, and seafood. Two of the favorites are the marinated octopus and the minced lamb rolled in sesame. If you're in the mood to splurge, you can go for the grilled octopus. ⊠ *U Lužického semináře 23, Malá Strana* ☎ *257–532–439* ⊟ *AE, MC, V* ☉ *Closed Mon.* Ⓜ *Line A: Malostranská.*

HRADČANY

ASIAN   ✕ **Malý Buddha.** Bamboo, wood, paper, incense—and the odd creepy mask
★ ¢–$$ on the wall—are all part of this funky New Age hideaway uphill from Nerudova Street. Spring rolls, vegetable and mixed stir-fries, fish, and

shark steaks come in generous portions. The drink list is unique, offering everything from ginseng wine to herbal drinks to mystery shots of exotic alcoholic concoctions. The restaurant has a no-smoking policy, so aromas are pure. You can buy much of what you see and smell, including Asian ceramics. ⊠ *Úvoz 46, Hradčany* ☎ *220–513–894* ⊟ *No credit cards* ⊘ *Closed Mon.* Ⓜ *Line A: Hradčanská.*

CONTINENTAL ✕ **U Zlaté hrušky.** A venerable institution in the castle-area dining scene
$$$–$$$$ since the early 1990s, "At the Golden Pear" reopened in 2004 under new ownership. The menu—Continental with international touches and an emphasis on traditional Czech cuisine—includes Bohemian soup with cinnamon gnocchi, rabbit in onion with new potatoes and stewed spinach, and grilled veal chop with nut purrée. The selection of fresh fish, including a winning skewer of sturgeon, is among the city's finest. You can find it down Nový Svět, one of Prague's prettiest cobblestone streets. ⊠ *Nový Svět 3, Hradčany* ☎ *220–514–778* ⊟ *AE, MC, V* Ⓜ *Line A: Hradčanská.*

CZECH ✕ **U Dragouna.** A true Czech restaurant, this neighborhood spot is also
¢–$$ a minor mecca for both Czechs and foreigners living in Prague. Among its specialties are the game dishes, such as wild boar gulaš and mountain rabbit, and it's one of best places to try them on this end of the city. Reasonably priced, clean, and with attentive service, it manages to please just about everyone. ⊠ *Parléřova 5, Hradčany* ☎ *220–511–282* ⊟ *No credit cards* Ⓜ *Line A: Hradčanská.*

STEAK ✕ **U Ševce Matouše.** In a district where restaurants rely on tourist traf-
$$ fic more than quality of food, this steak house, originally a shoemaker's shop (notice the centuries-old sign out front with the appropriate emblem), stands out. The thicker steaks (labelled *biftek* on the menu) are all the same price, but you can order them with different sauces and as rare or well-done as you like. Skip the boring desserts. ⊠ *Loretánské nám. 4, Hradčany* ☎ *220–514–536* ⊟ *MC, V* Ⓜ *Line A: Hradčanská.*

NOVÉ MĚSTO (NEW TOWN) & VYŠEHRAD

CONTEMPORARY ✕ **Zahrada v opeře.** These days, the concrete barricades and surly guards
$$–$$$$ on hand to protect the adjacent Radio Free Europe headquarters don't
Fodor'sChoice cause anyone living in the city to blink anymore. Inside, the inspired de-
★ sign by Barbora Skorpilova, with the pebbled floor and subdued lighting, make you forget what's outside anyway. With one of the most exceptional menus in the city, balancing creativity and price, Garden in the Opera, next to the Prague State Opera house at the top of Wenceslas Square is a sure bet. Grilled and roasted fresh fish, meat, and vegetables figure strongly, along with Asian and western ingredients. ⊠ *Legerova 75, Nové Město* ☎ *224–239–685* ⊟ *AE, MC, V* Ⓜ *Line C : Muzeum.*

$–$$ ✕ **Ultramarine.** Popular with the business-lunch crowd by day, and both the pre-club crowd and cozy couples in the evening, this restaurant has helped fill an important niche in offering affordable fare with international flair in a series of comfortably lit rooms, all under Gothic-style vaults. An added plus is that the kitchen is open 'til 1:30 AM for those

GOOD FOOD ON THE GO

THERE WAS A TIME NOT MANY YEARS AGO when a quick bite on the go in Prague was largely limited to the predictable fast food of two or three international chains and the fatty—albeit sometimes tasty—fare from the local sausage stands. These are still around, but if you're in the mood for something with a bit more pizzazz for that day-trip or picnic, keep an eye out for these specialty shops and bakeries in the downtown area, which offer freshly made sandwiches, salads, prepared meals, and pastries.

Bakeshop Praha (✉ Kozi 1, Staré Město ✉ Láeňska 19, Malá Strana) has fresh wonderful bread, good salads, and fantastic brownies. The sandwiches with English bacon have earned a patriotic following. Both locations have seating indoors if you're not looking to take your meal with you.

Culinaria (✉ Skořepka 9, Staré Město) has an ever-changing selection of salads, main courses, and desserts, which change regularly, but the display is always a painter's palette of color, and the staff are helpful. An herbal juice bar is complemented by a unique selection of the best western beverages. You can eat standing up at one of the few tables, or everything is available to go.

Paneria (✉ Kaprova 3, Staré Město ✉ Nekázanka 19, Nové Město ✉ Bělehradská 71, Vinohrady) shops are popping up in almost every district, some within two blocks of each other, and three in Old Town alone. The sandwiches are standardized but made fresh when you order, and they come with toppings such as green olives, mascarpone, and tomato. The desserts include some winners, such as the minicream flan with forest berries.

who like to eat really late. Small beers are a bit pricey by Prague standards, so quaffing is better done elsewhere, but the Thai soup and American-style burgers are local hits. Way, way down, the cellar houses more seating, as well as a bar and club. ✉ *Ostrovní 32, Nové Město* ☎ *224–932–249* ▭ *AE, MC, V* Ⓜ *Line B: Národní Třida.*

CONTINENTAL
$–$$$

✕ **Universal.** Universal is still able to serve up French and continental main courses, giant side orders of scalloped potatoes, and luscious lemon tarts or profiteroles at prices that have barely budged since it opened in the late 1990s. An affordable midday menu makes it an even more attractive lunchtime alternative. ✉ *V Jirchářích 6, Nové Město* ☎ *224–918–182* ▭ *MC, V* Ⓜ *Line B: Národní Třida.*

CZECH
¢–$$

✕ **Hospoda U Nováká.** A tourist-friendly Czech restaurant that is consistently filled with Czechs—always good sign—this spot in the city center is a very inexpensive place to try Czech dishes such as *smažený sýr* (fried cheese) or any one of a variety of chicken and pork cutlets. The starters, such as marinated *hermelín* (the Czech version of Camembert) and salted fish, are very representative and go well with beer. ✉ *V Jirchářích, Nové Město* ☎ *224–930–639* ▭ *No credit cards* Ⓜ *Line B: Národní Třida.*

¢–$ ✕ **V Krakovské.** At this clean, proper pub close to the major tourist sights, the food is traditional and hearty. This is the place to try *svíčková na smetaně* (sliced sirloin beef in cream sauce) paired with an effervescent pilsner beer. ☒ *Krakovská 20, Nové Město* ☏ *222–210–204* ▭ *No credit cards* Ⓜ *Line C: Muzeum.*

ECLECTIC ✕ **Dynamo.** Pale green walls decorated with framed arty posters, lots of
$–$$ glass, and cool wooden finishings give Dynamo a very funky feel, not unlike a futuristic-looking diner. The menu strikes a rare balance between vegetarian and carnivorous: eggplant with grilled vegetables, grilled feta with olives and sun-dried tomatoes, and a variety of grilled meats are just some of what's available. It's lively on unpredictable nights of the week. ☒ *Pštrossova 29, Nové Město* ☏ *224–932–020* ▭ *AE, DC, MC, V* Ⓜ *Line B: Národní Třida.*

$–$$ ✕ **Tulip.** The American owner of this restaurant likes to describe the cuisine as "casual gourmet." In this case, that means grilled duck breast with caramalized apples, almonds, and arugula, or Norwegian salmon with grilled fennel; fresh pasta is made right on the premises. Weekend brunches offer among the highest quality for price in town, and in a hot summer day, the courtyard patio beckons. ☒ *Opatovická 3, Nové Město* ☏ *224–930–019* ▭ *AE, MC, V* Ⓜ *Line B: Národní Třida.*

$–$$ ✕ **Vltava.** In this relative newcomer on the embankment, just down from the National Theatre, you get a little more than what you'd expect for the price. The location is convenient, near the center and the river, and the well-presented food, which includes everything from pasta with spinach-and-cream sauce to Tandoori chicken to beefsteak—seems a good match for the hip, clean-lined interior decor. Sunken a few steps down from street level, the dining room is surprisingly comfortable and bright; and in clear weather, you can watch the sun set behind the hills on the opposite side of the riverbank. ☒ *Masarykovo Nábřeží, Nové Město* ☏ *224–932–203* ▭ *AE, MC, V* Ⓜ *Line B: Národní Třida.*

¢–$$ ✕ **H2O.** Minimalist decor, featuring blond wood, big ferns, and nifty lighting, is soothing. Service, however, is sometimes on the slow side, though this may not be a problem if you're looking for a relaxing meal. The food covers Italian, French, and Asian territory, and you will be hardpressed to find a better-prepared piece of Norwegian salmon in the city for the price. ☒ *Opatovická 5, Nové Město* ☏ *776–390–292* ▭ *AE, DC, MC, V* Ⓜ *Line B: Národní Třida.*

FRENCH ✕ **Le Bistrot de Marlène.** Just outside of Prague's centre, this cozy French
$$$–$$$$ bistro, which began its life as an oasis in an area mostly bereft of restaurants—let alone good ones—is now one of the landmarks on a burgeoning local dining scene. Chef-owner Marlène is highly respected by many in the community for her dedication to authentic French cuisine such as duck liver with fresh figs and cherries, fried veal sweetbread with foie gras and Tokay wine sauce, and lobster canneloni with lemon confit. The restaurant has a strong loyal following, and it's a perfectly rewarding destination for a walk along the river. ☒*Plavecká 4, Nové Město* ☏*224–921–853* ▭*AE, MC, V* ☉ *Closed Sun. No lunch Sat.* Ⓜ *Line B: Karlovo Náměstí.*

$$–$$$$ ✕ **La Perle de Prague.** A calm, white interior and sturdy vases of fresh flowers complement the surprisingly large dining room on the top of

the famous "Fred and Ginger" building, designed by Frank Gehry. Though the controversy the building generated when it was erected in the mid-1990s is gradually dissipating (it replaced one of a very few buildings hit by a bomb in WWII), the quality of the restaurant is as fresh as ever, and French cuisine with an international influence is expertly prepared. Appetizers, including the lamb mosaic, are a blaze of color, with texture and flavor to match, while the main courses, such as poached John Dory filet with Champagne, or venison filet in red-wine sauce with celery puree, are superlative. On top of this, literally and figuratively, the upstairs semiprivate dining room and terrace offer a dazzling panoramic view of the city. ⊠ *Rašínovo nábř. 80, Nové Město* ☎ *221–984–160* ▤ *AE, DC MC, V* ✆ *Closed Sun. No lunch Mon.* Ⓜ *Line B: Karlovo Náměstí.*

RUSSIAN   ✕ **Tamada.** The word *Gruzinská* in the window means Georgian (the
¢–$$ country on the Black Sea coast, not the U.S. state). And in this case, that's a very good thing. Dishes on the menu at this fun spot with a woodsy-cabin interior carry a bit more tang, spice, and crunch than their Czech counterparts. *Pchali* (a piquant eggplant dish with spinach leaves and walnuts) and *chačapuri* (melted cheese on a soft, fragrant dough), are excellent, and they're only the beginning of an inexpensive and festive meal. ⊠ *Jenštejnská 2, Nové Město* ☎ *224–913–810* ▤ *No credit cards* Ⓜ *Line B: Karlovo Náměstí.*

THAI   ✕ **Lemon Leaf.** Located on what used to be a rather dusty, boring street,
★ $–$$$ Lemon Leaf helped cheer up this gradually gentrifying strip, which serves as the blurry edge of the dining ghetto behind the National Theatre. Airy and bright, with big pots of plants, tall windows, and funky lamps, this mostly Thai restaurant—with a few pasta dishes thrown in to satisfy more conservative tastebuds—is a great choice for authentic and exciting food at either lunch or dinner. Crunchy spring rolls and traditional Thai soups bursting with flavor are an almost essential opener to one of the noodle dishes or spicy curries, but keep an eye on the little flame symbols in the menu that denote the hotness of dishes. ⊠ *Na Zderaze 14, Nové Město* ☎ *224–919–056* ▤ *AE, MC, V* Ⓜ *Line B: Národní Třida.*

VINOHRADY

CZECH   ✕ **Myslivna.** The name means "Hunting Lodge," and the cooks at this
$–$$$ neighborhood eatery certainly know their way around venison, quail, and boar. Attentive staff can advise on wines: try Vavřinecké, a hearty red that holds its own with any beast. The roasted pheasant with bacon and the leg of venison with walnuts get high marks. ⊠ *Jagellonská 21, Vinohrady* ☎ *222–723–252* ▤ *AE, MC, V* Ⓜ *Line A: Jiřiho z Poděbrad.*

ECLECTIC   ✕ **Restaurace Zvonařka.** This restaurant has struggled with the scope of
$–$$ its cuisine and the theme of its decor over the years, but it has one thing all others lack: an enormous patio on the hillside of Prague's Nuslé Valley that even scores of Prague residents don't know about. Try the grilled vegetable salad, barbecued chicken wings, or tenderloin with spinach sauce while sitting in the shade of ivy-laden chestnut and ash,

and try to spot the occasional train that whistles by in the valley below. ⊠ *Šafaříova 1, Vinohrady* ☎ *224–251–990* ▭ *AE, MC, V* Ⓜ *Line C: I. P. Pavlova.*

ITALIAN   ✕ **Da Lorenzo.** Unpretentious Italian fare keeps food lovers coming back
¢–$$ to this humble hideaway in a mostly residential area of Vinohrady. The owner—also chef and storyteller extraordinaire—takes great pride in ensuring that all the ingredients come directly from Italy. Many of the meals are traditional family specialties, but generous portions of spaghetti Bolognese, lasagna al forno, and grilled trout with lemon and white wine are prepared with a deft hand. Ask about the Rat Pack. ⊠ *Chodská 7, Vinohrady* ☎ *222–521–716* ▭ *MC, V* Ⓜ *Line A: Náměstí Míru.*

¢–$$ ✕ **La Romantica.** This neighborhood pizzeria's patio, which offers dappled sunlight under a large tree on a quiet street, is the main draw here. Food is just average and the service consistently unenthusiastic, but it's very popular during the warm months, roughly from April to September, when you can take full advantage of the splendid setting. Even then, there's seldom a long wait for a seat. Most of the pizzas, such as chicken breast with gorgonzola, are safe bets while the dozen or so pasta dishes, some sporting unconventional combinations such as pork filet and Worchestershire sauce, are available for the more adventurous. ⊠ *Londýnská 22, Vinohrady* ☎ *224–257–812* ▭ *No credit cards* Ⓜ *Line A: Náměstí Míru.*

MEDITERRANEAN   ✕ **Artičok.** It's not easy to find grilled Mediterranean vegetables, St. Danielle
¢–$$ prosciutto, mussels with wine and garlic, and osso buco all in one place, let alone in Vinohrady, but Artičok has them, along with a tight selection of pizzas, pastas, and other meat and fish dishes. The owner, who brought in a French chef to do it right, can often be seen chatting with the regulars on the large patio in front. ⊠ *Londýnská 29, Vinohrady* ☎ *222–524–110* ▭ *No credit cards* Ⓜ *Line A: Náměstí Míru.*

MEXICAN   ✕ **Ambiente—The Living Restaurant.** The first of what has become a small
$–$$$ chain of successful restaurants helped champion the concept of attentive service, a foreign notion to Prague waitstaff when it opened in the late 1990s. This branch still retains the original Mexican theme that made it famous, but pasta and steaks also figure strongly on the expanded menu. It's a suitable stop before or after a stroll through Riegrovy sady, one of the city's grand hilltop parks, which is nearby. ⊠ *Mánesova 59, Vinohrady* ☎ *222–727–851* ▭ *AE, DC, MC, V* Ⓜ *Line A: Jiřiho z Poděbrad.*

¢–$ ✕ **Žluta Pumpa.** The menu at the "Yellow Pump," a popular neighborhood watering hole that's popular with students, but it also offers decent Mexican food at rock-bottom prices. The cocktails are good, too, and after a few, the crazy-colored wall murals being to take on a whole new meaning. ⊠ *Belgická 11, Vinohrady* ☎ *608–861–347* ▭ *No credit cards* Ⓜ *Line A: Náměstí Míru.*

VEGETARIAN   ✕ **Radost FX Café.** The service is of variable quality, and they still don't
★ $–$$ have draft beer, but this is likely the most popular vegetarian restaurant in the city thanks to its creative meals drawn from cuisines around the world. Appetizers such as marinara sauce with Lebanese cheese rolled

in pepper are small and flavorful, while the main courses, such as the grilled quesadilla, eggplant parmigiana, or Thai-style vegetables on rice, leave few people with room left for dessert, so plan for some sharing if you have a small stomach. The funky interior underwent a major renovation in 2004, which included moving the bar and converting the former art gallery into dining space, so now there's even more guild, mirror, and plush upholstery for a guaranteed cozy dining experience. ☒ *Bělehradská 120, Nové Město* ☎ *224–254–776* ⊟ *No credit cards* Ⓜ *Line C: I. P. Pavlova.*

LETNÁ & HOLEŠOVICE

CZECH   ✕ **U Počtů.** This charmingly old-fashioned neighborhood restaurant has
¢–$$ comparatively skilled service. Garlic soup and chicken livers in wine sauce are flawlessly rendered, and the grilled trout is delicious. ☒ *Milady Horákové 47, Letná* ☎ *233–371–419* ⊟ *AE, MC, V* Ⓜ *Line C: Vltavská.*

FRENCH   ✕ **La Crêperie.** Started by a Czech-French couple, this crêperie near the
¢–$ Veletržní palác (Trade Fair Palace) serves all manner of crêpes, both sweet and savory. (It may take at least three or four to satisfy a hearty appetite.) Make sure to leave room for the dessert crêpe with cinnamon-apple puree layered with lemon cream. The wine list offers both French and Hungarian vintages. ☒ *Janovského 4, Holešovice* ☎ *220–878–040* ⊟ *No credit cards* Ⓜ *Line C: Vltavská.*

MEDITERRANEAN   ✕ **Rhapsody Piano Bar.** It's all about the music. That's what the two broth-
$$–$$$ erly owners say about their establishment—and also the fact that you can walk in the footsteps of Eva Herzigová, Michael Douglas, and John Major. But really, it's also about the food: Prague's best (if not the country's only, true) piano bar has wonderful Lebanese, Indian, and Tunisian cuisine, thanks to resident and visiting chefs that have left their mark on the menu. ☒ *Dukelských hrdinů 46, Holešovice* ☎ *220–806–768* ⊟ *AE, MC, V* Ⓜ *Line C: Vltavská* ☉ *Closed Sun.*

ŽIŽKOV

ECLECTIC   ✕ **Palác Akropolis.** Though the club underneath is a popular night spot,
¢–$$ the restaurant is a draw in its own right. Steel-covered menus offer large portions of Czech fare such as pork cutlets and potato pancakes, but the menu has other things, including Mexican soup and Buffalo wings, all at reasonable prices. Aquariums containing industrial sculpture provide something to look at while the food arrives, though sometimes the staff is more interesting. The music, which ranges from hip-hop to Czech rock, can be quite loud. ☒ *Kubelíková 27, Žižkov* ☎ *296–330–911* ⊟ *No credit cards* Ⓜ *Line A: Jiřiho z Poděbrad.*

INDIAN   ✕ **Mailsi.** This neighborhood Pakistani restaurant is sometimes criticized
★ $–$$$ for its somewhat underdecorated interior, save the paintings of *Arabian Nights,* but it still offers decent vindaloos and kormas at prices lower than in the flashier Indian restaurants downtown, and the owner does his best to make sure everyone is happy. Take Tram 5, 9, or 26 to the

Lipanská stop, and then walk one block uphill. ⊠ *Lipanská 1, Žižkov* ☎ *222–717–783* ⊟ *No credit cards* Ⓜ *Line A: Jiřiho z Poděbrad.*

CAFÉS

Prague's cafés range from the historical to the literary to the trendy. Most cafés are licensed to sell alcohol, and are open until at least 11 PM, with some transforming into virtual bars by night. It only seems fair—espresso machines never had to rely on a chain of coffee bars to introduce the Czech Republic to quality coffee and can often be found in the dingiest of pubs. In all of the following you can sit down with a small snack and a java, and in most of them (except for the first two) you can order alcoholic beverages. As a general rule, the old-fashioned-looking cafés serve traditional Czech snacks, such as marinated cheese, while those with a splashy new façade carry a selection of more western-style desserts, from carrot cake to tiramisu.

Dahab. Walk in from the Dlouhá Street entrance and take in the effect of Persian rugs beneath Bohemian arches. This unique spot grew from a small couscouserie in the Roxy, which is next door. The food is authentically Middle Eastern, and definitely worth trying for a snack or a full meal. The occasional belly dancer has been sighted as well. ⊠ *Dlouhá 33, Staré Mešto* ☎ *224–827–375* ⊟ *AE, MC, V.*

Dolce Vita. A refined place to sit year-round, this Italian café on a quiet corner in Old Town makes a great spot to recharge with a latte and lemon torte. It draws a mix of regular clientele, who often emerge from nice cars parked nearby. ⊠ *Široká 15, Staré Mešto* ☎ *222–329–192* ⊟ *No credit cards.*

The Globe Bookstore & Coffeehouse. Prague's first English-language bookstore with a café draws both foreigners and Czechs for its books, brownies, and brunch—not to mention the bulletin board. The full menu includes marinated cheeses from Greece and the Balkans and other ingredients blended with a light-handed touch. Use the Internet or hook up your own laptop. ⊠ *Pštrossova 6, Nové Město* ☎ *224–934–203* ⊟ *AE, MC, V.*

James Bond Café. Silhouette images of Bond girls and funky molded furniture complement this cool café in Vinohrady. Stylish people sipping mojitos are a common sight, and occasionally, someone who looks like one of the silhouettes will walk by. ⊠ *Polská 7, Vinohrady* ☎ *721–449–732* ⊟ *No credit cards.*

Jazz Café č. 14. Marble floors, dim wall lamps, and old oak tables give this large but cozy café an old-fashioned Parisian charm. It's frequented by students from nearby Charles University. Marinated *hermelin* cheese makes a good snack. ⊠ *Opatovická 14, Nové Město* ☎ *224–920–039* ⊟ *No credit cards.*

Káva Káva Káva. If you like real Seattle-style arabica, this is the place to come. The beans are custom-roasted in this neck of the woods, and the barristas know what they are doing, so the coffee is good. You can also surf the Net for a few more crowns. ⊠ *Národní 37, Staré Město* ☎ *224–228–862* ▭ *No credit cards.*

Kavána Divadlo Komedie. Czechs—performers and otherwise—and a smattering of foreigners can usually be seen here sipping small coffees or holding big, thick glasses of Höegarten beer. The functionalist interior features duo-marble staircases, which lead to the theater downstairs. ⊠ *Jungmannova 1, Nové Město* ☎ *No phone* ▭ *No credit cards.*

Kavárna Obecní dům. Kill two birds with one stone by relaxing with a drink and taking in the opulent art nouveau surroundings in this famous building's magnificent café. ⊠ *Náměstí Republiky 5, Staré Město* ☎ *222–022–763* ▭ *AE, DC, MC, V.*

Medúza. Framed black-and-white photographs, burnished chairs, old lacquered tables, and cool music make anyone who drops into this charming and groovy café want to come again. The menu offers a selection of mostly vegetarian snacks and *palačinky* (filled pancakes) that go perfectly with a glass of wine. ⊠ *Belgická 17, Vinohrady* ☎ *222–515–107* ▭ *No credit cards.*

Shakespeare & Sons. Czechs and expats frequent this quiet café out of the city center, which offers Bernard beer and *medovina* (honey wine). The charming bookroom at the back has the strange power to make people linger longer than intended. ⊠ *Krymská, Vršovice* ☎ *271–740–839* ▭ *AE, MC, V.*

Vzpomínky na Afriku. At this tiny shop behind the Kotva department store you can find the widest selection of gourmet coffees in town, served at two tiny tables or to go. ⊠ *At Rybná and Jakubská, Staré Město* ☎ *603–441–434* ▭ *No credit cards.*

WHERE TO STAY

3

SING THE PRAISES
Aria Hotel, *Malá Strana* ⇨*p.81*

LOCATION, LOCATION
Hotel Roma, *Malá Strana* ⇨*p.85*

COZY & WELCOMING
Romantik Hotel U Raka, *Malá Strana* ⇨*p.85*

BEAUTIFUL & LUXURIOUS
Carlo IV, *Nové Město* ⇨*p.86*

COVETED ADDRESS FOR PAMPERING
Hotel Palace Praha, *Nové Město* ⇨*p.86*

MINIMALIST CHIC
Andel's Hotel Prague, *Smíchov* ⇨*p.89*

By Mindy Kay Bricker

THERE'S A GREAT DEAL OF GOOD NEWS on the lodging scene in Prague. A general rise in standards continues, as does a surge in options. A more Western standard of hospitality has seeped into local hotels, which means that room service and friendliness are becoming something you can expect rather than a pleasant surprise. And there's been a lot of development of top-end, international-standard hotels. Several opulent examples have been carved from historical buildings with high ceilings, frescos, and museum-quality antique furnishings. Definitely consider the more creative options before deciding to stay at the tried-and-true chain hotels.

On the more negative side, despite the wide choice of hotels, room rates are not so varied. In a word, Prague is expensive, especially during high season (basically, from May through the end of October, with some bargains appearing in the dog days of July and August). So don't expect to find the same kind of bargains in your accommodations as you will at local restaurants and expect few decent options in the city center under 3,500 Kč. Rates decrease as you move away from the city center; however, in most cases, the savings are so minimal that it's not worth the hassle of the commute by public transit from one of the outlying regions.

Most hotels have Web sites, and many of them offer deals online that are not offered once you're standing inside the hotel. The low season has the best lodging bargains, and if you can wait until November 1, rates will often drop by half, and rooms are pretty easy to come by. The high season, of course, is a different story. Make reservations 90 days in advance to secure the best rate, and—in cases of hotels on busy streets—the best and quietest rooms. If you make your reservation in person, ask about the occupancy. If the hotel has available rooms, managers are more likely to sell them at a discounted rate than to not sell them at all.

For devotees of star ratings, don't waste your time here. Since the Czech Republic does not have& an official rating system—as countries like Italy do—hotels take it upon themselves to rate themselves. Hence, hostelries often rate themselves one, if not two, stars above where they actually stand.

STARÉ MĚSTO (OLD TOWN)

The most convenient and atmospheric neighborhood in Prague, Old Town puts you in the heart of the city—and a beautiful heart it is with its narrow, cobblestone streets lined with baroque and Gothic architecture. Many of the hotels in this quarter are visually stunning and worth the extra cost. Anything that you could possibly need—outstanding restaurants, fashionable boutiques, trendy clubs, smoky pubs—are all at your doorstep. Overall, this area lacks the noise of trams and car traffic, but you might hear the occasional hoot and holler from a British stag party, which, at times, is louder than any noise from a freeway.

$$$$ 🏨 **Four Seasons Prague.** A new central building joins together a baroque house from 1737 and a renovated neoclassical former factory from

1846 into a large, modern luxury hotel with an unbeatable riverside location. Though a splendid hotel, it has the overly mannered, manicured appearance of a country club and attracts the same type of people. The expense of the rooms, which have attracted such movie stars as Sean Connery and Owen Wilson while they worked in Prague, may be worth it if you must have every small luxury—morning newspapers with your breakfast, in-room massages, twice-daily maid service, and views of the Prague Castle and the Charles Bridge. Service is consistently excellent, and the hotel's presentation along with the attention to the little things other hotels often overlook make this a top stay in Prague, even if it's an overly sanitized one. ⊠ *Veleslavinova 21, Staré Město, 110 00* ☎ *221–427–000* 🖶 *221–426–977* ⊕ *www.fourseasons.com* 🛏 *142 rooms, 20 suites ⚮ Restaurant, in-room safes, minibars, cable TV with movies, health club, massage, sauna, bar, concierge, Internet, business services, meeting rooms, parking (fee), some pets allowed (fee), no-smoking rooms* ☰ *AE, DC, MC, V* ⦿ *EP.*

$$$$ ⊞ **Grand Hotel Bohemia.** This beautifully refurbished art nouveau palace sits across the street from Obecní dům (Municipal House), near the Prašná brána (Powder Tower). During the Communist era it was a nameless, secure hideaway for ranking foreign party members. Once it was restored to private hands, the hotel was remodeled by its Austrian owners, who opted for a muted, modern look, which lacks a comfortable sense of interior design. Thus, the hotel is nice without being quite elegant, clean and comfortable but not homey. There are definite highlights, like the sumptuous Boccaccio ballroom left in its faux-rococo glory. In the rooms, sweeping, long drapes frame spectacular views of the Old Town. The location is unbeatable, and there are perks like having an answering machine in your room, but, overall, the rooms are a bit overpriced. ⊠ *Králodvorská 4, Staré Město, 110 00* ☎ *234–608–111* 🖶 *222–329–545* ⊕ *www.grandhotelbohemia.cz* 🛏 *73 rooms, 5 suites ⚮ Restaurant, café, in-room data ports, in-room fax, in-room safes, minibars, cable TV with movies, bar, meeting rooms, some pets allowed (fee), no-smoking floor* ☰ *AE, DC, MC, V* ⦿ *BP.*

★ **$$$$** ⊞ **Iron Gate Hotel.** This distinctive hotel near Old Town Square is an architectural gem offering apartment suites, and the luxurious details, location, and historical art make it an attractive choice. The building dates from the 14th century. During the 16th century, the building underwent a major renovation, adding balconies and terraces. In 2003 the building saw yet another face-lift when it was turned into a hotel, complete with original frescoes and decorative wooden ceilings discovered in most suites; they'd been covered over for hundreds of years. Sleigh beds, and other antique touches, fill the rooms and make them comfortable, and kitchenettes make the room your home. ⊠ *Michalská 19, Staré Město, 110 00* ☎ *225–777–777* 🖶 *225–777–778* ⊕ *www.irongate. cz* 🛏 *44 suites ⚮ Restaurant, room service, in-room data ports, in-room safes, kitchenettes, minibars, cable TV, concierge, meeting room* ☰ *AE, MC, V* ⦿ *BP.*

★ **$$$–$$$$** ⊞ **Josef.** This modern hotel with its all-white and glass lobby—flanked between an old police station and stone residential buildings—is just as visually arresting as it was when it opened in June 2002. Rooms are hip and simple, with minimalist furniture and glass walls separating bath-

3

Facilities
In most cases, cable TV, minibars, some kind of Internet connection, and breakfast are offered in hotels in all price ranges. Hotels at $$ and $$$ ranges usually have restaurants, cafés, room service, private baths and hair dryers. At $$$$ hotels, you can expect luxury amenities like bathroom toiletries, robes, sauna, steam bath, pool, concierge, and babysitting— oh, yes, and air-conditioning, which is often absent at cheaper hotels. Though many of Prague's older buildings are prohibited by city officials from installing air-conditioning for architectural reasons, many of the upscale hotels have somehow circumvented such concerns.

Reservations
During the peak season (May through October, excluding July and August) reservations are absolutely imperative; reserve 90 days in advance to stay in the hotel and room of your choice. For the remainder of the year, reserve 30 days in advance.

Prices
Many hotels in Prague go by a three-season system: the lowest rates are charged from November through mid-March, excluding Christmas and New Year's, when high-season rates are charged; the middle season is July and August; the high season, from the end of March through June and mid-August through the end of October, brings the highest rates. Easter sees higher-than-high-season rates, and some hotels increase the price for other holidays and trade fairs. Always ask first.

WHAT IT COSTS In koruna and euros				
$$$$	**$$$**	**$$**	**$**	**¢**
PRICES IN KORUNA over 7,000	5,000–7,000	3,500–5,000	1,500–3,500	under 1,500
PRICES IN EUROS over €225	€155–€225	€108–€155	47€–108 €	under 47€

Prices are for two people in a double room with a private bath and breakfast during peak season (March through October, excluding July and August).

room from bedroom. The clutter-free cleanliness is relaxing. In a superb location a few minutes' walk from Old Town Square, it's a perfect choice for those who want to admire the old architecture during the day but sleep in a choice urban atmosphere at night. And on those humid Prague evenings, you'll be glad that you chose a place with air-conditioning. ⊠ *Rybná 20, Staré Město, 110 00* ☎ *221–700–111* ⊟ *221–700–999* ⊕ *www.hoteljosef.com* ⇆ *110 rooms* ⌂ *Restaurant, café, in-room data ports, in-room safes, minibars, cable TV, in-room DVD, lobby lounge, dry cleaning, laundry service, Internet, business services, meeting rooms, parking (fee), some pets allowed (fee), no-smoking rooms* ⊟ *AE, DC, MC, V* ⊙⏐ *BP.*

★ **$$$** 🏨 **Leonardo.** On a quiet street a block away from Vltava River, this Old Town hotel is a comfortable and central place to stay. Newly opened in 2004, it has spacious rooms, but those in the back have a view of a wall. The furnishings are stately, with a splash of art deco, but the building begs for more creative decorative commotion, like the adjoining Renaissance-era restaurant. The price, staff, location, and comfortable beds make it worth a stay and better than its peers at the same price level. Apartment suites are equipped with kitchenettes. ⊠ *Karolíny Světlé 27, Staré Město, 110 00* ☎ *239–009–239* 🖷 *239–009—238* ⊕ *www.hotelleonardo.cz* 🛏 *50 rooms, 11 suites* ♨ *Restaurant, in-room safes, minibars, cable TV, some pets allowed (fee)* ▦ *AE, DC, MC, V* ⊚ *BP.*

$$$ 🏨 **Maximilian.** Oversize beds, classic French cherrywood furniture, and thick drapes make for a relaxing stay in this luxurious hotel. The hotel, which opened in 1995, is on a peaceful square, well away from traffic, noise, and crowds, yet within easy walking distance to Old Town Square and Pařížská Street. ⊠ *Haštalská 14, Staré Město, 110 00* ☎ *225–303–118* 🖷 *225–303–110* ⊕ *www.maximilianhotel.com* 🛏 *72 rooms* ♨ *Restaurant, room service, in-room fax, in-room safes, minibars, cable TV, dry cleaning, laundry service, business services, Internet, meeting rooms, parking (fee), some pets allowed (fee), no-smoking rooms* ▦ *AE, DC, MC, V* ⊚ *BP.*

$$ 🏨 **Haštal.** Built in 1850 and used as a brewery until 1903, this building does not have glamorous architectural statements like many other Prague hotels. However, others do not offer such cheap rates as this hotel, which is a few blocks from Old Town Square. Rooms are simply decorated with wooden furniture, but the windows have light-color curtains, making early-morning sun intrusive if you want to sleep in. ⊠ *Haštalská 16, Staré Město, 110 00* ☎ *222–314–335* 🖷 *222–314–336* 🛏 *24 rooms* ♨ *Café, minibars, cable TV, parking (fee), some pets allowed (fee); no a/c* ▦ *AE, DC, MC, V* ⊚ *BP.*

$–$$ 🏨 **Residence 7 Angels.** The best thing about this pension is the perfect location about halfway between Old Town Square and the Charles Bridge. This is definitely an apartment-like experience, so if you want a full-service hotel, keep looking. You do get daily maid service and your own keys (one set only), but there is no 24-hour front desk. The decor is a mixed bag of modern and antique, and rooms, which are built around a nice courtyard, are all different. A great cooked-to-order breakfast is served in the hotel restaurant, which also has tasty but too-pricey Czech cuisine accompanied by gypsy music in the evenings. ⊠ *Jilská 20, Staré Město 110 00* ☎ *224–226–955* 🖷 *224–234–381* ⊕ *www.7angels.cz* 🛏 *6 rooms, 4 suites* ♨ *Restaurant, some kitchenettes, refrigerators, cable TV, laundry service; no a/c* ▦ *AE, MC, V* ⊚ *BP* Ⓜ *Line A: Můstek.*

$–$$ 🏨 **U Zlatého Jalena.** Besides the killer location, there's little to attract you into this hotel, which looks like it was decorated more by your grandmother than a professional designer. If you're curious what most standard Prague apartments are like, this is a great example—high ceilings, parquet floors, and brass furniture. Despite the weak design judgment, rooms are comfortable enough and have private bathrooms; a continental breakfast is included. Most important, the staff are honest and helpful

Private Rooms

A private room can be a cheaper and more interesting alternative to a hotel. You can find agencies offering such accommodations all over Prague, including at the main train station (Hlavní nádraží), Holešovice station (Nádraží Holešovice), and at Ruzyně Airport. These bureaus usually are staffed with people who speak some English, and most can book rooms in hotels and pensions as well as private accommodations. Rates for private rooms start at around 400 Kč per person per night and can go much higher for better-quality rooms. In general, there's no fee, but you may need to try several bureaus to find the accommodation you want. Ask to see a photo of the room before accepting it, and be sure to pinpoint its location on a map—you don't want to wind up in an inconvenient location. You may be approached by (usually) men in the stations hawking rooms, and although these deals aren't always rip-offs, you should be wary of them. **Prague Information Service** arranges lodging from all of its central offices, including the branch in the main train station, which is in the booth marked TURISTICKÉ INFORMACE on the left side of the main hall as you exit the station.

Apartment Rentals

Apartment rentals are a great way to go if you want to be more independent. Several reliable agencies have an extensive network and can find you lower rates than you can generally find at a comparable hotel. Also, the apartments tend to be in the center of Prague with much better rates than nearby hotels. In some cases, a lengthy stay secures a cheaper rate. The downfall of the apartment stay is that you don't have the perks of cleaning services (though some arrange one) and other amenities like a restaurant, wake-up call, or even a phone for that matter. Some agencies, however, rent mobile phones, which require about a 3,000 Kč deposit.

If you're looking for an apartment, consider the following agencies:

Ariva Guesthouse. The owners reconstructed this house in 2003. In the trendy Žižkov neighborhood, the building has 16 apartments for rent, ranging from 1,650 Kč to 2,310 Kč per night. The rooms are beautiful, with original wood flooring and exposed brick walls, but the perks of televisions and air-conditioning aren't here. This spot boasts its gay friendliness. ⊠ *Vlkova 37, Žižkov, 130 00* ☎ *603–914–189* ⊕ *www.ariva-guesthouse.com.*

E-travel. Quick and easy, this Web-based company will find you cheap accommodation rates in the center of Prague—all via Internet. ⊠ *Ostrovní 7, Nové Město* ☎ *224–990–990* ⊕ *www.travel.cz.*

Mary's Travel & Tourist Services. This agency will do anything to give you everything you want. Primarily they arrange stays in Prague—hotels, apartments, hostels—so they can find you deals for as low as 700 Kč per night. Many of their apartments are in Old Town and come with cleaning services. Call on them to make your arrangements for out-of-town excursions, as well. ⊠ *Italská 31, Vinohrady, 120 00* ☎ *222–254–007* 🖷 *222–252–215* ⊕ *www.marys.cz.*

Prague Accommodation Service. The bluntly named agency can help you find a reasonably priced apartment in the center of town for even a short stay. ✉ *Opatovická 20, Nové Město* 🖷🖳 *233–376–638* ⊕ *www.accommodation-prague-centre.cz.*

Stop City. From rooms to apartments to hotels, this company in Prague 2 can score cheap deals for you in the Prague center. ✉ *Vinohradská 24, Vinohrady* ☎ *222–521–252* ⊕ *www.stopcity.com.*

Stop In. This company offers private apartments and rooms, some in the more residential areas. ✉ *V Holešovičhách 15, Libeň* 🖷🖳 *284–680–115* ⊕ *www. stopin.cz.*

Home Exchanges
If you would like to exchange your home for someone else's, join a home-exchange organization, which will send you its updated listings of available exchanges for a year and will include your own listing in at least one of them. It's up to you to make specific arrangements.

There are two major U.S.-based home exchange organizations. **HomeLink International** (✉ Box 47747, Tampa, FL 33647 ☎ 813/975–9825 or 800/638–3841 🖳 813/910–8144 ⊕ www.homelink.org); $110 yearly for a listing, online access, and catalog; $70 without catalog. **Intervac U.S.** (✉ 30 Corte San Fernando, Tiburon, CA 94920 ☎ 800/756–4663 🖳 415/435–7440 ⊕ www.intervacus.com); $125 yearly for a listing, online access, and a catalog; $65 without catalog.

Hostels
No matter what your age, you can save on lodging costs by staying at hostels. In some 4,500 locations in more than 70 countries around the world, Hostelling International (HI), the umbrella group for a number of national youth-hostel associations, offers single-sex, dorm-style beds and, at many hostels, rooms for couples and family accommodations. Membership in any HI national hostel association, open to travelers of all ages, allows you to stay in HI-affiliated hostels at member rates; one-year membership is about $28 for adults (C$35 for a two-year minimum membership in Canada, £14 in U.K., A$52 in Australia, and NZ$40 in New Zealand); hostels charge about $10–$30 per night. Members have priority if the hostel is full; they're also eligible for discounts around the world, even on rail and bus travel in some countries. For more information about hosteling, contact your local youth hostel office. In the Czech Republic, most hostels are geared to the college crowd. For further information, visit the Web site ⊕ Backpackers.cz.

At the Internet-equipped **Travellers' Hostel** (✉ Dlouhá 33, Staré Mešto, 110 00 ☎ 224–826–662 ⊕ www.travellers.cz) rates range from 370 Kč for a bed in a dormitory-style room to 1,300 Kč for a single room with a shower. The **Clown & Bard** (✉ Bořivojova 102, Žižkov, 130 00 ☎ 222–716–453 ⊕ www. clownandbard.com) is a perfect choice if you want to meet other up-all-night travelers. The rates start at 250 Kč for a dorm room and stop at 450 Kč for a two-person double room.

Hostelling International—USA (✉ 8401 Colesville Rd., Suite 600, Silver Spring, MD 20910 ☎ 301/495–1240 🖳 301/495–6697 ⊕ www.hiusa.org).

Hostelling International—Canada (✉ 205 Catherine St., Suite 400, Ottawa, Ontario K2P 1C3 ☎ 613/237–7884 or 800/663–5777 🖷 613/237–7868 ⊕ www.hihostels.ca). **YHA England and Wales** (✉ Trevelyan House, Dimple Rd., Matlock, Derbyshire DE4 3YH, U.K. ☎ 0870/870–8808, 0870/770–8868, or 0162/959–2600 🖷 0870/770–6127 ⊕ www.yha.org.uk). **YHA Australia** (✉ 422 Kent St., Sydney, NSW 2001 ☎ 02/9261–1111 🖷 02/9261–1969 ⊕ www.yha.com.au). **YHA New Zealand** (✉ Level 1, Moorhouse City, 166 Moorhouse Ave., Box 436, Christchurch ☎ 03/379–9970 or 0800/278–299 🖷 03/365–4476 ⊕ www.yha.org.nz).

when it comes to guiding you to the right places in Prague. The no-frills approach is refreshing because it means that you are able to stay in a clean room with furniture that's not from Ikea in the city center—but you don't have to exceed your credit limit in the process. ✉ *Celetná 11, Staré Město, 110 00* ☎ *222–317–237* 🖷 *222–318–693* ⊕ *www.beetletour.cz* ⌨ *10 rooms* ⌂ *Café, minibars, in-room safes, cable TV, in-room VCRs, some pets allowed (fee); no a/c* ⊟ *AE, DC, MC, V* ⊺⊙⊺ *CP.*

¢ 🏨 **Pension Unitas & Art Prison Hostel.** The spartan rooms of this former convent, now operated by the Christian charity Unitas, used to serve as interrogation cells for the Communist secret police. (Václav Havel was once a "guest.") Today the basement rooms maintain a prison theme, complete with steel bunk beds, for the Art Prison Hostel. The rest of the building is the pension, which is comfortable but certainly not as cozy as many of the pensions around. There's a common (but clean) bathroom on each floor. Cheap prices and a great location mean that you need to reserve well in advance, even in the off-season. ✉ *Bartolomějská 9, Staré Město, 110 00* ☎ *224–211–020* 🖷 *224–210–800* ⊕ *www.unitas.cz* ⌨ *40 rooms with shared bath* ⌂ *Restaurant; no a/c, no smoking, no room TVs* ⊟ *AE, DC, MC, V* ⊺⊙⊺ *BP.*

MALÁ STRANA (LESSER QUARTER)

The Lesser Quarter is one of the nicer areas to stay in; you can find Renaissance buildings and baroque churches that give this quarter its fairy-tale charm. The area not only inspired Franz Kafka when he lived in his sister's home on Golden Lane, but it continues to be Hollywood's backdrop for films like the Bourne Identity and Amadeus. Malá Strana is where you can find many of the city's best restaurants, which line the riverside, and some of the best sightseeing. Most people meandering in this part of town are tourists—locals tend to stay away, both in living and walking in this area.

$$$$ 🏨 **Aria Hotel.** The bland façade of the building gives no indication of
Fodor'sChoice the extravagance inside this music-theme hotel, which was once a print-
★ ing factory and is now the city's best luxury boutique hotel. Rooms are designed by Rocco Magnoli, the architect for the world's Versace stores. Each room is dedicated to a musical genre and equipped with DVDs and speakers so that you can hear music everywhere. Downstairs is a

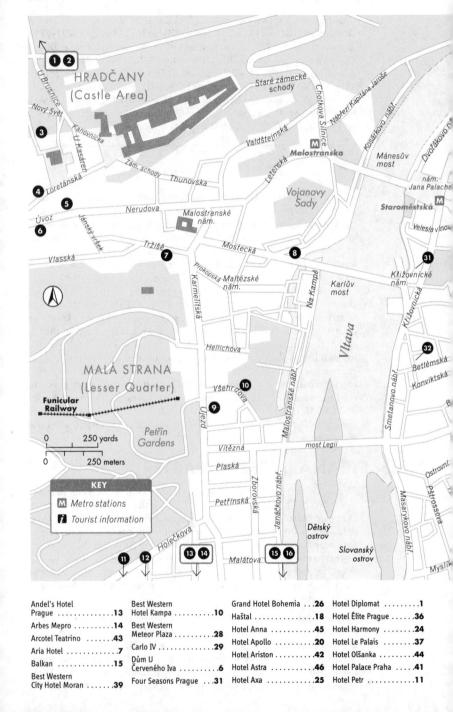

Andel's Hotel
Prague **13**

Arbes Mepro **14**

Arcotel Teatrino **43**

Aria Hotel **7**

Balkan **15**

Best Western
City Hotel Moran **39**

Best Western
Hotel Kampa **10**

Best Western
Meteor Plaza **28**

Carlo IV **29**

Dům U
Červeného Iva **6**

Four Seasons Prague . . .**31**

Grand Hotel Bohemia . . .**26**

Haštal **18**

Hotel Anna **45**

Hotel Apollo **20**

Hotel Ariston **42**

Hotel Astra **46**

Hotel Axa **25**

Hotel Diplomat **1**

Hotel Élite Prague **36**

Hotel Harmony **24**

Hotel Le Palais **37**

Hotel Olšanka **44**

Hotel Palace Praha **41**

Hotel Petr **11**

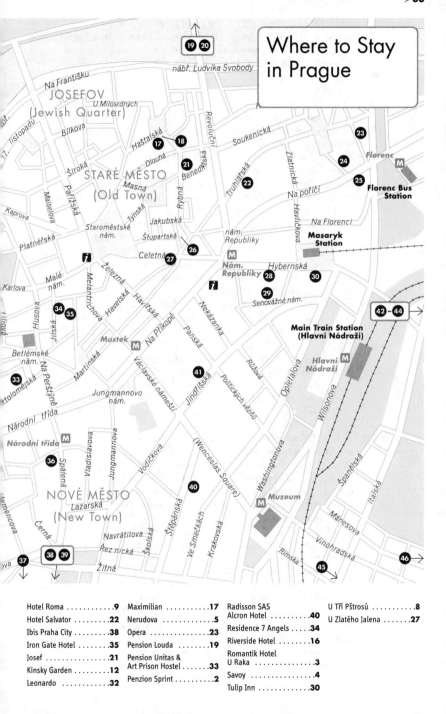

Where to Stay in Prague

Hotel Roma **9**

Hotel Salvator **22**

Ibis Praha City **38**

Iron Gate Hotel **35**

Josef **21**

Kinsky Garden **12**

Leonardo **32**

Maximilian **17**

Nerudova **5**

Opera **23**

Pension Louda **19**

Pension Unitas &
Art Prison Hostel **33**

Penzion Sprint **2**

Radisson SAS
Alcron Hotel **40**

Residence 7 Angels **34**

Riverside Hotel **16**

Romantik Hotel
U Raka **3**

Savoy **4**

Tulip Inn **30**

U Tří Pštrosů **8**

U Zlatého Jalena **27**

music library, offering anything from Johnny Cash to Mozart. Two private theaters are free for guests who would like to watch a movie or listen to tunes. The roof-top terrace, with its panoramic view of Prague, is simply the best there is to offer. ✉ *Tržiště 9, Malá Strana, 118 00* ☎ *225–334–111* 🖷 *257–535–357* ⊕ *www.ariahotel.net* 🛏 *52 rooms, 7 suites* ⚬ *Restaurant, café, room service, in-room safes, minibars, cable TV, in-room DVD, gym, massage, sauna, cinema, library, Internet, meeting rooms, parking (fee)* ▭ *AE, DC, MC, V* ⏺ *BP.*

$$$$ 🏨 **U Tří Pštrosů.** The location could not be better: a romantic corner a stone's throw from the river and within arms' reach of the Charles Bridge. The airy rooms of the centuries-old building still have their original oak-beam ceilings and antique furniture. Many have views over the river, but the view will cost you an extra €20. Massive walls keep out the noise of the crowds on the bridge. An excellent in-house restaurant serves traditional Czech dishes to guests and nonguests alike. Rates drop slightly in July and August—probably because there's no air-conditioning, though the building's thick walls generally help keep it cool. ✉ *Dražického nám. 12, Malá Strana, 118 00* ☎ *257–532–410* 🖷 *257–533–217* ⊕ *www.utripstrosu.cz* 🛏 *14 rooms, 4 suites* ⚬ *Restaurant, minibars, cable TV, Internet, laundry service, meeting room; no a/c* ▭ *AE, DC, MC, V* ⏺ *BP.*

$$$ 🏨 **Best Western Hotel Kampa.** This early-baroque armory-turned-hotel is tucked away on an abundantly picturesque street at the southern end of the Lesser Quarter, just off Kampa Island. Note the late-Gothic vaulting in the massive dining room. At one time, the bucolic setting and proximity to the city center made this lodging option a comparative bargain; now hotels within blocks offer the same, if not better, services and are a few euros cheaper. ✉ *Všehrdova 16, Malá Strana, 118 00* ☎ *257–320–508 or 257–320–404* 🖷 *257–320–262* ⊕ *www.bestwestern-ce.com* 🛏 *85 rooms* ⚬ *Restaurant, minibars, cable TV; no a/c* ▭ *AE, MC, V* ⏺ *BP.*

★ $$$ 🏨 **Dům U Červeného Lva.** (House at the Red Lion). This intimate, immaculately kept baroque building is right on the main, historic thoroughfare in the Lesser Quarter, a five-minute walk from Prague Castle's front gates. Guest rooms have parquet floors, 17th-century painted-beam ceilings, superb antiques, and all-white bathrooms with brass fixtures. The two top-floor rooms can double as a suite. There's no elevator, and the stairs are steep. ✉ *Nerudova 41, Malá Strana, 118 00* ☎ *257–533–832* 🖷 *257–532–746* ⊕ *www.hotelredlion.com* 🛏 *5 rooms, 3 suites* ⚬ *2 restaurants, in-room safes, minibars, cable TV, bar, some pets allowed; no a/c* ▭ *AE, DC, MC, V* ⏺ *BP.*

$$$ 🏨 **Nerudova.** Built in 1348, this building—now a small and modern hotel—is where Czech author Jan Neruda and his mother lived in 1860. As a tribute to the author, lines from his *Povídky malostranske* (Malá Strana stories) are painted in the stone hallways. The building is said to have a ghost—a woman who tried to burn her belongings so that her family could not have them but had a heart attack in the process; you might hear her and her jingling keys in the hallway. For a view other than a wall, request rooms facing the street. If you drive, the parking fee is quite expensive. ✉ *Nerudova 44, Malá Strana, 110 00*

☎ 257–535–557 🖶 257–531–492 ⊕ www.hotelneruda-praha.cz ⇝ 20 rooms ⚘ Restaurant, café, in-room safes, minibars, cable TV, parking (fee), some pets allowed (fee) ▤ AE, DC, MC, V ⏐⚬⏐ BP.

\$\$ 🏨 **Hotel Roma.** Down the hill from the Prague Castle, this hotel is in a great location and still shines after its debut in 2003. The atrium lobby is a bit bland and functionalist, but a few funky details, including an aquarium window in the lobby wall, give the place some character. Most rooms are simple and a bit spare, with blond wood furnishings and parquet floors, but the Roma also offers suites, which have regular wood floors and real antiques—however, that also means two single beds with bumping headboards are pushed together and don't really meet. The Roma has found its niche by offering comfort, cleanliness, and consistently friendly service at eminently fair rates, which makes this place a rarity in Prague. ✉ Újezd 24, Malá Strana, 110 00 ☎ 257–326–890 🖶 257–324–095 ⊕ www.hotelroma.cz ⇝ 62 rooms, 17 suites, 8 antique suites ⚘ Restaurant, in-room data ports, in-room safes, minibars, cable TV, gym, sauna, bar, laundry service, Internet, travel services, parking (fee), some pets allowed (fee); no a/c ▤ AE, DC, MC, V ⏐⚬⏐ BP.

FodorsChoice
★

HRADČANY

If you're coming to Prague to have a romantic getaway, complete with walks around the starlit castle and strolls through hilly parks that open into panoramic postcard views of Prague, Hradčany is the place for you. The area is peaceful and unexplored by rowdy pub crawlers. Barring the castle grounds and the adjoining Petřín Hill, there isn't much in this area in terms of solid shopping stops or bars. If you're a walker, however, Malá Strana is a downhill stroll away, and there you can find restaurants, artsy boutiques, and live music at the many bars.

★ **\$\$\$\$** 🏨 **Savoy.** A restrained yellow Jugendstil façade conceals one of the city's most luxurious small hotels. Once a budget hotel, the building was gutted and lavishly refurbished in the mid-1990s. A harmonious maroon-and-mahogany color scheme carries through the public spaces; some rooms are furnished in purely modern style, while others have a rococo look. The Restaurant Hradčany is among the city's better hotel dining rooms. The biggest disappointment: although Prague Castle is just up the road, none of the rooms have a view of it. ✉ Keplerova 6, Hradčany, 118 00 ☎ 224–302–430 🖶 224–302–128 ⊕ www.hotel-savoy.cz ⇝ 55 rooms, 6 suites ⚘ Restaurant, café, in-room data ports, in-room fax, in-room safes, minibars, cable TV, in-room DVDs, gym, sauna, concierge, meeting rooms, some pets allowed (fee), no-smoking floor ▤ AE, DC, MC, V ⏐⚬⏐ BP.

\$\$\$ 🏨 **Romantik Hotel U Raka.** This private guesthouse, since 1997 a member of the Romantik Hotels & Restaurants organization, has a quiet location on the ancient, winding streets of Nový Svět, just behind the Loreto Church and a 10-minute walk from Prague Castle. One side of the 18th-century building presents a rare example of half-timbering, and the rooms sustain the country feel with heavy furniture reminiscent of a Czech farmhouse. There are only six rooms, so if you can get a reservation you will have a wonderful base for exploring Prague. ✉ Černínská 10/93,

FodorsChoice
★

Hradčany, 118 00 ☎ *220–511–100* 🖷 *220–510–511* ⊕ *www. romantikhotels.com* ↘ *5 rooms, 1 suite* ⚲ *Cable TV, parking (fee), no-smoking rooms; no kids under 10* ▤ *AE, MC, V* ⦿ *BP.*

NOVÉ MĚSTO (NEW TOWN)

New Town is a bit grittier than aged Old Town. More modern build-ings are in this area, and the cheaper lodging options seem to be in these buildings. Let's just say that you can get more of an understanding of Communist design than of art nouveau in most of these places. Never-theless, New Town does have a few architectural gems. If you like to awake and immediately head out to shop, this is your place. The quar-ter includes Na Příkopě and Václavske náměstí, which are the two main shopping streets in the city. Also, when it comes to outdoor cafés and restaurant gardens, New Town is where it's at.

$$$$ 🏨 **Carlo IV.** Dripping with style and luxury, this Italian-owned hotel, both
Fodor'sChoice outside and inside, is one of the most beautiful in the city. High ceilings
★ present space for towering palm trees and playful design touches like a gargantuan bin with an umbrella and walking stick—such enormity lends a certain Alice-in-Wonderland quality. Attention to detail goes down to the cloudlike duvets in the rooms and the fountain in the indoor pool. Old-fashioned rooms are in the original building, which was once used as a bank, and modern rooms are available in the adjoining building. The only drawback is the snobby front-desk clerks; however, once past them, the rest of the staff are friendly and not so dense. ⊠ *Senovážné náměstí 13, Nové Město, 110 00* ☎ *224–593–090* 🖷 *224–593–000* ⊕ *www.boscolohotels.com* ↘ *130 rooms, 22 suites* ⚲ *Restaurant, in-room safes, minibars, cable TV, indoor pool, gym, hot tub, massage, sauna, steam room, 2 bars, babysitting, dry cleaning, laundry service, Internet, business services, meeting rooms, car rental, parking (fee), some pets allowed (fee), no-smoking rooms* ▤ *AE, DC, MC, V* ⦿ *EP.*

$$$$ 🏨 **Hotel Palace Praha.** For the well-heeled, this is a coveted address—a
Fodor'sChoice muted, pistachio-green art nouveau building perched on a busy corner
★ in the city center. The hotel's spacious, well-appointed rooms, each with a white-marble bathroom, are dressed in velvety pinks and greens cribbed straight from an Alfons Mucha print. The hotel's restaurant is pure continental, from the classic garnishes to the creamy sauces. A block from Wenceslas Square, and down the street from Na Příkopě, the ad-vantage that this hotel has is its location, and it's something that puts it ahead of other hotels in its class. Children 12 and under stay for free. ⊠ *Panská 12, Nové Město, 111 21* ☎ *224–093–111* 🖷 *224–221–240* ⊕ *www.palacehotel.cz* ↘ *114 rooms, 10 suites* ⚲ *2 restaurants, in-room data ports, in-room safes, cable TV, minibars, sauna, babysitting, dry cleaning, laundry service, concierge, meeting room, no-smoking floors* ▤ *AE, DC, MC, V* ⦿ *BP.*

$$$$ 🏨 **Radisson SAS Alcron Hotel.** Opened in 1932, the Alcron was one of Prague's first luxury hotels; a major renovation of the building in 1998 modernized the look but kept the dramatic white marble staircase. Rooms are elegant, updated art deco in style with all the amenities you'd expect in a business-centered hotel. However, the excellent location a block off Wenceslas Square makes it just as attractive to leisure travelers. Both restaurants are excellent, and monthly cooking classes by the young star chef are big draws. You get much more comfort for your more money here than at a typical chain hotel in Prague. ⊠ *Štěpánská 40, Nove Mesto 110 00* ☎ *222–820–000* 🖷 *222–820–120* ⊕ *www. radissonsas.com* ❑ *192 rooms, 19 suites* ᎒ *2 restaurants, in-room data ports, some in-room faxes, in-room safes, minibars, cable TV with movies, gym, sauna, bar, dry cleaning, laundry service, business services, Internet, meeting rooms* ⊟ *AE, MC, V* ⍟ *BP.*

$$$ 🏨 **Best Western Meteor Plaza.** This Best Western hotel offers modern conveniences in a historical building (Empress Maria Theresa's son, Joseph II, stayed here when he was passing through in the 18th century). The baroque building is five minutes on foot from downtown. Renovations have left most of the rooms with a surprisingly modern look that masks the hotel's history. To get a sense of the hotel's age, visit the original 14th-century wine cellar. ⊠ *Hybernská 6, Nové Město, 110 00* ☎ *224–192–130 or 224–192–159* 🖷 *224–213–005* ⊕ *www.hotel-meteor.cz* ❑ *90 rooms, 6 suites* ᎒ *Restaurant, minibars, cable TV with movies, gym, sauna, parking (fee); no a/c in some rooms* ⊟ *AE, DC, MC, V* ⍟ *BP.*

$$$ 🏨 **Hotel Élite Prague.** An extensive renovation preserved the 14th-century Gothic façade and many interior architectural details of this building while allowing for modern comforts. Rooms are furnished with antiques, and many have decorated Renaissance-style wooden ceilings and large desks. One of the suites has a mural ceiling. The central garden, with bar service in the daytime, makes a nice refuge from busy nearby Náodní třiADda. ⊠ *Ostrovní 32, Nové Město, 110 00* ☎ *224–932–250* 🖷 *224–930–787* ⊕ *www.hotelelite.cz* ❑ *77 rooms, 2 suites* ᎒ *Restaurant, room service, in-room data ports, in-room safes, minibars, cable TV with movies, hair salon, bar, laundry service, business services, meeting room, parking (fee), some pets allowed (fee)* ⊟ *AE, DC, MC, V* ⍟ *BP.*

$$ 🏨 **Best Western City Hotel Moran.** This renovated 19th-century town house has a bright, inviting lobby and equally bright and clean rooms that are modern, if slightly bland. Some upper-floor rooms have good views of Prague Castle. ⊠ *Na Moráni 15, Nové Město, 120 00* ☎ *224–915–208* 🖷 *224–920–625* ⊕ *www.bestwestern-ce.com* ❑ *57 rooms* ᎒ *Restaurant, cable TV, Internet, meeting room, some pets allowed, no-smoking floor* ⊟ *AE, DC, MC, V* ⍟ *BP.*

$$ 🏨 **Hotel Axa.** Funky and functional, this 1932 high-rise was once a mainstay of the budget-hotel crowd. Over the years, the rooms have certainly improved; however, the lobby and public areas are still decidedly tacky, with plastic flowers, lots of mirrors, and glaring lights. In the adjoining gym, there are scores of free weights and a swimming pool that costs 1 Kč a minute. ⊠ *Na Poříčí 40, Nové Město, 113 03 Prague 1* ☎ *224–812–580* 🖷 *224–214–489* ⊕ *www.hotelaxa.com* ❑ *126 rooms, 6 suites* ᎒ *Restaurant, cable TV, indoor pool, health club, hair salon, sauna, bar, laundry service, meeting room, some pets allowed; no a/c* ⊟ *AE, DC, MC, V* ⍟ *BP.*

$$–$$$ ▣ **Opera.** Once the lodging of choice for divas performing at the nearby Státní opera (State Theater), the Opera greatly declined under the Communists. The mid-1990s saw the grand fin-de-siècle façade rejuvenated with a perky pink-and-white exterior paint job. This exuberance is strictly on the outside, though, and the rooms are modern and easy on the eyes. Though the location is near the Old Town, the Opera house itself is not terribly near, however. ⊠ *Těšnov 13, Nové Město, 110 00* ☎ *222–315–609* 🖶 *222–311–477* ⊕ *www.hotel-opera.cz* 🗘 *65 rooms, 2 suites* ⚖ *Restaurant, minibars, in-room safes, cable TV, bar, gym, sauna, meeting room, parking (fee), some pets allowed (fee); no a/c* ☲ *AE, DC, MC, V* ⦿ *BP.*

★ **$$** ▣ **Tulip Inn.** This hotel has one foot in New Town and one foot in trendy Žižkov. Though technically in the city center, its location is between the best of both worlds—shopping and drinking. This inn is a three-star hotel with a four-star atmosphere, which comes as no surprise considering the general manager worked for Radisson in Prague and Germany for nearly six years. For the location and price, it's difficult to beat the deal. The only drawback, however, is that a highway runs along one side of the building. Windows are soundproof, but if you are a cat-light sleeper, it might be best to request a room away from the road. ⊠ *Hybernská 42, Nové Město, 110 00* ☎ *224–100–100* 🖶 *224–227–214* ⊕ *www.tulipinnterminus.com* 🗘 *65 rooms, 6 suites* ⚖ *Restaurant, in-room data ports, in-room safes, minibars, cable TV with movies, bar, meeting room, laundry services, dry cleaning, babysitting, parking (fee), no-smoking rooms* ☲ *AE, DC, MC, V* ⦿ *BP.*

$ ▣ **Hotel Harmony.** This is one of the renovated, formerly state-owned standbys. A stern 1930s façade clashes with the bright 1990s interior, but cheerful receptionists, comfortably casual rooms, and an easy 10-minute walk to the Old Town compensate for the aesthetic flaws. Ask for a room away from the bustle of one of Prague's busiest streets. ⊠ *Na Poříčí 31, Nové Město, 110 00* ☎ *222–319–807* 🖶 *222–310–009* ⊕ *www.hotelharmony.cz* 🗘 *60 rooms* ⚖ *2 restaurants, cable TV, meeting rooms, some pets allowed; no a/c* ☲ *AE, DC, MC, V* ⦿ *BP.*

★ **$** ▣ **Hotel Salvator.** An efficiently run establishment just outside the Old Town, this pension offers more comforts than most in its class, including cable TV and minibars in all rooms, and a combination breakfast room and bar with a billiard table. Rooms are pristine if plain, with the standard narrow beds. For those who must have air-conditioning, there are two rooms on the top floor with this luxury. ⊠ *Truhlářská 10, Nové Město, 110 00 Prague 1* ☎ *222–312–234* 🖶 *222–316–355* ⊕ *www. salvator.cz* 🗘 *28 rooms, 16 with bath; 7 suites* ⚖ *Restaurant, minibars, cable TV, bar, parking (fee), some pets allowed (fee); no a/c in some rooms* ☲ *AE, MC, V* ⦿ *BP.*

VINOHRADY

Welcome to wine country. At one time this section of Prague was full of vineyards (that's why it's called Vinohrady). Today, it's known as a choice place to live, with tree-lined streets, good restaurants, and great bars. Vinohrady is within walking distance of the city center, and convenient Metro stops (green line) and trams (No. 11) drop you off at the top of Václavské náměstí. Chances are, if you're staying here, after you've been to the center, you'll opt to relax in this swanky neighborhood, with its vast selection of wine bars, pubs, cocktail bars, and great restaurants.

$$$$ ⊞ **Hotel Le Palais.** Built in 1841, this venerable building served as the home and shop of Prague's main butcher (one of the front rooms was used to produce and sell sausage until 1991). Today, you will only find sausage in the distinctive hotel's restaurant. Rooms have original frescoes painted by Bohemian artist Ludek Marold, and a hallway has an original mosaic floor from 1897. Some rooms have fireplaces, making them especially cozy in winter, and all rooms have air-conditioning to make them comfortable in summer. Service is personal and welcoming, and the outstanding gym is a big plus. ⊠ *U Zvonařky 1, Vinohrady, 120 00* ☎ *234–634–111* 🖷 *222–563–350* ⊕ *www.palaishotel.cz* 🛏 *60 rooms, 12 suites* ⏦ *Restaurant, in-room data ports, minibars, cable TV, in-room DVD, gym, hair salon, indoor hot tub, massage, sauna, steam room, lobby lounge, library, meeting rooms, parking, some pets allowed (fee), no-smoking floors* ⊟ *AE, DC, MC, V* †⊙† *BP.*

$ ⊞ **Hotel Anna.** The bright neoclassical façade and art nouveau details have been lovingly restored on this 19th-century building. Although the street is quiet, a few minutes' walk will get you to bustling New Town. The suites on the top floors offer a nice view of the historic district. In 2002 the hotel opened an annex, the Dependance Anna, in the central courtyard of the block with 12 less-expensive rooms, but you must return to the main hotel for breakfast. ⊠ *Budečská 17, Vinohrady, 120 21* ☎ *222–513–111* 🖷 *222–515–158* ⊕ *www.hotelanna.cz* 🛏 *22 rooms, 2 suites, 12 annex rooms* ⏦ *Cable TV, Internet, meeting room, some pets allowed (fee); no a/c* ⊟ *AE, MC, V* †⊙† *BP.*

★ **$** ⊞ **Ibis Praha City.** The price and the location make this hotel a great pick. A few minutes' walking distance from Wenceslas Square, this is the cheapest air-conditioned place you can find this close to the center. Rooms are without frills but have everything you would expect from an international chain hotel, so if you are looking for a reasonably priced place to sleep but little else, it fits the bill quite nicely. ⊠ *Kateřinska 36, Vinohrady, 120 00* ☎ *222–865–777* 🖷 *222–865–666* ⊕ *www.ibishotel.com* 🛏 *181 rooms* ⏦ *Restaurant, minibars, cable TV, some pets allowed (fee), no-smoking rooms* ⊟ *AE, DC, MC, V* †⊙† *EP.*

SMÍCHOV

Smíchov means "mixed neighborhood" because, when the city had walls, the neighborhood was on the outside and all manner of people could live there. Although it's still a colorful, working-class area, lots of new construction has made it a shopping and entertainment hub as well, with relatively easy access—via tram, metro, or foot—to the city's historical center.

$$$$ ⊞ **Andel's Hotel Prague.** Simply and modernly minimalist, this is where
Fodor'sChoice many of the young, up-and-coming British trendsetters stay. And they
★ should feel right at home, considering the hotel, which opened in June

2002, was designed by British architects and designers Jestico + Whiles. With a nod to the Czech glass industry, the interior is an ode to glass, which is used liberally in the walls of conference rooms and within the hotel rooms. Close to the city center, this area is newly developed, boasting one of the most popular malls in Prague, which is this hotel's next door neighbor. ⊠ *Stroupežnického 21, Smíchov, 150 00* ☏ *296–889–688* 🖷 *296–889–999* ⊕ *www.andelshotel.com* ⇘ *231 rooms, 8 suites* ⚂ *Restaurant, café, room service, in-room data ports, minibars, in-room safes, cable TV, in-room DVDs, gym, hair salon, massage, sauna, bar, laundry service, meeting rooms, parking, no-smoking rooms* ⊟ *AE, DC, MC, V* ⫟⦿⫟ *BP.*

$$$$ 🖭 **Riverside Hotel.** On the Left Bank of the Vltava River, most rooms in this small hotel have enviable views of the Fred and Ginger building, the river, or the National Theater—and if the room faces into the courtyard, chances are you'll be compensated with a balcony. Decoration by French designer Pascale de Montremy, every detail was taken into consideration, down to the plush green bow for room service that reads "Please Make Up My Room." Though the hotel does not have room for a full restaurant, a buffet breakfast is included, and sandwiches are offered in the bar and via room service 24 hours. ⊠ *Janáčovo nabřeží 15, Smíchov, 150 00* ☏ *225–994–611* 🖷 *225–994–615* ⊕ *www. riversideprague.com* ⇘ *32 rooms, 13 suites* ⚂ *Restaurant, room service, in-room data ports, in-room safes, minibars, cable TV with movies, bar, dry cleaning, laundry service, meeting room, no-smoking floor* ⊟ *AE, DC, MC, V* ⫟⦿⫟ *BP.*

$$$ 🖭 **Kinsky Garden.** You could walk the mile or so from this hotel to Prague Castle entirely on the tree-lined paths of Petřín, the hilly park that starts across the street. Opened in 1997, the hotel takes its name from a garden established by Count Rudolf Kinsky in 1825 on the southern side of Petřín. The public spaces are not spaces, nor are some rooms, but everything is tasteful and comfortable. Try to get a room on one of the upper floors for a view of the park. ⊠ *Holečkova 7, Smíchov, 150 00* ☏ *257–311–173* 🖷 *257–311–184* ⊕ *www.hotelkinskygarden.cz* ⇘ *60 rooms* ⚂ *Restaurant, cable TV with movies, bar, Internet, meeting room, some pets allowed, no-smoking floor, parking (fee)* ⊟ *AE, DC, MC, V* ⫟⦿⫟ *BP.*

$ 🖭 **Arbes Mepro.** Renovations in 2001 redecorated and added fancier furniture and room safes to this hotel. The Smíchov neighborhood has several good restaurants (including the U Mikuláše Dačického wine tavern, across the street from the hotel), shopping at the Nový Smíchov mall (which is behind the hotel), and nice strolls along the river or up the Petřín hill. The wine cellar serves as a breakfast room and can be booked for group dinners. Trams to the historical center are a block away, or it's a 10-minute walk to the historic center. ⊠ *Viktora Huga 3, Smíchov, 150 00* ☏ *257–210–410* 🖷 *257–215–263* ⊕ *www.arbes-mepro.cz* ⇘ *27 rooms* ⚂ *In-room safes, cable TV, bar, meeting room, parking (fee), pets (fee); no a/c* ⊟ *AE, MC, V* ⫟⦿⫟ *BP.*

$ 🖭 **Hotel Petr.** Set in a quiet part of Smíchov, a few minutes' stroll from the Lesser Quarter, this is an excellent value. As a "garni" hotel, it does not have a full-service restaurant, but it does serve breakfast (included in the price). The rooms are simply but adequately furnished. It's a 10-minute walk from the closest metro stop and a five-minute walk from the closest tram stop. ⊠ *Drtinova 17, Smíchov, 150 00* ☎ *257–314–068* 🖷 *257–314–072* ⊕ *www.hotelpetr.cz* ⏎ *37 rooms, 2 suites* ⚘ *Restaurant, cable TV, Internet, parking (fee), some pets allowed (fee); no a/c* ☰ *AE, MC, V* ⦾ *BP* Ⓜ *Line B: Anděl.*

$ 📠 **Balkan.** A fresh coat of bright paint on the outside helps this bare-bones hotel to stand out from its run-down surroundings. Inside, the reception area smells like an ashtray due to a nearby bar, but rooms are clean and the staff is friendly. The spartan Balkan is on a busy street not far from the Lesser Quarter and the Národní divadlo (National Theater). ⊠ *Svornosti 28, Smíchov, 150 00 Prague 5* ☎☎ *257–327–180* or *257–322–150* ⏎ *30 rooms* ⚘ *Restaurant, cable TV, sauna, some pets allowed (fee); no a/c* ☰ *AE, MC, V* ⦾ *BP.*

ŽIŽKOV

It's hard to go for more than a block in this densely populated neighborhood without finding a pub or a nightclub. Several places offer live music, making it a center of nightlife. Plus, the restaurants here are generally quite good and a bit cheaper than those in the city center. This neighborhood is a 15- to 25-minute walk from the center, but trams can easily whisk you to both New Town and Old Town. As in all cities, some of the nightlife in this Prague area has a slightly seamy side. It's best to exercise a moderate amount of caution, especially on side streets, and avoid the seedier pubs that offer gambling machines or other more dubious attractions.

$–$$ 📠 **Arcotel Teatrino.** This building has been through many changes—in 1910 it was the city hall of Žižkove, then a theater, and during Communism the downstairs was a bar (rumor has it, the upstairs rooms were used as a sort of after-hours for couples to get acquainted). Today, this hotel, which was rebuilt in 2000, shines with class in a neighborhood that is not so classy, but it's still just two tram stops from the city center. The original art nouveau design was kept and paired with modern accoutrements. ⊠ *Bořivojova 53, Žižkov, 130 00* ☎ *221–422–111* 🖷 *221–422–222* ⊕ *www.arcotel.at* ⏎ *73 rooms* ⚘ *Restaurant, in-room safes, minibars, cable TV with movies, gym, sauna, steam room, meeting rooms, parking (fee), some pets allowed (fee); no a/c* ☰ *AE, DC, MC, V* ⦾ *BP.*

$ 📠 **Hotel Ariston.** Staff are proud to say that this hotel is always undergoing some type of renovation, at least every three years that is. The hotel, with its standard wooden furniture, green carpeting, and matching drapery, has rooms that are clean, cheap and often new, but lack any kind of creativity. The perk of staying here, however, is that the hotel is only three tram stops from the city center, or an easy 20-minute walk. The hotel fronts a tram road, so request a room in the back if you're a light sleeper. ⊠ *Seifertova 65, Žižkov, 130 00* ☎ *222–782–517* 🖷 *222–780–347* ⊕ *www.europehotels.cz* ⏎ *61 rooms* ⚘ *Restaurant, in-room safes, cable TV, some pets allowed (fee); no a/c* ☰ *AE, MC, V* ⦾ *BP.*

$ 🏊 **Hotel Olšanka.** The main calling card of this boxy modern hotel is its outstanding 50-meter swimming pool and modern sports center, which includes a pair of tennis courts and even aerobics classes. Rooms are clean and, though basic, have the expected amenities. There's also a relaxing sauna with certain nights reserved for men, women, or both. The sports facilities may be closed in August. The neighborhood is nondescript, but the Old Town is only 10 minutes away by direct tram. ⊠ *Táboritská 23, Žižkov, 130 87* ☎ *267–092–212* 🖷 *222–713–315* ⊕ *www. hotelolsanka.cz* ⬭ *200 rooms* ⬭ *Restaurant, cable TV, tennis court, pool, health club, bar, Internet, meeting rooms, some pets allowed (fee); no a/c* ▤ *AE, MC, V* ¶⊙¶ *BP.*

EASTERN SUBURBS

$ 🏨 **Hotel Apollo.** This is a standard, no-frills, square-box hotel, where clean rooms come at a fair price. The primary flaw is its location: roughly 20 minutes away by metro and tram from the city center. On the plus side, the city looks lovely from this vantage point. ⊠ *Kubišova 23, Libeň, 182 00 Prague 8* ☎ *284–680–628* ⊕ *www.avetravel.cz* ⬭ *35 rooms* ⬭ *Restaurant, cable TV; no a/c* ▤ *MC, V* ¶⊙¶ *BP* Ⓜ *Line C: Nádraží Holešovice; then Tram 5, 14, or 17 to Hercovka stop.*

$ 🏨 **Hotel Astra.** This modern hotel is best for drivers coming into town from the east, although the nearby metro station puts it within fairly convenient striking distance from the center (about a 15-minute trip on the Metro). The neighborhood is quiet, if ordinary, and the rooms are more comfortable than most in this price range. ⊠ *Mukařovská 1740/ 18, Stodůlky, 100 00* ☎ *274–813–595* 🖷 *274–810–765* ⊕ *www. hotelastra.cz* ⬭ *43 rooms, 10 suites* ⬭ *Restaurant, cable TV, nightclub, meeting room, parking (fee), some pets allowed; no a/c* ▤ *AE, DC, MC, V* ¶⊙¶ *BP* Ⓜ *Line A: Skalka; then walk south on Na padesátém about 5 min to Mukařovská.*

$ 🏨 **Pension Louda.** The friendly owners of this family-run guesthouse go out of their way to make you feel welcome. Large, spotless rooms are an exceptional bargain, and although the place is in the suburbs, the hilltop site offers a stunning view of greater Prague from the south-facing rooms. ⊠ *Kubišova 10, Libeň, 182 00 Prague 8* ☎ *284–681–491* 🖷 *284–681–488* ⬭ *9 rooms* ⬭ *Gym, sauna; no a/c, no room TVs* ▤ *No credit cards* ¶⊙¶ *BP* Ⓜ *Line C: Nádraží Holešovice; then Tram 5, 14, or 17 to Hercovka stop.*

WESTERN SUBURBS

$$–$$$ 🏨 **Hotel Diplomat.** This sprawling complex opened in 1990 and remains popular with business travelers thanks to its location between the airport and downtown. From the hotel, you can easily reach the city center by metro. The modern rooms may not exude much character, but they are tastefully furnished and quite comfortable, if fairly standard in a chain-hotel kind of way. ⊠ *Evropská 15, Dejvice, 160 00* ☎ *296–559–111* 🖷 *296–559–215* ⊕ *www.diplomatpraha.cz* ⬭ *369 rooms, 13 suites* ⬭ *2 restaurants, café, cable TV with movies, gym, sauna,*

bar, nightclub, Internet, meeting room, parking (fee), no-smoking floors
▱ *AE, DC, MC, V* ⎩◯⎭ *BP* Ⓜ *Line A: Dejvická.*

¢ ▦ **Penzion Sprint.** Decent though plain rooms, most of which have their own bathroom (tiny), make the Sprint a fine choice. Those rooms with bathrooms also have TVs. This pension is on a quiet residential street, next to a large track and soccer field in the outskirts of Prague. It's about 20 minutes from the airport. Tram 18 rumbles directly to the Old Town from the Batérie stop, which is two blocks away; travel time is about 20 minutes. ✉ *Cukrovárnická 62, Střešovice, 160 00* ☎ *233–343–338* 🖷 *233–344–871* ⊕ *web.telecom.cz/penzionsprint* ⇥ *21 rooms, 6 with bath* ⚘ *Restaurant, some pets allowed; no a/c, no TV in some rooms* ▱ *AE, MC, V* ⎩◯⎭ *BP.*

NIGHTLIFE & THE ARTS

4

BEST LOCAL JAZZ
AghaRTA, *Nové Město* ⇨*p.100*

WHERE MODERN IS BETTER
Pivovarský dům, *Nové Město* ⇨*p.103*

BEST SPOT FOR LIVE BANDS AND DJS
Roxy, *Staré Město* ⇨*p.105*

TOP VENUE FOR CLASSICAL MUSIC
Rudolfinum, *Staré Město* ⇨*p.114*

NEO-RENAISSANCE GEM
Národní divadlo, where the outside is as good as
the shows inside, *Nové Město* ⇨*p.114*

BEST VENUE FOR MODERN DANCE
Archa Theater, *Nové Město* ⇨*p.122*

By Raymond
Johnston

THERE ARE TWO DISTINCT SIDES TO PRAGUE NIGHTLIFE. On the one hand, world-class orchestras and opera troupes inhabit some of the finest concert halls and opera houses to be found anywhere in Europe. Classical musicians in tuxedos can be seen lugging instrument cases home on the tram after a performance, just as the younger crowd, in the latest club fashions, is heading out to dance clubs in converted factories and renovated former movie houses to hear the latest house tracks. That's the other side of Prague nightlife. Tickets to both high-culture events and dance clubs are rather cheap by international standards. And it's not unusual to see a few of the same faces in the audience of an opera and then later in the week at a drum 'n' bass concert.

Many people think of Prague's entertainment scene as almost a museum of old-fashioned productions and uninspired rock or jazz cover bands. That hasn't really been the case since the late 1990s. In all aspects of the performing arts, new talent has been coming to Prague, and local performers have been making a mark on the world stage. Because of its location right in the center of Europe, Prague ends up drawing most major acts, from touring modern dance companies to the Rolling Stones, which pass through Prague on their European tours. Since people tend to buy tickets at the last minute, shows are seldom sold out.

If one thing makes Prague unique, it's the way old and new blend together, often within a few feet of each other. While some tourists go looking for the church where Mozart played the organ, others now try to find the hangouts mentioned in songs by Nick Cave or Ritchie Blackmore. And everything can be found in the same small area.

For details of cultural and nightlife events, look for the English-language newspaper the *Prague Post* or one of the multilingual monthly guides available at hotels, tourist offices, and newsstands.

NIGHTLIFE

Nightlife for many in Prague means little more than drinking. The choices for alcohol used to be extremely limited once you got past beer and wine, but now the same brands of liquor are available here as in most of Europe. A recent addition to the nightlife scene is the fancy cocktail bar, so you can easily find a perfect Manhattan, the Martinim, or mojito. What are becoming harder to find—at least in the downtown area—are traditional, smoky Czech pubs, with long wooden tables, early closing hours, and typewritten menus, but they are worth seeking out if you'd like to have an authentic, old-fashioned Czech experience. Before the Velvet Revolution, the city had a thriving jazz scene that still continues (then, rock was frowned on as being too decadent). Many of the jazz clubs are in evocative, historical cellars and tend to fill up early if the band is any good. The years since the Velvet Revolution have brought a lot of diversity and competition, which have helped to keep entertainment prices fairly stable while upgrading the overall quality. Nightclubs in residential areas often get started early, so you can often find live rock, punk, and heavy metal shows playing well before you would expect them in other major cities. The same clubs stay open with DJs way into the night,

Prague Nightlife

KEY

M Metro stations

i Tourist information

HRADČANY (Castle Area)

MALÁ STRANA (Lesser Quarter)

Funicular Railway

Petřín Gardens

0 — 250 yards
0 — 250 meters

Abaton **25**
AghaRTA **53**
Alcohol Bar **16**
Angel Club **9**
Baráčnická rychta **4**
Bugsy's **15**
Caffrey's Irish Bar **19**
Casino Palais Savarin . . . **34**

Double Trouble **33**
DownTown Café Praha **38**
Drakes **12**
Duhová čajovna **43**
Duplex **39**
Escape to Paradise **50**
Face to Face **24**

First & Last **14**
Friends **46**
Futurum **11**
Gay Club Stella **57**
Gejeezer **59**
Happy Day Casino **40**
Jágr's Sports Bar **56**
Jáma **51**
James Joyce Pub **30**

Jazzboat **13**
Jazz Club U staré paní . . . **32**
Karlovy Lázně **29**
Klub Delta **1**
Kolkovna **17**
Lucerna Music Bar **52**
M1 Secret Lounge **20**
Malostranská Beseda . . . **5**

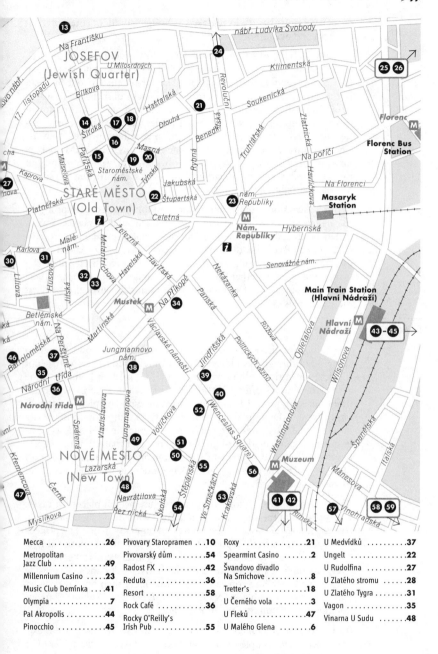

Mecca **26**

Metropolitan
Jazz Club **49**

Millennium Casino **23**

Music Club Demínka **41**

Olympia **7**

Pal Akropolis **44**

Pinocchio **45**

Pivovary Staropramen . . .**10**

Pivovarský dům **54**

Radost FX **42**

Reduta **36**

Resort **58**

Rock Café **36**

Rocky O'Reilly's
Irish Pub **55**

Roxy **21**

Spearmint Casino **2**

Švandovo divadlo
Na Smíchove **8**

Tretter's **18**

U Černého vola **3**

U Fleků **47**

U Malého Glena **6**

U Medvídků **37**

Ungelt **22**

U Rudolfina **27**

U Zlatého stromu **28**

U Zlatého Tygra **31**

Vagon **35**

Vinarna U Sudu **48**

though. Summer has the liveliest scene, bringing outdoor entertainment to parks and even to boats on the river.

The affordability of entertainment has a downside. Loads of tourists, mostly from Britain, come on special package tours that promise cheap beer and sleazy adult entertainment. They arrive throughout the year, but mostly in summer. Even before noon, packs of inebriated tourists in matching soccer jerseys can make walking past many parts of downtown very unpleasant. Nor are these rowdies all men. Bachelorette parties also draw loud groups of women in matching printed T-shirts. These groups are no longer as welcome as they used to be. Many bars now employ bouncers to keep away obviously inebriated groups, but the side-effect has been that particularly rowdy stag parties have resorted to drinking right on the street.

A word of caution. Adult entertainment establishments have sprung up to cater to this crowd, mostly on side streets around Wenceslas Square and in Žižkov. Although almost all forms of adult entertainment are legal in the Czech Republic, these places aren't always safe or cheap. Some establishments charge large sums of money for every quarter hour you stay in the place, whether you buy drinks and services or not. Others just charge outrageous fees for drinks. Professional thieves also frequent the same areas.

Discos

The number of discos in Prague is ever increasing and shows no sign of stopping. Although local house, techno, jungle, and trip-hop DJs—not to mention fairly well-known visitors—have made a home in some clubs, other places offer nights of campy Czech pop songs, which are often tunes from the 1960s British invasion with completely different Czech lyrics. Many discos open at 9 or 10 PM, but things don't really heat up until after midnight and then keep going until 4 or 5 AM. Unless there's a particularly well-known DJ, the cover charge is usually fairly nominal—30 Kč to 150 Kč. In summer, many of the nightclubs don't offer too much. The better DJs all flock to outdoor festivals held in smaller towns around the country.

Abaton. Abandoned factories like this one are perfect places for raves. Few signs point the way to this unadorned white building in an industrial area, and the street isn't even named on many maps. The place is only open once a week or so for techno parties with international DJs. Sometimes lineups of hardcore punk or heavy metal bands take the space over; less often it's world-music or alternative rock bands. The inside has several levels, and you can usually find more than one DJ or band playing at the same time. ⊠ *Na Košince 8, Libeň* ☏ *No phone* ⊕ *www. fanonline.cz/abaton* Ⓜ *Line B: Palmovka.*

Double Trouble. A vaulted basement that calls itself a "no blush music bar" encourages people to be a bit wild and dance on the tables. The younger crowd flocks to it. Those who want a mellower time think the club is aptly named and avoid it. The music varies but is seldom cutting edge. ✉ *Melantrichova 17, Staré Město* ☎ *221–632–414* ⊕ *www. doubletrouble.cz* Ⓜ *Line A: Staroměstská.*

Duplex. Mick Jagger booked this multilevel glass nightclub, which is on top of a building in the New Town's busiest shopping street, for his 60th birthday party. On weekend evenings, there's dancing and DJs with music that varies widely. Because of the location and aggressive marketing on the street level, the crowd is heavy with tourists who like to travel in large packs. ✉ *Václavské náměstí 21 Nové Město* ☎ *224–232–319* ⊕ *www.duplexduplex.cz* ⊕ *Line A or B: Můstek.*

Face to Face. With colored lights in the bar, two levels of dance floors, and recurring theme nights, this club in the middle of an island in the Vltava is going for the trendy disco crowd. Before thinking the island setting sounds romantic, you should be aware that the island is actually right by a very busy road, with entry to the club from the middle of a bridge. Scenes from the film *Everything Is Illuminated* were shot here. ✉ *Hlávkův most 1125, Štvanice ostrov* ☎ *607–180–331* ⊕ *www. nastvanici.cz* Ⓜ *Line C: Vltavská.*

Karlovy Lázně. A former bathhouse next to the Charles Bridge—its renovation left tiles and remnants from its former life still visible—claims on its gaudy neon sign to be the biggest club in central Europe. The four levels offer a variety of music from house to soul and old-fashioned disco. The crowd tends to be a mix of young locals sporting their club fashions as well as tourists. Lines to get in can be long on weekends. Bruce Willis once jammed with the band onstage when he was in town making a film. ✉ *Smetanovo nábřeží 198, Staré Město* ☎ *222–220–502* ⊕ *www.karlovylazne.cz* Ⓜ *Line A: Staroměstská.*

★ **Mecca.** This converted factory is the place you go to show off your expensive new club outfit. However, if you're not a night owl, be aware that the DJ action doesn't really get going until after midnight. Live acts tend to start around 10 PM. The club, which opened in 1998, has a good light system, a mirrored disco ball, and a downstairs lounge. Some nights feature live jazz or blues acts. ✉ *U Průhonu 3, Holesßovice* ☎ *283–870–522* ⊕ *www.mecca.cz* Ⓜ *Line C: Vltavská.*

Music Club Demínka. Although close to the city center, this club is just a little out of the way, on a side street, so people who come here tend to be regulars rather than those who were just passing by. Nothing much else distinguishes this renovated basement space with techno and pop DJs from several similar places that attract a mixed crowd of young locals, office workers, and tourists. ✉ *Škretova 1/a, Vinohrady* ☎ *603–185–699* ⊕ *www.deminka.com* Ⓜ *Line C: I. P. Pavlova.*

Radost FX. The city's original techno club still has a big following. Room on the dance floor can be kind of cramped, but other rooms have lots of seats and couches for hanging out. Posters for their theme nights can be found on lampposts and walls in the downtown area. ✉ *Bělehradská 120, Nové Město* ☎ *222–513–144* ⊕ *www.radostfx.cz* Ⓜ *Line C: I. P. Pavlova.*

Resort. Formerly called Industry 55, one of the less-touristy clubs near downtown is a converted cinema with fairly popular house and techno DJs. A redesign in 2004 added new bars and some sense of modern style, improving its appeal. On occasion there's a gay night. ☒ *Vinohradska 40, Vinohrady* ☎ *222–251–997* ⊕ *www.resort.cz* Ⓜ *Line A or C: Muzeum.*

U Zlatého stromu. You won't meet any local people at this somewhat cheesy nightclub with *Saturday Night Fever*–style lighted dance floors and, in some parts, bored go-go girls dancing and occasionally stripping. The same complex, right near the Charles Bridge, includes a restaurant and hotel. ☒ *Karlova 6, Staré Město* ☎ *222–220–441* ⊕ *www.zlatystrom. cz* Ⓜ *Line A: Staroměstská.*

Jazz Clubs

Jazz gained notoriety under the Communists as a subtle form of protest, and the city still has some great jazz clubs, featuring everything from swing to blues and modern. All listed clubs have a cover charge, usually around 100 Kč to 200 Kč.

Fodor'sChoice **AghaRTA.** The club itself is a small tunnel-shape affair, but many local
★ jazz acts call it home. The management also runs a jazz record label, and sell their CDs at the club's store. The place can't handle bigger acts, so the ongoing jazz festival often puts name acts into Lucerna Music Bar (see ⇨ Rock Clubs, *below*). Music starts around 9 PM, but come earlier to get a seat. ☒ *Krakovská 5, Nové Město* ☎ *222–211–275* ⊕ *www.agharta.cz* Ⓜ *Line A or C: Muzeum.*

Jazzboat. Be on time for the shows, as the ship does take off for a 2½-hour jazz cruise at the appointed hour. The Russian-made riverboat Kotva was refitted in 2001 and claims to be the fastest one on the Vltava. The bands are usually local. One obvious drawback is that if you don't like the show, it's very hard to leave. You can also buy food during the cruise, but no credit cards are accepted. ☒ *Usually takes off from pier No. 5, under Čechův most, Joefov* ☎ *731–183–180* ⊕ *www.jazzinprague. com* Ⓜ *Line A: Staroměstská.*

★ **Jazz Club U staré paní** (USP Jazz Lounge). This club, which is in a small hotel, hosts some of the better jazz acts in town. The interior is modern in design, which contrasts to the old-basement feel of most Old Town jazz clubs. DJs play after midnight. ☒ *Michalská 9, Staré Město* ☎ *224–228–090* ⊕ *www.jazzinprague.com* Ⓜ *Line A: Staroměstská.*

Metropolitan Jazz Club. Old-time swing and some blues are played by the house bands at this pleasant, unassuming courtyard club. It's pleasant if you just want live background music while you enjoy a few drinks. ☒ *Jungmannova 14, Nové Město* ☎ *224–947–777* ⊕ *mujweb.cz/www/ metropolitan* Ⓜ *Line A or B: Můstek.*

Reduta. The club's big claim to fame is that President Bill Clinton jammed on a saxophone here with Czech President Václav Havel in 1994. Pictures by the entrance commemorate the evening. That was a while ago, though. The club, founded in 1958, seems to have not been redecorated since the late 1980s and has garish furniture. It's also a little pricey and still holds onto the old-fashioned policy of forcing patrons to check all coats, just so they can get a few extra coins. ⊠ *Národní 20, Nové Město* ☎ *224–912–246* ⊕ *www.redutajazzclub.cz* Ⓜ *Line B: Národní třída.*

U Malého Glena. The historical basement of this building right off of Malostranské náměstí has a jazz-and-blues club with a number of decent house bands plus some visiting acts. Come early for a seat near the stage, as the tunnel-shape vault can be crowded. ⊠ *Karmelitská 23, Malá Strana* ☎ *257–531–717* ⊕ *www.malyglen.cz* Ⓜ *Line A: Malostranská.*

Ungelt. Hidden in the side streets behind Old Town Square, this basement has been around since the 15th century and has been a club since 2000. The house bands are pretty good and play jazz, blues, or fusion depending on the night. Few local jazz fans patronize the place, though, because it's in the heart of the historical area. ⊠ *Týn 2,, Staré Město* ☎ *224–895–748* ⊕ *www.jazzblues.cz* Ⓜ *Line A: Staroměstská.*

Pubs & Bars

Bars and lounges are not traditional Prague fixtures, but bars catering to a young crowd have elbowed their way in over the past few years. Still, most social life of the drinking variety takes place in pubs (*pivnice* or *hospody*), which are liberally sprinkled throughout the city's neighborhoods. Tourists are welcome to join in the evening ritual of sitting around large tables and talking, smoking, and drinking beer. There are plenty of popular pubs in the city center, all of which can get impossibly crowded.

Alcohol Bar. One of the largest selections of liquor, including 70 types of whiskey and some really rare rums, can be found in an upscale bar right near Old Town Square. Small tables and usually unobtrusive music make it a perfect spot for an intimate conversation. A bouncer by the door discourages large, boisterous groups from trying to enter. ⊠ *Dušní 6, Staré Město* ☎ *224–811–744* ⊕ *www.alcoholbar.cz* Ⓜ *Line A: Staroměstská.*

Bugsy's. This popular American-style cocktail bar was remodeled in 2002 and given a modern steel-and-glass, lights-in-the-bar look. The list of drinks has all the expected favorites, and sometimes there's live music. ⊠ *Pařížská 10, enter on Kostečná, Josefov* ☎ *224–810–287* ⊕ *www. bugsysbar.com* Ⓜ *Line A: Staroměstská.*

Caffey's Irish Bar. Caffey's is one of the less rowdy Irish bars in town, probably because it's a bit more expensive. The menu offers a full Irish breakfast in addition to burgers and salads. On St. Patrick's day, this bar is the headquarters of organized celebrations. ⊠ *Staroměstské náměstí, Staré Město* ☎ *224–828–031* ⊕ *www.caffreys.cz* Ⓜ *Line A: Staroměstská.*

First & Last. Fans of Nick Cave and the Bad Seeds, who might be looking for the Thirsty Dog, a grungy pub that Cave mentioned in a song, will be disappointed. The Thirsty Dog is gone, now, and the space has

CloseUp

PUB ETIQUETTE

Before venturing into a pub in Prague, it's best to familiarize yourself with a few points of pub etiquette. First, always ask if a chair is free before sitting down (Je tu volno?). To order a beer (pivo), do not wave the waiter down or shout across the room; he will often assume you want beer—most pubs serve one brand—and bring it over to you without asking. He will also bring subsequent rounds to the table without asking. To refuse, just shake your head or say "no thanks" (ne, děkuju). At the end of the evening, usually around 10:30 or 11, the waiter will come to tally the bill. In a traditional pub, for each beer the waiter will make one mark on a strip of paper. Don't lose the paper or doodle on it. Also, it's a good idea to ask how much each beer is before ordering and to keep track of how many you had. Waiters are adept at doctoring bills, especially for large groups. For tipping, the common practice is to round up the bill slightly when paying, rather than leaving extra money on the table. Only give a Western-style tip for exceptional service.

been spruced up to compete with other downtown pubs. The prices for food—pizza, Mexican specialties, and sandwiches—and drink are fairly reasonable to accommodate the young crowd that still goes here, and the music selection runs toward alternative rock. Beware of the spiral staircase after a few drinks. ⊠ *Elišky Krásnohorské 5, Staré Město* ☎ *222–310–039* Ⓜ *Line A: Staroměstská.*

Jágr's Sports Bar. The famous Czech hockey player runs a bar with many large TV screens and a decent menu. A roulette wheel is available, but watching sports is the main attraction. Celebrity guests have included Wesley Snipes and Michael Johnson. ⊠ *Václavské náměstí 56, Nové Město* ☎ *224–032–481* ⊕ *www.jagrsportbar.cz* Ⓜ *Line A or C: Muzeum.*

Jáma (The Hollow). An outdoor beer garden hidden from passersby on the street provides a nice temporary refuge from the noisy downtown crowds. The indoor part is decorated with old rock-and-roll posters. Beer and hard cider on tap go with Mexican food and some pretty good burgers. Internet access is available here for a reasonable price, and Wi-Fi access is free. ⊠ *V Jámě 7, Nové Město* ☎ *224–222–383* ⊕ *www. jamapub.cz* Ⓜ *Line A or B: Můstek.*

James Joyce Pub. An authentically Irish pub (it has Irish owners, who also own Caffey's) with Guinness on tap and excellent food of the fish-and-chips persuasion is a favorite hangout of large groups of young male tourists. ⊠ *Liliová 10, Staré Město* ☎ *224–248–793* ⊕ *www.jamesjoyce. cz* Ⓜ *Line A: Staroměstská.*

Kolkovna. Unpasteurized Pilsner beer is poured in an upscale pub that tries to capture a between-the-wars look. The name refers to tax stamps, which used to be printed here in the 1920s. On weekends, the place can be very crowded, and reservations are needed even for a small table near the bar. Czech food is also available. It has the same owners as Olympia. ✉ *V Kolkovně 8, Josefov* ☎ *224-819-701* ⊕ *www.kolkovna.cz* Ⓜ *Line A: Staroměstská.*

M1 Secret Lounge. Movie stars in town for a shoot have been known to stop by this slightly hidden lounge on a side street in Old Town. People like to dress up in their club fashions to pose in the sleek, under-decorated science-fiction setting while sipping their cocktails. ✉ *Masná 1, Staré Město* ☎ *221-874-256* Ⓜ *Line A: Staroměstská.*

Olympia. A hot spot from the 1930s has been returned to its former glory and provides a somewhat romanticized but enjoyable take on a Czech pub. The interior is quite large, with 250 seats, but still the place gets very busy. Like its sister pub Kolkovna, it serves unpasteurized Pilsner beer. ✉ *Vitežná 7, Malá Strana* ☎ *251-511-079* ⊕ *www.olympia-restaurant.cz* Ⓜ *Line B: Anděl.*

Fodor'sChoice
★ **Pivovarský dům.** Open since 1998, this brewpub offers less history but better beer than many of its rivals. The dark, light, and seasonal microbrew beers are outstanding. A small menu of Czech standards is printed on the placemats. The food is good, but a slight letdown when compared to the beer. Fermenting beer can be viewed through a window. ✉ *Lípová 15, Nové Město* ☎ *296-216-666* Ⓜ *Line A or B: Můstek.*

★ **Pivovary Staropramen** (Staropramen Brewery). For beer, why not go directly to the source? Staropramen means old source, and it's one of the most ubiquitous beers in the city. The brewery has its own bar that serves several varieties of beer including one that is only sold at the brewery. With advance reservations, tours are available. ✉ *Nádražní 84, Smíchov* ☎ *257-191-255 restaurant, 257-191-402 tours* ⊕ *www.pivovary-staropramen.cz* Ⓜ *Line B: Anděl.*

Rocky O'Reillys Irish Pub. Stag parties are welcome—if they keep it down to roar—at Prague's largest Irish pub, which also shows soccer matches on TV. In the cooler months, there's a burning fireplace. The decor is meant to suggest parts of an Irish village. Unless you're a soccer fan, it's best not to go when games are being shown on TV; other times, it's a mellower here. Weekday lunchtime is also much quieter than the evening. ✉ *Štepanská 32, Nové Město* ☎ *222-231-060* ⊕ *www.rockyoreillys.cz* Ⓜ *Line A or B: Můstek.*

Tretter's. The lost elegance of the 1930s, with clean lines on dark wood, is re-created in a bar that serves Manhattans, martinis, and other classic cocktails, sometimes with live jazz in the background. The staff is professional and competent. ✉ *V Kolkovně 3, Josefov* ☎ *224-811-165* ⊕ *www.tretters.cz* Ⓜ *Line A: Staroměstská.*

U Černého vola (At the Black Ox). The last old-fashioned pub in the Prague Castle area has long tables, a limited food selection, and cheap beer. It's almost impossible to find very many seats together at any time, though. Among the pub's many fans is Terry Jones of Monty Python fame. ✉ *Loretánské náměstí 1, Hradčandská* ☎ *220-513-481* Ⓜ *Line A: Hradčandská.*

U Fleků. The oldest brewpub in Europe has been open since 1499 and makes a tasty, if overpriced, dark beer. A steady stream of tours often makes it hard to find a seat. Cabaret shows have been added to the entertainment. A brewery museum (phone for reservations) opened in 1999. Beware of waiters trying to put unordered shots of liquor on your table. If you don't insist they remove them right away, they will be on your bill. ✉ *Křemencova 11, Nové Město* ☎ *224–934–019* ⊕ *www. ufleku.cz* Ⓜ *Line B: Karlovo náměstí.*

U Medvídků. A former brewery dating as far back as the 15th century now serves draft Budvar shipped directly from České Budějovice. Reservations are recommended as organized tours often fill the entire bar. The interior, including the tap, have a turn-of-the-20th-century flavor. ✉ *Na Perštýně 7, Staré Město* ☎ *224–211–916* ⊕ *www.umedvidku.cz* Ⓜ *Line B: Národní třída.*

U Rudolfina. Some people claim the way the beer is tapped here makes it the best in town, which probably explains the constant crowds. This was one of the first places to offer unpasteurized beer from tanks, rather than kegs. And the place still retains it old-fashioned charm, making it one of the best authentic Czech pubs in the heavily touristed area. Groups should make reservations, as whole free tables are rare. ✉ *Křížovnická 10, Josefov* ☎ *222–313–088* Ⓜ *Line A: Staroměstská.*

U Zlatého Tygra. The last of the old, smokey, surly pubs in the Old Town is famed as one of the three best Prague pubs for Pilsner Urquell. It also used to be a hangout for such raffish types as the writer Bohumil Hrabal, who died in 1997. Reservations are not accepted, so the best bet is to go in off hours. ✉ *Husova 17, Staré Město* ☎ *222–221–111* Ⓜ *Line A: Staroměstská.*

Vinarna U Sudu. While Prague is beer territory, a few places honor that other camp: wine. A mazelike, multilevel cellar makes a large wine bar in a baroque building. This is usually one of the first places to serve burčák, newly fermented grape juice used to make wine, in the fall. ✉ *Vodičkova 10, Nové Město* ☎ *222–232–207* Ⓜ *Line B: Karlovo náměstí.*

Rock & Live Music Clubs

Prague's rock, alternative, and world-music scene is thriving, although many of the concerts tend to begin early. Rock bands on reunion tours find enthusiastic crowds in clubs and arenas. Cover bands are pretty good (Lou Reed once mistook a recording by the local Velvet Underground's cover band for the real thing). World-music, especially Romany bands, usually draw big crowds and often sell out.

Baráčnická rychta. A patriotic society that formed in 1874 used this old-fashioned pub as a meeting hall. The upstairs has a pleasant beer garden with decent prices for the area. Downstairs is a concert venue that often hosts visiting world-music bands mixed in with local rock and funk. ✉ *Tržiště 23, Malá Strana* ☎ *257–532–461* ⊕ *www.baracnickarychta. cz* Ⓜ *Line A: Malostranská.*

Futurum. Video parties and punk or goth bands make the most of the schedule at this out-of-the-way club with a good video and sound system, 1950s sci-fi decor, and lots of beer-stained couches. ⊠ *Zborovská 7, Smíchov* ☏ *257–328–571* ⊕ *www.musicbar.cz* Ⓜ *Line B: Anděl.*

Klub Delta. Underground Czech bands quickly found a home here, far from the center of town, right after the Velvet Revolution. Although it's hard to find, the trip to this club can be rewarding since new, edgy bands share the program with famous dissident bands from the 1970s. ⊠ *Vlastina 886, Dejvice* ☏ *233–312–443* ⊕ *www.noise.cz/delta* Ⓜ *Line A: Dejvice, then a tram or bus.*

Lucerna Music Bar. Rock bands on the comeback trail like Slade, touring blues greats, plus Beatles and Rolling Stones cover bands make up the live schedule. Another big draw are the nights of 1980s or '90s music videos or campy old Czech pop songs. ⊠ *Vodičkova 36, Nové Město* ☏ *224–217–108* ⊕ *www.musicbar.cz* Ⓜ *Line A or B: Můstek.*

Malostranská Beseda. For a change, here's a club that's upstairs rather than in the basement. The building was a popular meeting place for writers and other artists in the 19th century. Over the years it's been a theater and since 1971 a folk and country club. Blues, rock, and ska bands make it onto the program these days. ⊠ *Malostranské nám. 21, Malá Strana* ☏ *257–532–092* ⊕ *www.mb.muzikus.cz* Ⓜ *Line A: Malostranská.*

★ **Palác Akropolis.** The city's best live music club is in Žižkov, its hippest neighborhood. When shows are sold out, though, this place can be pretty packed. The venue is home to an ongoing world-music festival called United Colors of Akropolis as well the ongoing EuroConections festival, which showcases mainly French bands. The main room closes at 10 PM due to noise concerns. DJs play in the two side bars until late in the evening. ⊠ *Kubelíkova 27, Žižkov* ☏ *299–330–913* ⊕ *www. palacakropolis.cz* Ⓜ *Line A: Náměstí Jiřího z Poděbrad.*

Rock Café. A somewhat dark and austere room, which tends to get pretty hot when it's full of people, hosts punk and alternative rock acts with the occasional screening of a movie on video. The bar is painted in orange and yellow, suggestive of giant glass of a whiskey, whose logo is featured prominently. ⊠ *Národní 20, Nové Město* ☏ *224–914–416* ⊕ *www.rockcafe.cz* Ⓜ *Line B: Národní třída.*

FodorśChoice **Roxy.** Part nightclub, part performance space, part Internet café, Roxy
★ is a residence for DJs and a popular venue for electronica and touring cult bands. The large former theater has a comfortable, lived-in feel. Complaints from neighbors have forced the owners to start and end live concerts relatively early. All exits from the club are final, and patrons are encouraged not to hang around the area, also because of noise. Upstairs, the NoD space has all manner of bizarre acts. Monday is free. ⊠ *Dlouhá 33, Staré Město* ☏ *224–826–296* ⊕ *www.roxy.cz* Ⓜ *Line B: Náměstí Republiky.*

Švandovo divadlo Na Smichove. Although primarily the programming in this theater consists of Czech-language plays, interesting avant-garde bands occasionally fill gaps in the schedule. The ongoing series of Scenic Interviews sometimes features English-speaking celebrities like Suzanne Vega. ⊠ *Štefánikova 57, Smíchov* ☎ *234–651–111* ⊕ *www. svandovodivadlo.cz* Ⓜ *Line B: Anděl.*

Vagon. When it fills up, this long and narrow room offers only a few good spots to actually see the band that's playing, so video projectors also show the action on the walls toward the back. The emphasis is on Czech rock bands, with concerts starting at 9 and DJs weekends at midnight. When the occasional touring rock or punk band comes here, the club can easily sell out. ⊠ *Národní třída 25, Staré Město* ☎ *221–085–599* ⊕ *www.vagon.cz* Ⓜ *Line B: Národní třída.*

Gay & Lesbian

There are a few prominent, openly gay, public figures in Prague, and registered partnerships have been seriously discussed several times in the Parliament. Overall, though, the gay community is fairly invisible, and the club scene depends very much on word of mouth. Clubs—at least on the street level—are fairly discreet, and a rainbow-color sign might be the only clue that a bar caters to a gay clientele. For more information on the Prague gay scene, check out the Web sites ⊕ prague.gayguide. net and ⊕ www.gay.cz.

Angel Club. Local gay men and women flock to this disco on a side street near the top of a hill. Tuesday is karaoke night, and the playlist has a good selection of Czech pop among the international hits. ⊠ *Kmochova 8, Smíchov* ☎ *256–316–127* ⊕ *www.clubangel.cz* Ⓜ *Line B: Anděl.*

DownTown Café Praha. Fresh fruit beverages, coffee drinks, sandwiches, and salads are available in this gay-friendly café. On Saturday, warm-up parties feature popular local DJs and alcoholic and nonalcoholic cocktails in the early evening before the other clubs get going. ⊠ *Jungmannovo náměstí 21, Nové Město* ☎ *724–111–276* ⊕ *www.downtowncafe.cz* Ⓜ *Line A or B: Můstek.*

Drakes. The admission price allows for multiple visits over 24 hours to this club, which is owned by gay porn director William Higgins and is open around the clock. Theme parties take place on a regular basis so be sure the check the schedule. The drinks and admission are pricey so most of the clientele is tourists. ⊠ *Zborovaská 50, Smíchov* ☎ *257–326–828* ⊕ *www.drakes.cz* Ⓜ *Line B: Anděl.*

Duhová čajovna. The relaxed teahouse sometimes has live music along with a selection of nonalcoholic beverages and light snacks. ⊠ *Chlumova 13, Žižkov* ☎ *608–521–821* ⊕ *www.duhova-cajovna.cz* Ⓜ *Line A: Náměstí Jiřího z Poděbrad.*

Escape to Paradise. This centrally located disco is popular with a primarily male clientele. Dinner in the restaurant is available from 7 PM, but the dancing and shows with go-go dancers don't really get going until midnight. ⊠ *V Jámě 8, Nové Město* ☎ *602–403–744* ⊕ *www.volny.cz/ escapeclub* Ⓜ *Line A or B: Můstek.*

Friends. This friendly bar in Old Town serves reasonably priced beer—and Western-priced mixed drinks—in a fairly roomy cellar space. There's plenty of seating most weeknights, but it does get busy on weekends. Videos play every night, and there's a DJ after 10 on weekends. Dancing is on a small dance floor. No cover. ⊠ *Bartolomějská 11, Nove Mesto* ☎ *224–236–772* Ⓜ *Line A or B: Můstek.*

Gay Club Stella. There are no DJs, but you will find a pleasant, homey bar with a few comfortable places to sit and chat. ⊠ *Lužická 10, Vinohrady* ⊕ *stellaclub.webpark.cz* Ⓜ *Line A: Náměstí Mirú.*

★ **Gejzeer.** One of the bigger gay clubs in town tends to open and stay open very late. The music is fairly cutting-edge, and the lighting and sound systems rival those in other popular discos. Although the disco does cater to a gay male crowd, other people have been known to go just for the music. ⊠ *Vinohradská 40, Vinohrady* ☎ *222–516–036* ⊕ *www.gejzeer.cz* Ⓜ *Line A or C: Muzeum.*

Pinocchio. Professional drag shows and even magicians sometimes come to this disco bar right at the edge of Žižkov. The complex also has a small pension and caters mostly to men. ⊠ *Seifertova 3, Žižkov* ☎ *221–710–773* ⊕ *www.volny.cz/pinocchio* Ⓜ *Line B or C: Florenc.*

Casinos

Gambling is legal in Prague. Many bars, especially those open around the clock, have a few slot machines and are distinguishable by a sign that says *herna bar.* For those who want a little more action, most of the big hotels provide some sort of gaming room. A few casinos downtown stand out among the rest.

Casino Palais Savarin. Old World charm and high betting limits are the trademarks of this gambling hall in a historical rococo palace. A private room is also available for those who wish to go incognito. Games include roulette and poker, plus slot machines. This one is the destination of choice for local high rollers. ⊠ *Na Příkopě 10, Nové Město* ☎ *224–221–636* ⊕ *www.czechcasinos.cz* Ⓜ *Line A or B: Můstek.*

Happy Day Casino. A little piece of Las Vegas seems to have gotten lost in the center of Prague. This casino has dozens of slot machines but just a few tables, plus blinking lights and some glitz. You can't walk past the place and not notice it. ⊠ *Václavské náměstí 35, Nové Město* ☎ *224–233–506* Ⓜ *Line A or B: Můstek.*

Millennium Casino. The modern and understated casino is near several upscale hotels. Your gaming choices include video slot machines and table games, including blackjack. ⊠ *V Celnici 10, Nové Město* ☎ *224–231–886* ⊕ *www.millenniumcasino.cz* Ⓜ *Line B: Náměstí Republiky.*

Spearmint Casino. This English-style casino has a view, if you care to look. Located right on the waterfront, its terrace is a good place to watch the lights of the Old Town reflected in the river. Roulette, blackjack, and pontoon are among the games available. The building was once a public bathhouse that has been heavily restored after the floods of 2002.

The casino also includes an adjacent "gentlemen's club," which offers adult entertainment in a fairly classy setting and welcomes stag parties. ✉ *U Plovárny 8, Malá Strana* ☎ *257–535–755* ⊕ *www.spearmintcasino. cz* Ⓜ *Line A: Malostranská.*

PERFORMING ARTS

Czech composers may be thought of as a bit of a footnote in the history of classical music, but in Prague, hardly a program is produced that doesn't include some Dvořák, Smetana, or Martinů; modern music programs often include Petr Eben, a living Czech composer. However tangential the native contribution, Prague played an important role in the development of classical music in Europe. Famous composers including Mozart, Beethoven, Liszt, Chopin, and Haydn all spent time in Prague and presented major works here as well. Usually they found the environment less stressful than Berlin or Vienna. Places where the composers performed still make note of that fact. The arts got a big boost during the late 1800s, when the national-awakening movement inspired the Czechs to build a National Theater (Národní divadlo) to compete with theaters that favored German-language productions. Composers and authors began to explore Czech mythology and history for themes to use in operas, plays, and classical music.

These days Prague has some of the most impressive venues for classical music in Europe, and they are in remarkably good condition. Prague escaped major damage in both World Wars, and has had few other catastrophes. The major classical venues were all built while Prague was part of the Austro-Hungarian Empire, and they reflect the opulence of the era. Only a few places were built between World War II and the fall of communism, and they are much less impressive functionalist structures. New venues such as Sazka Arena stress security over elegance. The cultural year has quite a few predictable highlights in the form of recurring festivals such as the Prague Spring and Prague Autumn festivals.

Live theater has had a long, fruitful history in Prague, with Shakespeare a surprisingly popular choice. Most theater is performed in Czech, but a few small local companies put on an occasional off-Broadway–style show in English, and some theater festivals have visiting companies. Národní divadlo (National Theater) has made a recent effort to add some modern dance to the ballet evergreens. Several other venues specialize in modern dance and physical theater, which are much less reliant on language and may be of more interest to non-Czech speakers.

Most people dress up for major classical concerts and the opera, with a jacket and tie for men and an evening dress for women being pretty much expected at most venues except those that cater exclusively to tourists. The Národní divadlo generally employs a no-jeans dress code.

FESTIVALS & EVENTS   One of the largest film festivals in Central Europe, **Febiofest** (⊕ www. febiofest.cz) runs for about a week at the end of January and start of February. Films—both premieres and retrospectives—come from virtually all over the world, and a number of directors and stars including Roman

Polanski have come to introduce their work. As a side to the festival, world-music bands also perform. The festival started in 1993 and has changed homes several times, but most recently has been in Slovanský dům.

The first sign of the coming of spring is the annual **Matějská pouť** (St. Matthew's Fair) (⊕ www.incheba.cz), which starts on February 24 every year and runs through the middle of April in Výstaviště. Although it started as a religious event in the Middle Ages, now it has carnival rides, food, and other family fun.

Fans of foreign films have a chance to catch up on recent English-sub-titled efforts in **Days of European Film** (⊕ www.eurofilmfest.cz), which happens every March in Prague and Brno. Approximately 10 days of films play at two cinemas; there are also some visiting guests. The Lucerna and Aero in Prague have been used most recently. One high-light is an all-night movie marathon.

Fans of documentaries look forward to the **One World Human Rights Film Festival** (Jeden svět; ⊕ www.oneworld.cz). The festival runs at various theaters, usually including Lucerna and Archa, at the end of April. For convenience, films in English or with English subtitles are grouped to-gether in one theater.

Modern physical theater is showcased in the **4+4 Days in Motion** (4+4 dny v pohybu; ⊕ www.ctyridny.cz), which often has shows in very un-usual venues like an old brickworks or disused factory as well as main-stream theaters. The festival usually happens at the end of May.

Romany (Gypsy) bands are becoming a hot item in the world-music scene. There's quite a bit of regional diversity in the music, and some groups now play jazz fusion with a Romany influence. The **Khamoro Festival** (⊕ www.khamoro.cz) gathers bands from across Europe at the end of May.

Lots of bands and theater troupes descend on the grounds of a mental health institution for **Mezi ploty** (✉ Ústavní ulice, Bohnice ⊕ www.meziploty.cz). The two-day festival has some of the best local bands, but be aware that only nonalcoholic beer can be sold on the grounds. The festival takes place at the end of May.

Since 1946, **Prague Spring** (Pražské jaro; ⊕ www.festival.cz) has been the main event of the classical season and usually runs from the end of May to the start of June. Conductors such as Leonard Bernstein and Sir Charles Mackerras have been among the guests. Important anniversaries of major composers, especially Czech ones, are marked with special con-certs. Orchestra concerts, operas, and church recitals make up the bulk of the schedule. Popular music, often in unusual venues, has been added to make the festival accessible to everybody. Bedřich Smetana's *Ma vlást* usually opens the festival. Major events can sell out months in advance.

Prague is known for its tradition of puppet theater, and puppets of var-ious qualities are ubiquitous at street markets. Visiting puppeteers put on shows in the annual **World Festival of Puppet Art** (⊕ www.puppetart.com), which runs from the end of May to the beginning of June at var-ious theaters.

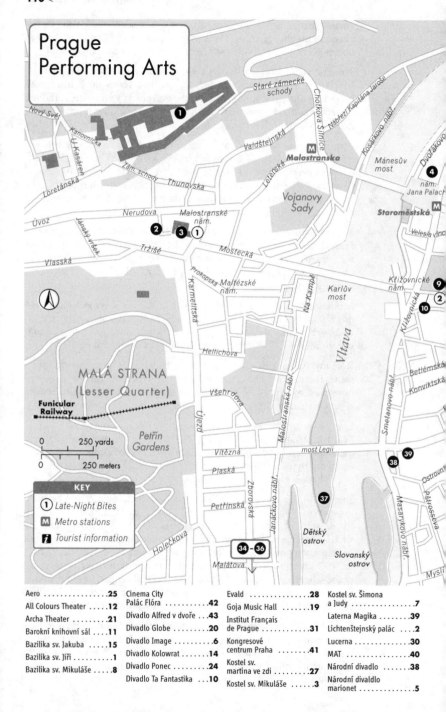

Aero **25**

All Colours Theater **12**

Archa Theater **21**

Barokní knihovní sál **11**

Bazilika sv. Jakuba **15**

Bazilika sv. Jiří **1**

Bazilika sv. Mikuláše ...**8**

Cinema City
Palác Flóra **42**

Divadlo Alfred v dvoře ...**43**

Divadlo Globe **20**

Divadlo Image **6**

Divadlo Kolowrat **14**

Divadlo Ponec **24**

Divadlo Ta Fantastika ...**10**

Evald **28**

Goja Music Hall **19**

Institut Français
de Prague **31**

Kongresové
centrum Praha **41**

Kostel sv.
martina ve zdi **27**

Kostel sv. Mikuláše **3**

Kostel sv. Šimona
a Judy **7**

Laterna Magika **39**

Lichtenštejnský palác **2**

Lucerna **30**

MAT **40**

Národní divadlo **38**

Národní divadlo
marionet **5**

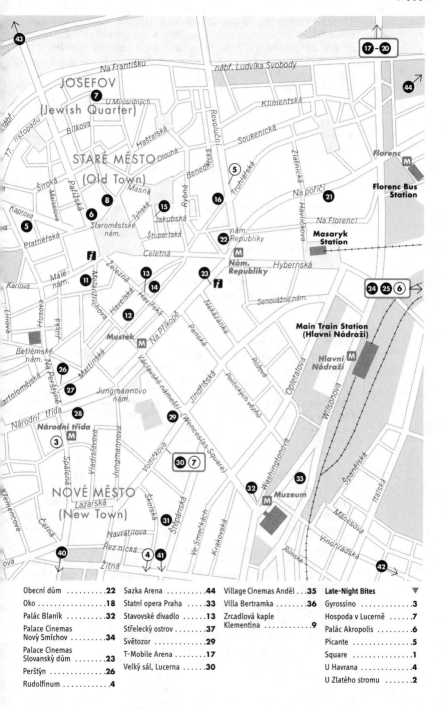

Obecní dům	22	Sazka Arena	44	Village Cinemas Anděl	35	**Late-Night Bites** ▼
Oko	18	Statní opera Praha	33	Villa Bertramka	36	Gyrossino	3
Palác Blaník	32	Stavovské divadlo	13	Zrcadlová kaple		Hospoda v Lucerně	7
Palace Cinemas		Střelecký ostrov	37	Klementina	9	Palác Akropolis	6
Nový Smíchov	34	Světozor	29			Picante	5
Palace Cinemas		T-Mobile Arena	17			Square	1
Slovanský dům	23	Velký sál, Lucerna	30			U Havrana	4
Perštýn	26					U Zlatého stromu	2
Rudolfinum	4						

There isn't much English-language theater in Prague. The annual **Prague Fringe Festival** (⊕ www.praguefringe.com), which began in 2002, has visiting acts from similar festivals in Scotland, New Zealand, Australia, and the United States. So far, each year has been bigger in terms of offerings than the one before. The venues change from year to year, but the festival always takes place in early June.

Modern dance is very popular in Prague and poses no language barrier. The monthlong **Tanec Praha** (⊕ www.tanecpha.cz) festival takes place in June and brings renowned companies from all over the world to several venues in the city.

The most important film festival is the Czech Republic in the spa town formerly known as Carlsbad. The **Karlovy Vary International Film Festival** (⊕ www.kviff.com) ranks with Cannes, Berlin, and Venice among important European festivals. Films compete for a main prize called the Crystal Globe. Visitors to the festival, which happens at the start of July, have included Lauren Bacall, Morgan Freeman, Michael Douglas, Gus van Sant, and Ivan Reitman.

The lovely organ in Bazilika sv. Jakuba attracts noted international musicians for the annual **International Organ Festival** (⊠ Malá Štuparská, Staré Město ⊕ www.auditeorganum.cz/festival.html), which runs from August to September with weekly concerts.

Young international classical musicians perform at **Mladá Praha** (Young Prague; ⊕ www.mladapraha.cz). A committee in Japan helps to search for Asian participants and some musicians come from the Americas and the rest of Europe as well. The festival runs from the end of August through early September, with some events out of town.

Beginning just after the Velvet Revolution, the annual **Prague Autumn** (Pražský podzim; ⊕www.pragueautumn.cz) emphasizes Czech composers and contemporary music. Visiting orchestras have included the BBC Scottish Symphony and Russian Philharmonia. The festival takes place in the second half of September.

TICKETS   The concierge at your hotel may be able to reserve tickets for you. Otherwise, for the cheapest tickets go directly to the theater box office a few days in advance or immediately before a performance. Ticket agencies may charge higher prices than box offices do. American Express offices sell tickets to many concerts.

Bohemia Ticket International. This agency specializes in mostly classical music, theater, and black-light theater. ⊠ *Na Příkopě 16, Nové Město* ☎ *224–215–031* ⊕ *www.ticketsbti.cz* ⊠ *Malé náměstí 13, Staré Město* ☎ *224–227–832.*

Sazka Ticket. The owners of Sazka Arena, major venue for large rock concerts and sporting events, distribute their own tickets exclusively through betting shops and street newspaper stands throughout the city. They sometimes have tickets for other events as well. ⊠ *Ocelářská 10, Vysočansky* ☎ *266–121–122* ⊕ *www.sazkaticket.cz.*

MOZART IN PRAGUE

ONSIDERING THAT WOLFGANG AMADEUS MOZART *visited Prague only four times, he left quite an impression on the city.* On his first trip, in early 1787, he visited Count Thun and his wife, whom he knew from Vienna. They lived in what is now the British Embassy in Malá Strana. Mozart stayed at an inn on Celetná Street. During this trip he conducted his Prague Symphony and a day later, on January 20, a performance of his opera The Marriage of Figaro, which had a more successful run in Prague than in Vienna. One legend from this time has the host of a party inviting him an hour before all the other guests and making him compose new dances for the evening.

His second trip is the most famous. The maestro came to visit composer F. X. Dušek and his new wife, opera singer Josephine, toward the end of 1787 at their rural villa Bertramka, although he also kept rooms at an inn at Uhelný třída. After several missed deadlines, he conducted the world premiere of Don Giovanni on October 29 at Stavovské divadlo. He tried out a number of church organs in his spare time.

His third visit was just a pass-through, but the fourth and final trip came just months before he died in 1791. He promised to write a new opera to mark the coronation of Leopold II as king of Bohemia. Unfortunately, La Clemenza di Tito, which premiered at the Stavovské divadlo on September 6, was written quickly and was not as well received as Don Giovanni. Once news of his death on December 5 reached Prague, his friends staged a memorial service that ended with church bells ringing all over town.

Ticketportal. The agency sells tickets for major classical and theater venues; they also provide tickets through some travel agents. On rare occasion, they have exclusive rights to a show. ⊠ *Politických vězňů 15, Nové Město* ☎ *224–091–437* ⊕ *www.ticketportal.cz.*

Ticketpro. The main outlet for tickets to all shows and clubs, especially stadium concerts, in Prague has several branches across the city. ⊠ *Salvátorská 10, Staré Město* ☎ *224–814–020* ⊠ *Rytířská 12, Staré Město* ⊠ *Václavské náměstí 38, Nové Město* ⊕ *www.ticketpro.cz.*

Ticketstream. Hotel desks and some restaurants carry tickets for classical and other events via this agency. ⊠ *Koubkova 8, Nové Město* ☎ *224–263–049* ⊕ *www.ticketstream.cz.*

Major Performance Venues

Divadlo Kolowrat. The least significant of three stages run by the National Theater features more experimental works and chamber operas that usually require a good grasp of Czech. The theater is upstairs in a baroque palace with Renaissance wooden ceilings that are worth seeing. ⊠ *Ovocný trh 6, Staré Město* ☎ *224–901–487* ⊕ *www.narodni-divadlo.cz* Ⓜ *Line A or B: Můstek.*

Kongresové centrum Praha (Congress Center). The former Palace of Culture, built in 1981, has never found a place in people's hearts. The large, functionalist, multipurpose building has several performance spaces that can seat thousands, but overall it has a very sterile feel. Plays—usually musicals—and special events come here. ⊠ *Třída 5. kvetna 65, Nusle* ⊕ *www.kcp.cz* Ⓜ *Line C: Vyšehrad.*

Lichtenštejnský palác (Lichtenstein Palace). The home of HAMU, the Czech music academy, this baroque palace from the 1790s has the large Martinů Hall for professional concerts and a smaller gallery that is sometimes used for student recitations. The courtyard sometimes has music in the summer months. ⊠ *Malostranské náměstí 13, Malá Strana* 🕾 *257–534–206* Ⓜ *Line A: Malostranská.*

FodorśChoice **Národní divadlo** (National Theater). The cornerstone of this neo-Renaissance building was laid in 1868 and the building was completed in 1881, only to almost immediately fall victim to a fire set by careless workmen. With a few modifications it was quickly rebuilt with murals and sculptures on historical themes by famous artists of their day. The theater has lost none of its late-19th-century splendor. The money for building came from coin collections. Foundation stones from various regions can be seen in the basement during the intermission. ⊠ *Národní třída. 2, Nové Město* 🕾 *224–901–448* ⊕ *www.narodni-divadlo.cz* Ⓜ *Line B: Národní třída.*

★ **Obecní dům** (Municpal House). Completed in 1911 on the site of a former royal residence, the Municipal House is where Czech politicians declared an independent Czechoslovakia in 1918. The interior has murals, reliefs, and glasswork by several artists, including Alfons Mucha. An expensive restoration in the mid-1990s has restored the impressive interior to its original condition. The main concert hall, a true art nouveau gem, is named in honor of composer Bedřich Smetana and is home to the Prague Symphony Orchestra. The Czech Radio Symphony Orchestra also makes occasional use of it. A few smaller halls, all named for famous figures, host chamber concerts. Private companies often organize classical concerts in period costumes, and costumed ticket sellers are often on the street in front of the building. ⊠ *Náměstí Republiky 5, Staré Město* 🕾 *222–002–100* ⊕ *www.obecnidum.cz* Ⓜ *Line B: Náměstí Republiky.*

FodorśChoice **Rudolfinum.** Austrian Crown Prince Rudolf lends his name to this neo-Renaissance concert space and exhibition gallery built in 1884. The large concert hall, named for Antonín Dvořák, hosts concerts by the Czech Philharmonic. The smaller Josef Suk Hall, on the opposite side of the building, is used for chamber concerts. The interior is not as ornate as its rivals, but the acoustics are excellent. ⊠ *Náměstí Jana Palacha, Staré Město* 🕾 *224–893–111* ⊕ *www.rudolfinum.cz* Ⓜ *Line A: Staroměstská.*

Sazka Arena. Security tends to be very high in this multipurpose arena that opened in 2004 for an ice-hockey championship and now hosts rock concerts and other events. The pride of the stadium is its beer delivery system, which uses a 30,000-liter tank, 3 kilometers of pipes, and 70 taps. ⊠ *Očáľařská 2, Vysočany* ☎ 266–121–122 ⊕ *www.sazkaarena. cz* Ⓜ *Line B: Českomoravská.*

★ **Statní opera Praha** (State Opera House). With the most ornate interior of any venue in Prague, the theater has more than a touch of *Phantom of the Opera.* Marble sculptures support the loges, and a fresco in need a good cleaning adorns the ceiling. The building started its life as the German Theater in 1887 and has undergone several name changes since. The rotating stage offers directors a chance to experiment, although the stage area is a bit cramped. ⊠ *Wilsonova 4, Nové Město* ☎ 224–227–266 ⊕ *www.opera.cz* Ⓜ *Line A or C: Muzeum.*

Stavovské divadlo (Estates Theater). It's almost impossible to leave Prague without knowing that Mozart conducted the world premiere of *Don Giovanni* on this stage way back in 1787. Fittingly, the interior was used for scenes in Milos Forman's movie *Amadeus.* The interior is stylish and refined without being distracting. Now the theater is a branch of the National Theater, and high-quality productions of Mozart are usually in the repertoire with other classic operas and plays. In summer, a private company often rents the theater for touristy productions of Mozart works. ⊠ *Ovocný tř. 1, Staré Město* ☎ 224–215–001 ⊕ *www.narodni-divadlo.cz* Ⓜ *Line A: Staroměstská.*

T-Mobile Arena. Most major rock acts use this large but somewhat run-down sports arena. It tends to get very smoky in spite of an indoor smoking ban. ⊠ *Za elektrárnou, Holešovice* ☎ 233–379–248 Ⓜ *Line: Nádraží Holešovice.*

Velký sál, Lucerna (Great Hall, Lucerna). A beautiful art nouveau ballroom with a big main floor and some loges hosts medium-size rock and pop bands like Lou Reed, Ritchie Blackmore, and Kraftwerk, from time to time. Swing orchestras also make use of it. When open, it's one of the more impressive venues. ⊠ *Vodičkova 36, Nové Město* ☎ 224–224–537 ⊕ *www.lucerna.cz* Ⓜ *Line A or B: Můstek.*

Villa Bertramka. A bit out of the way, the summer house of the Dušek family is where Mozart composed part of *Don Giovanni.* The building has period furniture, including musical instruments, although not much is original. Some programs to *Don Giovanni* are framed on the walls. Small ensembles give chamber and garden concerts throughout the year. ⊠ *Mozartova 169, Smíchov* ☎ 257–318–461 ⊕ *www.bertramka.cz* Ⓜ *Line B: Anděl.*

Classical Music

Classical concerts are held all over the city throughout the year. In addition to Prague's two major professional orchestras, classical ensembles are the most common finds, and the standard of performance ranges from adequate to superb, though the programs tend to take few risks. Serious fans of baroque music may have the opportunity to hear works of little-known Bohemian composers at these concerts. Some of the best chamber ensembles are the Martinů Ensemble, the Prague

Chamber Philharmonic (also known as the Prague Philharmonia), the Wihan Quartet, and the Agon contemporary music group.

Agon Orchestra. Bucking the trend for classical, one group specializes in contemporary music ranging from John Cage to Frank Zappa. Most often they play at Archa Theatre, but they have been in other venues including Národní divadlo. ⊕ *www.musica.cz/agon.*

Collegium Marianum. The members of this group go beyond the usual classical standards to revive seldom-heard works from archives and perform them on period instruments. Performances are usually organized around a historical or geographical theme. ⊠ *Melantrichova 971/19, Staré Město* ☎ *224–229–462* ⊕ *www.tynska.cuni.cz* Ⓜ *Line A: Staroměstská.*

Czech Philharmonic. Antonín Dvořák conducted the orchestra's first performance back in 1896. Guest conductors have included Gustav Mahler and Leonard Bernstein. Since 1990 there has been a rapid turnover in chief conductors, but the performances have been of consistently high quality. Most programs include some works by Czech composers. The orchestra also plans special concerts on the birthdays of various composers. ⊠ *Rudolfinum, Náměstí Jana Palacha, Staré Město* ☎ *224–893–111* ⊕ *www.czechphilharmonic.cz* Ⓜ *Line A: Staroměstská.*

Czech Radio Symphony Orchestra. As the name implies, this group started playing live on the radio in 1927. It hasn't been directly associated with the national radio system since the 1960s and has fewer concerts than its main rivals. The orchestra makes occasional appearances at the Rudolfinum and other venues. Besides Czech composers, the orchestra excels in Brahms and Mahler. ⊕ *www2.rozhlas.cz/socr.*

Nostitz Quartet. This youthful ensemble, whose name is a famous 18th-century patron of the arts, has won a few prestigious awards. They give well above-average performances of works by Mozart and Czech composers and are one of the better groups to apear in various church concerts around town. ⊕ *www.nostitzquartet.com.*

Prague Chamber Orchestra without Conductor. Since 1951 this ensemble has been famous for playing often (but not always) without a conductor. Their extensive repertoire covers the classics up through 20th-century composers. Usually they play in the Rudolfinum. ⊕ *www.pko.cz.*

Prague Philharmonia. A relative newcomer established in 1994 concentrates on classical and romantic-era pieces plus the work of 20th-century composers. The founding and principal conductor is Jiří Bělohlávek, who also conducted the orchestra when it appeared on BBC World Service radio with opera singer Magdelena Koẑená in 2004. Most concerts take place in the Rudolfinum. ⊕ *www.pkf.cz.*

Prague Symphony Orchestra (FOK). The group's nickname stands for Film-Opera-Koncert. They started in 1934, but it wasn't until 1957 that they became the official city orchestra. Although they don't do much opera and film anymore, they did do music for many Czech films in the 1930s. They tour extensively and have a large back catalog of recordings.

Frenchman Serge Baudo has been the principal conductor since 2001. The programs tend to be quite diverse. One of the guest conductors is Maxim Shostakovich, who conducts his father's works. ⊠ *Obecní dům, Náměstí Republiky 5, Staré Město* ☎ *222-002-100* ⊕ *www.fok.cz* Ⓜ *Line B: Náměstí Republiky.*

Stamic Quartet. Two members of the quartet were born in the same town as composer J. V. Stamic, so they chose this name. The group often plays some Britten and Bártok along with the classics and Czech composers and has made several recordings. ⊕ *www.stamicquartet.cz.*

Wihan Quartet. Many quartets borrow names from composers, but few choose the names of players. Wihan was a cellist who knew Dvořák. The quartet has won numerous awards since it started in 1985 and has participated in international broadcasts. Most of their sets include at least one Czech composer. ⊕ *www.wihanquartet.cz.*

Church Concerts

Churches often serve as venues for classical concerts, and sometimes coming to one of these concerts is the only way to have a look inside. Laws that now limit passing out leaflets on the street have made it easier to walk around Prague without being bothered, but a side-effect has also been a notable drop in the number of classical concerts aimed at tourists. It's too hard to get people to come through passive advertisements. There's not all bad news, of course, since most of the better concerts have managed to survive. Banners or signs at the churches usually announce when there's a concert. Usually weekend evenings are a safe bet. Listings can be found in English on the Web site ⊕ www.pis.cz.

Barokní knihovní sál (Baroque Library Hall). Impressive 18th-century frescoes and colorful stucco work in a monastery library hall make for one of the more charming, though lesser-used, concert halls. Music is usually played here on period instruments. ⊠ *Melantrichova 971/19, Staré Město* ☎ *224-229-462* ⊕ *www.tynska.cuni.cz* Ⓜ *Line A: Staroměstská.*

Bazilika sv. Jakuba (Basilica of St. James). Tacked up on the back wall of this very large church is the mummified hand of a thief. The frescoes and lavish sculptures make this a pleasant setting for classical concerts, assuming you have your back turned to the grim relic. Make sure that organ is one of the featured instruments. The organ, finished in 1709, was restored in the early 1980s to its original tone structure and is one of the best in town. ⊠ *Malá Štupartská 6, Staré Město* ☎ *No phone* ⊕ *www.auditeorganum.cz/organ.html* Ⓜ *Line A: Staroměstská.*

Bazilika sv. Jiří (Basilica of St. George). One of the churches at Prague Castle sometimes features small ensembles playing well-known Mozart tunes and Verdi's *Four Seasons* in a Romanesque setting. The building dates to the 11th century and has the tombs of some very early princes. ⊠ *Náměstí U sv. Jiří Pražský hrad* ☎ *No phone* Ⓜ *Line A: Hradčandská.*

Chrám sv. Mikuláše (Church of St. Nicholas, Staré Město). The chandelier inside this baroque landmark is based on the design for the Czar's crown. Private companies rent out the church for concerts by professional ensembles and visiting amateur choirs and orchestras. The quality and prices vary greatly. ⊠ *Staroměstské náměstí, Staré Město* ☎ 224–190–994 Ⓜ *Line A: Staroměstská.*

Kostel sv. Martina ve zdi (Church of St. Martin in the Wall). None of the town walls are left in this area, but the church, which was begun in the 12th century and rebuilt several times, was once right by the St. Martin Gate. On the outside corner of the roof is a statue of a small boy that legend has it was turned to stone for taunting a bishop. Now the church is run by the Evengelical Church of Czech Brethren and the interior is very plain. ⊠ *Martinská 8, Staré Město* ☎ *No phone* ⊕ *www. martinvezdi.cz* Ⓜ *Line B: Národní třída.*

Kostel sv. Mikuláše (Church of St. Nicholas). The interior of this beautiful Baroque church was featured as a ballroom in the movie *Van Helsing*. The building's dome was one of the last works finished by architect Kilian Ignatz Dientzenhofer before his death in 1751. Local ensembles play concerts of popular classics here throughout the year. ⊠ *Malostranské náměstí, Malá Strana* ☎ 257–534–215 ⊕ *www.psalterium. cz* Ⓜ *Line A: Malostranská.*

Kostel sv. Šimona a Judy (Church of Sts. Simon and Jude). This former church with a restored organ and frescoes is used by the Prague Symphony Orchestra for chamber concerts and recitals. The baroque altar is actually an elaborate painting on the wall. The building's musical legacy includes concerts by Haydn and Mozart. ⊠ *Dušní ulice, Josefov* ☎ 222–002–336 *for tickets* Ⓜ *Line A: Staroměstská.*

Zrcadlová kaple Klementina (Mirrored Chapel of the Klementinum). Now part of the National Library, this ornate little chapel in the middle of the Klementinum complex is worth a peek. The music offered is fairly standard selections played with skill if not a lot of enthusiasm. Different concert companies program the space; signs nearby usually have the day's schedule. ⊠ *Marianské náměstí, Staré Město* ☎ *No phone* Ⓜ *Line A: Staroměstská.*

Film

Nothing has changed more in the last few years than the cinema scene. New multiplexes have brought state-of-the-art screens along with popcorn and candy. Small one- and two-screen cinemas are now struggling to stay afloat by offering alternative programming or alternating films with live theater. Most films are shown in their original-language versions, but it pays to check. If a film was made in the United States or Britain, the chances are good that it will be shown with Czech subtitles rather than dubbed. (Film titles, however, are usually translated into Czech, so your only clue to the movie's country of origin may be the poster used in advertisements.) Movies in the original language are normally indicated with the note *českými titulky* (with Czech subtitles). Prague's English-language publications carry film reviews and full timetables. Many downtown cinemas cluster near Wenceslas Square.

Aero. Out of the way, but worth the trip, this small gem hidden (look for a vertical neon sign that says kino) in the middle courtyard of a residential block has the most ambitious schedule of two or three different films a day. Festivals and retrospectives sometimes feature films with English subtitles. Czech translations are done to headphones. Visiting guests have included Terry Gilliam, Godfrey Reggio, and Paul Morrisey. The theater also has an outdoor beer garden in the summer months and a lively indoor bar all year-round. ⊠ *Biskupcova 31, Žižkov* ☎ *271–771–349* ⊕ *www.kinoaero.cz* Ⓜ *Line A: Želivského.*

Bijásek. Partly owned by Czech actor Martin Dejdar, this small but well laid-out theater is hidden above a bingo hall and next to a movie-theme bar. The program is mostly second-run movies, alternating with live shows. ⊠ *Revoluční 1, Staré Město* ☎ *224–815–195* ⊕ *www.bijasek.cz* Ⓜ *Line B: Náměstí Republiky.*

Cinema City Palác Flóra. This venue has Oskar-IMAX, a large-format theater that shows many short films in 3-D and the occasional feature on a very large screen. Most IMAX shows are dubbed. Other screens offer the standard multiplex experience. ⊠ *Vinohradská 149, Vinohrady* ☎ *255–742–021* ⊕ *www.cinemacity.cz* Ⓜ *Line A: Flora.*

Evald. This small basement theater is run by a film distribution company. When they don't have a new film of their own, they show recent art films. Recently the company has even dabbled in production. New films can sell out, especially on weekends. There's no refreshment stand. Instead, a reasonably priced restaurant—also called Evald—in the same basement makes dinner and a movie a one-stop shopping opportunity. ⊠ *Národní 28, Nové Město* ☎ *221–105–225* ⊕ *www.cinemart.cz* Ⓜ *Line B: Národní třída.*

Institut Français de Prague. A full-size movie theater is tucked away in the basement here, and most of the programming consists of recent French films and retrospectives of classics (also French). About half of the films have English subtitles, and the admission fee is usually nominal. ⊠*Štěpanská 35, Nové Město* ☎ *221–401–011* ⊕ *www.ifp.cz* Ⓜ *Line A or B: Můstek.*

Lucerna. The city's handsomest old movie palace was designed by former President Vaclav Havel's grandfather and built in 1916. The art nouveau interior reminds one of cinema's glory days, but it could use a little more maintenance. The programming tends toward nonblockbuster releases. The café leading to the theater proper sometimes features a live piano player. ⊠ *Vodičkova 36, Nové Město* ☎ *224–216–972* Ⓜ *Line A or B: Můstek.*

MAT. The smallest theater in the city almost feels a private basement screening room, with a so-so program of classics and second-run mainstream releases. Older Czech films sometimes turn up with English subtitles. The adjacent bar has a few props from Czech films; upstairs is a DVD rental store. ⊠ *Karlovo náměstí 36, Nové Město* ☎ *224–915–765* ⊕ *www.mat.cz* Ⓜ *Line B: Karlovo náměstí.*

Oko. Most movie theaters in Prague lack marquees. Oko, which means eye, has a big blue neon sign on the outside with its name prominently displayed. The art house programming is a bit less adventurous than its rivals. ✉ *Fr. Křížka 15, Holešovice* ☎ *223–382–606* ⊕ *www.kinooko. cz* Ⓜ *Line C: Vltavská.*

Palác Blaník. Mainstream films alternate with live shows at this single-screen downtown theater run by a major film distributor. A renovation to upgrade the stage for theater also improved the seats. ✉ *Václavské nám. 56, Nové Město* ☎ *224–033–172* ⊕ *www.palacblanik.cz* Ⓜ *Line A or C: Muzeum.*

Palace Cinemas Nový Smíchov. Currently the largest multiplex in Prague, with 12 screens and 2,000 parking places, it's in a shopping mall and pretty much replicates the familiar mall theater you'd find anyplace else in the world. ✉ *Plzeňská 8, Smíchov* ☎ *257–181–212* ⊕ *www. palacecinemas.cz* Ⓜ *Line B: Anděl.*

Palace Cinemas Slovanský dům. The most central multiplex in Prague also has the highest ticket prices, not to mention the best digital projector. The draw for English-speaking visitors is that the cinema sometimes shows films in their original-language versions even when other theaters have them dubbed. ✉ *Na Příkopé 22, Nové Město* ☎ *257–181–212* ⊕ *www. palacecinemas.cz* Ⓜ *Line B: Náměstí Republiky.*

Perštýn. One of the stranger basement theaters has tables and chairs in the screening room but no real food on offer except chips and pretzels. It's owned by a mainstream film distributor, and the programming consists mainly of slightly artier mainstream selections. ✉ *Na Perštýně 6, Staré Město* ☎ *221–668–432* Ⓜ *Line B: Národní třída.*

Střelecký ostrov. In summer, a portable professional projection system makes its home on an island in the Vltava. The programming is generally fairly recent films, usually in English but sometimes Czech fare without subtitles. Tickets are less than at multiplexes. ✉ *Střelecký ostrov, Nové Město* ☎ *777–325–256* ⊕ *www.strelak.cz* Ⓜ *Line B: Národní třída.*

★ **Světozor.** Promising to show a Czech film with English subtitles every day, this centrally located, two-screen theater is hoping to find a niche. The management of Aero took the place over in 2004 and are trying to make an art house with wide appeal. One of the first special guests was John Cleese. The attitude is a bit more formal than at Aero, and the bar is much smaller, but it offers an exclusive brand of beer, also called Světozor. The theater has a long history that includes interactive cinema experiments back in the late 1960s. ✉ *Vodičkova 41, Nové Město* ☎ *224–946–824* ⊕ *www.kinosvetozor.cz* Ⓜ *Line A or B: Můstek.*

Village Cinemas Anděl. These theaters offer two so-called "Gold-Class" screening rooms, which have a small number of lounge chairs with buttons to summon a waitress to bring you fresh beverages or snacks. The rest of the theaters are standard-issue multiplex seating. ✉ *Plzeňská, between Radlická and Stroupežnického, Smíchov* ☎ *251–115–111* ⊕ *www.villagecinemas.cz* Ⓜ *Line B: Anděl.*

Opera

The Czech Republic has a strong operatic tradition. Unlike during the Communist period, operas are almost always sung in their original tongue, and the repertoire offers plenty of Italian favorites as well as the Czech national composers Janaček, Dvořák, and Smetana. (Czech operas are supertitled in English.) The major opera houses also often stage ballets. Appropriate attire is recommended for all venues. Suits and ties—or at least a sports coat—for men, and dresses for women are common. Shorts and T-shirts will probably generate odd looks from other patrons. The National and Estates theaters instituted a "no jeans" rule in 1998. Ticket prices are still quite reasonable, at 100 Kč–1,500 Kč.

Národní divadlo (National Theater). A slightly bigger budget and three different venues for operas give the National Theater's resident opera company a bit more flexibility than its rival, the Statní opera Praha. More ambitious productions are at the main Národní divadlo. They also program Stavovské divadlo with usually more mainstream works. Truly experimental and chamber operas wind up in Kolowrat. The productions run from excellent to slightly misconceived, but are always professional. ⌧ *Národní třída. 2, Nové Město* ☎ *224–901–448* ⊕ *www.narodni-divadlo.cz* Ⓜ *Line B: Národní třída.*

Statní opera Praha (State Opera House). Slightly fewer resources than are available to the National Theater are on hand for the productions at the State Opera. There's a tendency to crowd the chorus on the stage and try to make them look busy. Still, many directors have been very creative with the stage space, and the productions are every bit as good as those of Národní divadlo. The State Opera also commissions new works and tries to mix crowd-pleasing stagings of popular operas in with more challenging interpretations of obscure works. ⌧ *Wilsonova 4, Nové Město* ☎ *224–227–266* ⊕ *www.opera.cz* Ⓜ *Line A or C: Muzeum.*

Puppet Shows & Black Light Theater

Black-light theater, a form of nonverbal theater—a melding of live acting, mime, video, and stage trickery—was Czechoslovakia's contribution to Expo '58. The name comes from ultraviolet light, which is used to illuminate special makeup and details on the sets; this helps to create optical illusions. Some black-light shows have been running for thousands of performances. Puppetry also has a long tradition, but most of the shows are dialogue-intensive and aimed at a young audience.

All Colours Theater. Since 1993 this small theater has been presenting a small repertoire of nonverbal shows. Faust is the most popular, although they occasionally revive other works. Some legends claim that the real Faust lived in Prague, which gives the show some local connection. ⌧ *Rytiřská 31, Staré Město* ☎ *221–610–170* ⊕ *www.blacktheatre.cz* Ⓜ *Line A or B: Můstek.*

Divadlo Image. Home of a black-light and pantomine company that has a repertoire of long-running classics of the genre and a "best of" show.

✉ *Pařížská 4, Josefov* ☎ *222–329–191* ⊕ *www.imagetheatre.cz* Ⓜ *Line A: Staroměstská.*

Divadlo Ta Fantastika. A black-light show called *Aspects of Alice*, based loosely on *Alice in Wonderland*, has run here almost daily for more than 2,000 performances. Slightly campy musicals in Czech based on historical themes and starring popular local singers also play here. The theater was established in New York in 1981 and moved to Prague after the Velvet Revolution. It's been running at its current address, a minor Baroque palace, since 1993. ✉ *Karlova 8, Staré Město* ☎ *222–221–366* ⊕ *www. tafantastika.cz* Ⓜ *Line A: Staroměstská.*

★ **Laterna Magika.** The glass-block façade of the Nová scena (New Stage), which opened in 1983, stands out among the ornate 19th-century buildings in the area. The structure is the result of decades of planning to expand the adjacent National Theater. The program is almost exclusively made up of black-light and multimedia performances, which are popular with visitors because there's no language barrier. Laterna Magika takes its name from the original black-light presentation at Expo '58. ✉ *Národní třída 4, Nové Město* ☎ *224–931–482* ⊕ *www.laterna.cz* Ⓜ *Line B:* Národní třída.

Národní divadlo marionet (The National Puppet Theater). One puppet company has been presenting Mozart's *Don Giovanni* with string puppets set to recorded music sung in Italian since 1991. The opera is done with a slight sense of humor, and Mozart himself makes a guest appearance. ✉ *Žatecká 1, Staré Město* ☎ *224–819–322* ⊕ *www.mozart. cz* Ⓜ *Line A: Staroměstská.*

Theater

A dozen or so professional theater companies play in Prague to ever-packed houses. Visiting the theater is a vital activity in Czech society, and the language barrier can't obscure the players' artistry. Nonverbal theater also abounds: not only tourist-friendly mime and "Black Light Theater" but also serious (or incomprehensible) productions by top local and foreign troupes. Several English-language theater groups operate sporadically. For complete listings, pick up a copy of the *Prague Post*.

Fodor'sChoice **Archa Theater.** Both for its central location and eclectic programming,
★ Archa is the main venue for modern theater, dance, and avant-garde music. Some visiting troupes perform in English, and other shows are designated as English-friendly in the program. The theater opened in 1994 and had former Velvet Underground member John Cale perform one of its first concerts. ✉ *Na Poříčí 26, Nové Město* ☎ *221–716–333* ⊕ *www.archatheatre.cz* Ⓜ *Line B: Náměstí Republiky.*

Divadlo Alfred v dvoře. Most of the programming for this small, out-of-the-way theater is physical, nonverbal theater and dance. Visiting companies come often and take a more modern approach than can be seen in many of the more tourist-oriented nonverbal theaters. ✉ *Fr. Křížka 36, Bubeneč* ☎ *233–376–997* ⊕ *www.alfredvedvore.cz* Ⓜ *Line C: Vltavská.*

Divadlo Globe. Shakespeare's plays are remarkably popular here, so a fair replica of the famous Globe Theatre, where his plays were originally performed, was built in the Prague exhibition grounds. The wooden structure usually hosts Czech versions of the Shakespeare's work, though on rare occasion something is in English. ⊠ *Výstaviště, Holešovice* ☎ *No phone* Ⓜ *Line C: Nádraží Holešovice.*

Divadlo Ponec. The inside of this neoclassical building, a former cylinder factory and movie theater, was renovated into a modern dance venue in 2001, and the outside was finally spruced up in 2004 so it no longer feels as if you're seeing a show in an abandoned building. The dance pieces are fairly modern, with the house carrying a lot of premieres. Several dance festivals are based here. ⊠ *Husitská 24/a, Žižkov* ☎ *224–817–886* ⊕ *www.divadloponec.cz* Ⓜ *Line B or C: Florenc.*

GoJa Music Hall. A giant glass pyramid in the exhibition grounds was the first place to try Czech-language versions of Broadway hits. *Jesus Christ Superstar, Evita, Grease,* and *Les Miserables* have had runs here. The first part of the venue's name comes from Czech pop star Karel Gott. ⊠ *Výstaviště, Holešovice* ☎ *272–658–955* ⊕ *www.goja.cz* Ⓜ *Line C: Nádraží Holešovice.*

LATE-NIGHT BITES

When it comes to food, Prague is definitely a city with a curfew. Pubs used to close strictly at 10 PM. Even now, it's hard to find food even as late as midnight. Some fast-food branches have late-night windows near major tram stops. Václavské náměstí is lined with all-night food stands selling sausages on paper plates.

Gyrossino (Gyros Rossino). Two side-by-side storefronts without seating sell gyros, falafels, and cold slices of pizza until 5 AM, except Sunday when it closes at a more normal hour. All of the late-night trams stop down the street at Lazarská, so it's easy to reach. When this joint is closed, it's a hint to go home. ⊠ *Spalena 43, Nové Město* Ⓜ *Line B: Národní třída.*

Hospoda v Lucerně (Pub in Lucerna). This is a somewhat upscale version of the typical Czech pub, but the service can be really slow. The beer on tap is unpasteurized. The pub is open until 3 AM, but the kitchen closes a little earlier. ⊠ *Vodičkova 36, Nové Město* ☎ *224–215–186* Ⓜ *Line A or B: Můstek.*

Palác Akropolis. The corner restaurant in this nightclub serves a variety of reasonably priced meals, including a few vegetarian selections, until 1 AM. ⊠ *Kubelíkova 27, Žižkov* ☎ *299–330–913* ⊕ *www.palacakropolis.cz* Ⓜ *Line A: Náměstí Jiřího z Poděbrad.*

Picante. Mexican fast food is served nonstop in a location near several popular nightclubs and bars. Some seating is available. It's the best option in the area, and one of very few places open 24 hours a day. ⊠ *Revoluční 4, Nové Město* ☎ *222–322–022* Ⓜ *Line B: Náměstí Republiky.*

Square. A historical pub that was frequented by Kafka and Jan Neruda was renovated and turned into an upscale sushi and tapas bar in 2002. The kitchen is open until 12:30 AM and also cooks Mediterranean dishes. The bar stays open even later on weekends. ⊠ *Malostranské náměstí 5, Malá Strana* ☎ *257–532–109* Ⓜ *Line A: Malostranská.*

U Havrana (The Raven). A typical old-school Czech pub with guláš and fried cheese, it's the only one in town to cook really late, though the atmosphere is a bit smoky. The place used to be nonstop, but now it's open to at least 4 AM. ⊠ *Hálkova 6, Nové Město* ☎ *296–200–020* Ⓜ *Line C: I. P. Pavlova.*

U Zlatého stromu. The street-level restaurant of this hotel and nightclub serves pretty pricey international cuisine around the clock. ⊠ *Hotel U Zlatého stromu, Karlova 6, Staré Město* ☎ *222–220–441* Ⓜ *Line A: Staroměstská.*

SPORTS &
THE OUTDOORS

5

PLACE TO SPOT FUTURE STARS
HC Sparta Praha, *Holešovice* ⇨*p.130*

BEST PLACE TO PAMPER YOURSELF
Cybex, *Karlín* ⇨*p.129*

RATTLE 'ROUND THE CITY
City bike, *Staré Město* ⇨*p.128*

SUMMERTIME PLAYGROUND
Divoká Šárka, *Vokovice* ⇨*p.132*

BEST BILLIARDS
Kulečníkova Herna Billiard Centrum,
Nové Město ⇨*p.137*

By Tim Gosling **THE CITIZENS OF PRAGUE HAVE A PARTICULAR AFFINITY** for exertion and for the outdoor world. Come Friday afternoon, many are spotted sprinting out of the city toward the countryside to hide out at their country cottages, to hike in the scenic Czech countryside, or in winter to ski. Should the sun show its face, those remaining confined among the concrete apartment blocks are likely to head to one of the city's many parks for gentle recreation. (With the arrival of less glamorous weather, many keep themselves entertained with pub sports.)

All this activity appears to limit the time and enthusiasm Czechs find to commit to spectator sports. Certainly the city's sports teams have dedicated supporters, but it's rare that contests are sold out, and the atmosphere at many matches, save those between city rivals, can veer to the cool side. And then, as if out of the blue, international hockey and soccer championships catch the national consciousness by the tail.

At this level, hockey in particular takes on the character of an obsession. Huge screens appear in the center of Prague, beaming out the efforts of the national heroes, most of whom play in the U.S. leagues, and the screens are attended by thousands. Success breeds massive celebrations across the city, announced by car horns, fireworks, and, of course, a boost to the breweries' coffers. Around the turn of the 21st century, the streets were busy indeed as the Czechs won the 1998 Olympic title, and then went on to capture three consecutive World Championships.

If you're interested in seeing a hockey or soccer game during your stay, the best place to find out what's going on (and where) is the weekly sports page of the *Prague Post,* or you can inquire at your hotel.

PARKS & PLAYGROUNDS

Prague has numerous parks that play host to urban sportsmen and - women. Most are busy with in-line skaters rushing along the paths and the hazards of the Frisbee, and there are always beer gardens, of course. The city's two biggest parks, Letná and Stromovka, are both found in Prague 7.

Kampa. Under the noses of the throng on Charles Bridge: take the steps off the bridge onto Na Kampě and follow the wide cobbled street to the end; Kampa is a diminutive gem hidden in the heart of Malá Strana. A location for lazing in the sunshine or strolling to the quieter spaces of the Lesser Quarter, with a stop-off at the playground should the kids somehow have tired of gazing at the wonderful architecture. Activities here are often accompanied by the wish that the hippies will get tired of walloping drums. ⊠ *Malá Strana* Ⓜ *Tram to Malostranské náměstí.*

Letná. With a wonderful view over the city across the river, the park is always busy. It has a huge beer garden and restaurant when you need a break from your exertions; these are located around Letenský zámeček, near the intersection of Kostelní and Muzejní. The northern plateau often hosts large concerts, or acts as the meeting point for political rallies and similar events; otherwise, it hosts many amateur sports teams. An excellent playground sits in the center near the tennis courts, just to the west of Letenský zámeček. ⊠ *Holešovice* Ⓜ *Tram to Sparta.*

☺ **Riegrovy.** The lush park climbs sharply up the slopes of Vinohrady. On the east side of the park just off Chopinov, pretty landscaping surrounds one of the best beer gardens in Prague and a large playground. ⊠ *Vinohrady* Ⓜ *Line A: Jiřího z Poděbrad.*

Stromovka. The king of all Prague parks was formally a royal hunting ground. These days the deer have been usurped by horse-riders and dog-lovers, who are hauled along by Czech canines, which often tend to resemble rats on strings. Remarkably rustic for a city-based park, it's primarily a place for walking rather than lazing. The racket from the ramshackle amusements at Výstaviště exhibition grounds, found at the park's eastern entrance where Dukelských hrdinů meets U Výstaviště, connives to remind you that you remain city-bound. ⊠ *Holešovice* Ⓜ *Tram to Výstaviště.*

SPORTS & ACTIVITIES

Boating

Given the multitude of locks and weirs on the Vltava, you can't wander too far when boating under your own steam. Therefore, it's ideal for the lazy and those looking for a view of Charles Bridge from the ducks' perspective.

U Kotvy (⊠ Slovanský ostrov, Staré Město ☎ 603–523–371) rents out rowboats (60 Kč per hour, maximum four people per boat) and paddleboats (120 Kč per hour) from Slovanský ostrov, the island in the Vltava just south of the National Theater. It's usually open from 10 AM to sunset from May to September, but in high summer (usually late June through August) lanterns are provided for night cruising.

Bowling & Billiards

Given their love of beer it should come as no surprise that Czechs love pub sports almost as much. However, sticklers that demand professional standards from such facilities will have plenty to complain about. Remember, it's only a game.

Billiard Club Harlequin (⊠ Vinohradská 25, Vinohrady ☎ 224–217–240 ⊕ www.harlequin.zde.cz Ⓜ Line A: Náměstí Míru) offers billiards, pool, and snooker on decent tables. Prices range from 40 Kč to 120 Kč per hour, depending on the table and time of day. Housed in a huge, ★ somewhat tatty old ballroom, **Kulečníkova Herna Billiard Centrum** (⊠ V Cipu, Nové Město ☎ 224–009–235 Ⓜ Line A: Můstek) has three bowling lanes, many pool tables, table-tennis, and snooker. Ask for the activity you fancy at the entrance desk. A ticket will be provided to you where charges—either sporting or drinking—will be noted. Simply pay for the lot as you leave. Six newly constructed bowling lanes are available in Prague 7 at **Radava SC Praha** (⊠ Milady Horákové 37, Letná

CloseUp

DAY SPAS

AS DEEPLY AS THE CZECH CAPITAL can nourish the mind and the soul with its splendor, intellectual traditions, and arts, it can be also be a little rough on the body. Those miles of cobblestones that you tramp while sightseeing exert a toll on the soles, and plates of heavy fried food washed down by too many beers in smoke-filled pubs can strain the system. Recreational spas, where you can address the damage, are not yet well-established, but there's one or two select places to recharge your batteries.

Relaxation therapies abound in the posh pamper shop **Cybex** (⊠ Hilton Prague, Pobřežní 1, Karlín ☎ 224–842–375 ⊕ www.cybexprg.cz Ⓜ Line B or C: Florenc). By the time you finish, you may well feel like you're on the menu at some posh restaurant: duck in here to be rolled in yogurt and mud, smeared with mint gel or various oils, have your hide rubbed

with salt or pummeled with stones. Prices are steep by Prague standards, starting at 1,200 Kč for a massage, but the range of facilities matches up.

Awaiting your pains inside a shiny shopping center are the hands of experts from southeast Asia at **Sabai Studio** (⊠ Slovanský dům, Na Příkopě 22, Staré Město ☎ 224–451–180 ⊕ www.sabai. cz Ⓜ Line B: Náměstí Republiky). Thai massage costs 950 Kč an hour; aroma massage 1,250 Kč.

Overhaul the energy lines in your human body in the very center of the city. **Thai World** (⊠ Celetná 6, Staré Město ☎ 224–817–247 ⊕ www.thaiworld.cz Ⓜ Line B: Náměstí Republiky) offers Thai (499 Kč per hour), foot (499 Kč), or oil (699 Kč) massages to the weary.

☎ 233–101–213 ⊕ www.radava.cz Ⓜ Tram to Letenské náměstí) although booking ahead is advised.

Cycling

Much of the Czech Republic provides a pleasant and gently sloping track for peddlers. The capital, on the other hand, is hardly ideal for bicycles. There are few cycle paths in the city; none in the city center, and the cobbles can seriously shake you up, so make sure your saddle is well-padded. However, two-wheeled transport can be handy for speeding up sightseeing, and a bicycle allows you to roam farther with much less physical exertion. From April to October, two bike-rental companies provide locks, helmets, and maps; they will also store your bags for the duration, and each runs guided bike tours for around 450 Kč.

City Bike (⊠ Králodvorská 5, Staré Město ☎ 776–180–284 ⊕ www.pragueonline.cz/citybike Ⓜ Line B: Náměstí Republiky) offers guided tours leaving at 11, 2, 5, and a "Sunset" tour for which advance booking is needed. Your English-speaking guides concentrate on fun rather than in-depth history. One of the multicultural teams from **Praha Bike** (⊠ Dlouhá 15, Staré Město ☎ 732–388–880 ⊕ www.prahabike.cz

Ⓜ Line B: Náměstí Republiky) will casually guide you around one of two routes; tours at 11:30, 2:30, or 5:30.

Golf

On the weekend, expect to pay up to 2,500 Kč for a round of golf on an 18-hole course, possibly about half this amount during the week.

To polish your technique on a full-swing simulator, pop down to **Erpet Golf Centrum** (⊠ Strakonická 4, Smíchov ☎ 257–321–177 ⊕ www.erpet.cz Ⓜ Line B: Smíchovské nádraží).

Prague's only golf course is a 9-holer in the western suburbs at the **Hotel Golf** (⊠ Plzeňská 215, Motol ☎ 257–215–185). Take a taxi to the hotel or Tram 4, 7, or 9 from metro station Anděl to the Hotel Golf stop.

Praha Karlštejn Golf Club (⊠ Bělěc 280, Liteň ☎ 0/724–084–600 ⊕ www.karlstejn-golf.cz) offers a challenging course with a view of the famous Karlštejn Castle. It's 30 km (18 mi) southwest of Prague, just across the Berounka River from the castle. Trains to Karlštejn, costing about 50 Kč, leave Smíchov nádraží hourly. A short uphill walk or taxi (100 Kč max) will get you to the club.

Health Clubs

There are a number of high-end fitness centers around the city, as well as cheaper options, all of which you can visit on a day-pass. Expect to pay 80 Kč to 900 Kč.

FodorsChoice In the Hilton hotel **Cybex** (⊠ Hilton Prague, Pobřežní 1, Karlín
★ ☎ 224–842–375 ⊕ www.cybexprg.cz Ⓜ Line B or C: Florenc) provides superb high-tech fitness machines as well as pampering services.

Factory Pro (⊠ Nádražní 32, Smíchov ☎ 221–420–800 Ⓜ Line B: Smíchovské nádraží) offers numerous machines as well as aerobics and yoga classes; squash courts; a swimming pool; sauna; and solarium facilities.

Excellent and inexpensive facilities can be found at the **Hotel Axa** (⊠ Na Poříčí 40, Nové Město ☎ 224–812–580 ⊕ www.hotelaxa.com Ⓜ Line B: Náměstí Republiky), including an indoor pool.

Sportcentrum YMCA (⊠ Na Poříčí 12, Staré Město ☎ 224–875–811 Ⓜ Line B: Náměstí Republiky) is one of the cheaper options in Prague, which means it's a little more crowded than others, and facilities, although plentiful, may be well-used.

Hockey

Ice-hockey becomes a national obsession during international competitions. The hockey season runs from September to March. Tickets, which cost between 40 Kč and 100 Kč, are reasonably easy to secure, except for the big clashes between Prague's giants.

Although a relative giant in the Czech Republic, **HC Slavia Praha** (⊠ Zimní stadion Eden, Vladivostocká 10, Vršovice ☎ 267–311–417 ⊕ www.hc-slavia.cz Ⓜ Tram to Kubánské náměstí) usually find themselves chasing the leaders of the pack in international matches.

Fodor's Choice

★ Recently toppled from their perch at the top of the tree by a team of provincial upstarts **HC Sparta Praha** (✉ T-Mobile Arena, Za Elektrárnou 419, Holešovice ☎ 266–727–443 ⊕ www.hcsparta.cz Ⓜ Line C: Nádraží Holešovice) still attract many of the country's best young players. Until they are lured across the Atlantic, of course. Come to spot the next Jágr or Hašek.

Horse Racing

Horse racing has a small but dedicated following in the Czech Republic. If you just have to bet on the ponies, you're in luck.

Prague's horse-racing track, the **Velká Chuchle** (✉ Radotìnská 69, Velká Chuchle ☎ 257–941–431 ⊕ www.velka-chuchle.cz Ⓜ Bus 172 from Smíchovské nádraží to Dostihová) is on the southwestern edge of the city. Each Sunday from April to November—but with a rest in July—the course hosts almost all of the country's major-prize events; highlights include the Czech Derby in June and the Autumn Racing Festival in September. On race days, trains run regularly from Smíchovské nádraží to Velká Chuchle nádraží, which is right behind the main stands.

The Velké pardubické steeplechase, the most famous race in the Czech Republic—and the most dangerous horse-race in the world, according to many—takes place on the second weekend of October at the **dostihové závodiště Pardubice** (Pardubice Racecourse; ✉ Pardubice ⊕ www.pardubice-racecourse.cz) in eastern Bohemia.

Prague Marathon

Competitors from more than 55 countries run themselves ragged around the city center in late May or early June at the **Prague International Marathon** (⊕ www.pim.cz). Should the running bug bite you there are several noncompetitive races over more reasonable distances. All races start and finish in Old Town Square.

Skiing

Although it's not an everyday occurrence, you might even bump into skiers within the city limits after a heavy snowfall: after all, Prague is built on a series of hills. However, such folks are more likely to be commuting to work rather than engaging in leisure activities. Czechs are very enthusiastic skiers (note the three-year-olds whizzing past you), and the border regions of the country host many small resorts. The best area is generally acknowledged to be the Krkonoše Mountains, which straddle the border with Poland. Experienced skiers will find the mountains here small and the facilities rather poor. If you have the time, follow the Czech hordes down the highway to Austria. However, the Czech resorts can make for a decent day-trip from the capital and offer unbelievable prices of about 400 Kč to 500 Kč per day. All the area ski resorts are regularly served by buses leaving from Florenc.

Černá Hora (✉ Cernohorská 265, Janské Lázně ☎ 499–875–186 ⊕ www.cerna-hora.cz) is 180 km (about a four-hour drive) from Prague. The resort has a cable-car, one chair-lift and a couple of drag-lifts. The "Black Mountain" is not the biggest of ski resorts, but is often fairly quiet: meaning less waiting, and offers a nice unofficial run, with plenty of forest to explore, directly under the cable car.

On the weekends, if you fancy some space to breathe—let alone ski—head for **Harrachov** (✉ Harrachov ☎ 432–529–600 ⊕ www.harrachov.cz). In the west of the Krkonoše, around 120 km (a three-hour drive) from the capital, the resort offers red-and-blue runs served by two chair-lifts and 11 drag-lifts. This small and friendly resort is ideal for beginners and intermediates.

The biggest and most popular ski resort in the Czech Republic is **Skiareal Špindleruv Mlýn** (✉ Špindleruv Mlýn ☎ 499–467–102 ⊕ www.skiarealspindl.cz), which is 160 km (about a 3½-hour drive) from Prague. The twin slopes, Svatý Petr and Medvedín, gaze at each other over the small village and offer blue, red, and black runs served by four chair-lifts and numerous drag-lifts. Weekends here are mobbed to a point well past frustration.

Soccer

The domestic Czech league, the Gambrinus liga, runs from August to May with a break in December and January. Apart from certain matches between local or European rivals, the games and the fans tend to be somewhat lackluster. Tickets are plentiful enough on match days (except for tournaments) at 50 Kč to 150 Kč. Depending on the opposition, it can be tough to secure tickets for European and international matches, which are more expensive (usually between 200 Kč and 500 Kč). The Czech national team has punched well above its weight in the past decade or so, consistently rating in the top 10 in world rankings. Disciplined and with strong team-ethos, lower-profile Czech-based players form the steely spine that the few world stars dance upon. International matches are hosted at Sparta's stadium.

AC Sparta Praha (✉ Stadion AC Sparta Praha, Milady Horákové 98, Letná ☎ 220–570–323 ⊕ www.sparta.cz Ⓜ Line A: Hradčanská) has many skinhead fans that make their presence felt in sectors D3 and D4 behind the Milady Horackove goal at some games. Although Sparta has seen its fortunes dip a little recently, the team remains a domestic Goliath and a thorny David in European competition.

Reduced in the early 21st century to bringing up the rear in the capital are second-division **FC Bohemians Praha** (✉ Doliček stadion, Vršovická 31, Vršovice ☎ 271–721–459 ⊕ www.fc-bohemians.cz Ⓜ Tram to Vršovice Námestí).

Sparta's success is much to the chagrin of bitter rivals **SK Slavia Praha** (✉ Stadion Evžena Rošického, Zátopkova 2, Strahov ☎ 233–081–751 ⊕ www.slavia.cz Ⓜ Bus 176 to Stadion Strahov), which has been playing in Evžena Rošického stadium while waiting for a new one to be built in Prague 10. The former favorites of the First Republic and their fans have had to be very patient thus far. Then again, the team has been waiting to return to its position as the country's top dog since the 1950s.

These days the minnows of **Viktoria Žižkov** (✉ Viktoria Žižkov stadion, Seifertova, Žižkov ☎ 222–712–503 ⊕ www.fkviktoriazizkov.cz Ⓜ Tram to Husinecká) are becoming Prague's third team, often enjoying embarrassing supposedly superior teams in the UEFA cup, Europe's secondary cup competition.

Swimming

In high summer (primarily in July and August), Prague residents enjoy jumping into "natural" water. Lakes and quarries are variously adopted for bathing, many of them outside the city. However, within the confines of Prague are a few well-known spots.

★ At **Divoká Šárka** (✉ Divoká Šárka 1, Vokovice ☎ 235–358–022 Ⓜ Tram 20 or 26 to Divoká Šárka) your 40 Kč allows you to swim in the always-chilly, constantly flowing water then warm up by playing table-tennis. When you exit the tram at Divoká Šárka, walk behind McDonald's and take the steps to the right. At the bottom, turn left and walk 1 km through a green valley to find the two pools, fed by the streams you have walked alongside. Instead of turning left at the bottom of the steps behind the McDonald's, you can also turn right to get to **Džbán,** a murky brown lake surrounded by bars and hot-dog vendors. Entrance is 30 Kč. Those of a delicate nature should look out for and avoid the nude sunbathing section.

Hostivař (✉ K Jezeru, Hostivař ☎ 272–655–546 Ⓜ Line C: Háje) is a large brown lake that snakes through a forest and hosts folks into sunbathing, refueling, and occasionally falling into the water.

Hotel Axa (✉ Na Poříčí 40, Nové Město ☎ 224–812–580 ⊕ www.hotelaxa.com Ⓜ Line B: Náměstí Republiky) has a nice indoor pool.

Hotel Olšanka (✉ Táboritská 23, Žižkov ☎ 267–092–202 ⊕ www.hotelolsanka.cz) has a 25-meter pool open to the public every day. The hotel also offers a sauna (90 minutes for 120 Kč) and massage service (30 minutes for 220 Kč).

The busiest summer swimming pool in Prague is **Plavecký Stadión Podolí** (Podolí Swimming Stadium; ✉ Podolská 74, Podolí ☎ 241–433–952 Ⓜ Tram 3 or 17 to Kublov). An indoor pool is 50 meters long, but when the sun comes out, the focus is on the two open-air pools, the water slide, and an army of younger Czechs sunbathing and frolicking on the grass around them. A word of warning: Podolí, for all its attractions, is notorious as a local hot spot of petty thievery. Don't entrust any valuables to the lockers—it's best either to check them in the safe with the *vrátnice* (superintendent), or better yet, don't bring them at all.

Tennis

The most famous Czech tennis exports remain Ivan Lendl, and, by ethnicity at least, the great Martina Navratilova. Many Czechs have been inspired to the status of keen amateurs.

At **Bendvik** (⊠ Diskarská 1, Hradčany ☎ 251–611–129 Ⓜ Tram 15, 22, or 23 to Malovanka), indoor courts cost 250 Kč to 430 Kč per hour, outdoor courts 100 Kč to 200 Kč per hour.

Some of the city's best tennis courts are found right next door to the city's tennis stadium, **Česky Lawn Tennis Klub** (⊠ Ostrov Štvanice 38, Holešovice ☎ 222–316–317 Ⓜ Line C: Vltavská), which in its time has hosted ATP events. Open to the public for 300 Kč to–600 Kč per hour are 10 outdoor courts and 6 indoor courts, all hard-surface or clay despite the name.

Skateboarding

Directly above Čechův most on the southern edge of Letná Park, a huge metronome keeps the Vltava flowing to its beat. Behind the timepiece is an area of paving known as "Stalin," so called because a huge statue of the man stood here until it was blown up in 1964. The great dictator would probably have been enraged to spend his days watching the collection of scruffy youth that gathers here these days; the flagstones are home to one of the most popular unofficial skateboarding spots in the city.

In-line skates can be rented at **In-Line pujcovna** (⊠ Milady Horákové 98, Letná ☎ 603–938–328 ⊕ www.inlinespecial.cz Ⓜ Line A: Hradčanská) for 50 Kč an hour or 300 Kč a day.

★ Prague is host to the Mystic Skate Cup, part of the World Cup Skateboarding series. It's held annually in July at **Mystic Skatepark** (⊠ Stvanice Island, Holešovice ☎ 222–232–027 off-site office ⊕ www.mysticskates.cz Ⓜ Line C: Vltavská). The park is open to the public year-round. Skateboarders pay 50 Kč; those on a BMX or in-line skates have to cough up 80 Kč.

Squash

Squash has been growing in popularity in the last few years, and there are a few courts to choose from. Some of the courts do feature odd materials in their construction; in many cases, however, the changing rooms can be improved by better air circulation (or you could simply put a clothes pin on your nose).

The central location of **ABS Squash Centrum** (⊠ Václavské náměstí 15, Staré Město ☎ 224–217–789 ⊕ www.abssquash.cz Ⓜ Line A: Můstek) is the main advantage at these three courts, although prices (190 Kč–420 Kč per hour) give quite a wallop to the wallet.

Squash Centrum Haštal (⊠ Haštalská 20, Staré Město ☎ 224–828–561 Ⓜ Line B: Náměstí Republiky) has good prices, and the hollow construction of the walls does not even affect play too much, but the noise can be disconcerting.

Yoga

The mystical atmosphere of Prague, in combination with its reputation as a literary and arts center, ensures a steady supply of yoga classes. Of course, the trick is to find the ones that are taught in English. Good sources for temporary groups and classes are the message boards of prague.tv or www.expats.cz.

You can "harmonize your energy systems and manifest the universal law" and all that in English every Monday evening at 10 PM from April to September. Classes take place at **Lotus Centrum** (⊠ Dlouhá 2, Staré Město) for anyone over 15; cost is 100 Kč for 90 minutes.

SHOPPING

6

THROUGH THE LOOKING GLASS
Artěl, *Vinohrady* ⇨*p.151*

FASHION PLATE
Klára Nademlýnská, *Staré Město* ⇨*p.148*

INTERIOR DESIGNER HOME AWAY FROM HOME
Qubus Design, *Staré Město* ⇨*p.152*

CRYSTALS ARE A CZECH'S BEST FRIEND
Swarovski Bohemia, *Staré Město* ⇨*p.153*

BREAKFAST AT TATIANA'S
Tatiana, *Staré Město* ⇨*p.149*

BLAST FROM THE PAST
Art Deco Gallery Shop, *Malá Strana* ⇨*p.141*

By Mindy Kay
Bricker

THOUGH PRAGUE WAS CONSIDERED THE PARIS OF THE 1990S, that overused expression applied only to the city as a magnet for expatriot poets and writers, certainly not for shoppers. Although the choices available to the average consumer are improving, with the addition of trendy chains like H&M and luxury boutiques like Louis Vuitton, the broad range of stores in the major European capitals like Paris has not yet reached Prague. Attitudes, however, are similar. Czech shopkeepers—from the grocery store to the trendiest store—use the evil eye like a super power. Blame it, perhaps, on this country's numerous historical invasions, but for whatever reason shopkeepers assume that you are there to steal something from them, rather than to patronize their business. It's best to accept that fact, then you can ignore the glares and have fun.

Czech women have bird-like bodies, and you will find that clothing styles and sizes tend to cater to the smaller sizes. Don't be surprised if you go up one or two pants sizes while you're here—sizing is small in stores like Zara, Mango, and Benetton. Unfortunately for men, shopping in Prague is a woman's culture. Czech society pours all of its energy into ensuring that their women are the most beautiful, and the fashionable man is a forgotten breed. British chains like Marks & Spencer and Debenhams are helping out with casual buys for men; and of course, Hugo Boss has found its way here. Similarly, incredibly talented Czech designers have brought an old-meets-new style to their creations, much like the Czech approach to architecture. Unfortunately, as with the up-scale chains, the best designers are providing only for women.

But clothing isn't all there is to buy here. Czech glass artisans shine as brilliantly as the glass they create. Bohemian crystal and porcelain deservedly enjoy a worldwide reputation for quality, and plenty of shops offer excellent bargains. You will find the same modern-cut box vase in four stores on the same street, so shop around before you make an investment. Most high-end crystal stores will deliver your purchase to your hotel or even to your home, so opt for this rather than running the risk of it getting broken or, worse yet, stolen. And, of course, don't forget the marionettes. Even if you don't favor these arguably creepy puppets, it's interesting to take a peek in one of the shops and admire the craftsmanship. The most outstanding are the antique versions, which can be found at the more serious marionette stores.

The shopping hours for most chain stores, department stores, and boutiques are 10 AM to 7 PM every day. Shopping malls are open from 10 AM to 9 PM or, in some cases, 10 PM. Local boutiques, however, tend to take lunch breaks (so you'll find a sign indicating the shop is closed between noon and 2, or whenever the shop assistant decides it's time for lunch) and are closed on Sunday.

MAJOR SHOPPING DISTRICTS

Prague attempted to create an abbreviated copy of the Champs-Élyseés with **Pařížská ulice,** which is a tree-lined street lined with high-end fashion like Hugo Boss, Hermés, Louis Vuitton, and Salvatore Ferragamo.

The street's sidewalks are stuffed with outdoor tables, which are good havens to sit, breathe, and mull over whether you really need that silk peacock scarf. Serious shoppers will also want to poke around on the streets that cut through—you can find nice glass boutiques and interesting antiques shops in this area.

Dlouha is a feeder street into Old Town Square, so it's invariably simple to find. If you want to see the best in Czech fashion and home design, as well as the Czechs who buy the most fashionable products, head over to this area, where you can treat yourself to clothing boutiques by such local designers as Klára Nademlýnská, Tatiana, Timoure et Group, and Boheme. But the funky modern touch that Czechs have does not stop with a needle and thread. Home furnishings are also becoming part of their forte; be sure to check out Qubus Design and Sejto.

All of your favorite European clothing chains, including Zara, Mango, and Benetton can be found along **Na Příkopě**. And just off this main street, you'll find Versace, Ermenegildo Zegna, and Max Mara boutiques. Running into Na Příkopě is the famous **Václavské náměstí**, a tree-lined boulevard that is full of tourist kitsch but also such quality stores as Anima Tua and Accesorize.

DEPARTMENT STORES

The traditional Czech approach to large department stores was simply to house multiple kiosks under the same roof. The result, which you can still find in Prague, will allow you to make photocopies and buy a wig, all in the same room. But now that the British stores Tesco and Debenhams, and the French store Carrefour, have found their way to Prague, the choices are getting better.

Bílá Labuť. Electric-blue lava lamps, fake Miss Sixty–brand belts, mobile phones, and cheap cologne can be found at this store. It's interesting, for sure, as the overall shabbiness harks back to socialist times. ⊠ *Na Poříčí 23, Nové Město* ☎ *224–811–364* Ⓜ *Line B: Náměstí Republiky.*

Carrefour. The bonus of this French store, which is the anchor at one of the city's newest malls, Nový Smíchov, is that it's open until midnight. So look no farther than here if you have a toilet paper, hair product, underwear, or grocery emergency. ⊠ *Nový Smíchov, Plzeňská 8, Smíchov* ☎ *257–321–915* Ⓜ *Line B: Anděl.*

Debenhams. A new arrival in 2004, this British store gives shoppers trendy and durable clothing at fairly inexpensive prices. Stop here if you're looking for pink flip-flops smothered in hot-pink rhinestones, olive-green boxer shorts, or the latest Ralph Lauren perfume. There's also a home furnishings department upstairs. ⊠ *Václavské náměstí 21, Nové Město* ☎ *221–015–022* Ⓜ *Line A or B: Můstek.*

Kotva. This department store is nearly the only place in Prague where you can find New Balance running shoes; otherwise, the selection is small, but the prices are low. From striped tights to striped hats and all of the stationery and snorkels in between, this store has a large mix of items.

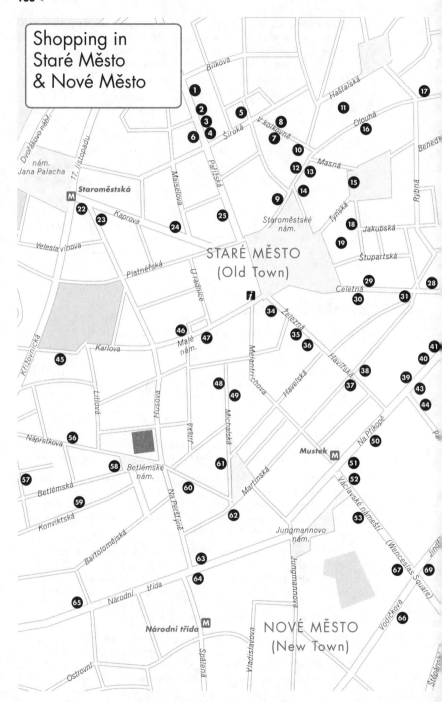

Shopping in Staré Město & Nové Město

STARÉ MĚSTO
(Old Town)

NOVÉ MĚSTO
(New Town)

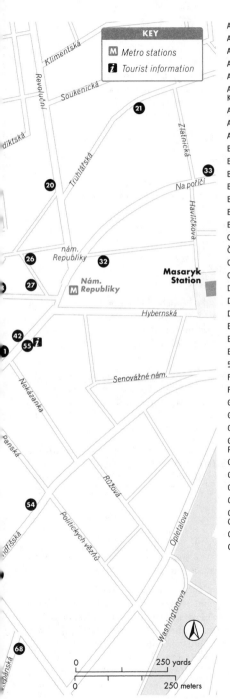

Accesorize	.52
Adidas	.43
Anagram Books	.19
Anima Tua	.52
Anne Fontaine	.15
Antikvariát Karil Křenek	.28
Art Deco Galerie	.48
Art Decoratif	.8
Arzenal	.22
Baťa	.53
Benetton	.51
Big Ben Bookshop	.18
Body Basics	.39
Bohème	.5
Botanicus	.61
Bric a Brac	.14
Cellarius	.66
Česky Garnat	.30
Christian Dior	.32
Coccinelle Accessories	.35
Debenhams	.69
Diva Center	.39
Dorotheum	.38
Ermenegildo Zegna	.26
Escada Sport	.55
Estee Lauder	.34
5 Avenue	.57
Francesco Biasia	.25
Fruits de France	.54
Galerie Bydlení	.21
Galerie JBK	.58
Galerie NoD	.17
Galerie Peithner-Lichtenfels	.49
Galerie Pyramida	.65
Galerie Tesar	.60
Galerie 'Z'	.47
Gianni Versace	.26
Globe Bookstore & Coffeehouse	.23
Golf & Leisure	.55
Granát	.16

Guess by Marciano	.2
Halada	.46
Hermès	.4
Hugo Boss	.3
Jan Kanzelsberger Bookshop	.68
JHB Starožitnosti	.44
Kenvelo	.52
Klára Nademlýnská	.12
Kotva	.20
Louis Vuitton	.6
Lush	.24
Mango	.50
Marks & Spencer	.39
Modernista	.59
Moser	.43
Nike	.67
Nový Svět	.7
Papillio	.19
Pietro Filipi	.63
Pohádka	.31
Promod	.69
Qubus Design	.11
Reporter	.7
Sejto	.13
Slovanský dům	.55
Sparkys	.37
Starožitnosti u sv. heleny	.33
Stefanel	.36
Swarovksi Bohemia	.29
Taiza	.42
Tatiana	.9
Tesco	.64
Timoure et Group	.10
U Karlova Mostu	.45
Vicini	.1
Villeroy & Boch	.62
Wilvorst	.27
Yanny	.41
Zara	.41
Zlatnictví František Vomáčka	.56

✉ *Náměstí Republiky 8, Nové Město* ☎ *224–801–111* Ⓜ *Line B: Náměstí Republiky.*

Tesco. The centrally located British chain is generally the best place for one-stop shopping to find fingernail polish remover or groceries. FYI: It has the best selection of English-language magazines if you find yourself craving an *Economist* or *Vanity Fair.* ✉ *Národní tř. 26, Nové Město* ☎ *222–003–111* Ⓜ *Line B: Národní třída.*

SHOPPING MALLS

Three malls with a Western flavor have popped up, giving Czech kids a new place to go when they're skipping school. These are also nice shopping havens for locals, who want to circumvent the tourist crowds and shop on the weekend.

Metropole. Although the selection of stores here is as large as that in Prague's other malls, the location is in a true suburb. If this piques your curiosity, make a day of this mall, which was completed in 2004, and IKEA, which is across the interstate. ✉ *Revnicka 1, Zličín* ☎ *257–111–511* Ⓜ *Line B: Zličín.*

Nový Smíchov. H&M, Zara, and a branch of Pietro Filipi are all here at this mall that was completed in 2003, but this is also the mall that has a giant Carrefour that stays open until midnight. For the kids, a video arcade is upstairs. ✉ *Plzeňská 8, Smíchov* ☎ *257–284–111* Ⓜ *Line B: Anděl.*

Palace Flora. Completed in March 2002, this mall was the first to bring an IMAX cinema to this country. Within the first year of its opening, the architects snagged a design award for this glass structure that houses Puma, Benetton, and Kenvelo (a local Old Navy look alike). ✉ *Vinohradská 149, Žižkov* ☎ *255–741–700* Ⓜ *Line C: Flora.*

Slovanský dům. Escada Sport, Mexx, and Diva have front windows at this small, trendy mall that's on the busiest shopping street in the city. Be sure to make it through the back doors, as the mall extends into the courtyard. ✉ *Na Příkopě 22, Nové Město* ☎ *257–181–212* Ⓜ *Line B: Náměstí Republiky.*

STREET MARKETS

It's better to hit Prague's two major street markets during the week since both are closed Saturday afternoon and all day on Sunday.

For fresh cherries, carrots, and handmade jewelry, the best street market in central Prague is on **Havelská ulice** in the Staré Mešto. The biggest and best market is the one in **Holešovice,** north of the city center on Bubenské nábřeží and Jateční streets; it offers Chinese food, cheap denim clothes shipped from Vietnam, and other surprises like antique lamps and paintings; to reach it, take the metro (Line C) to the Vltavská station and then catch any tram heading east (running to the left as you exit the metro station). Exit at the first stop and follow the crowds.

The **Easter Market,** held a week before and after the holiday, can be found where Václavské náměstí meets Na Příkopě in Nové Město. You can buy souvenirs and Easter switches (it's a Czech tradition for men to spank women on this holiday, an act that supposedly ensures a lady's fertility).

The **Christmas Market** stands out as the most exciting because of scheduled events for children and families, as well as booths stocked with wool scarves and *svařené vino or svařák,* which is warm wine. You can find the festivities and an enormous Christmas tree in Old Town Square, and this holiday market begins at the end of November and doesn't end until the first week of January.

SPECIALTY STORES

Antiques

For antiques connoisseurs, Prague can be a bit of a letdown. Even in comparison to other former Communist capitals such as Budapest, the choice of antiques in Prague can seem depressingly slim, as the city lacks large stores with a diverse selection of goods. The typical Prague *starožitnosti* (antiques shop) tends to be a small, one-room jumble of old glass and bric-a-brac. The good ones distinguish themselves by focusing on one particular specialty.

Art Deco Galerie. From a 1940s black lace slip dress to a funky art deco chair, there are many treasures to be found in this store, which is a few windy blocks away from Old Town Square. ⊠ *Michalská 21, Staré Město* ☎ *224–223–076* Ⓜ *Line A or B: Můstek.*

FodorśChoice **Art Deco Gallery Shop.** This shoebox-size shop has a great selection of
★ art deco tea sets from the 1930s that have "Made in Czechoslovakia" stamped on the bottom. Along with a good selection of jewelry, hats, and glass sets, the owner has English-language art books on hand so that you can read what collectors have to say about her items. The shop is only open from 2 to 7 PM most days (it opens at 11 AM on Wednesday and 2:30 on Sunday), so don't plan to make this an early-morning stop. ⊠ *Jánský vršek 8, Malá Strana* ☎ *257–535–801* Ⓜ *Line A: Malostranská.*

★ **Bric a Brac.** Antiques are stuffed on the shelves and even hang from the ceiling in this cluttered little shop that is the best store in Prague for small treasures such as a black-and-white picture book of Czech landmarks in Chicago (who knew?), candle holders, and a small selection of beaded or silver jewelry. The owner speaks perfect English and can answer any question you have about his merchandise. ⊠ *Týnská 7, Staré Město* ☎ *222–326–484* Ⓜ *Line A: Staroměstská.*

Dorotheum. On the pricey end of the scale is the Prague affiliate of the Austrian auction house, an elegant pawnshop that specializes in small things: jewelry, porcelain knickknacks, and standing clocks, as well as the odd military sword. ⊠ *Ovocný tř. 2, Nové Město* ☎ *224–222–001* Ⓜ *Line B: Náměstí Republiky.*

PRAGUE BLITZ TOUR

PUT ON YOUR WALKING SHOES AND PACK A BOTTLE OF WATER *because you're going to get your fair share of exercise today. Since most of the best shopping is in the heart of the city center, your feet are the most economical form of transport. Fuel yourself with a cup of espresso, and start this day by 10 AM sharp—this is extreme shopping.*

Start at the top of Václavské náměstí. See the National Museum? See the shops? Opt for culture on another day, today you're going to conquer the stores. Walk on the left side of the street, away from the museum, and head down the street. On Štěpánska, take a left and turn right into the Lucerna pasáž. Stop into **Cellarius** *for a bottle of Bohemian wine or champagne, and check out this building, which was once partly owned by former President Václav Havel. Once back on Václavské náměstí, look across the street to find* **Debenhams** *across the street. Stay on this side of the street, and walk until the street meets Na Příkopě.* **Kenvelo** *is on the corner, along with a currency-exchange booth—you can't get through this day without some cash, you know.*

Walk into the Koruna pasáž, where you will see **Accesorize** *to your right. Continue in the pasáž, and on the left is* **Anima Tua.** *At the end of the pasáž, take a right onto Na Příkopě.* **Benetton, Mango,** *and* **Moser** *are on your right. Walk farther up the street and* **Zara** *is on your left. Continue to the corner of Havířska, and then you have to make a choice: continue on and explore a few more stores or turn left and forge ahead.*

If you want to check out **Body Basics, Yanny,** *or* **Taiza,** *continue straight up Na Příkopě; they are up the street on your left. If you want to hit* **Mexx** *and* **Escada Sport,** *which are in the* **Slovanský dům** *mall, then go up the street and to the right. Either way, if you explore Na Příkopě further,*

you'll need to backtrack to Havířska, where you can turn right.

Back on Havířska, **Max Mara** *and the toy store* **Sparkys** *are on your left; both are worthy of your time. Walk to the end of this street, and take your first left, then your first right, and you find yourself on Železna. Walk up this street to find the dignified* **Coccinelle Accessories, Marina Rinaldi,** *and* **Estee Lauder** *on your left. Go farther and you see* **Benetton** *for children and* **Sergio Rossi** *on your right, and* **Stefanel** *to your left. Finally, after a few more steps, you're in Old Town Square—if you're here a few minutes before the hour is about to change, stick around and gawk at the Astronomical Clock with the other hundreds of gathered tourists.*

Do you see Týn church to your right, and the Jan Hus monument in the middle of the square? You're going to walk at a diagonal across the square between these landmarks. To the right of Jan Hus monument is a walkway, which will undoubtedly have a few vendor kiosks set up along it. Walk down this cobblestone path.

Once out of this path, notice the street on your left, Týnská, which is where you're going after you walk through the curved archway into the Týn courtyard, where you'll find adorable shops and the best coffee in town at **Ebel Coffee House**—*just in case you need to refuel. While you are here, check out the beautiful* **Botanicus** *store,* **Anagram Books,** *and the high-end antiques store* **Papillio.**

Retrace your steps out of the courtyard and turn right onto Týnská, where immediately on the left you can find **Bric a Brac.** *Go ahead and rummage through old, well, bric-a-brac. Continue down this street, turn left at the first opportunity, and the second shop to your left is* **Anne Fontaine.** *Continue down the street, take a* left and your first right. Now you are on Dlouha Street, which houses the heart of the creative Czech spirit.

Across the street and to your left is **Klára Nademlýnská.** After you check out her wares, walk back down the street, and your first left is Dušní, where you will find **Tatiana** and **Bohème.** Go back to Dlouhá street and turn left. **Sejto** is on your right, and across from the store is Rámová, where you will find **Qubus Design.** After this shop, return to Dlouhá and turn right, again backtracking. At the roundabout, look for V kolkovně, which is in front of you if Kozí is on your right. Go down V kolkovně to find **Timoure et Group.** Take a left on Vězeňská and head to Pařížská, where you will find **Hermès** on your right, along with **Vicini, Guess,** and **Hugo Boss.** Come back down the street on the opposite side and stop by **Louis Vuitton** and **Francesco Biasia.** Of course, in true Parisian style, this street is the best place to window shop if you don't want to pop in.

Backtrack one block, and take a left onto Široká, then take your first left onto Maiselova, and right onto Kaprova, where you will undoubtedly smell **Lush.** Follow your nose, and you'll see it on the right side. Cross the street, and take a left onto Žatecká, then take a right at the end of this street and walk about 30 feet. You're standing in front of the city library, with City Hall to your left on the square. Align yourself with the front doors of the library, and walk into the square, pass the parked cars and onto Husova street. At the end of this street, look up to see local artist David Černý's hanging man statue. After this, turn left onto Skořepka and stop by **Taizer Gallery,** which is on your right. Walk to the end of the street, and cross it into a brown open door that leads into a courtyard, which is the Platyž pasáž. Walk through the pasáž, and you will find yourself on Narodní. Turn right and walk

to the corner to find **Pietro Filipi,** a Czech clothing chain, where you are bound to find something that you like. Cross the street and walk toward **Tesco,** but unless you need something—more water, deodorant, an English-language magazine, new socks, or a candy bar— you can consider your Prague shopping blitz at an end.

JHB Starožitnosti. This is the place for old clocks: everything from rococo to Empire standing clocks and Bavarian cuckoo clocks. The shop also sells antique pocket watches. ✉ *Panská 1, Nové Město* ☎ *222–245–836* Ⓜ *Line A: Staroměstská.*

Nostalgie Antique. A shop that specializes in old textiles and jewelry, most of the textiles here are pre–World War II and include clothing, table linens, curtains, hats, and laces. ✉ *Jánský Vršek 8, Malá Strana* ☎ *257–530–049* Ⓜ *Line A: Malostranská.*

Papillio. In the elaborately refurbished medieval courtyard behind the Church of the Virgin Mary Before Týn, this is probably one of the best antiques shops in Prague, offering furniture, paintings, and especially museum-quality antique glass. Here you can find colorful Biedermeier goblets by Moser and wonderful Loetz vases. ✉ *Týn 1, Staré Město* ☎ *224–895–454* Ⓜ *Line A: Staroměstská.*

Starožitnosti u sv. heleny. Specializing in mostly clocks, scales, art, and jewelry from the 1940s, the women who own this shop run it brilliantly and with reasonable prices. They will also take care of shipping if you prefer. ✉ *Na Poříčí 35, Staré Město* ☎ *222–317–668* Ⓜ *Line B: Náměstí Republiky.*

Zlatnictví František Vomáčka. This is a cluttered shop that redeems itself with its selection of old jewelry in a broad price range, including rare art nouveau rings and antique garnet brooches. In the shop's affiliate next door, jewelry is repaired, cleaned, and made to order. ✉ *Náprstkova 9, Staré Město* ☎ *222–222–017* Ⓜ *Line A: Staroměstská.*

Art Galleries

The best galleries in Prague are quirky and eclectic affairs, places to sift through artworks rather than browse at arms' length. Many are also slightly off the beaten track and away from the main tourist thoroughfares.

Galerie JBK. A great gallery to find the talent of local artists, this is also the place to go if you're looking for original Pablo Picasso or Salvador Dali lithographs. In the basement you can find a nice selection of antique wooden furniture. ✉ *Betlémské náměstí 8, Staré Město* ☎ *222–220–689* Ⓜ *Line B: Národní třída.*

Galerie NoD. Above the Roxy, one of the most popular dance clubs in the city, this gallery shows an eclectic mix of the country's artistic talent. It's not as polished as others in the city, but the large space, young energy, and adjoining café make up for that. ✉ *Dlouhá 33, Staré Město* ☎ *No phone* Ⓜ *Line A: Staroměstská.*

★ **Galerie Peithner-Lichtenfels.** This deluxe gallery in Old Town specializes in modern Czech art. Paintings, prints, and drawings crowd the walls and are propped against glass cases and window sills. Comb through works by Czech Cubists, currently fetching high prices at international auctions. ✉ *Michalská 12, Staré Město* ☎ *224–227–680* Ⓜ *Line B: Náměstí Republiky.*

Books & Prints

Like its antiques shops, Prague's rare-book shops, or *antikvariáts*, were once part of a massive state-owned consortium that, since privatization, has split up and diversified. Now most shops tend to cultivate their own specialties. Some have a small English-language section with a motley blend of potboilers, academic texts, classics, and tattered paperbacks. Books in German, on the other hand, are abundant.

Anagram Books. If you're looking for a great nonfiction historical book about central Europe to read while you're here, head to this detailed store. The owner sells fiction and children's books, too. ⊠ *Týn 4, Staré Město* ☎ *224–895–737* Ⓜ *Line B: Náměstí Republiky.*

Antikvariát Karel Křenek. Near the Powder Tower, this shop specializes in books with a humanist slant. It has a good selection of modern graphics and prides itself on its avant-garde periodicals and journals from the 1920s and '30s. You can also find a small collection of English-language books. ⊠ *Celetná 31, Staré Město* ☎ *222–322–919* Ⓜ *Line B: Náměstí Republiky.*

Big Ben Bookshop. There's a great selection of new English-language books at this store. ⊠ *Malá Štupartská 5, Staré Město* ☎ *224–826–565* Ⓜ *Line B: Náměstí Republiky.*

Globe Bookstore & Coffeehouse. If you'd just like a good read, be sure to check out the longtime magnet for the local English-speaking community. ⊠ *Pšstrossova 6, Nové Město* ☎ *224–916–264* Ⓜ *Line B: Národní třída.*

Jan Kanzelsberger Bookshop. For hiking maps and road atlases, try the downstairs level of this shop on Wenceslas Square. ⊠ *Václavské nám. 42, Nové Město* ☎ *224–217–335* Ⓜ *Line A or B: Můstek.*

Shakespeare & Sons. The location is a bit out-of-the-city-center, but the trip is worth it for the great selection of new and used books, as well as one of the best literary vibes among local bookstores. From Náměstí Míru, hop on a tram to Krymská, and you'll be here. The bookstore doubles as a café, so this is a fantastic place to chill if the weather is not tourist-friendly. ⊠ *Krymská 12, Vršovice* ☎ *271–740–839* Ⓜ *Line C: Náměstí Míru, then a tram.*

U Karlova Mostu. The preeminent Prague bookstore has a suitably bookish location opposite the Klementinum; it's the place to go if you're looking for that elusive 15th-century manuscript. In addition to housing ancient books too precious to be leafed through, the store has a good selection of books on local subjects, a small foreign-language section, and a host of prints, maps, drawings, and paintings. ⊠ *Karlova 2, Staré Město* ☎ *224–229–205* Ⓜ *Line A: Staroměstská.*

Bags, Scarves & Accessories

Even though clothes tend to be expensive, stylish and trendy accessories can be found at low prices, especially at chain stores like Zara, H&M, and Mango. The following stores, however, are names of those that specialize in adding a little something to make a big statement, often at big prices.

Accesorize. The name says it all. Color-themed, this shop is where you will find purses, scarves, belts, earrings, bangle bracelets, and flip-flops to match your favorite color of sea-foam green. Prices are low, and quality is not bad, though some purses are overpriced. ✉ *Václavské nám. 1, Koruna pasáž, Nové Město* ☎ *257–951–950* Ⓜ *Line A or B: Můstek.*

Coccinelle Accessories. Chocolate brown and ivory scarves, and sidewalk-chalk blue leather handbags are made by this Italian designer, whose creations are always classic. ✉ *Železná 22, Nové Město* ☎ *224–228–203* Ⓜ *Line A or B: Můstek.*

Francesco Biasia. These soft leather purses in every shape and size imaginable are so beautiful you may want to eat them—even if you are a vegetarian. ✉ *Pařížská 5, Staré Město* ☎ *224–812–700* Ⓜ *Line A: Staroměstská.*

Hermés. Although the Prague boutique does not stock the famous Kelly bag, it does stock a wide selection of silk twill ties in a rainbow of colors, perfume, and perfectly crafted leather products. ✉ *Pařížská 12, Staré Město* ☎ *224–818–479* Ⓜ *Line A: Staroměstská.*

Louis Vuitton. Once this design house paired with Marc Jacobs, it gained a bit more street cred. Though the famous bags are still smothered in initials, now the designs go beyond brown and tan into a crayon-box mix of initials to little blue-and-gold totes. ✉ *Pařížská 11, Staré Město* ☎ *224–812–774* Ⓜ *Line A: Staroměstská.*

Clothing

FOR MEN & WOMEN **5 Avenue.** This boutique brings name-brand clothing, including such brands as DKNY, Tommy Hilfiger, and BCBG, among others, to Prague at discount prices. You can find a plethora of dresses in stock, in different brands, styles, and sizes, but there's generally only one of each. The store also stocks small selection of men's dress shirts. ✉ *Karolíny Světlé 22, Staré Město* ☎ *222–222–169* Ⓜ *Line A: Staroměstská.*

Benetton. Benetton defines international classics. You can count on finding any style sweater in any primary color here, and that goes for most any basics that you want. Of course, you can get your fill of Sissly jeans also. Upstairs, you'll usually find a great sale. ✉ *Na Příkopě 4, Nové Město* ☎ *224–236–744* Ⓜ *Line A or B: Můstek.*

Guess by Marciano. Jeans are the main course here, which you might expect from this well-known temple to the god of denim, though there's a nice selection of watches, light summer dresses for women, and beachside linen pants for men. ✉ *Pařížská 22, Staré Město* ☎ *222–328–649* Ⓜ *Line A: Staroměstská.*

H&M. One of Europe's biggest budget clothing retailers specializes in trendy, of-the-moment styles for both men and women, plus cheap and more timeless basics for everyone, including children. ✉ *Nový Smíchov, Plzeňská 8, Smíchov* ☎ *225–101–342* Ⓜ *Line B: Anděl.*

Kenvelo. This is the Old Navy of the Czech Republic, and it's mostly a place for teenagers to shop. Known for jeans and street wear, it always beats at the heart of casual Czech fashion. Some of the clothes might even be attractive to adults if they weren't ruined by the brand "Kenvelo" blasted across the chest of a button-down shirt or the back pockets of jeans. ✉ *Václavské náměstí 1, Nové Město* ☎ *221–111–711* Ⓜ *Line A or B: Můstek.*

Marks & Spencer. Also known as "Marks and Sparks," this is a British favorite. Ties, socks, underwear, hats, and dresses—you can find it all here. The store is known for durable quality, but basic, if not bland, clothing styles. ⊠ *Na Příkopě 19, Nové Město* ☎ *224-232-237* Ⓜ *Line A or B: Můstek.*

Pietro Filipi. The Czech fashion retailer has introduced reasonably priced clothing for the mainstream young professional. Conservative cuts and fabrics for both men and women, this store is a life saver when you are looking for seasonal staples, like black turtlenecks or beige jackets. ⊠ *Národní 31, Nové Město* ☎ *224-231-120* Ⓜ *Line B: Národní třída.*

Stefanel. This is a great place for ladies to find bubblegum-pink suede satchels and a banana-yellow wide-brimmed sun hat and other versatile accessories. For men, this is the place for those funky flowered summer shirts and mid-calf tan summer shorts. ⊠ *Železná 14, Nové Město* ☎ *224-226-546* Ⓜ *Line A or B: Můstek.*

Wilvorst. With plaid shirts for men and wool skirts for women, the clothing selection here is preppy. However, with brands like Joop!, the quality is the key here. There are also several spin-offs, including Wilvorst Sport & Casual (for men) and Vion by Wilvorst (for women). ⊠ *U Prašné brány 1, Nové Město* ☎ *222-323-573* Ⓜ *Line B: Náměstí Republiky* ⊠ *Wilvorst Sport & Casual* ⊠ *Obecni dum 2, Nové Město* ☎ *222-002-330* Ⓜ *Line B: Náměstí Republiky* ⊠ *Wilvorst-Women's* ⊠ *Obecni dum 1, Nové Město* ☎ *222-002-313* Ⓜ *Line B: Náměstí Republiky* ⊠ *Vion by Wilvorst* ⊠ *Pařižka 4, Staré Město* ☎ *224-814-438* Ⓜ *Line A: Staroměstská.*

Zara. Most clothes from this European chain aimed at youngish buyers are a fine line between classic and stylish, like a pink-and-white polka-dot summer skirt or black-and-white pumps that look like they came straight from the feet of Audrey Hepburn in *My Fair Lady*. Bags, scarves and the store-named perfumes are here, too. But men are a target audience upstairs, where they can find black-and-white pinstripe trousers, Zara cologne, and trendy brown leather ankle boots. ⊠ *Na Příkopě 25, Nové Město* ☎ *272-142-191* Ⓜ *Line A or B: Můstek.*

FOR WOMEN   With more chain stores and fashion boutiques opening in Prague, the selection of women's clothing is becoming more diverse and making a break from the skin-tight style that's more of a tattoo than a piece of clothing. Czech women love trends, so you'll see a majority of shops that cater to the ultrafashionable market, but more and more classic style shops are opening and are being taken seriously.

Anima Tua. A red string-bikini top covered in fake cloth roses can be found here among the miniskirts, lingerie, and accessories that have all the bling-bling you could ever want-want. Fashions are provocative and expensive. The staff is incredibly snobby, making shopping a bit uncomfortable in this tiny boutique. ⊠ *Koruna pasáž, Václavské náměstí 1, Nové Město* ☎ *224-473-074* Ⓜ *Line A or B: Můstek.*

Anne Fontaine. When you're not in Paris, it's always nice to shop like you are. This French designer handcrafts white—and only white—button-down blouses for women. Beautiful, detailed, expensive, and unique, they are worth every crown or euro. ⊠ *Masna 12, Staré Město* ☎ *224–808–306* Ⓜ *Line A or B: Můstek.*

Bohème. Simple, high-quality, and fashionable knitwear is what's in store for you at this boutique. Turtlenecks, sleeveless shirts, and drawstring pants will feel so comfortable that you'll crave a relaxing, but fashionable, weekend in the country. ⊠ *Dušní 8, Staré Město* ☎ *224–813–840* Ⓜ *Line B: Náměstí Republiky.*

Escada Sport. Classic and comfortable high-end fashion is in this store, where you can buy that cotton green-pastel collared shirt and wear it straight to your country club. ⊠ *Na Příkopě 22, Nové Město* ☎ *221–451–227* Ⓜ *Line B: Náměstí Republiky.*

Gianni Versace. Though the boutique is small, the Versace look is not diluted. Bright turquoise, electric pinks, and high-school-color purple are made to stretch over torsos in tight-fitting summery dresses. The shop also stocks a small selection of shoes. ⊠ *U Prašné brány 3, Staré Město* ☎ *224–810–016* Ⓜ *Line B: Náměstí Republiky.*

FodorśChoice **Klára Nademlýnská.** The darling of stylish Czech fashion, this designer
★ sells both funky and conservative clothes—everything from pin-stripe suits to floor-length halter dresses—in her Old Town boutique. Don't overlook the accessories case, which displays inexpensive costume jewelry. The store changes as often as the styles do, so look out for great end-of-the-season sales. ⊠ *Dlouhá 3, Staré Město* ☎ *224–188–769* Ⓜ *Line B: Náměstí Republiky.*

Mango. This Spanish chain makes shopping easy by color-coordinating everything, making this the perfect stop if you're looking for a black spaghetti-strap tank top. The cathedral-like building is packed with funky white business suits, ruffly black skirts, bow-clad kitten heels, red leather clutches, and other accessories. ⊠ *Na Příkopě 8, Nové Město* ☎ *224–218–884* Ⓜ *Line A or B: Můstek.*

Marina Rinaldi. A conservative, but stylish, shop, this is where trendy businesswomen go to add a butter yellow linen dress to their summer wardrobe or a black leather jacket to their winter wardrobe. ⊠ *Železná 22, Staré Mésto* ☎ *224–234–636* Ⓜ *Line A or B: Můstek.*

Nový Svět. With the sassy business woman in mind, this boutique stocks short, beige miniskirt suits that prove business does not have to be boring. There are more conservative options here, like pant suits, as well as evening wear. ⊠ *V kolkovné 5, Staré Město* ☎ *224–813–948* Ⓜ *Line A: Staroměstská.*

Presidents. Fashion designer Katarína Ihnátová dresses the younger Czech girls in sheer, black dresses sprinkled with silver stones and the more conservative woman in strapless Jackie Onasis–style gowns. When many female Czech spokespeople, singers, and television broadcasters are looking for elegance, they come here. ⊠ *Jana Masaryka 1, Vinohrady* ☎ *222–521–053* Ⓜ *Line C: I. P. Pavlova.*

Promod. This French clothing store offers three floors of clothing, jewelry, and shoes for going to work, hitting the town, or chilling at home. The second floor generally has some good bargains, so don't be afraid to get aggressive and tear through those racks. ⊠ *Václavské náměstí 2, Nové Město* ☎ *296–327–701* Ⓜ *Line A or B: Můstek.*

Taiza. You can find dresses covered in floral prints that explode, pinks that pop, and yellows that glow in this shop. The Cuban-born designer has fun with colors and knows how to make skirts show leg without sacrificing taste. ⊠ *Na Příkopě 31, Nové Město* ☎ *221–613–308* Ⓜ *Line B: Náměstí Republiky.*

Fodor'sChoice **Tatiana.** Whether you're looking for a black-silk obi, or a red corsage ★ the size of a man's fist, this local boutique has great accessories. The designer's specialty, however, is sexy evening and party wear; occasionally, you can find a piece or two that you can wear in view of your boss. ⊠ *Dušní 1, Staré Město* ☎ *224–934–850* Ⓜ *Line A: Staroměstská.*

Timoure et Group. Modern and simple, these two Czech designers don't push fashion into new directions with a fitted white tennis dress, but they're able to make women look smart and sophisticated. ⊠ *V kolkovné 6, Staré Město* ☎ *222–327–358* Ⓜ *Line A: Staroměstská.*

Yanny. With a selection of Dolce & Gabbana, Jean-Paul Gaultier, and other name-dropping designers, it's no surprise that this store's dresses, skirts, and tops can be found in many of the fashion spreads in magazines like *Elle* and *Dolce Vita.* ⊠ *Na Příkopě 27, Nové Město* ☎ *224–228–196* Ⓜ *Line B: Náměstí Republiky.*

FOR MEN The shopping in Prague is tremendously disappointing if you're a man. You can find mainly unstylish pleated and tapered-leg trousers. A handful of shops, however, save the day for men's fashion.

Ermenegildo Zegna. You'll have steam rising from your shoulders in a smoking, coal-black suit from this Italian designer. Here, you can find the highest-quality suits that this city has to offer—and also the most expensive. ⊠ *U Prašné brány 3, Staré Město* ☎ *224–810–018* Ⓜ *Line B: Náměstí Republiky.*

Golf & Leisure. For those gentlemen who have been unexpectedly invited for a game of golf, this is where you can buy the salmon-color Oscar Jacobson golf shirt, or a red, low-V-neck silk sweater. ⊠ *Na Příkopě 22, Nové Město* ☎ *221–451–775* Ⓜ *Line B: Náměstí Republiky.*

Hugo Boss. Depending on the occasion, Prague's trendiest men come here to buy tight leopard-print boxer briefs, tailored blue shirts, or drawstring white linen pants. ⊠ *Parízská 6, Staré Město* ☎ *222–324–536* Ⓜ *Line A: Staroměstská.*

Reporter. Smooth, black-leather wallets, star-silver Dandy-brand belts, and a room full of shirts, ties, and business suits are what you will find in this quality men's store. This Italian-owned shop brings Italian brands like Brioni, Canali, and Les Copains to the more fashionable streets of Prague. ⊠ *V kolkovné 5, Staré Město* ☎ *222–329–823* Ⓜ *Line B: Náměstí Republiky.*

FOR CHILDREN   Most of the quality children's clothing can be found at the mall, especially at Nový Smíchov, where you can find the cheapest and trendiest clothing for tykes at **H&M,** where half the store is devoted to children's clothing in the trendiest seasonal styles. See ⇨ For Men & Women, *above.*

Benetton. Tiny, tough jean vests and miniature white parachute pants are found here, where big trends are suited for little bodies at the company's store devoted to kids' fashions. ⊠ *Železna 1, Staré Město* ☎*224–221–910* Ⓜ *Line A or B: Můstek.*

Cosmetics & Perfume

Body Basics. So it isn't Czech-owned, but it is Czech-born. This seemingly ubiquitous shop sells cosmetics and bath goods that are similar to those found at the Body Shop. But, of course, the scents are different, so sniff around for that delicious avocado scrub. ⊠ *Na Příkopě 19, Nové Město* ☎ *224–231–271* Ⓜ *Line B: Náměstí Republiky* ⊠ *Vinohradská 50, Vinohrady* ☎ *222–097–105* Ⓜ *Line A: Jiřího z Poděbrad* ⊠ *Plzeňská 8 257322947, Smíchov* ☎ *257–322–947* Ⓜ *Yellow Line: Anděl.*

Botanicus. Every ingredient in the cosmetics and bath in this Czech-owned shop is organically grown and organically beautiful. Selling herbs, foods, oils, soaps, and even stationery, this is great proof of how green—and inventive—the Czech thumb can be. ⊠ *Michalská 2, Staré Město* ☎ *224–212–977* Ⓜ *Line A or B: Náměstí Republiky* ⊠ *Týnsky Dvůr 3, Staré Město* ☎ *224–895–446* Ⓜ *Line B: Náměstí Republiky.*

Christian Dior. Looking for lipstick that lasts for days or Ultimeyes mascara? Look no farther—you've found the spot in this dainty boutique, which also offers pedicures and manicures. ⊠ *V Celnici 4, Nové Město* ☎ *224–224–447* Ⓜ *Line B: Náměstí Republiky.*

Clinique. Just in case you are a Clinique-ophile and you forgot your face soap and moisturizing lotion, don't fret. A Clinique counter awaits you on the first floor of the Nový Smíchov mall, where you can find anything this brand sells. ⊠ *Nový Smíchov, Plzeňská 8, Smíchov* ☎ *257–329–230* Ⓜ *Line B: Anděl.*

Diva Center. After meandering through Prague's street on a hot day, this is a perfect place to freshen up or, rather, try to find a perfume that suits you. Czechs love perfumeries, and this is another one that offers hundreds of the usual suspects—Calvin Klein, Ralph Lauren, and all the other beautiful scents. ⊠ *Na Příkopě 19, Nové Město* ☎ *224–238–364* Ⓜ *Line B: Náměstí Republiky.*

Estee Lauder. A full store with full benefits is at this Old Town location. Find your favorites in make-up, cellulite cream, fingernail polish, perfume—or stop in and schedule a manicure. ⊠ *Železná 18, Staré Město* ☎ *224–232–023* Ⓜ *Line b: Náměstí Republiky.*

Lancôme. All of the usual finds are here, including Optimum smoothing moisturizer and other skin-softening products that make this French company famous. ⊠*Jungmannovo náměstí 20, Nové Město* ☎*224–217–189* Ⓜ *Line A or B: Můstek.*

Lush. All-natural with no animal testing—just people testing (folks actually eat each product to ensure its safety)—the products in this little shop are the best-smelling around. Like a cheese shop, Lush presents blocks of soaps that are sliced, weighed, wrapped, and ready for your bathtub. ⊠ *Kaprova 13, Staré Město* ☎ *603–164–362* Ⓜ *Line A: Staroměstská.*

Sephora. If you can't find the fire-engine red lipstick that you've been looking for here, it does not exist. This French store brings the best of cosmetics, perfumes, and beauty products under one roof with all of the brands that every fashion magazine in the world cherishes—Estee Lauder, Christian Dior, and the list goes on. ⊠ *Nový Smíchov, Plzeňská 8, Smíchov* ☎ *257–326–618* Ⓜ *Line B: Anděl.*

Food & Wine

Cellarius. This shop has a wide choice of Moravian and Bohemian wines and spirits, as well as products from more recognized wine-making lands. This is where you can pick up a bottle of Bohemia Sekt (champagne), which is inexpensive and perfect for celebrations. ⊠ *Lucerna Pasáž, Václavské nám., between Vodičkova and Štěpánská, Nové Město* ☎ *224–210–979* Ⓜ *Line A or B: Můstek.*

Fruits de France. This beautifully fresh shop charges Western-style prices for fruits and vegetables imported directly from France. ⊠ *Jindřišská 9, Nové Město* ☎ *224–220–304* Ⓜ *Line A or B: Můstek* ⊠ *Bělehradská 94, Vinohrady* ☎ *222–511–261* Ⓜ *Line C: I. P. Pavlova.*

Glass

Glass has traditionally been Bohemia's biggest export, and it was one of the few products manufactured during Communist times that managed to retain an artistically innovative spirit. Today Prague has plenty of shops selling Bohemian crystal, though much of it is tourist kitsch.

FodorśChoice
★
Artěl. Without any previous experience working with glass, the American owner of this store followed her instincts to pinpoint what was missing in the Czech glass scene—a combination of antique and modern. In her shop, you will find elegant, long-stemmed wine glasses and playful giraffe-series whiskey glasses. Her work has caught the attention of buyers like Whoopi Goldberg and fashion designer Marc Jacobs. ⊠ *Vinohradská 164, Vinohrady* ☎ *271–732–161* Ⓜ *Line A: Jiřího z Poděbrad.*

Galerie Pyramida. This is a good place to find modern works of art in glass from Czech and Slovak artists. The gallery is fairly large, and works with about 500 artists, so expect to find a wide range of work. ⊠ *Národní 11, Nové Město* ☎ *224–213–117* Ⓜ *Line B: Národní Třída.*

Galerie Tesar. Selling only clear glasses in a white-walled room with silver shelves, this shop does not look like it's open for business. Step inside, though, and admire this functional art, which is sold at reasonable prices. ⊠ *Skořepká 4, Staré Město* ☎ *572–695–476* Ⓜ *Line B: Národní třída.*

Galerie 'Z'. This gallery sells limited-edition mold-melted and blown glass. ⊠ *Michalská pasáž, Malé náměstí 11, Staré Město* ☎ *224–218–248* Ⓜ *Line A or B: Můstek.*

★ **Material.** You know that you're in a serious glass store when even the door's handle is artistically crafted from a vase. This eye-catching shop below the Charles Bridge sells glass homeware that is crafted from the Czech company Ajeto. There are many unique pieces here, including long-stem candlesticks with glass leaves that you will find nowhere else. ☒ *U Lužického semináře 7, Malá Strana* ☎ *257–533–663* Ⓜ *Line A: Malostranská.*

Moser. The opulent flagship store of the world-famous Karlovy Vary glassmaker, this shop offers the widest selection of traditional Bohemian glass. Even if you're not in the market to buy, stop by the store simply to look at the elegant wood-panel salesrooms on the second floor. The staff will gladly pack goods for traveling. ☒ *Na Příkopě 12, Nové Město* ☎ *224–211–293* Ⓜ *Line B: Náměstí Republiky.*

Villeroy & Boch. Though many engaged couples do their wedding registries here, that does not disqualify you from buying a little something for yourself. Delicate floral china patterns and a wide selection of crystal will make your dinner guests ask, "Where on earth did you find these glasses?" Prague, of course. ☒ *Ńrodní 37, Nové Město* ☎ *224–235–165* Ⓜ *Line B: Národní Třída.*

Home Design

Czech design is wonderfully rich both in quality and imagination, emphasizing old-fashioned craftsmanship while often taking an offbeat, even humorous approach. Strained relations between Czech designers and producers have reined in the potential selection, but there are nevertheless a handful of places showcasing Czech work.

Arzenal. A design shop that offers Japanese and Thai food in addition to funky, colorful glass vases and even beaded clothing, it exclusively sells work by Bořek Šípek, President Havel's official designer. ☒ *Valentinská 11, Staré Město* ☎ *224–814–099* Ⓜ *Line A: Staroměstská.*

Fast. Though a little bit off the beaten track, this store is worth the trek. Besides ultramodern furniture, there are ingenious (and more portable) pens, binders, and other office and home accoutrements. ☒ *Sázavská 32, Vinohrady* ☎ *224–250–538* Ⓜ *Line A: Jiřího z Poděbrad.*

Galerie Bydlení. This is a father-and-son operation focusing exclusively on Czech-made furniture. ☒ *Truhlářská 20, Nové Město* ☎ *222–312–383* Ⓜ *Line B: Náměstí Republiky.*

★ **Modernista.** Though you probably won't ship a restored 1960s-era, ruby-red armchair to your home, you might be interested in a black-and-white striped tea set that is gorgeously cubist. Treasures of all sizes are here, and the best part is that they are all modernly restored. ☒ *Konviktska 5, Staré Město* ☎ *222–220–113* Ⓜ *Line B: Narodní Třída.*

FodorśChoice **Qubus Design.** This home-design shop's idea of a vase is a ceramic white
★ galosh, men's size of course. Plenty of funky decorative items, sleek serving platters, and Yin-and-Yang salt-and-pepper shakers, are here. ☒ *Rámová 3, Staré Město* ☎ *222–313–151* Ⓜ *Line B: Náměstí Republiky.*

Sejto. Specializing in mostly silks for the home, this store also sells pillow covers, table cloths, and funky cloth napkins that are truly unique.

Modern, simple kitchenware is also sold here, along with shirts and purses. ⊠ *Dlouhá 24, Staré Město* ☎ *222–320–370* Ⓜ *Line B: Náměstí Republiky.*

Yves Delorme. Though Czech-made bedding is not known for class and comfort, the French are a different story. An egg-shell white linen duvet with airy pink honeysuckle flowers and pea-green stems makes for comfortable bedroom statement. If you're not interested in taking home a bed cover, the shop's namesake air fresheners are portable, stylish, and flowery scents. ⊠ *Ungelt 640, Staré* MeŇXtags error: Style name too longŇ Náměstí Republiky.

Jewelry

You won't find any jewelry steals in Prague. Garnets and amber are the hot commodities in the Czech Republic, but prices tend to be a bit steep, especially when the dollar is weak. Expect to pay the equivalent of at least $75 for a nice piece of silver jewelry with a stunning setting. Smaller pieces, amber bead bracelets, or stud earrings can be found for less than $40. Look around at jewelry stores before making a purchase—most sell the same items, so you generally can save a few dollars by being a patient shopper.

Art Decoratif. The creative Alfons Mucha torch passed to his granddaughter, Jarmila Mucha Plockova, who has produced designs inspired by her grandfather's work since 1992. This is where you can find a Sarah Bernhardt silver necklace or slender glass vase capped with a silver Mucha design. The designs are moderately expensive, but high inquality. The two branches do not have identical stock; the Josefov branch has a larger jewelry selection, for example. ⊠ *Široká 9, Josefov* ☎ *222–321–032* Ⓜ *Line A: Staromětská* ⊠ *Michalska 19, Staré Město* ☎ *225–777–156* Ⓜ *Line A or B: Můstek.*

Česky Garnat. Though the shop is flanked between kitschy tourist shops, it's among the best around, offering a wide selection of garnets and amber. Communistically organized, this store is divided by stone, so that hummingbird egg–sized amber stone ring ensconced in silver leaves will not be terribly difficult to locate. ⊠ *Celetná 4, Staré Město* ☎ *224–228–287* Ⓜ *Line A or B: Můstek.*

Granát. With a comprehensive selection of garnet jewelry, plus contemporary and traditional pieces set in gold and silver, this shop is fair with prices. ⊠ *Dlouhá 28, Staré Město* ☎ *222–315–612* Ⓜ *Line A: Staroměstská.*

Halada. This shop sells sleek, Czech-designed silver jewelry; an affiliate shop at Na Příkopě 16 specializes in gold, diamonds, and pearls. ⊠ *Karlova 25, Nové Město* ☎ *224–228–938* Ⓜ *Line B: Karlovo náměstí* ⊠ *Na Příkopě 16, Nové Město* ☎ *224–221–304* Ⓜ *Line B: Náměstí Republiky.*

Fodor'sChoice ★ **Swarovksi Bohemia.** Nicole Kidman donned a crystal dress, while Yves Saint Laurent sported a crystal heart for the cover of *Vogue*—both, of course, came from this Bohemian crystal designer. Crystal jewelry with a brilliant shine and mid-range prices make this a must if you're a jewelry aficionado. ⊠ *Celetná 11, Staré Město* ☏ *222–315–585* Ⓜ *Line A or B: Můstek.*

Marionettes

Marionettes have a long tradition in Bohemia, going back to the times when traveling troupes used to entertain children with morality plays on town squares. Now, although the art form survives, it has become yet another tourist lure, and you'll continually stumble across stalls selling almost identical marionettes.

Galerie Marionette. A small selection of puppets, which are one of a kind, can be found at this tiny shop in the Lesser Quarter. These beautiful marionettes differ from those typically seen around the city in that they are larger, with more exaggerated facial features. ⊠ *U Lužického semináře 7, Malá Strana* ☏ *257–535–091* Ⓜ *Line A: Malostranská.*

★ **Obchod Pod lampou.** The marionettes here are the real thing. These puppets—hand-crafted knights, princesses, and pirates—are made by the same artists who supply professional puppeteers. Prices may be higher than for the usual stuff on the street, but the craftsmanship is well worth it. ⊠ *U Lužického semináře 5, Malá Strana* ☏ *No phone* Ⓜ *Line A: Malostranská.*

Marionety. The owner of this shop has a discerning collection of new and antique marionettes. Find a modern devil or, if you prefer, an antique devi, which is from 1910 and comes with twice the painted eeriness and twice the price. ⊠ *Nerudova 51, Malá Strana* ☏ *257–533–035* Ⓜ *Line A: Malostranská.*

Miscellaneous

★ **Romen—The Little Shop.** Funded by European Union and other grants, this is the first shop in the country that exclusively sells Roma products, including everything from a black-and-white portrait shot of a crying, snotted child, to functional, handmade baskets made by Roma women in Southern Slovakia. Staff are friendly and speak a little English, so they can tell you what jovial CD is playing on the stereo or answer questions you might have about the shop or their culture. ⊠ *Nerudova 32, Malá Strana* ☏ *257–532–800* Ⓜ *Line A: Malostranská.*

La Perla Art. White silk fabrics that are sheer as a moth wing, and mint-green and cotton-candy pink Pashmina scarves are what you will find here. Much of the stock is from India, but the owner has selected only the best in quality and most interesting designs to sell in Prague. ⊠ *Malostranské náměstí 11, Malá Strana* ☏ *257–531–628* Ⓜ *Line A: Malostranská.*

Music & Musical Instruments

Capriccio. This is the place in Prague to find sheet music of all kinds. ⊠ *Újezd 15, Malá Strana* ☏ *257–320–165* Ⓜ *Line A: Malostranská.*

Dům Hudebnich Nastroju. You can find a comprehensive selection of quality musical instruments at reasonable prices at this four-story house of music. ⊠ *Jungmannova nám. 17, Nové Město* ☏ *224–222-501* Ⓜ *Line A or B: Můstek.*

Shoes

Shoes, even the low-quality variety, tend to be as expensive as electronics in Prague. In the past, they were expensive *and* tacky. Now, reputable local chains have improved their stock, and trendy shoe designers have added some competitive energy, which means that you'll pay top prices for shoes that, at least, will last longer than one season.

Baťa. Founded in 1894 in Bohemia, this local favorite has grown to be the largest shoe retailer in the world, which is recorded by the *Guinness Book of World Records*. Pumps, sneakers, boots, loafers, flip-flops—there are shoes for every occasion and for every foot size. There's also a branch in Nový Smíchov mall. ✉ *Václavské náměstí 6, Nové Město* ☎ *224–218–133* Ⓜ *Line A or B: Můstek* ✉ *Nový Smíchov, Plzeňská 8, Smíchov* ☎ *251–512–847* Ⓜ *Line B: Anděl.*

Beltissimo. Stylish, strappy shoes are sold here, but this is also one of the very few places where you can buy a pair of Campers, Italian shoes known for their durable leather, boxy presentation, and first-class comfort. Check out the branch in Slovanský dům. ✉ *U Prašné brány 1, Staré Město* ☎ *222–002–320* Ⓜ *Line B: Náměstí Republiky.*

Creation Elle de Motive. It's like walking into a crayon box when you enter this store, which is the exact image of a little girl's dress-up wonderland. Women's high-heels are given touches like hot-pink sequins and shiny silver buckles. These not just shoes—they're statements. This store is for the truly trendy at heart. ✉ *Pařížská 10, Staré Město* ☎ *222–315–182* Ⓜ *Line A: Staroměstská.*

Leiser. This is a fun store, where you can find those styles that are so funky that they almost seem vintage. What really makes this place so great is that they aren't even going for that approach. From sneakers to pumps, kids to adult, shoes are stocked according to size. ✉ *U Prašné brány 1, Nové Město* ☎ *224–810–431* Ⓜ *Line B: Náměstí Republiky.*

Salamander. This is where you can find the same shoes as in a midwestern American mall department store. Durable shoes, such as a pair of Tommy Hilfiger boat shoes, are here, but probably at a higher price than you would pay in the United States. There are two stores on one street, and though there isn't much of a difference between the two, they are worth checking out if you're in need of comfortable, quality shoes. ✉ *Na Příkopě 16, 23, Nové Město* ☎ *224–210–485 or 222–101–155* Ⓜ *Line B: Náměstí Republiky.*

Sergio Rossi. Designing for more than 40 years, this designer plays with stiletto shapes and leather designs to make shoes wearable and memorable. ✉ *Železná 1, Staré Město* ☎ *224–216–407* Ⓜ *Line B: Náměstí Republiky.*

Vicini. A shop that has a good selection of classic women's shoes with a stylish twist, this is where Prague's trendiest ladies buy their buckled boots and ankle-tied high heels. ✉ *Pařížská 24, Staré Město* ☎ *224–815–976* Ⓜ *Line A: Staroměstská.*

Sporting Goods

Adidas. Staff here are helpful and generally seem athletic rather than posing as athletes for fashion's sake. A colorful selection of sportswear, including shells and windbreakers and the other three-stripe Adidas staples, are in stock, along with shoes and socks. ⊠ *Na Příkopě 12, Nové Město* ☎ *224–210–204* Ⓜ *Line A or B: Můstek.*

Gigasport. This is where locals shop when they are serious about their sport. You can find diving fins and running shoes here, but it's best to know what you're looking for. Unless you get lucky, the staff tends to know only the basic elements about their department, so if you ask a staffer about running shoes and use the word "pronating," prepare yourself for a strange stare, followed by an awkward silence. ⊠ *Na Příkopě 19, Myslbek pasáž, Nové Město* ☎ *224–237–494* Ⓜ *Line B: Náměstí Republiky.*

Hudy Sport. This sport-goods store is a good source for quality hiking and camping equipment in case you find the urge to be one with nature. ⊠ *Na Perštýně 14, Nové Město* ☎ *224–218–600* ⊕ *www.hudy. cz* Ⓜ *Line B: Náměstí Republiky.*

Nike. Bright lights and loud music make this spot seem more like a club than a store—make your purchase, then use those new shoes to run out of here. Though standard sport shoes are sold here, the choice leans more toward fashionable than functional. ⊠ *Václavské náměstí 18, Nové Město* ☎ *224–237–921* Ⓜ *Line A or B: Můstek.*

Toys & Gifts for Children

Nearly every stationery store has beautiful watercolor and colored-chalk sets available at rock-bottom prices. The Czechs are also master illustrators, and the books they've made for young "pre-readers" are some of the world's loveliest. For the child with a theatrical bent, a marionette—they range from finger-size to nearly child-size—can be a wonder (see ⇨ Marionettes, *above*).

Hračky. For delightful and reasonably priced Czech-made wooden toys and wind-up trains, cars, and animals, look in this popular store. ⊠ *Pohořelec 24, Hradčany* ☎ *603–515–745* Ⓜ *Line A: Hradčanská.*

Pohádka. Right there among the tourist shops, you'll find this store that sells marionettes and hand puppets made for children to enjoy. Harry Potter, devils, and angels can all be found hanging from the ceiling and sitting on shelves at reasonable prices. ⊠ *Celetná 32, Nové Město* ☎ *No phone* Ⓜ *Line B: Nám. Republiky.*

★ **Sparkys.** It might be for little kids, but it isn't a little store. Probably the best known toy store in the city, this is where parents go when they don't want their children to play with the ubiquitous wooden toys tied to this country's history. Overstuffed animals that are child-size, Halloween costumes, games, and more are here. ⊠ *Havířská 2, Nové Město* ☎ *224–239–309* Ⓜ *Line B: Nám. Republiky.*

DAY-TRIPS FROM PRAGUE

7

MOST STRIKING CATHEDRAL
Chrám Svaté Barbory, *Kutná Hora* ⇨*p.160*

MOST UPBEAT CASTLE TOUR
Český Šternberk Castle ⇨*p.169*

LARGEST COLLECTION OF HUNTING TROPHIES
Konopiště Castle ⇨*p.171*

A FAIRY-TALE VIEW
Karlštejn Castle ⇨*p.164*

BONE-CHILLING!
Kostnice, *Sedlec* ⇨*p.162*

UNFORGETTABLE HISTORY LESSONS
Malá Pevnost, *Terezín* ⇨*p.175*

GOTHIC GEM IN THE FOREST
Great Hall, Křivoklat Castle ⇨*p.167*

By David
Friday

ALTHOUGH PRAGUE IS UNDENIABLY BEAUTIFUL, it's sometimes refreshing to get out of the city and its hustle and bustle for a day or even for a few hours. The wide choice of scenic towns lying within an hour or so of Prague makes getting away easy. Grand castles perched on hilltops, a quaint city with a strong medieval past, and moving World War II monuments represent the range of destinations that show you not only a different terrain but a different side of Czech life and history. An added bonus is that prices in village restaurants and hotels, should you choose to stay over, are much cheaper than in Prague. (It's a further bonus that the air is much cleaner, something you may not even notice until you get back to Prague.)

Karlštejn is the most popular day-trip from Prague, but it's by no means the outright best—that depends on your interests. If you go here, you very likely won't escape the large crowds, especially in summer. Křivoklát and Český Šternberk are a little more remote and certainly less touristy, though the latter is much more plush, if not posh, than the former.

Konopiště shares a grand history of hunting with Křivoklát, but it flaunts the tradition more shamelessly with an abundant taxidermy collection, all of which were killed by the famous Franz Ferdinand prior to World War I. Orlík is the most distant of the castles and therefore makes for the most remote day-trip of all, but you'll be rewarded by its splendid natural setting and the dramatic castle itself.

On a different note, Terezín and Lidice are both tributes to the Nazi atrocities of World War II. The former is the larger and more prominent, comprising several buildings (though you don't have to visit all of them). More sobering and educational than outright depressing, a visit to one of these places is recommended, particularly if you have not had the opportunity to visit a Holocaust site before.

Kutná Hora is a quiet town that, like many small towns in the Czech Republic, can look a little depressing on a rainy day. In the sunshine, however, it comes alive as the crumbling stucco building foundations and leftover examples of Communist retailing give way to the splendors of the ages that created the buildings. If you visit, you can see cobbled streets beneath medieval spires, as well as a few other surprises that can make your eyes widen.

With a few exceptions, most of these destinations are quite easy to visit on your own, by either car, train, or bus. Trains and bus fares do not differ greatly, though trains are usually a bit cheaper unless the destination is served by a local commuter bus. One advantage the train has over the bus is that it gives you a view of the countryside away from the noise and diesel fumes of the highways. You may also find it easier to get information and buy tickets for the train because the main train station is easier to negotiate than the Florenc bus station.

Numbers in the margin correspond to numbers on the Day-Trips from Prague and Kutná Hora maps.

About the Hotels & Restaurants
Although all the destinations in this chapter can be visited on a half- or full-day excursion from Prague, you may find yourself yearning for more

GERMANY

Ústí nad Labem

Střekov Castle

Litoměřice

Doksy

Turnov

Terezín ⑪

Mělník ⑫

Mladá Boleslav

Jičín

Louny

Žatec

Veltrusy Château and Gardens ◆

Zlonice

Neratovice

Lidice ⑩

Roztoky

Čelákovice

Poděbrady

Křikoklát ⑦

Kralovice

Beroun

Rudná

Prague

Říčany

Kolín

Labe

Zdice

⑥ Karlštejn

Uhlíře Janovice

Plzeň

Rokycany

Příbram

⑨ Konopiště

Sedlčany

⑧ Český Šternberk

Zbraslavice

Kutná Hora ①–⑤ see detail map

Dobřany

Nepomuk

⑬ Orlík

Milevsko

Pelhřimov

Klatovy

◆ Zvíkov Castle

peace and quiet than the capital can provide, particularly during the busiest months of the high season. There are decent options for an overnight stay near most of the day-trip excursion destinations, and the prices are certainly lower than in Prague itself. The same is true for food. However, be prepared for less choice and fewer English-speaking staff members.

	$$$$	**$$$**	**$$**	**$**	**¢**
WHAT IT COSTS in koruna and euros					
	HOTELS*				
IN KORUNA	over 7,000	5,000–7,000	3,500–5,000	1,500–3,500	under 1,500
	HOTELS*				
IN EUROS	over €225	€155–€225	€108–€155	€47–€108	under €47
	RESTAURANTS**				
	over 500	300–500	150–300	100–150	under 100

*Hotel prices are for two people in a double room with a private bath and breakfast during peak season (March through October, excluding July and August) and generally include 5% V.A.T. **Restaurant prices are per person for a main course at dinner and include 19% V.A.T.

KUTNÁ HORA

70 km (44 mi) east of Prague.

The long economic decline of this town, once Prague's chief rival in Bohemia for wealth and beauty, spared it the postwar construction that has blighted the outskirts of so many other Czech cities. Though it's undeniably beautiful, with an intact Gothic and baroque townscape, Kutná Hora feels a bit melancholy. The town owes its illustrious past to silver, discovered here during the 12th century. For some 400 years the mines were worked with consummate efficiency, the wealth going to support grand projects to rival those of Prague and the nearby Cistercian monastery of Sedlec. As the silver began to run out during the 16th and 17th centuries, however, Kutná Hora's importance faded. Since the early 1990s, the town has beautified itself to a degree, but despite a significant tourist industry, modern Kutná Hora is dwarfed by the splendors of the Middle Ages. The city became a UNESCO World Heritage Site in 1995.

When you arrive at Kutná Hora, it's best to get sense of centrality and orientation by first heading to the central town square, Palackého Náěstí. If you come into the town by bus, look for the spires and head downhill and to the left. If you come by train and get off at the Kutná Hora Město station, look at the map posted in the station and thread your way uphill and roughly to the right, through the somewhat crumbling streets until you reach Palackého Náměstí. The tourist office is here; it's small, but well-organized, and it also has a few Internet stations, which you can use to check e-mail.

❶ **Chrám svaté Barbory** (St. Barbara's Cathedral) is a 10-minute stroll from
FodorśChoice   the main Palackého náměstí along Barborská ulice. The approach to the
★   church, overlooking the river, is magnificent. Baroque statues line the road in front of a vast former Jesuit college as you near St. Barbara's, which is really just a parish church that is commonly granted the grander title. From a distance, the three-peaked roof of the church gives the impression of a large, magnificent tent more than a religious center. St. Barbara's is undoubtedly Kutná Hora's masterpiece and a high point of the Gothic style in Bohemia. Begun in the 1380s, it drew on the talents of the Peter Parler workshop as well as two luminaries of the late-Gothic of the late 15th century, Matyáš Rejsek and Benedikt Ried. The soaring roof was added as late as 1558, replaced in the 18th century, and finally restored, by Josef Mocker, in the late 1800s; the western façade also dates from the end of the 19th century. Once you arrive, you can see the romantic view over the town, marked by the visibly tilting 260-foot-tower of St. James's Church. Though the view is impressive, a few modern buildings intrude.

St. Barbara is the patron saint of miners, and silver-mining themes dominate the interior of the church. Gothic frescoes depict angels carrying shields with mining symbols. The town's other major occupation, minting, can be seen in frescoes in the **Mintner's Chapel**. A statue of a miner, donning the characteristic smock, stands proudly in the nave and dates from 1700. But the main attraction of the interior is the vaulting itself—attributed to Ried—which carries the eye effortlessly upward. ⊠ *Barborská ul.* ☏ *No*

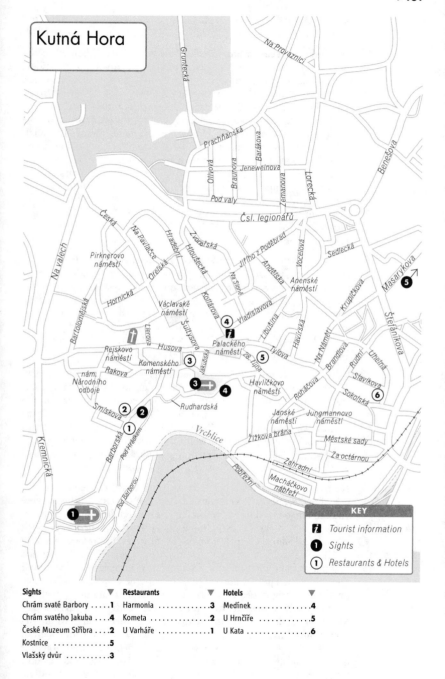

Kutná Hora

KEY

𝑖	*Tourist information*
❶	*Sights*
①	*Restaurants & Hotels*

Sights ▼	Restaurants ▼	Hotels ▼
Chrám svaté Barbory **1**	Harmonia **3**	Medínek **4**
Chrám svatého Jakuba **4**	Kometa **2**	U Hrnčíře **5**
České Muzeum Stříbra **2**	U Varháře **1**	U Kata **6**
Kostnice **5**		
Vlašský dvůr **3**		

phone ⌨ *30 Kč* ☉ *May–Sept., Tues.–Sun. 9–6:00; Oct. and Apr., Tues.–Sun. 9–noon and 1–4:30; Nov.–Mar., Tues.–Sun. 9–noon and 2–4.*

② The **České Muzeum Stříbra** (Czech Museum of Silver), housed in the Hrádek (Little Castle), which was once part of the town's fortifications, is a museum of mining and coin production. At one time, notably the 16th century, Kutná Hora boasted the deepest mines in the world, some going down as far as 500 meters. It's somewhat fitting, then, that the highlight of the Hrádek—and the focal point of the longer museum tours—is a hike down into a claustrophobic medieval mine tunnel. The small trek (you're inside for about 30 minutes) is more titillating than scary, though you may be happy you weren't a medieval miner. The cheapest tour, which doesn't include the mine, isn't very exciting, unless you're a fan of ore samples and archaeology. If it's available, go for the 1½-hour tour, which includes a portion of the displays from the museum proper, plus the mine. ⊠ *Barborská ul. 28* ☎ *327–512–159* ⊕ *www.cms-kh.cz* ⌨ *60 Kč–110 Kč* ☉ *Apr. and Oct., Tues.–Sun. 9–5; May–June and Sept., Tues.–Sun. 9–6; July–Aug., Tues.–Sun. 10–6.*

③ Coins were first minted at the **Vlašský dvůr** (Italian Court) in 1300, struck by Italian artisans brought in from Florence—hence the mint's odd name. It was here that the Prague groschen, one of the most widely circulated coins of the Middle Ages, was minted until 1726 and here, too, that the Bohemian kings stayed on their frequent visits. There's a **coin museum**, where you can see the small, silvery groschen being struck and buy replicas. ⊠ *Havlíčkovo nám.* ☎ *327–512–873* ⌨ *40 Kč* ☉ *Apr.–Sept., daily 9–6; Oct. and Mar., daily 10–5; Nov.–Feb., daily 10–4.*

④ If the door to the **Chrám svatého Jakuba** (St. James's Church), which is next door to the old mint, is open, peek inside. Originally a Gothic church dating from the 1300s, the structure was almost entirely transformed into baroque during the 17th and 18th centuries. The characteristic onion dome on the tower was added in 1737. The paintings on the wall include works of the best baroque Czech masters; the pietà is by the 17th-century painter Karel Škréta. The church is open only sporadically during the week and for Sunday mass. ⊠ *Havlíčkovo nám.* ☎ *No phone.*

No trip to Kutná Hora is complete without a visit to the nearby suburb of Sedlec, about 2 km from the center of the city. It's here where you can find one of Europe's most famous bone-chilling sights: a chapel decorated with the bones of some 40,000 people. The Kaple všech svatých (All Saints' Chapel), commonly known as the **Kostnice** (ossuary) or "Bone Church" is just up the road from the former Sedlec Monastery. The church came into being in the 16th century, when development forced the clearing of a nearby graveyard. Monks of the Cistercian order came up with the bright idea of using the bones to decorate the chapel; the most recent creations date from the end of the 19th century. The Sedlec Monastery is now a cigarette factory. Its run-down **Church of the Assumption of the Virgin** exemplifies the work of Giovanni Santini (1667–1723). A master of expressive line and delicate proportion, this one-of-a-kind architect fathered a bravura hybrid of Gothic and baroque. ⊠ *Zamecka 127, Sedlec* ☎ *327–561–143* ⊕ *www.kostnice.cz* ⌨ *30 Kč*

⑤ FodorśChoice ★

⊙ *Apr.–Sept., daily 8–6; Oct., daily 9–noon and 1–5; Nov.–Mar., daily 9–noon and 1–4. Church closed Sun. and Mon.*

Where to Eat

¢–$$ ✕ **U Varháře.** A good place to stop if you're walking up to St. Barbara's is directly across the street from Kometa, the other recommendable restaurant in this part of town. This is a slightly more upscale restaurant under the same ownership. The red-and-white tablecloth combination doesn't really do the dining room in this old villa justice, and the meals come with more elaborate sauces and presentations than Kometa. The large terrace perched on the edge of the valley has a beautiful view of the cathedral, arguably the best view in the city. ⊠ *Barborská 578* ☎ *327–512–769* ⊟ *AE, DC, MC, V.*

¢–$ ✕ **Harmonia.** The uninspired interior, which is characteristic of Kutná Hora restaurants, is completely vindicated by a small back patio, which you can enter from Komenského náměstí, near St. James's. Enclosed by charming shrubbery, it draws a small crowd of tourists when the weather is nice. It also draws a small crowd of wasps, but they seem happy enough trying to get into the sugar dispensers and rarely bother diners. Slightly more effort is put into the standard Czech cutlet-based fare than in many local spots, and the steaks are nicely done. ⊠ *Husova 104* ☎ *327–512–275* ⊟ *AE, MC, V.*

¢–$ ✕ **Kometa.** You can't miss the big wooden patio of this Czech restaurant on the corner leading up toward St. Barbara's. Under the shade of a huge, majestic tree—and looking across to the equally majestic form of the Jesuit College—it's one of the best places to stop for a coffee or snack on a nice day. The spacious interior is also more tolerable than many in the center of town. The menu includes the predictable array of chicken and pork cutlets typical of Czech restaurants, but the waitstaff are fast and attentive. ⊠ *Barborská 29* ☎ *327–515–515* ⊟ *AE, DC, MC, V.*

Where to Stay

$ ⌂ **Medínek.** A location right on the main square puts you an easy stroll from the sights, and the ground-floor restaurant offers decent Czech cooking in an atmosphere more pleasant than that found in the local beer halls. While the hotel's 1960s architecture blights the surrounding square, it does offer the advantages of larger windows and more spacious rooms than those found in many of the older hotels. ⊠ *Palackého nám. 316, 284 01* ☎ *327–512–741* ⊟ *327–512–743* ⊕ *www.medinek.cz* ⊡ *90 rooms, 43 with bath* ⌂ *Restaurant, café, cable TV, meeting rooms, some pets allowed (fee); no a/c* ⊟ *AE, MC, V* ⦿ *BP.*

¢ ⌂ **U Hrnčíře.** This quaint little inn is next to a potter's shop near the town center. The rooms are very plain and the stairs very steep, but the friendly staff gives the hotel a decidedly homey feel. The restaurant in the back garden has a beautiful view overlooking St. James's Church. ⊠ *Barborská 24, 284 01* ☎ *327–512–113* ⊡ *5 rooms* ⌂ *Restaurant, cable TV, some pets allowed (fee); no a/c* ⊟ *MC, V* ⦿ *BP.*

¢ ⌂ **U Kata.** If you're looking for something really cheap, this pension is the first one to try; though not nested in town with the monuments, it's about a 10-minute walk from them on the other side of Palackého Náměstí, in a part of town where the streets are still cobbled. The staff speaks German better than English, however, so don't rely on them for a bounty of tourist tips. ⊠ *Uhelná 596, 284 01* ☎ *327–515–096* ⌨ *30 rooms* ♿ *Restaurant, some pets allowed; no a/c* ☰ *No credit cards* ⍾ *EP.*

Kutná Hora Essentials

TRANSPORTATION   It's easy to get to Kutná Hora by either train or bus, and the trip in each case takes about an hour. If you take the train, you should be aware that attendants seldom bother telling tourists that the Kutná Hora main station is not in the town proper but in the suburb of Sedlec, about 2 km (1¼) away. If you're continuing into the town, you change to a tiny shuttle that goes the extra bit into the town center (it's scheduled to be waiting for many trains from Prague). However, since you're already in Sedlec, you also have the opportunity to take in the Bone Church in Sedlec, about 10 minutes away from the station, before walking to the town center about 2 km (1¼) away. When you're issued a ticket in Prague, it will say *město* in small print, meaning it goes to the station right in town, if the connection was available for your train time. If you don't want to walk to or from Sedlec, ask the attendant which trains are met by the shuttle.

By car, Highway 333, the westward extension of Vinohradská St., goes all the way to Kutná Hora. The drive takes about 50 minutes.

VISITOR   🏠 **Info-Centre Kutná Hora** ⊠ Palackého náměstí 377 ☎ 327-512-378 ⊕ www.
INFORMATION   kh.cz

KARLŠTEJN

★ ➏   *29km (18 mi) southwest of Prague*

Karlštejn, literally translated as "Charles Stone," is named after its founder in 1348, Holy Roman Emperor Charles IV, who also founded both Charles University and Prague's district of New Town (look at the similarity in shape of the Karlšstejn's tower and the New Town Hall). The castle was built for the express purpose of housing and guarding the crown jewels and was erected over the course of a decade or more— roughly speaking, from its lowest tower, the Well Tower, to its highest tower, the Great Tower. Within the Great Tower was constructed the **Chapel of the Holy Cross,** where the crown jewels—along with the most precious state documents, the Bohemian Archives—were held for almost 200 years, surviving attacks from the Hussites and their catapult bombardment. In 1619 the jewels were moved to the fisc chamber of St. Wenceslas Chapel in St. Vitus's Cathedral, where they remain to this day. Karlštejn, like most castles, underwent some architectural changes over the centuries. The late 1800s (under Franz Joseph I, father of Franz Ferdinand) saw a major effort to preserve the medieval origins of the castle, and much of the form we see today is a result of this valuable work. The Chapel of the Holy Cross is still the castle's greatest treasure, famous for the intensity of its workmanship. The walls are covered by 129 paintings by Master Theodoric, Charles's court painter, a stunning collection on the international stage. The arched canopy above is completely gilded and set with semiprecious stones. After 19 years of closure, it reopened to the public in 2000, but to see it you must take a guided tour. Tours are limited in order to preserve the microclimate inside the chapel, and you should reserve a time at least two weeks in advance to guarantee a spot on tour.

The cluster of street vendors at the main intersection at the foot of the hill signals the road up to the castle. Signs for change dealers and ceramics shops dwarf the simple sign indicating the direction of the castle and are telltale of how touristy things have become (Karlšteijn is the most-visited destination in the Czech Republic outside of Prague). Following the road up the hill you pass through a maze of street vendors, kiosks, and shops selling all manner of plastic toy swords, cell-phone covers, and hairy rubber spiders. Despite the somewhat trashy and repetitive quality of most of the kiosks, the handful of crystal shops on the route do give you a chance to buy a crystal vase for your favorite aunt or coworker, and the shop assistants are usually eager to cut a deal.

Around one of the uphill bends, the entire medieval profile of Karlštejn Castle suddenly comes into view, and it's simply breathtaking, a dramatic mass rising 319 meters above the rocks. It's probably your best photo opportunity, if you're looking to fit the whole castle in one snap.

If you haven't had your breakfast, you may need to refuel here; the walk uphill is a fair bit of exercise, taking about 15 to 20 minutes without breaks, and on a sunny summer day you're likely to see yourself reflected in the hot, flushed faces of tourists catching their breath after a long climb. Luckily, the dozen or so cafés and restaurants along the way offer plenty of opportunities for an ice cream, cappuccino, or beer. The Czech restaurants on this stretch are roughly similar in quality, so seating availability or a good view may be the main determinant of your choice.

Once you reach the top, take some time to walk the ramparts and take in the fabulous panorama of village and countryside far below. The interior tours are& time-consuming—55 minutes for the first circuit and 75 for the second. The Chapel of the Holy Cross, part of Tour 2, is undeniably the most compelling sight, so if you didn't reserve a spot and aren't a castle buff, you may wish to avoid the entry fee and just enjoy the scenery. If you like castles, the first-circuit tour does show some interesting spaces, including Charles's bedchambers and its royal fabrics. ⊠ Karlštejn 18, Karlštejn ☎ 311–681–617 castle information, 274–008–154 tour reservations ⊕ www.hradkarlstejn.cz ☜ Tour 1, 200 Kč, Tour 2, 300 Kč ☉ Apr. and Oct., Tues.–Sun. 9–4; May, June, and Sept., Tues.–Sun. 9–5; July and Aug., Tues.–Sun. 9–6; Nov.–Mar., Tues.–Sun. 9–3.

Where to Eat

\$–\$\$\$ ✕ **Restaurace a Pension Pod dračí skálou.** At the threshold of the ramp leading to the castle gate, look for the sign POD DRAČI SKÁKOU (Under Dragon's Hill) next to a footpath leading down the hill. The restaurant at the bottom is the most fun in the area and offers a large and very pleasant, partially sheltered terrace, in a rustic wooden style. The meal portions are huge, possibly fitting the exercise it takes to reach the place, if not the habitual cycling clientele. The small road that passes the restaurant can be followed to get back to the main highway so you

CloseUp
GUIDED DAY TOURS FROM PRAGUE

G UIDED BUS TOURS ARE AVAILABLE from several companies for Karlštejn, Konopiště, Kutná Hora, Český Šternberk, and Terezín. Although the tours make things easier, they cost several times as much as a bus or train fare. In the cases of Karlštejn and Konopiště, you'll see little extra convenience from taking a bus tour, as the buses cannot approach the castles any closer than regular traffic. In most cases, though, it's simply more fun to go on your own.

Martin Tours (☎ 224–212–473 ⊕ www. martintour.cz) tends to use smaller buses than other companies and is similarly priced, but some interesting sights, such as Kutná Hora's Kostnice, are not included.

Prague Sightseeing Tours (☎ 222– 314–661 ⊕ www.pstours.com) tends to be slightly cheaper than other companies, but it also uses large buses, so you're in a larger group.

Premiant Tours (☎ 606–600–123 ⊕ www.premiant.cz) tends to be the most expensive of the three major tour companies, though the tour content is roughly equivalent.

Wittmann Tours (☎ 222–252–472 ⊕ www.wittmann-tours.com), which does tours to Terezín and Lidice, is an exception to the rule about tour companies, giving you much more substance for your money. Though the prices are a little higher than those of other companies, the tour takes in both memorials in one day, and special personal insight is added thanks to founder Sylvie Wittmann, herself a Czech Jew. Buses leave Prague from the Inter-Continental Hotel, on Pařížská near the Staronová synagóga (Old-New Synagogue), daily from mid-March to December at 10 AM, returning around 5 PM, for a fare of 1,650 Kč.

don't have to climb back up to the castle again; it links with the main road up to the castle after about 10 minutes. Alternately, you can reach this restaurant by the same method. ⊠ *Karlštejn 130* ☎ *311–681–177* 🖃 *No credit cards.*

¢–$$ ✕🏠 **U Janů.** On the road up to the castle, this small pension's restaurant, which has a leafy beer garden out front, is the best option of the many touristy restaurants. The menu offers decent Czech-style food, including some game and fish options. The pension can also be a comfortable place to stay if you feel like being outside of Prague for a night but close to the action at the castle. ⊠ *Karlšejn 80, 267 18* ☎ *311–681–210* 🖷 *311–681–410* ⊕ *www.ujanu.cz* ⇄ *4 rooms* ⌂ *Restaurant, cable TV; no a/c* 🖃 *MC, V.*

Where to Stay

¢ **Penzion Irena.** This quaint B&B is on a road that links to the main road up to the castle. Rooms in the stately old villa are spacious and bright; three have balconies, but either way you generally get a pleasant view of the surrounding countryside, which is mostly green. The owner speaks German better than English, but attempts to be accommodating. ⊠ *Karlštejn 40, 267 18* ☎ *311–681–794* ⇄ *9 rooms* ⌂ *Cable TV, some pets allowed; no a/c* 🖃 *No credit cards* ⦿❙ *CP.*

Karlštejn Essentials

TRANSPORTATION There's no bus service to the castle from Prague, but it's an easy train journey. Several trains each day leave from both Hlavní Nádraží and Smíchovské Nádraží, and it's quite a pleasant ride. On reaching the Karlštejn station, you're faced with the somewhat surprising fact that the castle is nowhere in sight. When you get off the train, turn right, and walk back along the small lane parallel to the railway tracks. If it isn't raining or very cold, you'll normally see a smattering of people—or during sunny summer days throngs of people—all heading in the same direction. After a few minutes, you cross a bridge over the river; turn right onto the main road, which resembles a small highway (the absence of a pedestrian sidewalk doesn't seem to bother the locals). Be wary of traffic but continue for another two or three minutes until you reach a road going up the hill to your left. This is the main road up to the castle; it's hard to miss.

By car, take Highway 4—on the west side of the Vltava—to the edge of the city, then go right on Highway 115, southwest through Radotin. Take the Karlštejn exit, which puts you on Highway 116, and after a few more minutes you end up beside the Berounka River. You can find a large parking lot at the bottom of the hill below Karlsßtejn. No vehicles are allowed on the road up to the castle.

VISITOR
INFORMATION There's no tourist information center in the town of Karlštejn, but you can call the castle itself. Further information may be obtained from the booking office in Prague.

🎫 **National Monuments Institute for Central Bohemia** ✉ Sabinova 5, Žižkov, Prague ☎ 274-008-154

KŘIVOKLÁT

★ ❼ *43 km (27 mi) west of Prague*

If you really want to get away from the hustle and bustle of Prague for a few hours and feel a yearning for a touch of wilderness, a better choice than the well touristed Karlštejn may be Křivoklát. Situated in dense forest (the name means "twisted branches"), among the rolling green hills above the River Beroun, the castle makes for a more peaceful getaway than its more heavily touristed cousin. The area as a whole, which is often referred to in Czech literature, achieves its full beauty once the trees begin to bloom. Today, the remote complex, with its Gothic treasures, perches above a quiet, sleepy village, but in the Middle Ages it was strategically important, a place where political prisoners were held, and the scene of lavish festivities.

The roots of Křivoklát go back to the 12th century, when it was a hunting lodge for the nobility. It was King Wenceslas I who commissioned the castle in the 13th century and his son, Přemysl Otakar II, who finished it. In the 14th century, the future Emperor Charles IV was imprisoned here as a small boy by his father, John of Luxembourg. Charles later returned—in happier circumstances—to hunt, as did his son Wenceslas IV, who made significant alterations to the structure. Extensive alterations were also carried out by Polish King Vladislav II Jagiellon in the 1500s (the "W" insignia of Vladislav can be seen in several places). At the end of the 16th century Křivoklát began to lose its importance. It was damaged by fire several times and fell into disrepair. After the Thirty Years' War, Křivoklát was pledged to the Schwarzenbergs and then became the property of noble families including the Fürstenbergs, who owned it from 1733 until 1929, when it passed to the Czechoslovak state.

These days, the castle draws a combination of local hikers, a smattering of interested tourists, and film crews in search of historical authenticity. But it really comes alive on the night of April 30, when many Czech villages celebrate something called *Čarodejnice*. Roughly translated as "witch-burning"—a pagan-rooted festival to ward off the winter spirit and welcome the bounty of spring—it turns Křivoklát into the scene of Slavic festivities and mock Celtic battles, and hundreds of Czechs come from Prague and the surrounding countryside to enjoy the music, merriment, and cheap wine well into the wee hours. In Prague the ceremonies to mark this event are sometimes mentioned in the entertainment sections of local papers.

Walking up to the castle, stopping for a meal or drink, and enjoying the natural surroundings are enough to give you an impression, but if you go this far, you may as well do the longer tour, which is an hour, and see the best parts of the castle. One of the highlights is the Gothic chapel. Full of original details, its most conspicuous feature is a richly carved Gothic altarpiece (circa 1490), one of the finest still around. But even better—and the tour highlight—is the Great Hall. Notable for its great dimensions (28 meters long, 8 meters wide and 8.5 meters high), it's the second-largest Gothic hall in Central Europe (after Vladislav Hall in Prague Castle). Look out for the fragments of doodles on the walls; they were done by children in the Middle Ages and discovered only relatively recently. After the Gothic chambers come rooms housing the castle collections, including the library, which contains 53,000 volumes. The tour ends at the giant round tower, which was used as a prison until the 16th century. The infamous alchemist Edward Kelley, who claimed he could turn base metals into gold, was said to have been imprisoned here.

A number of shops near the main entrance to the castle and in buildings around the courtyard sell crafts. Among the products on sale are traditional carved wooden items and candles. Tours in English are available but have to be reserved in advance. ⊠ *Křivoklát* ☎ *313–558–440 castle information, 313–558–120 tour reservations* ⊕ *www.krivoklat. cz* ⬚ *160 Kč* ☉ *Apr. and Oct., Tues.–Sun. 9–3; May and Sept., Tues.–Sun. 9–4; June–Aug., Tues.–Sun. 9–5; Nov., Dec., and Mar., weekends 9–3.*

Where to Stay & Eat

¢ ✕⬚ **U Jelena.** Appropriate for a village where hunting was a popular pastime, game dishes are the specialty of the restaurant, which is just below the climb to the castle. Relatively upscale meals are served here in an old-world atmosphere, from the familiar *svíčková* (slices of beef loin in cream sauce) to more elaborate dishes such as venison steak with Cumberland sauce. The rooms upstairs are simply finished but have a cozy feeling thanks to wooden furnishings and pleasant lighting, and most have good views out the window to the woodsy surroundings. ⊠ *U Jelena 420, 27 023* ☎ *313–558–529* 📠 *313–558–233* ⊷ *6 rooms* ⚲ *Restaurant, cable TV, some pets allowed; no a/c* ⊟ *AE, MC, V* ⦾❘ *BP.*

Křivoklat Essentials

TRANSPORTATION If you have no car, a train is the best way to reach Křivoklát. Take the local train from Hlavní Nádraží or Smíchovské Nádraží to Beroun (the local train from these stations to Plzeň also stops here). From here, take another local train to Rakovník, getting off at the Křivoklát stop. Plan your journey carefully, as there are a only a few trains each day from Beroun to Rakovník.

If you're driving, the fastest way to Křivoklát is to follow Route 6 from Prague toward Karlovy Vary and after Jeneč turn onto Route 201 via Unhoště to Křivoklát. The trip is about 40 minutes. For a much more scenic drive—and an extra 15 minutes—take the E50 Highway from Prague toward Plzeň, then exit at Křivolklát to Route 116. Follow this highway, which goes along the Berounka River before veering up into the hills, to Route 201, which winds back south towards Křivoklát. Parking is just beneath the castle.

VISITOR INFORMATION There's no information center in Křivoklát, but the castle can provide some basic tourist information. Further information on the region is available from the tourist office in the nearby town of Rakovník.

🚩 **Rakovník Tourist Information** ⊠ Náměstí Svatopluka Čecha 82, Rakovník ☎ 313-585-263

ČESKÝ ŠTERNBERK

❽ *48 km (30 mi) southeast of Prague.*

Fodor's Choice ★

At night this 13th-century castle looks positively forbidding, occupying a forested knoll over the Sázava River. In daylight, the structure, last renovated in the 18th century, is less haunting but still impressive. For this one, a guided tour is essential—but don't worry about being paraded through musty stone hallways for hours—the interiors are beautiful and the guides are good, not only managing to teach you something but to fit the tour into 45 minutes.

The castle was founded in 1241 by Zdeslav of Divišov. Due to German influence and customs at the time, the coat of arms used by Zdeslav— an emblem bearing a gold, eight-pointed star—bestowed the name Šternberk on the castle, which is roughly translated as "star on the hill." After 1242, Zdeslav took on the name Zdeslav of Sternberg, and thus began the long lineage of the Sternberg family.

The castle itself was built in the early Gothic style. During the 15th and 16th centuries, following damage incurred during war, the castle underwent some architectural changes, preserving a few original details and making it stronger. The Swedes tried to conquer the castle in 1648 but failed; after the Thirty Years' War, other changes, particularly to the interiors, were made. In the first half of the eighteenth century the Lower Château was constructed; the French-style garden, across the river, was created in the same period.

Possibly the most interesting aspect of Český Šternberk is that the Sternberg family—one branch or another—has lived in the castle for most of this time. It gives a certain amount of credence to the interior, especially the gorgeous Knight's Hall, with its paintings and famous Italian stucco work. Though the castle is mostly given over to tours, the Sternbergs themselves live in the upper chambers and sometimes use the lower rooms for family gatherings. If you're feeling celebratory, you can rent out certain rooms; the royal dining room goes for only(!) 50,000 Kč an evening.

In 1948 the Sternberg family was moved to a small apartment in Prague when their castle, like all Czech castles, were nationalized by the Communist government, though the father, Jiři, agreed to work as a steward and guide for the property. Through property restitution, the castle was given back to his son Zdeněk in 1992. Zdeněk is over 80 years old today and is occasionally seen waving to tourists as he enters or leaves. ⊠ *Český Šternberk 1, Česky Šternberk* ☎ *317–855–101* ⊕ *www. hradceskysternberk.cz* ✉ *Guided tour 130 Kč* ☉ *Apr. and Oct., weekends 9–6; May and Sept., Tues.–Sun. 9–5; June–Aug., Tues.–Sun. 9–6; Nov.–Mar. by appointment only.*

Where to Eat

¢–$$ ✕ **Hradní Restaurace.** Keeping the same hours as the castle, the restaurant, which is accessible from the courtyard, is good place to stop for a snack. The prices are pretty much bargain-basement, and some harder-to-find traditional Czech dishes, such as potato dumplings with smoked meat, and yeast-raised pancakes with blueberries are humble but satisfying hits. ⊠ *Český Šternberk 1, Česky Šternberk* ☎ *317–855–101* ▭ *No credit cards* ☉ *Closed Mon.*

Where to Stay

¢ ⊞ **Párkhotel Český Šternberk.** For a somewhat upscale experience (though still way cheaper than in Prague) try the romantic-looking hotel, which is easily spotted from the castle heights. It's actually owned by the same company that runs the restaurant in the castle, and the menu items at the hotel's restaurant are similar to those in the castle restaurant. Located right beside the French Gardens across the river, it has a large summer terrace and its view of the castle is unparalleled. The rooms upstairs are spacious and quite bright. ⊠ *Český Šternberk 46, 257 27* ☎ *317–855–168* 🖷 *317–855–108* ⊕ *www.parkhoteldt.cz* ⇱ *19 rooms* ᗏ *Restaurant, cable TV, meeting rooms, pets allowed; no a/c* ▭ *No credit cards.*

Český Šternberk Essentials

TRANSPORTATION   Both trains and buses go daily to the Český Šterberk. Buses depart from Prague's southernmost bus station, Roztyly, which is about 15 minutes by metro from the city center on the Red line; purchase tickets directly from the driver.

Trains leave from Hlavní Nádraží and stop in many small towns on the way; you will have to change trains in Čerčany, about one hour out of Prague. Though the train ride is about 20 minutes longer than the trip by bus, it's a bit more scenic and doesn't require a rather boring metro ride to Prague's Roztyly metro station. The trip takes about two hours. If you're visiting in summer, you may be lucky enough to catch the old-fashioned steam train. It only runs on certain days, but seeing it pull up to the station down in the valley from the castle heights is a treat; ask for the *parní vlak* at the main station.

If you're driving, take the D1 Highway out of Prague (the main highway to Brno) and take the turnoff to Český Šternberk, following Route 111 to the castle, which perches over the highway. The drive takes just under an hour.

KONOPIŠTĚ

❾ *45 km (27 mi) southeast of Prague.*

Konopiště flanks the industrial town of Benešov. The town is best known for its 14th-century castle, which served six centuries later as the residence of the heir to the Austrian crown, Franz Ferdinand. Scorned by the Austrian nobility for marrying a commoner, Franz Ferdinand wanted an impressive summer residence to win back the envy of his peers, and he spared no expense in restoring the castle to its original Gothic form, filling its 82 rooms with outlandish paintings, statues, and curiosities. His dream came to a fateful end in 1914 when he was assassinated at Sarajevo, an event that helped precipitate World War I. The Austrian defeat in the war ultimately led to the fall of the Hapsburgs. Ironically, the destiny of the Austrian Empire had been sealed at the castle a month before the assassination, when Austrian emperor Franz Joseph I met with German kaiser Wilhelm II and agreed to join forces with him in the event of war.

Fodor'sChoice ★ Depending on how you get to **Zámek Konopiště** (Konopiště Castle), your trip will generally involve at least a ½-km walk through the woods. Before long, the rounded, neo-Gothic towers appear through the trees, and you reach the formal garden with its almost mystical circle of classical statues. Built by the wealthy Beneschau family, the castle dates from around 1300 and for centuries served as a bastion of the nobility in their struggle for power with the king. At the end of the 14th century, Catholic nobles actually captured the weak King Wenceslas (Václav) IV in Prague and held him prisoner in the smaller of the two rounded towers. To this day the tower is known affectionately as the Václavka. Several of the rooms, reflecting Archduke Franz Ferdinand's extravagant taste and lifestyle, are open to the public during the high season. A valuable collection of weapons from the 16th through 18th centuries can be seen in the Weapons Hall on the third floor. Less easy to miss are the hundreds of stuffed animals, rather macabre monuments to the archduke's obsession with hunting. The interior is only open to tours; the guides may not speak English, but there are English texts available. The castle is about 3 km (2 mi) west of Benešov's train and bus stations on red- or yellow-marked paths. ⊠ *Zámek Konopiště, Benešov* ☎ *317–721–366* ⊕ *www.zamek-konopiste.cz* ⛿ *Tours 130 Kč–260 Kč* ☉ *Apr. and Oct., Tues.–Sun. 9–3; May–Aug., Tues.–Sun. 9–5; Sept., Tues.–Sun. 9–4.*

Where to Stay & Eat

$ ✕▥ **Amber Hotel Konopiště.** Long a favorite with Prague-based diplomats, who come for the fresh air and outdoor sports, the motel is about 2 km

(1 mi) from Konopiště Castle, on a small road about 1 km (½ mi) from the main Prague–Tábor highway (E55). Rooms are small but well-appointed (ask for one away from the main road). Its lodgelike restaurant, Stodola ($$–$$$; open for dinner only), boasts a fine reputation for Bohemian-style grilled meats, chicken, and fish dishes. The live folk music in the evening is romantic rather than obtrusive; the wines and service are excellent. ✉ *Benešov, 256 01* ☎ *317–722–732* 🖷 *317–722–053* ⊕ *www.hotelkonopiste.cz* ⟳ *40 rooms* ♨ *2 restaurants, cable TV, miniature golf, tennis court, pool, gym, outdoor hot tub, massage, sauna, meeting room, some pets allowed (fee); no a/c* ▤ *AE, DC, MC, V* ⦾ *BP.*

Konopiště Essentials

TRANSPORTATION Several buses leave daily to Konopiště from Prague's Roztyly metro station (on the Red Line) and occasionally from Florenc. The trip lasts about an hour and lets you off about ½ km from the castle. Alternately, you can take the train, which is slightly faster but lets you off right in the town of Benešov. You must then catch a town bus to the castle.

By car, take the D1 Highway southwest toward Brno, (also named the E65); take the Benešov exit. Signs on this road lead you to Konopiště.

VISITOR 🚩 **Konopiště Tourist Information** ✉ Malé náměstí 1700, Benešov ☎ 317–726–004
INFORMATION ⊕ www.knihovna-benesov.cz

LIDICE

🔟 *18 km (11 mi) from Prague.*

The Lidice story really begins with the notorious Munich Pact of 1938, under which the leaders of Great Britain and France permitted Hitler to occupy the largely German-speaking border regions of Czechoslovakia (the so-called Sudetenland). Less than a year later, in March 1939, Hitler used his forward position to occupy the whole of Bohemia and Moravia, making the area into a protectorate of the German Reich. To guard his new possessions, Hitler appointed ruthless Nazi Reinhard Heydrich as Reichsprotektor. Heydrich immediately implemented a campaign of terror against Jews and intellectuals while currying favor with average Czechs by raising rations and wages. As a result, the Czech army-in-exile, based in Great Britain, soon began planning Heydrich's assassination. In the winter of 1941–42 a small band of parachutists was flown in to carry out the task.

The attack took place in the north part of Prague on May 27, 1942, and Heydrich died from his injuries on June 4. Hitler immediately ordered the little mining town of Lidice, west of Prague, "removed from the face of the earth," since it was alleged that some of the assassins had been sheltered by villagers there (this was later found to be untrue). On the night of June 9, a Gestapo unit entered Lidice, shot the entire adult male population (192 men), and sent the 196 women to the Ravensbrück concentration camp. A handful of the 103 children in the village were sent to Germany to be "Aryanized"; the others perished in death camps. On June 10, the entire village was razed. The Nazis found Heydrich's assassins and their accomplices a week later in the Orthodox

Church of Sts. Cyril and Methodius in Prague's New Town. There, the men committed suicide after a shoot-out with Nazi militia.

A new Lidice was built after the war on the initiative of a group of miners from Birmingham, England, who called their committee "Lidice Must Live."

The **Lidice Memorial** is an unforgettable and sobering sight. The meadow with the tall cross and small stream is where the town of Lidice stood until 1942. The monument is graphic in its depiction of the deportation and slaughter of the inhabitants. Hanging in the reception hall of the museum itself, a large painting of the Old Lidice helps put some perspective to the grassy field outside: it shows what the small village must have looked like, with the village church, meadow, and small stream. The museum is dedicated to those killed; there's a photograph of each person and a short description of his or her fate. You can also find reproductions of the German documents ordering the village's destruction, including the Gestapo's chillingly bureaucratic reports on how the massacre was carried out and the peculiar problems encountered in Aryanizing the deported children. The exhibits highlighting the international response (a suburb of Chicago was even renamed for the town) are heartwarming. The staff tend to speak German rather than English but are helpful and will play a short film (about 20 minutes) in English on request, between the other showings.

Outside, you can wander as much or as little as you like. The wooden cross in the field, starkly decorated with barbed wire, marks the place in Old Lidice where the men were executed. Remains of brick walls are visible here, leftover from the Gestapo's dynamite and bulldozer exercise. There are several moving sculptures made in tribute to the horror, including a very large one of 82 children with an unsettling inscription. It's worth walking to the far end of the meadow, where the town cemetery was, and back. ⊠ Ul. 10. června 1942 ⊕ www.lidice-memorial.cz ▧ 50 Kč ☉ Apr.–Oct., daily 8–6; Nov.–Mar., daily 9–3.

Where to Eat
A small stand in the parking lot, which you might recognize as being similar to those around Prague's out-of-center metro stations from the small cluster of old men eating párky (weiners) or knocking back a shot of vodka. The stand also sells beer, coffee, and a few other snacks. In other words, it's a good idea to get on the bus and go back to Prague for something to eat.

Lidice Essentials
TRANSPORTATION It's a shame that an important memorial so close to Prague's borders is not serviced better by public transportation. There's no train service to Lidice, although it's quite easy to get there by bus. However, the drivers rarely encounter tourists, seldom speak English, and make little effort to be helpful, regardless of language. If you decide to brave the buses and not let a possible smug response bother you, go to the bus stops on Evropska Street, about 100 meters from the turning circle at Dejvice. Several buses leave from here heading westbound, and those to Lidice and other small villages leave about every half-hour. It's necessary to ask the bus

driver if the bus goes to Lidice. (Buses heading to the larger town of Kladno pass nearby, but do not stop at Lidice.) Tickets are purchased directly from the driver. The trip should take about 20 minutes, and if all goes well, you'll be let off at an intersection across from the memorial itself.

By car Lidice is an easy 20-minute journey. From the Dejvice area, take Highway 7 out of Prague past the airport, then continue west on Route 551 until you see the well-marked memorial, with a parking lot, beside the highway.

VISITOR   There's no tourist information center in Lidice, but information may be
INFORMATION   obtained from the memorial's museum.

TEREZÍN

⑪ *48 km (30 mi) northwest of Prague.*

During World War II, the town of Terezín—called Theresienstadt by the Germans—served as a detention center for thousands of Jews and was used by the Nazis as an elaborate prop in a nefarious propaganda ploy. The large barracks buildings around town, once used in the 18th and 19th centuries to house Austrian soldiers, became living quarters for thousands of interred Jews. But in 1942, to placate international public opinion, the Nazis cynically decided to transform the town into a showcase camp—to prove to the world their "benevolent" intentions toward the Jews. To give the place the image of a spa town, the streets were given new names such as Lake Street, Bath Street, and Park Street. Numerous elderly Jews from Germany were taken in by the deception and paid large sums of money to come to the new "retirement village." Just before the International Red Cross inspected the town in early 1944, Nazi authorities began a beautification campaign: under Nazi command, the Jews painted the buildings, set up stores, laid out a park with benches in front of the town hall, and arranged for concerts and sports. The map just off the main square shows the town's street plan as the locations of various buildings between 1941 and 1945. The Jews here were able, with great difficulty, to establish a cultural life of their own under the limited self-government that was set up in the camp. The inmates created a library and a theater, and lectures and musical performances were given on a regular basis.

Once it was clear that the war was lost, however, the Nazis dropped any pretense and quickly stepped up transport of Jews to the Auschwitz death camp in Poland. Transports were not new to the ghetto; to keep the population at around 30,000, a train was sent off every few months or so "to the east" to make room for incoming groups. In the fall of 1944, these transports were increased to one every few days. In all, some 87,000 Jews from Terezín were murdered in this way, and another 35,000 died from starvation or disease. The conductor Karel Ančerl, who died in 1973, and the novelist Ivan Klíma are among the few thousand who survived imprisonment at Terezín.

The enormity of Theresienstadt's role in history is difficult to grasp at first because the Czechs have put up few signs to tell you what to see, but the **Památník Terezín** (Terezín Memorial) encompasses all the existing buildings that are open to the public. Buildings include the **Magde-burg Barracks,** where the Jewish Council of Elders met, and the **Jewish cemetery's crematorium** just outside the town walls.

The town's horrific story is told in words and pictures at the **Museum of the Terezín Ghetto** (⊠ Komenského ul. ☎ 416–782–577), just off the central park in town. A short documentary is also shown in many languages. If the staff know that you speak English, they'll let you roam the building and either tell you or flag you down when the next English-language video is being shown.

★ The **Malá Pevnost** (Small Fortress), the actual prison and death camp, is 1 km (½ mi) east of Terezín. In the strange redbrick complex you can see the prison more or less as it was when the Nazis left it in 1945. About 32,000 inmates came through the fortress, mostly POWs or political pris-oners; those that did not die here were shipped off to other concentra-tion camps. Above the entrance to the main courtyard stands the cynical motto ARBEIT MACHT FREI (Work Brings Freedom). Take a walk around the rooms, still housing a sad collection of rusty bed frames, sinks, and shower units. At the far end of the fortress, opposite the main entrance, is the special wing built by the Nazis when space became tight. The win-dowless cells are horrific; try going into one and closing the door—and then imagine being crammed in with 14 other people. In the center of the fortress is a museum and a small theater. ⊠ *Principova alej 304, Terezín* ☎ *416–782–225* ⊕ *www.pamatnik-terezin.cz* ✉ *One unit 160 Kč; all units 180 Kč* ☉ *Ghetto Museum and Magdeburg Barracks Apr.–Oct., daily 9–6; Nov.–Mar., daily 9–5:30. Small Fortress Apr.–Oct., daily 8–6; Nov.–Mar., daily 8–4:30. Crematorium Apr.–Nov., Sun.–Fri. 10–5.*

off the beaten path

STŘEKOV CASTLE – The Vltava River north of Litoměřice flows through a long, unspoiled, winding valley, packed in by surrounding hills. As you near heavily industrialized Ústí nad Labem, your eyes are suddenly assaulted by the towering mass of Střekov Castle, perched precariously on huge cliffs and rising abruptly above the right bank. The fortress was built in 1319 by King John of Luxembourg to control the rebellious nobles of northern Bohemia. During the 16th century it became the residence of Wenceslas of Lobkowicz, who rebuilt the castle in the Renaissance style. The lonely ruins have inspired many German artists and poets, including Richard Wagner, who came here on a moonlit night in the summer of 1842 and was inspired to write his romantic opera *Tannhäuser.* But if you arrive on a dark night, about the only classic that comes to mind is Mary Shelley's *Frankenstein.* Inside is a small historical exhibit about the Lobkowicz family and wine making. This is an interesting-looking castle, and it's probably worth a stop if you happen to be driving by, but it's not a destination unto itself. ⊠ *Na Zachazce, Ústí nad Labem* ☎ *475–530–682* ✉ *60 Kč* ☉ *May–Aug., Tues.–Sun. 9–5; Apr., Sept., and Oct., Tues.–Sun. 9–4.*

Where Eat

As most of the town is an exhibit, and a somber one at that, dining is best done elsewhere. The town of Litoměřice down the road about 2 km (1 mi) is a better option, offering several choices around the town square.

¢–$$ ╳ **Hotel Restaurant Salva Guarda.** This stately old building with arches and sgrafito, on the town square, dates back to the 14th century. The interior is comparatively plain, but in nice weather you can relax on the patio. Czech food of the cutlet category and several game dishes are served. There are rooms to rent upstairs. ⊠ *Mírové náměstí 12, Litoměřice* ☎ *416–732–506* ⊟ *AE, MC, V.*

Terezín Essentials

TRANSPORTATION   There's no train service directly to Terezín. Several buses leave the Florenc station daily, though weekends offer a bit more choice. The trip lasts about an hour and the bus stops twice: the first stop is in town, near the Museum of the Ghetto building; the bus also stops across town closer to the Small Fortress. Both of these have ticket desks. If you plan to visit both of these entities, it's better to visit the museum first as it will help put the entire sight and its history into perspective.

If you're driving, take the E55 north out of Prague (this is the main highway going to Dresden and Berlin) and head toward Lovosice. You can either take Exit 35 at Doksany and follow the country road straight to Terezín or continue to Lovosice, and from there, turn right and the road leads directly into Terezín. The trip takes about 50 minutes. To visit Střekov, follow the road signs from Terezín to Litoměřice, then take Highway 261 to Ústí nad Labem.

VISITOR   Information on Terezín can be found by contacting the office of the memo-
INFORMATION   rial itself; information on the area can be obtained from the tourist office in the neighboring town of Litoměřice.
🛈 **Litoměřice Tourist Information** ⊠ Mírové nám., Litoměřice ☎ 416–732–440 ⊕ www.litomerice.cz

MĚLNÍK

⑫ *About 40 km (23 mi) north of Prague.*

The town's **Zámek,** a smallish castle a few blocks from the main square, majestically guards the confluence of the Labe (Elbe) River and two arms of the Vltava. The view here is stunning, and the sunny hillsides are covered with vineyards. Indeed, the town is known best for its special Ludmila wine made from these grapes. As the locals tell it, Emperor Charles IV was responsible for bringing wine production to the area. Having a good eye for favorable growing conditions, he encouraged vintners from Burgundy to come here and plant their vines. Every autumn, usually in late September, MělniŇXtags error: Unexpected end of lineŇ

The courtyard's three dominant architectural styles, reflecting alterations to the castle over the years, fairly jump out at you. On the north side, note the typical arcaded Renaissance balconies, decorated with sgraffiti. To the west, a Gothic tract is still easy to make out. The southern wing is clearly baroque (although also decorated with arcades). Inside the castle at the back, you can find a *vinárna* with mediocre food but excellent views overlooking the rivers. On the other side is a **museum** of paintings, furniture, and porcelain belonging to the Lobkowicz family—an old aristocratic clan that has recovered quite a few castles and estates from the state. You can also tour the wine cellars under the castle. ⊠ *Náměstí Míru 54* ☎ *315–622–121* ⊕ *www.lobkowicz-melnik. cz* 🎫 *Castle 60 Kč, wine cellar tour 25 Kč, up to 220 Kč with wine tasting* ☉ *Castle daily 10–5. Wine cellar daily 10–6.*

Where to Eat

$–$$$ ✕ **Zámecká Restaurace.** The best place in town to eat is right in the castle itself. It certainly offers the best view. Choose the simpler but cheaper of two buffets that the castle offers. Then sip a glass of Ludmila wine and take in the scenery for a very reasonable price. ⊠ *Inside the Zámek, Náměstí Míru 54* ☎ *315–622–485* ⊟ *No credit cards.*

Where to Stay

¢ 🏨 **Ludmila.** Though the hotel is an inconvenient 4 km (2½ mi) outside the center of town, the pleasant, English-speaking staff keep the plain rooms impeccably clean, and the restaurant is better than many you will find in Mělník itself. ⊠ *Pražská 2639, 276 01* ☎ *315–622–423* 🖨 *315–623–390* ⌨ *79 rooms* ⚘ *Restaurant, cable TV, Internet; no a/c* ⊟ *AE, MC, V* ⏏ *BP.*

¢ 🏨 **Pension Hana.** Many of the better accommodations in the town are on the outskirts, but this small home with a garden is only a 10-minute walk from the center. The staff don't speak English very well, but they're friendly and will try to understand by throwing in the odd German word. The rooms are a reasonable size, and the plaid curtains and wooden tables give them a folksy warmth. ⊠ *Fügerova 714, 27 601* ☎ *315–622–485* 🖨 *315–622–485* ⌨ *10 rooms* ⚘ *Cable TV, meeting rooms; no a/c* ⊟ *No credit cards* ⏏ *BP.*

Mělník Essentials

TRANSPORTATION Bus service to Mělník is better than train service; it's also faster, cheaper, and more direct. The buses are run by a private company and leave throughout the day from Prague's Holešovice Station. Tickets can be purchased directly from the driver, and the ride is about 45 minutes.

If you're coming by car, take Highway 9, from Prague's northern tip, which heads all the way to Mělník. Park on the small streets just off the pretty but hard-to-find main square (head in the direction of the towers to find it).

VISITOR INFORMATION 🛈 **Mělník Tourist Information** ⊠ Nám. Míru 30, Mělník ☎ 315-627-503 ⊕ www. melnik.cz

ORLÍK

⑬ *70 km (44 mi) south of Prague*

Orlík is the most remote of the common day-trips from Prague, and it's especially popular in summer when the area is a beehive of activity, with Czech families taking small holidays, and ferry boats up and down the river. Plan ahead and bring your swimsuit if it's a hot summer day and join in the fun. What appears as a lake is really a large reservoir held back by the Orlík dam, part of a cascade of dams on the Vltava River. Its construction in the early 1960s was epic, consuming 1,250,000 cubic meters of concrete and 50,000 tons of reinforced steel. The lake behind the dam today is about 60 meters deep. This helps explain the perspective in most of the paintings and etchings of the ancient castle, at the time perched almost 50 meters above the Vltava River on a steep cliff. In fact, the name *Orlík* means young eagle. **Hrad Orlík** was always thought to be reminiscent of a young eagle in a nest far up in a rocky ledge. The castle dates back to the 13th century. Though the builders of the original structure are not known, the current castle was built in the early Gothic style by King Wenceslas II. The castle housed important figures in Czech history such as Jan Hus, after whom the Hussites are named, and Jan Žižka, the Hussite military leader after whom Prague's Žižkov district is named. It became the property of the Schwarzenberg family in 1719. The castle was nationalized by the Communist government after World War II, then, with the collapse of Communism, was returned to the Schwarzenbergs in the early 1990s. The rather dramatic appearance today is mostly due to renovations in the mid-1800s in the new Gothic style. Castle tours, like those of Český Šternberk, help you appreciate the history of the castle and what you're looking at. Tours last an hour and show you the portraits in the Small Empire Hall, the Napoleanic-era furnishings of the Great Empire Hall, and the incredible wooden sculpture by Jan Teska in the Teska Court. ⊠ *Hrad Orlík* ☎ *382–275–101* 🎫 *130 Kč* ⊙ *Apr. and Oct., Tues.–Sun. 9–3; May and Sept., Tues.–Sun. 9–4; June–Aug., Tues.–Sun. 9–5.*

Where to Eat

¢–$$ ✕ **Restaurace a ubytovna u Cvrků.** Dining and accommodation choices are almost nonexistent in Orlík, but this restaurant is only a kilometer or so south of the castle, in the village of Staré Sedlec. Czech food prevails and game is the specialty. A few rooms upstairs (¢) are no-frills, basic bedrooms, and the bathroom is in the hallway; they are popular among cyclers who appreciate the very cheap price. ⊠ *Staré Sedlo 61, 398 07* ☎ *777–160–515* ⊕ *www.ucvrku.cz* ▭ *No credit cards.*

Orlík Essentials

TRANSPORTATION Orlik is a difficult trip to manage by public transportation; however, it's an easy hour-long drive by car. Head south out of Prague on Highway 4, which roughly follows the Vltava, then turn right, after about 45 minutes, onto Highway 19. A final right turn brings you right into Orlík.

Getting to Orlík by bus is the problem—there are two or three direct connections every day leaving the Na Knížecí station, and the ride lasts a tolerable hour and 17 minutes. Returning to Prague is another story. The route back, which tours many more small villages than seems necessary and sometimes doubles back on itself, is a mildly cruel joke lasting from 2 to 3½ hours. If you decide to make it an adventure, the Na Knížecí bus station is accessible from the south exit (the far one from the city center) of the Anděl metro station. Make sure you ask the driver if you're on the right bus and buy the ticket from him directly. There are several buses coming back, which require a change in either Písek or Tábor; the Písek option is quicker and doesn't require a transfer from bus to train.

VISITOR There's no tourist information center in Orlik, but information on the
INFORMATION general area can be found by contacting the information center in Písek, about 30 km (19 mi) away.

🚩 **Písek Tourist Information** ⊠ Hejdukova 97, Písek ☎ 382-213-592 ⊕ www.icpisek.cz.

SOUTHERN BOHEMIA

8

THE BEST HOTEL IN ČESKÝ KRUMLOV
Hotel Růže, *Český Krumlov* ⇨*p.196*

PURE 19TH-CENTURY EXCESS
Hluboká nad Vltavou ⇨*p.189*

HOSPITABLE FAMILY-RUN PUB
Na Louži, *Český Krumlov* ⇨*p.195*

A HOTEL WITH ITS OWN CATACOMBS
Pension 189 Karel Bican, *Tábor* ⇨*p.183*

WHIMSICAL GRANDEUR
Kratochvíle, *Netolice* ⇨*p.191*

A HAUNTED CASTLE
Jindřichův Hradec ⇨*p.186*

By Tomáš
Kleisner

WITH PRAGUE AT ITS HEART—and powerhouses Germany and the former Austro-Hungarian Empire on its mountainous borders—the kingdom of Bohemia was for centuries buffeted by religious and national conflicts, invasions, and wars. But its position also meant that Bohemia benefited from the cultural wealth and diversity of Central Europe. The result is a glorious array of history-laden castles, walled cities, and spa towns set in a gentle, rolling landscape.

Southern Bohemia is particularly famous for its involvement in the Hussite religious wars of the 15th century, which revolved around the town of Tábor. But the area also has more than its fair share of well-preserved and stunning walled towns, built up by generations of noble families, who left behind layers of Gothic, Renaissance, and baroque architecture (particularly notable in Český Krumlov). Farther north and an easy drive east of Prague is the old silver-mining town of Kutná Hora, once a rival to Prague for the royal residence.

Český Krumlov (along with the spas of western Bohemia) offers some of the best accommodations in the Czech Republic outside the capital.

Numbers in the margin correspond to numbers on the Southern Bohemia and Český Krumlov maps.

About the Hotels & Restaurants

Outside of Prague, prices for food and hotels are lower, but service—and especially any level of functional English among the staff—sometimes lags behind. You are much more likely to find German-language menus in restaurants and German-speaking staff in both restaurants and hotels.

WHAT IT COSTS in koruna and euros				
$$$$	**$$$**	**$$**	**$**	**¢**
HOTELS*				
IN KORUNA	over 7,000	5,000–7,000	3,500–5,000	1,500–3,500	under 1,500
HOTELS*				
IN EUROS	over €225	€155–€225	€108–€155	€47–€108	under €47
RESTAURANTS**				
over 500	300–500	150–300	100–150	under 100

*Hotel prices are for two people in a double room with a private bath and breakfast during peak season (March through October, excluding July and August) and generally include 5% V.A.T. **Restaurant prices are per person for a main course at dinner and include 19% V.A.T.

TÁBOR

❶ *90 km (54 mi) south of Prague.*

It's hard to believe this dusty Czech town was built to receive Christ on his return to Earth in the Second Coming. But that's what the Hussites intended when they flocked here by the thousands in 1420 to construct

Southern Bohemia

Louny
Žatec   Zlonice
Mělník   Mladá
Boleslav
Neratovice
E48   Roztoky   Čelákovice   Poděbrady
Lidice
Rudná   Prague   E67   Kolín   Labe
Kralovice   Beroun   Říčany   12
Tepla   Zdice   Uhlířske   333   Kutná
Planá   Janovice   Hora
Tachov   Stříbro   Plzeň   Zbraslavice
Bor   Rokycany
Horšovský   Dobřany   Příbram   Sedlčany
Týn
Nepomuk   Milevsko
Domažlice   Zvíkov   19   Pelhřimov
Castle
Klatovy   Horažd'ovice   Písek ❷   ❶ Tábor   34
GERMANY   Sušice   Strakonice   Soběslav   Červená
Vodňany   Veselí   Lhota
Vimperk   Kratochvíle   ❺   ❹ Jindřichův
Hluboká nad Vltavou   ❻   ❸   Hradec
Regen   České Budějovice   Třeboň
Borovany
Česky   Trhové Sviny
Krumlov   Kaplice
Deggendorf   ❼ – ⓬   Gmünd
see detail   ⓭ Rožmberk
map   nad Vltavou
0   20 miles   Passau   AUSTRIA
0   30 km   Freistadt

a society modeled on the communities of the early Christians. Tábor's fascinating history is unique among Czech towns—it started out as a combination utopia and fortress.

Following the execution of Jan Hus, a vociferous religious reformer who railed against the Catholic Church and the nobility, reform priests drawing on the support of poor workers and peasants took to the hills of southern Bohemia. These hilltop congregations soon grew into permanent settlements, wholly outside the feudal order. The most important settlement, on the Lužnice River, became known in 1420 as Tábor. Tábor quickly evolved into the symbolic and spiritual center of the Hussites (now called Taborites) and, together with Prague, served as the bulwark of the reform movement.

The early 1420s in Tábor were heady days for religious reformers. Private property was denounced, and the many poor who made the pilgrimage to Tábor were required to leave their possessions at the town gates. Some sects rejected the doctrine of transubstantiation (the belief that the Eucharistic elements become the body and blood of Christ), turning Holy Communion into a bawdy, secular feast of bread and wine. Other reformers considered themselves superior to Christ—who by dying had shown himself to be merely mortal. Few, however, felt obliged to work for a living, and the Taborites had to rely increasingly on raids of neighboring villages for survival.

War fever in Tábor at the time ran high, and the town became one of the focal points of the Hussite wars (1419–34), which pitted reformers against an array of foreign crusaders, Catholics, and noblemen. Under the brilliant military leadership of Jan Žižka, the Taborites enjoyed early successes, but the forces of the established church and the moderate Hussite nobility proved too mighty in the end. Žižka died in 1424, and the Hussite uprising ended at the rout of Lipany 10 years later. Still, many of the town's citizens resisted recatholicization. Fittingly, following the Battle of White Mountain in 1620 (the final defeat for the Czech Protestants), Tábor was the last city to succumb to the conquering Hapsburgs.

Žižkovo náměstí (Žižka Square) is dominated by a large, 19th-century bronze statue of the gifted Hussite military leader. The stone tables in front of the Gothic town hall and the house at No. 6 date from the 15th century and were used by the Hussites to give daily communion to the faithful. Walk, if you dare, the tiny streets around the square, as they curve around, branch off, and then stop; few lead back to the main square. The confusing street plan was purposely laid during the 15th century to thwart incoming invasions.

The **Husitské muzeum** (Hussite Museum), just behind the town hall, documents the history of the reformers. You can visit an elaborate network of tunnels below the Old Town, carved by the Hussites for protection in case of attack. ⊠ *Žižkovo nám. 2* 🕾 *381–254–286* ⊕ *www.husmuzeum.cz* 🖼 *Museum and tunnel tours 40 Kč–60 Kč* ☉ *Apr.–Oct., daily 8:30–5; Nov.–Mar., weekdays 8:30–5.*

Pražská ulice, a main route to the newer part of town, is lined with beautiful Renaissance façades. If you turn right at Divadelní and head to the Lužnice River, you can see the remaining walls and fortifications of the 15th century, irrefutable evidence of the town's vital function as a stronghold.

Hrad Kotnov (Kotnov Castle), rising above the river in the distance, dates from the 13th century and was part of Tábor's earliest fortifications. The large pond to the northeast of the Old Town was created as a reservoir in 1492; since it was used for baptism, the fervent Taborites named the lake Jordán. ⊠ *Klokotská* 🕾 *381–252–788* ⊕ *www.husmuzeum.cz* 🖼 *Castle 40 Kč, tower 20 Kč* ☉ *May–Sept. 8:30–5; other times by appointment.*

Where to Stay

¢ 🕾 **Kapital.** A good bargain, this small hotel on the main street leading from the train and bus stations to the Old Town boasts of its "in-door toilets," but in truth offers more than most in its price range, such as a TV (and a bathroom) in every room and covered parking. ⊠ *Tř. 9 května 617, 390 01* 🕾 *381–256–096* 🖷 *381–252–411* ⊕ *web.quick.cz/hotel-kapital* 🛏 *24 rooms* ♧ *Restaurant, cable TV, bicycles, bar, parking (fee); no a/c* ⊟ *AE, DC, MC, V* ⭐ *BP.*

¢ 🖼 **Pension 189 Karel Bican.** At this lovely family-run pension, the service couldn't be nicer, nor could the soothing view of the river from some rooms. The premises date from the 14th century, and the Bicans will gladly show you the house's own catacombs, which once linked up to the medieval tunnel network. When it's hot outside, you can chill out in the cool basement lounge. Some rooms have cooking facilities. The level of comfort exceeds that found in many a Czech "luxury" hotel. ⊠ *Hradební 189, 390 01* 🖷 *381–252–109* ⊕ *www.globalnet.cz/ bican* 🛏 *6 rooms* ♨ *Some kitchenettes, minibars, cable TV, sauna, bicycles, some pets allowed; no a/c* 🖃 *AE, MC, V* 🍴 *BP.*

FodorśChoice
★

Tábor Essentials

TRANSPORTATION
Direct buses to Tábor leave Prague from the Na Knížecí station; the trip typically takes 90 minutes and costs 75 Kč. The train fare is nearly twice as much, and the journey can last for two hours, starting at the Hlavní nádraží (Main station). By car, the distance is about 90 km (56 mi) and should take a little more than an hour.

VISITOR
INFORMATION
🚩 **Tábor Tourist Information** ⊠ Žižkovo nám. 2 🖷 381–486–230 ⊕ www.tabor.cz

PÍSEK

❷ *44 km (28 mi) west of Tábor; 103 km (62 mi) south of Prague.*

If it weren't for Písek's 700-year-old **Gothic bridge,** peopled with baroque statues, you could easily bypass the town. Compared with the splendors of Český Krumlov or even Třeboň, Písek's main square, Velké náměstí, is plain, despite its many handsome Renaissance and baroque houses. The bridge, a five-minute walk from the main square along Karlova ulice, was commissioned in the 1260s—making it the oldest bridge in the Czech Republic, surpassing by 90 years Prague's Charles Bridge— by Přemysl Otakar II, who sought a secure crossing over the difficult Otava River for his salt shipments from nearby Prachatice. As early as the 9th century, Písek stood at the center of one of the most important trade routes to the west, linking Prague to Passau and the rest of Bavaria, and in the 15th century it became one of five major Hussite strongholds. The statues of saints weren't added to the bridge until the 18th century. One of the statues was damaged and all the paving stones washed away during the devastating floods of 2002, but the bridge itself survived and has now been restored.

Just off the main square, look for the 240-foot tower of the early-Gothic **Mariánský chrám** (Church of Mary). Construction was started at about the time the bridge was built. The lone surviving tower was completed in 1487. On the inside, look for the *Madonna of Písek,* a 14th-century Gothic altar painting. On a middle pillar is a rare series of early Gothic wall paintings dating from the end of the 13th century. ⊠ *Bakaláře at Leoše Janáčka.*

The **Prácheňské Museum** is in the 13th-century castle's frescoed medieval halls, documenting the history of Písek and its surroundings, including the Czech fishery industry (with the additional original touch of live fish in large aquaria). ⊠ *Velké nám. 114* ☏ *382–201–111* ⊕ *www. prachenskemuzeum.cz* 🎫 *30 Kč* ⊙ *Mar.–Sept., Tues.–Sun. 9–6; Oct.–Dec., Tues.–Sun. 9–5.*

off the beaten path	**ZVÍKOV –** If you've got room for still another castle, head for Zvíkov Castle, about 18 km (11 mi) north of Písek. The castle, at the confluence of the Otava and Vltava rivers, is impressive for its authenticity. Unlike many other castles in Bohemia, Zvíkov survived the 18th and 19th centuries unrenovated and still looks just as it did 500 years ago. ⊠ *Rte. 138, 18 km (11 mi) north of Písek* ☏ *382–285–676* 🎫 *90 Kč* ⊙ *May and Sept., Tues.–Sun. 9:30–4; June–Aug., Tues.–Sun. 9–5; Apr. and Oct., weekends 9:30–3:30.*

Where to Stay

$ 🏨 **Hotel America.** In a quiet area, the small, modern hotel somehow resembles an ocean liner with its round windows and terraces. The most expensive hotel in the town, it still looks rather ordinary inside but offers good rooms and many sporting options, including horseback riding, fishing, and hunting. ⊠ *Richarda Weinera 2375, 397 01* ☏ *382–219–357* 🖷 *382–212–361* ⊕ *www.interhotel-america.com* 🛏 *36 rooms* ⚘ *Restaurant, cable TV, golf, indoor pool, gym, sauna, bar, laundry service, Internet, some free parking, some pets allowed (fee)* ▤ *AE, DC, MC, V* ⭢◉ *CP.*

Písek Essentials

TRANSPORTATION There's no direct train from Prague to Písek. Buses leave from the Na Knížecí station and will take you there for 80 Kč–90 Kč in approximately two hours. If you drive, the trip should take no more than 90 minutes.

VISITOR INFORMATION 🚩 **Písek Tourist Information** ⊠ Heydukova 97 ☏ 382–213–592 ⊕ www. icpisek.cz

TŘEBOŇ

❸ *48 km (28 mi) south of Tábor; 138 km (83 mi) south of Prague.*

Amid a plethora of ponds rests a jewel of a town with a far different historical heritage than Tábor's. Třeboň was settled during the 12th century by the Wittkowitzes (later called the Rožmberks, or Rosenbergs), once Bohemia's noblest family. From the 14th to the end of the 16th century, the dynasty dominated southern Bohemia; they amassed their wealth through silver, real estate, and fish farming. You can see their emblem, a five-petal rose, on castles, doorways, and coats of arms all over the region. Their official residence was 40 km (25 mi) to the southwest, in Český Krumlov, but Třeboň was an important second residence and repository of the family archives, which still reside in the town château. Thanks to the Rožmberk family, this unlikely landlocked town has become the center of the Czech Republic's fishing industry. During the 15th and 16th centuries, the Rožmberks peppered the countryside with 6,000 enormous ponds, partly to drain the land and partly to breed fish. Carp breeding is still big business, and if you're in the area in late autumn, you may be lucky enough to witness the great carp harvests, when tens of thousands of the glittering fish are netted. The closest pond, **Rybník Svět** (Svět Pond), is on the southern edge of town; try to fit in a stroll along its banks. You can even swim here in summer (the pond has pleasant, sandy beaches), but it can get crowded.

Třeboň is an access point in the Czech Greenways network. Greenways is a Czech-American organization that is gradually establishing a chain of hiking, biking, and riding routes from Prague to Vienna, working with local authorities and property owners to develop "ecotourism" along the way. Around Třeboň, hiking and horseback trails snake through the area's ponds and peat bogs. For specific information, contact the local tourist office.

The partially intact town defenses, made up of walls, 16th-century gates, and three bastions, are among the best in the Czech Republic. Near the **Svinenská Gate**, there's an 18th-century brewery, still producing outstanding beer. First brewed in 1379, as the redbrick tower proudly boasts, beer enjoys nearly as long a tradition here as in Plzeň or České Budějovice. The main square, Masarykovo náměstí (Masaryk Square), has a typical collection of arcaded Renaissance and baroque houses. Look for the **Bílý Koníček** (Little White Horse), the best-preserved Renaissance house on the square, dating from 1544. It's now a modest hotel and restaurant. Stop by for some of the excellent local beer. Look for the castle-topped, white façade. ⊠ *Masarykovo nám. 97* ☎ *384–721–213* ⊕ *www. hotelbilykonicek.cz.*

The entrance to **Zámek Třeboň** (Třeboň Château) lies at the southwest corner of the square. From the outside it looks plain and sober, with its stark white walls, but the walls of the inner courtyard are covered with sgraffito. Several different tours of the interior feature sumptuous recreations of the Renaissance lifestyle enjoyed by the Rožmberks and apartments furnished in late-19th-century splendor. The last of the Rožmberks died in 1611, and the castle eventually became the property of the Schwarzenberg family, who built their family tomb in a grand park on the other side of Svět Pond. It's now a monumental neo-Gothic destination for Sunday-afternoon picnickers. ⊠ *Masarykovo nám.* ☎ *384–721–193* 📷 *Tour of family tomb 20 Kč. Tour of apartments 130 Kč* ☉ *Apr.–May, Sept., and Oct., Tues.–Sun. 9–4; June–Aug., Tues.–Sun. 9–5.*

The **Kostel svatého Jiljí** (Church of St. Giles), adjoining the former Augustine monastery just north of the main square, once held a set of altar paintings by the Master of the Wittingau Altar (Wittingau is the German name for Třeboň) that dates from the late 14th century). The paintings themselves, the most famous example of Bohemian Gothic art, are now in the Národní Galerie (National Gallery) in Prague. The church, with its row of slender columns dividing a double nave, exemplifies the Gothic style of southern Bohemia. ⊠ *Husova.*

Where to Stay

$ 🏨 **Zlatá Hvězda.** Although the façade of this hotel is less visually striking than the budget Bílý Koníček Hotel at the other end of the square, the "Golden Star" is a more comfortable alternative. Renovation in the late 1990s left the rooms still exuding a precapitalist spareness, while adding such conveniences as relatively spacious bathrooms and satellite TVs. ✉ *Masarykovo nám. 107, 379 01* ☎ *384-757-111* 🖷 *384-757-300* ⊕ *www.zhvezda.cz* ⇨ *42 rooms* ⚫ *Restaurant, cable TV, gym, pub, Internet, meeting room, some pets allowed (fee); no a/c* 🗖 *AE, DC, MC, V* ⦿| *BP.*

Třeboň Essentials

TRANSPORTATION A direct bus from the Florenc station goes to Třeboň in 2½ hours for 105 Kč. Although a train trip requires to change at Veselí, it takes the same time but it's more expensive (184 Kč). It's usually easier to stay overnight in České Budějovice and then to take a local bus to Třeboň because that trip takes only 30 minutes.

VISITOR INFORMATION 🚩 **Třeboň Tourist Information** ✉ Masarykovo nám. 103 ☎ 384-721-169 ⊕ www. trebon-mesto.cz.

JINDŘICHŮV HRADEC

❹ 28 km (17 mi) southwest of Trébon; 158 km (95 mi) south of Prague.

The ancient, picturesque town of Jindřichův Hradec, which dates to the end of the 12th century, is reflected in the waters of the Vajgar pond right in the middle of town. It came into existence as a market colony near the border between Bohemia and Moravia, so a castle was built to protect it. Under the protection of the castle, the town grew in size and importance. The surrounding countryside has its own special beauty—unspoiled, with more ponds, forests, hills, and numerous scattered granite outcrops—and is deservedly nicknamed "Czech Canada." A number of cultural events are held in the town every year, including the Concertino Praga (an international radio competition for young musicians), a folk music festival called "Folkloric Rose," the South Bohemian Music Festival, and occasional classical music concerts in castle Rondel.

Imposing Renaissance houses surround the **náměstí Míru** (Main Square). The open space in front of the late baroque town hall is dominated by the decorated column of the Holy Trinity. This fine example of local sculpture was paid for by the local postmaster in 1764, an unusual bequest from such a lowly functionary.

★ A short walk from the town square brings the visitor to the gates of the **castle.** Behind the courtyard and its lovely Italian arcades, the core of the castle is Gothic and its splendor is reflected not only in its thick defensive walls and round tower but also in the **murals** covering interior corridors. These date from 1338 and depict the legend of St. George as well as many colorful examples of medieval coats of arms. In the course of centuries, buildings of an adjoining Renaissance-era château were added to the early Gothic castle, forming together a large complex, the third-largest in size in the Czech Republic. There are three different marked routes through the castle for visitors to follow.

The most singular attraction within the Renaissance chateau must be the **Rondel,** a circular, domed jewel of a building decorated in the man-

GUIDED DAY TOURS TO SOUTHERN BOHEMIA

GUIDED BUS TOURS are available from several companies for some destinations in Southern Bohemia. Most need to be booked a day in advance.

Athos (☎ 244–003–203 ⊕ www.athos. cz) offers coach trips to Česky Krumlov, Hluboká Castle, Holašovice, and České Budějovice. The Athos coach leaves Prague from Na Příkopě street. Most trips to Southern Bohemia take about 10 hours and include lunch.

Čedok (☎ 224–197–111 ⊕ www.cedok. cz) offers the same and some longer trips as Athos and Martin, but the company also does longer itineraries. One three-day Čdok trip includes the highlights of Southern Bohemia with lodging at České Budějovice and Český Krumlov, or at Třebon, Jindřichův Hradec, and Telč. The main Prague departure point is náměstí Republiky (Republic Square) in central Prague, opposite the Prašná brána (Powder Tower). Čedok also offers spa and reconditioning programs at the Třebon Spa for a week or two.

Martin Tours (☎ 224–212–473 ⊕ www. martintour.cz) offers the same itineraries as Athos but uses mostly smaller minibuses. Departure poitns are Staroměstské náměstí (Old Town Square) and náměstí Republiky (Republic Square). All itineraries in Southern Bohemia are about 10 hours and include lunch.

---

nerist style of the late 16th century. It was designed by Italian architect Baldassare Maggio as a ballroom, and the delicate pink-and-white decorations summon up images of aristocratic dancers and musicians. The unique underground music chamber was connected to the main hall by a circular aperture in the center of the dance floor. A large decorative vase standing over this hole not only acted as a sound amplifier but also prevented the lordly dancers from falling in. Even without this peculiar feature, the acoustics of the Rondel remain especially good, and it's often still used for classical concerts in the summer. The castle is said to be haunted by the White Lady, who appears clad in diaphanous white but wearing long black gloves on her ghostly fingers; when she is seen, a member of the ruling Černín family is bound to die. ✉ *Dobrovského 1* ☎ *384–321–279* 🎟 *140 Kč* ☉ *June–Aug., Tues.–Sun. 9–5.30; Apr. and Oct., Tues.–Sun. 10–4; May and Sept., Tues.–Sun. 10–5.*

In the 13th century, a Franciscan monastery was built adjacent to the **Kostel svatého Jana** (Church of St. John). The extensive and fine murals in the clerestory of the church date from the first half of the 14th century and portray scenes from the lives of Christ, the Apostles, and various Czech saints. They clearly demonstrate the medieval necessity for pictorial stories to educate the illiterate population. On the south side of the sanctuary you can see the chapel of St. Nicholas, which was built in 1369. The vaulted ceiling is supported by a single central pillar and this is one of the earliest buildings of this sort of construction in Bohemia. Although the church is open to the public only in high summer season, there are occasional evening concerts in other months. ⊠ *Štítného* ⌑ *10 Kč* ⊙ *July and Aug., daily 9–noon and 12:30–4:30.*

Dominating Jindřichuv Hradec is the tall **Proboštský Kostel** (Church of the Assumption), which dates from the beginning of the 15th century. By coincidence, the corner of the church intersects with the earth's 15th meridian. A viewing gallery can be visited near the top of the church tower, and it provides extensive views across the surrounding area. However, this is achieved only after a climb of 157 steps. ⊠ *Za kostelem* ⌑ *Tower 10 Kč* ⊙ *June–Aug., daily 10–noon and 1–4; Apr., May, and Sept.–Jan., weekends 10–noon and 1–4.*

The local **Muzeum Jindřichohradecka** was founded in 1882. Its principal attraction is a quite extraordinary Christmas nativity scene. This huge, mechanical tableau in traditional style was created by one committed craftsman, Mr. Krýza, who dedicated more than 60 years to its creation in the latter part of the 19th century. The old mechanism has now been replaced with an electrical system, but the primitive charm of the moving figures remains. Altogether the scene contains 1,398 figures. Another unusual exhibit is the re-creation of a parlor from the home of the Czech opera star Emmy Destinn, who was famous in the early 20th century and was a popular partner with Enrico Caruso on the stage of the New York Metropolitan Opera. The taste of the time favored the eccentric, and you may find it remarkable that the diva should have reposed on a sofa made from so many antlers. ⊠ *Balbínovo nám. 19* ☎ *384–363–660* ⊕ *www.muzeum.esnet.cz* ⌑ *60 Kč* ⊙ *June–Sept., daily 8:30–noon and 12:30–5; Apr., May, and Oct.–Jan., Tues.–Sun. 8:30–noon and 12:30–5.*

off the
beaten
path

ČERVENÁ LHOTA – About 20 km (12 mi) north of Jindřichuv Hradec stands this fairy-tale chateau, unique for its red walls, which are mirrored in the beautiful surrounding lake. It's connected to the land by a stone bridge. The castle's current neo-Renaissance style dates from a renovation at the beginning of 20th century. Previously, the castle was a stronghold above a small river; the lake is artificial. The castle interiors are of great historical value, notably the dining room with its stucco decorations and the French drawing room. A small period garden adjoins the castle entrance and provides a calm setting from which to view the charming location. ⊠ *Kardašova Řečice 378 21* ☎ *384–384–228* ⌑ *120 Kč* ⊙ *May and Sept., Tues.–Sun. 9:30–4.30; June and Aug., Tues.–Sun. 9:30–5:15; Apr. and Oct. weekends 9:30–4:30.*

Where to Stay

$ ⊡ **Hotel Concertino.** At a safe distance from the castle and its spectral visitor, this hotel overlooks the town square. The façade suggests a charming period conversion, but once inside, modernity is the keynote. The hotel provides a series of up-to-date business services. ⊠ *Míru nám. 141, 377 01* ☎ *384–362–320* 🖷 *384–362–323* ⊕ *www.concertino. cz* 🛏 *33 rooms* ⚒ *Restaurant, minibars, in-room safes, cable TV, hair salon, bar, pub, billiards, paddle tennis, laundry service, meeting rooms, parking (fee); no a/c* ⊟ *AE, DC, MC, V.*

¢   🖭 **Hotel Bílá paní.** Right next to the castle, the "White Lady" hotel takes its name from the famous ghost who is reputed to haunt the castle itself. So far as we know, she does not appear in the hotel. The rooms themselves may not be up to her stately standards; however, they are presentable and clean, and from some of them a view can be had of the castle tower. They are certainly fine if you're just looking for an inexpensive place in the area for an overnight rest. ⊠ *Dobrovského 54, 377 01* ☎ *384–362–660* 🖷 *384–362–660* ⊕ *www.hotelbilapani.cz* 🛏 *9 rooms* ⚒ *Restaurant, cable TV, some pets allowed; no a/c* ⊟ *MC, V* ❢◯❢ *BP.*

Jindřichův Hradec Essentials

TRANSPORTATION Jindřichův Hradec is about three hours from Prague by bus; a bus from the Florenc station costs 115 Kč. The train from the Hlavní nádraží (Main station) will require a change at Veselí and takes 15 minutes more than the bus. It also costs more, at a fare of 184 Kč.

VISITOR   🖪 **Jindřichův Hradec Tourist Information** ⊠ Panská 136 ☎ 384-363-546 ⊕ www.
INFORMATION   jh.cz.

HLUBOKÁ NAD VLTAVOU

❺   *17 km (10½ mi) southwest of Trébon; 155 km (93½ mi) south of*
Fodor'sChoice   *Prague.*
★

This is one of the Czech Republic's most curious châteaux. Although the structure dates from the 13th century, what you see is pure 19th-century excess, perpetrated by the wealthy Schwarzenberg family as proof of their "good taste." If you think you've seen it somewhere before, you're probably thinking of Windsor Castle, near London, on which it was carefully modeled. Take a tour; the rather pompous interior reflects the no-holds-barred tastes of the time, but many individual pieces are interesting. The wooden Renaissance ceiling in the large dining room was removed by the Schwarzenbergs from the castle at Český Krumlov and brought here. Also look for the beautiful late-baroque bookshelves in the library.

If your interest in Czech painting wasn't satisfied in Prague, have a look at the **Galerie Mikolaše Alše** (Aleš Art Gallery; ☎ 387–967–041) in the Riding Hall, which displays a major collection of Gothic art and an exhibition of modern Czech works. The gallery is a popular spot for chamber concerts. ⊠ *Zamék 142, off Rte. 105 or 146, Hluboká nad Vltavou* ☎ *387–967–045 château* 🏷 *160 Kč castle, 30 Kč Aleš Art Gallery* ⊙ *Castle: Apr.–June, Sept., and Oct., Tues.–Sun. 9–4:30; July and Aug., daily 9–5. Aleš Art Gallery: May–Sept., daily 9–5; Oct.–Apr., Tues.–Sun. 9–3:30.*

☾   If you're in the mood for a brisk walk, follow the yellow trail signs 2 km (1 mi) to the **Lovecká chata Ohrada** (Ohrada Hunting Lodge), which houses a museum of hunting and fishing and also has a small zoo for children. ✉ *Zamék Ohrada 1, off Rte. 105, Hluboká nad Vltavou* ☎ *387–965–340* 🎟 *40 Kč* ⊘ *June–Aug., daily 9–5:30; May and Sept., Tues.–Sun. 9–5:30; Apr. and Oct., Tues.–Fri. 9–3; Nov.–Mar. by appointment.*

Hluboká nad Vltavou Essentials

TRANSPORTATION The journey from Prague to Hluboká—either by train from the Hlavní nádraží (Main station) or by bus from the Florenc coach—station is 2½ hours unless you get one of the local connections that stops everywhere (in which case the trip takes 3½ hours). The train ticket costs 184 Kč, the bus ticket 120 Kč. You may find it more convenient to stay overnight in České Budějovice and see the castle in the morning after a 20-minute trip either by local bus or train.

ČESKÉ BUDĚJOVICE

❻ *26 km (16 mi) southwest of Trébon; 164 km (99 mi) south of Prague.*

An industrial city of 100,000, České Budějovice is a much livelier scene than its more picturesque neighbors and has a large Old Town with several worthwhile sights, notably the well-preserved Gothic Dominican monastery and Church of the Virgin on Piaristické náměstí. The major attraction is the enormously proportioned main square—a rarity, it actually *is* square—named after King Přemysl Otakar II, lined with arcaded houses and worth an hour or two of wandering. However, the town is perhaps best known for its beer. For a bite to eat and a sampling of locally brewed Budvar beer in an atmospheric setting, stop by Masné Krámy on Krajinská 13, two blocks north of the square. Unfortunately, you can't tour the Budvar Brewery itself. The delicious local beer is known to Germans as Budweiser (they call the town Budweis)—but this is not the stuff made in St. Louis.

To get a good view over the city, climb the 360 steps up to the Renaissance gallery of the **Černá věž** (Black Tower), at the northeast corner of the square next to St. Nicholas's Cathedral. ✉ *Nám. Přemysla Otakara II* 🎟 *10 Kč* ⊘ *Apr.–June, Sept., and Oct., Tues.–Sun. 10–6; July and Aug., daily 10–6.*

The town is proud to possess **Koněspřežka**, the oldest railway station on the continent. Designed to transport salt to Bohemia from Linz in Austria, a horse-driven railway was built between 1825 and 1832. One of the first major industrial developments in Europe, it reduced the journey between Linz and České Budějovice from two weeks to four days. Public transport was introduced soon afterward. The station is now a part of the city museum. ✉ *Mánesova 10* ☎ *386–354–820* ⊕ *www. muzeumcb.cz* 🎟 *10 Kč* ⊘ *May–Sept., Tues.–Sun. 9–12:30 and 1–5.*

Founded in 1877, the **Jihočeské Museum** started with a couple of hundred donated items in three rooms in the town hall on the main square. Nowadays, the large collections are held and displayed in the main building and at four other locations outside the town. The major exhibits include themed collections portraying the history of the town and the region through an extensive variety of artifacts that include metalwork, ceramics, glass, and furniture. A fascinating large-scale model shows the Old Town and its picturesque medieval walls and towers. A regular series of temporary exhibitions also runs alongside the permanent ones. ⊠ *Dukelská 1* ☎ *386–356–447* ⊕ *www.muzeumcb.cz* ▨ *80 Kč* ☉ *Tues.–Sun. 9–12:30 and 1–5.*

off the beaten path

KRATOCHVÍLE – Thirty km northwest of České Budějovice, Kratochvíle is actually a punning title for this remarkable chateau since the Czech word suggests a caprice or whimsy. The modest scale and appearance of this summer residence for the lords of Rožmberk belies its charm and fascination, and the visitor will not be disappointed. Compared to the Rožmberk's main residence in Český Krumlov, this 16th-century manor complex seems to have been built on a dollhouse scale. The grounds include a small church, garden, and mock fortifications. The house itself contains splendid and colorful stucco decorations with motifs from mythology and the hunt. In addition to these period delights is a permanent exhibition of the work of Czech animator Jiří Trnka, whose magical puppets and designs create a unique world of their own and fit right into the setting. The animation exhibit is as entrancing for adults as for children. ⊠ *Netolice* ☎ *388–324–380* ▨ *120 Kč* ☉ *Apr. and Oct., weekends 9–4, May and Sept., Tues.–Sun. 9–4:15, June–Aug., Tues.–Sun. 9–5:15.*

HOLAŠOVICE – About 18 km (11 mi) west of České Budějovice, this small village is like a step back in time, filled with small houses, some of which date back to the town's founding in the 13th century; the town plan still follows the basic outlines of its medieval shape. The buildings around the spacious village green have changed little since the 18th century, and the town's heart has hardly been touched by the modern world. It's now being preserved as a unique example of the Czech rural environment and at the same time proof of the artistry of the architecture of the local inhabitants. A small exhibition at No. 60 offers an insight into the village life throughout the year. The exceptional completeness and excellent preservation of Holašovice and its buildings make it an outstanding example of traditional rural settlement in central Europe, a good example of the South Bohemian "folk baroque." For one weekend each summer the Selské slavnosti (Peasant Festival) unites the inhabitants and visitors with a whole range of musical entertainments and craft demonstrations. You can see the village easily in an hour, at which time the hungry traveler may be delighted to find genuine South Bohemian cooking in the village hopsoda. ☎ *387–982–145* ⊕ *www. holasovice.info* ☉ *Apr.–Oct., Tues.–Sun. 9–5.*

Nightlife & the Arts

As a regional capital, České Budějovice keeps its own theater, ballet, orchestra, and opera companies. Unlike theater, music knows no language barriers, and the local opera company is regularly praised for its charming productions. Summer performances are held in Česky Krumlov Castle park. It's worth noting that these tickets are very popular and are often sold out by the month before. They can be obtained from the theater box office in České Budějovice. ⊠ *Dr. Stejskala 23* ☎ *386–356–925* ⊕ *www.jihoceskedivadlo.cz.*

Where to Stay

$–$$ 🏨 **Grand Hotel Zvon.** Old-fashioned, well kept, and comfortable, the historic hotel has an ideal location right on the main square. A room with a view, however, costs extra, but these rooms are considerably larger and brighter and come with large period bathtubs. ⊠ *Nám. Přemysla Otakara II 28, 307 01* ☎ *387–311–384* 🖷 *387–311–385* ⊕ *www. hotel-zvon.cz* ⟿ *75 rooms* ⚭ *2 restaurants, café, some minibars, cable TV, pub, parking (fee), some pets allowed (fee); no a/c* ▤ *AE, DC, MC, V* ⭐ *BP.*

$ 🏨 **Hotel Bohemia.** The hotel has been created by combining two old burgher houses. Refurbishment resulted in a nicely designed hotel in a quiet part of the old town. The building has been modernized but still retains its centuries-old ceilings and original features and is a listed monument. ⊠ *Hradební 20, 370 00* ☎ *386–352–097* 🖷 *386–352–900* ⊕ *www.hotel-bohemia-cb.cz* ⟿ *18 rooms* ⚭ *Restaurant, minibars, cable TV, laundry service, free parking, some pets allowed; no a/c,* ▤ *AE, MC, V* ⭐ *BP.*

České Budějovice Essentials

TRANSPORTATION The trip to České Budějovice from Prague takes about 2½ hours by either bus or train. Be careful to choose a *rychlík* not a *osobní* (express, as opposed to passenger train), which would make your journey four hours. Trains go from the Hlavní nádraží (Main station) and cost 204 Kč; buses leave from both Florenc and Na Knížecí and cost 124 Kč. Car travel affords the greatest ease and flexibility. České Budějovice lies on the main artery through the region, the two-lane E55 south from Prague, which, though often crowded, is in relatively good shape. The journey by car should take no more than two hours.

VISITOR 🛈 **České Budějovice Tourist Center** ⊠ Nám. Přemysla Otakára II 1 ☎ 386–801–413
INFORMATION ⊕ www.c-budejovice.cz

ČESKÝ KRUMLOV

48 km (29 mi) southwest of Třeboň; 186 km (112 mi) south of Prague.

Český Krumlov, the official residence of the Rožmberk family for some 300 years, is an eye-opener. None of the surrounding towns or villages, with their open squares and mixtures of old and new buildings, will prepare you for the beauty of the Old Town. Here the Vltava works its wonders as nowhere else but in Prague itself, swirling in a nearly complete circle around the town. Across the river stands the proud castle, rivaling any in the country in size and splendor.

For the moment, Český Krumlov's beauty is still intact, even though the dilapidated buildings that lend the town its unique atmosphere are slowly metamorphosing into boutiques and pensions. Visitor facilities

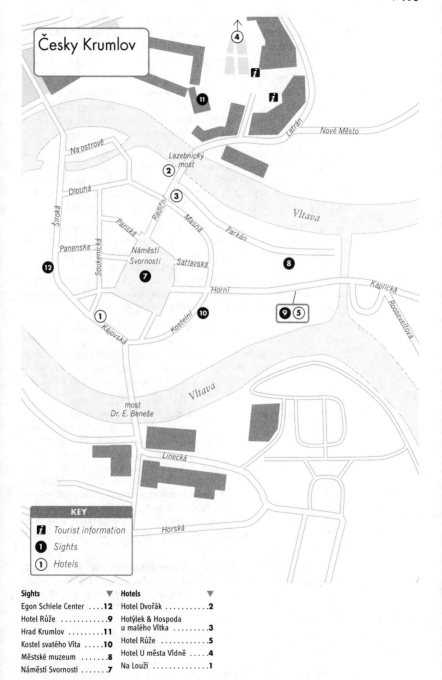

Česky Krumlov

KEY

🛈 *Tourist information*

❶ *Sights*

①　*Hotels*

Sights ▼

Egon Schiele Center **12**

Hotel Růže **9**

Hrad Krumlov **11**

Kostel svatého Víta **10**

Městské muzeum **8**

Náměstí Svornosti **7**

Hotels ▼

Hotel Dvořák **2**

Hotýlek & Hospoda
u malého Vítka **3**

Hotel Růže **5**

Hotel U města Vídně **4**

Na Louži **1**

are improving but can become overburdened during peak months. Overlook any minor inconveniences, however, and enjoy a rare, unspoiled trip in time back to the Bohemian Renaissance. Greenways trails lead to and from the town; for details, contact the tourist office.

What to See

❼ The town's main square, **náměstí Svornosti** (Unity Square), may not seem impressive at first sight, diminutive as it is. The **town hall**, at No. 1, built in 1580, is memorable for its Renaissance friezes and Gothic arcades. Tiny alleys fan out from the square in all directions.

❽ Just opposite the empty Hotel Krumlov, a street called Horní ulice leads off toward the **Městské muzeum** (City Museum). A quick visit will get you acquainted with the rise and fall of the Rožmberk dynasty. ☒ *Horní 152* ☎ *380–711–674* ☜ *50 Kč* ☉ *May, June, and Sept., daily 10–5; July and Aug., daily 10–6; Oct.–Apr., Tues.–Fri. 9–4, weekends 1–4.*

❾ Just opposite the City Museum are the Renaissance façades, complete with lively sgraffiti, of the former Jesuitská škola (Jesuit school)—now the semiluxurious **Hotel Růže**. Like many of Krumlov's most lordly edifices, it owes its abundance of Renaissance detailing to the town's location on the main trading routes to Italy and Bavaria—a perfect site for absorbing incoming fashions. The view over the Old Town and castle is most spectacular from the hotel parking lot. ☒ *Horní 154.*

❿ The tower of the Gothic **Kostel svatého Víta** (St. Vitus's Church), built in the early 1400s, rises to offset the larger, older tower of the castle across the river. Within the church, a marble-column baldachin shelters an elaborate baptismal font. At one time, it covered the tomb of Vilém von Rozemberk (1535–92), who was one of his line's most august heads and a great patron of the town. ☒ *Kostelní ul.*

⓫ To get to **Hrad Krumlov** (Krumlov Castle), cross the peaceful Vltava on the main street, Radniční, and enter via the staircase leading up from Latrán Street, or continue to the massive main gateway. The oldest and most striking part of the castle is the round, 13th-century **tower**, renovated in the 16th century to look something like a minaret, with its delicately arcaded Renaissance balcony. The tower is part of the old border fortifications, guarding the Bohemian frontiers from Austrian incursion. Now repainted in something like its Renaissance finery, from various perspectives it appears pompous, absurd, astonishingly lovely—or all of these at once. From dungeon to bells, its inner secrets can be seen from the interior staircase.

Vilém von Rožmberk oversaw a major refurbishment of the castle, adding buildings, heightening the tower, and adding rich decorations—generally making the place suitable for one of the grandest Bohemians of the day. The castle passed out of the Rožmberks' hands, however, when Vilém's brother and last of the line, the dissolute Petr Vok, sold both castle and town to Rudolf II in 1602 to pay off his debts. Under the succeeding Eggenberg and Schwarzenberg dynasties, the castle's transformation into an opulent palace continued. The Eggenbergs' prime addition was a **theater**, which was begun in the 1680s and completed in 1766 by

Josef Adam of Schwarzenberg. Much of the theater and its accou-trements—sets, props, costumes, stage machinery—survive intact as an extremely rare working display of period stagecraft. After a 30-year clo-sure, the theater reopened for tours in 1997.

As you enter the castle area, look into the old moats, where two play-ful brown bears now reside—unlikely to be of much help in protecting the castle from attack. In season, the castle rooms are open to the pub-lic. Be sure to ask at the ticket office about newly accessible areas of this enormous monument, as renovations and additional openings are ongoing. One sightseeing tour focuses on the Renaissance, baroque, and rococo rooms, taking in the delightful **Maškarní Sál** (Masquerade Hall), with its richly detailed 18th-century frescoes. A second tour highlights the seigneurial apartments of the Schwarzenbergs, who owned the cas-tle until the Gestapo seized it in 1940. (The castle became state prop-erty in 1947.)

The courtyards and passageways of the castle are open to the public year-round. After proceeding through the Renaissance-era third and fourth courtyards, you come to a wonderfully romantic elevated passageway with spectacular views of the huddled houses of the Old Town. The Aus-trian Expressionist painter Egon Schiele often stayed in Český Krumlov in the early 1900s and liked to paint this particular view over the river; he titled his now-famous Krumlov series *Dead City*. From the river down below, the elevated passageway is revealed as the middle level of **most Na plášti** (Cloaked Bridge), a massive construction spanning a deep ravine. Below the passageway are three levels of high arches, looking like a particularly elaborate Roman viaduct. On top runs a narrow three-story block of enclosed passages dressed in light blue and white. At the end of the passageway you come to the theater, then to the luxuriously appointed **castle garden**, formal at the near end, leafy and contemplative on the other. In the middle is an 18th-century summer house with a modern, revolv-ing open-air stage in front. Performances are held here in summer. ⊠ *Český Krumlov* ☎ *380–711–687* ☜ *Garden free, castle tours 150 Kč, tower 30 Kč, theater tours 180 Kč* ⊗ *Garden Apr.–Oct., daily. Castle interior Apr. and Oct., Tues.–Sun. 9–4; May and Sept., Tues.–Sun. 9–5; June–Aug., Tues.–Sun. 9–6. Tower May and Sept., daily 9–5; June–Aug., Tues.–Sun. 9–4. Theater May–Sept., daily 10–4; Oct., daily 10–3.*

⑫ The **Egon Schiele Center** exhibits the work of Schiele and other 20th-cen-tury and contemporary Austrian, German, and Czech artists in a ram-bling Renaissance building near the river. The museum closes occasionally during the winter season. ⊠ *Široká 70–72* ☎ *380–704–011* ⊕ *www. schieleartcentrum.cz* ☜ *180 Kč* ⊗ *Daily 10–6.*

Where to Eat

¢–$ ✕ **Na Louži.** Lovingly preserved wood furniture and paneling lends a tra-
Fodor'sChoice ditional touch to this warm, inviting, family-run pub. The food in the
★ pub is unfussy and satisfying; look for the *pstruh* (Vltava trout) with potatoes. The five country-style rooms upstairs (¢) are small but com-fortable enough for an overnight stay, breakfast included. ⊠ *Kájovská 66* ☎☎ *380–711–280* ▭ *No credit cards.*

Where to Stay

Český Krumlov is crammed with pensions and private rooms for rent, many priced as little as 250 Kč per person per night, though prices go up to 600 Kč. The best place to look is along the tiny Parkán ulice, which parallels the river just off the main street. A safe bet is the house at **Parkán No. 107** (☎ 380–716–396), blessed with several nice rooms and friendly management.

$$–$$$ 🏨 **Hotel Růže.** This Renaissance monastery has been transformed into **Fodor'sChoice** an excellent hotel, only a two-minute walk from the main square. The ★ decor is Ye Olde Bohemian but tastefully done, even extending to the bathroom "thrones." The rooms are spacious, and a few have drop-dead views of the castle, so ask to see several before choosing. Note that some double rooms have two narrow single beds, while some singles have beds large enough for two. The restaurant, too, is top-rate, and the elegant dining room is formal but not stuffy. ⊠ *Horní 154, 381 01* ☎ *380–772–100* 🖶 *380–713–146* ⊕ *www.hotelruze.cz* 🛏 *71 rooms* ⚴ *2 restaurants, café, cable TV, indoor pool, gym, hair salon, massage, sauna, bicycles, dry cleaning, laundry service, business services, meeting room, some pets allowed; no a/c* ⊟ *AE, MC, V* ⋈| *BP.*

$$ 🏨 **Hotel Dvořák.** Eminently comfortable, and completely modernized in 1999, this small hotel has three other things going for it: location, location, location. It's situated smack in the center of the historic district, right by the old Barber's Bridge. ⊠ *Radniční 101, 381 01* ☎ *380–711–020* 🖶 *380–711–024* ⊕ *dvorakck.genea2000.cz* 🛏 *17 rooms, 3 suites* ⚴ *Restaurant, in-room safes, cable TV, sauna, bar, dry cleaning, laundry service, business services; no a/c* ⊟ *AE, DC, MC, V* ⋈| *BP.*

$ 🏨 **Hotel U města Vídně.** The Vienna City hotel is easily found near the very center of Český Krumlov. Another charming old town house very tastefully reconstructed to a high standard as a modern hotel. The plush surroundings offer comfort and a touch of luxury at a reasonable price. ⊠ *Latrán 77, 381 01* ☎ *380–720–111* 🖶 *380–720–119* ⊕ *www.hmv. cz* 🛏 *46 rooms* ⚴ *Restaurant, café, cable TV, gym, sauna, laundry service, Internet, some free parking* ⊟ *AE, MC, V* ⋈| *CP.*

¢–$ 🏨 **Hotýlek & Hospoda u malého Vítka.** Not far from the river and on a quiet side street, this charming hotel has been thoughtfully renovated to a high standard. The rooms are tastefully plain with traditional wooden furniture and fittings. The most highly decorative feature must be the names of the rooms themselves. They are all named after titles of Czech fairy-tales. ⊠ *Radniční 27, 381 01* ☎ *380–711–925* 🖶 *380–711–937* ⊕ *www.vitekhotel.cz* 🛏 *19 rooms* ⚴ *Restaurant, bicycles, bar, wine bar, some pets allowed (fee); no a/c* ⊟ *AE, MC, V* ⋈| *BP.*

Nightlife & the Arts

Český Krumlov hosts numerous summertime cultural events, including Renaissance fairs, a chamber-music festival (in June and July), organ and piano festivals (July), and the top-notch International Music Festival in the castle (August), with performances by leading Czech and foreign classical ensembles. Theater and opera companies from České Budějovice perform in the castle garden in the summer.

Český Krumlov Essentials

TRANSPORTATION A direct bus to Česky Krumlov leaves Prague from both the Florenc and the Na Knížecí stations. The trip lasts three hours and costs 140 Kč. There's no direct train; with a change at České Budějovice, the trip clocks in at over four hours and costs 220 Kč.

VISITOR INFORMATION ▸ **Český Krumlov Tourist Information** ✉ Nám. Svornosti 2 ☎ 380-704-621 ⊕ www.ckrumlov.cz

ROŽMBERK NAD VLTAVOU

⑬ *22 km (13 mi) south of Český Krumlov; 208 km (125 mi) south of Prague.*

This little village, a few miles from the former Iron Curtain, was forgotten in the postwar years. It seems like a ghost town, especially at night. The darkened **Hrad Rožmberk** (Rosenberg Castle) keeps a lonely vigil atop the hill overlooking the Vltava River. The slender upper tower, the Jakobínka, dates from the 13th century, when the Rožmberk family built the original structure. Most of the exterior, however, is 19th-century neo-Gothic. In summer you can tour some of the rooms and admire the weapons and Bohemian paintings. Don't miss the painting of the White Lady; her ghost supposedly haunts the castle. ✉ *Rožmberk nad Vltavou* ☎ *380-749-838* ⊕ *www.hrad-rozmberk.cz* 🎟 *140 Kč* ☉ *May and Sept., Tues.–Sun. 9–4; June–Aug., Tues.–Sun. 9–5; Apr. and Oct., weekends 9–4.*

Rožmberk nad Vltavou Essentials

TRANSPORTATION The train trip from Prague to Rožmberk is not recommended. It requires two changes at České Budějovice and at Rybníkand takes 4½ hours, costing 274 Kč. The bus takes three hours and 45 minutes from Na Knížecí station for 155 Kč. Alternatively, you could take a bus from Český Krumlov (40 minutes) or from České Budějovice (90 minutes).

WESTERN BOHEMIA

9

GRANDEST SPA HOTEL
Grandhotel Pupp, *Karlovy Vary* ⇨*p.205*

BEST SPA HOTEL
Hotel Embassy, *Karlovy Vary* ⇨*p.226*

BEST PLACE TO GRAB A BITE
Tři Lilie, *Františkovy Lázně* ⇨*p.212*

BEST VIEW WITHOUT A ROOM
Jelení skok, *Karlovy Vary* ⇨*p.203*

BEST BREWERY TOUR
Pilsner Urquell Brewery, *Plzeň* ⇨*p.216*

By Philip
Traynor

UNTIL WORLD WAR II, WESTERN BOHEMIA WAS THE PLAYGROUND OF CENTRAL EUROPE'S RICH AND FAMOUS. Its three well-known spas, Karlovy Vary, Mariánské Lázně, and Františkovy Lázně (also known by their German names, Karlsbad, Marienbad, and Franzensbad, respectively), were the annual haunts of everybody who was anybody: Johann Wolfgang von Goethe, Ludwig van Beethoven, Karl Marx, and England's King Edward VII, to name but a few. Although strictly "proletarianized" in the Communist era, the spas still exude a nostalgic aura of a more elegant past and, unlike most of Bohemia, offer a basic tourist infrastructure that makes dining and lodging a pleasure.

The area is full of historic and natural features, the former stemming from the wealth accrued from the district's important trade routes into Germany and Italy, the latter from the region's distinct geological curiosities, including the numerous springs dotting the spa towns.

A strong Germanic influence can't be ignored, particularly in towns like Cheb, where the architecture and the German spoken on the streets and in shops are constant reminders of who the nearby border country is. To the southeast and away from the border, a different Germanic influence was laid upon Plzeň when the Nazis took over the town in the late 1930s. Prague and most of the rest of then-Czechoslovakia were liberated by the Soviet Army in May 1945, as agreed upon by Roosevelt, Stalin, and Churchill at the Yalta Conference, when it was also decided that Czechoslovakia would come under the Soviet sphere of influence after World War II. But the westernmost part of the country—from Plzeň to Karlovy Vary—was liberated by the Americans, led by General Patton. The toy shops in Plzeň are full of plastic models of World War II–era American tanks, jeeps, and other military hardware; the town itself has consistently held an annual liberation-day parade. Despite this history, the town is still strongly Czech. One need not look any further than the excellent Pilsner beer brewed there—and exported worldwide—to realize that the citizens are proud of their culture and heritage and have graciously taken part in opening Western Bohemia to those of us lucky enough to be able to visit it.

Numbers in the margins refer to the Western Bohemia and Karlovy Vary maps.

About the Hotels & Restaurants

The quality of hotels in Western Bohemia is on par with those in Prague, something that can't be said with most of the rest of the country, and most establishments have amenities you would expect, including satellite TV, room phones, and private bathrooms. There are two differences, however: the peak season is shorter, running from May through September, and the staff tend to speak a very limited amount of English—German and Russian are much more common, in keeping with the majority of visitors. Budget travelers can find some good deals, as rates in some of the lesser-known establishments can be a bargain compared to those in the capital. As in Prague, air-conditioning is a rarity found mostly in the global chains or top-tier hotels.

WHAT IT COSTS in koruna and euros				
$$$$	**$$$**	**$$**	**$**	**¢**
HOTELS*				
IN KORUNA over 7,000	5,000–7,000	3,500–5,000	1,500–3,500	under 1,500
HOTELS*				
IN EUROS over €225	€155–€225	€108–€155	€47–€108	under €47
RESTAURANTS**				
over 500	300–500	150–300	100–150	under 100

*Hotel prices are for two people in a double room with a private bath and break-fast during peak season (May through September). **Restaurant prices are per person for a main course at dinner and include 19% V.A.T.

KARLOVY VARY

132 km (79 mi) due west of Prague on Rte. 6 (E48).

Karlovy Vary, often known outside the Czech Republic by its German name, Karlsbad, is the most famous Bohemian spa. It's named for Emperor Charles IV, who allegedly happened upon the springs in 1358 while on a hunting expedition. As the story goes, the emperor's hound—chasing a harried stag—fell into a boiling spring and was scalded. Charles had the water tested and, familiar with spas in Italy, ordered baths to be established in the village of Vary. The spa reached its heyday in the 19th century, when royalty came here from all over Europe for treatments. The long list of those who "took the cure" includes Peter the Great, Goethe (no fewer than 13 times, according to a plaque on one house by the main spring), Schiller, Beethoven, and Chopin. Even Karl Marx, when he wasn't decrying wealth and privilege, spent time at the wealthy and privileged resort; he wrote some of *Das Kapital* here between 1874 and 1876, though much of it was written in the British Museum.

After decades of neglect under the Communists that left many buildings crumbling behind their beautiful façades, the town leaders today face the daunting task of carving out a new role for Karlovy Vary, since few Czechs can afford to set aside weeks or months at a time for a leisurely cure. To raise some quick cash, many sanatoriums have turned to offering short-term accommodations to foreign visitors (at rather expensive rates). By the week or by the hour, "classical" spa procedures, laser treatments, plastic surgery, and even acupuncture are purveyed to German clients or to large numbers of Russians, who bought property in town in the late 1990s. For most visitors, though, it's enough simply to stroll the streets and parks and allow the eyes to feast awhile on the splendors of the past.

Whether you're arriving by bus, train, or car, your first view of the town on the approach from Prague will be of the slightly run-down section on the banks of the Ohře River. Don't despair: continue along the main road—following the signs to the Grandhotel Pupp—until you reach the lovely main street of the older spa area, situated gently astride the banks of the little Teplá ("Warm") River. (Drivers, note that driving through or parking in the main spa area is allowed only with a permit obtainable from your hotel.) The walk from the new town to the spa area is about 20 minutes.

The Historická čtvrt (Historic District) is still largely intact. Tall 19th-century houses, with decorative and often eccentric façades, line the spa's proud riverside streets. Throughout, you can see colonnades full of people sipping the spa's hot sulfuric water from odd pipe-shape drinking cups. At night the streets fill with steam escaping from cracks in the earth, giving the town a slightly macabre feel.

What to See

❼ Karlovy Vary's jarringly modern **Vřídelní kolonáda** (Vřídlo Colonnade) is built around the spring of the same name, the town's hottest and most dramatic gusher. The Vřídlo is indeed unique, shooting its scalding water to a height of some 40 feet. Walk inside the arcade to watch the hundreds of patients here take the famed Karlsbad drinking cure. They promenade somnambulistically up and down, eyes glazed, clutching drinking glasses filled periodically at one of the five "sources." The waters, which range from 30°F to 72°F, are said to be especially ef-

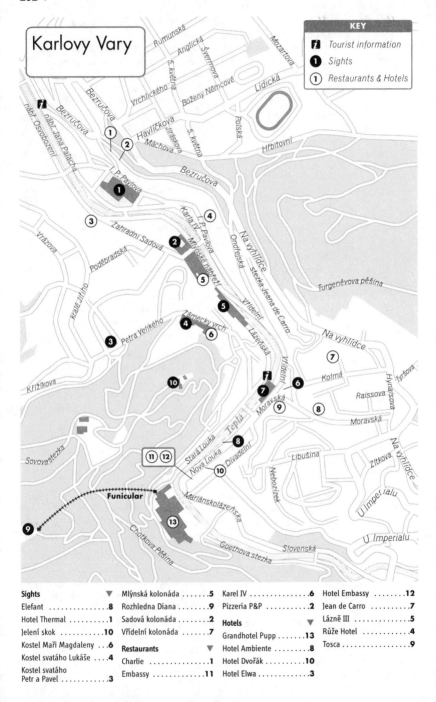

Karlovy Vary

Sights ▼	Mlýnská kolonáda **5**	Karel IV **6**	Hotel Embassy **12**
Elefant **8**	Rozhledna Diana **9**	Pizzeria P&P **2**	Jean de Carro **7**
Hotel Thermal **1**	Sadová kolonáda **2**		Lázně III **5**
Jelení skok **10**	Vřídelní kolonáda **7**	Hotels ▼	Růže Hotel **4**
Kostel Maří Magdaleny ...**6**		Grandhotel Pupp **13**	Tosca **9**
Kostel svatáho Lukáše **4**	Restaurants ▼	Hotel Ambiente **8**	
Kostel svatáho Petr a Pavel ...**3**	Charlie **1**	Hotel Dvořák **10**	
	Embassy **11**	Hotel Elwa **3**	

fective against diseases of the digestive and urinary tracts. They're also good for gout (which probably explains the spa's former popularity with royals). If you want to join the crowds and take a sip, you can buy your own spouted cup from vendors within the colonnade. ⊠ *Vřídelní ul., near Kosterní nám.*

★ ❻ To the right of the Vřídlo Colonnade are steps up to the white **Kostel Maří Magdaleny** (Church of Mary Magdalene). Designed by Kilian Ignaz Dientzenhofer (architect of the two Churches of St. Nicholas in Prague), this is the best of the few baroque buildings still standing in Karlovy Vary. ⊠ *Moravská ul.* ☎ *No phone* ☉ *Daily 9–6.*

❺ The neo-Renaissance pillared hall **Mlýnská kolonáda** (Mill Colonnade), along the river, is the spa town's centerpiece. Built from 1871 to 1881, it has four springs: Rusalka, Libussa, Prince Wenceslas, and Millpond. ⊠ *Mlýnské nábřeží.*

❷ The very elegant **Sadová kolonáda** (Park Colonnade) is a white, wrought-iron construction. It was built in 1882 by the Viennese architectural duo Fellner and Helmer, who sprinkled the Austro-Hungarian Empire with many such edifices during the late 19th century and who also designed the town's theater, the quaint wooden Tržní kolonáda (Market Colonnade) next to the Vřídlo Colonnade, and one of the old bathhouses. ⊠ *Zahradní.*

The 20th century emerges across the river from the historic district in
❶ the form of the huge, bunkerlike **Hotel Thermal,** built in the late 1960s as the Communist idea of luxury. Although the building is jarring to the eye, the view of Karlovy Vary from the rooftop pool and the Café Thermal is nothing short of spectacular. Even if you don't feel like a swim, it's worth taking the winding road up to the baths for the view. ⊠ *I. P. Pavlova 11* ☎ *359–001–111* 🏊 *40 Kč per hour* ☉ *Pool daily 8–8; café Tues.–Sun. 10–6.*

A five-minute walk up the steep Zámecký vrch from the Market Colon-
❹ nade brings you to the redbrick Victorian **Kostel svatého Lukáše** (St. Luke's Church), once used by the local English community. ⊠ *Zámecký vrch at Petra Velikého.*

From Kostel svatého Lukáše, if you take a sharp right uphill on the red-brick road. Then turn left onto a footpath through the woods, you can
❿ follow the signs to **Jelení skok** (Stag's Leap). After a while you can see
FodorśChoice steps leading up to a bronze statue of a deer looking over the cliffs, the
★ symbol of Karlovy Vary. From here a winding path leads up to a little red gazebo opening onto a fabulous panorama. ⊠ *Sovava trail in Petrova Výšina park.*

need a break? If you make it all the way to Stag's Leap, reward yourself with a light meal at the nearby restaurant **Jelení skok.** You may have to pay an entrance fee if there's a live band (but you'll also get the opportunity to polka). If you don't want to walk up, you can drive up a signposted road from the Victorian church.

CloseUp

GUIDED DAY TOURS TO WESTERN BOHEMIA

GUIDED ONE-DAY BUS TOURS FROM PRAGUE ARE AVAILABLE *from several companies to the larger spa towns of Karlovy Vary and Mariánské Lázně.*

Athos (☎ 244–003–203 ⊕ www.athos. cz) offers a Karlovy Vary itinerary similar to that of Martin Tour for the same price, 1,450 Kč. However, the tour runs one hour less than Martin's (9 hours), thus shaving valuable time. Tours are offered daily except Sunday, but the company offers the option of picking you up at your hotel.

Martin Tours (☎ 224–212–473 ⊕ www. martintour.cz) offers trips to Karlovy Vary on Tuesdays, Thursdays and Saturdays for 1,450 Kč. The price includes entry to the heated swimming pool atop the Hotel Thermal and lunch in the hotel. For those who feel like taking a dip and grabbing

some lunch, this setup is a good deal; however, these activities will cut into the total tour time, which is 10 hours. Martin Tours is one of the larger tour operators in the country, so expect to have plenty of others along with you.

Tip Top Travel (☎ 267–914–576 ⊕ www.tiptoptravel.cz) has a tour for those looking for a day-trip to Mariánské Lázně, though the tour is packaged along with a sightseeing stop in Karlovy Vary, for 1,100 Kč per person.

---

❸ The splendid Russian Orthodox **Kostel svatých Petra a Pavla** (Church of Sts. Peter and Paul) has six domes. It dates from the end of the 19th century and is decorated with paintings and icons that were donated by wealthy Russian visitors. ✉ *Tř. Krále Jiřího.*

❾ It's not necessary to walk to one of the best views of the town. Higher even than Stag's Leap is an observation tower, **rozhledna Diana**, accessible by funicular from behind the Grandhotel Pupp. There's an elevator to the top of the tower. ✉ *Výšina přátelství* 🚡 *Funicular 25 Kč one-way, 40 Kč round-trip; tower 10 Kč* ☉ *June–Sept., Mon.–Thurs. and Sun. 11–9, Fri. and Sat. 11–11; May and Oct., Tues., Wed., and Sun. 11–6, Fri. and Sat. 11–7; Mar., Apr., Nov. and Dec., Wed.–Sun. 11–5.*

❽ On one of the town's best shopping streets you can find **Elefant,** one of the last of a dying breed of sophisticated coffeehouses. Happily, the café as an institution is making a real comeback in the Czech Republic. ✉ *Stará louka 30* ☎ *353–222–544.*

Where to Eat

$$–$$$ ✕ **Charlie.** Normal Czech fare at abnormally high prices must help this restaurant meet the cost of being in a heavily-trafficked location. You most likely won't be dining with the locals, but having said that, the

central location, double outdoor patios, and attentive service help make up for the cost—at least a bit. Try the goulash—it's tasty. ⊠ *I. P. Pavlova 17* ☎ *353-225-283* ⊟ *MC, V.*

$$-$$$ ✕ **Embassy.** This cozy, sophisticated wine restaurant, conveniently near the Grandhotel Pupp, serves an innovative menu by local standards. Tagliatelle with smoked salmon in cream sauce makes an excellent main course, as does roast duck with cabbage and dumplings. The wine list features Czech varieties like the dry whites Rulandské bílé and Ryzlink Rýnský (the latter being the domestic version of the Riesling grape) and some pricey imports. Request one of the tables on the bridge over the river for a romantic evening. ⊠ *Nová louka 21* ☎ *353-221-161* ⊟ *AE, DC, MC, V.*

$$-$$$ ✕ **Karel IV.** This restaurant's location atop an old castle tower not far from the Market Colonnade gives diners the best view in town. Good renditions of traditional Czech standbys—*bramborák* (potato pancake) and chicken breast with peaches—are served in small, secluded dining areas that are particularly intimate after sunset. ⊠ *Zámecký vrch 2* ☎ *353-227-255* ⊟ *AE, MC, V.*

$$-$$$ ✕ **Pizzeria P&P.** Two patios on a busy thoroughfare make this pizzeria a good choice for people-watching while you wait on your order. Besides pizza, pasta such as gnocchi and lasagna are available. ⊠ *I. P. Pavlova 13* ☎ *602-414-765* ⊟ *No credit cards.*

Where to Stay

$$$ 🏨 **Hotel Dvořák.** Consider a splurge here if you're longing for Western standards of service and convenience. Opened in late 1990, this orange-and-white, Austrian-owned hotel occupies three renovated town houses that are a five-minute walk from the main spas. If possible, request a room with a bay-window view of the town. Weeklong spa packages here begin at €630 per person in high season. ⊠ *Nová louka 11, 360 21* ☎ *353-224-145* 🖷 *353-222-814* ⊕ *www.hotel-dvorak.cz* ⇥ *96 rooms, 10 suites* ⚐ *Restaurant, café, cable TV with movies, pool, gym, hair salon, spa, casino, Internet, some pets allowed (fee); no a/c in some rooms* ⊟ *AE, DC, MC, V* ⦿ *BP.*

$$-$$$ 🏨 **Grandhotel Pupp.** This enormous hotel (for Karlovy Vary, at least)—
Fodor's Choice which dates back well over 200 years—is one of Central Europe's most
   ★   famous resorts. Standards and service slipped under the Communists, but the highly professional management has more than made up for the decades of neglect. Some rooms are furnished in 18th-century period style. The vast public rooms exude the very best taste, circa 1913, when the present building was completed. Every July, the Pupp houses international movie stars in town for the Karlovy Vary International Film Festival. (The adjacent Parkhotel Pupp, under the same management, is a more affordable alternative.) ⊠ *Mírové nám. 2, 360 91* ☎ *353-109-111* 🖷 *353-109-620 or 353-224-032* ⊕ *www.pupp.cz* ⇥ *75 rooms, 34 suites* ⚐ *4 restaurants, in-room safes, minibars, cable TV with movies, health club, sauna, spa, lounge, casino, 2 nightclubs, Internet, some pets allowed (fee); no a/c in some rooms* ⊟ *AE, DC, MC, V* ⦿ *BP.*

$$ 🏨 **Hotel Elwa.** Renovations have successfully integrated modern comforts into this intimate, older, elegant spa resort midway between the old and new towns. Modern features include rooms with contemporary furnishings, including overstuffed chairs. There's also an on-site fitness center. The spa, like many in Karlovy Vary, specializes in treating digestive diseases. ✉ *Zahradní 29, 360 01* ☎ *353–228–472* 🖷 *353–228–473* ⊕ *www.hotelelwa.cz* ↘ *9 rooms, 8 suites* ⚒ *Restaurant, minibars, cable TV, health club, hair salon, spa, bar, some pets allowed (fee); no a/c* ⊟ *AE, MC, V* ¶◎¶ *BP.*

$$ 🏨 **Lázně III.** Neo-Gothic in style, this spa hotel serves the public as well as patients of the facility. The rooms are spartan, but classical-music lovers may love the place, as the Karlovy Vary Symphony Orchestra plays in a concert hall located in the same building. ✉ *Mlýnské nábřeží 5, 360 01* ☎ *353–223–473* 🖷 *353–225–641* ⊕ *www.lazneiii.cz* ↘ *16 rooms, 2 suites* ⚒ *Restaurant, bar, café, satellite TV, hair salon* ⊟ *AE, MC, V* ¶◎¶ *BP.*

$ 🏨 **Hotel Ambiente.** Situated on a curving cobblestone street uphill from the river—away from the tourist hustle and bustle—this spa hotel is perched on the edge of a tranquil neighborhood. Ambiente's rooms are modern and simply furnished; some have a commanding view of the town below. Packages include spa treatments and various meal plans. ✉ *Moravská 1A, 360 01* ☎ *353–365–111* 🖷 *353–365–102* ⊕ *www. premium-hotels.com* ↘ *32 rooms, 8 suites* ⚒ *Restaurant, minibars, cable TV, spa, bar, some pets allowed (fee); no a/c* ⊟ *AE, MC, V* ¶◎¶ *BP.*

$ 🏨 **Hotel Embassy.** On a quiet bend of the Teplá River, this family-run hotel's spacious, well-appointed rooms—one has a four-poster bed—usually include a sitting table and chairs or a couch with accompanying coffee table. The Embassy is more intimate and personal than the Grandhotel Pupp, with the same high level of quality in its restaurant, its rooms, and its staff. It also offers greens-fee discounts and starting times at four local courses for the golf-obsessed and massages and spa treatments for those who are not. ✉ *Nová Louka 21, 360 01* ☎ *353–221–161* 🖷 *353–223–146* ⊕ *www.embassy.cz* ↘ *18 rooms, 2 suites* ⚒ *Restaurant, bar, satellite TV, minibars, Internet, billiards, some pets allowed (fee); no a/c* ⊟ *AE, MC, V* ¶◎¶ *BP.*

Fodor's Choice
★

$ 🏨 **Jean de Carro.** Next to the Ambiente—and with a panoramic view—the three buildings that comprise the Jean de Carro stretch along a sloping walkway above the river. Grab a seat at one of the outdoor umbrella-covered tables to while away the hours picking out Karlovy Vary's landmarks and enjoying its lush, green surroundings. All of the hotel's rooms offer views of the town. ✉ *Stezka Jeana de Carro 4–6, 360 01* ☎ *353–505–111* 🖷 *353–505–151* ⊕ *www.premium-hotels. com* ↘ *25 rooms, 7 suites* ⚒ *Restaurant, bar, cable TV, some pets allowed (fee), parking (fee); no a/c* ⊟ *AE, MC, V* ¶◎¶ *BP.*

$ 🏨 **Růže Hotel.** More than adequately comfortable and well-priced given its location smack in the center of the spa district, this is a relatively inexpensive choice if you prefer a full hotel to a pension or private room. ✉ *I. P. Pavlova 1, 360 01* ☎☎ *353–221–846 or 353–221–853* ↘ *20 rooms* ⚒ *Restaurant, cable TV; no a/c* ⊟ *AE, V* ¶◎¶ *BP.*

Nightlife & the Arts

Lázně III. If you're looking to get a high-culture fix, the Karlovy Vary Symphony Orchestra plays regularly at this hotel. ✉ *Mlýnské nábř. 5* ☎ *353–225–641.*, a spa facility that is also an important cultural center for the town. Head to the Antonin Dvořák Music Hall on the first floor of the building to catch the concerts.

California Club. There's enough space for you and 249 of your closest friends in this West coast–theme club that features green, heavy wood tables and chairs and beige walls. DJs spin "oldies" (which usually means music from the 1970s on up) or disco, depending on the night. The kitchen is open late (3:30 AM, except for Sunday, when it closes at 12:30) for hungry night owls. There's no cover, and it's open from 1 PM until 5 AM. ⊠ *Tyšova 1753/2* ☎ *353–222–087.*

Calypso. Black leather, marble, and chrome mix with the mirrors and beats in this disco. Oldies are on the platters on Friday from 8 PM until 4 AM; Saturday features pop and disco during similar hours. Snacks can be had until midnight. ⊠ *Staromlýnská 31* ☎ *608–070–072.*

Club Propaganda. The club is noted for being the center of Karlovy Vary's underground music scene. Located in a former ballroom, it showcases DJs spinning nightly as well as the occasional live rock act. ⊠ *Jaltská 7* ☎ *353–233–792.*

Grandhotel Pupp. The upscale action centers on the two nightclubs and the casino of the biggest hotel in town. Gamble the night away within the mirrored walls and under the glass ceiling of the Pupp Casino Club, or settle into some live jazz at the English-themed Becher's Bar. ⊠ *Mírové nám. 2* ☎ *353–109–111.*

Inferno. Weekends heat up at this modern disco when a DJ is in the house. The rest of the week cools down with only a jukebox to push out tunes. Spend some of your money eating before you drop in between 5 PM and 5 AM—there's no kitchen or cover charge, but if you ask nicely, the staff will order a pizza for you from a nearby restaurant. ⊠ *Sokolovská 47* ☎ *353–540–266.*

Sports & the Outdoors

Opportunities abound in Karlovy Vary for staying active in the outdoors. For example, marked hiking trails snake across the beech-and-pine-covered hills that surround the town on three sides. If you walk past the Grand Hotel Pupp, away from the center, and follow the paved walkway that runs alongside the river for about 10 minutes, you will be rewarded with the discovery of a Japanese garden. A multiday canoeing competition, the Mattoni Canoe Race, is held in the Teplá river in front of the Thermal Hotel every May; it's the largest contest of its kind in the country.

Karlovy Vary's warm, open-air public pool on top of the **Thermal Hotel** (⊠ I. P. Pavlova) offers the experience of swimming comfortably even in the coolest weather; the view over the town is outstanding. Even if you are not staying at the hotel, you can still take a dip in the waters for 40 Kč per hour. Those with betting fever can head to the **Karlovařské zavodiště** (horse-racing track; ⊠ Kpt.Jarose 29 ☎ 353–592–122) outside of town from May to September to wager on their favorite steed. The **Karlovy Vary Golf Club** (⊠ Pražská 125 ☎ 353–331–101) is just out of town on the road to Prague; green fees are 1,300 Kč for 18 holes.

Shopping

The town's most exclusive shopping clusters around the Grandhotel Pupp and back toward town along the river on Stará louka. A number of outlets for lesser-known, although high-quality makers of glass and porcelain can be found along this street. If you're looking for an inexpensive but nonetheless unique gift from Karlovy Vary, consider a bottle of the ubiquitous bittersweet (and potent) Becherovka, a liqueur produced by the town's own Jan Becher distillery. Another neat gift would be one of the pipe-shape ceramic drinking cups used to take the drinking cure at spas; you can find them at the colonnades. You can also buy boxes of tasty *oplatky* (wafers), sometimes covered with chocolate, at shops in all of the spa towns.

For excellent buys in porcelain, try **Karlovarský porcelán** (⊠ Tržiště 27 ☎ 353–225–660) **Kolonáda** (⊠ I. P. Pavlova 15) sells boxes of melt-in-your-mouth spa wafers. Looking a bit like flattened-out manhole covers, the hazelnut- or chocolate-filled treats are the perfect confection on a sunny day. The store is generally closed from 12:30 to 1 for lunch. Karlovy Vary is best known to glass enthusiasts as the home of **Moser** (⊠ Tržiště 7 ☎ 353–235–303 ⊕ www.moser.cz), one of the world's leading producers of crystal and decorative glassware.

Karlovy Vary Essentials

TRANSPORTATION Frequent bus service between Prague and Karlovy Vary makes the journey only about two hours each way, and the ticket costs about 120 Kč. Train service is not nearly as convenient. The Prague–Karlovy Vary run takes far longer than it should—more than three hours by the shortest route—and costs more than double the price of a bus ticket. If you're driving, you can take the E48 directly from Prague to Karlovy Vary, a drive of about 1½ hours.

VISITOR INFORMATION 🛈 **Karlovy Vary Tourist Information** (Kur-Info) ⊠ Vřídelní kolonáda [Vřídlo Colonnade], Karlovy Vary ☎ 353–322–4097 ⊕ www.karlovyvary.cz ⊠ Nám. Dr. M. Horákové 18, near bus station, Karlovy Vary ☎ 353–222–833.

CHEB

⑫ *42 km (26 mi) southwest of Karlovy Vary; 174 km (105 mi) southwest of Prague.*

Known for centuries by its German name of Eger, the old town of Cheb lies on the border with Germany in the far west of the Czech Republic. The town has been a fixture of Bohemia since 1322 (when it was handed over to King Jan, or Johann, as thanks for his support of a Bavarian prince), but as you walk around the beautiful medieval square, it's difficult not to think you're in Germany. The tall merchants' houses surrounding the main square, with their long, red-tile, sloping roofs dotted with windows like droopy eyelids, are more Germanic in style than anything else in Bohemia. You can also hear a lot of German on the streets—more from the many German visitors than from the town's residents.

Germany took full possession of the town in 1938 under the terms of the notorious Munich Pact. But following World War II, virtually the entire German population was expelled, and the Czech name of Cheb was officially adopted. A more notorious German connection emerged in the years following the 1989 revolution: Cheb, like other border towns, became an unofficial center of prostitution. Don't be startled to see young women, provocatively dressed, lining the highways and roads into town.

The **statue** in the middle of the central square, náměstí Krále Jiřího z Poděbrad, similar to the Roland statues you see throughout Bohemia and attesting to the town's royal privileges, represents the town hero, Wastel of Eger. Look carefully at his right foot, and you can see a small man holding a sword and a head—this shows the town had its own judge and executioner.

On the lower part of náměstí Krále Jiřího z Poděbrad are two rickety groups of timbered medieval buildings, 11 houses in all, divided by a narrow alley. The houses, forming the area known as **Špalíček,** date from the 13th century and were home to many Jewish merchants. Židovská ulice (Jews' Street), running uphill to the left of the Špalíček, served as the actual center of the ghetto. Note the small alley running off to the left of Židovská. This calm street, with the seemingly inappropriate name ulička Zavražděných (Lane of the Murdered), was the scene of an outrageous act of violence in 1350. Pressures had been building for some time between Jews and Christians. Incited by an anti-Semitic bishop, the townspeople finally chased the Jews into the street, closed off both ends, and massacred them. Now only the name attests to the slaughter. ⊠ *Nám. Krále Jiřího z Poděbrad.*

need a break? Cheb's main square abounds with cafés and little restaurants, all offering a fairly uniform menu of schnitzel and sauerbraten aimed at visiting Germans. The **Kavárna Špalíček,** nestled in the Špalíček buildings, is one of the better choices and has the added advantage of a unique architectural setting.

The **Chebské muzeum** (Cheb Museum) in the Pachelbel House on the main square documents the history of Cheb, with particular emphasis on the Hapsburg era. It was in this house that the great general of the Thirty Years' War, Albrecht von Wallenstein, was murdered in 1634 on the orders of his own emperor, the Hapsburg emperor Ferdinand II, who was provoked by Wallenstein's increasing power and rumors of treason. According to legend, Wallenstein was on his way to the Saxon border to enlist support to fight the Swedes when his own officers barged into his room and stabbed him through the heart with a stave. In his memory, the stark bedroom with its four-poster bed and dark red velvet curtains has been left as it was. (The story also inspired playwright Friedrich Schiller to write the *Wallenstein* trilogy; he planned the work while living at the top of the square at No. 2.) The museum is interesting in its own right: it has a selection from the Wallenstein family picture gallery, a section on the history of Cheb, and a collection of minerals (including one discovered by Goethe). There's also the stuffed remains of Wallenstein's horse, who died in battle. ⊠ *Nám. Krále Jiřího z Poděbrad 3*

☎ *354–422–246* ⊕ *www.muzeumcheb.cz* ✉ *50 Kč* ⊙ *Mar.–Dec., Tues.–Sun. 9–noon and 1–5.*

The plain but imposing **Kostel svatého Mikuláše** (Church of St. Nicholas) was begun in 1230, when the church belonged to the Order of the Teutonic Knights. You can still see Romanesque windows on the towers; renovations throughout the centuries added an impressive Gothic portal and a baroque interior. Just inside the Gothic entrance is a wonderfully faded plaque commemorating the diamond jubilee of Hapsburg emperor Franz Joseph in 1908. ✉ *Kostelní nám.* ☎ *354–422–458.*

Follow Křižovnická, behind the Church of St. Nicholas, up to **Chebský hrad** (Cheb Castle), which stands on a cliff overlooking the Ohře River. The castle—now a ruin—was built in the late 12th century for Holy Roman Emperor Frederick Barbarossa. The square black tower was built with blocks of lava taken from the nearby Komorní Hůrka volcano; the redbrick walls are 17th-century additions. Inside the castle grounds is the carefully restored double-decker **Romanesque chapel,** which was restored in 2002, and notable for the many lovely columns with heads carved into their capitals. The rather dark ground floor was used by commoners. The bright, ornate top floor was reserved for the emperor and his family, who entered via a wooden bridge leading to the royal palace. ✉ *Dobrovského 21* ☎ *354–422–942* ⊕ *www.muzeumcheb.cz* ✉ *30 Kč* ⊙ *Apr. and Oct., Tues.–Sun. 9–4; May and Sept., Tues.–Sun. 9–5; June–Aug., Tues.–Sun. 9–6.*

Where to Eat

¢–$$ ✕ **Eva.** Of the many restaurants opened on and around the main square since the tourism boom began in the early 1990s, Eva is certainly one of the best. A decent array of mostly Czech and German dishes—with an emphasis on game—is served by a troop of attentive waiters. ✉ *Jateční 4* ☎ *354–422–498* ▤ *No credit cards.*

Where to Stay

¢–$ ⌂ **Hvězda.** Three charming baroque buildings, with bright pastel façades, were joined in 2000 into one of the few hotels in downtown Cheb. The location on a main square gives easy access to the city's sites and eateries. Some rooms offer spectacular views, and the hotel's sidewalk café is a pleasant place to watch the endless parade of strollers. One room has six beds. ✉ *Nám. Krále Jiřího z Poděbrad 5, 350 02* ☎ *354–422–705* 🖷 *354–422–546* ⊕ *www.hotel-hvezda.cz* ⤥ *90 rooms, 48 with shared bath* ⌂ *Restaurant, cable TV, parking (fee), some pets allowed (fee); no a/c* ▤ *AE, MC, V* ⏐◎⏐ *BP.*

Cheb Essentials

TRANSPORTATION The journey from Prague to Cheb is about 3½ hours each way, whether you are taking the bus or the train; expect to pay almost twice as much to ride the train, however. The price for the bus trip is 140 Kč, the price for the train ride 250 Kč. If you're driving, you can take the E50 and then the 21 from Prague to Cheb, a drive of about 2½ hours.

VISITOR INFORMATION 🖪 Cheb Tourist Information ✉ Nám. Krále Jiřího z Poděbrad 33, Cheb ☎ 354–434–385 or 354–422–705 ⊕ www.mestocheb.cz.

FRANTIŠKOVY LÁZNĚ

⑬ *6 km (4 mi) north of Cheb; 180 km (109 mi) southwest of Prague.*

Františkovy Lázně, or Franzensbad, the smallest of the three main Bohemian spa towns, isn't really in the same league as the other two (Karlovy Vary and Mariánské Lázně). Built on a more modest scale at the start of the 19th century, the town's ubiquitous kaiser-yellow buildings have been spruced up after their neglect under the Communist regime and now present cheerful façades, almost too bright for the few strollers. The poorly kept parks and the formal, yet human-scale, neoclassical architecture retain much of their former charm. This little spa town couldn't be a more distinct contrast to nearby Cheb's slightly seedy, hustling air and medieval streetscapes. Overall, a pleasing torpor reigns in Františkovy Lázně. There's no town to speak of, just **Národní ulice,** the main street, which leads down into the spa park. The waters, whose healing properties were already known in the 16th century, are used primarily for treating heart problems—and infertility, hence the large number of young women wandering the grounds.

You might enjoy walking the path, indicated with red markers, from Cheb's main square westward along the river and then north past **Komorní Hůrka.** The extinct volcano is now a tree-covered hill, but excavations on one side have laid bare the rock, and one tunnel is still open. Goethe instigated and took part in the excavations, and you can still—though barely—make out a relief of the poet carved into the rock face.

The most interesting sight in town may be the small **Lázeňský muzeum** (Spa Museum), just off Národní ulice. There's a wonderful collection of spa-related antiques, including copper bathtubs and a turn-of-the-20th-century exercise bike called a Velotrab. The guest books provide an insight into the cosmopolitan world of pre–World War I Central Europe. The book for 1812 contains the entry "Ludwig van Beethoven, composer from Vienna." ✉ *Ul. Doktora Pohoreckého 8* ☎ *354–542–344* 🎫 *20 Kč* ☉ *Tues.–Fri. 10–5, weekends 10–4; usually closed mid-Dec.–mid-Jan.*

The main spring, **Františkův pramen,** is under a little gazebo filled with brass pipes. The colonnade to the left was decorated with a bust of Lenin that was replaced in 1990 by a memorial to the American liberation of the town in April 1945. The oval neoclassical temple just beyond the spring (amazingly, *not* painted yellow and white) is the **Glauberova dvorana** (Glauber Pavilion), where several springs bubble up into glass cases. ✉ *Národní ul.*

Where to Stay & Eat

Most of the establishments in town do a big trade in spa patients, who generally stay for several weeks. Spa treatments usually require a medical check and cost substantially more than the normal room charge. Walk-in treatment can be arranged at some hotels or at the information center. Signs around town advertise massage therapy and other treatments for casual visitors.

$ ✕▥ **Slovan.** This gracious place is the perfect complement to this relaxed little town. The eccentricity of the original turn-of-the-20th-century design survived a thorough renovation in the 1970s. The airy rooms are clean and comfortable, and some have a balcony overlooking the main street. The main-floor restaurant serves above-average Czech dishes such as tasty *svíčková* (beef sirloin in a citrusy cream sauce) and roast duck. ✉ *Národní 5, 351 01* ☎ *354–542–841* 🖷 *354–542–843* ⬅ *25 rooms, 19 with bath* ⚭ *Restaurant, café, refrigerators, cable TV, bar, Internet, meeting room, some pets allowed (fee); no a/c* ▤ *AE, MC, V* ⑈ *BP.*

$ ▥ **Centrum.** Rooms in this barnlike building are well-appointed, if a bit sterile. Still, it's among the better-run hotels in town and only a short walk from the main park and central spas. ✉ *Anglická 392, 351 01* ☎ *354–543–156* 🖷 *354–543–157* ⬅ *30 rooms* ⚭ *Restaurant, cable TV, bar, some pets allowed; no a/c* ▤ *AE, MC, V* ⑈ *BP.*

$$ ▥ **Tři Lilie.** Reopened in 1995 after an expensive renovation, the "Three
Fodor'sChoice Lilies," which once accommodated the likes of Goethe and Metternich,
★ immediately reestablished itself as the most comfortable spa hotel in town. Situated in the center of the spa quarter, the yellow, three-story building has what many others lack—air-conditioning. Some of the rooms have balconies with French doors. It is thoroughly elegant, from guest rooms to brasserie. ✉ *Národní 3, 351 01* ☎ *354–208–900* ⬅ *31 rooms* ⚭ *Restaurant, café, cable TV, some pets allowed (fee)* ▤ *AE, MC, V* ⑈ *BP.*

Františkovy Lázně Essentials

TRANSPORTATION Expect to spend about four hours each way traveling between Prague and Františkovy Lázne via bus or train, and you'll pay almost double for riding the rails. Costs are 150 Kč one-way for the bus, 270 Kč for the train. If you're driving, you can take the E50 and then the 21 from Prague to Františkovy Lázne, a drive of about three hours.

VISITOR ⓕ **Františkovy Lázně Tourist Information** ✉ Tři Lilie Travel Agency, Národní 3,
INFORMATION Františkovy Lázně ☎ 354–542–430 ⊕ www.franzensbad.cz.

MARIÁNSKÉ LÁZNĚ

⑭ *30 km (18 mi) southeast of Cheb; 47 km (29 mi) south of Karlovy Vary.*

Your expectations of what a spa resort should be may come nearest to fulfillment here. It's far larger and more active than Františkovy Lázně and greener and quieter than Karlovy Vary. This was the spa favored by Britain's Edward VII. Goethe and Chopin also repaired here frequently. Mark Twain, on a visit in 1892, labeled the town a "health factory" and couldn't get over how new everything looked. Indeed, at that time everything was new. The sanatoriums, most built during the 19th century in a confident, outrageous mixture of "neo" styles, fan out impressively around a finely groomed oblong park. Cure takers and curiosity seekers alike parade through the Empire-style Cross Spring pavilion and the long colonnade near the top of the park. Buy a spouted drinking cup (available at the colonnades) and join the rest of the sippers taking the drinking cure. Be forewarned, though: the waters from the Rudolph,

Ambrose, and Caroline springs, though harmless, all have a noticeable diuretic effect. For this reason they're used extensively in treating disorders of the kidney and bladder.

A stay in Mariánské Lázně can be healthful even without special treatment. Walking trails of varied difficulty levels surround the resort in all directions, and one of the country's few golf courses lies about 3 km (2 mi) to the east of town. Hotel staff can also help arrange activities such as tennis and horseback riding. For the less intrepid, a simple stroll around the gardens, with a few deep breaths of the town's clean air, is enough to restore a healthy sense of perspective.

For information on spa treatments, inquire at the main **spa offices** (⊠ Masarykova 22 ☎ 354–623–061 ⊕ www.marienbad.cz). Walk-in treatments can be arranged at the **Nové Lázně** (New Spa; ⊠ Reitenbergerova 53 ☎ 354–644–111).

off the beaten path

CHODOVÁ PLANÁ – If you need a break from the rigorous healthiness of spa life, the Pivovarská restaurace a muzeum ve skále (Brewery Restaurant & Museum in the Rock) is a few miles south of Mariánské Lázně in an underground complex of granite tunnels that have been used to age beer since the 1400s. Generous servings of Czech dishes including a whole roast suckling pig can be ordered to accompany the strong, fresh Chodovar beer tapped directly from granite storage vaults. Giant tanks of aging beer and brewing memorabilia can be seen through glass windows on the way in. You can tour the brewery, but at this writing, tours were conducted in German only. ⊠ Pivovarská 107, Chodová Planá ☎ 374–798–122 ⊕ www.chodovar.cz ⊠ Museum free, tour 50 Kč ⊙ Daily 11–11; brewery tours daily at 2.

Where to Eat

The best place to look for a private room is along Paleckého ulice and Hlavní třída, south of the main spa area. Private accommodations can also be found in the neighboring villages of Zádub and Závišín, in the woods to the east of town.

★ $$–$$$ ✕ **Churchill's.** Dark-wood paneling, a serpentine bar, and a mixture of tables and booths give this restaurant the feel of a comfortable British pub. In the same building as the Excelsior hotel—but with a separate entrance—Churchill's is a good place to go if you need a break from Czech cooking. Steaks, fish, and salads are all available, as are vegetarian options. ⊠ Hlavní tř. 121 ☎ 354–697–235 ▭ AE, MC, V.

★ $$–$$$ ✕ **Koliba.** This combination hunting lodge and wine tavern, set in the woods roughly 10 minutes on foot from the spas, is an excellent alternative to the hotel restaurants in town. Grilled meats and shish kebabs, plus tankards of Moravian wine (try the dry, cherry red Rulandské červené), are served with traditional gusto while fiddlers play rousing Moravian tunes at lunchtime. Exposed wooden ceiling beams add to the rustic charm of the inn's 15 rooms that face the surrounding nature preserve. ⊠ Dusíkova 592, in the direction of Karlovy Vary ☎ 354–625–169 ▭ MC, V.

¢–$$ ✕ **Filip.** This bustling wine bar is where locals come to find relief from the sometimes large hordes of tourists. There's a tasty selection of traditional Czech dishes—mainly pork, grilled meats, and steaks. ⊠ *Poštovní 96* ☎ *354–626–161* ⊟ *No credit cards.*

¢–$$ ✕ **Piccolo.** If you're pressed for time, the service at this pizza and pasta restaurant is quicker than many other joints in town. Keep your pizza simple—ham or just cheese are recommended—for the best result, as too many toppings tend to make for a soggy pie. ⊠ *Nerudova 1* ☎ *354–626–039* ⊟ *No credit cards.*

Where to Stay

★ $$ ▦ **Hotel Bohemia.** At this gracious, late-19th-century hotel, beautiful crystal chandeliers in the main hall set the stage for a comfortable and elegant stay. The crisp beige-and-white rooms let you spread out and *really* unpack; they're spacious and high ceilinged. (If you want to indulge, request one of the enormous suites overlooking the park.) The helpful staff can arrange spa treatments and horseback riding. A renovation in 2001 brightened up the façade and modernized the kitchen. An annex, Dependence, has added 12 additional suites. ⊠ *Hlavní tř. 100, 353 01* ☎ *354–610–111* 🖨 *354–610–555* ⊕ *www.orea.cz/bohemia* ⤳ *72 rooms, 4 suites, 12 additional suites in Dependence* ⌂ *Restaurant, café, cable TV, lounge, some pets allowed (fee); no a/c* ⊟ *AE, MC, V* ⦿ *BP.*

$$ ▦ **Hotel Excelsior.** This lovely older hotel is on the main street and is convenient to the spas and colonnade. Rooms have traditional cherrywood furniture and marble bathrooms, and the views over the town are enchanting. The staff is friendly and multilingual. Although the food in the restaurant, 1900, is average, the romantic setting provides adequate compensation. ⊠ *Hlavní tř. 121, 353 01* ☎ *354–622–705* 🖨 *354–625–346* ⊕ *www.orea.cz/excelsior* ⤳ *64 rooms* ⌂ *Restaurant, café, minibars, cable TV with movies, massage, sauna, some pets allowed (fee); no a/c* ⊟ *AE, DC, MC, V* ⦿ *BP.*

$$ ▦ **Parkhotel Golf.** Book in advance to secure a room at this stately villa situated 3½ km (2 mi) out of town on the road to Karlovy Vary. The large open rooms are cheery and modern. The restaurant on the main floor is excellent, but the big draw is the 18-hole golf course on the premises, one of the few in the Czech Republic. The course was opened in 1905 by King Edward VII. ⊠ *Zádub 55, 353 01* ☎ *354–622–651* 🖨 *354–622–655* ⊕ *web.telecom.cz/parkhotel-golf* ⤳ *28 rooms* ⌂ *Restaurant, minibars, cable TV, 18-hole golf course, tennis court, pool, spa. nightclub, Internet, meeting room, some pets allowed (fee); no a/c* ⊟ *AE, DC, MC, V* ⦿ *BP.*

$$ ▦ **Villa Butterfly.** The interior and exterior of this modern, angular art nouveau–style hotel are decorated with the works of some of the country's top artists. Female figurines stand on the roof, arms outspread like a butterfly's wings, seemingly about to take flight. Ask for a room in the front, as the view of the forested hills that make up the town is outstanding. ⊠ *Hlavní třída 655, 353 01* ☎ *354–654–111* 🖨 *354–654–200* ⊕ *www.marienbad.cz* ⤳ *88 rooms, 8 suites* ⌂ *2 restaurants, room service, some in-room hot tubs, minibars, cable TV, spa, bar, library, game room, Internet* ⊟ *AE, MC, V* ⦿ *BP.*

★ **$–$$** 🏨 **Hotel Nové Lázně.** Opened in 1896, this neo-Renaissance, multitowered hotel and spa lines a large part of one side of the park. In the center of the building, a cast-iron sculpture of the donor of health, Hygiea, is carried by the sea god Triton, the son of Neptune, who stands on top, stressing the importance of water in spa treatments. Inside, the complex of Roman baths is decorated with marble and houses period frescoes. ✉ *Reitenbergerova 53, 353 01* 🕿 *354–644–111* 🖷 *354–644–044* ⊕ *www.marienbad.cz* ✍ *97 rooms, 1 suite* ⚒ *Restaurant, café, minibars, cable TV, gym, spa, bar; no a/c in some rooms* 🖃 *AE, MC, V* ❏❘ *BP.*

$ 🏨 **Centrální Lázně.** Near the colonnade and Ambrose Spring, this eggshell-white spa hotel offers some more unique treatments such as magnetotherapy and peat packs. The wooden pavilion of the Mary Spring, used in special "gaseous" therapy, stands opposite the entrance to the courtyard. Patients enter the pavilion and stand in the carbon-dioxide-laden vapors while being supervised by health-care specialists. Judging by the number of seniors sitting around the lobby, this hotel appears to be a favorite of the over-70 set. ✉ *Goethovo náměstí 1, 353 43* 🕿 *354–634–111* 🖷 *354–634–200* ⊕ *www.marienbad.cz* ✍ *98 rooms, 1 suite* ⚒ *Restaurant, café, refrigerators, cable TV, hair salon, spa; no a/c in some rooms* 🖃 *AE, MC, V* ❏❘ *BP.*

¢–$ 🏨 **Grandhotel Pacifik.** This spa hotel's balcony-studded yellow façade, with a black-handed clock on the top floor, dominates the main street in Mariánské Lázně. From the windows, there's a commanding view of the colonnade and the spa quarter. Treatments such as gas injections, cryotherapy, and lavaterm are offered in-house. For the less daring, individual and group remedial gymnastics are available, as well as classic massages. ✉ *Mírové náměstí 84, 353 48* 🕿 *354–651–111* 🖷 *354–651–200* ⊕ *www.marienbad.cz* ✍ *98 rooms, 7 suites* ⚒ *Restaurant, coffee shop, some minibars, some refrigerators, cable TV, spa; no a/c* 🖃 *AE, MC, V* ❏❘ *BP.*

Nightlife & the Arts

The West Bohemian Symphony Orchestra performs regularly in the New Spa (Nové Lázně). The town's annual Chopin festival each August brings in pianists from around Europe to perform the Polish composer's works.

Casino Lil (✉ Anglická 336 🕿 354–623–293) is open daily from 2 PM to 7 AM. For late-night drinks, try the **Parkhotel Golf** (✉ Zádub 55 🕿 354–622–651 or 354–622–652), which has a good nightclub with dancing in season.

Mariánské Lázně Essentials

TRANSPORTATION Regular bus and train service between Prague and Mariánské Lázně makes the journey about three hours each way. While similar in travel time, the train costs almost twice as much as the bus. Expect to pay 130 Kč one-way for the bus, 230 Kč for the train. If you're driving, you can take the E50 and then the 21 from Prague to Mariánské Lázně, a drive of about two hours.

VISITOR 🛈 **Mariánské Lázně Tourist Information** (Cultural and Information Center) ✉ Hlavní INFORMATION 47, Mariánské Lázně 🕿 354–625–892 or 354–622–474 ⊕ www.marianskelazne.cz.

PLZEŇ

⑮ *92 km (55 mi) west of Prague.*

The sprawling industrial city of Plzeň, liberated by American troops just before the end of World War II, is ideal for either a day-trip or a laid-back, overnight stay. Two sights here are of particular interest to beer fanatics, the city's famous brewery and its beer museum.

Fodor's Choice The **Pilsner Urquell Brewery** is east of the city near the railway station.
★ The first Pilsner beer was created in 1842 using the excellent Plzeň water, a special malt fermented on the premises, and hops grown in the region around Žatec. On a group tour of the 19th-century redbrick building you can taste the valuable brew, exported around the world. You can only visit the brewery on one of the daily guided tours, weekdays at 12:30 PM (sometimes also at 2 PM in the summer). You can only visit via the tour, however. ⊠ *U Prazdroje 7* ☎ *377–061–111* ⊕ *www.pilsner-urquell.com* 🕙 *120 Kč* ☾ *Tours Apr., May, and Sept., daily at 12:30; July and Aug., daily at 12:30 and 2; Oct.–Mar., weekdays at 12:30.*

need a break? If you visit the Pilsner Urquell Brewery, you can continue drinking and find some cheap traditional grub at the large **Na Spilce** (⊠ U Prazdroje 7) beer hall just inside the brewery gates. The pub is open weekdays and Saturday from 11 AM to 10 PM, Friday from 11 AM to 11 PM, and Sunday from 11 AM to 7 PM.

The **Pivovarské muzeum** (Brewery Museum) is in a late-Gothic malt house one block northeast of náměstí Republiky. All kinds of paraphernalia trace the region's brewing history, including the horse-drawn carts used to haul the kegs. ⊠ *Veleslavinova 6* ☎ *377–235–574* ⊕ *www.pilsner-urquell.com* 🕙 *100 Kč* ☾ *Daily 10–6.*

★ The **Plzen Historical Underground,** dating from the 13th century, is a network of multilevel tunnels that were used for storing food and producing beer and wine. Many of the labyrinthine passageways are dotted with wells and their accompanying wooden waterpipe systems. ⊠ *Perlova 4–6* ☎ *377–225–214* 🕙 *45 Kč* ☾ *Apr.–Nov., Wed.–Sun. 9–4; June–Sept., Tues.–Sun. 9–4.*

The city's architectural attractions center on the main **náměstí Republiky** (Republic Square). The square is dominated by the enormous Gothic **Chrám svatého Bartoloměje** (Church of St. Bartholomew). Both the square and the church towers hold size records: the former is the largest in Bohemia and the latter, at 335 feet, the tallest in the Czech Republic. Around the square, mixed in with its good selection of stores, are a variety of other architectural jewels, including the town hall, adorned with sgraffiti and built in the Renaissance style by Italian architects during the town's heyday in the 16th century. The Moorish **synagogue,** one of the largest in Europe, is four blocks west of the square, just outside the green strip that circles the old town.

Where to Eat

$–$$ ✕ **Dominik Café.** Blue papier-maiché lights, stained-glass cubes, and columns etched with Keith Haring–inspired figures make this funky upstairs café an attractive spot to park yourself for pizzas, salads, and some meat-based dishes. ⊠ *Dominikánská 3* ☎ *377–323–226* ⊘ *Closed Sun.*

$–$$ ✕ **Maxim Cafe.** A wraparound bar forms the center of this restaurant with iron candleholders and copies of French artwork on the walls. Italian food and many varieties of chicken are available. If it's cool outside, ask for a table in the heated and covered patio, which is comfortably set in between the café and an adjacent building. ⊠ *Martinská 8* ☎ *377–323–076* ▤ *AE, MC, V.*

$–$$ ✕ **Rango.** Arched stone ceilings and wood-and-iron decor—all lit with the help of candles—make this subterranean restaurant a relaxing place to stop for lunch or dinner. Of the traditional Italian specialties, the gnocchi gorgonzola stands out. ⊠ *Pražská 10* ☎ *377–329–969* ▤ *AE, MC, V.*

$–$$ ✕ **U Mansfeld.** Fresh 12-degree Pilsner Urquell and variations on classic Czech dishes draw diners to this Pilsner Urquell–sponsored restaurant. A copper hood floats above the taps, and the patio invites visitors to spend the day sipping cold beer and enjoying treats such as turkey escalope in a potato pastry or roasted goose livers in red wine and almonds. ⊠ *Dřevěna 9* ☎ *377–333–844* ▤ *AE, MC, V* ⊘ *Closed Mon.*

¢–$$ ✕ **Continental.** Five minutes on foot from the main square, this late-19th-century restaurant remains a good choice, and the current owners are still working to return the hotel ($) to its former glory, when movie stars like Ingrid Bergman and Marlene Dietrich stayed there. The restaurant serves dependably satisfying traditional Czech dishes such as *cibulka* (onion soup) and *svíčková* (beef sirloin in a citrusy cream sauce). ⊠ *Zbojnická 8, 305 31* ☎ *377–236–477* ▤ *AE, DC, MC, V.*

¢–$$ ✕ **El Cid.** Mojitos and tapas are the order of the day at this Spanish restaurant. Pictures of bullfighters line the yellow walls, while a patio overlooks the sprawling Křižíkovy park. ⊠ *Křižíkovy sady 1* ☎ *377–224–595* ▤ *AE, MC, V.*

¢–$ ✕ **Cafe Bar Praga.** Lots of chrome and black mixed with wood accents create a modern setting for this sleek café. The menu lists some Czech specialities, but judging from the orders coming from the kitchen, the emphasis is on desserts, including rich slices of cake. A lengthy list of juices helps wash it all down. ⊠ *Rooseveltova 9* ☎ *777–199–142* ▤ *AE, MC, V.*

¢–$ ✕ **Caffe Fellini.** Right across from St. Bartholomew Church, this dessert spot, with its outdoor patio overlooking the square, is a great place to cool down. Order some ice cream or a piece of cake and take in the front-row views. ⊠ *Náměstí Republiky* ☎ *377–423–965* ▤ *No credit cards.*

¢–$ ✕ **Klec.** This bar, with its mottled blue and orange walls and a metal balcony, is a hangout for the teens-to-twentysomething set, with music to match. Cocktails, coffee, wine, and Krušovice are on tap. ⊠ *Dřevěna 6* ☎ *602–457–288* ▤ *No credit cards.*

¢ ✕ **Slunečnice.** This vegetarian café is a good place to grab a ready-made sandwich or a cheap buffet meal of rice and fresh vegetables. Vegan products and bio juices are also available. The sunny interior further emphasizes its name, which means sunflower. ⊠ *Jungmannova 4* ☎ *377–236–093* ⊘ *Closed weekends.*

Where to Stay

$ ⊞ **Hotel Central.** This angular 1960s structure is recommendable for its sunny rooms, friendly staff, and great location, right on the main square. Indeed, even such worthies as Czar Alexander of Russia stayed here in the days when the hotel was a charming inn known as the Golden Eagle. Breakfast costs a few koruna extra. ⊠ *Nám. Republiky 33, 305 31* ☎ *377–226–757* 🖷 *377–226–064* ⊕ *www.central-hotel.cz* ☜ *77 rooms* ♨ *Restaurant, café, cable TV, bar, Internet, some pets allowed (fee); no a/c* ☰ *AE, DC, MC, V* ♦⦿♦ *EP.*

$ ⊞ **Hotel Continental.** Large rooms with space for all your bags and double doors that block out sound are the features that help this hotel stand out. In addition, the furnishings, which include antique mirrors and armoires, make for a comfortable atmosphere. A slow but steady renovation is ongoing. ⊠ *Zbrojnická 8, 305 04* ☎ *377–235–292* 🖷 *377–221–746* ☜ *44 rooms, 3 suites* ♨ *Restaurant, café, cable TV, bar; no a/c* ☰ *AE, MC, V* ♦⦿♦ *BP.*

$ ⊞ **Hotel Slovan.** You may feel like you just entered a private mansion after seeing the 40-foot ceilings and broad winding staircase adorned with white ironwork and sgraffito in this hotel's lobby. The rooms are simply furnished—no tassles on the drapes; however, some offer a great view of the lush Smetanova Park in front of the hotel. Ask for a reconstructed room, as the originals share the bathrooms in the hall. ⊠ *Smetanovy sady 1, 301 37* ☎ *377–227–256* 🖷 *377–227–012* ⊕ *hotelslovan.pilsen.cz* ☜ *111 rooms, 77 with shared bath, 2 suites* ♨ *Restaurant, cable TV; no a/c* ☰ *AE, MC, DC, V* ♦⦿♦ *BP.*

¢ ⊞ **Pension Sandra.** A great choice for the low-budget traveler, this pension faces Kopeckého park and is in Plzen's center. The rooms are basic, the staff friendly and willing to help with any needs. ⊠ *Kopeckého 15, 301 36* ☎ *377–325–358* ✉ *sandra101@volny.cz* ☜ *4 rooms with shared bath* ♨ *Restaurant, café, bar; no a/c* ☰ *AE, MC, V* ♦⦿♦ *BP.*

Nightlife

House of Blues (⊠ Černická 10 ☎ 377–224–294), which is related to the American chain in name only, showcases live blues and rock acts. Ignore the mirrored disco ball on the ceiling—ashtrays on every table let you know you're in a real joint. **Jazz Rock Cafe** (⊠ Sedláčkova 18 ☎ No phone) gives you a license to party. Drop by on Wednesday to catch some live blues or jazz music. **Maxim Music Club** (⊠ Martinská 8 ☎ 377–221–271) features different music every night of the week. Call first to check if that evening's performance will be jazz, rock, blues, dance music, or some other genre. Doors open at 6; closing time is around 5 AM. **Zach's pub** (⊠ Palackého náměstí ☎ 377–223–176) highlights various live acts, including Latin and blues, outdoors in its summer patio.

Plzeň Essentials

TRANSPORTATION Frequent bus and train service between Prague and Plzeň makes the journey about 1½ hours each way. Train fares are almost twice as much as bus fares. Expect to pay 80 Kč for the bus, 140 Kč for the train. If you're driving, you can take the E50 directly to Plzeň, a drive of about one hour.

VISITOR
INFORMATION   ▮ **Plzeň Tourist Information** ✉ Nám. Republiky 41, Plzeň ☎ 378-032-750 ⊕ info. plzen-city.cz.

MORAVIA

10

THE COUNTRY'S ONLY MINARET
Château Lednice na Moravé, *Lednice* ⇨*p.231*

LEAST EXPECTED MODERN LANDMARK
Villa Tugendhat, *Brno* ⇨*p.238*

CHÂTEAU THAT EQUALS ITS GARDENS
Kroměříž Château, *Kroměříž* ⇨*p.243*

BEST CAVE
Punkevní jeskyně, *Moravský Kras* ⇨*p.244*

TALLEST BAROQUE COLUMN
Morový sloup, *Olomouc* ⇨*p.245*

By Raymond
Johnston

LACKING THE TURBULENT HISTORY OF BOHEMIA to the west or the stark natural beauty of Slovakia farther east, Moravia, the easternmost province of the Czech Republic, is frequently overlooked as a travel destination. Although Moravia's cities do not match Prague for beauty and its gentle mountains hardly compare with Slovakia's strikingly rugged Tatras, Moravia's colorful villages and rolling hills certainly do merit a few days of exploration. Come here for the good wine, good folk music, friendly faces, and a languid pace.

Moravia has a bit of both Bohemia and Slovakia. It's closer culturally to Bohemia: the two were bound together as one kingdom for some 1,000 years, following the fall of the Great Moravian Empire (Moravia's last stab at Slavonic statehood) at the end of the 10th century. All the historical and cultural movements that swept through Bohemia, including the religious turbulence and long period of Austrian Hapsburg rule, were felt strongly here as well. But, oddly, in many ways Moravia resembles Slovakia more than its cousin to the west. The colors come alive here in a way that is seldom seen in Bohemia. The subdued earthen pinks and yellows in towns such as Telč and Mikulov suddenly erupt into the fiery reds, greens, and purples of the traditional folk costumes farther to the east. Folk music, all but gone in Bohemia, is still very much alive in Moravia.

Southern Moravia's highlands define the "border" with Bohemia. Here, towns such as Jihlava and Telč are virtually indistinguishable from their Bohemian counterparts. The handsome squares, with their long arcades, bear witness to the prosperity enjoyed by this part of Europe during the 16th and early 17th century, until the Hapsburg crackdown on the Czech lands at the outset of the Thirty Years' War. In the south along the frontier with Austria—until the late 1980s a heavily fortified expanse of the Iron Curtain—the towns and people on both sides of the border seek to reestablish ties going back centuries. One of their common traditions is wine making. Znojmo, Mikulov, and Valtice are to the Czech Republic what the small towns of the *Weinviertel* on the other side of the border are to Austria. Although it's possible to do a quick day-trip to Moravia, the distance is better suited to an overnight trip.

Numbers in the margin correspond to numbers on the Moravia and Brno maps.

About the Hotels & Restaurants

Moravia, especially beyond Brno, has changed at a much slower pace than Prague has since 1990. Prices for food and hotels are lower, but service—and especially any level of functional English among the staff—truly lags behind. You're much more likely to find German-language menus in restaurants and German-speaking staff in both restaurants and hotels. Many hotels in this region often still try to charge foreigners more for rooms, even though this practice should have stopped once the Czech Republic joined the European Union. On a positive note, hotel and restaurant workers tend to be a whole lot friendlier in Moravia and a bit more attentive than they are in Prague.

Don't expect gastronomic delights in Moravia. The choices—especially outside Brno—are usually limited to roast pork with sauerkraut and

Moravia

POLAND

AUSTRIA

SLOVAKIA

dumplings, ho-hum chicken dishes, and the ever-reliable trout. In mountainous areas, inquire locally about the possibility of staying in a *chata* (cabin). These are abundant, and they are often a pleasant alternative to the faceless modern hotels. Many lack modern amenities, though, so be prepared to rough it a bit.

WHAT IT COSTS in koruna and euros				
$$$$	**$$$**	**$$**	**$**	**¢**
HOTELS*				
IN KORUNA	over 7,000	5,000–7,000	3,500–5,000	1,500–3,500	under 1,500
HOTELS*				
IN EUROS	over €225	€155–€225	€108–€155	€47–€108	under €47
RESTAURANTS**				
	over 500	350–500	150–350	100–150	under 100

*Hotel prices are for two people in a double room with a private bath and breakfast during peak season (March through October, excluding July and August) and generally include 5% V.A.T. **Restaurant prices are per person for a main course at dinner and include 19% VAT.

JIHLAVA

❶ *124 km (75 mi) southeast of Prague.*

On the Moravian side of the rolling highlands that mark the border between Bohemia and Moravia, just off the main highway from Prague to Brno, lies the old mining town of Jihlava, a good place to begin an exploration of Moravia. If the silver mines here had held out just a few more years, the townspeople claim, Jihlava could have become a great European city. There are several interesting churches clustered on or around the town's main square.

During the 13th century, the town's enormous main square, **Masarykovo náměstí** (Masaryk Square), was one of the largest in Europe, rivaled in size only by those in Cologne and Kraków. But history can be cruel: the mines went bust during the 17th century, and the square today bears witness only to the town's once oversized ambitions. Some of the town walls and gates are still in place, and old tunnels under the main square are sometimes accessible to the public. The town is also becoming famous for its annual international festival of documentary films, held at the end of October. A plague column marks the north end of the square. The column was built in 1690 to give thanks because an epidemic bypassed the town. A pillory stood there for many years, and it was the site for executions. Lower down in the square, two elaborate stone fountains, both dedicated to Roman gods, were built in 1797. On the eastern side of the square is the Municipal Hall, which was built in 1425 and renovated in 2004. The outer rim of the square shows some unfortunate buildings from the 1980s that don't fit in with the rest of the historical structures.

The **Kostel svatého Ignáce** (St. Ignatius Church), in the northwest corner of the town square, is relatively young for Jihlava. It was built at the end of the 17th century. Look inside to see a rare Gothic crucifix, created during the 13th century for the early Bohemian king Přemysl Otakar II. The ceiling frescoes, altar, stucco work and pulpit are all fine examples of 17th-century baroque craftsmanship. The church courtyard has an entrance to the town's underground tunnel system, which are open April through December. ✉ *Masarykovo náměstí.*

The town's most striking structure is the Gothic **Kostel svatého Jakuba** (St. James the Greater Church), which is east of the main square. The church's exterior, with its uneven towers, is Gothic; the interior is baroque; and the font is a masterpiece of the Renaissance style, dating from 1599. Note also the baroque Chapel of the Holy Virgin, sandwiched between two late-Gothic chapels, with its oversize 14th-century pietà. The tower, which offers a good view, is sometimes open the public. ✉ *Farní ul.* 🎫 *10 Kč* ⊗ *Tower: June and Sept., weekends, 10–1 and 2–6; July and Aug., Tues.–Sun., 10–1 and 2–6.*

Where to Stay & Eat

¢ ✕🏨 **Zlatá Hvězda.** Centrally located on the main square, this reconstructed old hotel in a beautiful Renaissance house is comfortable and surprisingly elegant. In keeping with the building, rooms are modestly harmonious, with wood ceilings and down comforters. You're a short walk from Jihlava's restaurants and shops, though the on-site café (¢–$$$) and wine bar are among the best in town. Breakfast is not included in the rates. ⊠ *Masarykovo nám. 32, 586 01* ☎ *567–309–421* 🖷 *567–309–496* ⊕ *www.zlatahvezda.cz* 🛏 *17 rooms, 1 apartment* 🍴 *Restaurant, café, cable TV, bar, meeting room, some pets allowed; no a/c* ☰ *AE, MC, V* 🍽 *EP.*

Jihlava Essentials

TRANSPORTATION Visiting Jihlava from Prague is easiest if you drive. By car, take Highway E65, and change to E59 at Exit 112. Jihlava is on the main road. With good traffic, the trip is well under an hour.

A bus is usually your best option to Jihlava. Direct buses to Jihlava leave from the Florenc bus station in Prague and cost around 100 Kč; if you take a direct bus, your travel time to Jihlava will be around 1½ to 2 hours.

Train service fron Prague's main train station, Hlavní nádraži, requires at least one change, usually in Hlavičkův Brod; depending on your connection, the trip can take from just under two hours to well over three hours. The price for the trip varies, but it's generally around 200 Kč.

VISITOR ☎ Jihlava Tourist Information ⊠ Masarykovo nám. 19 ☎ 567-167-120 ⊕ www.
INFORMATION jihlava.cz

TŘEBÍČ

❷ *27 km (16 mi) southeast of Jihlava; 35 km (21 mi) east of Telč; 151 km (91 mi) southeast of Prague.*

Partway between Telč and Brno, Třebíč has a Jewish Quarter and basilica that became UNESCO World Heritage Sites in 2003. There was a substantial Jewish population in the town up until World War II. The town is first mentioned in 1101, but it was almost completely destroyed in a war in 1468 and then rebuilt. Though known for its historic buildings, TrŇXtags error: Unexpected end of lineŇ

★ A virtual maze of winding streets, the **Zámostí** (Jewish Quarter) has two synagogues and other buildings formerly used by the town's Jewish community. The **Front Synagogue** on Tiche náměstí is now used for Protestant services. The **Rear Synagogue** (⊠ Blahoslavova 5 ☎ 568–896–120) sometimes has concerts or exhibitions, for which it charges a small admission. The **Jewish Cemetery** (⊠ Hradek 14 ☎ 568–827–111) has 3,000 tombstones dating from the Renaissance up to the 20th century. It's free to enter. Several houses in the district are quite interesting, including a pink Renaissance house with an overhanging second floor at Pokorný 5. A trail of signs in English point out the remarkable spots. Remember your manners, as most houses in the area are not museums and people actually live in them. ☉ *Rear Synagogue: June–Sept., weekdays 9–noon and 1–5, weekends 1–5; Oct.–May, weekends 1–5. Jewish Cemetery: May–Sept., daily 8–8; Oct., Mar., and Apr., daily 8–6; Nov. and Feb., daily 9–4* 🎫 *Rear Synagogue 30 Kč. Jewish Cemetery free.*

The late Romanesque and early Gothic **Bazilika sv. Prokupa** (St. Procopius Basilica) retains much of its original layout from when it was begun in 1260, although new sections were added up to the 1950s. The oldest parts are easy to spot. They have a very heavy look, with lots of stone and few windows. Two baroque towers at the front were added in the early 1700s by architect F. M. Kaňka. One of the oldest sections is the crypt, with Romanesque pillars and arches. The adjoining château, which has a separate admission charge, displays a collection of Nativity scenes, 250 tobacco pipes, folk art items, and even some mineral samples. ⊠ *Zámek 1* ☎ *568–840–518* 🖆 *Basilica: 10 Kč. Château: 20 Kč* ⊙ *Apr.–Sept., Tues.–Fri., 8–11:30 and 1–5; weekends 1–5.*

Třebíc Essentials

TRANSPORTATION It's best to combine Třebíč with a visit Jihlava or Telč. Direct train travel to Třebíč from Jihlava takes around 45 minutes to more than an hour and costs around 65 Kč; there's no direct train service to Jihlava from Telč. A direct bus from Jihlava to Třebíč takes about the same amount of time but costs around 40 Kč; from Telč, the bus trip takes less than 45 minutes and costs less than 30 Kč.

Car travel from Telč is direct on Route 23 and takes about 20 minutes. From Jihalva, it's fastest to get back on Highway E50 and go east to Velké Meziříčí, and then go south on Route 360; the trip should take about 30 minutes.

VISITOR ℹ️ **Třebíč Tourist information** ⊠ Karlovo nám. 53 ☎ 568-896-120 ⊕ www.
INFORMATION mkstrebic.cz.

TELČ

③ *30 km (19 mi) south of Jihlava; 154 km (94 mi) southeast of Prague, via Rte. 406*

The little town of Telč has an even more impressive main square than that of Jihlava—it has been on the UNESCO World Heritage list since 1992, but what strikes the eye most here is not its size but the unified style of the buildings. On the lowest levels are beautifully vaulted Gothic halls, just above are Renaissance floors and facades, and all the buildings are crowned with rich Renaissance and baroque gables.

★ **Náměstí Zachariáše z Hradce,** the main square, is so perfect you feel like you've entered a film set, not a living town. The town allegedly owes its architectural unity to Zacharias of Neuhaus, and the square is named after him. During the 16th century, so the story goes, the wealthy Zacharias had the castle—originally a small fort—rebuilt into a Renaissance château. But the contrast between the new castle and the town's rather ordinary buildings was so great that Zacharias had the square rebuilt to match the castle's splendor. Luckily for architecture fans, the Neuhaus dynasty died out shortly thereafter, and succeeding nobles had little interest in refashioning the town according to the vogue of the day.

It's best to approach Telč's main square on foot. If you've come by car, park outside the main walls on the side south of town and walk through the **Great Gate,** part of the original fortifications dating to the 13th century. As you approach on Palackého ulice, the square unfolds in front of you, with the château at the northern end and beautiful houses, bathed in pastel reds and golds, gracing both sides. If you're a fan of Renaissance reliefs, note the black-and-white sgraffito corner house at No. 15, which dates from the middle of the 16th century. The house at No. 61, across from the Černý Orel Hotel, is also noteworthy for its fine detail.

Statní zámek Telč (Telč château) forms a complex with the former **Jesuit college** and **Kostel svatého Jakuba** (Church of St. James). The château, originally Gothic, was built during the 14th century, perhaps by King John of Luxembourg, the father of Charles IV. Credit its current Renaissance appearance to Italian masters, who oversaw a renovation between 1553 and 1568. In season, you can tour the castle and admire the rich Renaissance interiors. Given the reputation of nobles for lively, lengthy banquets, the sgraffito relief in the dining room depicting gluttony (in addition to the six other deadly sins) seems odd indeed. Other interesting rooms with sgraffiti include the Treasury, the Armory, and the Blue and Gold chambers. A curious counterpoint to all this Renaissance splendor is the castle's permanent exhibit of paintings by leading Czech modernist Jan Zrzavý. There are two tours: the first goes through the Renaissance chambers; the second displays the rooms that were used as recently as 1945. ⊠ *Statní zámek Telč, nám. J. Kypty* ☎ *567–243–943* ⊕ *www.zamek-telc.cz* ⌑ *Tours 140 Kč each, with English printed text; gallery 30 Kč* ☉ *Apr. and Oct., Tues.–Sun. 9–noon and 1–4; May–Sept., Tues.–Sun. 9–noon and 1–5.*

> **need a break?**
>
> If you're looking for sweets, you can get good homemade cakes at **Cukrárna u Matěje,** a little café at Na baště 2, on the street leading past the château to a small lake.

A tiny street leading off the main square takes you to the 160-foot Romanesque tower of the **Kostel svatého Ducha** (Church of the Holy Spirit). This is the oldest standing structure in Telč, dating from the first quarter of the 13th century. The interior, however, is a stylistic hodgepodge, as it was given a late-Gothic make-over and then, due to fire damage, refashioned through the 17th century. ⊠ *Palackého ul.*

Where to Stay & Eat

★ $ ✕☒ **Černý Orel.** Here you can get a very rare treat: an older, refined hotel that puts modern amenities in a traditional setting. The public areas mix architectural details such as vaulted ceilings with plush, contemporary armchairs, and the basic but inviting rooms are well balanced and comfortably furnished. Ask for a room overlooking the square, as the baroque façade provides a perfect backdrop from which to view it. Even if you don't stay here, take a meal at the excellent hotel restaurant ($$–$$$$), a great spot for straightforward beef or pork dishes. ⊠ *Nám. Zachariáše z Hradce 7, 588 56* ☎ *567–243–222* 🖷 *567–243–221* ⊕ *www.cernyorel. cz* ⇝ *30 rooms, 25 with bath* ⌂ *Restaurant, cable TV, bar, meeting room, some pets allowed (fee); no a/c* ⊟ *AE, MC, V* ⊙ *BP.*

¢–$ ⊞ **Telč.** This is a slightly upscale alternative in town, even though the bright, polished appearance of the reception area doesn't quite carry over to the functional but pleasant rooms. (Some rooms open onto a court-yard.) The location, however, in a corner of the main square, is ideal. ⊠ *Na Můstku 37, 588 56* ☎*567–243–109* 🖷*567–223–887* ↩*10 rooms* ⊕ *www.hoteltelc.cz* ⟐ *Restaurant, cable TV, some pets allowed (fee); no a/c* ⊟ *AE, DC, MC, V* ⦿| *BP.*

Telč Essentials

TRANSPORTATION A car is your best option, and makes it easy to combine a trip to Telč with a stop en route in Jihlava. From Prague, take Highway E50 and E59 through Jihlava south to Route 23 and then east. The trip takes less than two hours without stops.

Direct bus service leaves from Prague's Florenc bus station and takes just under three hours; the fare is approximately 110 Kč. From Jihlava, a direct bus can take from 40 to 90 minutes and costs around 40 Kč.

Train service from Prague requires several changes and takes more than four hours, so it isn't a practical option for most people. It's recommended only for those who want the scenic route. Train service from Jihlava also requires a change and takes more than an hour. The cost from Jihlava is less than 60 Kč.

VISITOR 🔠 **Telč Tourist Information** ⊠ nám. Zachariáše z Hradce 10 ☎ 567–112–407 ⊕ www. INFORMATION telc-etc.cz/en/homeen.html.

CHÂTEAU VRANOV NAD DYJÍ

❹ *55 km (34 mi) southeast of Telč; 209 km (128 mi) southeast of Prague.*

As a swimming and boating center for southern Moravia, Vranov might be a good place to stop in its own right. But what makes the town truly noteworthy is the enormous and colorful **Château Vranov nad Dyjí** (Vra-nov Château), rising 200 feet from a rocky promontory. For nearly 1,000 years this was the border between Bohemia and Austria, and thus it re-quired a fortress of these dimensions. In the foreground, the solemn Re-naissance tower rises over some Gothic fortifications. On its left is a golden baroque church, and there's a beautiful pink-and-white baroque dome to the back. Each unit is spectacular, but the overall effect of so many styles mixed together is jarring. Take your eyes off the castle's motley exterior and tour its mostly baroque (and more harmonious) interior. The most impressive room is certainly the 43-foot-high elliptical Hall of Ancestors, the work of the Viennese master Johann Bernhard Fischer von Erlach (builder of the Clam-Gallas Palace in Prague and the Hof-burg in Vienna). From June to August you can look inside the castle church as well. The rotunda, altar, and organ were designed by Fischer von Er-lach at the end of the 17th century. ⊠ *Zámecka ul. 93, Vranov* ☎ *515–296–215* ⬚ *Château 65 Kč. Château with English-language text 130 Kč. Church 15 Kč* ⊕ *www.pamatkybrno.cz* ☉ *Castle Apr. and Oct., weekends 9–4; May, June, and Sept., Tues.–Sun. 9–5; July and Aug., Tues.–Sun. 9–6. Church June, weekends 9–5; July and Aug., Sun.–Tues. 9–6; other times by arrangement.*

Vranov Essentials

A visit to Vranov should be combined with a trip to Telč or Znojmo. Although it's possible to get to Vranov by bus, a car is much more convenient. By car from Telč, Vranov is about 50 km (30 mi) on Highway E59; the trip takes about 30 minutes. From Znojmo, take Highway E59 northwest to Route 398, where you continue southwest to Vranov; the trip from Znojmo is 25 km (15 mi) and takes less than 30 minutes.

Bus travel from anywhere requires a change in Znojmo. Buses leave from the main bus depot or from Dr. Horákové in Znojmo. The trip takes half an hour and costs around 20 Kč. There's no train service to Vranov.

ZNOJMO

❺ *20 km (12 mi) east of Vranov; 229 km (140 mi) southeast of Prague.*

Znojmo enjoys a long history as an important frontier town between Austria and Bohemia and is the cultural center of southern Moravia. The Přemyslid prince Břetislav I had already built a fortress here in the 11th century, and in 1226 Znojmo became the first Moravian town (ahead of Brno) to receive town rights from the king. But modern Znojmo, with its many factories and high-rises, isn't really a place for lingering. Plan on spending no more than a few hours walking through the Old Town and visiting the remaining fortifications and churches that stand between the New Town and the river.

Znojmo's tumbledown **main square,** now usually filled with peddlers selling everything from butter to cheap souvenirs, isn't what it used to be when it was crowned by Moravia's most beautiful town hall. Unfortunately, the 14th-century building was destroyed in 1945, just before the end of the war, and all that remains of the original structure is the 250-foot Gothic tower you see at the top of the square—looking admittedly forlorn astride the modern department store that now occupies the space. From here, you can follow the run-down Zelinářská ulice, which trails from behind the town hall's tower to the southwest in the direction of the Old Town and the river.

The grand Gothic **Kostel svatého Mikuláše** (Church of St. Nicholas; ✉ Nám. Mikulášské) dates from 1338, but its neo-Gothic tower was not added until the 19th century. If you can get into the church (it's often locked), look for the impressive sacraments house, which was built around 1500 in late-Gothic style. Just behind the Kostel svatého Mikuláše is the curious, two-layer **Kostel svatého Václava** (Church of St. Wenceslas; ✉ Nám. Mikulášské), built at the end of the 15th century. The upper level of this tiny white church is dedicated to St. Anne, the lower level to St. Martin. Along the medieval ramparts that separate the town from the river stands the original 11th-century **Rotunda svaté Kateřiny** (St. Catherine's Rotunda; ✉ Hradní), still in remarkably good condition. Step inside to see a rare cycle of restored frescoes from 1134 depicting various members of the early Přemyslid dynasty.

Where to Stay & Eat

Znojmo has two claims to fame that have endeared the town to the hearts (and palates) of Czechs everywhere. The first is the Znojmo gherkin, first cultivated in the 16th century. You can find this tasty accompaniment to meals at restaurants all over the country. Just look for the *Znojmo* prefix—as in *Znojemský guláš*, a tasty stew spiced with pickles. Znojmo's other treat is wine. As the center of the Moravian wine industry, this is an excellent place to pick up a few bottles of your favorite grape. The best designations to look for, in addition to Znojmo, are Mikulov and Valtice. Some of the best varieties of grapes are Rulandské and Vavřinecké (for red) and Ryzlink and Müller Thurgau (for white).

¢ ✕⊡ **Hotel Morava.** A pretty, moderately ornate pink-and-yellow building on one of the town's squares in the historic district offers exceptionally large rooms with folksy furnishings. The rooms, which can comfortably hold up to four people, have pleasant views of the square's fountain. The hotel restaurant (¢–$$) offers outdoor dining in the summer and a selection of local wines. ⊠ *Horní nám. 16, 669 01* ☎ *515–224–147* ⊕ *www.znojman.cz/morava* ⟋ *2 rooms* ♲ *Restaurant, some pets allowed (fee); no a/c, no room phones* ⊟ *AE, MC, V* ⍩ *BP.*

★ ¢ ⊡ **Penzion Kim-Ex.** A family home with a terrace in a quiet residential neighborhood offers a relaxed atmosphere right on the Dyje River, facing a national park. Znojmo's historical center is about a mile away, but public transportation is close by. The wood-panel rooms are bright and airy. ⊠ *Vinohrady 26, 669 02* ☎ *515–222–580* ⊕ *penzionkimex.cz* ⟋ *4 rooms* ♲ *Cable TV, some pets allowed; no a/c* ⊟ *No credit cards* ⍩ *BP.*

Znojmo Essentials

TRANSPORTATION Znojmo, which is along the main route to Vienna, is easily reached by car from from Prague or Brno. Take Highway E50 southeast from Prague, then turn south on Highway E59 near Jihlava. The trip is just under 200 km (120 mi) and takes about two hours. From Brno, the trip is about 70 km on Highway E461 and Highway 53 and takes under an hour.

Direct buses leave from Prague's Florenc bus station for the 210-km (126-mi) trip, which takes at least three hours; the cost is about 150 Kč. From Brno, the 67-km (40-mi) trip by direct bus takes 1 hour and 15 minutes and costs around 60 Kč.

Train travel requires a change in Brno and at least one more change. From Brno, the trip takes about two hours and costs around 110 Kč.

VISITOR 🚩 **Znojmo Tourist information** ⊠ Karlovo nám. 53 ☎ 568-896-120 ⊕ www.
INFORMATION mkstrebic.cz.

MIKULOV

❻ *54 km (34 mi) east of Znojmo; 283 km (174 mi) southeast of Prague.*

In many ways, Mikulov is the quintessential Moravian town. The soft pastel pinks and yellows of its buildings look almost mystical in the afternoon sunshine against the greens of the surrounding hills. But aside from the busy wine industry, not much goes on here, even though this is the main border crossing on the Vienna–Brno highway. It's as though the waning of the town's Jewish community left a breach that has never been filled.

If you happen to arrive at grape-harvesting time in October, head for one of the many private *sklípeks* (wine cellars) built into the hills surrounding the town. The tradition in these parts is simply to knock on the door; more often than not, you'll be invited in by the owner to taste a recent vintage. If you visit in early September, try to hit Mikulov's renowned wine-harvest festival, which is celebrated with traditional music, folk dancing, and much quaffing of local Riesling.

The striking **Mikulov zámek** (Mikulov château) dominates the tiny main square and surrounding area. The château started out as the Gothic-era residence of the noble Liechtenstein family in the 13th century and was given its current baroque appearance some 400 years later. The most famous resident was Napoléon Bonaparte, who stayed here in 1805 while negotiating peace terms with the Austrians after winning the Battle of Austerlitz (Austerlitz is now known as Slavkov, and is near Brno). Sixty-one years later, Bismarck used the castle to sign a peace treaty with Austria. The castle's darkest days came at the end of World War II, when retreating Nazi SS units set fire to it. The château now houses the **Regionální Muzeum** (Regional Museum). Along with the expected rooms of period furniture, objects related to local wine-making are displayed. The most remarkable exhibit is a wine cask made in 1643, with a capacity of more than 22,000 gallons. This was used for collecting the vintner's obligatory tithe. ⊠ *Zámek 5* ☎ *519–510–255* ⊕ *www.rmm.cz* ✉ *40 Kč* ☽ *May–Sept., Tues.–Sun. 8–6; Apr., weekends 9–4.*

Mikulov has a prominent **Jewish Cemetery.** During the 19th century, Jews constituted nearly half the population of Mikulov. The town was the seat of the chief rabbi of Moravia from the 17th to the 19th centuries and a center of Jewish learning. Great Talmudic scholars, including Rabbis Jehuda Loew and David Oppenheimer, lived and taught here, and they ultimately died here. The cemetery gate is usually locked, but the key may be borrowed from the Částek family at Brněnská 28 (ring the buzzer). Out of respect for Jewish customs, the key is not lent out on Saturday. ⊠ *Off Brněnská ul.*

Only a few of the structures that served the Jewish community are left intact. One is the 16th-century **Altschul** (Old Synagogue), which has been restored and now houses a small exposition and gallery. ⊠ *Husova 11* ✉ *10 Kč* ☽ *May–Sept., Tues.–Sun. 1–5.*

Where to Stay & Eat

★ ¢–$ ╳⌂ **Rohatý Krokodýl.** This is a prim, nicely renovated hotel in the old chief rabbi's house, under the castle. The doubles are on the small side, but the suites, which cost just a little more, are quite roomy. The facilities are the best in Mikulov, particularly the ground-floor restaurant (¢–$$), which serves a typical but delicately prepared selection of traditional Czech dishes. The front desk can arrange for hot-air balloon rides. ⊠ *Husova 8, 692 01* ☎ *519–510–692* 🖷 *519–511–695* ⊕ *www.*

rohatykrokodyl.cz 🔗 *14 rooms* ⚫ *Restaurant, cable TV, pub, some pets allowed (fee); no a/c* 🖃 *AE, MC, V* 🍴 *BP.*

Mikulov Essentials

TRANSPORTATION Mikulov is best combined with a trip to Brno. Direct bus service from Brno's Zvonařka bus station to Mikulov, a 50-km (30-mi) trip, takes under an hour and costs less than 50 Kč.

Train service from Brno requires a change, usually at Břeclav. It takes a little more than an hour and costs 170 Kč.

By car, the trip is south of Brno on Highway E65 to Breclav and then east on Rte. 40. The trip takes a little over 30 minutes.

VISITOR 🎫 **Mikulov Tourist Information** ⊠ Nám. 1, Mikulov ☎ 625-510-855 ⊕ www.
INFORMATION mikulov.cz.

VALTICE

❼ *13 km (8 mi) east of Mikulov along Hwy. 414; 296 km (182 mi) southeast of Prague.*

This small town of Valtice would be wholly nondescript except for the fascinating **Valtice zámek** (Valtice Château), just off the main street, which was built for the Liechtenstein family by a group of leading baroque architects, among them Fischer von Erlach. There are some 365 windows as well as painted ceilings and much ornate woodwork. But best of all is the lure of spending the night—a rare practice in the Czech Republic. The left wing of the castle has been converted into the Hubertus hotel. You can also tour more than a dozen rooms, the chapel, and a picture gallery. ⊠ *Zámek 1* ☎ *519-352-423* ⊕ *www.pamatkybrno. cz* 🎫 *50 Kč; guided tour in German, occasionally in English, 100 Kč* ⊙ *Apr., Sept., and Oct., Tues.–Sun. 9–4; May–Aug., Tues.–Sun. 8–5.*

Fodor'sChoice Just 7 km (4 mi) northeast of Valnice is the **Château Lednice na Moravé.**
★ As a display of their wealth and taste, the Liechtenstein family sprinkled neoclassical temples and eclectic follies across a huge swath of parkland around Valtice and Lednice throughout the 18th and 19th centuries. The extravagantly neo-Gothic château, which is slowly being repaired after decades of neglect during the Communist era, has a sumptuous interior; particularly resplendent are the blue-and-green silk wall coverings embossed with the Moravian eagle in the formal dining room and bay-window drawing room. The grounds, now a pleasant park open to the public, have a 200-foot-tall minaret and a massive greenhouse filled with exotic flora. The landscaped area has been on the UNESCO World Heritage list since 1996. ⊠ *Lednice* ☎ *519–340–128* ⊕ *www. pamatkybrno.cz* 🎫 *Tours 60 Kč–100 Kč; minaret 10 Kč* ⊙ *Apr. and Oct., Tues.–Sun. 9–4; May–Sept., Tues.–Sun. 9–6.*

Where to Stay & Eat

★ ¢ ✕🏨 **Hotel Hubertus.** This comfortable hotel is not hard to find. Just look for the only palace in town; the hotel is on the left-hand side. Though the rooms are neither palatial nor furnished in period style, they are nevertheless inviting, with high ceilings and fresh flowers. Book ahead in summer, as the hotel is popular with Austrians who like to slip across the border for an impromptu holiday. ⊠ *Zámek 1, 691 42* ☎ *519–352–537* 🖷 *519–352–538* ⊕ *www.hotelhubertus.cz* ⇥ *29 rooms, 22 with bath* ⚒ *Restaurant, bar, meeting room, some pets allowed; no a/c, no TV in some rooms* ▤ *AE, MC, V* ⋈ *BP.*

Valtice Essentials

TRANSPORTATION Lednice and Valtice are less than 10 km (6 mi) apart. You'll find frequent bus service, a 17-minute ride, between the main square of Lednice and the Besední dům of Valtice for around 12 Kč.

By car, Valtice is 12 km (7 mi) southeast of Mikulov via Route 40. The trip takes less than 10 minutes. Valtice is also reachable by car from Brno via Highway E65 southeast to Břeclav, which you switch to Route 40 and continue west for about 15 km (9 mi). The trip is about an hour.

Direct bus service from Brno's Zvonařka bus station to Lednice is a 77-km (46-mi) trip that takes 90 minutes and costs about 65 Kč; from there, you take the local bus to Valtice.

VISITOR INFORMATION 🛈 **Valtice Tourist Information** ⊠ Nám. Svobody 4, Valtice ☎ 519–352–977 ⊕ www.valtice.cz.

BRNO

202 km (122 mi) southeast of Prague via Hwy. E65

Moravia's cultural and geographic center, Brno (pronounced *burr*-no) grew rich in the 19th century and has a different feel from any other Czech or Slovak city. Beginning with a textile industry imported from Germany, Holland, and Belgium, Brno became the industrial heartland of the Austro-Hungarian Empire during the 18th and 19th centuries—hence its nickname Manchester of Moravia. You'll search in vain for an extensive old town; you'll also find few of the traditional arcaded storefronts that typify other historic Czech towns. Instead you'll see fine examples of the Empire and neo-Renaissance styles, their formal, geometric facades more in keeping with the conservative tastes of the 19th-century middle class.

In the early 20th century, the city became home to the best young architects working in the cubist and constructivist styles. Experimentation wasn't restricted to architecture. Leoš Janáček, an important composer of the early modern period, lived and worked in Brno, as did Austrian novelist Robert Musil. The modern tradition continues even today, and the city is considered to have the best theater and performing arts in Moravia, as well as a small but thriving café scene.

It's best to avoid Brno at trade-fair time (the biggest are in early spring and early autumn), when hotel and restaurant facilities are strained. If the hotels are booked, the accommodation services at the town hall or main station will help you find a room.

Numbers in the text correspond to numbers in the margin and on the Brno map.

Exploring Brno

Begin the walking tour at the triangular **náměstí Svobody** ❽ in the heart of the commercial district. Then walk up Masarykova ulice toward the train station and make a right through the little arcade at No. 6 to see the animated Gothic portal of the **Stará radnice** ❾. Leave through the portal and turn right into the old **Zelný trh** ❿. On the far side of the market, dominating the square, stands the severe Renaissance Dietrichsteinský palác at No. 8. Go through an archway into the palace garden, from where stairs lead down to the baroque **Kostel Nalezení svatého Kříže** ⓫.

Towering above the church and market is the **Chrám svatých Petra a Pavla** ⓬, Brno's main church and a fixture of the skyline. The best way to get to it is to return to Zelný trh (via the little street off Kapucínské náměstí), make a left, and walk up narrow Petrská ulice, which begins just to the right of the Dietrichsteinský palác. Before leaving the church area, stroll around the pretty park and grounds. Return to the juncture of Petrská and Biskupská and follow Biskupská to Starobrněnská ulice. Turn left and cross the busy Husova třída onto Pekařská ulice. At the end of the street you come to a square named for Gregor Mendel (Mendlovo náměstí) and a medieval monastery with a large Gothic church, Starobrněnský klášter.

Continue the tour along the busy and somewhat downtrodden Úvoz ulice. Take the first right and climb the stairs to the calmer residential street of Pellicova. If there's a unique beauty to Brno, it's in neighborhoods such as this one, with its attractive houses, each in a different architectural style. Many houses incorporate cubist and geometric elements of the early modern period (1920s and 1930s). Begin the ascent to the **Špilberk hrad** ⓭. There's no direct path to the castle; just follow your instincts (or a detailed map) upward, and you'll get there. After taking in the view, stroll back down one of the windy paths to Husova třída and have a look in two of the Czech Republic's finest museums: the **Uměleckoprůmyslové muzeum** ⓮ and, a block farther down Husova, Brno's modern-art museum, the **Pražákův palác** ⓯. For old art culled from Moravian churches and estates, make sure to pay a visit to the **Místodržitelský palác** ⓰. It's also worth it to find a way to Ludwig Mies van der Rohe's **Villa Tugendhat** ⓱, the city's most famous work of architecture. The house is a bit off the beaten track, so you will need to travel there by car, taxi, or tram. **Muzeum Romské kultury** ⓲ is about halfway between the historical sights of the city center and Villa Tugendhat, accessible by the same tram lines as Villa Tugendhat.

TIMING A walking tour of Brno should take two to three hours at a leisurely pace. Allow a couple of hours to fully explore the Špilberk castle. Museum enthusiasts could easily spend a half-day or more browsing through the city's many collections. Brno is relatively busy on weekdays, surprisingly slow on weekends.

What to See

⓬ **Chrám svatých Petra a Pavla** (Cathedral of Sts. Peter and Paul). This is one church that probably looks better from a distance. The interior, a

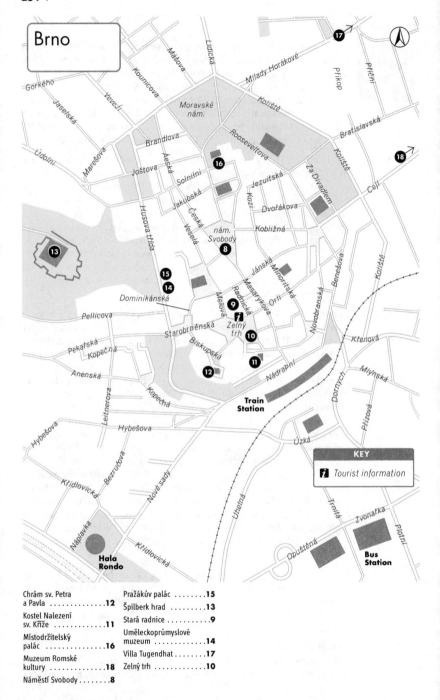

Brno

Chrám sv. Petra
a Pavla 12

Kostel Nalezení
sv. Kříže 11

Místodržitelský
palác 16

Muzeum Romské
kultury 18

Náměstí Svobody 8

Pražákův palác 15

Špilberk hrad 13

Stará radnice 9

Uměleckoprůmyslové
muzeum 14

Villa Tugendhat 17

Zelný trh 10

blend of baroque and Gothic, is light and tasteful but hardly mind-blowing. Still, the slim neo-Gothic twin spires—added in the 20th century to give the cathedral more of its original Gothic dignity—are a nice touch. Don't be surprised if you hear the noon bells ringing from the cathedral at 11 AM. The practice dates from the Thirty Years' War, when Swedish troops were massing for an attack outside the town walls. Brno's resistance had been fierce, and the Swedish commander decreed that he would give up the fight if the town could not be taken by noon the following day. The bell ringer caught wind of the decision and the next morning, just as the Swedes were preparing a final assault, rang the noon bells—an hour early. The ruse worked, and the Swedes decamped. Ever since, the midday bells have been rung an hour early as a show of gratitude. Although the city escaped, the cathedral caught a Swedish cannon shot and suffered severe damage in the resulting fire. The church can be seen on the face of the 10-Kč coin. ☒ *Petrov at Petrská ul.* ☎ *Free* ☉ *Daily dawn–dusk; closed during services.*

★ ⑪ **Kostel Nalezení svatého Kříže** (Church of the Holy Cross). Formerly part of the Capuchin Monastery, this church combines a baroque silhouette with a rather stark façade. If you've ever wondered what a mummy looks like without its bandages, then enter the door to the monastery's *krypta* (crypt). In the basement are the mummified remains of some 200 nobles and monks from the late 17th and 18th centuries, ingeniously preserved by a natural system of air circulating through vents and chimneys. The best-known mummy is Colonel František Trenck, commander of the brutal Pandour regiment of the Austrian army, who, at least in legend, spent several years in the dungeons of Špilberk castle before finding his final rest here in 1749. Experts have concluded that his head is real, contrary to stories of its removal by a thief. A note of caution about the crypt: the graphic displays may frighten small children, so ask at the admission desk for the small brochure (20 Kč) with pictures that preview what's to follow. ☒ *Kapucínské nám. 5* ☎ *542–213–232* ⊕ *www. volny.cz/kapucini.brno* ☒ *40 Kč* ☉ *May–Sept., Mon.–Sat. 9–11:45 and 2–4:30, Sun. 11–11:45 and 2–4:30; Oct.–mid-Dec. and mid-Jan.–Apr., Tues.–Sat. 9–11:45 and 2–4:30, Sun. 11–11:45 and 2–4:30.*

⑯ **Místodržitelský palác** (Governor's Palace). Moravia had much stronger artistic ties to Austria than Bohemia did, as can be seen in the impressive collection of Gothic, baroque, and 19th-century painting and sculpture found in this splendid baroque palace. Particularly fetching are Austrian painter Franz Anton Maulbertsch's ethereal rococo pageants. ☒ *Moravské nám. 1A* ☎ *542–321–100* ⊕ *www.moravska-galerie.cz* ☒ *40 Kč* ☉ *Apr.–Sept., Wed. and Fri.–Sun. 10–6, Thurs. 10–7; Oct.–Mar., Wed. and Fri.–Sun. 10–5, Thurs. 10–6.*

⑱ **Muzeum Romské kultury** (Museum of Romani Culture). Halfway on the way from Brno's historical center to the Villa Tugendhat, Brno has a small but unique museum. The Roma, as Gypsies prefer to be called, are often the victims of discrimination in the Czech Republic. To bridge cross-cultural understanding, a museum dedicated to their culture and history opened in 1991. Exhibits deal with traditional occupations, dress, and lifestyles. A study room has documents and photographs.

✉ *Bratislavská 67* ☎ *545–571–789* ⊕ *www.rommuz.cz* 🎫 *20 Kč* ⊙ *Tues.–Fri. 10–5.*

❽ Náměstí Svobody (Freedom Square). The square itself is architecturally undistinguished, but here and along the adjoining streets you can find the city's best stores and shopping opportunities. Anyone who has been to Vienna might experience a feeling of déjà vu here, as many of the buildings were designed by 19th-century Austrian architects. Especially noteworthy is the stolid Klein Palace at No. 15, built by Theophil Hansen and Ludwig Foerster, both prominent for their work on Vienna's Ringstrasse.

❻ Pražákův palác (Pražák Palace). This handsome, 19th-century neo-Renaissance building houses the largest collection of modern and contemporary Czech art outside of Prague. Although works by many of the same artists represented in Prague's major galleries can be seen here, the emphasis is on Moravian artists, who tended to prefer rural themes—their avant-garde concoctions have a certain folksy flavor. ✉ *Husova 18* ☎ *542–215–758* ⊕ *www.moravska-galerie.cz* 🎫 *40 Kč* ⊙ *Apr.–Sept., Wed. and Fri.–Sun. 10–6, Thurs. 10–7; Oct.–Mar., Wed. and Fri.–Sun. 10–5, Thurs. 10–6.*

⓭ Špilberk hrad (Spielberg Castle). Once among the most feared places in the Hapsburg Empire, this fortress-cum-prison still broods over Brno from behind its menacing walls. The castle's advantageous location was no secret to the early lords of the city, who moved here during the 13th century from neighboring Petrov Hill. Successive rulers gradually converted the old castle into a virtually impregnable fortress. Indeed, it successfully withstood the onslaughts of Hussites, Swedes, and Prussians over the centuries; only Napoléon, in 1809, succeeded in occupying the fortress. But the castle is best known for its gruesome history as a prison for enemies of the Austro-Hungarian monarchy and, later, of the Nazis in World War II. Although tales of torture during the Austrian period are probably untrue (judicial torture had been prohibited prior to the first prisoners' arrival in 1784), conditions for the hardest offenders were hellish: they were shackled day and night in dank, dark catacombs and fed only bread and water. The most brutal corrections ended with the death of the harsh, rationalist ruler Joseph II in 1790. The castle complex is very large, and the various parts generally require separate admissions. The **casemates** (passages within the walls of the castle) have been turned into an exhibition of the late-18th-century prison and their Nazi-era use as an air-raid shelter. You can see the entire castle grounds as well as the surrounding area from the **observation tower.** Above ground, a **museum** in the fortress starts off with more displays on the prison era, installed in a row of cells on the ground floor, with detailed English texts. Included in the tour of the museum is an **exhibition** on the history of Brno, including several panoramic paintings showing the city in the 17th century, and photos showing then-and-now views of 19th- and 20th-century redevelopment in the Old Town. Displays of local artists and modern architecture complete the castle's exhibits. ✉ *Špilberk 1* ☎ *542–214–145* ⊕ *www.spilberk.cz* 🎫 *Casemates 30 Kč, museum 30 Kč; Casemates, tower, and exhibitions, 100 Kč* ⊙ *Casemates and tower May–June and Sept., Tues.–Sun. 9–6; July and Aug., daily 9–6; Oct.–Apr.,*

Tues.–Sun. 9–5. Museum Apr.–Sept., Tues.–Sun. 9–6; Oct.–Mar., Wed.–Sun. 10–5.

need a break?

After a long walk and a good climb in Špilberk Castle, what could be better than one of the best beers you'll ever have? The **Stopkova pivnice** (✉ Česká 5) will set you up with one, or a soft drink. If you're hungry, try the house goulash, a tangy mixture of sausage, beef, rice, egg, and dumpling. For something more substantial, head for the restaurant on the second floor.

❾ Stará radnice (Old Town Hall). The oldest secu!ar building in Brno has an important Gothic portal. The door is the work of Anton Pilgram, architect of Vienna's St. Stephen's Cathedral. It was completed in 1510, but the building itself is about 200 years older. Look above the door to see a badly bent pinnacle that looks as if it wilted in the afternoon sun. This isn't the work of vandals but was apparently done by Pilgram himself out of revenge against the town. According to legend, Pilgram had been promised an excellent commission for his portal, but when he finished, the mayor and city councillors reneged on their offer. Pilgram was so angered by the duplicity that he purposely bent the pinnacle and left it poised, fittingly, over the statue of justice.

Just inside the door are the remains of two other famous Brno legends, the **Brno Dragon** and the **wagon wheel.** The dragon—a female alligator, to be anatomically correct—apparently turned up at the town walls one day in the 17th century and began eating children and livestock. A gatekeeper came up with the novel idea of filling a sack with limestone and placing it inside a freshly slaughtered goat. The dragon devoured the goat, swallowing the limestone as well, and went to quench its thirst at a nearby river. The water mixed with the limestone, bursting the dragon's stomach (the scars on the preserved dragon's stomach are still clearly visible). The story of the wagon wheel, on the other hand, concerns a bet placed some 400 years ago that a young wheelwright, Jiří Birk, couldn't chop down a tree, fashion the wood into a wheel, and roll it from his home at Lednice (53 km [33 mi] away) to the town walls of Brno—all between sunup and sundown. The wheel stands as a lasting tribute to his achievement. (The townspeople, however, became convinced that Jiří had enlisted the help of the devil to win the bet, so they stopped frequenting his workshop; poor Jiří died penniless.)

No longer the seat of the town government, the Old Town Hall holds exhibitions and performances. To find out what's on, ask in the information center just inside Pilgram's portal. The view from the top of the tower is one of the best in Brno, but the climb (five flights) is strenuous. ✉ *Radnická 8* ⊕ *www.kultura-brno.cz* ☎ *Tower 20 Kč* ⊙ *Apr.–Sept., daily 9–5.*

⓮ Uměleckoprůmyslové muzeum (Museum of Applied Arts). Open again after a long renovation that ended in 2001, this is doubtless the best arts-and-crafts museum in the Czech Republic. It has an assemblage of artifacts far more extensive than the truncated collection in Prague's museum of the same name. The collection includes Gothic, art nouveau, and secessionist pieces, as well as an excellent, comprehensive overview of Bohemian and Moravian glass. Keep an eye out for the elegant furniture from Josef Hoffmann's Wiener Werkstätte (Vienna Workshop). A jagged, candy-color table by Milan Knížák is a striking example of contemporary work. ✉ *Husova 14* ☎ *532–169–111* ⊕ *www.moravska-galerie. cz* ✉ *40 Kč* ☉ *Tues.–Sun. 9–5.*

⑰ Villa Tugendhat. Designed by Ludwig Mies van der Rohe and completed
Fodor'sChoice in 1930, this austere, white Bauhaus villa counts among the most im-
★ portant works of the modern period and is now a UNESCO World Heritage Site. The emphasis here is on function and the use of geometric forms, but you be the judge as to whether the house fits the neighborhood. The Tugendhat family fled before the Nazis, and their original furnishings vanished during the war or the house's subsequent heavy-handed remodeling. Replicas of Mies's cool, functional designs have been installed in the downstairs living area. Some of the original exotic wood paneling and an eye-stopping onyx screen remain in place. The best way to get there is to take a taxi or Tram 3, 5, or 11 to the Dětská nemocnice stop and then walk up unmarked Černopolní ulice for 10 minutes or so; you'll be able to see the modernist structure up on the hill. Advance reservations for tours are highly recommended. The building is undergoing a long-term renovation, and is sometimes closed to the public. ✉ *Černopolní 45* ☎ *545–212–118* ⊕ *www.tugendhat-villa.cz* ✉ *80 Kč* ☉ *Wed.–Sun. 10–6; last tour starts at 5:15.*

⑩ Zelný trh (Cabbage Market). The only place where Brno begins to look like a typical Czech town, the Cabbage Market is immediately recognizable, not just for the many stands from which farmers still sell vegetables but also for the unique **Parnassus Fountain** that adorns its center. This baroque outburst (you either love it or hate it) couldn't be more out of place amid the formal elegance of most of the buildings on the square. But when Johann Bernhard Fischer von Erlach created the fountain in the late 17th century, it was important for a striving town like Brno to display its understanding of the classics and of ancient Greece. Thus, Hercules slays a three-headed dragon, while Amphitrite awaits the arrival of her lover—all incongruously surrounded by farmers hawking turnips and onions.

off the
beaten
path

MORAVSKÝ KRUMLOV – Admirers of art nouveau master Alfons Mucha may want to make a 50 km (30 mi) detour off the main highway linking Mikulov and Brno. The town château is the unlikely home of one of Mucha's most celebrated works, his 20-canvas *Slav Epic.* This enormous work, which tells the story of the emergence of the Slav nation, was not well received when it was completed in 1928; painters at the time were more interested in imitating modern movements and considered Mucha's representational art to be old-fashioned. The city of Prague owns the paintings and has from time to time said it was going to relocate them, but so far no concrete action has been taken. A music festival takes place there in June. ✉ *Zámecká 1* ☎ *515–322–789* ☉ *Apr.–June, Sept., and Oct., Tues.–Sun. 9–4; July and Aug., Tues.–Sun. 9–5* ✉ *50 Kč.*

Where to Stay & Eat

¢–$$$ ✕ **U Královny Elišky.** Few restaurants can match this 14th-century wine cellar for historical atmosphere. Local specialties including wild game and fish are served in rooms with names such as "The Musketeer" and "The Napoléon." In summer you can sit in the garden and order roast suckling pig or lamb while watching fencers in historical dress cross swords. The adjacent pension (¢) offers eight reasonably comfortable rooms at a good price (rates double during major trade fairs, however). Breakfast for pension guests is extra, however, which is unusual here. ⊠ *Mendlovo nám. 1A, 603 00* ☎ *543–212–578 restaurant, 543–216–898 pension* ▤ *No credit cards* ⊗ *Restaurant closed Sun. and Mon. No lunch.*

$$ ✕ **Černý Medvěd.** Decorated in cottage fashion with down-home Moravian floral upholstery, this is one of Brno's most comfortable dining rooms. Wild game is the key ingredient in a traditionally Czech menu. ⊠ *Jakubské nám. 1* ☎ *542–214–548* ▤ *AE, MC, V* ⊗ *Closed Sun.*

¢–$$ ✕ **Indická restaurace Taj.** One of the few places in the city to make a real try at any kind of ethnic food, this eatery hidden upstairs in a Victorian house creates a nice atmosphere as well. Once you cross the tiny bridge over a man-made indoor stream, you can sit in the Indian-theme main room and choose from the vegetarian or meat dishes. Some dishes can be prepared on a lava grill, which is brought out to your table. Lunch specials are a real value. ⊠ *Běhounská 12* ☎ *542–214–372* ▤ *AE, DC, MC, V.*

¢–$ ✕ **Zemanova kavárna.** This contemporary re-creation of a landmark 1920s coffeehouse (the original was razed by the Communists to make way for a theater) is extremely stylish. Everything from the light fixtures to the furniture is faithfully copied from the original interior. The lofty ceilings provide pleasant, lilting acoustics, and the food isn't bad either: the few main courses are Czech with a dash of French, such as pepper steak with fries. ⊠ *Jezuitská 6, between Za Divadlem and Koliště* ☎ *542–217–509* ⊕ *www.1926-zemanovakavarna.cz* ▤ *DC, MC, V.*

$$$$ ▦ **Grandhotel Brno.** Though not really grand, this hotel, built in 1870 and thoroughly remodeled in 1988, is certainly comfortable and convenient. High standards are maintained through the hotel's association with an Austrian chain. Service is attentive; the rooms, though small, are well-appointed, with coffered ceilings and leather sofas. Ask for a room at the back, facing the town, as the hotel is on a busy street opposite the train station. ⊠ *Benešova 18/20, 657 83* ☎ *542–518–111* 🖷 *542–210–345* ⊕ *www.grandhotelbrno.cz* ⇴ *116 rooms* ⬧ *3 restaurants, minibars, cable TV with movies, gym, sauna, casino, nightclub, Internet, meeting rooms, some pets allowed (fee); no a/c* ▤ *AE, DC, MC, V* ⧗❙ *BP.*

$$ ▦ **Holiday Inn.** Opened in 1993, this handsome representative of the American chain has become the local hotel of choice for business travelers. It has all you'd expect for the price, including a well-trained, multilingual staff. Executive rooms have some extra perks, such as a modem line and trouser press. The location, at the exhibition grounds about a mile from the city center, is inconvenient for those who don't have a car. Prices go up significantly during trade fairs and conventions.

✉ *Křížkovského 20, 603 00* ☎ *543–122–111* 🖷 *543–236–990* ⊕ *www. hibrno.cz* ⟶ *202 rooms* ⚬ *2 restaurants, room service, some in-room data ports, some minibars, some in-room safes, cable TV with movies, sauna, shop, bar, dry cleaning, laundry service, Internet, meeting rooms, car rental, some pets allowed (fee)* ⊟ *AE, DC, MC, V* ⏀ *BP.*

★ $ 🏨 **Hotel Pegas.** This little inn makes an excellent choice given its reasonable price and central location. The plain rooms are snug and clean, with wood paneling and down comforters, and the staff is helpful and friendly (and speak English). Even if you don't stay here, be sure to have a meal and home-brewed beer at the house microbrewery. ✉ *Jakubská 4, 602 00* ☎ *542–210–104* 🖷 *542–211–232* ⊕ *www.hotelpegas.cz* ⟶ *14 rooms* ⚬ *Restaurant, minibars, pub, some pets allowed; no a/c* ⊟ *DC, MC, V* ⏀ *BP.*

$ 🏨 **Slavia.** The century-old Slavia, just off the main Česká ulice, was thoroughly renovated in 1987. The grace of the fin-de-siècle façade and stucco-ceiling lobby is now oddly paired with utilitarian (though relatively spacious) rooms. The café, with adjacent terrace, is a good place to enjoy a cool drink on a warm afternoon. ✉ *Solniční 15/17, 622 16* ☎ *542–215–080* 🖷 *542–211–769* ⊕ *www.slaviabrno.cz* ⟶ *81 rooms* ⚬ *Restaurant, café, minibars, in-room safes, cable TV, no-smoking rooms, some pets allowed; no a/c* ⊟ *AE, DC, MC, V* ⏀ *BP.*

Nightlife & the Arts

Brno is renowned throughout the Czech Republic for its theater and performing arts. There are a couple of main venues for jacket-and-tie cultural events, both slightly northwest of the center of town, a five-minute walk from náměstí Svobody. Check the schedules at the theaters or pick up a copy of *Do města/Downtown*, Brno's free fortnightly bulletin of cultural events. For more sophisticated entertainment than a conversational evening at the local *pivnice* or *vinárna,* head for one of Brno's casinos. The tables usually stay open until 3 or 4 AM. In Brno you can buy tickets for performing arts productions at individual theater box offices or at the central **Předprodej vstupenek** (Ticket office ✉ Běhounská 17).

One of the country's best-known fringe theater companies, **Divadlo Husa na provázku** (Goose on a String Theater; ✉ Zelný tř. 9, at Petrská ulice ☎ 542–211–630), has its home in Brno. Opera and ballet productions are held at the modern **Janáček Theater** (✉ Rooseveltova 7 ☎ 542–158–252 ⊕ www.ndbrno.cz). The **Mahen Theater** (✉ Rooseveltova 1 ☎ 542–158–252 ⊕ www.ndbrno.cz) is the city's principal venue for dramatic theater.

The **Grandhotel Brno** (✉ Benešova 18/20 ☎ 542–518–111) has the Grand Casino. The Star Club Casino at the **Hotel International** (✉ Husova 16 ☎ 542–122–111) has roulette, blackjack, and poker tables, among others.

A few blocks north of the city center, **Klub Alterna** (✉ Kounicova 48 ☎ 541–212–091 ⊕ www.alterna.cz) hosts good Czech jazz and folk performers.

Shopping

Moravia produces very attractive folk pottery, painted with bright red, orange, and yellow flower patterns. You can find these products in stores and hotel gift shops throughout the region. For sophisticated artwork, including paintings and photography, stop by **Ambrosiana** (⊠ Jezuitská 11 ☎ 542–214–439). For rare books, art monographs, old prints, and a great selection of avant-garde 1920s periodicals, stop by **Antikvariát Alfa** (⊠ Jánská 11, in the arcade ☎ 542–211–947). You can buy English-language paperbacks and art books at **Knihkupectví Jiří Šedivý** (⊠ Masarykova 6 ☎ 542–215–456). **S: Lukas** (⊠ Kapucínské nám. 5 ☎ 542–221–358) stocks handmade textiles, ceramics, and glass.

Brno Essentials

If you've arrived at Brno's main train station and are stuck for a room, try the accommodations service on the far left of the main hall, nominally open around the clock; you can place a sports bet there, too.

TRANSPORTATION TO BRNO
It's possible to fly from Prague to Brno on Air Ostrava, but the distance between the cities is short, and it's ultimately cheaper and quicker to travel by road or rail. During the two large Brno trade fairs, in April and September, foreign carriers also connect the city with Frankfurt and Vienna. These flights are usually crowded with businesspeople, so you have to book well in advance.

Bus connections from Prague's Florenc terminal to Brno are frequent, and the trip is a half-hour shorter than by train. Most buses arrive at the main bus station, a 10-minute walk from the train station. Some buses stop next to the train station. Buses also run between Brno and Vienna's Wien-Mitte station, stopping at Mikulov. Departures leave Brno for Vienna at 7:30 AM daily and at 5:30 PM every day except Tuesday.

Brno, within easy driving distance of Prague, Bratislava, and Vienna, is 196 km (122 mi) from Prague and 121 km (75 mi) from Bratislava. The E65 highway links all three cities.

Six comfortable EuroCity or InterCity trains daily make the three-hour run from Prague to Brno's station. They depart either from Prague's main station, Hlavní nádraží, or the suburban nádraží Holešovice. Trains leaving Prague for Bratislava, Budapest, and Vienna normally stop in Brno (check timetables to be sure).

🛪 **Air Ostrava** ⊠ Prague ☎ 220–113–406 ⊕ www.airport-brno.cz. **Hlavní nádraží** ⊠ Nádražní 1 ☎ 542–214–803 ⊕ www.jizdnirady.cz or www.idos.cz. **Main bus station (ÚAN Zvonařka)** ⊠ Zvonařka 1 ☎ 543–217–733.

TRANSPORTATION AROUND BRNO
Trams are the best way to get around the city. Tickets cost 8 Kč–24 Kč, depending on the time and zones traveled, and are available at newsstands, yellow ticket machines, or from the driver. Single-day, three-day and other long-term tickets are available. Most trams stop in front of the main station (Hlavní nádraží). Buses to the city periphery and nearby sights such as Moravský Kras in northern Moravia congregate at the

main bus station, a 10-minute walk behind the train station. To find it, simply go to the train station and follow the signs to ČSAD.

The nominal taxi fare is about 20 Kč per km (½ mi). There are taxi stands at the main train station, Výstaviště exhibition grounds, and on Joštova Street at the north end of the Old Town. Dispatchers tend not to understand English.

TRAVEL AGENCIES ☑ **Čedok** ✉ Nádražní 10/12 ☎ 542-321-267 ⊕ www.cedok.cz.

VISITOR INFORMATION ☑ **Brno Tourist Information** ✉ Radnická 8, Old Town Hall ☎ 542-211-090 ⊕ www. kultura-brno.cz ✉ Nádražní 6, across from train station ☎ 542-221-450.

SLAVKOV U BRNA

⑲ *20 km (12 mi) east of Brno; 216 km (134 mi) southeast of Prague.*

Slavkov, better known as Austerlitz, was the scene of one of the great battles of European history, where the armies of Napoléon met and defeated the combined forces of Austrian emperor Franz II and Czar Alexander I in 1805. If you happen to have a copy of *War and Peace* handy, you can find no better account of it anywhere. Scattered about the rolling agricultural landscapes between Slavkov and Brno are a number of battle monuments linked by walking paths. Napoléon directed his army from Žuráň Hill, above a small town called Šlapanice (which can be reached from Brno by train or bus). Several miles southeast of Šlapanice an impressive memorial to the fallen of all three nations, the Mohyla míru (Cairn of Peace), crowns a hill above the village of Prace. Alongside the cairn is a small museum devoted to the battle. Several days of events commemorate the battle every year around December 2.

★ The **Historické muzeum** (History Museum) in Slavkov is housed in the baroque château, where you can find exhibits of memorabilia about the battle of Austerlitz; it's well worth visiting, particularly if you're interested in European history. The building itself is rather plain as a château and is less impressive than either the displays on the Three Emperors, the gardens, or the battlefield itself. ✉ *Palackého nám. 126* ☎ *544-221-685* ⊕ *www.zamek-slavkov.cz* ✎ *Château tour 45 Kč. Napoléonic history tour 50 Kč* ☉ *Apr., Oct., and Nov., Tues.–Sun. 9–4; May and Sept., Tues.–Sun. 9–5; June, daily 9–5; July and Aug., daily 9–6; Dec.–Feb. by appointment.*

Slavkov u Brna Essentials

TRANSPORTATION Slavkov u Brna is best visited as a side-trip from Brno. By car, the trip is 22 km (13 mi) via Highway E50 and takes about 15 minutes.

Direct trains leave from Brno several times a day for the 27-km (16-mi) trip that takes 25 minutes and costs around 40 Kč.

Direct bus service leaves from Brno's Zvonařka bus station for a 22-km (13 mi) trip, which takes 30 minutes and costs around 25 Kč.

KROMĚŘÍŽ

20 *100 km (60 mi) east of Brno, 40 km (24 mi) south of Olomouc; 296 km (182 mi) southeast of Prague.*

Fodor'sChoice
★
Kroměříž Château, one of Moravia's UNESCO World Heritage Sites, is the former summer palace of archbishops of Olomouc. The building dates back to 1260, but the current romantic and neoclassical look comes from a 1752 renovation. In keeping with its use as a summer palace, weapons and hunting trophies make up part of the objects on display. Most of the objects come from one hunt when Russian Czar Alexander III came in 1885 and met with Emperor Franz Josef. The room where they talked still has furniture from the time and portraits of the two rulers, though it's by no means the most impressive room. The library hall has thousands of rare books plus a lovely allegorical ceiling fresco. Pages of some of the books can be seen on the château's Web site. Even more opulent is the Assembly Hall, which housed Austria's parliament in 1848, and has another ceiling fresco and several chandeliers. The painting gallery includes a masterpiece by Titian. The château is also renowned for its two gardens. The Podzámecká Garden is a fairly wild park with a river flowing through it. The Libosad, the more famous of the two, is about a kilometer from the château; it's a mathematically laid-out flower garden with rotunda in the middle and statue-filled colonnade on the side. The complex also has a mint with a coin display, located a few hundred yards from the main house. Three different tours are offered. ⊠ *Směnovní náměstí 1* ☎ *573–502–011* ⊕ *www.azz.cz* ✉ *Tours: Historical halls 80 Kč, 160 with English explanation; art gallery 30 Kč, 60 with English explanation; sala terrena 10 Kč, 20 with English explanation. Tower: 40 Kč. Podzámecká Garden free. Libosad 10 Kč. Mint: 10 Kč* ☉ *Apr. and Oct., weekends 9–5; May, June, Sept., Tues.–Sun. 9–5; July and Aug., Tues.–Sun. 9–6.*

Kroměříž Essentials

TRANSPORTATION It's best to combine a trip to Kroměříž with Brno or Olomouc; it's somewhat closer to Olomouc.

By car from Brno, Kroměříž is east on Highway E462 to Vyškov, where you turn onto Route 41. The trip is about 50 km (30 mi) and takes about 90 minutes.

Direct bus service from Brno's Zvonařka bus station takes 1¼ hour and costs around 55 Kč. Direct bus service from Olomouc's main bus station takes between 60 and 90 minutes and costs around 40 Kč.

Train service from Brno is inconvenient and expensive, requiring at least one change, usually at Kojetín; the trip takes almost two hours and costs around 100 Kč. Train service from Olomouc's main station requires at least one change, usually at Hulín, and takes at least 1¼ hours; the 45-km (27-mi) trip costs around 65 Kč.

MORAVSKÝ KRAS

🕐 **㉑** *30 km (19 mi) north of Brno; 226 km (141 mi) southeast of Prague.*

If it's scenic rather than military tourism you want, take a short trip north from Brno up the Svitava Valley and into the Moravský Kras (Moravian Karst), an area of limestone formations, underground stalactite caves, rivers, and tunnels. The most interesting part of the karst is in the vicinity of Blansko and includes several caves. You can arrange tours 8 km (5 mi) from the outskirts of Blansko at the Skalní Mlýn Hotel or the Moravian Karst information office.

Kateřinská jeskyně (Catherine Cave; Skalní mlýn) is set amid thickly forested ravines, and visitors taking the half-hour tour are serenaded by recorded opera tunes. ⊠ *Skalní mlý* ☎ *516–418–602, 516–413–57 information, 516–410–024 advance tickets* ⊕ *www.cavemk.cz* ✉ *40 Kč* ☉ *Apr.–Sept., daily 8–4; Mar. and Oct., daily 8–2, hrs vary depending on number of visitors.*

Fodor'sChoice The most interesting of the Moravian caves is **Punkevní jeskyně** (Punkva
★ Cave). A tour includes a boat trip along an underground river to the watery bottom of **Macocha Abyss,** the deepest drop of the karst (more than 400 feet). On this tour, a little motorized "train" links the Skalní Mlýn Hotel to the Punkva Cave, from where a funicular climbs to the lip of Macocha Abyss. Punkva Cave is normally open year-round, but check with the information service for up-to-date information. It's always advisable to arrive at least an hour before scheduled closing time in order to catch the day's last tour. ⊠ *Skalní mlýn* ☎ *516–418–602, 516–413–57 information, 516–419–701, 516–410–024 advance tickets for both caves* ⊕ *www.cavemk.cz* ✉ *Cave 100 Kč, funicular 50 Kč* ☉ *Punkva Cave Apr.–Sept., daily 8–3:30; Oct.–Mar., daily 8–2. Funicular Apr.–Sept., daily 8–5; Oct.–Mar., hrs vary depending on number of visitors.*

Moravský Kras Essentials

TRANSPORTATION The caves are accessible from Blansko, which is just north of Brno. Direct train service from Brno's main train station leaves several times a day for the 22-km (13-mi) trip that takes 30 minutes and costs around 35 Kč.

Bus service requires a change at Lipůvka and takes 1 hour and 10 minutes for a 32-km (19-mi) trip that costs 22 Kč. The caves are a 5-km (3-mi) hike outside of Blansko.

By car, take Highway E461 north of Brno to Route 379, and then go east, just past Blansko. The trip is about 25 km (15 mi) and takes less than a half hour.

Underground or on the surface, the walking is excellent in the karst, and if you miss one of the few buses running between the town of Blansko and the cave region, you may have to hoof it. Try to obtain a map in Brno or from the Moravian Karst information office in the settlement of Skalní Mlýn. Look for Čertův most (Devil's Bridge), a natural bridge high over the road just past the entrance to Catherine Cave. You can follow the path, indicated with yellow markers, from the cave for another couple of miles to the Macocha Abyss. Before setting out, check with the information office or at the bus station for current bus schedules; for much of the year the last bus from Skalní Mlýn back to Blansko leaves at around 3 PM.

OLOMOUC

★ ㉒ *77 km (48 mi) northeast of Brno; 275 km (165 mi) southeast of Prague.*

Olomouc is a paradox—so far from Austria yet so supportive of the empire. The Hapsburgs always felt at home here, even when they were being violently opposed by Czech nationalists and Protestants throughout Bohemia and much of Moravia. During the revolutions of 1848, when the middle class from all over the Austro-Hungarian Empire seemed ready to boot the Hapsburgs out of their palace, the royal family fled to Olomouc. Mozart, Mahler, and other famous composers stopped by on occasion, and the resulting musical heritage they left behind means that the city has an active classical music scene to this day. A discount card called the **Olomouc card** is valid for most tourist sites in and around the city and is available for 150 Kč for 24 hours or 220 Kcfor 72 hours. Included are the Town Hall tower, botanical gardens, zoo, Hrad Bouzov, Hrad Šternberk, and other sites. The card also provides discounts at some restaurants, pools, fitness centers, and hotels. You can buy the card—and get more information on discounts and deals—at the main tourist information center at Horní náměstí 1.

Despite being overshadowed by Brno, Olomouc, with its proud square and prim 19th-century buildings, still has the feel of a provincial imperial capital, not unlike similarly sized cities in Austria. The Old Town, situated on a slight rise over a tributary of the River Morava, luckily managed to escape damage during the July 1997 floods that inundated a huge swath of Moravia, Poland, and eastern Germany. The most prominent open space in Olomouc is the triangular Horní náměstí (Upper Square). Four of the city's half-dozen renowned **baroque fountains,** depicting Hercules (1687), Caesar (1724), Neptune (1695), and Jupiter (1707), dot the square and the adjacent Dolní náměstí (Lower Square) to the south.

Fodor'sChoice ★ The eccentric **Morový sloup** (Trinity Column), in the northwest corner of Horní náměstí, is one of the best surviving examples of the Olomouc baroque style, which was prevalent in this region of Moravia after the Thirty Years' War. At 35 meters, it's the tallest plague column in the Czech Republic and houses a tiny chapel. The column—but not the rest of the square (or the city)—is a UNESCO World Heritage Site. Its construction was begun in 1717, but it was not completed until 1754, long after the death of its principal designer, Václav Render, who left all his wealth to the city of Olomouc so that the column could be completed. Inside is a small chapel, that is unfortunately never open. ⊠ *Horní náměstí.*

Olomouc's central square is marked by the bright, spire-bedecked Renaissance **Radnice** (Town Hall) with its 220-foot tower. The tower was begun in the late 14th century and given its current appearance in 1443; the Astronomical Clock on the outside was built in 1422 and once rivaled the one in Prague. It was mostly destroyed by an artillery shell on the last two days of World War II. The modern social-realist mosaic decorations of the current clock date from 1955. Be sure to look inside the town hall at the beautiful stairway. You can also visit a large Gothic banquet room in the main building, with scenes from the city's history, and also a late-Gothic chapel. Tours of the tower and chapel are given several times daily; contact the tourist office in the town hall. ⊠ *Horní nám.* ☎ *585–513–385 tourist office* 🎟 *Tours 10 Kč* ☉ *Mar.–Oct., daily 9–7; Nov.–Feb., daily 9–5.*

> **need a break?** The wooden paneling and floral upholstery in the **Café Mahler** (⊠ Horní nám. 11) recall the taste of the 1880s, when Gustav Mahler briefly lived just around the corner while working as a conductor at the theater on the other side of the Upper Square. It's a good spot for ice cream, cake, or coffee.

The original **Chrám svatého Mořice** (Church of St. Maurice) stood just north of the Horní náměstí in 1257, but nothing is left of that structure. A new church was started in 1412 on the same site and remodelled many times. Its current fierce, gray exterior dates from the middle of the 16th century. A sculpture of Christ on the Mount of Olives dates to the 15th century. The baroque organ inside, the largest in the Czech Republic, originally contained 2,311 pipes until it was expanded in the 1960s to more than 10,000 pipes. An international organ festival takes place in the church every September. ⊠ *Jana Opletalova ul.* ☉ *Hrs are sporadic, but church is often open during the day.*

The interior of triple-dome **Kostel svatého Michala** (St. Michael's Church) casts a dramatic spell. The frescoes, the high and airy central dome, and the shades of rose, beige, and gray trompe-l'oeil marble on walls and arches blend to a harmonious, if dimly glimpsed, whole. The decoration followed a fire in 1709, only 30 years after the original construction. Architect and builder are not known, but it's surmised they are the same team that put up the Church of the Annunciation on Svatý Kopeček (Holy Hill), a popular Catholic pilgrimage site just outside Olomouc. ⊠ *Žerotínovo nám., 1 block uphill from Upper Sq. along Školní ul.* ☉ *Hrs are sporadic, but church is often open during the day.*

Between the main square and the **Dóm svatého Václava** (Cathedral of St. Wenceslas) lies a peaceful neighborhood given over to huge buildings, mostly belonging either to the university or the archbishopric. As it stands today, the cathedral is just another example of the overbearing neo-Gothic enthusiasm of the late 19th century, having passed through just about every other architectural fad since its true Gothic days. ⊠ *Václavské nám.* ☉ *Daily 9–6.*

Next to the cathedral is the entrance to the **Palác Přemyslovců** (Přemyslid Palace), which houses a museum where you can see early-16th-century wall paintings decorating the Gothic cloisters and, upstairs, a wonderful series of two- and three-arch Romanesque windows. This part of the building was used as a schoolroom some 700 years ago, and you can still make out drawings of animals engraved on the walls by early vandals. You can get an oddly phrased English-language pamphlet at the entrance to help you around the building. ⊠ *Václavské nám.* 🎫 *15 Kč* ⊘ *Apr.–Oct., Tues.–Sun. 9–12:30 and 1–5.*

The **Děkanství.** (Deacon's House), opposite the cathedral, now part of Palacký University, has two unusual claims to fame. Here, in 1767, the young musical prodigy Wolfgang Amadeus Mozart, age 11, spent six weeks recovering from a mild attack of chicken pox. The 16-year-old King Wenceslas III suffered a much worse fate here in 1306, when he was murdered, putting an end to the Přemyslid dynasty. The house is not open to the public. ⊠ *Václavské nám.*

off the beaten path

★

HRAD BOUZOV (Bouzov Castle) – One of Moravia's most impressive castles—30 km (18 mi) west of Olomouc—has been featured in several fairy-tale films; it also stood in as a school for the Nazi elite in the 2004 German film *Napola*. Its present romanticized exterior comes from a remodeling at the turn of the 20th century, but the basic structure dates back to the 1300s. It was owned by the Order of Teutonic Knights from the late 1600s up to the end of World War II, when it was confiscated by the state. Inside, the knights' hall has extensive carved-wood decorations and wall paintings that look old, even if many are reconstructions. Other rooms have collections of period furniture. The castle kitchen, which was used up to 1945, is one of the best preserved examples. Four tours are available, with the grand tour offering most of the highlights. The supplementary tour (doplňková trasa) includes a secret passage. You can easily arrange a tour from the tourist information office in Olomouc; the castle is included in the Olomouc card. ⊠ *Bouzov 8, Bouzov* ☎ *585–346–201* ⊕ *www.hrad-bouzov.cz* 🎫 *Classic tour 80 Kč; grand tour 120 Kč; supplementary tour 120 Kč; château room tour 120 Kč* ⊘ *Apr. and Oct., weekends 9–3; May–Sept., daily except Mon. 9–4.*

HRAD ŠTERNBERK (Sternberg Castle) – Part of the tower and walls of this castle—which is 18 km (11 mi) north of Olomouc—date to the late 13th century, but several conflicts left marks on the structure. The building was all but ruins before an extensive reconstruction in the late 19th and early 20th century. One of the main attractions is a set of Renaissance tile stoves. An architectural point of interest is the well-preserved medieval privy. It's admission is included in the Olomouc card. The short tour covers the castle; a long tour includes the entirety of the short tour plus some objects collected from other Moravian castles. ⊠ *Horní náměstí 6, Šternberk* ☎ *585–012–935* ⊕ *www.sternberk.cz* ⊘ *Apr. and Oct., weekends 9–3; May–Sept., Tues.–Sun. 9–4; Nov. and Dec., weekends 10–2* 🎫 *Short tour 60 Kč; long tour 80 Kč.*

Where to Stay & Eat

$–$$$ **Moravská restaurace a vinárná.** Traditional Moravian dishes like roast duck with cabbage, chicken breast stuffed with almond butter, or roast piglet are served in an interior decorated with rustic images and motifs. The wine cellar, open Monday through Friday, is a bit homier than the street-level restaurant. The staff wears folk costumes, and live musicians sometimes perform folk music of the region. International wines are available alongside a large selection of Moravian wine. ⊠ *Horní náměstí 23* ☎ *585–222–868* ▤ *AE, MC, V.*

$ ⊡ **Flora.** Don't expect luxury at this 1960s cookie-cutter high-rise, about a 15-minute walk from the town square. To its credit, the staff is attentive (English is spoken), and the pleasant, if anonymous, rooms are certainly adequate for a short stay. ⊠ *Krapkova 34, 779 00* ☎ *585–422–200* 🖷 *585–421–211* ⊕ *www.hotel-flora.cz* ↝ *140 rooms, 4 suites* ⌂ *Restaurant, cable TV, some pets allowed (fee); no a/c* ▤ *AE, DC, MC, V* ⏺ *BP.*

$ ⊡ **U Dómu svatého Václava.** This pleasant place represents a new class of Czech hotel and pension: you can find modernized fittings installed in the old house. The six small suites all have kitchenettes. It's just down the street from the sleepy Václavské náměstí, where the Cathedral of St. Wenceslas is. ⊠ *Dómská 4, 772 00* ☎ *585–220–502* 🖷 *585–220–501* ↝ *6 rooms* ⌂ *Kitchenettes, cable TV; no a/c* ▤ *AE, MC, V* ⏺ *BP.*

Olomouc Essentials

It's a wash in terms of travel time between taking a train or driving yourself to Olomouc. Car travel is usually faster to Olomouc from Prague via Brno, as much more of the trip is by highway. Take Highway E65 (also called E50) to Brno and then Highway E462 to Olomouc. The trip takes three hours.

Direct train travel from Prague takes at least 3¼ hours and costs around 300 Kč for the 250-km (150-mi) trip.

Direct bus service from Prague's Florenc bus station takes between four and five hours and costs around 170 Kč for the 262-km (157-mi) trip. Bus service with a change in Brno can be faster, however, at 3½ hours; the 300-km (180-mi) trip costs about 280 Kč.

🛈 **Olomouc Tourist Information** ⊠ Radnice, Horní nám., Olomouc ☎ 585–513–385 ⊕ www.olomouc-tourism.cz, www.olomoucko.cz.

UNDERSTANDING PRAGUE

PRAGUE AT A GLANCE

TIME'S MAGPIE

A SHORT HISTORY OF THE CZECH REPUBLIC

THE CZECHS AND THEIR BEER

BOOKS & MOVIES

CZECH VOCABULARY

PRAGUE AT A GLANCE

Fast Facts

Nickname: City of a Hundred Spires, the Golden City, Paris of the Twenties in the Nineties, the Heart of Europe
Type of government: Democratic self-governed municipality with 57 districts, each with elected bodies and administrative offices and a municipal assembly, with 70 members elected according to a system of proportional representation. Members of the Assembly elect the mayor of the city and 11 members of the City Council.
Population: 1.2 million

Population Density: 2,419 people per square km (6,250 people per square mi)
Median age: 38.6
Ethnic groups: Czech 93%; other (Moravian, Slovak, Polish, German, Ukrainian, Vietnamese) 7%
Religion: Unaffiliated 67%; Roman Catholic 18%; other 8%; Hussite 2%; evangelical 1%

If not us, who? If not now, when?
— Slogan by Czech university students in Prague, November 1989

Geography & Environment

Latitude: 50° N (same as Amiens, France; Krakow, Poland; Vancouver, Canada)
Longitude: 14° E (same as Valletta, Malta; Tripoli, Libya)
Elevation: 245 meters (803 feet)
Land area: 496 square km (192 square mi)
Terrain: Straddles the Vltava River
Natural hazards: Floods
Environmental issues: Air pollution from Prague's traffic is a problem, with sulfur dioxide and lead on the decrease, but still at levels far above government goals. The city estimates that about one-third of its population lives with excessive noise, mostly road traffic. The vibration and pollution from traffic is also damaging the city's famous old buildings.

Prague is like a vertical Venice . . . steps everywhere.
— Penelope Gilliatt

Economy

Unemployment: 2.8%
Major industries: Aircraft engines, automobiles, beer, chemicals, diesel engines, furniture, machine tools, optical instruments, processed food, railroads, streetcars

Did You Know?

• Nicknamed "the heart of Europe," Prague is almost exactly in the center of the continent. The city is the same distance from the Baltic Sea, North Sea, and the Adriatic Sea.

• The 18-acre Prague Castle is the world's largest ancient castle. Its 9th-century polygon design is an average of 128 meters (420 feet) wide.

• The average tourist stays in Prague for almost four days.

• In August 2002 the Vltava River swelled to flood Prague. The Charles

Bridge closed, so did the metro, the Four Seasons, the Inter-Continental, and the Hilton. By the time the river level dropped, more than a dozen people were dead, and the city was hit with nearly $3 billion in damage.

• Since 1995, several services have driven drunk drivers home in Prague. The companies send two men in a car to wherever an inebriated driver is, using one of the employees to get the driver home, while the other follows in a car. The service costs about 30 koruna (a bit more than $1). One of the largest companies makes 200 trips per night. The Czech Republic has a zero-tolerance policy for drunk driving.

• Prague's U Fleku brewery is one of the world's oldest, operating since 1499. The city's ties to beer include the world's first beer museum, printing of first brewing textbook, and the world's first president, Prague native Vaclav Havel, to have written a play based on his experiences working in a brewery.

• The Vltava River reaches its widest point of 330 meters (1,080 feet) in Prague. Many of the city's bridges were put in over ancient fords.

TIME'S MAGPIE

FORGET THE LONG DAYS. When the days are long, bands of Germans and Italians and Japanese and British mob the narrow streets of Old Town, and herds of American college students in velvet jester hats and PRAGUE DRINKING TEAM T-shirts stampede across the Charles Bridge singing Pearl Jam songs. But in March or April, the worst of the winter is over and tourist hoards have yet to descend; by early September the summer crowds have dispersed. On the edge of a season it is still possible to duck onto a narrow, cobbled side street to find it deserted and to feel time straddling centuries the way Prague straddles its river. So many of Europe's cities have been bombed and burnt and torn down and rebuilt again that their physical history survives in stray fragments or not at all, but Prague is time's magpie, hoarding beautiful, eclectic bits from each successive era. In Prague, Gothic towers neighbor eleventh-century courtyards, which lead to Baroque and Renaissance houses with twentieth-century bullets embedded in their walls. Art Nouveau hotels abut formerly socialist department stores that now sell French perfume and American sneakers. Through a combination of luck, circumstance, and obstinance, Prague has stockpiled ten centuries of history.

The city's unrelenting profusion of stimuli forces the brain to screen things out, until one day a new sort of detail will ambush an unconscious filter and then appear everywhere, remaking once-familiar streets. Almost every city block displays a plaque commemorating Prague's countless martyrs from across the centuries—resistance fighters and outspoken nationalists, religious heroes and fallen soldiers. Usually these plaques are placed over doorways, or just above eye level on a building's edge. Small and made of dark, weathered metal, they are easily over-looked but upon noticing one the rest appear, Prague's long, sad memory emerging with each additional step. It becomes impossible to go anywhere without noticing more names; Prague becomes a city overrun by death. Then, the eye will be diverted from the funereal by an ornamental frog decorating a doorway or a marble frieze of a violinist fronting an apartment building that was a music school a century before. It becomes apparent that almost every building is charmingly adorned—even in the shabbier neighborhoods lion heads roar above doorways or cherubs recline below windows. The memorial plaques fade into the background.

The nemesis of ornament, Prague's graffiti also exists at first as visual static, soft and persistent and easily glossed over. Spray paint crawls across delicate Art Nouveau façades; black tags mar eighteenth-century marble; names are keyed into granite landings and wooded window sills. In the wake of the Velvet Revolution, graffiti has spread like mold along the city's edifices, leaving practically no surface untouched. Here, where old beautiful buildings are the default rather than the treasured exceptions to time's entropic rule—and where rich architecture belies an impoverished budget—it's impossible to safeguard everything. Freed from Communism's straitjacket, the entire city is now wrapped in scrawl.

But the beauty of Prague's youth almost excuses their penchant for vandalism. Preternaturally appealing creatures with sculptural faces, creamy skin, and long, supple limbs, they lean against buildings, cigarettes dangling from their lips. They sip slow drinks in cafes; they spill onto the streets in acid-washed jeans. They cultivate looks of boredom that highlight their full lips and Slavic cheekbones. Their attractiveness is alarming in its universality and in its disappearance at the earliest intimation of middle age. Prague's denizens breathe coal-laced air, drink polluted water, and live on boiled dumplings and pork cutlets, beer and cigarettes—a diet that generally allots a person only three good decades. Faces become haggard and loose-skinned; bellies grow and arms become flaccid; spines curve; strange lumps and moles appear.

In Prague there is no culture of continuing care facilities or retirement communities. The old are not shunted away, nor do they move to sunny locales with more golfing opportunities. Prague is home to stooped old ladies with necks crooked like canes, and old ladies with perfect posture. There are old ladies in sensible, square-toed shoes and old ladies with sagging pantyhose stuffed inside bright red Mary Janes, old ladies with large handbags and fuzzy wool caps they knit themselves, and old ladies in ratty fur coats. In Prague the blue-haired old lady is no less common than the violet-haired old lady or the scarlet-haired old lady—punk rock dye-jobs hallucinatory in their vibrancy, and which are still commonplace a decade after the arrival of Western cosmetics might have been expected to impose a certain refinement of hue. Sometimes old ladies are in the company of old men but mostly old ladies are alone, or with old lady friends, or with small, unfriendly dogs. Husbands die, and perhaps there is a small pension, but old ladies still carry baskets filled with groceries. They still make their painstaking way down sidewalks and hold their breath as they risk the first stair of a speeding escalator.

The velocity and intensity with which Prague's inhabitants age merely mirrors time's unlikely acrobatics from one city block to the next. A street frequently occupies two centuries at once. In the city center, a TGI Friday's inhabits an eighteenth-century mansion; signs posted on elegant, antique streetlamps display the word CASINO in Czech, English, Japanese, and Hebrew; a fourteenth-century boulevard contains a McDonald's, a Pizza Hut, and numerous discos, its sidewalk hucksters proclaiming the virtues of nearby strip clubs.

Prague's magpie instincts are not strictly temporal. The mad rush toward Westernization has resulted in a spectacular street mélange of consumer culture, international tourism, and incipient capitalism. In Old Town, a restaurant tout sports an oversized sombrero and a Mexican poncho on which are emblazoned the words PIZZA and FELAFEL, while a restaurant named Chicago advertises Mexican cuisine. A gaggle of schoolgirls squawks, in accented English, "We're from Belgium, mighty mighty Belgium." their voices echoing through the streets. A flock of Japanese tourists photographs the clock tower from the opposite side of Old Town Square, their flashes impotent against the deepening night. Kerchiefed, thick-fingered snack-stand proprietors vend—in addition to the traditional sausages and fried cheese—a frozen treat called "Rentgen!" a fluorescent yellow Popsicle on a black skeleton-shaped stick, bearing a radioactive symbol on its wrapper. On a pedestrian plaza, a street vendor waves a crumpled piece of paper at a cop in desperation, blocking his briefcase of fake Soviet artifacts with his body. From a loudspeaker fronting a downtown bingo hall, a voice drones each successive number in a robotic monotone that suggests imminent death from boredom. At a tram stop, a stray mutt trots back and forth before a woman eating a roll until she feeds him some crumbs. Prague's human beggars opt for complete prostration, face down on their elbows and knees, hands proffered in supplication, a square of newspaper tucked under their legs for cushioning, but the dogs have better luck.

In the years since Communism's demise, gambling has become as common as graffiti. Along neighborhood streets, twenty-four-hour *hernas* advertise the day's accumulated jackpot on digital street displays, while inside the door, catatonic men feed coins into slot machines. Off-track betting parlors inhabit every major subway station. It's easy to become disheartened. Hopefully, discouragement will cast the gaze downward to Prague's sidewalks. They are not concrete or slate, but marble mosaics that stretch from the city's touristed center to its most ordinary neighborhoods; they are part of the city's fabric, nearly daring to be overlooked. There are never more than two colors of stone to a sidewalk, but those colors change. Sometimes the stones are gray and white, sometimes roseate and white, marble cubes the size of children's blocks forming patterns that shift from block to block— sometimes diamonds, sometimes a checkerboard, sometimes squares of varying shape. Who decides the pattern? Is there a plan in a municipal building somewhere mandating which city block receives nesting squares and which lines of diamonds? Occasionally small piles of marble cubes rest beside a patchy sidewalk,

waiting to be set in place by a sidewalk fixer in blue overalls. Oblivious to the street traffic, he will patiently tap each stone into place with a metal mallet and a bricklayer's hammer, his methods no different from the pavers of 1763. In the intervening years, empire has been replaced by Communism, which has been supplanted by capitalism, each passing era leaving its mark but not obscuring what came before. The sidewalks persist in their mosaic geometrics. Whether ruled by emperor or dictator or venture capitalist, Prague is simply too old and its habits too engrained not to remain faithful to itself.

— Myla Goldberg

From TIME'S MAGPIE: A Walk in Prague by Myla Goldberg. Copyright 2004 Myla Goldberg. Illustrations copyright 2004 Ken Nash. Published by Crown Journeys, member of the Crown Publishing Group, a division of Random House, Inc.

A SHORT HISTORY OF THE CZECH REPUBLIC

BEING AT THE HEART OF THINGS CAN BE A GREAT ADVANTAGE, but not always. For the Czechs, their place in the center of Europe has been a mixed blessing at best. Over the years, several of their neighbors have marched merrily into their land and set up shop. The current phase of independence since the so-called "Velvet Revolution" of 1989 is only the third short period of self-determination for the Czech Republic since 1526.

On May 1, 2004, the Czech Republic entered the EU. Given the concerns over national sovereignty exhibited in many other countries, one may be surprised that the Czechs made little fuss over their impending membership. However, the road they have taken is the expedient one, and pragmatism is a Czech specialty, along with a tradition of liberal democracy, intellectualism, and tolerance. Centuries have been spent crafting these skills; the training program has been arduous, and it may continue for some time still as the country enters the European free-for-all.

Beginnings

The Celts are the first modern humans known to have settled the area. Between the 3rd and 7th centuries they were assimilated by the influx of Slavs migrating westward into much of central and southeastern Europe. During the 8th and 9th centuries the Great Moravian Empire occupied the area and was the first political structure approximating a state in Europe to accept Christianity.

Czech legend has it that Prague was first seen in a vision by the beautiful Queen Libuse, who predicted the rise of a great city as she stood at Vysehrad. Libuse is also said to be the fount of the Přemysl Dynasty, a bloodthirsty bunch that would rule Bohemia until the 14th century. Václav I was killed by his brother "Boleslav The Cruel" around 930, thus becoming not only a Czech saint but also the world-famous

Good King Wenceslas of the Christmas carol.

A Kingdom Grows in Power

Throughout the 12th and 13th centuries the Czech kingdom steadily grew, in large part thanks to its position on several continental trade routes. Under Karel IV (1316–78) the medieval Czech state reached the height of its powers. Many of the best known buildings in Prague were constructed under his direction, including St. Vitus's Cathedral (1344), the Charles Bridge (1357), and Charles University (1348), which was the first center of higher education in Central Europe.

Prague's development into a European center brought new ideas, knowledge, and customs to the country, including the writings of church reformer John Wycliffe. Wycliffe's views strongly influenced the young priest Jan Hus, who preached in Czech at Betlémská kaple. Predictably less than impressed, Catholic authorities burnt Hus at the stake on July 6, 1415. This only served to radicalize his followers, the Hussites, even further. In 1419 the Hussites introduced the traditional Czech practice of defenestration by throwing seven town councillors out of the New Town Hall windows.

Five crusades were sent by the pope to crush the Hussites, but the Czech reformers, led by the one-eyed Jan Žižka (1360–1424) repelled them all. Their nemesis however was within. The Hussites stumbled under the weight of infighting and promptly pressed the self-destruct button; the Battle of Lipany on May 30, 1434, saw the defeat of the radical "Taborite" Hussites by the moderate "Utraquists," who were composed mostly of the Protestant Czech nobility, also known as the "Estates." The Utraquists reached agreement with the Catholic Church in 1436, strengthening the Estates' own political position at the same time.

Enter the Hapsburgs

In 1526, thanks to the weakness of central authority, the vacant Bohemian throne was taken by the Austrian Hapsburgs. This dominion would continue for the next four centuries. The Hapsburgs' first move was to gather power back to the throne. The Estates launched a rebellion in 1547 to reclaim the throne for the Czechs, but it was unsuccessful.

Hapsburg Emperor Ferdinand II moved his court to Prague for the period of his reign (1576–1611). Variously described as an inspired eccentric or a soft-headed fool, Ferdinand enthusiastically sponsored the arts and sciences, and Prague filled with painters, physicists, architects, and alchemists. This period is considered to have provided much of the city's mystical character; it also produced many of Prague's precious baroque architecture. It was also Ferdinand II who first introduced artists working with glass to the Czech lands, and from them the famous Bohemian crystal evolved. Crystal is still a mainstay of today's tourist industry, as a brief wander through Prague confirms.

As the Hapsburgs rescinded the religious freedom of Protestants, 1618 saw Prague's citizens orchestrated the second defenestration in 1618, which sparked another rebellion by the Estates. The rebels were crushed in 1620 at the Battle of Bílá Hora (White Mountain) on the western edge of Prague.

These events ignited the Thirty Years' War, which engulfed much of Europe. The defeat of the Protestant forces, coupled with the ire of the Austrian Empire toward their troublesome northern territory led to harsh repercussions and a clampdown on religious and political freedoms.

In the 18th and 19th centuries, the Czech lands, especially the border regions, developed into the industrial base of the Austrian power bloc. As in many parts of Europe in the mid-19th century, however, along with the urbanization that accompanied the industrial revolution came revolutionary impetus of a different complexion. Writers and philosophers, stressing the importance of the Czech language—then practically defunct—were at the forefront of the Czech National Revival movement, which called for greater autonomy within the Empire.

Liberation and a New Dictator

World War I served to unite the factions pushing for liberalization. The U.S.-based Czech National Council, led by philosophy professor Tomáš Masaryk (1850–1937), gained Allied recognition as the valid voice of the country. In November 1918, Masaryk became the President of the Czechoslovak Republic (these days known as the "First Republic"). It was one of the few genuinely democratic states in Europe during the period between the two world wars.

After much agitation of the large German minority, who lived in the "Sudenten" border regions, Adolph Hitler browbeat the Allied powers into ceding to him parts of Czechoslovakia in September 1938. Most of the Republic's other neighbors then chimed in to snatch pieces of territory.

Throughout World War II, the Czech lands were occupied by the Nazis; Slovakia, meanwhile, became an "independent" Nazi state. Czechoslovak President Edvard Beneš (1884–1948) fled to England in 1940, where he faced an uphill battle with the Western leaders who continued for some time to advocate Hitler's appeasement.

The Czech resistance movement was small but dedicated. Their greatest success was the assassination of the vicious *Reichsprotektor* Reinhard Heidrich in 1942. The Czechs suffered terrible retributions for this, particularly the small central-Bohemian villages of Lidice and Ležáky, both of which were completely obliterated.

A few days ahead of the arrival of Allied forces, the Czechs fought the occupiers in the Prague Uprising. While U.S. forces paused at Plzeň, Prague was officially liberated by Soviet troops, as agreed between the Allies at the Yalta Conference. Shortly after the end of the war, the Beneš Decrees were signed; these expelled the majority of the German population from Czechoslovakia, an issue that has recently returned to the forefront at the behest of Austria and some German regions, and which the Czechs refuse to countenance.

Communists Take Hold

The Communists gained a foothold of power in the May 1946 elections. In 1948 the communists staged the so-called "February Coup," taking full control and banning opposition parties. Klement Gottwald (1896–1953) became the first "working class President" of Czechoslovakia. Industry and agriculture were instantly nationalized, and a series of purges and show trials, under the auspices of Soviet "advisers," began.

As has so often been the case in the Czech Republic, the liberalization that started to creep in throughout the 1960s was prompted by the intellectual community: writers, musicians, and filmmakers all helped to push the official limits. Meeting them halfway was the recently appointed First Secretary of the Communist Party: Slovak Alexander Dubček (1921–92), whose program to create what he called "Socialism with a human face" became synonymous with the "Prague Spring" of 1968.

The Soviet Union was less than impressed with the reforms taking place in their small socialist brother land. On the night of August 20, 1968, forces from all Warsaw Pact nations (except Romania) entered Czechoslovakia to put an end to the intellectual uprising. As Russian tanks roamed the streets, the Czechoslovak leaders were invited to Moscow, where a memorandum was signed requesting the extended presence of Soviet troops to pro-

tect against further insurgency. Protesting against the invasion of his country, Jan Palach (1948–69), a philosophy student, burnt himself to death in Wenceslas Square in January 1969.

For the next two decades Czechoslovakia was to experience some of the most repressive conditions in the Eastern Bloc. "Normalization" did not depend on show trials and executions, as in the 1950s, but steadily ground the population down through economic and bureaucratic oppression. Once again it was the scholarly types that led what resistance there was, the best known organization being Charter 77.

A Real Nation

At the end of the 1980s, with Mikhail Gorbachev's stewardship of the Soviet Union, Communist regimes around Eastern Europe were falling. In Czechoslovakia, the "Velvet Revolution," a peaceful overthrow of the Communists, started on November 17, 1989. Strikes were punctuated by huge demonstrations around the country. As ever, in Prague, Wenceslas Square was at center stage: the crowds would jangle their keys, telling the Communists that it was time to leave.

Heading the negotiations with the government was an amalgamation of non-Communists known as the Civic Forum, headed by absurdist playwright Václav Havel (b. 1936), who was then elected to the presidency in 1990. In 1992 election results paved the way for the split of the Czechoslovak union, for the most part over the rate and method of economic reforms. Divorce was the politically expedient course, and despite protestations and eventually a resignation by Havel, on January 1, 1993, the two went their separate ways.

Havel was subsequently elected the first President of the Czech Republic. His dual role as intellectual artist and spokesman for a globalized humanitarian political ideal helped stimulate a vision of Prague as an artistic city, an image that, along with cheap beer, did much to attract the thousands of foreigners that reside here today.

Since the amicable split with Slovakia, the Czech Republic—and Prague in particular—has gone on to firmly establish itself as a hub of the region. The country's traditional role as a high-tech center and aggressive free-market policies (which have led to both successes and failures), and its position at the heart of Europe have all helped to attract investment from abroad and the establishment of many international businesses. While the picture isn't entirely rosy—an overburdened health-care system is not helped by the chronic pollution that is the fallout of the Czech role as the engineers of central Europe—the country's entrance in the EU is a hopeful sign that real sovereignty will continue.

— Tim Gosling

THE CZECHS & THEIR BEER

IN SOME PRAGUE PUBS, the minute you sit down a waiter comes and puts a beer (*pivo*) in front of you, making a little stroke-mark on a long, thin piece of paper. What else would anybody want but a beer? And why would anybody leave before the paper is filled with stroke marks? After all, Czech beer is, arguably, some of the best in all of Europe, and the Czechs are devoted consumers. Local consumption per capita is the highest of any country, with each person drinking about 43 gallons per year. Beer is much more popular in Bohemia than in Moravia, which means some thirsty Bohemians are picking up the slack for their vinophilic Moravian co-citizens.

Beer has been an integral part of Czech culture since the Dark Ages. Hops were an important crop as early as AD 900. In 1088 there's mention of a tax on hops in the foundation charter of Vyšehrad signed by Czech ruler Vratislav II. Laws originally only allowed home brewing, but by 1118, a communal brewery was established in Cerhenice, halfway between Prague and Kutná Hora. Special permission was needed to establish breweries for a long time after.

Holy Roman Emperor Rudolf II, who emptied Prague's royal coffers trying to turn lead into gold, made at least one sensible investment during his reign. In 1583 he sunk some money into the already existing Krušovice brewery, which is still running as a "royal brewery" and uses his name and likeness in their ad campaigns. His physician maintained that beer was good for health, a notion that is still widely held among the local population.

Other breweries have equally historical roots. Regent beer, for example, has been made in Třeboň since 1379; the brewery was founded by Augustinian monks and expanded in 1482 by the noble Rožmberk—

or Rosenberg—family, which explains the five-petal rose on the label. Other beers claim an even older heritage but are seldom seen outside of a small area where they are produced. In Prague the brewpub U Fleků has been making dark beer since 1499, although the current recipe dates from the turn of the 20th century.

Brewpubs used to be much more common in the country, but beer quality wasn't always good or consistent. One legend has it that a *vodník,* a kind of water sprite from fairy tales, went into a pub on Prague's Kampa island. He declared the beer to be little more than the river water he was used to drinking and put a curse on the place. The exact location of the cursed pub is unknown. The importance of the breweries is much less in question. In most beer-making towns (including Prague), special messengers were always ready at the main water towers to notify the breweries first in case a fire or other catastrophe was going to disrupt the water supply.

Almost all of the beer currently made in the Czech Republic is Pilsner-style beer, a light, golden-hue variety that was developed in 1842 in Plzeň, also known as Pilsen, in the west of Bohemia. Even if a beer label claims that the brewery has been around for centuries—and it very well may have been—the flavor of its beer is probably of more recent vintage. Before the 1840s, wheat beers were popular, especially dark brews in the Prague area. Dark beers (*černé* or *tmavé*) now make up only a few percentage points of the country's beer production and consumption. What gives Czech beer its distinctive bitter flavor are the hops from the Žatec region. The town of Žatec has a hops museum. Historically, trying to smuggle out hop seeds or cuttings, which would have threatened Bohemia's monopoly, carried very stiff penalties.

One step to standardizing beer quality was the development of the Balling Scale, by Czech chemist Karl Josef Napoleon Balling in the mid-19th century, to designate the amount of malt sugar at the start of fermentation. Most Czech pubs still designate beer as 10, 12, or more degrees. Some beers go as high as 24 degrees, but those are mostly high-alcohol novelty brews. A 10-degree beer has between 3 and 4 percent alcohol. The degree mark sometimes is printed as a percentage mark, which causes a bit of confusion; the alcohol content is about a quarter to a third of the Balling Scale degree. The degrees still appear in popular usage, with a 10-degree beer being called a *desítka*, and a 12-degree beer a *dvanáctka*. Although most breweries still use the Balling scale, a 2003 law requires that beer also be labeled with less specific terms of *výčepní, ležák,* or *speciální* for different strengths; further, the actual alcohol content of a beer must now be listed in the fine print on the label. Purists complain that the new labeling laws allow producers to be less strict with the quality of the malt.

The country's largest and most famous beer producer, Pilsner Urquell is still based in Plzeň. It has swallowed up a lot of its competition, though it still keeps the formerly independent brand names of Radegast and Kozel alive. The international conglomerate SABMiller now owns Pilsner Urquell, and the company has started to produce some Pilsner Urquell in Poland. Aggressive marketing has made the 12-degree Pilsner Urquell and its 10-degree sister brew Gambrinus the most common beers in Czech pubs.

Staropramen, brewed in Prague, is served in many central Bohemian pubs and has a large following. Staropramen is now owned by Belgian-based Interbrew. Pubs that carry Staropramen have recently started to carry imported Belgian beer on tap as well, but the reception for milder-flavor imports has been a bit slow, to say the least. Budvar, or Budweiser, is based in the southern Bohemian city of České Budějovice, and is one of the best-known names in beer-making. The company is involved in a long-running international legal dispute with Anheuser-Busch of the U.S. over the use of the name Budweiser. In German, České Budějovice was called Budweis. The Czech brand has won the rights to the name Budweiser in several important European markets. Budvar is less bitter than its main rivals.

A recent trend in Czech pubs has been a return to unpasteurized beer. Pasteurizing beer helps it to last longer, but heating the beer also damages its flavor. Several pubs with a high turnover have installed special tanks. Most carry Pilsner Urquell, but other brands are getting in on the trend as well. The unpasteurized beer is slightly cloudy and has a more pronounced hops flavor. Look for a sign near the door proclaiming the pub a *tankovná* if you'd like to try some unpasteurized beer.

If you had any doubts about the importance of beer in Czech culture, you can easily see its influence in popular literature and movies. Playwright and former President Václav Havel set one of his most famous plays, *Audience,* in a small-town brewery. Havel, who eschewed most pomp, also liked to take visiting dignitaries to local pubs. Jaroslav Hašek's main character in *The Good Soldier Švejk* spends most of his free time either in pubs or looking for pubs around the time of World War I. Švejk tells another soldier to meet him at a certain pub at 6 o'clock after the war, since he basically intends on being in the pub every night once his service is over. The pub he mentions, U Kalicha, is still around, and like several others it capitalizes on the image of the carefree, beer-guzzling, harmless soldier. The book also warned that any government that altered the price of beer would not last long. Jan Neruda's characters also typically frequented pubs in his *Malá Strana Stories.* He tried to paint fairly sympathetic pictures of the common man.

Much of Bohumil Hrabal's fiction also addresses pub culture. *The Snowdrop Festival*, based on his stories, was filmed in 1983 by Jiří Menzel. Menzel's Oscar-nominated *My Sweet Little Village*, based on an early script Kolya writer Zdeněk Svěrák, has a famous bit about storing beer on the proper step on the stairs. The

musical romantic comedy *The Hop Pickers* (*Starci na chmelu*) has been one of the most popular Czechoslovak films since it was released in 1964, and has been adapted into a musical stage play.

— Raymond Johnston

BOOKS & MOVIES

ENGLISH READERS have an excellent range of both fiction and nonfiction about the Czech Republic at their disposal. The most widely read Czech author of fiction in English is probably Milan Kundera, whose well-crafted tales illuminate both the foibles of human nature and the unique tribulations of life in Communist Czechoslovakia. *The Unbearable Lightness of Being* takes a look at the 1968 invasion and its aftermath through the eyes of a strained young couple. *The Book of Laughter and Forgetting* deals in part with the importance of memory and the cruel irony of how it fades over time; Kundera was no doubt coming to terms with his own forgetting as he wrote the book from his Paris exile. *The Joke*, Kundera's earliest work available in English, takes a serious look at the dire consequences of humorlessness among Communists.

Born and raised in the German-Jewish enclave of Prague, Franz Kafka scarcely left the city his entire life. *The Trial* and *The Castle* strongly convey the dread and mystery he detected beneath the 1,000 golden spires of Prague. Kafka worked as a bureaucrat for 14 years, in a job he detested; his books are, at least in part, an indictment of the bizarre bureaucracy of the Austro-Hungarian Empire, though they now seem eerily prophetic of the even crueler and more arbitrary Communist system that was to come.

In contrast, Jaroslav Hašek wandered far and wide, from childhood to his early death. Often described as an anarchist, Hašek was big and bawdy, often drunk, and fond of practical jokes. His unfinished novel *The Good Soldier Svĕjk* (often found with extended title *The Good Soldier Svĕjk and His Fortunes in the World War*) stars an idiot savant, who, by obeying orders to the letter, undermines the authority of the Austro-Hungarian army during World War I. Svĕjk has commonly

been heralded as typical of the Czech character by surviving absurd situations through his subversive wit and by thumbing his nose behind authority's back.

The most popular Czech authors at the close of the 20th century were those banned by the Communists after the Soviet invasion of 1968. Václav Havel and members of the Charter 77 group illegally distributed self-published manuscripts, or *samizdat* as they were called, of these banned authors—among them, Bohumil Hrabal, Josef Škvorecký, and Ivan Klíma. Many claim to have shared a table with Hrabal, perhaps the most beloved of all Czech writers, at his favorite pub in Prague, U Zlatéyho tygra. Hrabal's books include *I Served the King of England* and the lyrical *Too Loud a Solitude*, which is narrated by a lonely man who spends his days in the basement compacting the world's greatest works of literature along with bloodied butcher paper into neat bundles before they get carted off for recycling and disposal. Škvorecký sought refuge and literary freedom in Toronto in the early 1970s; his book *The Engineer of Human Souls* reveals the double censorship of the writer in exile—censored in the country of his birth and unread in his adopted home. Still, Škvorecký did gain a following thanks to his translator, Paul Wilson—who lived in Prague in the 1960s and '70s until he was ousted for his assistance in dissident activities. Wilson also set up 68 Publishers, which is responsible for the bulk of Czech literature from that period that is translated into English. Novelist, short story writer, and playwright Ivan Klíma is now one of the most widely read Czech writers in English; his books include the novels *Judge on Trial* and *Love and Garbage*, and *The Spirit of Prague*, a collection of essays about life in the post-Communist Czech Republic.

Václav Havel, onetime dissident playwright turned president of the Czech

Republic, is essential nonfiction reading. The best place to start is probably *Living in Truth,* which provides an absorbing overview of his own political philosophy and of Czechoslovak politics and history since 1968. Other recommended books by Havel include *Disturbing the Peace* (a collection of interviews with him) and *Letters to Olga.* Havel's plays explore the absurdities and pressures of life under the former Communist regime; the best example of his absurdist dramas is *The Memorandum,* which depicts a Communist bureaucracy more twisted than the streets of Prague's Old Town.

Among the most prominent of the younger Czech writers is Jáchym Topol, whose *A Visit to the Train Station* documents the creation of a new Prague with a sharp wit that cuts through the false pretenses of American youth occupying the city.

Prague figures in the work not only of Czech authors but also American and British writers, who have flocked to Prague to lead the expat life since 1990. Novelist Myla Goldberg revisits Prague in her short essay-book *Time's Magpie.* The characters of *Prague,* a novel by Arthur Phillips, have settled for Budapest, but it's Prague where they wish they lived. Or you can revisit Prague in the 1970s in Philip Roth's *The Prague Orgy.*

Film

Since the end of World War II, the Czech film industry has experienced two vastly differing conditions that have influenced its output. Until the fall of Communism the industry was state-run, which meant no box-office issues but strong censorship. Hand-in-hand with such freedom from commercial concerns, the famous FAMU school in Prague produced many cerebral filmmakers. The best-known period of Czech film came in the 1960s, when the Czech New Wave was at the forefront of the movement for liberalization. In addition, Czech animation has long been widely respected for its formal invention and haunting mix of fantasy

and black humor, as seen in Jan Švankmajer's *Little Otik,* an adaptation of a Czech fairy tale starring a tree stump that comes to life as a ravenous baby.

Miloš Forman is perhaps the best known Czech director. He emigrated to the United States in 1968, returning to Prague briefly in the early 1980s to film *Amadeus.* His New Wave films tend to involve everyday characters that are neither hero nor villain and include the satirical farce *Fireman's Ball* and the somewhat more sober *Loves of a Blonde.*

The tragicomic themes that many films of the New Wave investigate are exemplified in *The Shop On Main Street* (which received an Academy Award for best foreign-language film in 1966). Jan Kadar's and Elmar Klos's film concerns the predicament of a simple man who is caught between his conscience and his ability to ensure his personal safety from totalitarian authorities, in this case the occupying Nazis.

Jiří Menzel joined Forman in his exploration of a magnified realism, dallying on ostensibly mundane details. Menzel was another Oscar winner in 1968 with *Closely Observed Trains.* Adapted from Hrabal's novel by Menzel and the author himself, the tale follows a young railway dispatcher who is far more concerned with losing his virginity than resisting the Nazi occupation.

At the other end of the style spectrum were formal experimenters. Věra Chytilová's *Daises* features the crazed and destructive antics of two young girls, and it's either a bold expression of the director's flair for groundbreaking structure or a jumble of haphazard images. Possibly both. Meanwhile Jan Němec made his biggest impression, both on audiences and the censors, with the menacing and highly stylized *The Party and the Guests,* a condemnation of surrender to dominant ideology. Jaromil Jireš's starkly political version of Kundera's novel *The Joke* contrasts with his surreal vampire story: *Valerie and Her Week of Wonders.*

In 1990 Czech filmmakers were freed from the state censors but also suddenly cast into the free-market jungle. The older generation have struggled under these conditions, but younger directors have managed to produce a healthy number of thoughtful yet commercially viable films. Most successful of these has been Jan Svěrák, thanks in part to his saccharine tooth. *Kolya* (Academy Award for best foreign-language film in 1996), set in the final days of Communism, follows the transition of an aging bachelor when he inherits a young Russian "son." A more recent film, *Dark Blue World*, is an awkward yet somehow satisfying concoction of numerous story lines spanning fractured time lines and two languages.

In contrast, Petr Zelenka offers a darkly ironic sense of humor. *Year of The Devil* is a mock documentary following a local folk-rock band; the six disparate stories in *Buttoners* are only cobbled together at the finale. Jan Hřebejk is apparently working his way through contemporary history in chronological order, his films grounded in the gentle self-depreciation and humanism inherent in Czech humor. *Divided We Fall* is set in World War II; *Cozy Dens* deals with the period leading up to the 1968 invasion, and in *Pupendo* we are plunged back into "normalization" in the 1980s.

Recently, the historic locations of the city have become the darlings of Hollywood, and recent films, as disparate as *Van Helsing* and *Everything is Illuminated* have been shot in Prague. Keep yourself amused in Prague by spotting stars, and later amaze your friends by pointing out which Prague street the particular action hero or be-wigged dandy is pacing in each scene. Spot your favorite pub in *Mission Impossible, XXX,* or Terry Gilliam's *The Brothers Grimm* to name but three.

— Tim Gosling

CZECH VOCABULARY

Czech is considered a difficult language, but it is pronounced phonetically.

Consonants

c = a "ts" sound, as in *its*
č = a "ch" sound, as in *chair*
ch = a hard "ch" sound, as in *loch*
j = a "y" sound, as in *yes*
ň = an "ny" sound, as in *canyon*

r = a combination of "r" and
   "z," as in *Dvorak*
š = an "sh" sound, as in *shine*
z = a "z" sound, as in *zero*
ž = a "zh" sound, as in *pleasure*

Vowels

a = a short sound, as in *lamb*
e = a short sound, as in *best*
ě = a short "ye," as in *yes*
i, y = a short sound, as "i" in *city*
o = a short sond, as in *book*
u = pronounced as "oo" in *book*

á = a long sound, as in *father*
é = pronounced as "ai" in *air*
í, ý = as a long "e" sound, as in
   meet
ó = pronounced as "o" in *more*
ú, uŷ = prounced as "oo" in
   boom

English	Czech	Pronunciation

Basics

English	Czech	Pronunciation
Yes/no	Ano/ne	**ah**-no/neh
Please	Prosím	**pro**-seem
Thank you (kindly)	Děkuji	**dyek**-oo-yee
Excuse me	Pardon	**par**-don
Sorry [for doing something]	Promiňte	**proh**-meen-yteh
I'm sorry [about something]	Lituji	**liht**-oo-yee
Hello [during the day]	Dobrý den	**dohb**-ree den
Good evening	Dobrý vecer	**dohb**-ree veh-chehr
Goodbye [formal]	Na shledanou	**nas**-khleh-dah-noh-oo
Goodbye [informal]	Ahoj	**ah**-hoy
Today/During the day	Dnes	dnes
Tonight	Dnes večer	**dnes** veh-chehr
Tomorrow	Zítra	**zee**-trah
Do you speak English?	Mluvíte anglicky?	**mloo**-vit-eh ahng-**glit**-ski?
I don't speak Czech.	Nemluvím česky.	**neh**-mluv-eem **ches**-ky
I don't understand.	Nerozumím	**neh**-rohz-oom-eem
Please speak slowly.	Prosím, mluvte pomalu.	**pro**-seem, **mloov**-teh **poh**-mah-lo
Please write it down.	Prosím napište to.	**pro**-seem nah-**peesh**-teh toh
Please show me.	Ukažte mně	oo-**kazh**-te mnye

I am American (m/f).	Jsem Američan/ Američanka	sem ah-**mer**-i-chan/ ah-**mer**-i-chan-ka
I am English (m/f).	Jsem Angličan/ Angličanka	sem **ahn**-gli-chan/ **ahn**-gli-chan-ka
I am Australian (m/f).	Jsem Australan/ Australanka	sem **aus**-trah-lahn/ **aus**-trah-lahn-ka
I am Canadian (m/f).	Jsem Kanaďan/ Kanaďanka	sem **Kah**-nahd-yan/ **Kah**-nahd-yank-a
Right/left	Vlevo/ vpravo	**vleh**-voh/ **vprah**-voh
Open/closed	Otevřeno/ Zavřeno	**Oh**-tev-rzh-ehn-oh/ **zav**-rzh-ehn-oh
Arrival/departure	Příjezd/ Odjezd	**przhee**-yeezhd/ **oh**-dy eezhd
Where is . . . ?	Kde je . . .?	g-deh yeh
. . . the train station?	. . . Nádraží?	nah-**drah**-zee
. . . the bus station?	. . . Autobus?	**au**-toh-boos
. . . the bus stop?	. . . Autobus?	**au**-toh-boos
. . . the airport?	. . . Letiště?	**leh**-tish-tyeh
. . . a post office?	. . . Pošta?	**po**-shta
. . . a bank?	. . . Banka?	**bahn**-ka
. . . a hotel?	. . . Hotel?	**hoh**-tel
. . . an internet café?	. . . Internetová kavárna?	in-ter-net-oh-vah kah-**ver**-na
. . . a restroom?	. . . Toaleta?	**toha**-leh-tah
Stop here.	Zastavte tady.	**zah**-stahv-teh **tah**-dee
I would like . . .	Chtěl bych . . .	kh-tyel bihk
How much does it cost?	Kolik to stojí?	ko-**lik** toh **stoy**-ee
Letter/postcard	Dopis/pohlednice	doh-**pis**-ee/**poh**-hled-nit-seh
By airmail	Letecky	**leh**-tet-skee
Help!	Pomoc!	**po**-motz

Meeting people

My name is . . .	Jmenuji se . . .	ymen **weh**-seh
What is your name?	Jak se jmenujete?	yahk seh ymeh-**noo**-yeh-teh
Where do you live?	Odkud jste?	**od**-kood ysteh
What do you study?	Co studujete?	tsoh **stud**-yeh-teh
What is your major?	Jaký obor?	ya-**kee** oh-bor
What is your occupation?	Kde pracujete?	kdeh **prats**-oo-yet-eh
What music do you like?	Jakou hudbu posloucháte?	ya-koo hood-boo **pos**-loots-hat-eh

Let's have a coffee.	Půjdeme na kávu?	**pood**-yuh-deh-meh nah **kah**-voo
You are beautiful.	Jste krásná/ krásný (f/m)	yes-teh **krahs**-nah **krahs**-nee
You have lovely eyes.	Máte krásné oči.	**mah**-teh **krahs**-neh oats-ee
I like you.	Líbíte se mi.	lee-bee-teh seh mee
I love you.	Miluji Vás.	mee-lu-yee vahs
Stop harassing me!	Neobtěžujte mne!	neh-ohb-tyeh-zhyuy-teh muh-neh
I've got to go.	Musím jít	**moo**-seem yeet

Numbers

One	Jeden	ye-**den**
Two	Dva	dvah
Three	Tři	tshree
Four	Čryři	ch'**ti**-zhee
Five	Pět	pyet
Six	Šest	shest
Seven	Sedm	**sed**-oom
Eight	Osm	**oh**-soom
Nine	Devět	**deh**-vyet
Ten	Deset	**deh**-set
Eleven	Jedenáct	yeh-**deh**-nahtst
Twelve	Dvanáct	**dvah**-nahtst
Thirteen	Třináct	trzhee-**nahtst**
Fourteen	Čtrnáct	chtihr-**nahtst**
Fifteen	Patnáct	pat-**nahtst**
Sixteen	Šestnáct	shest-**nahtst**
Seventeen	Sedmnáct	sedm-**nahtst**
Eighteen	Osmnáct	ohsm-**nahtst**
Nineteen	Devatenáct	**deh**-vah-teh-**nahtst**
Twenty	Dvacet	**dvah**-tset
Thirty	Třicet	**trzhee**-tset
Fourty	Čtyřicet	**chtee**-rzhee-tset
Fifty	Padesát	**pah**-deh-saht
Sixty	Šedesát	**sheh**-deh-saht
Seventy	Sedmdesát	**sedm**-deh-saht
Eighty	Osmdesát	**ohsm**-deh-saht
Ninety	Devadesát	**deh**-vah-deh-saht
One hundred	Sto	stoh
One thousand	Tisíc	**tee**-seets

Days of the Week

Sunday	Neděle	**neh**-dyeh-leh
Monday	Pondělí	**pon**-dye-lee
Tuesday	Úterý	**oo**-teh-ree
Wednesday	Středa	**stshreh**-da
Thursday	Čtvrek	**ch't'v'r**-tek
Friday	Pátek	**pah**-tek
Saturday	Sobota	**so**-boh-ta

Where to Sleep

A room	Pokoj	**poh**-koy
The key	Klíč	kleech
With a bath/a shower	S koupelnou/sprchou	s'**ko**-pel-noh/**sp'r**-khoh

Food

A restaurant	Restaurace	**reh**-stau-rah-tseh
The menu	Jídelní lístek	yee-dell-nee **lis**-tek
The check, please.	Účet, prosím.	oo-chet **pro**-seem
I'd like to order this.	Chtěl bych tohle	khteel bikh **toh**-leh
Breakfast	Snídaně	**snyee**-dan-ye
Lunch	Oběd	**ob**-yed
Dinner	Večeře	**ve**-cher-zhe
Bread	Chléb	khleb
Butter	Máslo	**mah**-slo
Salt/pepper	Sůl/pepř	sool/pepsh
Bottle	Láhev	**lah**-hev
Red/white wine	Cervené/bílé víno	**cher**-ven-eh/**bee**-leh vee-no
Beer	Pivo	**piv**-oh
(Tap) water	Voda	**vo**-da
Sparkling water	Sodovka	**soh**-dohv-ka
Mineral water	Minerálka	min-eh-**rahl**-ka **vo**-da
Milk	Mléko	**mleh**-koh
Coffee	Káva	**kah**-va
Tea (with lemon)	Čaj (s citrónem)	tchai (se tsi-**tro**-nem)
Chocolate	Čokoláda	cho-koh-**lah**-da

INDEX

A

Accessories shops, *145–146*
Addresses, *F33*
AghaRTA, *F29, 100*
Airports and transfers, *F36–F37*
Air travel, *F33–F36*
booking your flight, *F34*
carriers, *F34*
check-in and boarding, *F34–F35*
with children, *F40*
complaints, *F36*
cutting costs, *F35*
discount reservations, *F44*
enjoying the flight, *F35–F36*
flying times, *F36*
luggage concerns, *F50*
reconfirming, *F36*
Alcron ✕, *63*
Allegro ✕, *F29, 62*
Altschul, *230*
Amber Hotel Konopiště ✕⊡, *171–172*
Ambiente–Pasta Fresca ✕, *57*
Ambiente–The Living Restaurant ✕, *70*
Andel's Hotel Prague ⊡, *F28, 89–90*
Antiques shops, *141, 144*
Apartment rentals, *79–80*
Arbes Mepro ⊡, *90*
Archa Theater, *F29, 122*
Arcotel Teatrino ⊡, *91*
Aria Hotel ⊡, *F28, 81, 84*
Art Deco Gallery Shop, *F30, 141*
Artěl, *F30, 151*
Art galleries and museums
commercial galleries, *144*
Hradčany, *29*
Josefov, *17*
Letná and Holešovice, *49, 50*
Malá Strana, *23*
Moravia, *238*
Nové Město, *42*
Pražský hrad, *35*
Southern Bohemia, *195*
Staré Město, *8*
Artičok ✕, *70*
Astronomical clock, *12*
ATMs, *F48*
Austerlitz, battle of, *242*

B

Babysitting services, *F40*
Balkan ⊡, *91*

Bank hours, *F37*
Barock ✕, *54*
Bars, *101–104*
Basilika svatého Vavřince, *45–46*
Bazaar ✕, *64*
Bazilika svatého Jiří, *F30, 32*
Bazilika sv. Prokupa, *225*
Beer, *F26–F27, 259–261*
Bellevue ✕, *57*
Best Western City Hotel Moran ⊡, *87*
Best Western Hotel Kampa ⊡, *84*
Best Western Meteor Plaza ⊡, *87*
Betlémská kaple, *6–7*
Bicycling, *F25, 128–129*
Billiards, *127–128*
Bílý Koníček, *185*
Black light theater, *121–122*
Bludiste na Petřína, *25*
Boating and sailing, *F25, 127*
Boat tours, *F52–F53*
Bohemia. ⇨ See Southern Bohemia; Western Bohemia
Bohemia Bagle ✕, *65*
Books about Czech Republic, *262–263*
Bookstores, *F45, 144–145*
Botanická zahrada, *50*
Bowling, *127–128*
Bretfeld Palace, *24*
Breweries
Southern Bohemia, *185*
Western Bohemia, *213, 216*
Bridges
Malá Strana, *21–22*
Southern Bohemia, *183*
Brno
dining, *239*
exploring, *232–238*
lodging, *239–240*
nightlife and the arts, *240*
shopping, *241*
transportation and services, *241–242*
visitor information, *242*
Brno Dragon, *237*
Brno-Tuřany Airport, *F36*
Business etiquette, *F45–F46*
Business hours, *F37*
Bus tours, *F53.* ⇨ *also* Sightseeing tours
Bus travel, *F37*

C

Cafe Bar Praga ✕, *217*
Cafés, *72–73*
Caffe Fellini ✕, *217*
Cameras, *F37–F38*
Čapek, Karel, *47*
Carlo IV ⊡, *F28, 86*
Car rentals, *F38–F39*
discount reservations, *F44*
Car travel, *F39–F40*
Casinos
Moravia, *240*
Prague, *107–108*
Western Bohemia, *215*
Castles and châteaux, *F25*
day-trips from Prague, *164–165, 167–168, 169–170, 171, 175, 176–177, 178*
Fodor's Choice, *F31–F32*
Moravia, *226, 227–228, 230, 231, 236–237, 238, 243, 247*
Nové Město, *44–46*
Pražský hrad, *30–39*
Southern Bohemia, *182, 184, 185, 186–187, 188, 191, 194–195, 197*
Troja, *50*
Western Bohemia, *210*
Caves, *244*
Celetná ulice, *7*
Cemeteries
Josefov, *17–18*
Moravia, *224, 230*
Nové Město, *46*
Vinohrady, *48*
Centrální Lázně ⊡, *215*
Centrum ⊡, *212*
Černá věž, *190*
Černý Medvěd ✕, *239*
Černý Orel ✕⊡, *226*
Červená Lhota, *188*
Česká kancelář, *36–37*
České Budějovice, *190–192*
České Muzeum Stříbra, *162*
Český Krumlov, *192–197*
Český Šternberk, *F31, 169–171*
C'est La Vie ✕, *F29, 63*
Chapel of the Holy Cross, *164*
Charlie ✕, *204–205*
Château Lednice na Moravé, *F31, 231*
Château Vranov nad Dyjí, *227–228*
Châteaux. ⇨ See Castles and châteaux

Cheb, *208–210*
Chebské muzeum, *209–210*
Chebský hrad, *210*
Chez Marcel ✕, *62*
Children and travel, *F40–F41*
Children's attractions, *F41*
Letná and Holešovice, 49—50
*Malá Strana, 20–21, 24–25, 26,
27*
Moravia, 244
Nové Město, 44–46
*parks and playgrounds,
126–127*
*Southern Bohemia, 189–190,
194–195*
toy and gift shops, 156
Troja, 51
Chodová Planá, *213*
Chrám svaté Barbory, *F30,
160, 162*
Chrám svatého Bartoloměje,
216
Chrám svatého Jakuba, *162*
Chrám svatého Mikuláše, *F30,
20*
Chrám svatého Mořice, *246*
Chrám svatého Víta, *F30,
32–34*
Chrám svatých Petra a Pavla,
233, 235
Church concerts, *117–118*
Churches. ⇨ *also*
Monasteries and convents
*day-trips from Prague, 160,
162, 164*
Fodor's Choice, F30
Hradčany, 29
Malá Strana, 20, 22–23
*Moravia, 223, 225, 226, 228,
233, 235, 246*
Nové Město, 45, 46
Pražský hrad, 32–34, 37
*Southern Bohemia, 183, 185,
187–188, 194*
Staré Město, 6–7, 9, 10
Vinohrady, 47–48
*Western Bohemia, 203, 204,
210, 216*
Churchill's ✕, *213*
Church of the Assumption of
the Virgin, *162*
Císařská konírna, *35*
Clam-Gallas palác, *7–8*
Classical music, *115–118*
Clementinum, *8*
Climate, *F21*
Clothing shops, *146–150*
Concierges, *F41*
Consumer protection, *F41*

Continental ✕, *217*
Convents. ⇨ *See*
Monasteries and convents
Cosmetics shops, *150–151*
Credit cards, *F48*
Cubist buildings, *41*
Currency, *F48*
Customs, *F41–F43*
Cybex, *F32, 129*

D

Da Lorenzo ✕, *70*
Day-trips from Prague,
158–178
Děkanství, *247*
Dentists, *F45*
Department stores, *137, 140*
Dining, *F25–F26, 53–54.*
⇨ *also* Price categories;
*specific Prague
neighborhoods; specific
cities and towns*
cafés, *72–73*
with children, F40
fast food, 67
Fodor's Choice, F29
late-night bites, 123–124
restaurant know-how, 55–57
symbols related to, F14
tipping, F55–F56, 57
traditional Czech food, 58–59
vocabulary for, 268
Disabilities and accessibility,
F43–F44
Discos, *98–100*
Discounts and deals, *F44*
Divinis ✕, *62–63*
Doctors, *F45*
Dominik Café ✕, *217*
Dóm svatého Václava, *246*
Druhé nádvoří, *34–35*
Dům U černé Matky Boží, *8*
Dům U Červeného Lva 🏨, *84*
Duties, *F41–F43*
Dvořák, Antonín, *48*
Dynamo ✕, *68*

E

Egon Schiele Center, *195*
El Cid ✕, *217*
Electricity, *F44–F45*
Elefant, *204*
Embassies, *F45*
Embassy ✕, *205*
Emergencies, *F45*
road service, F39
English-language media, *F45*
Etiquette and behavior,
F45–F46

Eva ✕, *210*
Exchanging money, *F48–F49*

F

Festivals and seasonal events,
F22–F24, 108–109, 112
Filip ✕, *214*
Film, *118–120*
Films about Czech Republic,
263–264
Flora 🏨, *248*
Fodor's Choice, *F28–F32*
Food shops, *151*
Fountains
Letná and Holešovice, 49
Moravia, 238, 245
Four Seasons Prague 🏨,
75–76
Františkovy Lázně, *211–212*
Františkův pramen, *211*
Franz Kafka Exposition, *8*
Free attractions, *7*
Front Synagogue, *224*

G

Galerie Rudolfinum, *17*
Gardens
Malá Strana, 20–21, 23, 26–27
Pražský hrad, 36
Troja, 50
Gasoline, *F39*
Gas stations, *F37*
Gay and lesbian clubs,
106–107
Gay and lesbian travel, *F46*
Gift shops, *156*
Gitanes ✕, *65*
Glass shops, *151–152*
Golf
Prague, 129
Western Bohemia, 207, 214
Gothic bridge, *183*
Grand Hotel Bohemia 🏨, *76*
Grandhotel Brno 🏨, *239*
Grandhotel Pacifik 🏨, *215*
Grandhotel Pupp 🏨, *F28,
205*
Grand Hotel Zvon 🏨, *192*

H

Harmonia ✕, *163*
Haštal 🏨, *78*
Havel, Václav, *45*
HC Sparta Praha, *F32, 130*
Health clubs, *129*
Health concerns, *F46*
Hiking, *F26*
Historické muzeum, *242*

History of the Czech Republic, 255–258
Hluboká nad Vltavou, F31, 189–190
Hockey, 129–130
Holašovice (Bohemian village), 191
Holešovice (Prague neighborhood). ⇨ See Letná and Holešovice
Holiday Inn ⌧, 239–240
Holidays, F46
Home design shops, 152–153
Home exchanges, 80
Horse racing
Prague, 130
Western Bohemia, 207
Hospitals, F45
Hospoda U Nováka ✕, 67
Hostels, 80–81
Hotel Ambiente ⌧, 206
Hotel America ⌧, 184
Hotel Anna ⌧, 89
Hotel Apollo ⌧, 92
Hotel Ariston ⌧, 91
Hotel Astra ⌧, 92
Hotel Axa ⌧, 87
Hotel Bílá paní ⌧, 189
Hotel Bohemia ⌧ (České Budějovice), 192
Hotel Bohemia ⌧ (Mariánské Lázně), 214
Hotel Central ⌧, 218
Hotel Concertino ⌧, 188–189
Hotel Continental ⌧, 218
Hotel Diplomat ⌧, 92–93
Hotel Dvořák ⌧ (Český Krumlov), 196
Hotel Dvořák ⌧ (Karlovy Vary), 205
Hotel Élite Prague ⌧, 87
Hotel Elwa ⌧, 205–206
Hotel Embassy ⌧, F28, 206
Hotel Excelsior ⌧, 214
Hotel Harmony ⌧, 88
Hotel Hubertus ✕⌧, 231–232
Hotel Le Palais ⌧, 89
Hotel Morava ✕⌧, 229
Hotel Nové Lázně ⌧, 215
Hotel Olšanka ⌧, 92
Hotel Palace Praha ⌧, F28, 86
Hotel Pegas ⌧, 240
Hotel Petr ⌧, 90–91
Hotel Restaurant Salva Guarda ✕, 176
Hotel Roma ⌧, F28, 85

Hotel Růže ⌧, F28, 194, 196
Hotels. ⇨ See Lodging
Hotel Salvator ⌧, 88
Hotel Slovan ⌧, 218
Hotel Thermal, 203
Hotel U města Vidně ⌧, 196
Hotýlek & Hospoda u malého Vítka ⌧, 196
Hrad Bouzov, 247
Hradčanské náměstí, 29
Hradčany (Castle Area), F15
dining, 65–66
exploring, 27–30
lodging, 85–86
Hrad Kotnov, 182
Hrad Krumlov, 194–195
Hradní Restaurace ✕, 170
Hrad Orlík, 178
Hrad Rožmberk, 197
Hrad Šternberk, 247
Hřbitov, F31, 46
H2O ✕, 68
Hus, Jan, 9
Husitské muzeum, 182
Hvězda ⌧, 210

Ibis Praha City ⌧, 89
Indická restaurace Taj ✕, 239
Informační středisko, 35
Insurance
for car rentals, F38
travel insurance, F46–F47
Iron Gate Hotel ⌧, 76
Itineraries, F18–F20

Jan Hus monument, 9
Jazz clubs, 100–101
Jean de Carro ⌧, 206
Jelení příkop, 35
Jelení skok, F32, 203
Jewelry shops, 153–154
Jewish Cemetery (Mikulov), 230
Jewish Cemetery (Třebíč), 224
Jewish cemetery's crematorium, 175
Jewish Quarter. ⇨ See Josefov
Jezdecké schody, 37
Jihlava, 223–224
Jihočeské Museum, 190–191
Jindřichův Hradec, 186–189
John Lennon Peace Wall, 26
John of Nepomuk, St., 33
Josef ⌧, 76–77
Josefov (Jewish Quarter), F15
exploring, 14–18

K
Kafka, Franz, 8, 38–39, 48
Kampa, 20–21
Kampa Park ✕, F29, 63
Kapitál ✕, 182
Kapitulní kostel svatých Petra a Pavla, 46
Kaple všech svatých, 37
Karel IV ✕, 205
Karlovo náměstí, 41–42
Karlovy Vary
dining, 204–205
exploring, 200–204
lodging, 205–206
nightlife and the arts, 206–207
shopping, 208
sports and the outdoors, 207
transportation and services, 208
visitor information, 208
Karlovy Vary Airport, F36
Karlštejn, 164–167
Kateřinská jeskyně, 244
Kavárna Slavia ✕, F29, 62
Kinsky Garden ⌧, 90
Klára Nademlýnská, F30, 148
Klášter Emauzy, 42
Klášter svaté Anežky České, 9
Klášter svatého Jiří, 35–36
Klausová synagóga, 16
Klec ✕, 217
Koliba ✕, 213
Kolkovna ✕, 57, 62
Kometa ✕, 163
Komorní Hůrka, 211
Koněspřežka, 190
Konopiště, 171–172
Korunní kamora, 33
Kostel Maří Magdaleny, 203
Kostel Nalezení svatého Kříže, 235
Kostel Nejsvětějšího Srdce Páně, 47–48
Kostel Panny Marie před Týnem, 9
Kostel Panny Marie vítězné, 22–23
Kostel svatého Ducha, 226
Kostel svatého Ignáce, 223
Kostel svatého Jakuba (Jihlava), 223
Kostel svatého Jakuba (Telč), 226
Kostel svatého Jana, 187–188
Kostel svatého Jiljí (Prague), 10
Kostel svatého Jiljí (Třeboň), 185

Kostel svatého Lukáše, 203
Kostel svatého Martina ve zdi, 10
Kostel svatého Michala, 246
Kostel svatého Mikuláše (Cheb), 210
Kostel svatého Mikuláše (Prague), 10
Kostel svatého Mikuláše (Znojmo), 228
Kostel svatého Václava, 228
Kostel svatého Víta, 194
Kostel svatých Petra a Pavla, 204
Kostnice, F30, 162–163
Královská zahrada, F31, 36
Kralovské mausoleum, 33
Kralovské oratorium, 33
Královský letohrádek, 36
Královský palác, 36
Kratochvíle, 191
Křivoklát, 167–169
Křižikova fontána, 49
Kroměříž, F32, 243
Kutná Hora, 160–164

L

La Crêperie ✕, 71
Language, F47
Czech vocabulary, 265–268
La Perle de Prague ✕, 68–69
Lapidárium, 49
La Romantica ✕, 70
Last Judgment mosaic, 34
Lázeňský muzeum, 211
Lázně III ⛬, 206
Le Bistrot de Marlène ✕, 68
Ledeburská zahrada, 23
Lemon Leaf ✕, 69
Leonardo ⛬, 78
Letenské sady, 49
Le Terroir ✕, 54
Letná and Holešovice, F15
dining, 71
exploring, 49–50
Libraries, 30
Libuše's Bath, 46
Lidice, 172–174
Lidice Memorial, 173
Live music clubs, 104–106
Lobkovický palác, F32, 37
Lodging, 75. ⇨ also Price categories; specific Prague neighborhoods; specific cities and towns
alternatives to hotels, 79–81
with children, F40
for disabled travelers, F43
discount reservations, F44

facilities and reservations, 77
Fodor's Choice, F28–F29
suburbs of Prague, 92–93
symbols related to, F14
tipping, F55–F56
vocabulary for, 268
Loreta, 29
Lovecká chata Ohrada, 189–190
Ludmila ⛬, 177

M

Magazines, F45
Magdeburg Barracks, 175
Mail and shipping, F47–F48
Mailsi ✕, 71–72
Maiselova synagóga, 16
Malá Pevnost, 175
Malá Strana (Lesser Quarter), F16
dining, 63–65
exploring, 18–27
lodging, 81, 84–85
Malé náměstí, 10
Malostranské náměstí, 23
Malý Buddha ✕, 65–66
Maps for driving, F39
Marathon races, 130
Mariánské Lázně, 212–215
Mariánský chrám, 183
Marionette shops, 154
Matyášova brána, 37–38
Maxim Cafe ✕, 217
Maximilian ⛬, 78
Medínek ⛬, 163
Mělník, 176–177
Městské muzeum, 194
Mikulov, 229–231
Mikulov zámek, 230
Minting operations, 162
Mintner's Chapel, 160
Místodržitelský palác, 235
Mlýnská kolonáda, 203
Monasteries and convents
Hradčany, 30
Nové Město, 42
Pražský hrad, 35–36
Staré Město, 9
Money matters, F48–F49
Moravia, 221–248
price categories, 221–222
Moravská restaurace a vinarná ✕, 247–248
Moravský Kras, 244–245
Moravský Krumlov, 238
Morový sloup, F31, 245
Morzin Palace, 24
Mozart, W. A., 27, 113, 247
Mucha Museum, 42

Museum Kampa, 23
Museum of the Terezín Ghetto, 175
Museums. ⇨ also Art galleries and museums
arts-and-crafts, 237–238
Austerlitz battle, 242
brewing, 213, 216
business hours of, F37
coins, 162
day-trips from Prague, 162, 175, 176–177
Dvořák, 48
fishery industry, 183–184
Fodor's Choice, F32
history, 12, 37, 43, 190–191, 194, 209–210, 236
in Hradčany, 30
hunting and fishing, 189–190
Hussites, 182
Kafka, 8
in Letná and Holešovice, 49–50
literature, 30
in Malá Strana, 27
military history, 30
in Moravia, 230, 236, 237–238, 242
Mozart, 27
in Nové Město, 43
in Pražský hrad, 37, 38
prisons, 236
Romani culture, 236
silver, 162
in Southern Bohemia, 182, 183–184, 188, 190–191, 194
spa-related antiques, 211
in Staré Město, 8, 12
technology, 49–50
Terezín ghetto, 175
toys, 38
in Vinohrady, 48
in Western Bohemia, 209–210, 211, 213, 216
wine-making, 230
Music and musical instrument shops, 154
Muzeum Antonína Dvořáka, 48
Muzeum Hlavního Města Prahy, 12
Muzeum hraček, 38
Muzeum Jindřichohradecka, 188
Muzeum Romské kultury, 235
Myslivna ✕, 69

N

Na Louži ✕, F29, 195
Na Příkopě, 10–11

Národní divadlo, F29, 42–43, 114
Národní galerie, 29
Národní muzeum, 43
Národní Technické muzeum, 49–50
National Memorial, 51
Nazi concentration camp, 174–175
Nerudova 🖫, 84–85
Nerudova ulice, 23–24
Newspapers, F45
Nightlife
Fodor's Choice, F29–F30
Moravia, 240
Prague, 95–108
Western Bohemia, 207, 215, 218
Nové Město (New Town), F15–F16
dining, 66–69
exploring, 39–46
lodging, 86–88
Novoměstská radnice, 43
Nový Svět, 29–30
Nový židovský hřbitov, 48

O

Obecní dům, F31, 11
Obrazárna, 35
Observatories, 25
Office hours, F37
Olomouc, 245–248
Opera, 121
Opera 🖫, 88
Orange Moon ✕, 54
Orlík, 177–178
Ossuaries, 162–163
Ostrava Airport, F36

P

Package deals, F44, F56
Packing, F49–F50
Palác Akropolis ✕, 71
Palaces
Hradčany, 29, 30
Malá Strana, 24, 25, 27
Moravia, 235, 236, 246–247
Pražský hrad, 36, 37
Staré Město, 7–8, 11
Palác Kinských, 11
Palác Přemyslovců, 246–247
Pálffy Palác ✕, 63–64
Památník národního písemnictví, 30
Památník Terezín, 174–175
Párkhotel Český Šternberk 🖫, 170
Parkhotel Golf 🖫, 214

Parking, F39
Parks, 126–127
Letná and Holešovice, 49
Malá Strana, 24–25
Parnassus Fountain, 238
Pasha ✕, 65
Passports, F50–F51
Pavilon, 48
Pension Hana 🖫, 177
Pension Louda 🖫, 92
Pension 189 Karel Bican 🖫, F28–F29, 183
Pension Sandra 🖫, 218
Pension Unitas & Art Prison Hostel 🖫, 81
Penzion Irena 🖫, 166
Penzion Kim-Ex 🖫, 229
Penzion Sprint 🖫, 93
Performance venues, 113–115
Performing arts
Fodor's Choice, F29
Moravia, 240
Prague, 108–123
Southern Bohemia, 191–192, 196
Western Bohemia, 206–207, 215
Perfume shops, 150–151
Petříinská razhelda, 25
Petřín sady, 24–25
Pharmacies, F45
business hours, F37
Philosophical Hall, 30
Photography, F37–F38
Piccolo ✕, 214
Pilsner Urquell Brewery, F31, 216
Pinkasova synagóga, 16
Písek, 183–184
Pivovarská restaurace a muzeum ve skále, 213
Pivovarské muzeum, 216
Pivovarský dům, F29, 103
Pizzeria P&P ✕, 205
Pizzeria Rugantino ✕, 63
Playgrounds, 126–127
Plzeň, 216–219
Plzen Historical Underground, 216
Prácheňské Museum, 183–184
Prague. ⇨ also specific neighborhoods
facts about, 250–251
nightlife, 95–108
performing arts, 108–123
shopping, 136–156
sports and the outdoors, 126–134
suburban areas, 92–93

Prague Marathon, 130
Prašná brána, 11–12
Pravda ✕, F29, 57
Pražákův palác, 236
Pražský hrad (Prague Castle), 30–39
Price categories
day-trips from Prague, 158–159
Moravia, 221–222
Prague dining, 56
Prague lodging, 77
Southern Bohemia, 180
Western Bohemia, 199–200
Private guides, F53
Private rooms, 79
Proboštský Kostel, 188
První nádvoří, 38
Public transit, F51
Pubs, 101–104
Punkevní jeskyně, F32, 244
Puppet shows, 121–122

Q

Qubus Design, F30, 152

R

Radisson SAS Alcron Hotel 🖫, 86–87
Radost FX Café ✕, 70–71
Railway stations, 190
Rango ✕, 217
Rear Synagogue, 224
Regionální Muzeum, 230
Residence 7 Angels 🖫, 78
Restaurace a Pension Pod dračí skálou ✕, 165–166
Restaurace a ubytovna u Cvrků ✕, 178
Restaurace Zvonařka ✕, 69–70
Restaurants. ⇨ See Dining
Restrooms, F51–F52
Rhapsody Piano Bar ✕, 71
Riverside Hotel 🖫, 90
Road conditions, F39
Rock clubs, 104–106
Rohatý Krokodýl ✕🖫, 230–231
Romanesque chapel, 210
Romanesque rotunda, 45
Romanský palác, 37
Romantik Hotel U Raka 🖫, F28, 85–86
Rotunda svaté Kateřiny, 228
Roxy, F30, 105
Royal crypt, 33
Rozhledna Diana, 204
Rožmberk nad Vltavou, 197
Rudolfinum, F29, 16–17, 114

Růže Hotel, *206*
Ruzyně Airport, *F36*
Rybník Svět, *185*

S

Sadová kolonáda, *203*
Safety, *F52*
Savoy ☒, *85*
Sbírka moderního a
 soucasného umění, *50*
Scams, *F52*
Schönbornský palác, *25*
Schwarzenberský palác, *30*
Senior-citizen travel, *F52*
Shoe shops, *155*
Shopping, *F26, F52*
 blitz tour, 142–143
 business hours, F37
 Fodor's Choice, F30
 Moravia, 241
 Prague, 136–156
 Western Bohemia, 208
Shopping malls, *140*
Sightseeing tours, *F52–F54*
 day-trips from Prague, 166
 Southern Bohemia, 187
 Western Bohemia, 204
Skateboarding, *133*
Skiing, *F26, 130–131*
Slavia ☒, *240*
Slavkov u Brna, *242*
Slovan ✕☒, *212*
Slunečnice ✕, *218*
Smetanova síň, *11*
Smíchov, *F16*
 lodging, 89–91
Soccer, *131–132*
Southern Bohemia, *180–197*
 price categories, 180
Souvenirs, *F52*
Španělská synagóga, *17*
Spas
 Prague, 128
 *Western Bohemia, 200–208,
 211–215*
Špička, *45*
Špilberk hrad, *236–237*
Sporting goods shops, *156*
Sports and the outdoors
 Fodor's Choice, F32
 Prague, 126–134
 Western Bohemia, 207
Square ✕, *64*
Squares of Prague
 Hradčany, 29
 Malá Strana, 23, 26
 Nové Město, 41–42, 44
 Staré Město, 10, 13
Squash, *133–134*

Stará radnice, *237*
Stará sněmovna, *37*
Staré Město (Old Town), *F16*
 dining, 54, 57, 62–63
 exploring, 2–14
 lodging, 75–78, 81
Staroměstská mostecká věž,
 22
Staroměstská radnice, *12*
Staroměstské náměstí, *F31,
 13*
Staronová synagóga, *17*
Starý židovský hřbitov, *F31,
 17–18*
Statní zámek Telč, *226*
Statue of St. Wenceslas, *43*
Stavovské divadlo, *13–14*
Štefánik Observatory, *25*
Šternberský palác, *29*
Strahov Library, *30*
Strahovský klášter, *30*
Street markets, *140–141*
Střekov Castle, *175*
Student travel, *F54*
Sushi Bar ✕, *65*
Svinenská Gate, *185*
Swarovksi Bohemia, *F30,
 153–154*
Swimming
 Prague, 132
 Western Bohemia, 207
Symbols, *F14*
Synagogues
 Josefov, 16, 17
 Moravia, 224, 230
 Western Bohemia, 216

T

Tábor, *180–183*
Tamada ✕, *69*
Tatiana, *F30, 149*
Taxes, *F54*
Taxis, *F54–F55*
 tipping, F55–F56
Telč, *225–227*
Telč ☒, *227*
Telephones, *F55*
Tennis, *133*
Terezín, *174–176*
Theater, *121–123*
Theater buildings
 Josefov, 16–17
 Nové Město, 42–43
 Staré Město, 13–14
Theresienstadt, *174–176*
Thun-Hohenstein Palace, *24*
Ticket outlets, *112–113*
Time, *F55*
Tipping, *F55–F56, 57*

Tourist traps, *15*
Tour operators, *F56*
Towers
 Malá Strana, 22
 Moravia, 245–246
 Southern Bohemia, 190
 Staré Město, 11–12
 Western Bohemia, 204
 Žižkov, 51
Town Hall Tower, *12*
Toy shops, *156*
Train travel, *F56–F57*
 for disabled travelers, F43
Trančicí dům, *44*
Travel agencies
 for disabled travelers, F43–F44
 selecting an agent, F57–F58
 for tour bookings, F56
Traveler's checks, *F49*
Travel insurance, *F46–F47*
Třebíč, *224–225*
Třeboň, *184–186*
Třeti nádvoří, *38*
Tři Lilie ☒, *F28, 212*
Troja, *50–51*
Trojský zámek, *50*
Tulip ✕, *68*
Tulip Inn ☒, *88*

U

U Dómu svatého Václava ☒,
 248
U Dragouna ✕, *66*
U Hrnčíře ☒, *163*
U Janů ✕☒, *166*
U Jelena ✕☒, *168–169*
U Kata ☒, *163–164*
U Královny Elišky ✕, *239*
Ultramarine ✕, *66–67*
U Maltézských rytířů ✕, *64*
U Mansfeld ✕, *217*
U Mecenáše ✕, *64*
Uměleckoprůmyslové muzeum,
 237–238
Universal ✕, *67*
U Pačtů ✕, *71*
U Sedmi Švábů ✕, *64–65*
U Ševce Matouše ✕, *66*
U tří housliček, *24*
U Tří Pštrosů ☒, *84*
U Varháře ✕, *163*
U Zlatého Jalena ☒, *78, 81*
U Zlaté hrušky ✕, *66*

V

Václavské náměstí, *44*
Valdštejnská kaple, *34*
Valkoun House, *24*
Valšský dvůr, *162*

Valtice, *231–232*
Valtice zámek, *231*
Value-added tax (V.A.T.),
  F54
Veletržní palác, *50*
Velkopřevorské náměstí, *26*
Villa Bertramka, *27*
Villa Butterfly ⚑, *214*
Villa Tugendhat, *F32, 238*
Vinohrady, *F16–F17*
  dining, 69–71
  exploring, 47–48
  lodging, 88–89
Visas, *F50–F51*
Visitor information, *F58*
V Krakovské ✕, *68*
Vladislavský sál, *36*
Vltava ✕, *68*
Vocabulary words, *265–268*
Vojanovy sady, *26*
Vojenské historické muzeum,
  30
Volcanoes, *211*
Vřídelní kolonáda, *201, 203*

Vrtbovská zahrada, *26–27*
Vyšehrad, *F17, 44–46*
V Zátiší ✕, *57*

W
Wagon wheel, *237*
Walking tours, *F53–F54*
W. A. Mozart Museum, *27*
Web sites, *F58*
Western Bohemia, *199–219*
  price categories, 199–200
When to go, *F21*
Wine, *F27, 55–56*
Wine shops, *151*
Women traveling alone, *F52*

Y
Yoga, *134*

Z
Zahrada Valdštejnského palác,
  27
Zahrada v opeře ✕, *F29, 66*

Zámecká Restaurace ✕, *177*
Zámek Konopiště, *F32, 171*
Zámek Třeboň, *185*
Zelný trh, *238*
Zemanova kavárna ✕, *239*
Židovská radnice, *18*
Žižkov, *F17*
  dining, 71–72
  exploring, 51
  lodging, 91–92
Žižkov TV Tower, *51*
Zlatá Hvězda ✕⚑ (Jihlava),
  223–224
Zlatá Hvězda ⚑ (Třeboň),
  185–186
Zlatá ulička, *38–39*
Žluta Pumpa ✕, *70*
Znojmo, *228–229*
Zoologická zahrada v Praze,
  51
Zoos
  Southern Bohemia, 190
  Troja, 51
Zvíkov, *184*

NOTES

Praise
UNDER PRESSURE

BY DAVID FAUST

STANDARD
PUBLISHING
Cincinnati, Ohio

Library of Congress Cataloging-in-Publication Data

Faust, David.
    Praise under pressure : a new look at David / by David Faust.
            p.   cm.
    Includes bibliographical references.
    ISBN 0-7847-0489-9
    1. David, King of Israel.   2. Stress (Psychology)—Religious aspects—
Christianity.   3. Christian life.
I. Title.
BS580.D3F38   1996
222'.4092—dc20
                                                            96-14641
                                                            CIP

Edited by Theresa C. Hayes.
Cover design by Dale E. Meyers.

The Standard Publishing Company, Cincinnati, Ohio.
A division of Standex International Corporation.

    03   02   01   00   99   98   97   96   5   4   3   2   1

To my parents, Paul and June Faust,
who have praised God together for fifty years

Contents

Introduction 7

Chapter One 13
Pressure-Tested: How God Prepares a Leader

Chapter Two 25
Overcoming Giant Problems

Chapter Three 35
Target Practice: Coping With Angry People

Chapter Four 47
Friends in Need, Friends in Deed

Chapter Five 59
Staying Sane in a Crazy World

Chapter Six 69
Don't Cave In

Chapter Seven 79
Why Worry When You Can Worship?

Chapter Eight 91
Fit for a King

Chapter Nine 103
Dining at the King's Table

Chapter Ten 113
The High Price of Giving In

Chapter Eleven 125
Heartbreak in the Household

Chapter Twelve 137
Mighty Men

Chapter Thirteen 147
Famous Last Words

Notes 155

Praise Under Pressure

Pressure. The very word can make us cringe.

To a quarterback, pressure is a three-hundred-pound lineman closing in for a crushing tackle.

To a young mother or dad, it's a sick baby crying at 3:00 A.M. for the fifth night in a row.

To a factory worker, it's an unreasonable boss who wants the job done twice as well in half the time.

To a busy executive, pressure means eighty-hour work weeks and a phone that never stops ringing.

To a teenager, it's peer pressure and never-ending schoolwork.

We are not exempt from pressure just because we believe in God. In fact, the Christian life has its own unique pressures. It's hard to wrestle against temptation in our increasingly complicated, sin-infested world. And if our own lives aren't stressful already, the Bible tells us to "bear one another's burdens," so there's always plenty of pressure to go around! The apostle Paul faced the daily pressure of his concern for God's people (2 Corinthians 11:28).

PRESSURE-PACKED LIVES

Did you ever watch a pressure cooker on the kitchen stove? My mother used one when I was a boy. A tightly-sealed pressure cooker uses high temperatures (up to 266 degrees Fahrenheit) to tenderize meat and vegetables.

Do you ever feel as though you live in a pressure cooker? High heat. High stress. No escape. Is your daily life filled with deadlines, responsibilities, burdens, and hassles?

Modern conveniences don't always help. Cars are

useful; traffic jams are not. Computers are time-savers;
but as humorist Gary Apple says, "Now I know why they
call that computer program 'Windows'; you get so frustrated, you want to throw your computer out one!"

Since 1990 the Week-at-a-Glance planning calendars
have added two extra hours to each day's schedule.
They now begin at 7:00 A.M. and end at 7:30 P.M., since
as a company representative noted, "We're not a nine-
to-five society anymore." It's a pressure-cooker world.

Of course, pressure isn't all bad. When the weather-
man predicts an approaching "high pressure system,"
we can expect clear skies and sunny weather.
Sometimes we actually perform better under pressure.
The pressure of an upcoming exam motivates students
to study harder. Athletes relish the chance to play in a
World Series or an Olympic medal round, and many of
them perform at a higher level when the pressure is
on.

Though we may not like to admit it, most of us probably need the healthy pressure of deadlines and
accountability. But the problem is, too much pressure
can make us collapse. And too much pressure can dis-
tract us from serving God.

Financial pressure weighs us down: "How can I pay
my credit card bills? Can I afford that expensive car
repair? How am I going to pay for college?"

There's *family* pressure: "How should we handle our
teenage son? How can we keep our marriage strong?
How shall we care for our aging parents?"

Add to that some *friendship* pressure: "Why do I feel
lonely even when I'm in a crowd of people? How can I
find time just to laugh, listen, and pray with others?"

Above all, Christians experience *faith* pressure; "How
can I stay close to the Lord when my life is busy and
stressful? Where does God fit in all of this? How can I
find time to pray?" Soul-stress may be the toughest pressure of all.

DAVID'S PRESSURE-PACKED LIFE

Fortunately, the Bible tells us about real people who faced the same problems we face today—people who managed to trust and obey God in a pressure-cooker world.

Tucked away in the middle of the Old Testament is the interesting historical account of David. I may be biased (since my own name is David), but for years I have felt a deep fascination with this faithful but flawed man of God. As a child, I enjoyed hearing how David used a sling, a smooth stone, and a strong faith to kill a giant no one else dared to confront. Later I memorized David's masterpiece, the Twenty-third Psalm. I pictured him penning those words while sitting on a sunlit hillside, with his sheep grazing nearby.

But there's a lot more to David's story than green pastures and quiet waters. David climbed from rags to riches—from the pasture to the palace—from humble beginnings as a shepherd to a forty-year reign as king over Israel. There were times when David desperately ran for his life, pursued by the angry and paranoid King Saul. Later, David found himself at the pinnacle of success, enjoying victories over his enemies and the comforts of royal life. Then he nearly threw it all away by engaging in a scandalous affair with another man's wife.

David was "a man after God's own heart" whose weaknesses were just as obvious as his strengths. Sometimes he stumbled, but he kept walking with God. He was a less-than-perfect man with a less-than-ideal family, but his faith was strong and authentic.

David illustrates what it's like to serve God in a high-pressure world.

PRAYER ON THE RUN

David was multitalented: a shepherd, a harpist, a poet and songwriter, a military strategist, and a statesman. But one of David's greatest skills was his ability to "pray on the run." Even as he balanced the pressures of work, family, and national leadership, he was a man of unceasing prayer and devotion to God. As many godly people have done throughout history, David took the time to write down his personal prayers, many of which are preserved as part of our Old Testament.

Not only do we possess the historical accounts of David's life (in 1 and 2 Samuel, 1 Kings, and 1 Chronicles), we also can read David's spiritual reflections on these events. Psalms, the longest book of the Bible, contains one hundred and fifty great songs of praise—and nearly half of them (seventy-three chapters) bear a subtitle identifying them as "Psalms of David."[1]

Many of the psalms are linked with specific events in David's life. For example, Psalm 3:3 says, "But you are a shield around me, O Lord; you bestow glory on me and lift up my head." The chapter begins with a subtitle informing us that David penned these words "when he fled from his son Absalom." No wonder he needed the Lord's protection and care—his own son was pursuing him and trying to kill him! According to another subtitle, David wrote Psalm 51—a heartfelt confession of sin—when the prophet Nathan confronted him about his adultery with Bathsheba.

When we read David's psalms, we are peering into his spiritual journal.[2] We catch a glimpse of how David coped with the ups and downs of a pressure-packed life. He loved God deeply, but sometimes he felt distant from God.

The same man who wrote, "The Lord is my shepherd" (Psalm 23:1) also wrote, "My God, my God, why have you forsaken me?" (Psalm 22:1). He could blurt out, "How long, O Lord? Will you forget me forever?" and then conclude the same prayer song with, "I will sing to the Lord, for he has been good to me" (Psalm 13:1, 6). David knew how it felt to be rich and famous, but he also endured times of ridicule and failure. Early in his career, the crowds literally sang David's praises;

later people cursed his name. The daring warrior who brought down Goliath eventually was reduced to tears by the death of his rebellious son Absalom.

But through it all, David offered God praise under pressure. He was no artificial hero, no religious smart aleck offering flippant answers to life's hard questions. His problems were genuine, but so were his prayers. Even in the midst of hardships, David came to God with heartfelt praise and honest questions.

This is a book about David's life and prayers. It's a book for broken people who dare to trust in the unbroken promises of God. It's a message of encouragement for people under pressure—for those who believe God holds the answer to life's puzzles, but who sometimes wonder exactly how all the pieces fit together. It's a book for people who want to follow Jesus, "the Son of David."

Are you feeling burned out? Then learn from David who prayed, "You, O Lord, keep my lamp burning; my God turns my darkness into light" (Psalm 18:28).

Are you stumbling under a heavy load of work, hardship, or responsibility? Listen to the counsel of David who wrote, "Praise be to the Lord, to God our Savior, who daily bears our burdens" (Psalm 68:19).

Like David, we can learn to praise God—even when under pressure.

CHAPTER ONE

Pressure-Tested: How God Prepares a Leader

1 SAMUEL 16; PSALM 139

It's always good to be prepared.

Before guests come over for dinner, you prepare the food, dust the furniture, and make sure there are no dirty dishes in the sink. Before you face the world in the morning, you wash your face and comb your hair.

Before the members of a ball team take the field, they practice the fundamentals and scout out the strengths and weaknesses of the opposing team.

Before the hospital aides wheel you into the operating room for surgery, the doctor explains the procedure and prepares you for the operation.

Before a college professor enters the classroom, he spends many hours studying and preparing his lecture notes.

A farmer prepares the soil before he plants his crop.

A preacher prepares his sermon before he stands behind the pulpit to preach. (At least his congregation hopes he does.)

Sometimes we aren't as prepared as we think we are. For years I carried a dime in my wallet just in case I needed to use a public phone. Finally, one day I was stranded in an airport in a distant city, and I needed to make that phone call—but the price had gone up to a quarter!

Our heavenly Father believes in preparation. He waited centuries until "the time had fully come" before sending His Son Jesus to earth (Galatians 4:4). Then John the Baptist came as a forerunner to prepare the way for the Lord (Mark 1:2-4). Jesus spent three years teaching His twelve apostles by word and example, preparing them for service.

Do you ever wonder what the Lord has been doing to prepare *you* for service? How does God prepare a servant-leader, anyway? Nothing is wasted in God's economy. Our childhood experiences, our hurts, practical skills we develop, wise teachers and advisers we encounter along the way, lessons learned in the school of hard knocks—all play a part in preparing us for useful service.

David eventually became one of the greatest leaders of all time. But first he had to be "pressure-tested." What experiences in his early life made him "a man after God's own heart"? How did God prepare him for leadership?

GOD GAVE DAVID A FAITHFUL FAMILY

David's family had a lot to do with his preparation. God's hand was on his life even during the prenatal stage as he developed in his mother's womb. David wrote: "For you created my inmost being; you knit me together in my mother's womb. I praise you because I am fearfully and wonderfully made; your works are wonderful, I know that full well" (Psalm 139:13, 14).

David grew up within a rich heritage of faith that stretched back several generations. It wasn't by chance that he grew up in Bethlehem. His great-grandmother was Ruth, whose story of faith appears in the Old Testament book bearing her name. Ruth faced a lot of pressure and hardship: famine, widowhood, poverty. But God's hand of providence was at work through it all.

Eventually Ruth married Boaz, a landowner and leader in Bethlehem. No one paid much attention as these two newlyweds settled into their rustic life together, but "big doors turn on little hinges." Something big "clicked" in the plan of God as Ruth and Boaz passed along a heritage of faith to their son Obed, then to their grandson Jesse (who was the father of David).

Many years later, Jesus Christ was born there in Bethlehem (the "city of David"). In terms of His human genealogy the Son of God was descended from the lineage of Ruth, and Jesse, and David (Matthew 1:5, 6). Never underestimate the influence of a faithful family!

When former First Lady Barbara Bush delivered a commencement address at Wellesley College, she remarked, "Your success as a family, our success as a society, depends not on what happens in the White House, but on what happens in your house."[1] Likewise, our personal success depends not merely on what happens in Sunday school or public school classrooms, but in the classroom of the home as moms, dads, and grandparents prepare the next generation for leadership.

A doctor friend specializes in family medicine. During medical school he received some of his training in an office called a "Family Practice Center." In a way, that's what every home is: a family practice center, a training ground for the practice of godliness, a place where we practice love, faith, patience, gentleness, and self-control. As the word "hospitality" suggests, our homes can be "hospitals" where hurting people find healing and help.

What if you grew up in a troubled family? Remember: by God's grace it's possible to rise above a difficult home life to become a strong Christian leader. (As we will see, King David's own family was far from perfect.) Sometimes a painful past is part of the "pressure-testing" God uses to prepare us for greater growth and service.

GOD SAW IN DAVID A COMMITTED HEART

After the Lord rejected Saul as king over Israel, He sent the prophet Samuel to Jesse's home in Bethlehem. The Lord said, "I have chosen one of his sons to be king," but at first He did not reveal to Samuel which of the young men He had selected (1 Samuel 16:1-3).

When Samuel arrived in Bethlehem, he invited Jesse
and his sons to join him in offering a sacrifice to God.
The eldest son, Eliab, was an impressive-looking fellow.
Samuel sized him up and thought, "Surely the Lord's
anointed stands here before the Lord" (1 Samuel 16:6).

First impressions are not always correct, however.
Eliab might have been man's pick, but he was not
God's. Instead, the Lord told Samuel, "Do not consider
his appearance or his height, for I have rejected him.
The Lord does not look at the things man looks at. Man
looks at the outward appearance, but the Lord looks at
the heart" (v. 7).

How our society needs to hear this message! Concern
with outward appearance seems to dominate our culture. In 1993, Americans spent $293 billion on clothing,
accessories, and jewelry—$25 billion on barbershops,
beauty parlors, and health clubs.[2]

Often we ask the wrong questions about people:

> "Is she pretty? Is he strong?
> Is that hairstyle slightly wrong?
> Does he wear his jacket right?
> Does she have an overbite?
> Does he drive a fancy car?
> Does she own a VCR?
> Is her voice too soft? Too loud?
> Does he fit in with the crowd?
> Is he wealthy? Funny? Cool?"
> Perhaps all these . . . yet still a fool.
> "Is she godly, pure, and wise?"
> Look closer, then . . . for she's a prize.

Men and women are equally guilty: Jesus denounced
the scribes and Pharisees who were like cups and dishes,
scrubbed and shining on the outside but full of greed
and self-indulgence on the inside. He compared them
to whitewashed tombs, "which look beautiful on the
outside but on the inside are full of dead men's bones
and everything unclean" (Matthew 23:25-28).

Don't misunderstand. Outward beauty is not wrong, it just isn't enough. David himself was a nice-looking man. He was "ruddy" (that is, he probably had auburn or reddish hair, and possibly a fair or reddish complexion), "with a fine appearance and handsome features" (1 Samuel 16:12). But the Lord was more interested in the condition of his heart than with the curl of his hair or the breadth of his shoulders.

"The Lord does not look at the things man looks at" (1 Samuel 16:7).

Men saw a baby born to a family of slaves and taken away from his mother at an early age—but God saw Moses.

Men saw a strange bald-headed fellow who wore an old cloak—but God saw the prophet Elisha.

Men saw an unrefined, unsophisticated fisherman with little patience and a quick mouth—but the Lord saw Simon Peter.

Men saw a poor widow drop a couple of copper coins into the temple treasury—but Jesus saw the woman's faith and generous spirit.

Men saw a woman with a tainted past—but Jesus saw Mary Magdalene, who was one of the first to witness His resurrection from the dead.

Even Jesus himself didn't impress people with His outward appearance. "He had no beauty or majesty to attract us to him, nothing in his appearance that we should desire him" (Isaiah 53:2). Yet there was glory in this "Word [who] became flesh . . . full of grace and truth" (John 1:14).

If God allows us to experience pressure-testing, it's because the pressures of life can purify and refine our character and faith (James 1:2-4; 1 Peter 1:6, 7). David welcomed God's inspection of his heart. He prayed, "Search me, O God, and know my heart; test me and know my anxious thoughts. See if there is any offensive way in me, and lead me in the way everlasting" (Psalm 139:23, 24).

GOD TAUGHT DAVID DISCIPLINE
THROUGH HUMBLE SERVICE

One by one, Jesse's sons passed in front of Samuel—first Eliab, then Abinadab, then Shammah, then four more younger brothers. Scripture doesn't tell us their state of mind as these men walked through this awkward audition. Did they realize what hung in the balance? Did each one secretly hope to be chosen by the Lord's prophet? Were they afraid? Did their hearts beat a little faster, did their palms perspire, as Samuel examined each one and listened for the Lord's voice of approval?

Finally Samuel announced the disappointing verdict: none of these men were chosen by the Lord. Puzzled, Samuel asked Jesse, "Are these all the sons you have?"

Jesse was bewildered too. Altogether he had eight sons, but only seven accompanied him to Samuel's sacrifice. Almost as an afterthought, Jesse told Samuel, "There is still the youngest, but he is tending the sheep" (1 Samuel 16:11).

Why wasn't David invited to the sacrifice? As the youngest of eight brothers, he probably seemed the least likely to be selected for important service. Besides, someone had to watch Jesse's flock. The sheep couldn't be left unattended, so David was the logical choice to supervise the flock while his brothers met with the prophet Samuel.

Maybe you can identify with David. Were you ever stuck with a boring job while everyone else was out having fun? Were you bypassed for a well-deserved promotion at work? Did you change diapers in the church nursery while the rest of the congregation shared an uplifting worship service?

Tending sheep sounds dull and unspectacular, but it was part of the discipline of humble service through which God prepared David for leadership. Instead of wallowing in self-pity, David learned valuable lessons through those long, unglamorous days and nights watching his flocks.

1. He learned patience. Herding sheep takes time; so does leading people. A sheepherder needs lots of patience; so does a leader of men. A shepherd's rewards are not immediate. Eventually he will eat the meat from his flock and turn the wool and sheepskin into warm clothes, but first he must feed the sheep, search for strays, and protect the lambs from thieves and wolves.

Thumbtacked to the bulletin board near my desk is an old, yellowing piece of paper containing this piece of wisdom: "Waiting is often the providential discipline for those to whom exceptional work has been given."3 When we feel impatient, we need to remember that the Lord may simply be preparing us for greater work in the future.

2. He learned responsibility. I didn't tend flocks as David did, but I did grow up on a farm. My dad assigned chores to each of his sons. My brothers and I fed the hogs and calves, gathered the eggs, and helped with other tasks around the farm. We were expected to complete our chores every morning before school (and before breakfast).

There were plenty of times I would rather have slept late, skipped the chores, or simply goofed off with my friends. But looking back, I'm glad Dad insisted on those chores. I learned valuable lessons about hard work and responsibility, which I probably wouldn't have learned without handling that pitchfork and loading those heavy bales of hay.

As Jesus taught, we need to learn faithfulness in small things before we are given greater responsibility: "Whoever can be trusted with very little can also be trusted with much, and whoever is dishonest with very little will also be dishonest with much" (Luke 16:10). Why should God let David lead his nation if he couldn't even handle a flock of sheep?

It's important to honor God in the small tasks. Get up in the morning and go to work. Go to class. Pay the bills. Be faithful in the small things. God prepares us to reach our long-term goals through the "ordinaries" of everyday tasks.

3. David learned how to be quiet. David's obscure years with the sheep were not wasted. They provided time for uninterrupted prayer and communion with God. Would David ever have written the Twenty-third Psalm ("The Shepherd's Psalm") if not for those long days and nights with the sheep?

Some lessons can be learned only when we slow down, scale down, and quiet down. Our lives tend to be too busy, too noisy, too cluttered to hear God's still, small voice. The world says, "Stay noisy and busy at all times." The Lord says, "Be still, and know that I am God" (Psalm 46:10). The apostle Paul urged, "Make it your ambition to lead a quiet life, to mind your own business and to work with your hands" (1 Thessalonians 4:11).

David's isolation in the hills of Judea was not wasted. He learned how to take care of himself. His perceptive eyes memorized the terrain. Years later David's survival skills and his familiarity with the hills, caves, and cliffs proved useful when he hid from Saul, and led his own men into battle.

4. He learned humility. In God's order of things, "humility comes before honor" (Proverbs 18:12). David wasn't born a powerful king; he was the eighth son of a humble shepherd. While his brothers auditioned before Samuel, David toiled away on some obscure hillside, outside the spotlight of public view. This was all part of his pressure-testing.

Anyone who is a baseball fan knows that some of the greatest baseball managers endured rather unspectacular careers as players. For example, Sparky Anderson won more than two thousand games as a manager, but as a player he had an unimpressive .218 batting average.

Hall of Famer Connie Mack won 3,776 games as a manager (more than any other manager in the history of baseball). But before becoming a manager, he spent several painful years behind home plate as a little-known catcher for four different teams. The fact is, "Connie Mack" wasn't even his real name. His full name, Cornelius Alexander McGillicuddy, wouldn't fit on the scoreboard! These men did not earn high accolades for their playing, but they were watching (often from the bench), learning, and preparing—being pressure-tested—for the time when eventually they would lead others.

The discipline of humble service was part of the pressure-testing that prepared David for leadership.

GOD REFINED DAVID'S GIFTS AND TALENTS

Finally David came in from the fields and stood before Samuel. The Lord said, "Rise and anoint him; he is the one" (1 Samuel 16:12). A short time later David entered the service of King Saul. When a musician was needed to help soothe Saul's bad temper, David's ability as a harpist caught the king's attention. His musical skill made a favorable impression and brought considerable relief to a royal atmosphere poisoned by Saul's increasingly-common fits of rage. In fact, David impressed the king so much that, in time, he became one of Saul's personal armor-bearers. One of King Saul's attendants described David as "a brave man and a warrior" who "speaks well and is a fine-looking man" (1 Samuel 16:18).

David possessed an unusual combination of skills. He was tough—a courageous warrior in a time of violent hand-to-hand combat. He also was thoughtful and sensitive—a writer of prayers and songs. He was an outdoorsman who could survive alone in the wilderness, but he was also an inspiring leader of men and a good public speaker. Perhaps his most surprising skill was his capability as a musician. Somehow, when you picture a rugged warrior, you don't expect him to play the harp![4]

Whatever our gifts and talents may be, the Lord wants us to develop and refine them to use for His glory: "Each one should use whatever gift he has received to serve others" (1 Peter 4:10).

When I was a boy, my home church encouraged everyone—even the children and youth—to use and refine our gifts. (And believe me, mine needed a lot of refining!) Each year on Father's Day, the church sponsored Youth Sunday, a day when the youth group led worship. I'll never forget the hot, steamy Father's Day in 1969 when a nervous fifteen-year-old boy delivered a short sermon about Jesus entitled, "The Light of the World." I'll never forget it because I was that fifteen-year-old boy. My sermon lasted only eight minutes. (I don't know if my sermons are better today, but they're definitely longer!)

More than a quarter of a century later, I'm still a preacher of the gospel of Christ. I'm glad someone gave me a chance to test the waters and develop my skills years ago.

GOD STRENGTHENED DAVID THROUGH THE SPIRIT'S PRESENCE AND POWER

In the end, however, David's success as a leader did not depend on his looks, his physical strength, his musical skill, or any of his other talents. The key was the presence and power of God.

As a sign of God's call to service, Samuel took a horn of oil and anointed David in the presence of his brothers, "and from that day on the Spirit of the Lord came upon David in power" (1 Samuel 16:13). Even others who met David recognized "the Lord is with him" (v. 18).

David was keenly aware of the Lord's presence in his life. He asked God, "Where can I go from your Spirit? Where can I flee from your presence?" (Psalm 139:7).

God had a special reason for granting His Spirit's

presence and power to David. But it's good to remember that the very same Holy Spirit is at work in our lives if we have accepted Jesus as Savior and Lord! In Christ we receive not only the gift of forgiveness; we also receive the empowering gift of the Holy Spirit (Acts 2:38; Romans 8:9-11). Through the Spirit's power we can find new strength in our inner being as we face the pressures of life (Ephesians 3:16).

My daughter Michelle runs on her high school cross-country team. One Saturday morning in September, I sat on top of a hill as more than one hundred runners gathered at the starting line in the valley below. It was a spectacular sight. The runners were wearing their multicolored school uniforms. The race course followed a riverbank, and the water sparkled in the morning sun.

Even though I wasn't running in the race, I sensed the pressure the runners felt as a whistle blew and then a gun sounded to start the 3.1-mile race. A few swift runners quickly moved into the lead, and I was pleased to see my daughter running near the front of the pack. By the end, most of the exhausted but happy runners staggered across the finish line, falling into the arms of their coaches and teammates, who offered congratulations and comfort.

But soon I noticed another girl who got off to a poor start. By the race's halfway point, she was far behind everyone else except for one other girl from another team. I felt sorry for both of them, for each runner surely wanted to avoid finishing last.

The last-place runner slowly advanced toward the next-to-last-place runner. Soon they were running together side-by-side. To my surprise, neither girl tried to pass the other. As the long race continued, they just kept pace with one another.

And that's how they crossed the finish line—last, but together.

Like David, you and I face a lot of pressure. We have

a long hard race to run. But even when we limp, even when we fall, even when it seems as though we're coming in last, we have Someone by our side to the very end. The Lord will never let us down.

CHAPTER TWO

Overcoming Giant Problems

1 SAMUEL 17; PSALM 20

If you were asked to name a great battle, what would come to mind? The Battle of Gettysburg? The Alamo? The Battle of the Bulge?

Some battles are closer to home. Sometimes neighbors disagree, quarrel, and fight. After my wife and I were married, our first apartment was located across the street from a tavern. Many times we watched men come tumbling out of the bar, punching each other in a drunken brawl.

Sometimes people war, not with fists but with words. Have you heard the old saying, "Sticks and stones will break my bones, but words can never harm me"? Not true! Some bruising verbal battles take place at home and at work, and usually someone walks away wounded.

There are also battles of ideas. If you believe in God and the Bible, you may find your beliefs under attack in the college classroom or in conversations with friends.

Some of us fight private battles with physical illness, depression, financial difficulties, grief, worry, frustration, or loneliness. These problems can appear so huge, so overwhelming, we seem to be no match for them. Maybe you feel like the lion tamer who placed an advertisement in the newspaper: "Lion tamer wants tamer lion."[1]

We all face some giant problems. That's why we need to look again at the familiar Bible story about David and Goliath. It's one of the best-known battles ever fought— a life-and-death struggle between a young man and a mighty giant whose very name, "Goliath," has become a synonym for something enormous and intimidating. On the surface, it's a gripping story even children can

25

appreciate—a story of bravery and adventure, of good versus evil, of the weak overcoming the strong. From a historical perspective, it reveals important developments in the ongoing military struggles between Israel and their enemies, and helps explain David's rise to prominence.

But this is far more than a drab piece of history or a story for kids. From David's adventure we can learn how to conquer our own giant problems.

RECOGNIZE THE ENEMY

1 Samuel 17 paints a vivid picture of the battle scene: "The Philistines occupied one hill and the Israelites another, with the valley between them" (1 Samuel 17:3). The two rival armies stared menacingly across the valley like two angry children daring each other to throw the first punch. It was a bizarre standoff—an ancient game of "chicken." No one wanted to make the first move. But then Goliath lumbered onto the scene like an armored tank.

Goliath was *physically powerful.* He stood over nine feet tall (v. 4). That's two feet taller than the center on your favorite professional basketball team. He would make Shaquille O'Neal look short. If Goliath could stand flat-footed under one of today's basketball hoops, his head would touch the net!

Let's put it this way: if the Philistines had a Big and Tall Men's Shop, that's where Goliath bought his clothes. His wardrobe probably outweighed David! Goliath wore a heavy bronze helmet to protect his head. On his legs he wore greaves (shin guards) made of bronze, and the armor covering his upper body weighed about 125 pounds.

Goliath's extra-large spear had a shaft "like a weaver's rod" (v. 7)—at least two inches thick. The spear's iron point weighed about fifteen pounds. Also (as if he needed any extra help), Goliath had an assistant who walked ahead of him to carry his shield.

Goliath was a walking arsenal! His bronze leg-gear clanked as he walked, and his armor glittered under the rays of the sun. Goliath typifies everything many people value: physical fitness, a spirit of self-reliance, the best equipment money could buy. He appeared invincible.

Goliath was also *verbally abusive.* Some big men have big hearts, but Goliath was just big—a bully, a loudmouth, a trash-talker, a master of the put-down. Defiantly Goliath taunted the Israelites: "Choose a man and have him come down to me. If he is able to fight and kill me, we will become your subjects; but if I overcome him and kill him, you will become our subjects and serve us" (vv. 8, 9).

Proverbs 12:18 says, "Reckless words pierce like a sword, but the tongue of the wise brings healing." Some people speak words that comfort and soothe; but others, like Goliath, use words as weapons. They fill their sentences with ridicule, sarcasm, and profanity (see 1 Samuel 17:41-44).

Sadly, most of us probably know someone whose tongue is a lethal weapon. Some face the giant problem of verbal abuse in their own homes from a parent or spouse.

No doubt Goliath was capable of violence. But nowhere does the biblical text say he actually laid a hand on any of the Israelites. Psychological warfare was working just fine. Why should Goliath fight with his spear when he could defeat the Israelites with words?

Goliath created an atmosphere of fear and intimidation. "On hearing the Philistine's words, Saul and all the Israelites were dismayed and terrified" (1 Samuel 17:11). The Israelites were like the comic strip character, Charlie Brown, who said, "There's no problem so big that I can't run from it."

Even King Saul was afraid! If anyone was big enough to overcome Goliath it was Saul, who stood a head taller than the other Israelites (1 Samuel 9:2). But the king was filled with fear.

No football player wants his quarterback to walk into the huddle and say, "Look, guys, we may as well give up. We're going to lose!" People are looking for courageous, faith-filled leaders who are not easily intimidated and who are willing at least to try.

Another important point to notice about Goliath is his *persistence.* "For forty days the Philistine came forward every morning and evening" (1 Samuel 17:16). How demoralizing it was for the Israelites to hear Goliath's defiant challenge twice a day for nearly a month and a half! You could set your watch by this guy! He came back every morning and every evening to make the Israelites miserable.

The worst "giant problem" is the one that just hangs on and never seems to go away. It stares you in the face every morning when you wake up—and it's still there in the evening—and it will still be there tomorrow, and next week, and next month.

We can become so preoccupied with surface-level irritations (rainy weather, personality conflicts, cars that need repair, annoying coworkers) that we fail to recognize the real enemy behind our giant problems. "For our struggle is not against flesh and blood, but . . . against the spiritual forces of evil in the heavenly realms" (Ephesians 6:12). Our enemy the devil is like a roaring lion seeking someone to devour (1 Peter 5:8).

Like Goliath, the devil tries to paralyze God's army. Satan is a deceiver, a demoralizer, a divider, a discourager. Too many churches are like Israel's army, paralyzed by fear. Too many Christians are like King Saul, paralyzed by fear. We need to recognize the enemy's tactics, and act boldly.

REFUSE TO BE DISCOURAGED

The three oldest of Jesse's eight sons (Eliab, Abinadab, and Shammah) joined Saul's army and stood in the battle line facing the Philistines. Meanwhile David stayed at home tending his father's sheep. When Jesse decided to send his sons a "care package" of bread, cheese, and roasted grain, David took the food and made his way to the Israelite camp. He arrived just in time to hear Goliath shout his daily defiant challenge to the Israelite army. To David's dismay, none of his countrymen—not even his brothers—dared to respond. "When the Israelites saw the man, they all ran from him in great fear" (1 Samuel 17:24).

The soldiers' reluctance to fight Goliath surprised and angered David, especially since King Saul was offering substantial rewards to anyone who could solve this giant problem. Whoever killed Goliath would receive great wealth, he could marry the king's daughter, and his father's family would be exempt from taxes in Israel (v. 25). If the large cash bonus and marriage into the royal family weren't enough, surely the idea of a permanent tax exemption would motivate someone to tackle this giant problem!

But discouragement reigned, and the more David spoke about fighting the Philistine, the more others tried to discourage him. Eliab, his oldest brother, exploded in anger at David. Maybe Eliab was still jealous and hurt because he had been passed over when Samuel anointed David (1 Samuel 16:6, 7). Whatever his reasons, Eliab spewed out a torrent of resentment: "Why have you come down here? And with whom did you leave those few sheep in the desert?" (Angry people can be very petty; the kingdom of Israel was at stake, and Eliab was taking a cheap jab at David!) Even more hurtful, Eliab questioned David's motives and integrity: "I know how conceited you are and how wicked your heart is." And instead of being grateful for David's visit and the food he brought, Eliab added another insult: "You came down only to watch the battle" (1 Samuel 17:28).

Eventually David's willingness to fight Goliath became known to King Saul, who proceeded to offer his own discouraging words: "You are not able to go out against this Philistine and fight him; you are only a boy, and he has been a fighting man from his youth" (v. 33).

"You aren't able!" Words like those can drain the life out of a willing volunteer.

Any time you undertake a noble act of faith, there will be people who will try to discourage you. A friend of mine became a Christian when he was fifteen during a mission trip he took with a church youth group. He was baptized in the Gulf of Mexico, and came home thrilled with his new life in Christ. But instead of encouraging him, his family and friends had only negative things to say: "It won't last." "What happened? Did those folks brainwash you?"

To overcome giant problems, we must refuse to accept the gloomy predictions of the skeptics who question our motives and who have no faith in the power of God.

I like the old Chinese proverb: "Man who say it cannot be done should not disturb man doing it."

As motivational speaker John Maxwell says, "The size of the person is more important than the size of the problem."[2]

Some looked at Goliath and said, "That guy is too big to hit!" David looked at him and said, "He's too big to miss!"

As hockey star Wayne Gretzky says, "You miss 100 percent of the shots you never take."

If you volunteer to serve God, don't be surprised when skeptics tell you why you won't succeed, why you should quit, why your plans won't work. It happened to David, but he refused to give in to discouragement.

REMEMBER PAST TRIUMPHS

David was confident to face Goliath because he recalled how God helped him overcome other giant problems in the past.

David was no stranger to danger. He made his case to King Saul: "Your servant has killed both the lion and the bear; . . . The Lord who delivered me from the paw of the lion and the paw of the bear will deliver me from the hand of this Philistine" (vv. 36, 37).

Has God helped you win some victories in the past? Have you been in a tough spot, but, by the grace of God, made it through? Were you rescued from "the paw of the lion" or "the paw of the bear"?

Past victories can give us confidence to fight today's battles. Smaller triumphs can help us face big battles with boldness and confidence.

When my youngest daughter, Mindy, was six years old, my family attended a Christian convention in Louisville, Kentucky. I stood talking with my friend, Chuck Lee (one of my former Bible college professors), while Mindy picked up free samples from the various display booths.

Soon Chuck and I saw Mindy smiling excitedly as she ran toward us carrying a bright red helium balloon on a string. "Look what I have, Daddy!" she called—just as the string slipped from her fingers and the balloon floated up to the convention center ceiling. Disappointed, Mindy burst into tears. I comforted her and assured her that the loss of one balloon wasn't the end of the world!

After Mindy calmed down, we watched as she headed back into the display area to find another balloon. Chuck commented, "Isn't that the way God sees us sometimes? We come to Him in tears, feeling like our whole world is falling apart and things are slipping out of our hands. But God knows everything is going to be OK!"

He was right. God has helped us in the past. He will help us with the giant problems we face today.

REJECT INADEQUATE SOLUTIONS

Finally David persuaded King Saul to give him a chance. Saul agreed that David could confront Goliath, and told him (still with plenty of reservations), "Go, and the Lord be with you" (v. 37).

Trying to be helpful, Saul put some of his own special battle gear on David to prepare him for combat: a tunic, a coat of armor, and a bronze helmet.

This is a humorous scene. Saul was unusually large, a head taller than other men. David was younger and smaller, unaccustomed to the accompaniments of war. Saul was a size 58 long; David was a 34 regular. The armor didn't fit, nor did this whole approach to battle. It was like preparing a farmer to work in his fields by replacing his jeans and work boots with a starched white shirt and tie and an oversized suit.

Like an ill-at-ease shopper in a men's clothing store, David walked around for a while, trying to get comfortable in his new "duds." Finally he told King Saul, "'I cannot go in these because I am not used to them." If David was going to defeat the giant, he had to be himself! He had to go with his own God-given strengths. Saul may have meant well, but his garments just didn't fit David (v. 39).

Instead, David chose to face the giant with simpler tools: his shepherd's staff, five smooth stones, and a leather sling (v. 40).[3]

When you face a giant problem, be sure to reject inadequate solutions. Unbelievers try to pile on plenty of "Saul's armor." Are you struggling in your marriage? Some will be quick to counsel, "Just get a divorce." Are you unhappy in your church? Some will be quick to advise, "Just quit. Don't bother trying to work things out. Who needs the hassle?" If you're facing giant financial problems, some will recommend a "get-rich-quick scheme" that has nothing in common with authentic Christian stewardship.

Don't buy it. Often the "easy" way isn't the right way. In fact, sometimes the "easy" way isn't even easy! Saul's armor simply didn't fit David. It was too bulky, too unnatural for a man with a young shepherd's quickness and skill. David was wise to put it aside.

When we're faced with the world's inadequate solutions, we must choose God's way—the way of faith.

REJOICE IN GOD'S VICTORY

From a human perspective, David was headed for disaster. There was no way David could win this fight on his own. It was the world heavyweight champion against an untested rookie; the Dallas Cowboys against the local Pee Wee football team. It was Mario Andretti's Indianapolis race car against my 1988 Ford Tempo!

As David bravely stepped out from the battle lines, surely he wondered, *Can faith bring down that hulking mountain of a man sneering across the valley?* Sure, faith can move mountains. But we want to know, can it move *my* mountain?

His armor-bearer walking in front for protection, Goliath approached David and he "despised him." To fight a young whippersnapper like David seemed beneath his dignity. Noticing the shepherd's staff in David's hand, Goliath exclaimed, "Am I a dog, that you come at me with sticks?" Calling on the name of his Philistine gods, Goliath cursed and threatened David: "Come here," he said, "and I'll give your flesh to the birds of the air and the beasts of the field!" (vv. 41-44).

No doubt David's heart was pounding hard. But he didn't shrink from the confrontation. This wasn't merely David's battle; it was the Lord's (1 Samuel vv. 45-47).

As Goliath drew closer to begin his attack, David reached into his bag, took one of the smooth stones he had chosen, and slung it at Goliath's head. Since Goliath was wearing protective headgear (a bronze helmet) David had to make a perfect shot, and he did. It was a direct hit, and Goliath slumped to the ground. Triumphantly, David stood over the fallen Philistine and used Goliath's own huge sword to cut off the giant's head as proof of his death.

It wasn't David's skill that won the battle that day, it was God's power. It wasn't a smooth stone that made the difference, it was a strong faith.

Someone has said, "If you never undertake more

than you can possibly do, you'll never accomplish all that you possibly can." Scripture says it better: "With God all things are possible" (Matthew 19:26). "I can do everything through him who gives me strength" (Philippians 4:13).

David's victory over Goliath had far-reaching effects. The previously self-confident Philistines panicked and ran once they realized their hero was dead. The previously immobilized Israelites now surged ahead and fought with new confidence and success. One man's faith inspired confidence and renewed faith in a whole nation.

Perhaps David looked back on this great victory when he wrote Psalm 20:6-8: "Now I know that the Lord saves his anointed; he answers him from his holy heaven with the saving power of his right hand. Some trust in chariots and some in horses, but we trust in the name of the Lord our God. They are brought to their knees and fall, but we rise up and stand firm."

So what is your giant problem? Whatever it is, it's not as big as the power of God.

One giant problem we all have in common is our sin problem, "for all have sinned and fall short of the glory of God" (Romans 3:23). But through Jesus Christ, God casts our mountain of sin into the sea of His grace. We are forgiven—free to rejoice in God's victory.

A five-year-old prayed at bedtime: "Dear God, please wash away all our sins. And wash away everyone's sins, God. And God just wash away the devil. And just drown him, God. Amen."[4]

Sometimes it's hard to approach our problems with childlike confidence in God. But "this is the victory that has overcome the world, even our faith" (1 John 5:4).

When Jesus died on the cross and rose from the dead, He won life's most important battle. He broke Satan's death grip. God "gives us the victory through our Lord Jesus Christ" (1 Corinthians 15:57).

With God's help, David overcame a giant problem. With God's help, you can too.

CHAPTER THREE

Target Practice: Coping With Angry People

1 SAMUEL 18, 19; PSALM 55

I could be wrong, but I think people today are angrier than they used to be.

Hostility lies just beneath the surface of our society like a submarine armed with deadly torpedoes ready to fire at any moment.

People have short fuses. They are like "T.N.T." (Touchy Nasty Temper), ready to explode at the slightest provocation.

Uptight drivers curse, yell, and jockey for a position on the highway. Angry words pour out on the ball field or the basketball court when an official makes a questionable call. Tempers flare at home when parents and teenagers disagree. Brothers and sisters quarrel and exchange words that cut like knives. Instead of working out their differences in a positive way, coworkers blow up and tell one another off with a torrent of hateful words.

As someone has pointed out, "Anger is just one letter short of danger."

Angry people can be found in churches too. According to Marshall Shelley, frequent author on church leadership issues, some Christians are "well-intentioned dragons." They act like adversaries, not allies. They are quick to criticize, slow to apologize. They destroy enthusiasm and morale, and fill the church atmosphere with tension and suspicion. They are the reason church leaders need to have "the mind of a scholar, the heart of a child, and the hide of a rhinoceros."[1]

Anger presents a difficult dilemma for Christians. How can you deal with your angry feelings and still be kind, gentle, Christlike, and self-controlled?

Even if you manage to keep your own anger under control, you still have to cope with the anger of others. Do you ever encounter hostile people who take out their frustrations on you? Do others try to make you the scapegoat for their anger, even when you've done nothing to harm them? How can you keep your cool when others try to use you for target practice?

As David struggled to praise God under pressure, he frequently faced hostile enemies. He cried out to God, "I am distraught at the voice of the enemy, at the stares of the wicked; for they bring down suffering upon me and revile me in their anger" (Psalm 55:2, 3). David could have been describing today's world when he wrote, "I see violence and strife in the city . . . malice and abuse are within it. Destructive forces are at work in the city; threats and lies never leave its streets" (vv. 9-11).

David became a target of the rage and temper tantrums of his angry employer, King Saul. Their story can help us cope with the angry people in our lives.

CAUSES OF UNHEALTHY ANGER

Ironically, David's problems began right on the heels of his great victory over Goliath. Almost as soon as his military conflict with Goliath ended, his interpersonal conflict with Saul began.

At first, David received a hero's welcome. He was the toast of the town, the center of attention. A spontaneous victory parade sprang up, with David as guest of honor. Women celebrated David's victory with songs and dancing (1 Samuel 18:6, 7). If it happened today, someone would probably print T-shirts bearing David's face and a slogan like "David 1, Goliath 0."

But when Saul heard the women singing about David, he "was very angry; this refrain galled him" (v. 8). Saul's attitude reveals several causes of unhealthy anger.

Saul's first problem was *jealousy.* He was unhappy to see someone else honored above him. He reasoned, "They have credited David with tens of thousands, but me with only thousands"—in other words, "They are more impressed with him than they are with me." As a result, "from that time on Saul kept a jealous eye on David" (vv. 8, 9).

While playing basketball with some friends, I watched two men grab a rebound under the basket. They began wrestling for the ball. There was only one problem; the two guys were both on the same team. One of their teammates began shouting, "Same team! Same team!" Finally the two men realized what was happening, and one allowed the other to control the ball.

Christians need to learn that we're on the "same team" with other believers. Why not be happy when someone else enjoys the spotlight? Why not rejoice with others instead of secretly envying them?

King Saul wanted to be the center of attention. He could not rejoice at David's achievements. He resented his young rival and envied the accolades David received.

A second factor in Saul's unhealthy anger was a deep sense of *insecurity.* Saul began to worry that David would take away his throne: "What more can he get but the kingdom?" (v. 8).

When I was in high school, one of my classmates bullied and intimidated everyone around him. He created the impression that he wasn't afraid of anyone or anything. But one day he received a disciplinary suspension that prevented him from playing basketball for two games. He sat on the bench in the locker room and cried like a baby. Despite his angry, belligerent exterior, he was insecure and immature on the inside.

All of us want to feel secure and significant, but we don't need to put others down in order to feel better about ourselves. We need to find our security and significance in Christ.

Spiritual factors were also involved in Saul's anger.

Earlier, Saul disobeyed God and displayed an impatient, impetuous attitude that grieved the Lord and hurt the nation of Israel. God rejected Saul as king, and removed His Spirit from Saul (1 Samuel 15; 16:1-14).

Even strong believers go through discouragement and "faith stress." But Saul's heart was filled with a dark despondency and discontentment. He brooded. He fretted. He plotted to get revenge. His mind became clouded and pessimistic, his moods became frighteningly unpredictable.[2]

Spiritually, Saul was running on empty. And he was running scared. Repeatedly the Scripture states that "Saul was afraid of David," while David's popularity with the people continued to grow (1 Samuel 18:12, 15).

RESULTS OF UNHEALTHY ANGER

Saul embarked on an angry vendetta against David— and the results were devastating.

EMOTIONAL WOUNDS

Anyone who has experienced emotional suffering can identify with David's plight. Saul's angry behavior created an atmosphere of confusion and tension.

Not long ago I found a hornet's nest as big as a basketball on a tree limb in my front yard. My neighbor called his friend (a professional exterminator) who took one look at said, "Stay away from that tree! Those are baldfaced hornets." I'm a novice when it comes to insects, but baldfaced hornets sounded scary to me! The exterminator removed the nest, but within a week the few surviving hornets had built another nest as large as a baseball. I didn't realize how tenacious and determined a group of hornets could be.

Dealing with angry people is like trying to get rid of a hornet's nest. It's dangerous. One mistake, and you can get really hurt. And just when you think you've solved the problem, it comes back again.

What hurt David the most was that his pain was being

inflicted by someone who ought to have been his friend. "If an enemy were insulting me, I could endure it; if a foe were raising himself against me, I could hide from him. But it is you, a man like myself, my companion, my close friend, with whom I once enjoyed sweet fellowship as we walked with the throng at the house of God" (Psalm 55:12-14).

PHYSICAL VIOLENCE

But for David, there was more at stake than simply getting his feelings hurt. His very life was in danger as he labored in the house of King Saul. More than once, Saul flew into such a rage that he took a spear in his hand and hurled it at David, trying to pin him against the wall. David narrowly escaped with his life, managing to elude the spear each time (1 Samuel 18:10, 11; 19:9, 10).

There's a connection between smoldering inner anger and violent acts like murder (Matthew 5:21, 22). The first man ever born (Cain) killed the second man ever born (Abel) because of hatred and jealousy (Genesis 4:1-8, 1 John 3:11-15).

Unhealthy anger causes physical harm, not only to others, but also to the one who is angry!

Slobodan Jankovic, a six-foot eight-inch basketball player for a Greek national team, fumed at a referee's call that fouled him out of the game. In a rage, Jankovic rammed his head against the cement blocks supporting the backboard, and in the process broke his neck and paralyzed his body from the neck down.[3]

Fortunately, the consequences of our anger are usually not as tragic, but we may pay the price of excessive anger through high blood pressure, headaches, and stomach problems. As Carl Pruitt points out, "The connection of anger to physical problems can be observed in such expressions as 'he is a pain in the neck,' 'he makes me sick to my stomach,' 'a blinding rage,' or 'itching to get our hands on someone.'"[4]

FAMILY COMPLICATIONS

Saul's next tactic was to offer his daughter in marriage to David, but he was motivated by anger, not love;
he didn't really want David for a son-in-law! Saul simply
wanted to maintain his own credibility as king. Earlier,
he had promised that whoever slew Goliath could
marry his daughter (1 Samuel 17:25). At the same time,
Saul secretly hoped David would die in battle at the
hand of the Philistines. So he said to David, "Here is my
older daughter Merab. I will give her to you in marriage; only serve me bravely and fight the battles of the
Lord" (1 Samuel 18:17).

At first David was too modest to accept the honor of
being the king's son-in-law. When he hesitated to marry
Merab, Saul gave her to another man instead. However,
eventually David married Michal, another of Saul's
daughters (1 Samuel 18:18-27).

Talk about a rough start to a marriage! The bride's
manipulative, angry father was scheming plots for the
groom's death (1 Samuel 18:25). Anger poisons the
roots of many a family tree. Unresolved, it can rot relationships between in-laws, spouses, and children.

LONG-LASTING BITTERNESS

Like a pot simmering on a hot stove, Saul's unhealthy
anger toward David stayed at a slow boil. Saul
"remained his enemy the rest of his days" (v. 29).

If you're always angry with others, you'll make yourself miserable. As Benjamin Franklin once said, "He that
scatters thorns, let him not go barefoot." Brooding and
bitterness poison the soul with toxic memories: "You
hurt me." "You disappointed me." "You let me down." "I
will never forgive or forget what you did to me."

Strangely, the person preoccupied with hatred gives
his enemies *more* power, not less, for much of his time
and energy are consumed by angry thoughts and plots
of revenge.

Bitterness can reduce grownups to silly, childish

behavior: giving someone "the silent treatment," refusing to sit in the same church pew, avoiding social contact because of old grievances.

I remember hearing the story of two women who attended the same church, but never spoke to one another. The preacher investigated and soon found out the reason for their disagreement. Years before, the ladies lived in a rural area where no refrigeration was available, so they shared a spring house where the cold water cooled their milk and butter. One day one of the women accidentally dumped a large pan of butter into the spring, wasting the butter and giving the water an unpleasant taste.

It was a small mistake, but no apologies were offered and no forgiveness granted. So for years the two women remained "bitter over the butter"! They allowed an old grudge to ruin their Christian fellowship.

Unresolved anger bears bitter fruit.

DEALING WITH ANGRY PEOPLE

David was under a lot of pressure. His father-in-law was volatile, unpredictable—and wanted David dead. Besides, Saul still reigned as king. He could use his royal authority to crush anyone who threatened his throne.

How should we respond to the mean-spirited, angry people we encounter? How can we handle the "Sauls" in our lives?

DO THE RIGHT THING, NOT THE REVENGE THING

What should we do with our own anger?

Should we just "stuff it"? Just hold it all inside and never express any anger at all?

Should we "fluff it"? Make light of it, joke around but never deal with the real issues, act as if our angry feelings are no big deal?

Or should we "puff it"? Blow our anger all over everyone, like Saul of Tarsus who breathed out murderous threats against the disciples (Acts 9:1)?

The Lord shows us a healthier, wiser way to deal with anger. If others mistreat us, we must do the right thing, not the revenge thing!

SIX PRACTICAL STEPS

Scripture tells us how David reacted, and in the process shows how we can respond to the angry people in our lives.

1. Examine yourself first. All Saul did was blame David. David took the healthier route: instead of blaming others, he opened his heart to God and admitted his own anguish and fears (Psalm 55:1-8). Turning *to God* is healthier than turning *against others.*

While working at my desk at home recently, I couldn't find my scissors. I searched all around my desk, but I still couldn't find the scissors. I felt angry because I thought someone must have borrowed the scissors without asking. Even though it was a small irritation, I began to feel really upset! Angry questions grew in my mind: "Why do the kids always take my stuff? Why doesn't everybody just leave my things alone?"

Sure enough, I found the scissors lying on the dresser in my son's room. Settling back into my desk chair in a self-righteous huff, I took a closer look at those scissors. Then it hit me. Do you know where I got those scissors? They belonged to my mother! I "borrowed" them when I went to college twenty-three years ago, and never gave them back!

As a husband, it's easy to point out my wife's failings. But God doesn't command me to judge and correct her; He calls me to love her "as Christ loved the church and gave himself up for her" (Ephesians 5:25). It's easy to find fault with our parents, but our first responsibility is to honor them (Ephesians 6:2). It's easy to criticize our church leaders, but our first task is to obey them, submit to their authority with proper respect, and make their work a joy (Hebrews 13:17).

2. Don't give up too soon. David was remarkably patient with Saul. He didn't pout, whine, and lash back. He did what he was supposed to do. He kept serving in the Israelite army and defending his nation against the Philistines. He even continued playing the harp for Saul as long as he could (1 Samuel 19:8, 9).

When my daughter Mindy was six years old, she wrote me a letter. Still learning to spell, she printed her thoughts in dark pencil lead on a wrinkled sheet of notebook paper. Around the margins Mindy drew a row of hearts, and in her letter she wrote:

> To Daddy,
>   I love you. I will owys [always] love you all though you get angry.
>   But that will not stop me.
>   Love, Mindy

I'm glad she won't stop loving me, even though I sometimes get angry! We can't stop loving just because others are difficult to deal with. We must approach them with a spirit of forbearance, long-suffering, and forgiveness. Don't give up too soon.

3. When possible, confront the offender. Don't engage in backbiting and gossip. Jesus instructs us to seek reconciliation and to confront offenders directly and in person (Matthew 5:23-26, 18:15-17).

If you swim in the ocean, you need to watch out for the undertow. This strong current, though not obvious on the surface of the water, can pull you under. Likewise, we need to watch out for the undertow in our relationships with others. Strong but invisible undercurrents of gossip and unresolved anger can pull people down, divide churches, and drown morale.

4. When necessary, enlist the help of friends. Jonathan, one of Saul's sons, recognized David's innocence and tried to intervene. Although Saul eventually rejected Jonathan's pleas on David's behalf, at least David had a friend who understood his dilemma and tried to help (1 Samuel 19:1-7).

True friends are one of God's greatest gifts. If you are trying to cope with an angry person, why not enlist the support of a few trusted Christians who will support you through prayer, listening, and wise advice? Don't go it alone. Get involved in a small group, talk with a counselor, share your burden with an elder or a minister who can encourage you. "As iron sharpens iron, so one man sharpens another" (Proverbs 27:17).

5. When necessary, remove yourself from the situation. David was patient, but he wasn't foolish. When Saul threw his spears, David eluded them.

One night Saul sent his men to watch David's house. They intended to kill him at daybreak. But David's wife, Michal, helped him escape through a window under cover of darkness. David ran until he found the prophet Samuel who had anointed him months before, and he told Samuel all that had happened (1 Samuel 19:11-18).

Escaping from an abusive situation need not be an act of cowardice. Sometimes it's a sign of wisdom and courage. If a hurricane is coming, it's wise to evacuate!

On more than one occasion Jesus avoided arrest because it was not yet time for Him to die (Luke 4:28-30; John 8:59; 10:39; 11:53, 54). Saul of Tarsus (the apostle Paul) once escaped from his enemies in Damascus by night, huddling inside a basket his friends lowered through an opening in the wall (Acts 9:23-25).

Sometimes it's wise to run. Don't play around with temptation; "flee from sexual immorality" (1 Corinthians 6:18). Don't flirt with the devil; "avoid every kind of evil" (1 Thessalonians 5:22). Prayerfully set boundaries and be brave enough to stand firm.

David wisely took action to protect himself from Saul's vicious attacks. For us, it might mean changing jobs, finding a different roommate, breaking off an unhealthy relationship, or firmly confronting someone.

6. Trust God. David didn't face Saul's anger alone. He said, "But I call to God, and the Lord saves me. Evening, morning and noon I cry out in distress, and he hears my voice. He ransoms me unharmed from the battle waged against me, even though many oppose me. . . . Cast your cares on the Lord and he will sustain you; he will never let the righteous fall" (Psalm 55:16-18, 22).

If you want to grow a healthy lawn, you can go around and try to pull out all the dandelions and other weeds one by one. But the better way is to plant lots of healthy grass so there's no room for the weeds. In the same way, a heart filled with praise has no room for bitterness.

We live in an angry world; but God can replace the roots of bitterness with the good fruit of love, joy, peace, patience, kindness, goodness, faithfulness, gentleness and self-control (Galatians 5:22, 23). He can help us go the extra mile, turn the other cheek, and pray for our enemies instead of engaging in an unproductive cycle of revenge (Matthew 5:41-44).

Remember: Jesus encountered a lot of angry people too. He was often a target. Hostile crowds belittled Him and challenged His teaching. At first Jesus' own brothers refused to believe in Him. Eventually Judas betrayed Him. When He died on the cross His disciples fled and the religious leaders mocked Him.

It's hard to live in an angry world. But it helps to know you are at peace with God. When Jesus suffered and died on the cross, He took upon himself God's righteous anger against our sin (Romans 5:1-9).

Because of Jesus, we can have peace where it counts the most—in our relationship with God.

Angry people do not have the last word—God does. And it's not a word of anger, but of grace.

CHAPTER FOUR

Friends in Need,
Friends in Deed

1 SAMUEL 20; PSALM 133

Garry Barr was my first real friend. His sister's name (I'm not making this up!) was Candy Barr. When I was a young boy, Garry and I played together almost every day.

We built snow forts and tree houses. We played hockey in the winter, baseball in the summer, and basketball in the fall. We wrestled, argued, and stuck up for each other—because we were friends.

Friendship, however, is a lot more than child's play. Adults need friends too. In the past, many television shows featured famous friendships: Lucy Ricardo and Ethel Mertz; Wally Cleaver and Eddie Haskell; Andy Taylor and Barney Fife. More recent shows have focused on the interaction of larger groups of friends (Friends, Seinfeld, and others). Unfortunately, the friends on these programs often portray unhealthy attitudes about biblical values like honesty, faithfulness, and sexual purity.

The Bible has a lot to say about friendship. Job's friends offered questionable advice, but at least they were there when he was hurting. Moses depended on his trusted aide, Joshua. Daniel had a lot in common with his friends, Shadrach, Meshach, and Abednego.

Men like Peter, Matthew, and James, called Jesus "Lord," yet Jesus didn't hesitate to call them "friends" (John 15:14, 15). John was "the disciple whom Jesus loved." Mary, Martha, and their brother Lazarus, opened their home to the Lord and invited him to dinner.

The apostle Paul labored alongside trusted coworkers

47

like Barnabas, Luke, Silas, Timothy, Priscilla, and Aquila. Paul was a busy man, driven to fulfill God's mission in his life; but he was no lone ranger. He invested the time and energy to develop supportive relationships with the Ephesian elders and other members of the churches he planted (Acts 20:36-38; 1 Thessalonians 3:6-10).

In his book, *Restoring Your Spiritual Passion,* Gordon MacDonald writes, "Many of us would be tempted to think that cultivating special friends is something done over and above our work. I have come to believe that the developing of special friends is part of our work."[1]

THE NEED FOR TRUE FRIENDSHIP

David and Jonathan enjoyed one of the greatest friendships described in the Bible.

On the surface, it's surprising that these men would need friends at all. Both of them were rugged individualists—masculine, courageous warriors, unafraid to stand apart from the crowd. They first became acquainted after David killed Goliath. David's victory earned him widespread respect in Israel, but Jonathan was especially impressed. He and David were kindred spirits, and they soon developed a close bond (1 Samuel 18:1). Like all of us, they needed friends.

Friends provide accountability. Do you know anyone who works as an accountant? Reliable accountants are important, helpful—and sometimes irritating! After all, we could upgrade our computer or remodel the office—except the accountant reminds us that those items are not in the budget.

Just as a business corporation depends on its accountants to keep the books straight, we need friends to hold us accountable to a Christian lifestyle. All of us are accountable to God (Romans 14:12), but human friends can help us stay on the right path.

Friends provide encouragement. One of my friends is a bicyclist who thinks it's fun to ride in one-hundred-mile races. There are many advantages, he says, to riding with others in a "pack." Not only will the other bicyclists motivate you to keep up the pace; as alternating riders take the lead, the pedaling actually becomes easier because you can draw on the "draft" created by the other riders.

All of us, even individualists like David and Jonathan, need the support of friends. "But encourage one another daily, as long as it is called Today, so that none of you may be hardened by sin's deceitfulness" (Hebrews 3:13).

Friends help us grow. Do you ever find it difficult to pray? Find a small group of supportive friends who will pray with you and for you. Do you have some rough edges on your personality that need polishing, or some fruit of the Spirit that hasn't ripened yet? Find friends who can challenge and stretch you.

Friendships can even improve our physical wellbeing. Dr. Leon Eisenberg, a professor at Harvard Medical School, studied the relationship between social isolation and illness. A nine-year survey of nearly five thousand adults found that the risk of illness was two to three times greater for those who experienced low levels of social contact. Similar studies have confirmed that significant friendships in the home, church, and other groups actually can increase resistance to disease.[2]

Friends make us more productive. "Two are better than one, because they have a good return for their work" (Ecclesiastes 4:9).

I serve as preaching minister for a young urban congregation located near the University of Cincinnati. For the first five years of our existence, the church rented space in a local community center and the YMCA. As the church grew, we decided to purchase a nearby church building. At the end of our final worship service in the YMCA, the entire congregation picked up our chairs, sound equipment, flower pots, tables, Bibles, and office supplies, and marched down the sidewalk to our new building three blocks away. We laughed and rejoiced together, celebrating God's provision of a permanent meeting place. Passing motorists stopped to stare at our strange parade. One of our members said it was like "Christian looting"!

Within forty-five minutes all the equipment was deposited onto the floor of our new building, and we sat amid the clutter singing "Amazing Grace." A sizable moving job was finished in less than an hour because the whole congregation was involved. Great things happen when people work together.

THE QUALITIES OF TRUE FRIENDSHIP

David and Jonathan illustrate several important qualities of true friendship.

COMMITTED LOVE

"Jonathan became one in spirit with David, and he loved him as himself" (1 Samuel 18:1). The King James Version translates this verse as, "The soul of Jonathan was knit with the soul of David." They were more than mere acquaintances. Repeatedly the Scripture refers to their friendship as a "covenant"—a solemn, binding promise (18:3; 20:8, 16; 23:18). Four times Scripture emphasizes the love Jonathan and David had for each other (18:1, 3; 20:17; 2 Samuel 1:26).

This is the kind of sacrificial self-giving that moved Jesus to die on the cross for us (Romans 5:6-8). It's the kind of love that holds marriages and families together (Ephesians 5:33). Jesus said that love is the distinguishing mark of His disciples (John 13:35), and that the greatest love is demonstrated when someone lays down his life for his friends (John 15:13).

Too often—even in the church—it's hard to get beyond surface-level conversation to heart-level commitment. Like passengers riding on a bus or subway, people enter our lives and travel with us awhile, then depart with barely a meaningful word spoken.

Real friendship requires an active, intentional interest in others. To paraphrase John F. Kennedy's famous words, we should "ask not what our friends can do for us; ask what we can do for our friends" (see Philippians 2:1-4).

SHARED RESOURCES

As a sign of their friendship, Jonathan gave David his robe, tunic, sword, bow, and belt (1 Samuel 18:4).

These items were more than token gifts. Jonathan was a prince, the oldest son of King Saul. His robe was a symbol of royalty. The tunic was a shirt-like garment, probably part of Jonathan's military dress (as in 1 Samuel 17:38, 39). Weapons were highly valued and sometimes in short supply (13:16-22). It was no small gesture for a warrior like Jonathan to give up his sword, bow, and belt. It's comparable to a fisherman giving away his favorite rod and reel, a farmer giving away his best tractor, or a professional baseball player giving up his well-worn glove.

What resources are we willing to share with our friends? "If anyone has material possessions and sees his brother in need but has no pity on him, how can the love of God be in him?" (1 John 3:17).

It sounds noble to say, "I'd give up my life for my friends." But most of the time we give up our lives, not in major acts of martyrdom, but in small pieces. Usually it's not, "I'll lay down my life." It's "I'll give you a ride," "I'll write you a check," "I'll visit you in the hospital," "I'll help you find a place to live," "I'll try to see your point of view," or "I'll help you find a job."

True friends put "LEGS" on our faith. We:

> L isten,
> E ncourage,
> G ive, and
> S erve.

Jonathan was willing to give up even his most prized possession—his claim to his father's throne. As the

king's oldest son, he was the heir to succeed Saul as
Israel's king. But instead of being jealous of David (as
Saul was), Jonathan willingly recognized David's right to
the throne and said, "You will be king over Israel, and I
will be second to you" (1 Samuel 23:17).

CONSISTENT LOYALTY

Jonathan remained loyal to David despite Saul's opposition and angry outbursts. He was even willing to intervene and speak in David's defense (1 Samuel 19:4-7).

Fake friends are like fickle sports fans who cheer
their favorite player when he plays well, but boo him
mercilessly as soon as he makes an error. True friends
are consistently faithful, even when the pressure rises.
"A friend loves at all times, and a brother is born for
adversity" (Proverbs 17:17).

HONEST EMOTIONS

Running for his life, David found Jonathan and
explained that King Saul was trying to kill him. Together
they devised a plan to save David's life (1 Samuel 20:1-
23).

Ordinarily David would join the king for dinner during the Israelites' New Moon festival. Instead, he hid in
a field while Jonathan tried to explain David's absence
to King Saul. Saul, however, erupted in anger and
hurled his spear at Jonathan, confirming his intent to
kill David.

Filled with anger and grief, Jonathan took a young
boy with him to the field where David was hiding.
Jonathan shot an arrow into the distance—a prearranged warning signal. After the boy retrieved the
arrow, Jonathan sent him away so he and David could
talk in private (vv. 4-40).

What unfolded next was a touching scene. David and
Jonathan were warriors, hard-nosed veterans of military
conflict. Yet they were willing to express honest emo-
tions with one another. In a gesture filled with respect

in their Middle Eastern culture, David bowed three times before Jonathan, pressing his face to the ground. The men kissed each other and cried together, and David (evidently the more emotional of the two) wept the most (v. 41).

Tears are not a sign of weakness. Sometimes they are a sign of great love. Jesus cried when His friend Lazarus died (John 11:35). The apostle Paul reminded the Ephesian elders that he "served the Lord with great humility and with tears," and Paul wept unashamedly when these men knelt together in prayer and exchanged tearful good-byes (Acts 20:19, 36-38).

Christian love has to go deeper than a casual hand-shake at the door on Sunday morning. In your church, do the preachers and elders sometimes weep together because of their concern for one another and for the Lord's work? Do those who attend your church services really experience the compassion of Christ? Are we really bearing one another's burdens? Have we forgotten how to "rejoice with those who rejoice" and "mourn with those who mourn" (Romans 12:15)?

David and Jonathan's friendship was not emo-tionalism. They simply were two people who were will-ing to become vulnerable and allow God's love to touch their hearts deeply. True friendship goes beneath the surface. It can say without embarrassment, "I have you in my heart . . . I long for all of you with the affection of Christ Jesus" (Philippians 1:7, 8).

SPIRITUAL DEPTH

Sadly, David and Jonathan prepared to go their sepa-rate ways. But their common faith brought them com-fort. This was more than just "male bonding" between two guys with similar interests. As Jonathan said, they could "go in peace" because their friendship was "in the name of the Lord" (1 Samuel 20:42). Later Jonathan found David again and "helped him find strength in God" (1 Samuel 23:16).

For a believer, friendship moves to a new level, which the New Testament calls koinonia—"participation or fellowship," sharing a common life in God's family (Acts 2:42, 1 Corinthians 10:16). In Christ we are joined in spiritual kinship even with people we might not otherwise choose for friends. "Here there is no Greek or Jew, circumcised or uncircumcised, barbarian, Scythian, slave or free, but Christ is all, and is in all" (Colossians 3:11).

Should we cultivate friendships with unbelievers? Of course! Jesus did this (and was criticized for it). Friendships with non-Christians provide useful bridges for sharing our faith, but we must beware of unhealthy friendships that weaken our faith. "He who walks with the wise grows wise, but a companion of fools suffers harm" (Proverbs 13:20).

If you've ever had to bid farewell to a close friend, you can understand what David and Jonathan were feeling as they said good-bye. It's sad when a friend moves away. But for Christians, the bond of fellowship remains strong even when we are separated by miles. The word "good-bye" is just a contracted form of the blessing, "God be with you."

A couple of years ago, the members of our church said good-bye to Dan and Sue Burton, who had labored with us for years in an effective campus ministry. The Burtons now serve the Lord as missionaries in Ethiopia. We seldom see them anymore, but the Burtons are still our dear friends. We pray for them daily. We stay in touch through letters, faxes, and phone calls. In the future we plan to send a delegation from our church to visit them in Ethiopia.

Friendship endures when it is grounded in the Lord.

THE BLESSINGS OF TRUE FRIENDSHIP

Perhaps David had Jonathan in mind when he described the blessings of unity and friendship in Psalm 133.

UNITY IS GOOD AND PLEASANT

"How good and pleasant it is when brothers live together in unity!" (Psalm 133:1).

Unity is good and pleasant because it's a mark of spiritual maturity (Ephesians 4:13-16). It honors the Lord Jesus who prayed for our oneness (John 17:20-23). It helps the church live out our calling as a "care corps" (from the Latin *corpus*, "body")—a caring body reflecting Christ's love. Non-Christians are impressed by Christian unity, but they are repulsed by unfriendly and cliquish church members.

Just as unity is good and pleasant, division is ugly and unpleasant. Petty jealousy and religious wrangling repel those who seek true friendship.

Joe's One Visit

Joe, the non-Christian, once went to church,
For he was engaged in a spiritual search.
A tired, hungry soul who wanted release—
Joe needed to learn of the Lord, Prince of Peace.

One Sunday he walked to the church and went in,
Searching for love and forgiveness of sin.
Inside he was met by a man with a frown,
Who glumly said, "Come, I'll show you around."

"Your name is Joe? Well, Joe, here's the scoop:
We really are quite a diversified group.
Mrs. Smith never speaks to old Mrs. Jones.
The preacher is rotten clear down to his bones.

"Some sit in pews while the rest prefer chairs.
Our elders are known for their long-winded prayers.
The sermons are boring, our building is cold.
We need some new flooring, our hymns are too old.

"This woman's too stubborn, that man is headstrong.
The preacher's wife's wardrobe and hairstyle are wrong!

This child is too loud, that man is too quiet . . .
But it's great to be a Christian, Joe! You really should try it!

"Our keyboardist frequently misses a chord,
And no one can trust the men on the board.
And, oh, yes, our church dinners—how very sublime!
We picnic and nitpick at the very same time!

"We argue and fight, and it's easy to see:
On doctrine and methods we seldom agree.
But, Joe, in spite of all of this fuss,
We hope you feel right at home here with us!"

But Joe wasn't listening. He had walked out the door.
In a world filled with quarrels, Joe didn't need more.
He longed for true friendship; instead, he found fights.
Why didn't God's people just point him to *Christ?*

UNITY IS LIKE PRECIOUS OIL

Unity, David says, "is like precious oil poured on the head, running down on the beard, running down on Aaron's beard, down upon the collar of his robes" (Psalm 133:2).

What does this mean? Oil running all over someone's beard and clothes doesn't sound "good and pleasant." It sounds like a mess! In Exodus 30:32, 33, the Lord told Moses to make a special oil for anointing the priests. This sweet-smelling oil (made of cinnamon, fragrant cane, olive oil, and various spices) was never to be worn as an ordinary perfume. Only priests could use it. It was a privilege—a special mark of the priesthood—to be anointed with this aromatic oil.

Under God's New Covenant, all Christians are priests (1 Peter 2:9, 10; Revelation 1:6). When we live and serve together in harmony, our unity (like precious oil) is fragrant and pleasing to God, and to others it's a breath of fresh air in a world polluted by division and selfishness.

UNITY IS LIKE THE MORNING DEW

"It is as if the dew of Herman were falling on Mount Zion, for there the Lord bestows his blessing, even life forevermore" (Psalm 133:3).

The Israelites thought of dew as a mysterious gift from God—quiet, cool, refreshing. Like the morning dew, true friendship blankets us with God's blessing.

Both the oil and the dew are pictured as descending, flowing down from the top to the bottom. Mount Hermon is a large mountain (over nine thousand feet high) located about twenty miles north of the Sea of Galilee. The Jordan River originates at the base of Mount Hermon. Likewise, Christian unity flows from the top down, originating with the head of the church, Jesus Christ.

Healthy friendships are a precious gift from God. We can learn a lot from the human friendship of David and Jonathan. But in the end, Jesus is the greatest friend. He laid down His life for us, and He will be there even if every other friend lets us down. He is "a friend who sticks closer than a brother" (Proverbs 18:24).

He will help us when we're under pressure.

CHAPTER FIVE

Staying Sane in a Crazy World

1 SAMUEL 21; PSALM 34

What makes you feel stressed? Eleven thousand people responded to a National Stress Survey conducted by *Prevention* magazine. According to the survey, the number-one cause of stress is personal finances, followed by job stress, responsibilities and chores, and marriage or other relationship issues.[1]

The survey included space for people to write down some of the frustrations that recently caused them to feel stressed. The list included:

* "My husband signed up for $4,000 in flying lessons after I took a second job to pay bills."
* "A boat trailer and truck took up eleven spaces at a parking lot."
* "My neighbor had a leaf blower and two lawn mowers going at the same time."
* "My daughter had her tongue pierced."
* "The bowler next to me kept running up just as I was ready to bowl."
* "Mother sued us after falling on our deck."
* "While cleaning out my closets and drawers, my husband accidentally gave away all my winter clothes."
* "I was shortening a new pair of slacks—and cut the same leg twice."[2]

A major league batting coach once said, "There are two theories on hitting the knuckleball. Unfortunately, neither of them works." Sometimes life is like facing a knuckleball pitcher—and every day, you step up to the plate again.

Maybe you can relate to the bumper sticker that says, "When my ship finally comes in, I'll probably be at the airport."

Life doesn't always make sense. Puzzling over an English assignment, my daughter asked me, "If you have more than one mouse, why are they called mice? If you have more than one house, you don't call them hice!" It's a crazy world.

Of course, most of the time when we say something is "driving us crazy," we aren't talking about certifiable insanity. We just mean we're feeling pressured and stressed, anxious and worried, burdened and hassled.

Sometimes, even our spiritual lives don't make sense. Many believers go through times when life feels joyless, when spiritual clarity is replaced by confusion, when God's blessings seem to give way to the blues and the blahs.

It happened to David. Just when he was on the verge of greatness, his life turned upside down. David was fast becoming one of Israel's best-known warriors. But King Saul angrily set out to kill him. Instead of ruling from a throne, David was on the run. He was feeling desperate.

In one of the lowest moments of his life, David acted like a madman to escape capture and death. But he still managed to give God praise under pressure. First Samuel 21 provides the historical details, while Psalm 34 contains David's spiritual journal of the incident.

David illustrates how to stay clear-minded and spiritually strong in the midst of our crazy world.

CRAZY-MAKING CONDITIONS

According to 1 Samuel 21:1, David fled from Saul to a village called Nob. "Nob" probably meant a "hill" or "knoll." Nob probably was located on a high ridge of ground just a mile or two north of present-day Jerusalem. So many priests lived in Nob the village was known as "the town of priests" (1 Samuel 22:18, 19). There David found a priest named Ahimelech.

Ahimelech trembled with fear when he saw David (1 Samuel 21:1). It must have been highly unusual to have the king's son-in-law suddenly appear at your door asking for help! Besides, news travels fast; perhaps Ahimelech had already heard that David was a marked man. If Ahimelech helped David, he would be guilty of aiding a fugitive. On the other hand, he may have feared David's reaction if he refused to assist.

David's own nervousness did little to put Ahimelech at ease. Throughout 1 Samuel 21 we do not see David at his best. It's almost embarrassing to read about David's weaknesses and subtle deceptions. Scripture describes even its main characters "warts and all." This chapter portrays David as a pretty unheroic hero.

But, come to think of it, David acted the way many of us do when we're under pressure. He was thinking fast, trying to survive. He bent the truth, implying that the king had sent him on a secret mission. He was upset and off balance as he struggled with several crazy-making conditions.

NO FRIENDS

Just days before, David said a tearful good-bye to his friend Jonathan (1 Samuel 20:41, 42).

Problems grow more intense when we have to face them without the support of friends. "Pity the man who falls and has no one to help him up!" (Ecclesiastes 4:10).

NO FOOD

Weak and famished after days of hiding, David asked Ahimelech for bread or whatever else he could find (1 Samuel 21:3). Problems seem amplified when we're hungry, sick, or physically exhausted. David was desperate for food. How humbling it was for this great warrior to beg for bread!

In a relatively prosperous nation like the United States, it's easy to take food for granted. We shop in supermarkets that stock thousands of foods plus other products from cosmetics to videotapes. For breakfast alone, a typical American can enjoy Florida orange juice, bananas from the Caribbean, a New York bagel, and Wisconsin cream cheese; then wash it all down with a cup of South American coffee or Chinese tea. But in biblical times most people could not take food for granted. In fact, much of their time was spent simply growing and preserving enough basic food to survive—which is still the case many places in today's world.

No matter how crazy things seem, we can be thankful for basic blessings. Contentment is a great coping mechanism in a crazy world. As the apostle Paul said, "Godliness with contentment is great gain" (1 Timothy 6:6). When life is going eighty miles per hour, it's good to slow down and pray, "Give us today our daily bread" (Matthew 6:11). Thank God for a simple meal, a healthy body, another day of life.

The only bread Ahimelech could offer David was some special consecrated bread ("shewbread") baked specifically for use only in the tabernacle. According to the Law of Moses, twelve loaves of bread were to be arranged in two straight rows on a golden table. Fresh bread was set out each week, and the old bread was eaten by the priests (Leviticus 24:8, 9). Technically David and his men had no right to eat this bread, but the priest allowed it. The ceremonial aspect of the law paled in comparison with the need to save and sustain a man's life.[3]

NO SWORD

Not only was David hungry. He also was unarmed. He asked Ahimelech, "Don't you have a spear or a sword here?" (1 Samuel 21:8).

David must have been feeling desperate and vulnerable. Normally you would ask him for advice on spiritual matters, but you wouldn't ask a priest to arm you for battle! Ahimelech owned no arsenal of weapons. Ironically, though, the extra-large sword previously owned by Goliath was wrapped in a cloth and hidden away somewhere in the tabernacle. Ahimelech offered David the huge weapon and said, "If you want it, take it; there is no sword here but that one." And David replied, "There is none like it; give it to me" (v. 9).

Just when David felt utterly defenseless and vulnerable, he ended up with the granddaddy of all weapons: Goliath's huge sword. When this world is driving us crazy, and we feel defenseless and vulnerable, it's good to remember that we Christians have a sword too: the "sword of the Spirit, which is the word of God" (Ephesians 6:17). God's Word is "living and active," and "sharper than any double-edged sword" (Hebrews 4:12). If we know the Scriptures, we're well-equipped to fight our spiritual battles. We can say of the Bible what David said of Goliath's sword: "there is none like it; give it to me."

NO PRIVACY

David faced yet another problem. He was no longer an unknown shepherd boy from the backwoods. Like today's celebrity who cannot go out in public without being swarmed by photographers, David was now so well known that nearly everyone recognized his face. Just as Michael Jordan can't walk through a crowded Chicago street without someone noticing him, David the giant-killer found it difficult to escape notice in Israel. There was no place to hide.

While David talked with Ahimelech , he caught the eye of a bystander who happened to be one of Saul's advisers. "Now one of Saul's servants was there that day, detained before the Lord; he was Doeg the Edomite, Saul's head shepherd" (1 Samuel 21:7). This fellow, Doeg, was high on the list of people David didn't want to see right then! Doeg recognized David, and reported to King Saul everything that happened. Eventually Doeg caused even greater harm. Saul, angry that the priests had come to David's aid, commanded Doeg to kill the eighty-five priests and slaughter the whole population of Nob. And he did (1 Samuel 22:9-23).

David left Ahimelech the priest and sought asylum in a town called Gath (located near the Philistine border) which was ruled by a king named Achish. Again, David could run but not hide. The king's servants recognized him and told Achish, "Isn't this David, the king of the land? Isn't he the one they sing about?" (1 Samuel 21:10, 11).

Lack of privacy can be a serious problem, especially in a city. Today many folk work in crowded factories or offices. Others live in overcrowded apartment buildings or dormitory rooms. We all need friends (and some personality types require more people-contact than others do), but everyone also needs a time and place to be alone. Too much noise, too many demands, too much contact with people can put us on the edge of craziness. Maybe that's why Jesus often slipped away to lonely places and prayed (Luke 5:16). Maybe that's why He said to pray in a "closet," an inner room where no one sees us but our heavenly Father (Matthew 6:6). Moments of sustained privacy can nurture our souls and restore our spiritual sanity.

When I was a boy, I complained because I had to share a room with one of my brothers. Somehow my plight seemed less harsh when I visited a friend whose family had twice as many children living in a house half the size of mine. In Haiti and Mexico, I've been amazed to see how many people can crowd into a tiny home. My missionary friends in Africa struggle to find any "alone time." Many of us need to be more grateful for the private times God provides.

NO DIGNITY

Now that Achish, the king of Gath, knew who he was, David grew even more afraid. What if Achish decided to kill him rather than risk the wrath of Israel's King Saul? Quickly David found a strange but effective solution to his predicament: "So he pretended to be insane in their presence; and while he was in their hands he acted like a madman, making marks on the doors of the gate and letting saliva run down his beard" (1 Samuel 21:13).

What a humiliating scene! David, the great hero of faith, was acting like a raving lunatic. Even Achish seemed embarrassed. Sarcastically he said to his servants, "Look at the man! He is insane! Why bring him to me? Am I so short of madmen that you have to bring this fellow here to carry on like this in front of me? Must this man come into my house?" (v. 14). If the situation weren't so serious, the king's words could sound humorous: what his city didn't need was a few more imported madmen!

But this incident certainly wasn't funny for David, and it's not funny to anyone who has ever experienced great mental or emotional distress. Crazy conditions can bring us to the breaking point.

HOW TO KEEP YOUR HEAD

What was David thinking when this terrible trauma finally ended? Psalm 34 tells us.

According to the subtitle appearing before verse one, David wrote this psalm "when he pretended to be insane before Abimelech" (another name for Achish, king of Gath).[4] Evidently David wrote the psalm soon after he made his escape.

This chapter is an acrostic poem, one of the so-called "alphabetical psalms." That is, each verse of the psalm begins with a different letter of the Hebrew alphabet, in consecutive order. The Israelites sometimes wrote this way to express poetic beauty and as an aid to memorization.[5]

Psalm 34 is filled with encouragement for people under pressure. Inspired by God, David shows us how to keep our heads when the world is going crazy.

LEARN TO FOCUS ON GOD

Sixteen of the twenty-two verses in this psalm refer to "the Lord." It begins with praise: "I will extol the Lord at all times; his praise will always be on my lips." Even at such a low point in his life, David could find reasons for praise. This was not just spiritual escapism. David made a conscious choice to recognize the reality of God at all times.

It's fairly easy to praise God on Sunday morning when we're together in a church building with sunlight streaming through the windows—when prayers, songs, and friendly greetings fill the air. When your family is getting along, and the physician gives you a clean bill of health, and the boss gives you a raise—it's easy to praise God then.

But what about the other times? When you feel foolish or discouraged? When you're tempted to sin? When God doesn't seem to be leading anywhere? When you're under pressure? Even when the pressure mounts and crazy things happen, you can decide to praise God.

David continues, "My soul will boast in the Lord; let the afflicted hear and rejoice. Glorify the Lord with me; let us exalt his name together" (vv. 2, 3).

Usually none of us enjoy hearing someone else boast—especially when we're afflicted! If you catch the flu, you don't want to hear someone else boast about his perfect health. If you strike out every time you bat, you don't want to hear your teammate brag about his five-for-five day. If you failed a test at school, you don't appreciate hearing a friend brag about making an "A."

But David wasn't boasting about himself. Whatever else David may have learned from his experiences in Gath, he clearly learned a lesson in humility. His life nearly fell apart. He acted like a madman. His pride, dignity, and self-importance stripped away, David now was boasting "in the Lord."

It's easy to exaggerate our own importance. In one of Aesop's fables, a fly clinging to a chariot wheel brags, "My, what a dust cloud I have caused!" In our lives, it isn't our strength and talent that make a difference, it is God's. Instead of "glorify the Lord with me," the King

James Version translates "magnify the Lord with me."
Magnify Him! Put the magnifying glass on God's goodness. The closer you look, the more there is to see of
God's character and greatness. You can't over exaggerate the importance of God.

Magnify Him *with me!* When we worship Him together
with other believers, God's praise is amplified. Alone I
don't have "a thousand tongues to sing my great
Redeemer's praise," but together we do. Some experiences are more meaningful when they are shared.
Imagine going to an important ball game where you
were the only person in the stands rooting for the
home team. Imagine going to a concert performed by a
great symphony orchestra, and you were the only person in the audience.

Even when life doesn't make sense, we must not give
up meeting together (Hebrews 10:25), for something
special happens when we exalt his name together.

GIVE YOUR FEARS TO GOD

David writes, "I sought the Lord, and he answered
me; he delivered me from all my fears" (Psalm 34:4).

I lived in New York when Hurricane Gloria hit the
coast of Long Island in 1985. Our church building was
located just a quarter of a mile from the shore of the
Atlantic Ocean. Nervous neighbors and business owners
boarded up their windows as the storm approached. My
friend Tom, a deacon in the church, helped me pull
important files and books out of my office as we tried to
do everything possible to protect our belongings from
the storm's high winds and high tides. As we slid into
my car and drove to higher ground, I said, "Tom, we
need to pray, 'Lord, it's in Your hands now.'" Tom
replied, "Dave, it always *was* in the Lord's hands!"

When David was at a low point in his life, he didn't
just whine, "Oh, poor me." He realized that his life
always was in God's hands. He said, "This poor man
called, and the Lord heard him" (Psalm 34:6). It does

no good to sit around feeling sorry for yourself. But when we pray, God helps us overcome fear.

1. He removes shame (v. 5).
2. He saves from troubles (v. 6).
3. His angels protect the faithful (v. 7, cf Hebrews 1:14).
4. He is good, a place of refuge (v. 8).
5. He meets needs; those who fear him "lack nothing" (vv. 9, 10).

Maybe you've heard the Woody Allen line, "The lion and the lamb may lie down together, but the lamb won't get much sleep." But according to David, even lions sometimes "grow weak and hungry, but those who seek the Lord lack no good thing" (v. 10). We don't need to be afraid.

FIND COMFORT IN GOD

When life was driving David crazy, he found comfort in the Lord. He realized "the Lord is close to the broken-hearted and saves those who are crushed in spirit" (v. 18). David says the Lord protects all the bones of the one who trusts in Him (v. 20). This doesn't mean a believer will never suffer a bone injury! It's just another way of emphasizing God's concern for us. Our bodies contain more than two hundred bones. But since the heavenly Father knows even the number of hairs on our heads (Matthew 10:30), bones should be no problem! God watches over our lives—all the parts, all the details.

In a deeper sense, David is alluding to the flawless Passover lamb—a symbol of innocent suffering—whose bones were not to be broken (Exodus 12:46), and deeper still, to Jesus' perfect sacrifice on the cross, when none of His bones were broken (John 19:36).

Think of it. Jesus Christ, the sinless Son of God, hung helplessly on a cross, suffering for sins He did not commit. On the surface it seems crazy, insane, senseless. But sometimes when life doesn't seem to make sense, God is doing His greatest work.

CHAPTER SIX

Don't Cave In

1 SAMUEL 22-26; PSALM 57

When I was a freshman in college, one autumn afternoon a group of friends persuaded me to go "spelunking" with them. Spelunkers, they explained, are people
who explore caves and underground caverns.

I love being outdoors—especially as the air turns
cooler and the leaves change colors in the fall. But I
was a novice when it came to caves. I had never
"spelunked" before. I barely knew a stalactite from a
stalagmite. But my friends reassured me that caving was
great fun, so I drove with them to Carter Caves State
Park in eastern Kentucky. One by one my friends disappeared through a tiny opening in the ground. A little
uncertain, I took one last breath of fresh air and followed them into the cave.

Now, no offense to anyone who loves spelunking, but
caves are not pleasant places! Caves are dark, damp,
and chilly. They are confining and claustrophobia-pro-
ducing. At one point in our expeditions my friends and
I pressed through a section of the cave that grew
increasingly compressed. At first we walked, then we
stooped, and finally we crawled on our hands and
knees along the smooth cold rock. I will never forget
how relieved I felt when we saw a flicker of sunlight up
ahead. Finally we squeezed through a small opening
and emerged into the fresh air.

I wonder if David liked caves. Probably not. He was a
shepherd, an outdoorsman, accustomed to the open
fields. On the other hand, he probably knew the caves
around Judea very well. Shepherds often took shelter in
caves during rainy weather. It's easy to imagine young

David and his older brothers playing in the caves near their home in Bethlehem.

According to 1 Samuel 22:1, David fled to a cave in a place called Adullam. This cave—which some think was actually a large network of underground caverns—became David's unofficial headquarters while he was forced to hide from King Saul. David's gloomy surroundings in the cave seem almost fitting. He was down. He was in a pit. Saul's heart was as hard and unyielding as the cave's cold walls.

If you've ever been so discouraged you felt like "crawling in a hole," you can appreciate David's state of mind. He was destined to become king, but at the moment he could hardly show his face in public.

We can learn from David some valuable truths about "spiritual spelunking." Eventually most of us spend time in the cave. (Maybe you're there right now.) We fall into pits of depression, caverns of grief, dark holes of doubt.

Sometimes it feels as though we will never escape from the cave. But eventually we do, and in the process God uses our spiritual spelunking to build our faith. Even some of the great heroes of faith "wandered in deserts and mountains, and in caves and holes in the ground" (Hebrews 11:38).

According to an explanatory note above Psalm 57, David wrote this psalm of praise "when he had fled from Saul into the cave." When David was most low, he called out to God most high. Even when life was caving in on him, David gave God praise under pressure.

FINDING PURPOSE IN THE PITS

1 Samuel 22–26 tells the story of David's continuing flight from King Saul. Imagine how it felt to live every waking moment as a fugitive from a jealous, hostile king, trying to escape arrest and death. David could never let down his guard. He was under constant pressure. During the day he constantly had to watch over

his shoulder. At night, it was difficult to close his eyes and sleep in peace.

But God took care of David even when he was in the pit of despair. 1 Samuel 23:14 offers this summary statement, "David stayed in the desert strongholds and in the hills of the Desert Ziph. Day after day Saul searched for him, but God did not give David into his hands."

ATTACKED, BUT NOT ALONE

God provided David a new set of friends when he was in the cave. "All those who were in distress or in debt or discontented gathered around him, and he became their leader. About four hundred men were with him" (22:2).

This band of supporters doesn't seem like the greatest group to have around. David's support group was dysfunctional with a capital "D." All who came to him were in Distress, in Debt, or Discontented. These were not the popular, the rich, the people who had everything together. At first glance, these men appear to be misfits, losers, failures, malcontents, castoffs. This group was living proof that "misery loves company."

But notice what happened when these folk gathered around David. "He became their leader." David didn't say, "I'm too good to associate with people like you." He didn't say, "Look, I have enough problems of my own." Despite their problems, he saw their potential; and as time passed, David's leadership turned this bunch of so-called misfits into a makeshift army clever and strong enough to protect David from the far larger army of Saul. In fact, some of these troubled followers eventually became known as "David's mighty men."

Never underestimate what God can do for people— especially when they receive the right kind of godly leadership. The Lord can turn losers into winners, sinners into saints, the confused into the committed, the hurting into the hopeful.

Isn't that what Jesus did? Those who came to Jesus
were distressed, discontented, and owed a debt of sin.
He never shunned them. Lepers, tax-collectors, the
chronically ill, people with scarred and ugly pasts—Jesus
taught them, touched them, transformed them. Suffering
people flocked to Jesus. He met them with open arms
and said, "Come to me, all you who are weary and burdened, and I will give you rest" (Matthew 11:28).

Some might regard Jesus' twelve apostles as a bunch
of misfits—a stormy combination of personalities (uned-
ucated fishermen, tax collectors, doubters, political
activists). But under Jesus' leadership they blossomed
into a band of missionaries who changed the course of
history.

VICTIMIZED, BUT NOT VENGEFUL

1 Samuel 24 tells how David and his men were hiding deep inside a cave near an unpleasant-sounding
place called "the Crags of the Wild Goats." Saul was still
in hot pursuit with an army of three thousand select
soldiers searching for David.

As David and his men huddled quietly in the inner
recesses of the cave, who should come walking in but
Saul himself! And he was alone—an easy mark if David
wanted to kill him. You can almost hear David's men
whispering, "Now's your chance, David! Go ahead, kill
King Saul! Get revenge on your enemy. Get rid of him
so you can be king!"

But David didn't kill Saul. Instead, while Saul was
preoccupied in the cave, David crept up quietly and cut
off the corner of the king's robe, then retreated unnoticed into the cave. Without realizing he had just experienced a close brush with death, Saul nonchalantly left
the cave unharmed, oblivious to David's presence there
(vv. 3-7).

David came out of the cave and called out to Saul,
"My lord the king!" Imagine Saul's amazement to find
that David had been in the cave with him! David

explained that he had no intention of harming Saul. He posed no more danger to Saul than a dead dog or a flea! David even felt conscience-stricken because he had dared to cut off a corner of Saul's robe. David said to Saul, "May the Lord judge between you and me. And may the Lord avenge the wrongs you have done to me, but my hand will not touch you" (v. 12).

David was victimized but not vengeful. He confronted Saul with the truth, but not with violence, or a spirit of revenge. David reasoned, "No matter what Saul has done to me, he's still God's anointed king. I have no right to take his life. If God wants him out of the way, I'll wait for God to take care of things in His own time."

David's gracious approach touched the heart of his enemy. Saul wept and told David, "You are more righteous than I. You have treated me well, but I have treated you badly" (vv. 16, 17). David's problems with Saul were not over; but he had won a major victory for the sake of his own personal integrity. And, in the long run, David was vindicated. God eventually did remove Saul, and David became king—not right away, but when the time was right.

How should you respond when life is caving in around you? When you're stuck with family problems, financial pressures, illness, or other burdens? When you feel unfairly hassled, unappreciated, and mistreated? David reacted with patience and grace. Instead of repaying evil for evil, he tried to "overcome evil with good" (see Romans 12:17-21).

ANGRY, BUT ABLE TO ACCEPT ADVICE

1 Samuel 25 tells about David's close encounter with a woman named Abigail and her husband, Nabal, who was a wealthy farmer. Talk about a mismatched and incompatible couple! Abigail was "an intelligent and beautiful woman, but her husband, a Calebite, was surly and mean in his dealings" (v. 3). "Nabal" means "fool," and unfortunately the man's name was a good

description of his character! According to Abigail, her husband was "just like his name—his name is Fool, and folly goes with him" (v. 25).

It was sheepshearing time—an annual social event that often included large feasts, shearing contests, and other festivities. Since Nabal owned a thousand goats and three thousand sheep, his shearing party was bigger than most, and David's men could use some "R & R." David politely asked Nabal to permit his men to attend the sheepshearing festival and to receive some of Nabal's provisions. This was a reasonable request, since earlier David's men had treated some of Nabal's shepherds kindly (vv. 4-9).

When Nabal heard David's request, however, he reacted with anger. "Who is this David?" he asked. "Who is this son of Jesse? . . . Why should I take my bread and water, and the meat I have slaughtered for my shearers, and give it to men coming from who knows where?" (vv. 10, 11). When David heard about Nabal's insult, he was furious. He and four hundred of his men put on their swords and headed toward Nabal's farm. No doubt there would have been a bloody confrontation if not for the intervention of Abigail.

Abigail was very wise. She brought a large gift (enough bread, wine, meat, grain, and fruit to feed David's men) and she brought a peacemaking message. She asked David to forgive her husband's reckless insults. ("He's like that with everybody," she said.) David did not need to engage in pointless bloodshed, she argued, for God would take care of the situation.[1]

David listened to Abigail's advice, and decided not to harm Nabal. As it turned out, any action on David's part would have been unnecessary anyway. Eventually Nabal died and the widowed Abigail became David's wife (vv. 35-44).[2]

Sometimes it's hard to accept wise advice. When we're angry and upset, it's hard to accept the counsel of cooler-headed friends. It can also be hard to intervene.

I remember seeing a videotape of a boxing match. At one point in the fight, the referee attempted to step between the boxers. One of the boxers accidentally landed a crushing right jab to the jaw of the referee, who crumpled unconscious to the floor. Intervention can be dangerous!

Abigail dared to intervene, and despite David's anger, he was willing to heed her wise advice. If we're going to survive our times in the spiritual deserts and caves, we must do the same.

BURDENED, BUT STILL BOLD

Though David was still on the run, he had lost none of his courage. First Samuel 26 records yet another time when David boldly approached King Saul. Saul set up camp with his three thousand soldiers. When night came, Saul was sleeping inside the camp surrounded by his armed guards, with his own spear stuck in the ground near his head.

David and a friend named Abishai decided to sneak into the campground. Silently, they crept unnoticed past the sleeping soldiers until they saw where Saul was sleeping on the ground. In an excited whisper, Abishai offered to kill Saul while he had the perfect opportunity. But David wouldn't allow it. He told Abishai, "Don't destroy him! Who can lay a hand on the Lord's anointed and be guiltless?" (vv. 5-9).

Sometimes courage makes us speak up and take action. But at times the braver course of action is to refrain from acting and to wait on the Lord.

At His trial, Jesus refused to answer the charges of the false witnesses. The supreme example of courage, He was like a silent sheep before its shearers. Though He could have called thousands of angels to rescue Him from the cross, Jesus bravely endured the suffering and trusted His Father's plan.

David could have killed Saul. But he boldly trusted God's power and timing. Instead of taking Saul's life,

David took the king's water jug and his spear. Before anyone woke up, David and Abishai slipped outside the camp. Once a safe distance away, David woke the king and his men with a shout, displayed Saul's water jug and spear, and told Saul, "As surely as I valued your life today, so may the Lord value my life and deliver me from all trouble" (vv. 12-24).

Even Saul was impressed by David's bravery and fairness. He told David, "May you be blessed, my son David; you will do great things and surely triumph" (v. 25).

And triumph David did. Eventually Saul's sons were killed in battle with the Philistines, Saul took his own life, and David was anointed king (1 Samuel 31:1-13; 2 Samuel 2:4). David was blessed because he trusted in the Lord. He went from the cave to the crown, from the pit to the palace.

PRAISE FROM THE DEPTHS OF THE CAVE

David wrote Psalm 57 "when he had fled from Saul into the cave." In this song of praise we catch a glimpse of the faith that sustained David during those long days and nights he spent in the caves and deserts.

WHEN YOU ARE MOST LOW, GOD IS STILL MOST HIGH

From the depths of the cave, David wrote, "I cry out to God Most High, to God, who fulfills his purpose for me" (Psalm 57:2).

This title for God, the Hebrew *Elohim 'Elyon,* meaning "God Most High," has a long history. Back in Abraham's day, Melchizedek was known as "priest of God Most High" (Genesis 14:18-20). When the angel Gabriel appeared to Mary, he said that her Son, Jesus, would be great and would "be called the Son of the Most High" (Luke 1:32).

The Lord God is most high. He is superior to all else. He towers above any other physical or spiritual power in the universe. No human idol comes close. No problem is too big for God. No human philosophies can match His wisdom. God says, "As the heavens are higher than the earth, so are my ways higher than your ways and my thoughts than your thoughts" (Isaiah 55:9). Yet God Most High is willing to stoop down and hear our prayers when life caves in on us.

It's ironic that the drug culture picked up the phrase "getting high." Drugs make you "high" at first, but eventually they bring you down. An exciting ball game can make you feel "pumped up," a gripping movie can get your adrenaline flowing, a fast jog on a brisk morning can give you "runner's high," and get your blood pumping. But eventually you come down from physical and emotional highs—sometimes into a cave! What then? What will you do? Where can you turn in the down times?

David turned to the Most High God. In Psalm 27:4, David wrote, "One thing I ask of the Lord, this is what I seek." What was this "one thing"? Constant comfort? A spiritual high? No, it was simply to know God Most High! "That I may dwell in the house of the Lord all the days of my life, to gaze upon the beauty of the Lord and to seek him in his temple."

I've been to the top of tall buildings like New York's World Trade Center. I've been on tall mountains like Wyoming's Grand Teton. I've flown over the ocean on powerful jets, thousands of feet above the earth. Astronauts have walked on the moon and lived on a space station in outer space. But nothing in our human experience can surpass the greatness of knowing God Most High.

WHEN YOU ARE EXHAUSTED, GOD IS STILL EXALTED
Like many of the hymns and praise choruses we use today, Psalm 57 contains a short refrain repeated word-for-word (in verses 5 and 11), "Be exalted, O God, above the heavens; let your glory be over all the earth."

David was exhausted. His life was caving in. But

while he hid under the ground, he prayed for God's glory to be displayed above the heavens.

In July, 1995, the Sampoong Department Store in Seoul, Korea, collapsed and trapped hundreds of people. More than two weeks after the building collapsed, a rescue worker heard a faint voice in the rubble. To everyone's amazement, a nineteen-year-old woman named Park Sung-hyun was found still alive. For sixteen days she lay buried face down under concrete slabs and crumbled boulders. She persevered, and the rescue workers didn't give up, even when all hope of survival seemed past.[3]

When we feel exhausted, and hope seems lost, God is still exalted. He can display His glory and power even during our weakest moments.

WHEN OTHERS ARE HATEFUL, GOD IS STILL FAITHFUL

David's enemies were like "lions" and "ravenous beasts—men whose teeth are spears and arrows, whose tongues are sharp swords" (v. 4). David felt pursued and pressured, hounded and harassed, wounded and weakened, tripped and trapped.

But notice how David describes the Lord: "He sends from heaven and saves me, rebuking those who hotly pursue me; God sends his love and his faithfulness" (v. 3). Continuing in prayer, David sings, "For great is your love, reaching to the heavens; your faithfulness reaches to the skies" (v. 10).

When life threatens to crush you, don't cave in. God is faithful. You can praise Him, even when you're under pressure.

CHAPTER SEVEN

Why Worry When You Can Worship?

2 SAMUEL 6; PSALM 8

My family has taken several memorable vacations together, but none surpasses the summer when we camped out in Yellowstone National Park and the Grand Teton Mountains. Far from the pressures of the daily grind, it was easy to put aside our worries for a few days. The air was crisp and clear. The mountain scenery was spectacular, bathed in unpolluted sunshine and the scent of pine. Old Faithful gushed up right on schedule.

On chilly nights, my wife and I, along with our son and two daughters, slept in tents. We roasted marshmallows over a campfire beneath a cloudless, star-filled Wyoming sky. We spent our days hiking along tree-lined mountain trails leading past towering waterfalls, lakes formed by melting snow, and prairies covered with graceful ferns and red, yellow, and purple wildflowers. We saw deer, elk, chipmunks, and trumpeter swans. We watched a moose swim across a lake. We laughed when a herd of buffalo surrounded our car. We watched in awe when a light rain produced a bright double rainbow over the mountains.

One afternoon we climbed a steep trail to a place in the Grand Teton Range known as Inspiration Point, a high rocky ledge overlooking beautiful Jenny Lake. From there we ventured deeper into Cascade Canyon, where rugged cliffs and boulders surrounded a briskly-flowing creek. We decided to scatter out so each member of the family could spend a few minutes alone.

I climbed about fifty yards above the trail and sat on a

large chunk of granite. In every direction I could see God's creative splendor. Towering behind me was a gray wall of rock. Before me was a tree-lined, snow-capped peak jutting into the blue sky. Below me was a cascading stream flowing swiftly along the rocks. And from my high vantage point I could see my wife and children near the trail below, sitting on logs and rocks, taking in the scene.

Reaching into my backpack, I pushed past the water bottles, mosquito repellent, and sunscreen until I found the Bible I had brought along. I turned to Psalm 8 and read David's words of praise:

> O Lord, our Lord,
>   how majestic is your name in all the earth!
> You have set your glory above the heavens.
> From the lips of children and infants
>   you have ordained praise.
>
> . . . .
>
> When I consider your heavens,
>   the work of your fingers,
> the moon and the stars,
>   which you have set in place,
> what is man that you are mindful of him,
>   the son of man that you care for him?
>
> . . . .
>
> You made him ruler over the works
>   of your hands;
>   you put everything under his feet:
> all flocks and herds, and the beasts of the field,
> the birds of the air, and the fish of the sea,
> all that swim the paths of the seas.
> O Lord, our Lord,
>   how majestic is your name in all the earth!
>
> Psalm 8

WHY GOD DESERVES OUR WORSHIP

Sitting on that mountainside, I realized how David must have felt. David's adventures brought him many up-close encounters with nature. He spent lots of time on rugged mountain trails. He noticed the wildlife, the quiet streams, the star-filled night sky—all the things my family described with adjectives like "majestic" and "awesome" and "spectacular." But above all, what took David's breath away was the majesty and glory of God!

GOD'S CHARACTER

Psalm 8 begins and ends with identical exclamations of joyful praise: "O Lord, our Lord, how majestic is your name in all the earth!" God is our royal ruler, our sovereign king, who deserves to be addressed as "Your Majesty." Instead of "majestic," some translations say, "how excellent is your name," for God's name excels over all others. He is worthy of our highest honor. His character is flawless.

My grandfather's name was Worth Faust. It's unfortunate that the name "Worth" has fallen out of fashion today. I like to picture two parents looking down at their wiggling baby son and saying, "That child is Worth!" Every human being possesses great worth and value. But no human worth compares with that of God himself. When we praise the Lord we acknowledge His supreme value. We adore Him. We affirm His majesty and greatness. He is worthy of our worship ("worth-ship").

Instead of giving God the priority He deserves, it's easy to be distracted by worries. Instead of "O Lord, our Lord!" we say, "O job, my job!" or "O money, my money!" or "O schoolwork, my schoolwork!" or "O car, my car!"

Why worry when you can worship? Jesus said not to worry about our food, drink, and clothes, or even about our very lives; but He didn't stop there. Jesus went on to show that worship is a positive alternative to worry: "Seek first his kingdom and his righteousness, and all these things will be given to you as well" (Matthew 6:25-34). The apostle Paul did not merely say, "Do not be anxious about anything." He continued, "But in everything, by prayer and petition, with thanksgiving, present your requests to God" (Philippians 4:6).

Why worry when you can worship? God's character holds the answers to our anxieties. Why worry about the future? God is timeless, eternal, the giver of hope. Why worry about finances? God is omnipotent, all-powerful, the giver of every perfect gift. Why worry about difficult relationships? God is love; He is the peacemaker and healer of wounds. Why worry even about death? We worship the immortal one, "the living God," the Almighty who has conquered sin and death through the resurrection of His Son.

GOD'S CREATIVITY

David was filled with awe when he considered how God created the heavens, the moon, and the stars (Psalm 8:3).

Abraham Lincoln expressed a similar sense of awe when he said, "I never behold the stars that I do not feel that I am looking in the face of God."

There's a tendency today to explain everything through purely natural causes; to ignore theology (the science or study of God) and deify technology. But the more we know about nature, the more we must stand in awe of the creator who designed and formed it.

On the clearest night, David could see only about one thousand stars with the naked eye. With today's telescopes we can see countless stars, and yet we have not begun to comprehend the depths of God's wisdom. God has not somehow gone out-of-date in our day of computers, lasers, satellites, fax machines, and nuclear physics. He is not surprised by any of our discoveries. He created the materials and processes in the first place! Science brings us many benefits, but it merely scratches the surface of the creator's awesome power.

Have you put aside your worries today long enough to marvel at God's creative handiwork?

GOD'S CONCERN

Since God is so powerful and the universe so immense, David wonders, "What is man that you are mindful of him, the son of man that you care for him?" (Psalm 8:4).

Do you ever feel this way? Do you ever gaze out the window of an airplane and notice how tiny and unimpressive the houses and cars appear—like plastic pieces on a Monopoly game board? Do you ever glance at a phone book and think, "I'm just one of thousands upon thousands of names—just another number"? Billions of people live on the earth today; why should God care about me?

Some folk conclude that God doesn't care. Zen Buddhists say, "Man enters the water and causes no ripple." In his autobiography, Mark Twain wrote that when you die, you leave a world where you were of no consequence—where you were nothing but a mistake. The world, he said, "will mourn you a day and forget you forever."[1] The philosopher, John Stuart Mill, cynically wrote, "If the maker of the world can [do] all that he wills, he wills misery."[2]

Are these people right? Does your life cause any ripples? Does God care? Does He want us to be miserable?

David ponders a marvelous fact: God is "mindful" of us (v. 4). Think of it: God has us on His mind! He is constantly aware of us, concerned for our well-being. Before we even thought of Him, God had us on His mind. He had us in mind two thousand years ago when Jesus Christ was born in a manger. He had us in mind when He was nailed to the cross, paying hell's penalty for us.

In fact, Jesus has us in mind right now as He reigns at the right hand of God, interceding for us and speaking to the Father on our behalf. He has us in mind every day when we face another challenge at school or at work. The details of God's creation are amazing. But even more amazing is the fact that we are some of the details!

GOD'S COMMISSION

David continues his prayer: "You have made him ruler over the works of your hands; you put everything under his feet" (v. 6). It's amazing to realize what God has entrusted to His people: His earth, His gospel, His truth, His church, His mission.

Almighty God is willing to join with us in a great "co-mission"—we are His partners, called to do His work in the world. God deserves our praise.

THREE WAYS TO MAKE WORSHIP MEANINGFUL

What does it mean, then, to really worship God? How can we worship Him "in spirit and in truth" (John 4:24)? Worship is a choice, an action, a lifestyle of constant praise, an ongoing awareness that we live in the presence of God. "Whatever you do, do it all for the glory of God" (1 Corinthians 10:31). We offer our bodies to Him as "living sacrifices." Every word and deed, every act of kindness to others, becomes a sacrifice of praise (Romans 12:1; Hebrews 13:15, 16).

Although David faced many pressures, we know him more for his worship than for his worries. Eventually David's chief nemesis, King Saul, died in battle along with his sons—including David's close friend Jonathan (1 Samuel 31:1-6). David mourned their deaths (2 Samuel 1:1-27), but as time passed he continued to win more battles over the Philistines and he gained increasing recognition. Eventually the leading citizens of Judah and Israel anointed David as their king (2 Samuel 2:4; 5:3-5).

One of David's first official acts as king had to do with worship. The ark of the covenant had been stored for safekeeping in the house of a man named Abinadab.[3] David decided to bring the ark to his new capital city of Jerusalem (now known as the City of David). This was no small undertaking. David selected thirty thousand men to accompany the ark and assure its safe passage to Jerusalem.

Second Samuel 6 tells what happened, and reveals several important facts about meaningful worship.

HOLD GOD'S NAME IN AWE

The ark of the covenant was a symbol of God's presence, protection, and mercy. It was "called by the Name, the name of the Lord Almighty, who is enthroned between the cherubim that are on the ark" (2 Samuel 6:2). When the Israelites carried the ark from place to place, in a sense they were carrying the name of God with them.

We carry God's name with us too. We don't carry His name in a gold-covered box, but in our hearts! "We have this treasure in jars of clay to show that this all-surpassing power is from God and not from us" (2 Corinthians 4:7).

Imagine if all Christians wore name tags that said in bold letters: "BELIEVER IN JESUS," "CHILD OF GOD," or "FOLLOWER OF CHRIST." We don't wear name tags, but we are responsible to wear the Lord's name with dignity and reverence. "If you suffer as a Christian, do not be ashamed, but praise God that you bear that name" (1 Peter 4:16). Do those around you catch a glimpse of the majesty of God's name?

OBEY GOD'S WORD WITH REVERENCE

David's men placed the ark on a new cart and made their way toward Jerusalem. Suddenly, the oxen pulling the cart stumbled. A man named Uzzah, seeing the cart lurch to one side, reached out to steady it—but "the Lord's anger burned against Uzzah because of his irreverent act; therefore God struck him down and he died there beside the ark of God" (2 Samuel 6:7).

At first glance God's abrupt death sentence seems unusually harsh. Why did God strike Uzzah down when he was only trying to help? David was angry, puzzled, and afraid. He suspended movement of the ark for three months while he pondered the situation (vv. 8-11).

A closer examination of the circumstances makes it clear that God acted fairly—in fact, with remarkable patience. It's surprising, not that the Lord punished one lawbreaker, but that He didn't punish more of them! In the Law of Moses, God gave specific instructions for the care of the ark. The Kohathites, a branch of the tribe of Levi, were supposed to take care of the holiest of the tabernacle furnishings. This responsibility was given to them alone. According to Numbers 4:15-20, the Kohathites were to carry the holy articles. They were not to touch the holy things or even look at them, or they would die. (See also Numbers 3:27-31.) Even Aaron and his sons were not actually to touch the ark. The ark was made with special rings on the sides. Poles were inserted through the rings, then the Kohathites were to carry the poles.

David's men flagrantly disregarded these guidelines. Placing the ark onto a new oxcart may have seemed like a nice gesture, but they weren't doing things the way God had prescribed. By using no poles, and by allowing ordinary men to touch the ark, they displayed too casual an attitude toward the holiness of God. Eventually David realized the root of the problem, and made sure that the ark was moved in accordance with God's instructions (1 Chronicles 15:1-15).

Worship is not something to take lightly. Scripture warns, "Guard your steps when you go to the house of God" (Ecclesiastes 5:1). The first-century church "grew in numbers, living in the fear of the Lord" (Acts 9:31). The fear of God is a church growth principle! Churches thrive in an atmosphere of heartfelt worship and holy reverence.

CELEBRATE GOD'S PRESENCE WITH JOY

Reverent obedience doesn't have to be dull, however. In fact, obedience to God's Word opens the door to an experience of joy we could not otherwise know.

When David and his men followed God's instructions

for carrying the ark, they found the freedom to worship with exuberance and joy. "David, wearing a linen ephod, danced before the Lord with all his might, while he and the entire house of Israel brought up the ark of the Lord with shouts and the sound of trumpets" (2 Samuel 6:14, 15). Sacrifices were offered, and every man and woman present that day went home with a loaf of bread, a cake of dates, and a cake of raisins to eat. This worship celebration was anything but boring! God's people were filled with joy and excitement as they praised Him from their hearts.

One of the Hebrew words for praise is "hal," which means a shout. Today when we are filled with exuberance or overwhelmed with joy, we might lift our voices and say, "Yea! All right! Great!" But the Hebrew people included God in their exclamations of joy. They shouted "Hallelujah," which means "shout to Jehovah" or "praise the Lord." Praise is a "holy hurrah." It is "lauding God."[4]

Of course, joy in worship needs to be balanced with reverence and decency. In public worship assemblies, "everything should be done in a fitting and orderly way" (1 Corinthians 14:40). God is not honored by confusion and disorder. Loud music and unstructured services do not guarantee true worship. But, on the other hand, stiff formality and silence do not guarantee true worship either. It's sad when formalism stifles faith; when our gatherings leave no room for spontaneity; when the order printed in the bulletin takes precedence over a heart-level response to God's Word.

David himself was criticized for expressing so much joy in worship. Michal, to whom David had been married years before, watched from a window as the procession moved toward Jerusalem, and "when she saw King David leaping and dancing before the Lord, she despised him in her heart."[5] Later when he arrived at home, ready to cheerfully "bless his household" (2 Samuel 6:20), she greeted him with a few choice words of biting sarcasm:

"How the king of Israel has distinguished himself today, disrobing in the sight of the slave girls of his servants as any vulgar fellow would!" (vv. 16-20). At the very moment when David was filled with joy, someone close to him threw a wet blanket onto his enthusiasm.

David's dancing was a vigorous physical expression of praise, but it was not merely for his own entertainment, and there was nothing immoral about it. When Michal accused David of "disrobing," she meant that he had taken off his outer garments and was wearing an "ephod"—a sleeveless pullover garment normally worn by the priests. David's behavior was not indecent, though it was unusual for a king to dress like this. Michal, who was raised in the home of her father, King Saul, was concerned that David conduct himself with royal dignity. David's unbridled enthusiasm—dancing vigorously as ordinary people might do—seemed like no way for a king to act. (Maybe we can relate to how she felt. We can picture the President of the United States attending a baseball game; but it's hard to imagine him standing and cheering wildly or doing "the wave"!)

The problem was, Michal didn't seem to understand why the return of the ark was so significant, or why David loved God so much. She reminds us of Martha, who Jesus said was "worried and upset about many things," but whose worries made her overlook the one thing most needed—to worship at the feet of her Lord (Luke 10:38-42). David responded firmly to Michal's criticism. He insisted, "I will celebrate before the Lord" (2 Samuel 6:21). He was not worried about his own sense of dignity. Most of all, he just wanted to worship God.

This chapter compels us to take an honest look at our own attitudes about worship. It's good to ask, "Who is most like me in 2 Samuel 6?"

Am I like Uzzah—playing with fire, not taking God's commands seriously? Am I too casual about my obedience?

Am I like Michal—playing the critic's role? Instead of worshiping God myself, do I merely criticize the way others choose to worship?

Am I like David? Do I say firmly, "I will worship the God who created me, who cares for me, who commissioned me to do His work"? Dare I say, "I'll worship Him with my whole heart, even if others criticize and don't understand"?

Eventually my family vacation in Wyoming came to an end. When we arrived home in Cincinnati, our city was under a smog alert. Instead of clear blue skies, a thick smelly haze enveloped us and made it hard to breathe. Instead of sitting on a mountainside surrounded by wildflowers and a flowing stream, I came back to a desk stacked with bills to pay and unfinished work to do.

But the same God who was with me on the mountain also is with me in the valley. "O Lord, our Lord, how majestic is your name in *all* the earth"—even the earth's low points.

Why worry when you can worship?

CHAPTER EIGHT

Fit for a King: Honoring God in Times of Personal Success

2 SAMUEL 7, 8; PSALM 16

In his book, *Living the Psalms,* Maxie Dunnam tells about three men who were discussing what it means to be successful. One said, "Real status is when you're invited to the White House for a personal conversation with the President." The next man responded, "No, you know you've arrived when you're invited to the White House, and while you're talking with the President, the Hot Line rings, and the President decides to ignore it so he can give you his undivided attention." Finally the third man said, "No, you're both wrong. Real status means you're invited to the White House, the Hot Line rings, the President answers it, and he says, 'Here, it's for you.'"[1]

How do you measure success? How will you know when you've attained it? As one fellow said, "I'm already over the hill . . . and I don't ever remember being on top of it!"

Did you ever see a dog chase a car? What will happen if the dog ever *catches* a car? We spend a good portion of our lives pursuing things we consider important, but what will happen once you finally catch what you're chasing? How will you handle it when you finally accomplish your goals?

Eventually, many of us achieve some measure of success. After years of expensive study, you finally graduate from college. You meet the right person and marry. You buy a house, or receive a long-awaited promotion, or enjoy that dream vacation you've always talked about. What then? What will happen when you finally attain the success you've been pursuing for so long?

DAVID'S ROAD TO SUCCESS

David encountered many problems and stresses. But 2 Samuel 7 describes a time in David's life when everything was going well. He finally caught what he had been chasing.

FROM RAMS TO RICHES

Career? No problem. David now occupied the top position in his nation, and was firmly established as king. Housing? No problem. Instead of living in the open fields with the sheep or hiding in a cave, now he lived in a palace large enough to accommodate his growing family. Standard of living? Comfortable—very comfortable. When King Saul pursued him, David barely managed to find enough food to survive, but now he was healthy and prosperous. Servants stood ready to do his bidding. A rich variety of foods adorned the royal table. Everything around him was fit for a king.

David became king in the prime of his life and reigned over Israel forty years (2 Samuel 5:4). By the age of thirty, he achieved what many of us only dream of—money, power, prestige, a sense of accomplishment. He had it made.

As 2 Samuel 7 begins, David "was settled in his palace and the Lord had given him rest from all his enemies around him" (v. 1). Oddly, though, David still felt restless. It bothered him to think that he was living in a comfortable palace paneled with cedar, while the ark of the covenant remained stored in a tent. He conferred with the prophet Nathan, who passed on to David specific instructions he received from the Lord: "Now then, tell my servant David, 'This is what the Lord Almighty says: I took you from the pasture and from following the flock to be ruler over my people Israel'" (v. 8).

For some people, success is a case of "rags to riches." David's success story was literally a case of "rams to riches." God took him from the poverty of the pasture to the pomp of the palace.

FROM A "NO-NAME" TO A KNOWN NAME

Nathan continued God's promise to David: "'Now I will make your name great, like the names of the greatest men of the earth'" (v. 9).

There was a time when the name of David was virtually unknown, yet this obscure shepherd boy became so famous that now we recognize him even without a surname; "David" says it all. Altogether, his name appears more than one thousand times in the Bible. The Messiah was called the "Son of David." God made David's name great.

Are you ever tempted to "make a name for yourself"? What athlete doesn't enjoy hearing the crowd cheer when his name is introduced in the starting lineup? What author doesn't like to see her name in print? What actor doesn't want to see his name in lights on a theater marquee? Even the Bible says, "A good name is more desirable than great riches; to be esteemed is better than silver or gold" (Proverbs 22:1).

But you can't measure success by the number of people who know your name. In the final analysis, the most important thing is for your name to be written in the Lamb's book of life (Revelation 20:15; 21:27). One day Jesus' disciples excitedly reported the success of their preaching expedition. They were so filled with spiritual power, they even cast out demons. But Jesus warned them, "Do not rejoice that the spirits submit to you, but rejoice that your names are written in heaven" (Luke 10:20).

When Judgment Day arrives, it won't matter if anyone knows your name except the Lord. Many will point to their accomplishments on that day, saying, "Lord, Lord, look what I did! I was successful in the world's eyes. I made a name for myself. I was a model citizen. I was listed in *Who's Who.* Aren't You impressed, Lord?" And He will say, "Depart from me. I never knew you."

Even if a billion people know your name, no amount of human recognition can compare with the importance of knowing the Lord and His salvation. And even if no one else on earth knows who you are, it's enough that your heavenly Father knows your name and includes you among the saved.

FROM AN UNCERTAIN FUTURE TO A GLORIOUS FUTURE

David's accomplishments were more than just a temporary flash of fame. This was no fly-by-night success story. The Lord said, "Your house and your kingdom will endure forever before me; your throne will be established forever" (2 Samuel 7:16).

Ironically, this chapter begins with David proposing to build a house for the Lord; but instead, the Lord promises to establish a house for David—a lasting royal dynasty. As years passed, David's descendants continued to reign, beginning with his son Solomon and extending through twenty kings in all who ruled in Jerusalem. Figuratively speaking, Christ himself came to occupy David's throne, since He was descended from "the house and line of David" (Luke 2:4-7). David's influence extended centuries into the future as God unfolded His plan.

Whatever success we achieve during our short lifetimes pales in comparison with the surpassing importance of the long-range purposes of God. Sometimes faith means trusting God's wisdom even when we do not live to see the full fruit of our earthly goals and ambitions. God is "able to do immeasurably more than all we ask or imagine, according to his power that is at work within us," and this promise is not limited to our own lifetime, but extends "throughout all generations" (Ephesians 3:20, 21).

FROM CONSTANT HARDSHIP TO CONSTANT VICTORY

Over and over again, the biblical narrative emphasizes David's success: "The Lord gave David victory wherever he went. David reigned over all Israel, doing what was just and right for all his people" (2 Samuel 8:14, 15).

Does this mean that David no longer faced any pressure? Hardly! Success brings its own pressures. Now that David was wealthy and well-known, the pressures didn't go away—they simply took a different form.

BUMPS ON THE ROAD TO SUCCESS

There are several "bumps" on the road to success.

1. Success can make you lazy. As someone has said, "The road to success is dotted with many tempting parking places." When things are going well, it's easy to become too comfortable. Complacency replaces commitment. Golfer Chi Chi Rodriguez said, "It's a lot harder to get out of bed in the morning when you're sleeping in silk pajamas."

2. Success makes you vulnerable. More people want to tackle you if you're the one carrying the ball. The more successful you become in the world's eyes, the more vulnerable you will be to criticism and jealousy. Others will make more demands of you. As John Maxwell says, "Success is relative; once you have it, all the relatives come!"[2]

3. Success brings temptation. As one Christian said, "If I had more money, I'd just be tempted to sin more extravagantly!" Success breeds an attitude of self-sufficiency. We begin to think we don't really need God. Such pridefulness is poison. It's spiritual high cholesterol that clogs our souls and chokes the flow of faith and grace.

4. Success will not satisfy your soul. As someone has said, "Many people spend their lives climbing the ladder of success, only to come to the end and realize it was leaning against the wrong wall!"

Several years ago, successful TV newsman Harry Reasoner reflected on his career in a televised interview. Looking back on his life, Reasoner commented, "I envy the people with clear eyes." I think I know what he meant. No matter what rewards life brings you, there's no substitute for a clear-eyed sense of purpose and faith.

Financial analyst Jon Talton wrote:

> The truth? All the work in the world, the most glamorous job with the most money and the best chance to accumulate human and material trophies—all of it can't make up for our great deficit of the soul. All of it can't buy the simple shelter of love and trust and integrity.
>
> So here we are: rich and smart and lost. We can't go back to anybody's old-time religion or misty Ozzie and Harriet memory.
>
> We know too much. And not enough.[3]

Jesus said it best: "What good is it for a man to gain the whole world, yet forfeit his soul?" (Mark 8:36).

DAVID'S RESPONSE TO SUCCESS

In June, 1995, the *American Queen,* the largest river steamboat ever constructed, began its maiden voyage up the Mississippi River. Unfortunately, the huge boat became stuck in the mud and sat immobilized for days while work crews labored to get it moving again.

Was the boat a "success"? Not when it was stuck in the mud! The *American Queen* was built to be a masterpiece of craftsmanship—but it fulfilled its purpose only when it moved its passengers up the river. The boat's designers did not intend for it to sit there unmoving, going nowhere.

Sadly, sometimes churches resemble that steamboat; instead of fulfilling their God-given potential and moving full steam ahead, it's as if they are stuck in the mud, going nowhere. Like the church at Sardis, they "have a reputation of being alive," for they have achieved respectability and success in society, but from the Lord's perspective they are lethargic and dead (Revelation 3:1, 2).

Maybe God seldom allows people to achieve a great deal of success precisely because so few are able to handle it well! Samson possessed great physical strength, but he was careless and reckless. The wise and wealthy Solomon foolishly allowed his wives to pull his heart away from the Lord. Brash Simon Peter bragged about his loyalty to Jesus, but just a few hours later, he denied the Lord three times.

David, on the other hand, seems to have handled success well at this point in his life.

HE PRAYED ABOUT IT

As soon as he heard Nathan's encouraging words, "King David went in and sat before the Lord" (2 Samuel 7:18).

His first response to success was not to gloat, pat himself on the back, or brag to a friend. He didn't even take his family out to dinner to celebrate! His first response was to pray.

Prayer is the right response to any circumstances, good or bad. "Is any one of you in trouble? He should pray. Is anyone happy? Let him sing songs of praise" (James 5:13).

We need to put the Lord first in our times of joy and victory. If you land a good job, thank God for it and ask Him to use it as an opportunity for ministry. When you get an "A" on that big test, thank the Lord. If you preach an effective sermon or sing a well-received song in church, don't just bask in the limelight—pray! When you graduate from high school or college, spend time in prayerful reflection on God's purpose for your life. Make your wedding ceremony more than a party; make it a worship experience.

HE WAS HUMBLE ABOUT IT

David prayed, "Who am I, O Sovereign Lord, and what is my family, that you have brought me this far?"

(2 Samuel 7:18). He realized, "apart from [the Lord] I have no good thing" (Psalm 16:2).

David's success didn't swell his head with pride. He wasn't arrogant and boastful. He felt deeply unworthy of God's blessing.

Humility is the "humus," the fertile soil in which God grows the seed of fruitful service.

I once read about a fellow named Leon Huffstutter who dreamed of opening a Christian bookstore. With meager start-up funds, he rented a small vacant building and opened the store with a total inventory on the shelves of three Bibles and fifteen books. From this tiny beginning, the bookstore grew into a sizable business, touching hundreds of lives with Christian literature.

Leon described his success this way: "With pride I often say, 'See what I did.' In more rational moments I say, 'See what I did with God's help.' When I'm really seeing the big picture, I say, 'See what God did.' After even more thought I say, 'See what God did in spite of me.'"[4]

David responded to success by singing God's praises: "Lord, you have assigned me my portion and my cup; you have made my lot secure. The boundary lines have fallen for me in pleasant places; surely I have a delightful inheritance" (Psalm 16:5, 6). Have you thanked God recently for drawing pleasant "boundary lines" around your life?

HE VIEWED HIS SUCCESS
AS AN OPPORTUNITY TO HONOR GOD

David's prayer continued: "And now, Lord God, keep forever the promise you have made concerning your servant and his house. Do as you promised, so that your name will be great forever. Then men will say, 'The Lord Almighty is God over Israel!'" (2 Samuel 7:25, 26).

David's goal was not just to make a name for himself. He wanted the Lord's name to be glorified.

For a Christian, our noblest purpose in life is not just

to enjoy pleasures "fit for a king." Our purpose is to be *servants* "fit for a King"—to pour out our lives in dedication to the King of kings, whether this brings us fame or obscurity, wealth or poverty.

REDEFINING SUCCESS

During a visit to New York City, I noticed a poster thumbtacked to a message board on the Staten Island Ferry. The poster said, "Who cares whether knowledge is power or money is power (as long as you end up with both)?" Christians choose a different route.

David's song of praise in Psalm 16 reveals a healthier and more biblical understanding of success.[5]

SUCCESS COMES
WHEN YOU'RE SECURE IN THE LORD

> I will praise the Lord, who counsels me;
> even at night my heart instructs me.
> I have set the Lord always before me.
> Because He is at my right hand,
> I will not be shaken.
>
> Psalm 16: 7, 8

I like those words, "I will not be shaken!" Around six o'clock one Saturday morning, my family awoke to find our windows rattling and the floor trembling. It was a small earthquake. No damage resulted, but it was an unsettling experience, to say the least. It's scary to be shaken.

Think how the people in Jerusalem felt on the day Jesus died. The Bible says the earth shook so much that the rocks split. Again, three days later, a violent earthquake accompanied Jesus' resurrection from the dead (Matthew 27:51; 28:2). God shook the earth when Jesus died and rose again, so that in the long run His people could be secure and unshakable no matter what hardships life brings. As Christians "we are receiving a kingdom that cannot be shaken" (Hebrews 12:28). What security, what success, what safety there is in Christ who overcame sin and the grave!

> Therefore my heart is glad and my tongue rejoices;
>   my body also will rest secure,
> because you will not abandon me to the grave,
>   nor will you let your Holy One see decay.
>   Psalm 16:9, 10

Several years ago, my wife, Candy, and I visited missionary friends in Mexico. They took us into the crowded marketplaces of Saltillo and the smoggy streets of Monterrey. Every place we went was unfamiliar territory. I can assure you, we stayed close to Juan and Brenda, our guides! It was reassuring to know that we could trust our friends who knew their way around.

No earthly success can compare with the grand reality of God's never-failing love. He will never abandon or forsake us. We are never left to flounder alone through life's unfamiliar twists and turns. We are secure in Him.

SUCCESS COMES WHEN YOU'RE SAVED

No one celebrates success in hell. All earthly goals and accomplishments pale in comparison with the surpassing importance of being right with God. David's psalm of praise ends on a joyful note:

> You have made known to me the path of life;
> you will fill me with joy in your presence,
> with eternal pleasures at your right hand.
>   Psalm 16:11

But the story doesn't end in the Old Testament. Psalm 16 is a messianic psalm filled with prophetic significance about the work of Christ. Peter quoted from this psalm in his sermon on the Day of Pentecost. Jesus Christ is the ultimate fulfillment of David's words about the "Holy One" who would not be abandoned to decay in the grave (Acts 2:24-28). The greatest picture of success is Jesus!

Jesus turned the cross—a dreaded symbol of pain and humiliation—into a mark of triumph. Crucifixion was a gruesome sign of failure, but Jesus turned it into a success story.

And Jesus radically redefined success for all of us when He said, "Whoever wants to save his life will lose it, but whoever loses his life for me and for the gospel will save it" (Mark 8:35).

What will happen when you finally catch what you've been chasing all your life? You'll find joy and eternal pleasures in the presence of Jesus—but only if your life's ambition has been to follow the One who said, "Take up your cross and follow me."

Let's be servants fit for a King.

CHAPTER NINE

Dining at the King's Table

2 SAMUEL 9; PSALM 23

Do you ever feel frustrated by some physical limitation your body places upon you (too short, too tall, too heavy, too thin, too weak)? If you try, you probably can find something less-than-perfect about your physical appearance, your personality, or your status in life.

Healthy self-esteem is an elusive quality. Do you ever feel sorry for yourself and wallow in self-pity? Do you ever feel overworked and under appreciated? Do you ever feel inferior or inadequate when you compare your talents and accomplishments with those of others? Maybe you can relate to the words of baseball player Larry Anderson who remarked, "If at first you don't succeed, failure may be your thing."

Instead of being on top of the world, do you sometimes feel like the world is on top of you? As the cartoon character, Ziggy, said, "I've been here and there. I've been up and I've been down. I've been in and I've been out. I've been around and I've been about. But not once, not even once, have I ever been 'where it's at'!"

OUR NEED FOR GOD'S GRACE

Life's demands can seem overwhelming. Parents sometimes feel inadequate to handle the demands of child-rearing. My wife, Candy, went back to school at age forty to become a registered nurse. On her first day of chemistry class, she came home looking a little dazed, saying, "I think I've gotten in over my head!"

My friend, Joe Cluff, talked with me recently about his plans to do missionary work in Africa. Joe will be teaching schoolchildren and helping start a new church. As we discussed his plans, Joe said, "I've been thinking about how inadequate I feel to do something in a different culture that is hard to do even in my own culture."

Much of the pressure we face in life comes from the outside—for example, as we deal with angry people or problems outside our control. Many times, however, the pressure comes from inside ourselves. A lot of stress is self-inflicted.

To a certain extent, it's good to recognize our weaknesses and imperfections. "Blessed are the poor in spirit, for theirs is the kingdom of heaven" (Matthew 5:3). Happy are those who sometimes feel unhappy with themselves, for only a humble, repentant heart can discover Heaven's kind of happiness!

The fact is, we really aren't worthy—but we're not worthless. We can never do enough, work enough, or be good enough to earn God's favor—but God shows us kindness anyway. The apostle Paul rejoiced because of God's "glorious grace, which he has freely given us in the One he loves [Jesus Christ]" (Ephesians 1:6).

God has lavished His grace on us through Jesus Christ! None of us deserves such kindness. What we could never do in our weakness, God has done by His power. God turns paupers into princes. He takes us from the gutter of sin and seats us at the king's table.

DAVID AND MEPHIBOSHETH:
AN EXAMPLE OF GRACE

Second Samuel 9 tells a tender story of compassion and kindness. On the surface it's a straightforward historical narrative about how David handled personal matters early in his reign as king. But if we look deeper, we can find encouragement in this chapter for anyone who struggles with self-esteem and feelings of inadequacy. David's kindness to Mephibosheth provides a helpful illustration of the way God, our gracious King, treats us.

A WEAK MAN

Mephibosheth was the son of David's friend, Jonathan, and the grandson of David's old nemesis, King Saul. Earlier, the Philistines nearly wiped out Saul's entire family (1 Samuel 31:2). Mephibosheth survived, but he had serious physical complications. He was "crippled in both feet" (2 Samuel 9:3), the result of an accident that occurred when he was five years old. According to 2 Samuel 4:4, Mephibosheth's nurse picked him up and attempted to flee when she heard the news of Saul and Jonathan's deaths, but in her haste she dropped him and permanently injured his feet.

A bone injury like this one was especially serious in ancient times. There were no physical therapists or orthopedic surgeons, no leg braces, wheelchairs, or even crutches as we know them today. There were no cars or buses to make travel easier. The lame had to make their way around by using sticks or canes, or persuade some friends to carry them around (see Mark 2:3).

Life wasn't easy for Mephibosheth. He couldn't run for fun and exercise. He couldn't run from his circumstances either. I wonder if he felt resentful or bitter as he recalled the childhood accident—someone else's mistake—that left him physically challenged.

Mephibosheth also faced some social limitations. In those days, newly-crowned kings had a nasty habit of killing relatives of the previous king to prevent anyone from making a claim to the throne. Unsure what King David's policy would be or how others loyal to David might treat a descendant of King Saul, Mephibosheth lived under a cloud of anxiety. His father, Jonathan, was dead, and his grandfather, King Saul, died in dishonor. Instead of enjoying the life of a prince, Mephibosheth found a place to live outside the public eye in an obscure village called Lo Debar. The village's very name suggests how undesirable this place was. In Hebrew, "Lo Debar" means "no pasture."

Mephibosheth probably faced some social stigma because of his inability to walk. Tragically, people with obvious physical weaknesses often encounter prejudice and misunderstanding. William J. Diehm, a clinical psychologist who was stricken with poliomyelitis at the age of five, has pointed out the negative effects of thoughtless words and stereotypes. "Handicap" is from the Old English expression, "cap in hand," as used in reference to a beggar. "Cripple" is derived from the old English "to creep." "Invalid" suggests that a person is "not valid." Words like "abnormal" and "deformed" diminish personhood and communicate disrespect.[1]

Joni Eareckson Tada became a quadriplegic as a result of a swimming accident when she was a teenager. According to Joni, sometimes the church tends to view those who struggle with physical challenges as projects, not people. She says, "When we don't view people with disabilities as just that—people—but as the disabled or retarded, we're missing a big dimension as to who they really are. They are people, not with problems, but with gifts and abilities, with hobbies, interests, and opinions, with tastes in fashion, with ideas about politics and current events."[2]

As someone has asked, "Who is handicapped, the person who can't see or the one who doesn't look? The one who can't hear or the one who won't listen? The one who reaches with one hand or the one who is afraid to reach at all?"

Mephibosheth's problems chipped away at his self-esteem until he ended up with limited expectations. He had lost hope. He described himself as nothing but "a dead dog" (2 Samuel 9:8). In those days, dogs symbolized the unclean and the unacceptable. In Jewish society it was hard to think of anything more disgusting and untouchable than a dead dog. When David summoned him to the palace, Mephibosheth came with fear and trembling, feeling unworthy and unwanted, not knowing what to expect.

A KIND KING

But David intended no harm to Mephibosheth (as other kings might have done). Instead of vengeance and hatred, David had a gracious goal in mind. He asked his servants, "Is there anyone still left of the house of Saul to whom I can show kindness?" (2 Samuel 9:1).

It's amazing the difference a little kindness can make. Alice Peter was born with cerebral palsy. She was unable to roller skate, swim, ride a bike, or drive a car. But her parents' love sustained her through the hardships. Alice wrote:

> They encouraged and shared my prayer life, opened His holy Word to me daily, worshiped with me in Sunday school and church, and never left any doubt in my mind that I was loved by them as well as the Lord who made me. Not once in all those growing-up years did they allow me to blame someone else for my aches and pains or for my being different. Always, when I became frustrated and discouraged (as I often did), the two who loved me the most suggested I look at my situation from another angle.
>
> If people had difficulty understanding my speech, maybe I should write the things I felt. Since I was unable to ride a bike or drive a car, maybe I should learn to enjoy God's world by taking walks through the countryside. Because of my slower pace, they taught me to observe the waxy yellow buttercup and the thorny wild rose, the oak and the willow tree, the specks of precious color preserved in each troublesome pebble along the path. . . .
>
> Every once in a while, I dig out my college diploma, or slides I took while traveling in Europe, or baby pictures of my three sons, and I have a deep sense of satisfaction. It is true I have . . . pain, discomfort, and frustration, but most of the time I really can thank the Lord that He hasn't forgotten me.[3]

Indeed, the Lord doesn't forget. Neither should we. Kindness is a gift anyone can give.

David was *a king who kept his promises.* He wanted
to show kindness "for Jonathan's sake" (2 Samuel 9:1).
Long before, David and Jonathan tearfully agreed to a
covenant of friendship that included their future descendants (1 Samuel 20:42). Although Jonathan was dead,
David remembered his promise and kept his word.

It took some effort even to locate Mephibosheth, but
David was *a king searching for someone to bless.* David
found a man named Ziba (who had been one of Saul's
leading servants) and told him of his desire to find a
survivor from Saul's family. After learning that Jonathan's
son was still alive, David sent some of his servants to Lo
Debar to bring Mephibosheth back to the palace.

When Mephibosheth came trembling before David,
he bowed down to honor the king. Like the prodigal
son returning home, he felt unworthy to be considered
part of the family. Mephibosheth expected nothing good
from the king. After all, David had endured long-lasting
hostility and ill-treatment from the household of Saul,
so why should he show any kindness to Saul's relatives?

But David reassured Mephibosheth. David was *a
loving king who treated people like family.* He said,
"Don't be afraid . . . for I will surely show you kindness
for the sake of your father Jonathan. I will restore to
you all the land that belonged to your grandfather Saul,
and you will always eat at my table" (2 Samuel 9:7).

This was far more than Mephibosheth hoped for! In
those days it was an act of grace for the king simply to
spare his life. No king would treat a former enemy as if
he were a member of the family!

David could have shown his generosity some other
way. He could have presented Mephibosheth a nice
engraved plaque to hang on the wall, or a large sum of
money to take care of him the rest of his life. David
could have invited Mephibosheth to make an annual
visit to the palace. But instead, David insisted,
"Mephibosheth will always eat at my table."

Some of my family's greatest memories have taken

place around our kitchen table. Our table has been the site of countless meals, spirited arguments and debates, games of checkers and Monopoly, corny jokes, and painful tears. Our children learned to pray there, uttering solemn words of thanks over bowls of Cheerios®. Folk from our church have joined us around the table for Bible studies, Christmas open houses, ministry team meetings, premarriage counseling sessions, Thanksgiving dinners, and youth group pizza parties.

The family table is more than just a place of physical nourishment. In a way, it represents all that is healthy and wholesome about a family. It's a safe place where you don't have to worry about impressing anyone, a place of acceptance, encouragement and peace. Maybe that's why one of the biblical descriptions of Heaven is a great feast around God's banquet table. Jesus often used the dinner table as a pulpit of sorts. He turned meals into teaching times at the homes of Matthew, Zacchaeus, Mary and Martha, Simon the Leper, Simon the Pharisee, and others. When Jesus taught about the kingdom, He used parables about wedding feasts and great banquets prepared by benevolent hosts (Luke 12:35-38; 14:16-24). John's vision of Heaven includes the angel's exciting message, "Blessed are those who are invited to the wedding supper of the Lamb!" (Revelation 19:9).

Actually, we have a lot in common with Mephibosheth, don't we? He was weak. He was unworthy. He had no reason to expect any royal favors. Neither do we. In our sin we have treated God like an enemy. We are unworthy servants who do not deserve any special favors from God.

But Christ our King is faithful to His promises. He is kind and gracious. He seeks the lost. He adopts us into His family and treats us like one of His own. He welcomes us to the family table, saying, "Here I am! I stand at the door and knock. If anyone hears my voice and opens the door, I will come in and eat with him, and he with me" (Revelation 3:20).

To refuse the Lord's offer would be just as foolish as if Mephibosheth had told David, "No thanks, I'd rather stay in Lo Debar." Mephibosheth knew a good thing when he saw it! Second Samuel 9 concludes: "And Mephibosheth lived in Jerusalem, because he always ate at the king's table, and he was crippled in both feet."

SECURE IN GOD'S GRACE

When G. Campbell Morgan sought a license to preach, a group of church leaders denied his application. He sent a one-word telegram to his father: "Rejected." Immediately his father wired back: "Rejected on earth. Accepted in Heaven. Dad." Morgan went on to become an effective preacher to a church of thousands.[4] The person who feels rejected and unimportant in the world's eyes is still valuable and useful to God. God's grace makes all the difference.

Captain Scott O'Grady was an Air Force fighter pilot shot down over Bosnia. For a week he hid in the mud, with enemy soldiers walking within a few feet of his hiding place. He survived by eating grass and ants, and by squeezing water to drink out of his own socks. But eventually O'Grady was rescued, and upon his return to the United States he dined at the White House on macadamia-crusted lamb chops and other gourmet dishes. In a few days' time he went from huddling in the mud to dining at the President's table.

No matter how desperate your circumstances, Heaven's King has a place for you at His table.

Why was David so kind to Mephibosheth? Maybe it's because he himself had learned to rest in God's grace.

David knew what it meant to be a shepherd. But in David's most famous Psalm—his masterpiece—he portrays himself as a sheep and the Lord as the shepherd. Psalm 23 describes the confident security we can find in the Lord who "prepares a table before us in the presence of our enemies."

When I am helpless and hurting inside,
The Lord is my shepherd to guard and to guide.
When my heart's empty—my wounded soul bleeds,
   I shall lack nothing; the Lord meets my needs.
When life seems confusing and out of control,
He leads by the waters that quiet my soul.

When the road is too rough and I'm tired of the game,
He guides me in paths that will honor His name.
When fear chokes my vision and shortens my breath,
He's with me to walk through the shadow of death.
Dejected, discouraged, unable to laugh—
I find comfort beneath the Lord's rod and His staff.

I'm weak and unworthy, with nothing to bring—
But He prepares me a table! I dine with the King!
I'm safe in His presence, unhurt by my foes,
For His oil soothes my head, and my cup overflows.
Through pressures and problems, in stresses and strife,
His goodness and love fill the days of my life.
The Lord's watchful care will not weaken or cease
And forever I'll dine at His table in peace.
Forever I'll dwell with my Shepherd in peace.

CHAPTER TEN

The High Price of Giving On

2 SAMUEL 11, 12; PSALM 51

According to U.S. State Department figures, there are one hundred million land mines deployed worldwide, and another two million land mines are set in place each year. Land mines are a serious problem in nations plagued by guerrilla warfare and terrorism. Some land mines are quite sophisticated and are laid out in carefully-planned patterns. Others are scattered randomly along the ground. But any land mine is a serious threat. One false step can cause an unsuspecting passerby to lose his leg or his life.[1]

Our world is littered with spiritual land mines as well. Some of Satan's weapons are easy to recognize, but others are like land mines hidden beneath the surface.

The apostle Paul warned, "Be very careful, then, how you live—not as unwise but as wise, making the most of every opportunity, because the days are evil" (Ephesians 5:15, 16).

A few years ago, a fellow in New Jersey found a shiny object lying in his front yard near the highway. Evidently the heavy, oblong piece of metal had fallen from a passing car or truck. The man liked the way it looked, so he took it into his garage, spray-painted it silver, and attached it to the front of his car. Eventually someone noticed his unusual hood ornament. It turned out to be a live grenade from a nearby military base! Unwittingly, that fellow played around with something explosive that could have harmed himself and others.

That's what happened to King David. Just when he

was enjoying great success, he stepped on a spiritual land mine that nearly destroyed him—the land mine of sexual sin.

A famous statue of David stands on display in Florence, Italy. In the early 1500s, Michelangelo took two and a half years to carve this great work of art out of a thirteen and a half-foot-high block of marble. Next to the Statue of Liberty, Michelangelo's David is perhaps "the most famous statue in the world."[2] Michelangelo saw David as the true Renaissance man, the ideal human being, strong, confident, rock-like, determined, heroic.

But 2 Samuel 11, 12 reveal a disappointing side of David's life. This great man wasn't chiseled out of marble after all. In a weak moment David yielded to sexual temptation and committed adultery, then engaged in a deadly cover-up scheme. It's a true-life story of a sin committed (2 Samuel 11), a sin confronted (2 Samuel 12), and a sin confessed (Psalm 51).

A SIN COMMITTED

Like cancer, sin begins small and grows rapidly. The Bible compares the deadly cycle of sin with the way a person grows from a tiny embryo to a full-grown adult. "He who is pregnant with evil and conceives trouble gives birth to disillusionment" (Psalm 7:14). "Then, after desire has conceived, it gives birth to sin; and sin, when it is full-grown, gives birth to death" (James 1:15).

David's problems began small and became tall. He had conquered the giant Goliath with a tiny stone, but now he fell victim to his own lust for a beautiful woman. Small indiscretions grew into huge life-changing decisions.

DAVID FLIRTED WITH TEMPTATION

Like most sins, this one started not in David's actions, but in his mind. As David flirted with sin and imagined himself involved in it, gradually his moral defense system broke down.

It happened "in the spring, at the time when kings go off to war" (2 Samuel 11:1). This sounds odd to us—somehow I don't think kings just woke up some warm morning and said, "It's springtime, so I think I'll go to war." Most battles happened in the spring when weather conditions were favorable for troop movements. David sent his men out to fight, as he had done so many times before. But this time, he "remained in Jerusalem."

Have you noticed how temptation seems to increase when you have extra time on your hands? When you have a free evening to fill, or you're staying in a lonely motel in a distant city? "An idle mind is the devil's workshop."

"One evening David got up from his bed and walked around on the roof of the palace. From the roof he saw a woman bathing. The woman was very beautiful, and David sent someone to find out about her" (vv. 2, 3). In those days, the flat roof of a house was a pleasant place to rest or pray, especially in the cool of the evening. David's palace was high enough to provide a wide view of the surrounding homes. We can only speculate about Bathsheba's motives. Maybe she was an innocent, unintentional object of David's lust who had no idea she was being observed. Or perhaps, in her husband's absence, this beautiful young woman was purposely enticing the handsome king. Either way, David not only caught a brief glimpse of her beauty, he took a long look, and sent one of his trusted friends to find out about her.

If "the eye is the window of the soul," many of us probably need to do some window washing! Our eyes are bombarded by television shows, billboards, magazine ads, and movie scenes deliberately calculated to arouse sexual passion and curiosity. A short look can become a long look; a long look can become a lustful look; a lustful look can become an immoral act; immoral acts lead to physical, emotional, and spiritual harm.

Job understood this. He said, "I made a covenant with my eyes not to look lustfully at a girl" (Job 31:1). Jesus understood it. He warned that lustful looks can be just as serious as outward acts of adultery (Matthew 5:27, 28). Paul understood it. He wrote, "Flee from sexual immorality. All other sins a man commits are outside his body, but he who sins sexually sins against his own body" (1 Corinthians 6:18).

The only prescription for really "safe sex" is within the God-given boundaries of the marriage covenant. David was straying into unsafe territory. Bathsheba was already married to a soldier, Uriah the Hittite, who was one of David's most dependable warriors (2 Samuel 23:39). David was already married to the beautiful and intelligent Abigail, and despite God's desire for monogamous marriages, David had taken other wives and concubines as well (1 Samuel 25:3, 42, 43; 2 Samuel 5:13).

What was going on in David's mind? What twisted logic (or nonlogic) could make a man jeopardize his reputation, his integrity, and his family for the sake of a forbidden fling? Was this some sort of a midlife crisis? Was David bored now that he had accomplished many of his life's goals?

What was lacking in David's life? Accountability with other men? A sense of closeness to God? Did his marriages seem stale compared with the excitement of someone new? Did David really think this through, or did his feelings simply overrule his better judgment?

DAVID MADE A WRONG CHOICE

David didn't spend a lot of time analyzing the situation. He acted quickly, impulsively—foolishly. Exercising his power as king, he sent some of his messengers to get Bathsheba. They brought her back, and he slept with her (2 Samuel 11:4). Instead of looking for a positive way to escape temptation (1 Corinthians 10:13), David gave in. It could have been a "no-sin" situation, but instead it turned into a "no-win" situation.

There's a subtle sadness about the way the Scripture describes the aftermath for Bathsheba. It just says flatly, "Then she went back home." David sent for her, used her, then sent her home—as if nothing had happened. But something had happened which drastically changed both their lives.

David appears to have been in denial, while we are left to wonder how Bathsheba felt as she walked back into her empty house. Was she an unwilling participant, now filled with anger and shame? Did she cry herself to sleep? Did she long for the comforting arms of her husband Uriah? Or, was she filled with pride, delighted that she'd succeeded in seducing the king of Israel?

Sin stains and scars people. An impulsive sin is like a flash flood that rises up quickly, then leaves mud and debris strewn along the riverbank after the rushing waters recede. Sin leaves behind a residue of emptiness and betrayal.

The Bible uses only one short verse to describe the way David actually committed this sin. But it requires roughly the next fifty verses to tell what resulted from this one act of sinful passion. In many ways, David's life was never the same again. Family problems and internal conflicts weakened David's kingdom from this point on.

It's hard to resist temptation. But the consequences of sin are harder. "Can a man scoop fire into his lap without his clothes being burned? Can a man walk on hot coals without his feet being scorched? So is he who sleeps with another man's wife; no one who touches her will go unpunished" (Proverbs 6:27-29).

DAVID TRIED TO COVER UP THE CONSEQUENCES

At first, it seemed David's deed would go undiscovered. By now, David was accustomed to success. He was used to having his way, and perhaps felt invincible, as if he could get away with anything. But no one can disobey God's law without consequences. "Do not be deceived: God cannot be mocked. A man reaps what he sows" (Galatians 6:7).

If David assumed there would be no repercussions to his sin, Bathsheba shattered any such illusions when she sent him this message: "I am pregnant" (2 Samuel 11:5).

The devil has a way of twisting things around so that what should be good news becomes bad news. What could be better news than the announcement that a baby is going to be born? But this wasn't good news to David. Besides the spiritual implications of what he'd done (which seemed far from David's consciousness at this moment), this was a political disaster too. If the news of his affair became known, it would weaken his credibility as king.

Thinking fast, David came up with a scheme to cover up what he had done. He sent for Bathsheba's husband Uriah. With shameless hypocrisy, David made small talk with Uriah about how the war was going, then sent Uriah home for the night (so it would appear that Uriah had fathered Bathsheba's baby). But Uriah was such a noble gentleman and a loyal soldier, he could not in good conscience enjoy the comforts of home while his fellow soldiers were suffering on a distant battlefield; so he slept at the entrance to the palace and refused to go to his own house.

David then resorted to Plan B. He invited Uriah to eat and drink with him. (What hypocrisy! David slept with the man's wife, but now he's pretending to be his best friend.) David attempted to lower Uriah's resistance by getting him drunk; but still Uriah refused to go home to his wife.

Finally David resorted to drastic measures to make this problem go away. He wrote a letter to Joab (the military general in charge of David's army) with instructions to put Uriah in the front line of battle and then withdraw the troops so that he would be certain to die. Uriah himself carried the letter back to Joab. In other words, without realizing it, Uriah delivered his own death warrant. Joab obeyed David's instructions, and a few days later, Uriah was killed in battle (vv. 14-17).

For a while, David was off the hook once again—or so it seemed. After Bathsheba mourned the death of her husband, "David had her brought to his house and she became his wife and bore him a son" (vv. 26, 27). But there is no real peace when guilt remains unresolved, and David's sins were mounting up. He committed adultery, he was dishonest, he abused the power of his office as king, and in effect he committed murder by placing Uriah in mortal danger.

All this did not go unnoticed in the courts of Heaven. The chapter ends with ominous words that rumble like distant thunder from an approaching storm: "But the thing David had done displeased the Lord" (v. 27).

No one can escape the gaze of God. No cover-ups. No excuses. He knows and sees it all. You can run, but you can't hide. "Nothing in all creation is hidden from God's sight. Everything is uncovered and laid bare before the eyes of him to whom we must give account" (Hebrews 4:13).

SIN CONFRONTED

As 2 Samuel 12 begins, "The Lord sent Nathan to David." Earlier, Nathan conveyed the good news about God's promise to bless the throne of David and his descendants (2 Samuel 7:1-17). But this time Nathan came to speak a hard but necessary truth. He came alone, for a one-on-one confrontation with David.

Confrontation is never easy, but it must have been especially difficult to confront a king! To correct a brother requires prayerful forethought, a humble attitude, a combination of honesty and tact. "Brothers, if someone is caught in a sin, you who are spiritual should restore him gently"(Galatians 6:1). "He who rebukes a man will in the end gain more favor than he who has a flattering tongue" (Proverbs 28:23).

NATHAN'S STORY

Nathan used a clever parable to make his point. It was a story to which a former shepherd like David could relate:

> There were two men in a certain town, one rich and the other poor. The rich man had a very large number of sheep and cattle, but the poor man had nothing except one little ewe lamb he had bought. He raised it, and it grew up with him and his children. It shared his food, drank from his cup and even slept in his arms. It was like a daughter to him.
>
> Now a traveler came to the rich man, but the rich man refrained from taking one of his own sheep or cattle to prepare a meal for the traveler who had come to him. Instead, he took the ewe lamb that belonged to the poor man and prepared it for the one who had come to him (2 Samuel 12:1-4).

David listened intently to Nathan's story, and his temper flared at the thought of such injustice inflicted upon a powerless victim. David "burned with anger" against the rich man in the parable. Filled with righteous indignation, David exclaimed, "As surely as the Lord lives, the man who did this deserves to die! He must pay for that lamb four times over, because he did such a thing and had no pity" (vv. 5, 6).

Little did David realize that the parable was about him. Nathan jolted David with an eye-opening, soul-stirring sentence: "You are the man!"

Have you ever gone through a time of spiritual unmasking when you realized in the depths of your soul that you were wrong, desperately wrong? Have you experienced the deep level of repentance that comes when there's no more game-playing, no more hiding behind excuses, no more jokes and evasions—just the sobering realization, "I am the man"? Most great servants of God eventually came to such a point of brokenness. Think of Moses, a fugitive from Egypt because he

killed an Egyptian, stammering at the burning bush
about his inability to speak. Think of Peter, weeping bitterly after denying Jesus three times, just hours after
boasting, "I'll stay with You even if all the others run
away." Think of proud Saul of Tarsus, humbled and
blinded on the Damascus road, led around by the hand,
helpless and suddenly submissive to the Lord he previously persecuted.

Like a sharp arrow, Nathan's pointed story found its
mark in David's heart. Like a surgeon's scalpel, God's
powerful Word began the painful process of cutting
away David's sin and self-deception.

DAVID'S RESPONSE

Stunned and heartbroken, David stammered, "I have
sinned against the Lord" (v. 13). What else could he say?
He could only cast himself on God's mercy and seek
forgiveness. Though David's life was collapsing around
him, there was still hope as he returned to the Lord and
the familiar moral compass that had guided his life for
years.

As the consequences of David's poor choices continued to unfold, *there was tragedy.* The son born to
David and Bathsheba became deathly ill (vv. 13-15).

There was earnest prayer. David pleaded with God to
spare the child's life. He fasted, and spent long nights
lying on the ground agonizing in prayer. Nevertheless,
the baby died.[3]

There was acceptance. Upon hearing the news of the
baby's death, David bathed and dressed, worshiped
God, and asked for something to eat. Though David
certainly wasn't finished grieving, he accepted the reality
of his son's death and realized he couldn't undo what
had happened.

There was hope. Though David couldn't bring the
child back from the dead, he said with confidence, "I
will go to him." He looked forward to a reunion with
his departed son with a glimmer of resurrection hope,

which glows ever brighter in light of New Testament teaching about the peace and joy of Heaven.

Another indication of hope is that David and Bathsheba later had another son (Solomon). Scripture says "the Lord loved him," and as the story comes full circle, the same prophet, Nathan, who earlier brought bad news and a message of judgment this time brought good news; Solomon was to be nicknamed "Jedidiah," which means "loved by the Lord."

THE CONFESSION OF SIN

The subtitle of Psalm 51 says this chapter was written "When the prophet Nathan came to him after David had committed adultery with Bathsheba." This psalm allows us to peer into David's state of mind during this dark hour of his life, and it serves as a model of confession for any sinner.

HE ADMITTED HIS GUILT

David prayed, "For I know my transgressions, and my sin is always before me. Against you, you only, have I sinned and done what is evil in your sight" (vv. 3, 4).

Some of the hardest words to say are simply, "It's my fault. I was wrong." But until we're honest with God and admit our shortcomings, guilt drags us down like a heavy ball and chain. Living with unforgiven sin is like trying to drive a car with four flat tires—it takes a lot of effort to move forward, with little real progress.

Remember the land mines mentioned earlier in this chapter? According to military experts, land mines are very difficult to locate and remove. The only way to be 100 percent certain is to do manual clearing—get down on your hands and knees and probe the soil around you with long skewers.[4]

Spiritual land mines are cleared in much the same way, down on our knees in prayer.

HE ASKED FOR CLEANSING

"Wash me, and I will be whiter than snow. . . Hide your face from my sins and blot out all my iniquity" (vv. 7, 9).

Ultimately only God can make us clean. We can't do it ourselves. But the wonderful message of the gospel is that through Jesus Christ we can be clean again. Jesus brought hope to a Samaritan woman whose checkered past included five husbands and a live-in partner. He refused to condemn a woman caught in the very act of adultery, warning her, "Go now leave your life of sin" (John 8:11).

If you've been involved in sexual sin, Christ can help you make a clean break from the past. Commit yourself to sexual purity from this day forward. Seek the help of godly leaders and friends who can help hold you accountable. Break off any relationship that may drag you back into sexual immorality. It's not an impossible battle. When you're baptized into Christ you receive both pardon ("forgiveness of sins") and power ("the gift of the Holy Spirit") to be victorious (Acts 2:38).

There is a high cost to giving in. Our sin cost Jesus His life! He suffered and shed His blood to make us clean. "If we confess our sins, he is faithful and just and will forgive us our sins and purify us from all unrighteousness" (1 John 1:9).

HE TURNED HIS FAILURE INTO A TESTIMONY

Once forgiven, David promised, "Then I will teach transgressors your ways, and sinners will turn back to you" (Psalm 51:13). David's failure actually became an important part of his testimony. He serves as a living example of how God can still use people who have been wounded and broken by sin.

On a hot afternoon in early July, I took my daughters berry picking at a farm called Raspberry Acres. The landowner turned out to be a kindhearted fellow who brought us lemonade while we picked our berries. As we struck up a friendly conversation about his farm, the man told me, "You know, there's a lot more to raising good raspberries than meets the eye. Every year you have to get rid of the old, dead canes so the plants will bear fruit next summer."

Somehow I think it's true of more than raspberries! God can help us get rid of the old dead canes of sin. Pruned, clean, fresh, and forgiven, we can bear much fruit.

CHAPTER ELEVEN

Heartbreak in the Household: When Your Family Brings You Pain

2 SAMUEL 13-18; PSALM 3

When you hear the word "family," what comes to mind? For some, "family" means babies in high chairs with spaghetti all over their faces. It means romping on the floor with a playful child, and sitting by her bedside when she's burning with fever. Family means birthday parties, holiday dinners, graduations, weddings, and funerals. It's first steps, first haircuts, and first days of school.

Family also means arguing with your brothers and sisters, teasing your mother-in-law, and listening to your uncle tell corny jokes at reunions. It's having someone share your joy when you remember your lines in the school play, hit a home run in Little League, or get a promotion at work.

Unfortunately, for many people "family" isn't a happy word anymore. Fractured families abound. In the United States, the number of couples who live together without marriage has increased by 400 percent since 1970.[1] The number of out-of-wedlock births more than doubled between 1978 and 1990.[2] According to *American Demographics,* "If current rates of divorce continue, the majority of today's children will spend some of their childhood in a single-parent home."[3]

Robert Frost wrote, "Home is the place where, if you have to go there, they have to take you in." Humorist Tom Mullen said homeowners define "home" differently:

125

"For them, it is the place where, if you live there, something has to be fixed!"[4]

Clearly, a lot needs to be fixed in today's homes. The pressure on Christian parents grows as our culture becomes increasingly confused about right and wrong. Peer pressure and secularism tug at the hearts and loyalties of our children. Politicians talk about family values—but who really accepts responsibility for shaping the moral fabric of our children? Not the entertainment industry. NBC television executive Don Ohlmeyer flatly states, "It's not the role of network television to program for the children of America," and CBS entertainment president Leslie Moonves admits that even during the early evening hours there are TV shows "that I find terribly objectionable for my children to watch."[5]

In the rush to gain material prosperity, it's easy to overlook the need for spiritual guidance. As James Dobson says, "Sometimes we're so concerned about giving our children what we never had growing up, we neglect to give them what we did have growing up."[6] Today folk seem to have more clothes in their closets, but less security in their hearts. More freedom, less faith. More comforts, less commitment. More convenience, less conviction.

Fortunately, positive things are happening too. Christian couples still pursue the goal of a strong, lasting marriage. Singles are realizing the wisdom of a commitment to sexual purity. People wounded by divorce are finding healing and grace in Christ. Through programs like "True Love Waits," hundreds of thousands of teenagers have pledged to exercise self-control and remain sexually abstinent until marriage.

There's still plenty of hope for the family. God's way still works, and now more than ever we need His help. "Except the Lord build the house, they labor in vain that build it" (Psalm 127:1, *King James Version*).

Along the way, however, many of us experience pain in our households. Some of our deepest wounds come from our nearest relatives. For many folk, the word "family" brings to mind a lot of pressure, frustration, and guilt.

God's Word is bluntly honest about this. Parental favoritism (Isaac and Rebekah), sibling rivalry (Jacob and Esau), infertility (Hannah), sexual promiscuity (Eli's sons), marital cruelty (Nabal and Abigail), and widowhood (the widow at Zarephath) are among the family problems mentioned in Scripture. But King David's family provides one of the most vivid examples of heartbreak in the home.

A FAMILY IN TURMOIL

David fathered many offspring. His multiple marriages (at least eight wives are named in Scripture) resulted in a complex "blended family" filled with half brothers and half sisters. This definitely was not "the Brady Bunch"! Altogether, Scripture mentions at least twenty of David's children by name, and implies there were others whose names were not listed (2 Samuel 3:2-5; 1 Chronicles 14:3-5). Evidently, at least some of David's wives and children lived under the same roof in his large palace. Imagine the problems!

Amnon was David's firstborn son, the product of David's marriage to a woman named Ahinoam (1 Samuel 25:43). Absalom was his third son, born to a woman named Maacah who was the daughter of a foreign king (2 Samuel 3:3).

AMNON'S SIN

The tragic story of Amnon is almost too terrible to tell—a sordid tale of lust, lies, violence, and hatred.

By most estimates, Amnon was about twenty years old when the events described in 2 Samuel 13 took place. Like many men his age, Amnon wrestled with sexual temptation. To further complicate matters, the object of his romantic fantasies was his own half sister, a beautiful young woman named Tamar. The longer Amnon toyed with this forbidden love, the more it bothered him.

Finally when he became "frustrated to the point of illness" over Tamar, he followed the advice of his cousin, a shrewd fellow named Jonadab. Amnon pretended to be sick, and asked King David's permission for Tamar to come to his bedroom and prepare some special food for him. When Tamar came with the food, Amnon urged her to come to bed with him. She resisted, but Amnon's greater strength prevailed, and he raped her.

Immediately afterward, "Amnon hated her with intense hatred. In fact, he hated her more than he had loved her. Amnon said to her, 'Get up and get out!'" (v. 15). What an honest commentary on the emptiness that results from an immoral sexual relationship! Amnon's "love" really was no more than selfish lust. After he used Tamar to satisfy his sexual desires, he felt disgusted with her (and should have been disgusted with himself as well).

Inside the security of a committed marriage, sexual intimacy is a wholesome bond of love—a figurative picture of love and unity between the Lord and His people (see Ephesians 5:31-33). But outside its proper bounds, sexual intimacy diminishes people into lust objects and leaves behind an ugly residue of hurt feelings, resentment, and guilt. Notice the results of Amnon's sin:

1. His victim was devastated. "And Tamar lived in her brother Absalom's house, a desolate woman" (v. 20).

2. His father was dismayed. "When King David heard all this, he was furious" (v. 21). Oddly, though, there is no indication that David took any direct action to punish Amnon or correct the situation. Thus he neglected his duty both as a father and as a king.

3. His brother hated him. Amnon's sin, and David's reluctance to deal justly with the situation, created a lingering resentment that smoldered in his brother's heart. "Absalom never said a word to Amnon, either good or bad; he hated Amnon because he had disgraced his sister Tamar" (v. 22).

4. Eventually, Absalom killed Amnon. For two years, Absalom plotted to avenge his sister's rape. His opportunity finally came when all the king's sons attended a sheepshearing festival. Absalom waited until Amnon was distracted by the festivities and wine, then ordered his men to strike Amnon down. When it was clear that Amnon was dead, David and his sons wept bitterly and Absalom went into hiding for three years (vv. 23-39).

As evangelist Ravi Zacharias points out, disruption in the family is a prime cause of violence in society. "If . . . fatherless homes can become the breeding grounds for violent children, what else can we expect in a world at large that has been told it has no [heavenly] Father?"[7]

DAVID'S MISTAKES

How much of this heartache was David's fault? Sometimes a wayward child goes astray despite his parent's best efforts. The general rule for parenting is, "Train a child in the way he should go, and when he is old he will not turn from it" (Proverbs 22:6). But the child himself must follow another Proverb: "Listen, my son, and be wise, and keep your heart on the right path" (Proverbs 23:19). No matter how hard a parent tries, a child still may make foolish choices that bring anguish to his loved ones.

But in this case, there's little doubt David's own parenting errors contributed to his sons' problems. Where did he go wrong?

First, *he set a poor example in his home.* David was a great man in many ways, but his family was his Achilles' heel. He married multiple wives, committed adultery with Bathsheba, and tried to cover up his sin. David's poor choices weakened his parental authority.

When the actor Charles Coburn was young, he loved the theater and went to plays whenever possible. His father warned him, "One thing, son, you must never do. Don't go to burlesque houses."

"Why?" the boy asked.

His father answered, "Because you would see things you shouldn't."

Later, Charles visited a burlesque house, and sure enough, he saw something he shouldn't have seen; his father![8]

Surely there is no sharper pain than the sight of our own faults reappearing in the lives of our children.

Only the heavenly Father is a perfect parent. None of us are perfect parents. When two streams converge into one, there will be turbulence; likewise, when two imperfect people join in marriage, there will be turbulence. Add a few children to the mix, and the turbulence grows. Let them grow into their teen years, and white-water rafting looks easy compared to rearing a family!

God will help us survive the turbulence, but parents must remember that our example is the greatest teaching tool, the most powerful visual aid our children will ever see—and often it is the one strong rope that prevents young people from going completely overboard during their times of rebellion.

Another problem was that *David allowed an unhealthy distance to develop between himself and his sons.* He was easily deceived by Amnon's faked illness, and naive when he failed to see Amnon's real motive in inviting Tamar to visit his bedroom. After Tamar was raped, David became angry but did not get involved. Then Absalom killed Amnon and went into hiding for three years in a place called Geshur. Though "the king longed to go to Absalom," there was no contact between them for a long time. Later, Absalom moved back to Jerusalem, but "Absalom lived two years in Jerusalem without seeing the king's face" (2 Samuel 13:38, 39; 14:28). At least five years passed with little or no contact between David and Absalom. Meanwhile, old grievances grew, unhealed wounds festered, and angry feelings remained unresolved.

Perhaps David's most glaring fault as a father was that

be neglected to offer needed guidance and correction.
When the Bible tells about Adonijah, another of David's
sons, it says, "His father had never interfered with him
by asking, 'Why do you behave as you do?'" (1 Kings 1:6).

Doesn't it seem strange that this mighty leader of
men failed to lead his own sons well? Was he too ten-
derhearted to be firm with those he loved? Did he
assume that his job as a father was mainly just to provide material things for his children? Was he simply too
busy—distracted by all the demands of his job as king?

The Bible tells about a fellow named Hiel who rebuilt
a city's foundations "at the cost of his firstborn son
Abiram, and he set up its gates at the cost of his
youngest son Segub" (1 Kings 16:34). No matter what
we accomplish in life, it's done at too high a price if we
do it at the expense of our children.

ABSALOM'S REBELLION

In some ways David's problems were only beginning.
As time passed, his son Absalom caused increasing grief.
Like toxic waste pouring into a river, Absalom's rebellious attitude spread its poison throughout his family
and his nation—with devastating effects.

He wasted his opportunities. Absalom was born a
prince, and he was remarkably good-looking. "In all
Israel there was not a man so highly praised for his
handsome appearance as Absalom. From the top of his
head to the sole of his foot there was no blemish in
him" (2 Samuel 14:25).

Heads turned when the Absalom walked by with his
movie-star looks. Perfect skin. No blemishes. A perfect
physique. A thick head of hair. In fact, the Bible makes
special mention of Absalom's haircuts, "Whenever he
cut the hair of his head—he used to cut his hair from
time to time when it became too heavy for him—he
would weigh it, and its weight was two hundred shekels
[about five pounds] by the royal standard" (v. 26). That
was one heavy head of hair!

Absalom had three sons, and a daughter who "became a beautiful woman" (v. 27). Money, good looks, children to be proud of—Absalom had it all. His life was filled with opportunities. But he threw it all away.

He deceived others. Absalom knew how to smooth talk and manipulate people for his own advantage. Today's politician rides around in a limousine accompanied by campaign workers; Absalom rode in a fancy chariot with fifty men running ahead of him. Today's office-seeker shows up early at the train station and shakes hands with potential voters; Absalom arrived early by the city gate. Pretending to be genuinely concerned, he extended his hand and even kissed people as they entered the city.

Absalom used flattery and rumors to undercut his father's leadership. He sowed seeds of discord by hinting that King David was negligent. He told people, "Look, your claims are valid and proper, but there is no representative of the king to hear you," then he would add slyly, "If only I were appointed judge in the land! Then everyone who has a complaint or case could come to me and I would see that he gets justice." Thus Absalom "stole the hearts of the men of Israel" (2 Samuel 15:1-6).

He dishonored his parents. By the time David realized what was going on, Absalom's rebellion was gaining momentum. David and his followers fled from the palace and escaped from Jerusalem. What a humiliating moment for proud King David—chased out of his palace by his own son! "A foolish son brings grief to his father and bitterness to the one who bore him" (Proverbs 17:25).

Absalom's conspiracy turned the great King David into a homeless fugitive. Barefoot and weeping, David and his family traveled up the Mount of Olives in a sad procession into exile (2 Samuel 15:30). A fellow named Shimei cursed and belittled David, and pelted him with dirt and rocks (2 Samuel 16:5-14).

He disregarded God's standards. When the Scripture describes Absalom, there is a notable lack of any reference to his faith in God. Though David had many faults, he was so sensitive to the will of God that he repented when confronted with his sin. Absalom, on the other hand, seems devoid of spiritual depth. He was like an out-of-control semi-trailer with no brakes, plunging full speed ahead on a mountain road.

Absalom not only violated God's command to "honor your father and your mother" (Exodus 20:12), he had his servants pitch a tent on the palace roof, and there "he lay with his father's concubines in the sight of all Israel" (2 Samuel 16:22). By this degrading public act of immorality, Absalom thumbed his nose at his father David and showed utter disregard for God's standards of decency.

He lost his life. Absalom's thick head of hair eventually contributed to his undoing. "Now Absalom happened to meet David's men. He was riding his mule, and as the mule went under the thick branches of a large oak, Absalom's head got caught in the tree. He was left hanging in midair, while the mule he was riding kept on going" (2 Samuel 18:9). As Absalom hung there helplessly in the oak tree, David's general Joab and some of his men struck him with javelins and killed him (vv. 14, 15).

Earlier, Absalom had erected a stone pillar as a monument to himself; but his life ended in disgrace and he was buried in a pit in the forest, with a heap of rocks thrown over his body (vv. 17, 18).

He broke his father's heart. If David had been clinging to a shred of hope that Absalom would repent, now there was nothing left but grief. Despite all the harm Absalom had done, David still felt his son's loss with anguish only a parent can fully understand.

With tears streaming down his cheeks, David grieved the loss of his wayward but beloved son, "O my son Absalom! My son, my son Absalom! If only I had died instead of you—O Absalom, my son, my son!" (v. 33).

WHAT CAN WE LEARN FROM DAVID'S FAMILY?

Like other Old Testament events, "These things happened to them as examples and were written down as warnings for us" (1 Corinthians 10:11). We can learn several important lessons from David's heartbreaking household.

A WARNING: THE HIGH COST OF REBELLION

The sins of Amnon and Absalom cost them their lives, disgraced their loved ones, and threw their nation into turmoil. Unless sin is repented of and forgiven, it leads to tragedy. "A man reaps what he sows" (Galatians 6:7).

In a larger sense, sin and rebellion disrupted the entire human family, and cost perfect Jesus His life (Romans 5:6-11).

Out of a broken heart, David cried out to his rebellious son Absalom, "If only I had died instead of you!" Out of a loving heart, Jesus told all of God's rebellious children, "I *will* die in your place!" And He did.

A CHALLENGE:
THE NEED FOR STRONG, ATTENTIVE PARENTING

When my son, Matt, was six years old, we were talking about what his life might be like as a grownup. I told him he could look forward to adulthood. I said I was confident he'd grow up strong and capable, ready to live on his own someday—although, I added, we definitely would miss him around our house. Matt thought for a moment, shrugged his shoulders and said, "Well, Dad, I guess you just have to enjoy me while you can!"

As parents we do need to enjoy our kids—and love, accept, and guide them—while we can. Did you ever watch bricklayers at work? Bricklayers give a lot of attention to the first row of bricks on a wall, because they know if the first row is level, the rest of the wall will go up straight and strong. Likewise, parents need to give special attention to our children during their earliest years as the foundation is laid for their future.

AN ENCOURAGING WORD:
GOD STILL WORKS THROUGH IMPERFECT FAMILIES

David's family was far from perfect. In many ways, his household is an example of what *not* to do; yet God still accomplished His purposes through David and his descendants.

David offered God praise under pressure even "when he fled from his son Absalom," as the subtitle of Psalm 3 states. In spite of his troubles, David prayed, "But you are a shield around me, O Lord; you bestow glory on me and lift up my head. . . . I lie down and sleep; I wake again, because the Lord sustains me" (Psalm 3:3, 5).

Despite severe family problems, David found peace in the Lord; and the Lord found a useful servant in David.

When family problems make us feel vulnerable, God is still our shield. When we're bowed down, He lifts up our heads. When we're exhausted, He provides rest.

When we feel like giving up, He will help us keep going until we enter Heaven's household, where there are no broken hearts.

CHAPTER TWELVE

Mighty Men

2 SAMUEL 23, 24; PSALM 22

My grandmother was an excellent gardener. When I was a little boy playing in her yard, I knew almost nothing about flowers. I was more interested in playing basketball in the driveway where Grandpa had installed a backboard and hoop, exploring the dusty hay-filled barn where chickens roamed free, and searching for tadpoles in the creek.

But on sunny days in June, Grandma's towering sunflowers, fragrant sweet peas, and rows of bright orange marigolds demanded attention. Near the flower garden was an old well with a rusty hand pump, and a stone birdbath where my cousin and I kept our tadpoles.

One day Grandma headed out toward the flower garden saying, "Do you want to help me, David? I'm going to plant some glads!" Now, I didn't know what a "glad" was, but this sounded like fun! "Glads" turned out to be flowers called gladiolas, and planting them was no special thrill. But I've never forgotten that phrase, "planting glads."

Come to think of it, God has planted a lot of "glads" in my life. How about yours? Despite all the problems and pressures, God quietly plants blessings in our lives.

God's presence and power bring gladness. In dark nights of the soul and on the happiest days of our lives, He is there. He's there in times of sickness and health, victory and failure. To comfort and strengthen. To reassure and encourage. To love. Jesus promised, "I am with you always, to the very end of the age" (Matthew 28:20).

God's people bring gladness. I am glad when I sit at the kitchen table playing checkers with my daughter

(even when she beats me). I am glad to take my son to
his football games, and listen to my other daughter sing
in her high school choir. I find joy in seeing friends at
church each week, and spending time with the small
group my wife and I lead.

King David faced a lot of pressure. But David offered
God praise because the Lord had planted "glads" in his
life too. One of David's biggest reasons for gladness was
a group of supportive friends who assisted him, fought
for him, and sacrificed themselves for his benefit. Some
of these fellows, known as David's mighty men, probably rose from the ranks of the four hundred "in distress
or in debt or discontented" who originally gathered
around David while he was being pursued by Saul (1
Samuel 22:2). Under David's leadership they became
strong leaders themselves, and some of them became
notable heroes.[1]

Second Samuel 23 records the exploits of David's
mighty men. One short story in this chapter stands out,
for it provides a glimpse of what it takes to be a "mighty
man" or a "mighty woman" who brings gladness to God
and to others.

MIGHTY MEN ARE WILLING TO HELP

Many things in life are uncontrollable. I didn't choose
to have brown eyes, but I do. I didn't choose to be left-
handed, but I am. I didn't decide to be born in
Wilmington, Ohio, in 1954, but I was. No one asked me
how tall I would like to be, or whether I'd prefer dark or
blonde hair. Someone else even gave me my name.
Many times we can't control what happens to us. But we
do have a choice about life's most important question:
"Am I willing to serve the Lord?" Every day we must
choose either "Thy will be done," or "My will be done."

David's mighty men made themselves available to
serve. These were dangerous times. David was hiding in
a cave, and the Philistines occupied Bethlehem (2
Samuel 23:13, 14). The mighty men easily could have

found an excuse to stay away. It was "harvest time"—the busiest time of year in an agricultural nation like Israel. Food supplies of wheat and barley had to be stored up for the entire year. Every able-bodied man, woman, and child went to work in the harvest field. But instead of reasoning, "We're too busy to help David right now," or "It's just too dangerous," David's mighty men chose to serve their leader. When there's a need to meet, mighty men don't just stand around.

Did you hear about the man who fell into a pit? A self-righteous person came by and said, "People who fall into a pit probably deserve it."

A college professor noticed the man and commented, "We should do a study on pits."

A reporter came on the scene and said, "This would make a great human interest story! I'll write an article about the man in the pit."

A lawyer leaned over and said, "You should sue the person who dug that pit!"

An optimist told the man, "Cheer up, the pit could be deeper than it is!"

A pessimist told him, "It's probably going to rain, and you'll get really muddy in there."

An inspector came by and said, "Did you get a permit to dig that pit?"

A religious person passed by and said, "I'll pray that your time in the pit will enhance your spiritual growth."

An IRS agent said, "If you stay there long enough, you must pay taxes on your pit."

But then Jesus came by and said, "Here, take my hand." And Jesus lifted the man out of the pit.[2]

Mighty men are willing to help.

MIGHTY MEN GO THE EXTRA MILE

While he was hiding in the cave, "David longed for water." Perhaps he was sick or feverish, or it simply was too dangerous for him to go out looking for water. Whatever the reason for his thirst, David said, "Oh, that someone would get me a drink of water from the well near the gate of Bethlehem!" (v. 15).

Remember, David grew up in Bethlehem. He had fond memories of the water from Bethlehem's well. How sweet it tasted at the end of a long hot day in the fields! We long remember the little pleasures we enjoyed as children. No doughnuts ever tasted better than the ones my mother made by hand, deep-fried and sprinkled with powdered sugar. No sweet corn surpasses the tender ears plucked fresh from Dad's garden. I've eaten more expensive desserts, but nothing tops the Dairy Queen ice cream cones I enjoyed as a boy.

I loved drinking from the old well on my grandfather's farm. My brothers and I drank from a dented tin cup that hung on a nail on a nearby fence post. Sharing one cup probably wasn't very sanitary, but who cared? How good that ice-cold, rust-flecked water tasted on a hot summer day! Even now I would enjoy a drink of water from that old well. (I wonder if the old tin cup is still there.)

As David grew older, memories of his boyhood days seemed pleasant and nostalgic. Aside from his thirst, he probably felt a little homesick as he thought about the well by Bethlehem's gate. Besides, Bethlehem was under enemy occupation. It must have broken David's heart to see the cruel Philistines living in his hometown.

But notice: David didn't command his men to get him a drink from Bethlehem's well. He just "longed" for it. He didn't say, "Men, this is an order! I command you to get me some water!" Sometimes a wish motivates people more effectively than a command. If you order your friend, "Give me a piece of your candy bar!" he's likely to say no (and he will conclude that you have a lot of nerve to boss people around that way)! But if you gently say, "I sure wish I could have a bite of candy," your friend will usually comply! (One time I tried that technique, and along with giving me several bites of her

Hershey's bar, my youngest daughter also smeared gooey chocolate-covered fingers all over my shirt!)

David seems to be thinking, "Oh, I know this isn't practical at all. There's no way I would ever order my followers to put their lives in danger for such a trivial thing as a drink of water. But how I would enjoy a drink from the well that refreshed me as a child!"

David's men didn't need a command. Their leader's wish was their command. These mighty men loved David, and love gladly goes the extra mile. Love motivates us to do even more than what's asked, and consider it a privilege.

MIGHTY MEN ARE COURAGEOUS

Bringing David a drink from Bethlehem's well was no small accomplishment. Philistine soldiers surrounded the town, and the well was located right by the gate, which no doubt was heavily guarded.

But three of David's mighty men "broke through the Philistine lines, drew water from the well near the gate of Bethlehem and carried it back to David" (v. 16). We're left to wonder exactly how they pulled off this feat. It's the stuff action-adventure movies are made of: three men endangering their lives to bring a drink of water to their leader. They took a very big risk to do a very small kindness, and the Bible doesn't even tell all the details.

But that's how courage acts. Courageous deeds aren't always the ones you read about in the newspaper. Do you want to see a "mighty man" in action? Watch the Christian husband who quietly earns the respect of his coworkers because he is faithful to his wife and devoted to his children. Look at the teenage boy who says no when his friends offer him a puff of marijuana. Watch the elderly gentleman who stays by his wife's side through a prolonged illness.

Do you want to see a "mighty woman"? Watch the medical professional who cares for AIDS patients.

Notice the young mom who sacrifices years of her life to meet the needs of her children. Look at the woman who courageously overcomes a difficult childhood to become a productive adult.

It was a tense moment as David's three mighty men approached Bethlehem's city gate—perhaps crawling on their bellies, ducking behind rocks, gesturing to one another with hand signals. With adrenaline flowing and hearts pounding, they swiftly made their move toward the well. Maybe two of them created a diversion or fought the Philistine guards, while their partner quickly drew water from the well. Before the rest of the Philistine camp realized what was happening, David's men accomplished their mission and made their escape. Tired and bruised but triumphant, they painstakingly carried their precious trophy (a leather canteen of water) back to David.

THEIR EFFORTS BECAME A SACRIFICE TO GOD

David's men must have felt proud. I picture them slapping one another on the back as they made their way to David, retelling their adventure over and over again. Finding David in the cave, they excitedly explained what they had done, and then, bursting with pride, they handed him the container of water. Surely they expected David to gulp down this refreshing drink. Isn't that what blessings are for—to be enjoyed to the fullest?

But David "refused to drink it; instead, he poured it out before the Lord. 'Far be it from me, O Lord, to do this!' he said. 'Is it not the blood of men who went at the risk of their lives?' And David would not drink it" (vv. 16, 17). Not only did David refuse to drink the water himself, he made sure no one else would drink it—he poured it out!

I wonder how his three mighty men reacted at first. If I were one of them, I would have felt surprised and angry. What ingratitude! I would have protested, "Wait a minute, David! Don't you appreciate what we did for you? How could you be so ungrateful? Don't you realize we risked our lives to give you the luxury of a drink from Bethlehem's well? How could you just pour it out?"

But David *was* grateful. In fact, he appreciated his mighty men's effort so much, his conscience wouldn't allow him to drink water acquired at such a high price.

By pouring out the water, David didn't insult his men, he honored them. Their loyalty and love were more refreshing than any water could be. He might be thirsty still, but no longer discouraged. If David had been feeling tired, weak, sick, or lonely there in the cave, think how he felt now! Why, a leader could overcome any enemy with brave, devoted followers like these on his side! The water was sweeter to David as he poured it out than it would have been if he had gulped it down.

Notice, David didn't just pour the water out aimlessly. He "poured it out before the Lord." He prayerfully offered that precious water as a sacrifice to God. Is it too much to picture David and his three mighty men praying together, perhaps embracing each other, with tears in their eyes?

Blessings are ours to share, not to hoard. At that moment in the cave, the water was David's most valuable possession, and he offered it up to God. His mighty men watched as the precious water dripped from the rocks and soaked into the clay cave floor. They needed no more recognition and applause for their gallant act. It was enough just to pour it out before the Lord. When Mary poured expensive perfume on Jesus' feet and wiped His feet with her hair, some complained that she was wasteful; but Jesus commended her faith (John 12:1-8). It's never a waste to give your best to God.

Evidently personal sacrifice was very important to David. According to 2 Samuel 24, the Israelites suffered from a severe plague. Looking for solutions, David talked with a prophet named Gad. Gad's instructions?

Build an altar on the site where a fellow named
Araunah owned a threshing floor.[3]

David offered to buy the land, but Araunah didn't
want the king's money. He volunteered to give David
everything needed for the sacrifice. Thanks to Araunah's
generous offer of the threshing floor, plus free oxen
and wood, David could have offered a cheap, easy, no-
cost sacrifice. But instead, David told Araunah, "No, I
insist on paying you for it. I will not sacrifice to the
Lord my God burnt offerings that cost me nothing" (v.
24). David refused to take the easy way. A sacrifice that
cost nothing really wasn't a sacrifice at all.

David paid Araunah fifty shekels of silver for the
threshing floor and oxen, and six hundred shekels of
gold for the site itself (1 Chronicles 21:25). After David
offered his gifts on the altar, "the Lord answered prayer
in behalf of the land, and the plague on Israel was
stopped" (2 Samuel 24:25).

Personal sacrifice isn't a popular concept in our day
of "easy believism," when "Find a church where you feel
comfortable" often takes precedence over "Take up your
cross and follow me." Today we don't need to offer
oxen; we offer ourselves as "living sacrifices, holy and
pleasing to God" (Romans 12:1).

But none of our personal sacrifices could ever make
us right with God. No amount of silver and gold could
remove the plague and penalty of sin. No matter how
noble and gallant our efforts, on our own we are not
mighty men and mighty women. We need the mightiest
of men, Jesus Christ.

THE MIGHTIEST OF MEN

Several years later, David's son, Solomon, built a
beautiful temple dedicated to the worship of God on
the very site of the threshing floor David purchased
from Araunah (2 Chronicles 3:1). Though he probably
didn't realize it at the time, David's costly sacrifice purchased a piece of ground where God's people would be

blessed for years to come as they worshiped and offered sacrifices there.

Centuries later, Jesus himself walked these grounds, and offered himself as a perfect sacrifice on the hill called Golgotha (or Calvary) a short distance away.

David wrote a psalm about the mightiest of men. Though not as well-known as the Twenty-third Psalm, Psalm 22 paints a powerful prophetic portrait of the suffering Messiah who gave himself as a sacrifice for sin.[4]

Psalm 22's best-known words appear in its opening verse: "My God, my God, why have you forsaken me?" Not only did Jesus quote these words as He died on the cross (Matthew 27:46), His death corresponded closely to numerous other details in the psalm:

> Insulted and scorned by the mocking crowd (Psalm 22:6-8; Matthew 27:41-43)
>
> Intense pain, diminished strength, overpowering thirst (Psalm 22:14, 15; John 19:28-30)
>
> Hands and feet pierced by evil men (Psalm 22:16; Acts 2:23; John 20:24-29)
>
> Garments divided and treated as a gambling prize (Psalm 22:18; Mark 15:24).

Psalm 22 begins with suffering, but it ends with rejoicing. It starts with hurt and ends with hope. David learned that God can be trusted even when He seems distant. "For he has not despised or disdained the suffering of the afflicted one; he has not hidden his face from him but has listened to his cry for help" (v. 24).

Jesus Christ, the mightiest one of all, redefines what it means to be mighty. When He died on the cross, He showed that the true measure of greatness is self-sacrifice.

Our mighty Savior is also a suffering servant, the good shepherd who leads the flock, and He's the lamb of God who identifies with the flock.

He understands your weaknesses, and He's the source of unlimited strength.

Aren't you glad?

CHAPTER THIRTEEN

Famous Last Words

2 SAMUEL 23:1-7; PSALM 103:13-22

Greg Allen leads worship in one of America's largest churches, Southeast Christian Church in Louisville, Kentucky. One Sunday morning, while belting out a high note at the top of his voice, Greg burst a blood vessel in his throat. Doctors later explained he had developed two polyps on his vocal cords, and there was danger he had permanently impaired his ability to sing—a terrible problem for someone who leads thousands of people in worship every week.

Surgeons removed the polyps in December, and they told Greg he couldn't say a word for two weeks—including Christmas. On Christmas morning he couldn't say a word as his two young daughters opened their presents. Greg eventually made a full recovery, but his doctors insisted that he should resume speaking very carefully. They allowed him to speak just five minutes a day at first. Greg says he used all his allotted speaking time "to tell his wife and daughters how much he loved them."[1] If you had only five minutes a day to express what is on your heart, what would you say?

What if you had only five minutes left to live? What would be your last words?

In the second century, Polycarp died as a martyr for his faith—burned at the stake at the age of eighty-six. He died with a prayer on his lips, thanking God that he was counted worthy to die in the service of Christ. In 1415, the reformer John Huss was burned at the stake. At the place of execution, he sang psalms of praise to God and prayed, "Lord Jesus Christ, assist and help me,

that, with a firm and present mind, by thy most powerful grace, I may undergo this most cruel . . . death."[2]

When the French skeptic Voltaire was dying, however,
he was filled with terror and told his doctor, "I will give
you half of what I am worth, if you will give me six
months' life." In his writings Voltaire argued the merits
of atheism, and repeatedly referred to Jesus Christ as a
"wretch," but as death neared, he was filled with regret
and even called out to Christ, complaining that he felt
"abandoned by God and man." Thomas Paine, who
expressed disdain for Christian faith in his book, *The
Age of Reason,* was filled with remorse in his last days.
His attending physician wrote that Paine cried out
repeatedly, "O Lord, help me! God, help me!"[3]

The Bible contains many famous (and encouraging)
last words. As the old patriarch Jacob neared death, he
gathered his twelve sons (and Joseph's sons) around
him and offered words of blessing and warning
(Genesis 49; Hebrews 11:21). Moses blessed the twelve
tribes of Israel (Deuteronomy 33). Joshua used his last
speech to offer a challenge: "Choose for yourselves this
day whom you will serve . . . But as for me and my
household, we will serve the Lord" (Joshua 24:15).
When he was being stoned to death, Stephen prayed,
"Lord Jesus, receive my spirit," and he asked the Lord to
forgive the people who were killing him (Acts 7:59). As
Paul approached death, he said with confidence, "I have
fought the good fight, I have finished the race, I have
kept the faith" (2 Timothy 4:7).

In 2 Samuel 23, the Bible records the last words of
King David. As David neared death, he was no longer a
young, vigorous shepherd strong enough to fight lions,
bears, and giants. Now he was a weary veteran, shiver-
ing in the cold no matter how many blankets his servants piled on him (1 Kings 1:1). He was only seventy
years old; but David's years as a warrior had worn him
down. His family problems and the pressures of serving as king had taken their toll. As a "Frank & Ernest"

cartoon caption says, "You're only young once, but it makes you tired for the rest of your life."

My guess is that David felt frustrated by his physical limitations. Perhaps he felt like the fellow who complained that he had reached the "metallic age"—silver in his hair, gold in his teeth, iron in his vitamins, and lead in his shoes! But David, "Israel's singer of songs" (or as the *King James Version* calls him, the "sweet psalmist of Israel") still had the presence of mind to voice some final words of praise, inspired by the Holy Spirit (2 Samuel 23:1, 2).

A HOUSE RIGHT WITH GOD

David asked, "Is not my house right with God?" (2 Samuel 23:5)—an urgent question when you consider the brevity of life. "As for man, his days are like grass, he flourishes like a flower of the field; the wind blows over it and it is gone, and its place remembers it no more" (Psalm 103:15, 16).

People say that time flies. If so, it doesn't float along like a hot-air balloon. It speeds by like a rocket on supersonic wings.

Bob Russell tells about a man who had only six months to live. This man's doctor suggested he marry a widow with twelve children. "Will that make me live longer?" the man asked. "No," the doctor replied, "but it will seem longer."

Our schedules can become so fast-paced, there's little time to reflect on the significance and purpose of our lives. Maybe you've seen the Calvin and Hobbes cartoon that says, "God put me on this earth to accomplish a certain number of things, and right now I'm so far behind that I will never die."

But we will die. In *The Denial of Death,* Ernest Becker argues that "the idea of death, the fear of it, haunts the human; . . . it is a mainspring of human activity . . . to avoid the fatality of death, to overcome it by denying in some way that it is the final destiny for man." According to Becker, "Modern man is drinking and drugging himself out of awareness, or he spends his time shopping, which is the same thing. . . . Or, alternatively, he buries himself in psychology in the belief that awareness all by itself will be some kind of magical cure for his problems."[4]

When Jerry Garcia died at the age of fifty-three, fans and nonfans of his rock and roll music pondered the paradoxical name of his band, "The Grateful Dead." Grateful to die? Only if your house is right with God.

David didn't deny the reality of death. He made sure his house was right with God. At the urging of his wife Bathsheba and his old friend Nathan the prophet, David made sure his son Solomon would succeed him as king (1 Kings 1:11-53). He gave Solomon some final instructions, and charged him to be faithful to God (2:1-12).

What kind of legacy will you leave to the next generation? Is your house right with God?

A COVENANT ARRANGED BY GOD

David faced death calmly because he trusted God's promises. "Has he not made with me an everlasting covenant, arranged and secured in every part?" (2 Samuel 23:5).

Years before, God made a special covenant (a solemn, binding agreement) to bless David and his descendants forever (7:12-17). Despite all David's failures and faults, he relied on God's faithfulness. "But from everlasting to everlasting the Lord's love is with those who fear him, and his righteousness with their children's children— with those who keep his covenant and remember to obey his precepts" (Psalm 103:17, 18).

God is willing to enter into a covenant with us, too. It's not a covenant for only one person or one ethnic group, but for all people in every nation who accept the Lord (Galatians 3:26-29; Revelation 7:9). It's a new and wonderful covenant guaranteed by the blood of Jesus Christ (Hebrews 7:22; 8:6).

It doesn't matter whether you're old or young, rich or poor. Your skin color doesn't matter, nor does the language you speak, or even what you have done in the past. You can live forever in a covenant relationship with God! On the day you die, nothing will matter as much as this.

Why reject God's promise of forgiveness and eternal life? Why ignore God's warnings of judgment? In 1902, a volcano called Mount Pele erupted on the West Indian island of Martinique. The entire population of Saint-Pierre, one of Martinique's largest towns, died when the volcano unleashed its fury. Roughly thirty thousand people perished, but even more tragic, this massive loss of life could have been avoided. Scientists had advised everyone to evacuate the island; but because city officials wanted people to vote in an election, they ignored the warnings and urged everyone to stay. When the volcano finally erupted, there was no time to escape.[5]

God's judgment is real. The day will come when "we must all appear before the judgment seat of Christ" (2 Corinthians 5:10). In light of this coming event, God has provided for our salvation through the sacrifice of His Son. We can join in a covenant of love with the God of grace!

A HOPE GUARANTEED BY GOD

Death is the great equalizer. By one account, when Queen Elizabeth I was dying, she said she would give all she owned for a moment of time. But even a powerful monarch can't buy time. In the words of Thomas Gray,

> The boast of heraldry, the pomp of power,
>   And all that beauty, all that wealth ever gave,
> Awaits alike the inevitable hour:
>   The paths of glory lead but to the grave."[6]

Though he was a mighty king, David had to die as everyone else does. As he told his son Solomon, "I am about to go the way of all the earth" (1 Kings 2:2). Ever since sin entered the world, death has been "the way of all the earth" (see Genesis 2:15-17; 3:19; Romans 5:12-21). But Jesus came to bring a new way to the earth—a way of life and hope.

David's last words contained a lasting message of hope: "Will he not bring to fruition my salvation and grant me my every desire?" (2 Samuel 23:5). David's faith looked ahead with a glimmer of hope that spanned the centuries toward the one "who as to his human nature was a descendant of David, and who through the Spirit of holiness was declared with power to be the Son of God by his resurrection from the dead: Jesus Christ our Lord" (Romans 1:3, 4).[7]

Dan Eynon is ninety years old. Most of his life he's been a preacher. I went to visit Dan at the funeral home after his wife died. They had been married sixty-five years. As I began to offer some words of sympathy, Dan waved his hand at me reassuringly and said, "Of course I miss my wife. But we don't have to worry about her." A tear came to his eye as he looked at me, but then said with much conviction in his voice, "You know, I haven't been preaching fairy tales all these years!"

No, Jesus isn't a fairy tale. Salvation isn't a religious pipe dream. Jesus' resurrection is a fact, not a myth. Empty hearts can find comfort in the Lord's empty tomb. He is alive!

Scripture describes David's death by saying he "rested with his fathers" (1 Kings 2:10). What a beautiful thought! For believers, death means rest, and it means reunion with the faithful saints of God who have died in the past. In Heaven we will enjoy restful fellowship with Abraham, Isaac, and Jacob . . . with Peter, John, and Paul . . . and most of all, with Jesus! "'Blessed are the dead who die in the Lord from now on.'" "'Yes,' says the Spirit, 'they will rest from their labor, for their deeds will follow them'" (Revelation 14:13).

David "died at a good old age, having enjoyed long

life, wealth and honor" (1 Chronicles 29:28). But as David prepared to die, his greatest satisfaction came not from his possessions or the honors he received, but simply from the assurance that his life mattered to God.

It's interesting to think that David, who wrote so many songs of praise, now abides in eternity where God's praises never cease. Can you picture him there in Heaven? Is he playing his harp? Is he singing at the top of his voice?

> Praise the Lord, you his angels,
>   you mighty ones who do his bidding,
>   who obey his word.
> Praise the Lord, all his heavenly hosts,
>   you his servants who do his will.
> Praise the Lord, all his works everywhere in his
>   dominion.
> Praise the Lord, O my soul.
>
> Psalm 103:20-22

Throughout his life, David offered God praise under pressure. He was merely practicing for eternity. In Heaven the pressure is gone, but the praise is ongoing.

It's estimated that John Wesley preached more than forty thousand sermons during his lifetime. Before he died on March 2, 1791, several of his friends gathered for prayer and songs of praise to God. Though weak and aware of his impending death, Wesley sang the lyrics of a hymn:

> I'll praise my Maker while I've breath,
> And when my voice is lost in death
> Praise shall employ my nobler powers.
> My days of praise shall never be past,
> While life, and thought, and being last,
> Or immortality endures.[8]

As his strength continued to wane, Wesley could no longer sing the song in its entirety. He could only utter the song's opening words: "I'll praise . . . I'll praise." His last words were, "Best of all, God is with us."[9]

Sometimes we may feel that life is mainly about pressure. But life is really about worship. Life's pressures will finally come to an end. The earth itself will come to an end someday. But God lives on forever. Whoever "does the will of God lives forever" (1 John 2:17). Worship and praise will go on forever.

For a Christian, death isn't the closing benediction of life. It's more like an opening call to worship.

Let the praise begin.

Notes

NOTES: INTRODUCTION

[1]Some scholars suggest that the phrase "A Psalm of David" does not require that David himself authored the psalm, but simply that it was written "for David" or under his supervision. Long-standing Hebrew tradition, however, supports the idea that David himself wrote the psalms that bear his name, and numerous Scriptures plainly state that David was a musician and psalm writer (for example, 2 Samuel 22. See also Mark 12:35-37, where Jesus named David as the author of Psalm 110.)

[2]In a sense, the psalms are everyone's spiritual journal. The Jewish people grouped the psalms into five books, each of which ends with a doxology of praise (see Psalms 41, 72, 89, 106, and 150). Just as the Bible begins with five books of Law, the psalms include five books of prayer and praise. All of God's Word speaks *to* us; but in a sense, the psalms also speak *for* us, expressing our response to God's Word and our circumstances.

NOTES: CHAPTER ONE

[1]"Choices and Change," speech delivered by Barbara Bush at Wellesley College on June 1, 1990. Published in *The Art of Public Speaking,* 5th edition, by Stephen E. Lucas (New York: McGraw-Hill, 1995), p. 450.

[2]Robert Famighetti, *The World Almanac and Book of Facts: 1995* (Mahwah, NJ: Funk & Wagnalls, 1994), pp. 128 and 379.

[3]Cam Floria, *The Apostle* (Lexicon Music, Inc., 1973), p. 35.

[4]In those days, harps were not the large bulky instruments familiar to us. Usually they were smaller wood-framed instruments with strings made from sheep intestines. We tend to think of harps as delicate, gentle-sounding instruments. But in the Bible, harps were used to express joyous, cheerful worship of God (Psalm 33:1-3; 98:4, 5; Revelation 5:8-14).

NOTES: CHAPTER TWO

[1]John C. Maxwell, *Developing the Leader Within You* (Nashville: Thomas Nelson, 1993), p. 73.

[2]Maxwell, p. 73.

[3]In those days a sling was not merely a child's toy. It was a deadly weapon made of ropes fastened to a leather thong. Most armies contained a number of "slingers," and some were so proficient in their craft they could sling a stone at a hair and not miss (see Judges 20:16).

[4]Mary Alice Parks, "Tell Me It's Just a Phase!" *Focus on the Family* magazine, October, 1986, p. 12.

NOTES: CHAPTER THREE

[1]Marshall Shelley, *Well-Intentioned Dragons: Ministering to Problem People in the Church,* The Leadership Library, Vol. 1 (Waco, Texas: Word Books, 1985), pp. 35, 41.

[2]It's puzzling to read that "an evil spirit from God came forcefully upon Saul" (1 Samuel 18:10; see also 16:14-23, 19:9). While God does not desire that anyone fall into evil (James 1:13, 14), God did allow Saul to experience the negative results of his own sinful choices. Also, the word "evil" in this context may carry the connotation of "injurious" or "hurtful." Instead of enjoying the strength and assistance of the Lord, Saul felt the painful consequences of his disobedience.

[3]*The Cincinnati Enquirer,* April 30, 1993, p. D3.

[4]Carl W. Pruitt, *God's Answers to Personal Problems* (Joplin: College Press, 1982), pp. 224-225.

NOTES: CHAPTER FOUR

[1]Gordon MacDonald, *Restoring Your Spiritual Passion* (Nashville: Thomas Nelson, 1986), p. 176.

[2]*New York Newsday,* September 22, 1980, II, 7.

NOTES: CHAPTER FIVE

[1]*Prevention,* March, 1995, p. 75.

[2]*Prevention,* p. 78.

[3]Jesus pointed to this incident when He responded to the Pharisees' criticism of His disciples who picked some grain on the Sabbath Day. The Pharisees considered the disciples' actions a violation of the Law against working on the Sabbath. But Jesus is "the Lord of the

Sabbath." He insisted that Sabbath laws, like the other laws of God, were intended to benefit people, not enslave them to traditions and rituals (Mark 2:23-28).

[4]Achish also was known as Abimelech, this name he is given in the superscription above Psalm 34. Apparently his actual name was Achish, while Abimelech was his title. "Abimelech" (which means "father of a king") was a long-standing designation for Philistine kings (see Genesis 26:1-16). The matter is further complicated by the similar spelling of "Ahimelech" ("brother of a king"), the name of the priest also mentioned in 1 Samuel 21:1.

[5]The acrostic technique was also used in Psalms 25, 119, and the book of Lamentations.

NOTES: CHAPTER SIX
[1]Abigail used an interesting metaphor when she said David would be "bound securely in the bundle of the living" (1 Samuel 25:29). In the ancient world, people carried bags made of leather or cloth, somewhat like backpacks or duffel bags we use today. Evidently Abigail meant that the Lord would take care of David, carry him along, keep him safe. Christians can rest secure in our living Savior. As long as we belong to Him, our Lord keeps us "bound securely in the bundle of the living."

[2]Why did David have more than one wife? The Old Testament mentions several examples of this practice, despite the fact that God warned of its folly. Not only did polygamy lead to resentment and bitter rivalry within the home (as in the case of Hannah and Peninnah in 1 Samuel 1:1-8), the Law of Moses specifically warned that multiple marriages could result in tragic consequences for kings and the nations they led (Deuteronomy 17:17). This very problem led to Solomon's downfall (1 Kings 11:1-6). By God's grace, He used men like David in spite of their imperfect home life, but it was His intention that a man should cleave to his *wife,* not his many *wives,* and that the *two* (not three, or five or eight) should become one flesh in marriage. (Compare Genesis 2:24; Matthew 19:4-6; 1 Timothy 3:2).

[3]*The Cincinnati Enquirer,* July 16, 1995, p. A5.

NOTES: CHAPTER SEVEN
[1]*The Autobiography of Mark Twain,* Charles Neider, ed. (New York: Harper & Brothers, 1959), p. 191.

[2]John Stuart Mill, "Nature and Utility of Religion," in *The Existence of God,* John Hick, ed. (New York: Macmillan, 1964), p. 119.

[3]The ark of the covenant was a wooden box covered with gold that contained the stone tablets on which the Ten Commandments were written, along with other items of sacred value to God's people. See Exodus 37:1-5 and Hebrews 9:4.

[4]Mitch Simpson, *What the Bible Says About Prayer* (Joplin, MO: College Press, 1987), p. 303.

[5]Michal's negative attitude becomes a bit more understandable— though not excusable—when we consider what she had been through. According to 1 Samuel 25:44, her angry father Saul took her from David and gave her to a man named Paltiel.

NOTES: CHAPTER EIGHT

[1]Maxie Dunnam, *Living the Psalms* (Nashville: Upper Room Books, 1990), p. 124.

[2]John Maxwell, *Developing the Leader Within You* (Nashville: Thomas Nelson, 1993), p. 109.

[3]Jon Talton, "Slogans Can't Compensate What's Lost," *The Cincinnati Enquirer,* May 28, 1995.

[4]Leon Huffstutter, "Are You Rolling Marbles or Moving Mountains?" *The Lookout,* July 30, 1989, p. 7.

[5]For a more extensive look at the subject of redefining success, see my earlier book, *Growing Churches, Growing Leaders,* (Joplin, MO: College Press, 1994).

NOTES: CHAPTER NINE

[1]William J. Diehm, "Handicapped," *Christian Standard,* February 9, 1986, p. l0.

[2]Joni Eareckson Tada, "Losing the Winner Mentality," *Moody Monthly,* February 1987, p. 31.

[3]Alice C. Peter, "Has God Forgotten the Handicapped?" *The Lookout,* March 8, 1987, p. 7.

[4]LeRoy Lawson, *Lord of Victory* (Cincinnati: Standard, 1988), p. 35.

NOTES: CHAPTER TEN

[1]"Military Confetti: The Global Curse of Land Mines," *Context,* May 1995, p. 11.

[2]Will Durant, *The Story of Civilization,* Vol. V, "The Renaissance" (New York: Simon and Schuster, 1953), pp. 467-469.

[3]It's painful to consider the death of David's infant son. Suffering and death are not easily explained, especially when an innocent child is involved. While there is no simple answer, this incident serves as a solemn reminder that one person's sinful decisions can have a tragic effect on others (for example, King Herod's wicked edict resulted in the deaths of many young boys; see Matthew 2:16). God is just, but life is often painful in our fallen world.

[4]"Military Confetti," p. 11.

NOTES: CHAPTER ELEVEN

[1]*Single Adult Ministries Journal,* March-April, 1992.

[2]*Newsweek,* June 21, 1993.

[3]"Life Without Fathers," *American Demographics,* July, 1995, p. 60.

[4]Tom Mullen, *Seriously, Life Is a Laughing Matter* (Waco, Texas: Word, 1978), p. 73.

[5]John Kiesewetter, "The Passing of TV's Family Hour," *The Cincinnati Enquirer,* August 20, 1995.

[6]Dr. James Dobson, "Focus on the Family Bulletin" (March, 1990).

[7]Ravi Zacharias, "The Haunts of Violence Filling the Land," *Just Thinking* (Spring/Summer, 1995), p. 3.

[8]LeRoy Lawson, "Privileged Persons: A Father's Formula for Enjoying Teenagers," *The Lookout,* June 19, 1983, p. 14.

NOTES: CHAPTER TWELVE

[1]Many exploits of the "mighty men" are recounted in 2 Samuel 23:8-39. For example, a man named Eleazar stood his ground against the Philistines even when his fellow soldiers retreated, and fought until his hand grew cramped and "froze to the sword." A fellow named Benaiah "went down into a pit on a snowy day and killed a lion." Another of David's men was famous for defeating a huge man from

Gath who had "six fingers on each hand and six toes on each foot" (2 Samuel 21:20, 21).

[2]The "man in the pit" illustration is my own adaptation of a similar story by an unknown author.

[3]A threshing floor was a large wooden platform where wheat or barley was spread out, then a team of oxen pulled a heavy wooden sledge over the surface to separate the grain from the chaff.

[4]What makes this prophetic description of Jesus' death especially remarkable is that David had never seen a crucifixion before (for this method of execution was not common in his day). The reference to piercing of the hands and feet is particularly striking (Psalm 22:16).

NOTES: CHAPTER THIRTEEN

[1]Ninie O'Hara, "Silence," *The Southeast Outlook,* October 6, 1995, pp. Al, A9.

[2]Davis W. Clark, *Death-Bed Scenes: Dying With and Without Religion* (New York: Hunt & Eaton, 1851), p. 55.

[3]Clark, *Death-Bed Scenes,* pp. 523-528.

[4]Ernest Becker, *The Denial of Death* (New York: Macmillan, 1973), pp. ix, 284.

[5]"Montserrat Braces for Double Blow," *The Cincinnati Enquirer,* August 26, 1995, p. A2.

[6]Thomas Gray, "Elegy Written in a Country Churchyard," from *The Literature of England* (Glenview, IL: Scott, Foresman and Company, 1967), p. 643.

[7]See also Acts 2:29-36.

[8]John Wesley adapted this song from Isaac Watts' Psalms of David (1719). See The Works of John Wesley, Vol. 7, Franz Hildebrandt and Oliver A Beckerlegge, eds. (Nashville: Abingdon, 1983), pp. 349-350.

[9]Clark, *Death-Bed Scenes,* pp. 163-165.